Handbook of Special Education

Research and Practice

Volume 3

Other titles of interest

WANG et al.	Handbook of Special Education, Volume 1: Learner Characteristics and Adaptive Education
WANG et al.	Handbook of Special Education, Volume 2: Mildly Handicapped Conditions
WANG et al.	Handbook of Special Education, Volume 4: Emerging Programs
WANG et al.	Special Education: Research and Practice: Synthesis of Findings
DUNKIN	The International Encyclopedia of Teaching and Teacher Education
PSACHAROPOULOS	Economics of Education: Research and Studies
POSTLETHWAITE	The Encyclopedia of Comparative Education and National Systems of Education
KEEVES	Educational Research, Methodology, and Measurement: An International Handbook
TITMUS	Lifelong Education for Adults: An International Handbook
ERAUT	International Encyclopedia of Educational Technology
WALBERG	The International Encyclopedia of Educational Evaluation
THOMAS	Encyclopedia of Human Development and Education
LEWY	The International Encyclopedia of Curriculum
REYNOLDS	Knowledge Base for the Beginning Teacher

Handbook of Special Education
Research and Practice
Volume 3

Low Incidence Conditions

Edited by

MARGARET C. WANG
Temple University, Philadelphia, USA

MAYNARD C. REYNOLDS
University of Minnesota, Minneapolis, USA

HERBERT J. WALBERG
University of Illinois at Chicago, USA

PERGAMON PRESS

OXFORD · NEW YORK · BEIJING · FRANKFURT
SEOUL · SYDNEY · TOKYO

U.K.	Pergamon Press plc, Headington Hill Hall, Oxford OX3 0BW, England
U.S.A.	Pergamon Press Inc., Maxwell House, Fairview Park, Elmsford, New York 10523, U.S.A.
PEOPLE'S REPUBLIC OF CHINA	Maxwell Pergamon China, Beijing Exhibition Centre, Xizhimenwai Dajie, Beijing 100044, People's Republic of China
GERMANY	Pergamon Press GmbH, Hammerweg 6, D-6242 Kronberg, Germany
KOREA	Pergamon Press Korea, KPO Box 315, Seoul 110-603, Korea
AUSTRALIA	Maxwell Macmillan Pergamon Publishing Australia Pty Ltd, Lakes Business Park, 2 Lord Street, Botany, NSW 2019, Australia
JAPAN	Pergamon Press, 8th Floor, Matsuoka Central Building, 1-7-1 Nishi-Shinjuku, Shinjuku-ku, Tokyo 160, Japan

Copyright © 1989 Pergamon Press plc

First edition 1989
Reprinted 1991

Library of Congress Cataloging in Publication Data

Handbook of special education.
(Advances in education)
Vol. 3 has imprint: Oxford; New York: Pergamon Press.
Series statement from vol. 1, jacket.
Vol. 3 lacks series statement.
Includes bibliographies and indexes.
Contents: v. 1. Learner characteristics and adaptive education— —v. 3. Low incidence conditions.
1. Special education. 2. Special education—United States.
I. Wang, Margaret C. II. Reynolds, Maynard Clinton.
III. Walberg, Herbert J., 1937–
IV. Series.
LC3965.H263 1987 371.9'0973 87–18965

British Library Cataloguing in Publication Data

Handbook of special education: research and practice.
Vol. 3: Low incidence conditions
1. United States. Special education
I. Wang, Margaret C. II. Reynolds, Maynard C.
III. Walberg, Herbert J.
371.9'0973

ISBN 0-08-033385-0

Information included in this publication is the result of a project funded at least in part through Federal funds from the U.S. Department of Education under contract number 300–84–0194. The contents of this publication do not necessarily reflect the views or policies of the U.S. Department of Education; nor does the mention of trade names, commercial products or organizations imply endorsement by the U.S. Government.

Printed in Great Britain by BPCC Wheatons Ltd, Exeter

Contents

v

SECTION 3: HANDICAPPED INFANTS

Preface

In the United States, as in many other parts of the world, we are engaging in a new wave of education reform efforts, particularly the improvement of schools' capabilities to serve students who have greater-than-usual needs for educational support but were often either left out of earlier reform movements or kept on the sidelines. The term "students with special needs" is used here to refer to students with physical, behavioral, or cognitive disabilities; students from economically, culturally, or language disadvantaged backgrounds; and students with chronic low achievement or those who otherwise can be considered academically at risk.

Significant progress has been made, especially in the past decade, in providing equal access to free and appropriate schooling for students. At this point in our history, nearly all school-age children in the United States and other industrialized countries attend school. This effort to achieve universal and effective education is based on a recognition of the rights of children to basic education that enables them to thrive in a complex society, as well as a realization that technological and economic growth is facilitated by increasing the numbers of students, even those with poor academic prognoses, who are, in fact, successful in school learning. Thus, recent and current efforts to improve schooling serve both private and social interests.

This three-volume publication, *The Handbook of Special Education: Research and Practice*, represents a commitment to examine the research base, broadly defined to represent current knowledge or the "state of the art," that can be used in formulating plans to improve the chances of schooling success for all students, especially students with special needs. Each of the 45 chapters comprising the *Handbook* summarizes the well-confirmed knowledge in a particular area, giving attention first to the research literature, broadly defined, and then to the tested experience and practices of leading professionals. The authors include in their reviews estimates of the state of practice in their respective topic areas and then proceed to recommend improvements for effectively linking practice with the state of the art. Thus, the research syntheses provide state-of-the-art standards against which the state of practice can be judged.

Several perspectives provided the specific context for this *Handbook*. First, the reviews of research and practice mark the impact of a decade of intensive research and program development in the United States aimed at improving the chances of educational success for students with special needs. Since 1975, the year of the enactment of The Education for All Handicapped Children Act (PL 94–142), schools have made major advances in providing for handicapped students and others with special needs. Consequently, there is reason to celebrate the 10th anniversary of what has proven to be an extremely powerful and influential piece of legislation. During the same period, there have been important advances in educational research, thus adding to the impetus for careful review of both research and practice at this time.

The second perspective derives from the movement to provide more inclusive arrangements for disabled persons and for others who often find themselves at the margins of schools and other institutions. These efforts are variously described as deinstitutionalization, normalization, and mainstreaming. Even persons with severe impairments are less often segregated in special enclaves and more often mainstreamed into ordinary community situations. As a result, it is critical that the findings from research on persons with special needs be made available to broader groups than ever before, and that future research be conducted in new settings and on the specific processes of change involved in implementing new policies. In a sense, research needs to be "mainstreamed." Accordingly, the reviews reported here join the work of special education researchers with that of the broader community of researchers in general education and human behavior.

The need to coordinate services across a wide range of caretakers and agencies provided a third perspective for the research syntheses. Specifically, special education must be coordinated with services such as health and welfare, family services, correction, rehabilitation, and employment assistance. Many of the "new morbidities," such as child abuse, drug addiction, and the erosion of "natural" support systems as a consequence of broken family structures and incomplete mother–child attachments, have grave effects on school children. Often, children who are referred to special education programs come from unsupportive families and disordered communities. Schools must respond by linking up with other community agencies in order to construct high-quality, broadly coordinated programs for students and families with special needs. At the same time, it is necessary to recognize and delimit the special functions of the schools. In this context, the research reviews reported in this *Handbook* were designed to be instructionally relevant, while also acknowledging the larger networks of service to which educational processes can be linked.

The dependence of special education on public policy and legal imperatives is yet another perspective that guided the research syntheses. Several reports, court decisions, and policies have enlarged this perspective in recent years. Examples include Nicholas Hobbs' 1975 work entitled, *The Futures of Children* (San Francisco, CA: Jossey-Bass); and the 1982 report by the National Academy of Sciences Panel on Selection and Placement of Students in Programs for the Mentally Retarded, entitled *Placing Children in Special Education: A Strategy for Equity* (K. A. Heller, W. H. Holtzman, and S. Messick, Editors, Washington, DC: National Academy Press). These and other reports by leading scholars cast doubt on some of the traditional practices of special education.

The courts, moreover, have had far-reaching effects on educational policy. For instance, the 1972 decision of *Larry P. v. Riles* (Civil action N.L.-71-2270, 343 F. Supp. 1306, N.D. Cal., 1972) held that the use of intelligence tests as a prime determiner of the classification and placement of children as educable mentally retarded is unconstitutional. Similar court decisions have been the basis for many program changes. Clearly, the field of special education is held accountable to the procedural standards and practices outlined by binding court decisions. Thus, the research reviews reported in this work were sensitive to studies of policy and policy related developments.

Finally, the research syntheses took account of the rising public concern over the general quality of schools, as expressed in the widely heralded 1983 report by the National Commission on Excellence in Education entitled, *A Nation at Risk: The Imperative for Educational Reform* (Washington, DC: U.S. Department of Education), as well as at least a dozen other recent and significant national reports. They reflect growing public demand for better instruction and for a greater focus on all forms of school accountability, including a commitment to provide the greater-than-usual educational interventions required by students who are difficult to teach. Because recent developments in special education (e.g., more individualized planning, closer partnerships with parents, better measurements of instructional outcomes) are congruent with the increasing general demands made of schools, it should be possible, as we see it, for special educators to complete the necessary reforms. To this end, the authors of the chapters in these volumes sought to define the knowledge

base and extend its application in the field of special education in the broadest and most helpful way. Just as students with special needs are no longer isolated in the schools, research in special education should no longer be treated in isolation.

As we have noted, 1986 is a year in which schools in the United States entered into a second decade under the mandates of changed national policy concerning special education and related services for students with special needs. However, the authors of the research syntheses were also mindful of the international scope of the research literature and of the similarity in trends and problems surrounding special education throughout the world.

This publication was initiated, in part, as a culminating activity of a project entitled, "Research Integration of Selected Issues in the Education of Handicapped Children," which was funded by the Office of Special Education and Rehabilitative Services of the United States Department of Education. The 45 chapters are organized in three volumes under nine major topic areas or sections. Volume I includes chapters in the topic areas, Learning Characteristics of Handicapped Students and the Provision of Effective Education, Effectiveness of Differential Programming in Serving Handicapped Students, and Noncategorical Programming for Mildly Handicapped Students. Volume II consists of writings in the areas of Mild Mental Retardation, Behavioral Disorders, and Learning Disabilities. The chapters in Volume III focus on the topic areas, Education of Deaf Children and Youth, Education of Visually Handicapped Children and Youth, and Handicapped Infants.

An eight-member advisory board played a major role at important stages in the substantive development and preparation of the research syntheses. They participated in the initial selection of areas of research in special education and related fields, in the identification of authors who would conduct the research syntheses, and in the reviewing of manuscripts. The members of the advisory board were Joseph Fischgrund from the Lexington School for the Deaf in New York; James Gallagher from the University of North Carolina; Reginald Jones from the University of California, Berkeley; Stephen Lilly from Washington State University; Daniel Reschly from Iowa State University; Judy Schrag from the Washington State Department of Education; Phillip Strain from the University of Pittsburgh; and Martha Ziegler from the Federation for Children with Special Needs based in Boston, Massachusetts.

A group of scholars, each of them nationally and internationally known and active in research, provided substantive leadership to the authors in the nine topic areas. These scholars assisted the editors of this *Handbook* in overseeing the quality and breadth of the content coverage. They also wrote Introductions that provide overviews of the topics addressed in the nine areas. The names of these individuals and the topic areas in which they worked are Verna Hart from the University of Pittsburgh—Handicapped Infants; Kenneth Kavale from the University of Iowa—Effectiveness of Differential Programming in Serving Handicapped Students; Barbara Keogh from the University of California, Los Angeles—Learning Disabilities; Daniel Reschly from Iowa State University—Mild Mental Retardation; Maynard Reynolds from the University of Minnesota—Noncategorical Programming for Mildly Handicapped Students; Geraldine Scholl from the University of Michigan—Education of Visually Handicapped Children and Youth; E. Ross Stuckless from the National Technical Institute for the Deaf—Education of Deaf Children and Youth; Margaret Wang from Temple University—Learning Characteristics of Handicapped Students and the Provision of Effective Education; and Frank Wood from the University of Minnesota—Behavioral Disorders.

The chapters were reviewed during various draft stages by persons representing a broad range of expertise in research, personnel preparation, curriculum development, and educational practice. The contributions of these reviewers helped to enhance the comprehensiveness and relevance of the individual research syntheses. Lists of reviewers for the chapters included in individual volumes are provided at the end of the volumes.

The comprehensiveness of the research syntheses was further enhanced by making available to all authors the findings from computerized literature searches. These covered the two major indices of the Educational Resources Information Center (ERIC)—the Resources in Education Index and the Current Index to Journals in Education. In addition, the authors made use of technical reports and other documentation on more than 100 research projects in special education that were conducted in the United States in recent years.

As a final note, we wish to acknowledge the contributions of several others who played important roles in facilitating the development and production of this *Handbook*. Funding from the Office of Special Education and Rehabilitative Services provided the necessary support to commission the writing of most of the chapters. Judy Fein and Nancy Safer from that agency's staff were the source of continuing advice and encouragement. Special acknowledgments go to Mary Kay Freilino for her efficient orchestration of the myriad administrative details involved in the manuscript reviewing process and her efforts in overseeing the substantive and technical details of conducting computerized literature searches for authors; to K. Charlie Lakin whose substantive input during the reviewing of many of the manuscripts was consistently insightful; to Rita Catalano for her editorial and administrative leadership throughout the preparation of this work; to Jackie Rubenstein for her technical editing expertise and her diligence in monitoring the details of a Herculean editing assignment; and to Regina Rattigan for her contribution as a member of the technical editing team. Finally, we are grateful to Barbara Barrett from Pergamon Press for her constant support and guidance throughout the editing and production process.

Margaret C. Wang
Maynard C. Reynolds
Herbert J. Walbert
Editors

SECTION 1

Education of Deaf Children and Youth

Introduction

E. ROSS STUCKLESS

National Technical Institute for the Deaf
Rochester Institute of Technology

It is common to introduce literature on the psychological and educational implications of deafness by saying that deafness is a communication handicap. Although this statement has become a cliché, it remains a fundamental fact about deafness, and it is most evident in deaf children. Communication, its development and means of expression among deaf children and the effect of its deprivation, constitute the themes of the collection of chapters in this section. The research literature is organized and discussed in five topical areas, each of which has a bearing on and is influenced by the others. The respective chapter authors are to be commended for observing the topical parameters, artificial though the boundaries may be. Together, the writings in this section reference the major issues and known variables of interest in the education of deaf students to the extent that salient research literature exists.

This is not to say that readers would give the same attention to, or draw the same interpretations from, all the literature as presented by the various authors. Nor will prospective and knowledgeable readers necessarily agree with the authors on every point. It would have been disappointing if the authors had chosen to develop chapters on which they expected to find full consensus among readers. Suffice it to say that the choice of authors was not made casually, but on the basis of their authority on the given topics.

In the chapter, "English Language Development," Quigley and Paul examine the effects of deafness on the acquisition of English literacy skills. The acquisition of language is a critical element in a deaf student's education, both for active participation in society and as a requisite for success in academic content areas. However, as the authors conclude from their review of empirically-based studies, literacy in English remains beyond the grasp of many, if not most, deaf students. A typical 18- to 19-year-old, prelingually deaf student reads and writes at the level of a typical 8- or 9-year-old hearing student. Quigley and Paul discuss this low level of achievement—as well as exceptions to it—and stress the need for further investigation of literacy problems and instructional practices in the education of deaf students.

A relatively small proportion of prelingually deaf students acquire what can be considered intelligible speech and most probably do not profit as they might from appropriate amplification. Yet responsible educators of deaf children recognize the value of functional oral and aural communication skills. There should be no question that the development of a deaf child's potential for oral/aural communication is a legitimate and necessary educational responsibility regardless of the prevailing mode of communication or the type of school placement. In his chapter, entitled "Speech and Hearing in Communication," Levitt explicates the effects of hearing impairment on understanding and producing speech. He also discusses the methods used to improve communication skills, including the use of modern technical aids.

The next chapter in this section, by Lowenbraun and Thompson, is on the topic, "Environments and Strategies for Learning and Teaching." Two major movements have dominated the education of deaf students for more than a decade. The first movement is toward the broad adoption of "total communication" within educational programs for deaf students at all educational levels. Recognizing that there are individual differences among students, there is a need to examine the contributions made by total communication. The second movement is in the direction of mainstreaming. It is driven by the need to bring more objectivity to school placement decision and the need to examine more closely the levels and kinds of support required by deaf students in various educational environments. In their chapter, Lowenbraun and Thompson address four specific topics related to environments and strategies for learning and teaching: changing demographics, total communication, technologies and media, and adoption/adaption of other educational technologies. For each topic, they synthesize research, note how each topic has influenced and been influenced by current practices, and make recommendations for future work.

Lang's chapter on "Academic Development and Preparation for Work" pays particular attention to the subject matter areas of science, mathematics, and social studies. He notes the serious dearth of research on instructional materials development for hearing-impaired students and on the potential of the contextual bases provided by these subjects for the language, communication, cognitive, social/moral, and career development of these students. Educational and communication researchers have traditionally focused their investigations on the hypothetical factors contributing to the educational lags of hearing-impaired students; empirical research studies that examine pedagogical strategies are scarce. Lang points out that the absence of a research base is reflected in the quality of teaching and materials development, and he calls for increased work in the area.

This section's final chapter, by Mark Greenberg and Carol Kusché, is entitled, "Cognitive, Personal, and Social Development of Deaf Children and Adolescents." The underlying premise of this chapter is that the hearing deficit common to all deaf students can have broad implications for development along each of these three dimensions. There is considerable concern among many educators of deaf students about a developmental lag in the reasoning, problem-solving, and decision-making skills among their students that cannot be attributed to intelligence per se. Similar lags have been reported in social maturation. Emotional and personality development has also been the subject of considerable concern. Numerous systematic efforts have been

introduced into curricula at all levels to foster development in these areas. The relevance of family, peers, and the community to this topic is also important. Greenberg and Kusché review the literature in this area, comment on the processes and structures that support research on deafness, and recommend improvements in the ability of the research to contribute to the education and support of deaf children and their families.

In closing, it is important to remember that deaf students, like other students with special needs, are often the victims of stereotyping. Unfortunately, it is common for investigators to be neglectful in adequately defining their terms and describing their populations, and it is even more common for readers to ignore the definitions and descriptions that are provided. This makes the task of reviewing and synthesizing published research very difficult. Readers of chapters in this section are urged not to become impatient with the authors' reluctance to draw conclusive inferences from inconclusive information or to draw generalizations from data specific to a small subset of deaf students.

English Language Development

STEPHEN P. QUIGLEY

College of Education, University of Illinois at Urbana-Champaign

PETER V. PAUL

Department of Educational Services and Research, The Ohio State University at Columbus

Abstract—This chapter delineates some effects of deafness on the acquisition of English literacy skills. The review of the published literature is intended to be representative, with an emphasis on empirical-based studies. It is concluded that the typical 18-to-19-year-old prelinguistic deaf student is reading and writing at a level commensurate with the typical 8-or-9-year-old hearing student. Exceptions to this low level of achievement are also discussed. Not much is known about the merits of instructional practices. There is a pressing need to investigate the English literacy problems of deaf students on an intersentential or connected discourse level. Finally, current instructional practices need to be evaluated, and teachers should receive more theoretical-based training in language and reading development.

The primary purpose of this chapter is to depict the impact of deafness on the acquisition of English literacy skills, that is, reading and writing. After operationally defining deafness, a critical integrative review of research and theory in reading and written language development is presented. Also discussed is the relationship between data-based knowledge and currently-employed instructional practices. Finally, needs and recommendations are suggested for personnel preparation programs and for further research endeavors.

The selection of the literature is intended to be representative of the issues being considered, rather than exhaustive. Some selectivity is necessary due to the limitations imposed on space and the adequateness of sample selection and research design. Priority is given mainly to primary sources, that is, empirical-based studies. Significant secondary sources, for example, earlier syntheses of research, are also included.

At present, it is appropriate to review the research literature pertaining to secondary language development of English. Since the Chomskyan revolution, the language, reading, and writing abilities of deaf students have been studied by linguists, psycholinguists, and cognitive psychologists as well as by those investigators more directly involved in the field of deafness. The available findings provide some insights on the effects of certain variables, for example, communication approaches, on the development of secondary English language skills (King & Quigley, 1985; Quigley & Paul, 1984b). The disproportionate amount of space devoted to reading here is representative of much of the recent available research information.

Definitional Issues

To synthesize the findings of research, there must be, at least, agreement that the various samples in the studies were drawn from the same population. The importance of defining the population under consideration to avoid the generalization of findings to dissimilar populations cannot be overemphasized (Quigley & Kretschmer, 1982). A few descriptive variables which have been found to influence significantly the language comprehension abilities of deaf students are: type of communication input and educational program, socioeconomic status (SES), intelligence (IQ), the hearing status of parents and siblings, type of hearing impairment, etiology, age at onset, and degree of hearing impairment. While the salient effects of several of the above on secondary language development are considered in this chapter, it is necessary to highlight two variables, that is, degree and age at onset of hearing impairment, which play the most essential roles in our definition of deafness.

The term hearing impairment refers to all degrees of hearing losses measured in decibels (dB) across a range of frequencies from 125 to 8000 hertz (Hz). An individual's hearing impairment is typically reported as the average hearing threshold level of pure audiometric tones in the better unaided ear for the three frequencies deemed to be essential for speech reception: 500, 1,000, and 2,000 Hz. The label deaf should be reserved for those persons whose impairment is in the extreme or profound range, that is, with a loss of 90 dB or greater. Even with the use of amplification, there is evidence to suggest that, at this level, the individual's primary avenue for

3

the development of language and for communication is through vision rather than audition (Conrad, 1979; Quigley & Kretschmer, 1982). Thus, for most deaf persons, the use of residual hearing or audition is a secondary and supplemental channel. As much as possible, the studies included here employed hearing impaired subjects in the extreme or profound range. A few significant investigations with severely hearing-impaired subjects (i.e., 70 dB to 89 dB) were also considered.

The second major variable in defining deafness is the age at onset of hearing impairment. Along with the degree factor, the age at which a profound hearing impairment is sustained pervasively affects the exposure to normal aural/oral interactions which form the foundation of an auditorally-based, internalized linguistic system. Children incurring a profound hearing impairment prior to 2 or 3 years of age have been found to perform significantly inferior to those deafened after this age on certain language tasks. Consequently, this critical period has been designated as the dividing line between prelinguistic and postlinguistic deaf individuals. This paper is mainly concerned with typical (nonmultiply handicapped), prelinguistic deaf students since their language and communication problems are significantly different from those of typical, postlinguistic deaf students.

Reading

Assessment

The construction and classification of evaluation tools are inextricably related to theoretical viewpoints regarding the nature of reading (Pearson 1985; Pearson & Gallagher, 1983). Evidence is accruing to support the contention that reading is an interactive process involving reader-based (e.g., linguistic competence), text-based (e.g., text readability), and situation-based (e.g., home or school environment) variables (Anderson, 1981). In relation to assessment, there is lack of agreement on whether reading should be viewed as a global, holistic, unitary entity or as a set of discrete subskills. Even if reading comprehension is defined as a set of discrete skills, there is no conclusive evidence depicting the exact nature and number of these skills (Mason, Osborn, & Rosenshine, 1977; Rosenshine, 1980). In addition, while there may be enough evidence to demonstrate that word knowledge is related to reading comprehension (e.g., Davis, 1944, 1968; Spearritt, 1972) the reasons for this relationship are not well understood (Anderson & Freebody, 1979). Nevertheless, subtests of vocabulary knowledge play a major role in a majority of formal reading tests.

Assessment tools can be classified into three general areas: formal tests, informal tests, and record-keeping procedures related to instructional activities (Gronlund, 1981; Salvia & Ysseldyke, 1978). These tasks may require free (e.g., recall of events in stories) and/or controlled (e.g., multiple-choice questions) responses.

Most formal reading tests contain only two subtests: vocabulary and comprehension. Others may center on a specific domain or skill such as decoding or locating the main idea. There are also diagnostic tasks which focus on certain language-related variables suspected of affecting reading comprehension ability, for example, syntactic structure, idiomatic expressions, and multiple meanings of words. Much of the research literature contains reports of the results of deaf students on general achievement and diagnostic tests.

Present Status of Reading Achievement

A review of the research literature reveals that most deaf students do not read as well as their hearing counterparts (Allen, 1986; Di Francesca, 1972; Trybus & Karchmer, 1977). There is even evidence to suggest that general achievement batteries give spuriously high estimates of reading ability and that the true reading levels may be even lower (Moores, 1982). Generally, it has been reported that the average 18-to-19-year-old deaf student is reading no better than the average 8-or-9-year-old normally-hearing student (Babbini & Quigley, 1970; Pintner & Paterson, 1916, 1917).

These results have been obtained from tests standardized on nondeaf students and thus have been questioned. It has been argued that general achievement batteries normed on hearing students are assessing the English language abilities rather than the educational levels of deaf students (Babbini & Quigley, 1970). The construction of a standardized achievement tool which can provide reliable estimates of educational achievement in various academic areas, including reading, for hearing-impaired students has been undertaken by the Center for Assessment and Demographic Studies (CADS; Allen, White, & Karchmer, 1983). The work of the CADS researchers resulted in an *adapted* version of the Stanford Achievement Test (SAT).

Despite special adaptations, the reading level of most severely-to-profoundly hearing-impaired students has been reported to be not much different than that measured by nonadapted instruments, and indeed, not much different from the results of Pintner and his collaborators in 1916 and 1917. Trybus and Karchmer (1977), for example, reported a median reading grade level of about 4.5 and an annual growth rate of 0.3 grade, and that less than 10% of the 16-years-old-and-older group were reading at or above the eighth-grade level. Using statistical conversion measures, it was found that the reading levels of the 1983 sample were higher than those for the 1974 sample (Trybus & Karchmer, 1977) at every age level compared (Allen, 1986). Nevertheless, the mean reading grade of the total 1983 sample was still below fourth grade. Indeed, there appeared to be a leveling off (plateau) at this level; however, this may be attributed to a higher proportion of students with additional handicaps in the upper ages.

The findings of these national surveys should be interpreted with caution. The surveys obscure performances of certain subgroups within the hearing-impaired student population. For example, the reading achievement of oral deaf students in highly structured, comprehensive oral programs (Lane, 1976a, 1976b; Ogden, 1979), students in integrated classrooms (Pflaster, 1980), and those in some Total Communication programs (Delaney, Stuckless, & Walter, 1984) is higher than that reported in the national surveys. These good deaf readers, however, may be a select group (e.g., having high socioeconomic status, involved parents, and verbal communication skills).

The poor reading performance of most deaf students may be viewed within an interactive theoretical framework in which the reader uses specific skills (e.g., decoding and inference) to hypothesize at various linguistic levels (e.g., lexical, syntactic, semantic, textual) about the information contained in the text (Anderson, 1981). In relation to this, the reading difficulties of deaf students may be attributed to deficits in experiential (e.g., world knowledge), cognitive (e.g., inferencing), and linguistic (e.g., word knowledge) variables. Other variables of equal importance are educational and socioeconomic in nature. The specific difficulties of deaf students with respect to reading ability are examined in the following sections.

Linguistic Aspects of the Text

Vocabulary

A number of investigations and research reviews on the reading vocabulary development of deaf students have led to similar conclusions: the vocabulary growth of the population is quantitatively reduced and slower in rate than that of hearing peers (Cooper & Rosenstein, 1966; Paul, 1984; Walter, 1978). Specifically, it was found that deaf students not only comprehend fewer words from print, but also their receptive and expressive distributions of words in the various form classes (e.g., nouns, verbs, connectives) are quantitatively reduced when compared to hearing counterparts. Attempts have been made to study some linguistic variables which might influence the acquisition of word knowledge.

It has been shown, for example, that the frequency of a word in print affects the difficulty of a word, and consequently, reading comprehension. Walter (1978) examined the relationship between word knowledge and word frequency and found that the hearing students outperformed the deaf students at each age level tested. The difference between the two groups increased as the frequency of word usage decreased.

The importance of a reader knowing several meanings of a word has been established by investigations on hearing (Mason, Kniseley, & Kendall, 1979) and deaf (Letourneau, 1972; Paul, 1984) students. Paul (1984) reported that hearing students significantly outperformed deaf students on selecting two meanings of multimeaning words and on selecting at least one meaning for the same words on a picture vocabulary test. For both groups, however, choosing two correct meanings was found to be more difficult than choosing only a single meaning. Paul concluded, as have others, that deaf and hearing students have difficulty with the notion that a word may have more than one meaning. This may contribute to comprehension difficulties if the secondary or less common meanings of words are used in reading materials.

Syntactic Structures

It is possible to understand the meanings of individual words and still misunderstand the meaning of a sentence as a whole due to problems with syntax (Chomsky, 1957, 1965). This simple, yet complex, notion generated an intellectual revolution in linguistics giving birth to several linguistics-related disciplines and a theory labeled *tranformational generative grammar* (Slobin, 1979). The study of syntax within a psycholinguistic framework not only has shed some light on the reading difficulties of deaf students, but also has shown that syntactic competence is related to the ability to recall temporal-sequential, linguistic information (Lake, 1980; Lichtenstein, 1984).

An extensive national study of English syntactic development of deaf students was conducted by Quigley and his collaborators (Quigley, Wilbur, Power, Montanelli, & Steinkamp, 1976). The results of this longitudinal research led to the conclusion that the comprehension and production of syntactic structures in the language of deaf students was quantitatively reduced but qualitatively similar (i.e., order of difficulty) in comparison to normally-hearing students. It was found that most of the oldest deaf students (18- to 19-year-olds) in these studies performed at a significantly inferior level to the 8-year-old hearing students on all structures assessed. The importance of knowledge of syntax to the comprehension of print on a sentential level has been supported also by a research review on hearing students (Adams, 1980) and by the more recent investigations on deaf students (Hatcher & Robbins, 1978; Robbins & Hatcher, 1981).

Another related area of equal importance was the comparison of deaf students' knowledge of syntax with the frequency of appearance of the specific structures in reading materials. A huge mismatch was found between the appearance of specific syntactic structures and their understanding by deaf students. The problem was of such a magnitude that modifications of existing reading materials were deemed to be of limited value. Subsequently, the work of Quigley and his associates provided the research base for the construction of a reading series specifically designed for deaf students (Quigley & King, 1981, 1982, 1983, 1984).

Figurative Language

One of the most complex and colorful aspects of a language and another area of difficulty for most deaf students is the presence of figurative expressions. These ambiguous phrases and statements are "one of the most productive sources of linguistic change" (Sadock, 1979, p. 48). Examples include figures of speech (metaphor: John is a fox) and various kinds of idioms (fixed idiom: it's raining cats and dogs). Boatner and Gates (1969) estimated that figurative expressions comprise approximately two-thirds of the English language. Makkai (1972) found that idioms with the verb-particle structure (e.g., run up the bill) occur more frequently in the English language than any other type. Dixon, Pearson, and Ortony (1980) asserted that the beginning reader encounters many of these expressions in commonly used reading materials.

Several researchers have reported that deaf students have difficulty with certain aspects of figurative language (Conley, 1976; Giorcelli, 1982; Payne, 1982). Conley (1976) for example, developed and administered an idiom test to deaf and hearing students matched for reading levels. The hearing students had significantly superior scores; however, it is not clear whether the deaf students experienced difficulty with the idioms or with the complex syntactic structures in which they were expressed.

Payne (1982) focused on the verb-particle combinations in five types of syntactic structures. He established three types of combinations with respect to semantic difficulty: literal (e.g., *the boy walked up the stairs*), semi-idiomatic (e.g., *the girl tore the paper up*), and idiomatic (e.g., *the woman ran into a friend*). Even with the vocabulary selected from first- and second-grade levels, the scores of the hearing students were significantly superior to those of the deaf students on all three types of verb-particle combinations and for all syntactic structures.

From another perspective, Iran-Nejad, Ortony, and Rittenhouse (1981) presented evidence to suggest that deaf students can comprehend some aspects of figurative language *with training*. They showed that some students can be taught to understand metaphorical expressions if the variables of vocabulary and syntax are experimentally controlled. It is clear that the comprehension of some expressions is somewhat dependent on an understanding, at least, of the vocabulary and syntactic structures used in expressing them.

This can be inferred also from a more recent study by Fruchter, Wilbur, and Fraser (1984). They studied the comprehension of 20 English idioms by deaf students whose reading levels ranged from Grade 1 to 10 on achievement tests. Two sets of four illustrations each accompanied each idiom; one set contained the literal picture and the other, the figurative picture. It was found that selecting the literal meaning posed little difficulty for the students. The scores on the figurative meaning part were lower, and more importantly, correlated significantly with reading achievement levels.

Discourse Analysis

Some researchers, notably McGill-Franzen and Gormley (1980) and Ewoldt (1981) have studied the reading ability of deaf students on a connected discourse level. Influenced by top-down theories of reading (e.g., Goodman, 1967; Smith, 1978), these researchers argued that the emphasis should be on what the deaf reader brings to the task of reading rather than on linguistic weaknesses. The essence of the argument is that inadequate knowledge of certain linguistic factors exists on the sentential level only. On the paragraph level, the reader accumulates a sufficient amount of cues which permits the revision of falsely interpreted sentences.

McGill-Franzen and Gormley (1980) found that an improvement in comprehension occurred when truncated passives (e.g., *The boy was hit*) were embedded in meaningful discourse rather than presented in isolated sentences. They argued that the use of highly familiar reading material reduces the mismatch between English syntax and the English language competence of deaf readers, thereby allowing them to interact with print on the basis of world knowledge.

Ewoldt (1981) assessed four deaf students' comprehension of stories by miscue analysis, cloze procedures, and recall analysis (retelling of stories). She concluded that the strategies employed by deaf readers were similar to those identified in hearing readers in miscue research. For example, hearing readers rely heavily on graphic information when encountering difficult reading material. For the deaf readers, there was evidence of an increase in finger spelling. On the whole, however, the deaf readers were able to comprehend the stories by constructing hypotheses and revising and refining them as they gathered more syntactic and semantic cues beyond the sentence level.

Top-down processes are important; however, there is a growing body of research supporting an interactive view of reading which entails the use of both top-down and bottom-up (e.g., understanding linguistic aspects) strategies (Anderson, 1981; Pearson, 1985). The major criticism of top-down theories is that the information related to the highly familiar stories is not text dependent. The reader is so familiar with the story that general information can be understood or questions answered *without reading*. In fact, beginning readers, poor readers, and readers with limited experiences are heavily dependent on top-down strategies which may cause them to misinterpret or not comprehend important details in a story which are dependent, in part, upon a knowledge of language variables on a sentential or intrasentential level (e.g., vocabulary syntax).

Reader-Based Variables

Research on some reader-based variables (e.g., meta-cognitive and inferencing strategies) in deaf students is virtually non-existent (King & Quigley, 1985; Kretschmer, 1982). Other reader-based variables uniquely attributed to deaf students can be roughly categorized as personal characteristics, communication modes, and internal coding strategies. Obviously these variables are not mutually exclusive. Furthermore, it is probably best to discuss some personal characteristics (e.g., use of hearing aids, speech intelligibility) in the context of communication modes, which is, of course, related to type of educational program and all of these may be inextricably connected to socioeconomic and cultural factors (e.g., education level of deaf students' parents).

Modes of Communication

One of the most enduring issues in the education of deaf students has been termed the manual/oral controversy (Moores, 1982). It should be emphasized that this issue contains two major aspects: type of language and form of communication (Quigley & Kretschmer, 1982). Specifically, there are two languages, American Sign Language and English, and two communication forms, manual and oral. The debate focuses on the form of language and communication that should be used with deaf students in educational programs.

The intent, here, is to discuss the reading comprehension abilities of deaf students exposed to the various communication methods. The two languages and communication forms can be combined to produce a variety of approaches, and these can be categorized into three broad areas: Manually Coded English (MCE), American Sign Language (ASL), and Oral English (OE). In-depth descriptions of the various approaches within these categories can be found elsewhere (Quigley & Kretschmer, 1982; Quigley & Paul, 1984b). In essence, it is shown that the poor reading skills of most deaf students are inextricably related to their inadequate primary English language development.

Manually Coded English. In recent years, a number of morphologically-based sign systems have been developed for the purpose of teaching English literacy skills, that is, reading and writing. The creators of these systems employed ASL-like signs, contrived sign markers, and for some uses, finger spelling, to represent the structure of standard English in a manual manner. The selection of the various manual signs and markers varies according to the arbitrary rules assigned to the systems. The representation of the approaches to the grammar of English has been discussed in detail by Quigley and Paul (1984b). In relation to their viewpoint, the effects of the MCE approaches are presented in the order of their placement on a continuum ranging from least representative to most representative of English.

1. *Pidgin Sign English (PSE).* In the early 1970s, PSE was referred to as American Sign English (Ameslish), Sign English (Siglish), Manual English, and simultaneous communication (Quigley & Paul, 1984b). The effects of PSE on secondary English language development have not been explored extensively. The dearth of research findings may be due, in part, to the difficulty of providing an operational definition of PSE to ascertain which educational programs are actually employing this method. The two studies discussed here, however, do provide some insights as long as the reader keeps in mind what is meant by PSE.

Brasel and Quigley (1977) studied deaf students who were assigned to one of four communication groups: Manual English (i.e., PSE), Average Manual (AM), Intensive Oral (IO), and Average Oral (AO). The Manual English (ME) students were reported to be using signs and some inflectional sign markers in an English word order. The oral groups were established in relation to the type of oral training the students received in the home and school environments. The parents of the students in the manual groups were deaf whereas those of the oral groups had normal hearing.

Analyzing the scores on certain language-related tests, it was found that, on the whole, the two manual groups performed better than the two oral groups. In addition the ME (PSE) group performed significantly better than all other groups. The reading level of the ME group was approximately 6.2 grades, and this was nearly two grades higher than the AM and IO groups.

The benefits of using simultaneous communication (i.e., speaking and signing in an English word order) has also been reported by the more recent work of Delaney, Stuckless, and Walter (1984). They investigated the educational achievement and communication skills (e.g., speech reading) of students in a school which was gradually adopting a Total Communication (TC) philosophy. Three groups of students were established: one was exposed to Aural/Oral (A/O) only, one to Aural/Oral and then to TC, and one to TC methods only (i.e., the use of simultaneous communication). The results indicated that the TC group obtained the highest scores, followed by the group exposed to A/O and TC and the one exposed to A/O only. The mean reading grade level of the TC was nearly equivalent to the ME group in the Brasel and Quigley (1977) study. More importantly, Delaney et al. suggested that the higher achievement of the TC group may not be due only to the use of TC (this is interpreted to mean the use of simultaneous communication). They proffered other suspected factors discussed previously, namely, the increased involvement of parents and school personnel, and improvements in the curriculum.

2. *Signed English (SE).* Bornstein and his associates have extensively investigated the effects of SE on primary English language development (Bornstein, 1982; Bornstein & Saulnier, 1981; Bornstein, Saulnier, & Hamilton, 1980). A group of hearing impaired (mean = 88 dB) students from residential and day

school programs were followed for approximately 5 years. The results indicated that vocabulary growth was less than one-half the rate reported for hearing children of similar ages, and that the levels of morpho-syntactic expressive abilities were equivalent to average normal-hearing children at 3 to 4 years old. At the conclusion of the longitudinal study, it was reported that the 10-year-old students were producing only half of the 14 sign markers which exist in this system. The effects of SE on the development of English literacy skills have not been investigated.

3. Signing Exact English (SEE II). This system has been heavily promoted (Gustason, 1983; Gustason, Pfetzing, & Zawolkow, 1980), yet only one study was found which evaluated its effects on secondary English language development. Babb (1979) studied deaf students, half of whom were exposed to SEE II in the home and school environments and half in the school environment only. He reported that the students exposed to SEE II in the home and in school performed significantly better than the group whose exposure to SEE II was in school only. It was also noted that the former group did as well as the Manual English (i.e., PSE) group in the Brasel and Quigley (1977) study (and as well as the TC group in the Delaney et al. study). The SAT scores of the deaf students exposed to SEE II in the school only were no better than the national norms reported for hearing-impaired students (Di Francesca, 1972).

4. Seeing Essential English (SEE I). Seeing Essential English has been investigated by Raffin and his collaborators (Gilman, Davis, & Raffin, 1980; Raffin, 1976; Raffin, Davis, & Gilman, 1978). The focus was on deaf students' comprehension of eight of the most common English morphemes on a morphology test administered in SEE I. In general, the results of these studies indicated that deaf students, ages 5 to 12 years, acquire these morphemes in nearly the same order, albeit at a slower rate, as that reported by hearing children in Brown's study (1973). In addition, the researchers noted that the receptive and expressive uses of the morphemes were influenced by the ability of teachers to use them consistently. The latter finding is important in light of the finding by several investigators that some teachers do not consistently express the sign markers of certain systems while speaking and signing simultaneously (Kluwin, 1981; Marmor & Pettito, 1979; Reich & Bick, 1977).

5. Finger Spelling. In the 1950s and 1960s, the Rochester Method (i.e., simultaneous use of finger spelling and speech) was used widely (Quigley, 1969); however, by the late 1970s, it was present only in a few educational programs, particularly at the junior high and high school level (Jordan, Gustason, & Rosen, 1979). Quigley (1969) studied the effects of this approach on deaf students' language and reading abilities for approximately 5 years. He reported that the students exposed to the Rochester Method had significantly higher reading and language levels than those exposed to other methods of instruction.

Later studies centered on the processing of print and finger spelling by deaf students. Stuckless and Pollard (1977) found that the ability to process was related to English competence level and that print was easier than finger spelling for the college-age deaf students. Looney and Rose (1979), on the other hand, concluded that both finger spelling and print can be used to teach morphological structures of English. Due to its diminishing use, there have been no further investigations of the reading abilities of deaf students exposed to the Rochester Method since the work of Quigley (1969).

6. Summation. Despite 15 years or more of use, little research has been conducted and little educational success has been reported for most deaf students through the use of the various MCE approaches. While it has been found that certain aspects of English grammar, notably morphology, can be taught, the rate of acquisition becomes slower in the later years. Knowledge of English morphology, obviously, is not enough to develop adequate reading skills. Several studies have indicated other factors of importance such as active involvement of parents and teachers, improved curricula, and the presence of verbal primary language skills in the target language upon which the secondary language forms are based. Finally, it is difficult to evaluate the merits of approaches most representative of English (e.g., SEE I, SEE II) since many practitioners may not adhere to the rules for expressing the manual aspects of these approaches.

American Sign Language. As a language, American Sign Language (ASL) is different from English in two important ways: form and grammar (Lane & Grosjean, 1980; Wilbur, 1979). In relation to form, English is a *spoken* language whereas ASL is a *signed* language expressed without the accompaniment of speech. While the grammar of ASL has been influenced somewhat by English, it is, nevertheless, *not derived* from English. In addition, it must be emphasized that ASL is also different from the contrived MCE codes which were designed to reflect the morpho-syntactic structure of English. Even though the lexicon of American Sign Language forms the basis for most of the signed codes, the use of ASL-like signs in the syntax of English *is not* ASL since the meanings of the signs may not reflect their original meanings in the context of ASL (Stokoe, 1975; Wilbur, 1979). Thus, deaf children for whom ASL is a first language should probably be taught English in a bilingual or second-language situation (Quigley & Paul, 1984a).

To assess the effects of knowing ASL as a first language on the acquisition of English literacy skills, most of the early investigations employed the paradigm of comparing deaf students of deaf parents (*dsdp*) to deaf students of hearing parents (*dshp*). On measures of overall academic achievement, intelligence, psychosocial development, reading, vocabulary, written language, speech reading, finger spelling, and signing abilities, the consistent finding was that *dsdp* were significantly superior to *dshp* (Balow & Brill, 1975; Meadow, 1968; Quigley & Frisina, 1961; Stuckless & Birch, 1966). In some cases, the mean reading level was nearly two grades higher. Even having only one deaf parent was enough to produce certain advantages on English psychoeducational measurements. These advantages were said to be the result of early exposure to manual communication which, in retrospect, referred to American Sign Language, and to parental acceptance which was supposedly higher in *dsdp*.

The two factors, parental acceptance and type of manual communication, have been further investigated. Parental acceptance is essential for academic success in school; however, it is not limited to deaf students of *signing* deaf parents. It can be found in home environments where deaf parents used *speech* with their deaf children and in *dshp* (Corson, 1973; Messerly & Aram, 1980). In relation to type of manual communication, the work of Brasel and Quigley (1977) discussed previously has substantiated its importance. Given the findings of several studies (e.g., Babb, 1979; Delaney et al., 1984), it is still equivocal as to the manner in which English should be (if at all) represented manually. It should be clear, however, that the ability to read is not dependent on one, all-encompassing factor such as manual communication *in any form*. As discussed in the next section, one extremely important factor appears to be well-developed verbal primary English language skills.

Oral English. To evaluate the effects of oral English on English secondary language development, care must be exercised in the selection of studies. The deaf students in these studies should be those who have been exposed *primarily* to an oral approach, particularly in a highly structured, comprehensive oral program, for example, Central Institute for the Deaf (CID), or in integrated regular education programs. Within these restrictions, it is safe to conclude that very few deaf students are exposed to these approaches (Quigley & Paul, 1984b). In general, it is shown that the oral English approaches have been successful mainly with deaf students with select characteristics, for example, those reared in high SES home environments (Ogden, 1979). In relation to the paucity of data, however, there is still a need for "well-documented research, demonstrating the value and need for oral methods" (Lane, 1976b, p. 137).

Lane and Baker (1974) compared the reading comprehension scores of former students of Central Institute for the Deaf (CID) with those in the Wrightstone, Aronow, and Moskowitz study (1963) reported by Furth (1966), and with those in the Vernon and Koh study (1970). It was found that the reading achievement level of the former students was higher than that reported by the other studies for comparison, including the one with a group of oral students (Vernon & Koh, 1970). More importantly, the graph of the growth in reading depicted a continuous upward trend with no evidence of asymptote or a plateau.

In another study, Doehring, Bonnycastle, and Ling (1978) evaluated the language and reading abilities of hearing-impaired students integrated in regular education classrooms. The results indicated that the deaf students performed below grade level on most of the language-related measures; however, the poor scores were argued to be an artifact of the inappropriate tasks. In relation to reading, the students were on or above grade level when compared to normal-hearing peers.

Pflaster (1980) conducted a factor-analytic study to determine the factors most conducive to high levels of language and reading achievement in hearing-impaired students in integrated classrooms. Most of the students were in the severe and profound impairment categories. Three major categorical groups of factors were identified, namely, personality, linguistic competence, and oral communication skills. The latter group was considered to be most influential, and this has been supported by other studies of oral deaf students (Lane, 1976a; Ogden, 1979; Reich, Hambleton, & Houldin, 1977).

Internal Coding Strategies

Another perspective on the language and reading difficulties of deaf students has been provided by the research on the nature of their internal mediating systems. It is suspected that a relationship exists between internal coding strategies and reading comprehension abilities (e.g., Conrad, 1979). It appears that normal-hearing children develop an internal representation of the spoken language to which they are typically exposed. This internalized, primary language representation is used for cognitive activities such as memory and inferencing tasks, and these also play a role in secondary language development.

In relation to reading, a phonological or speech-based recoding strategy appears to be of importance for facilitating the process of proceeding from print to meaning. It seems that speech-based codes and print share cross-modal properties. Thus, a reader is able to proceed from speech to print and vice versa. In addition, the use of speech-based codes has been shown to be related to working memory capacity which, in turn, may affect the understanding of hierarchical, temporal-sequential information in reading materials (Conrad, 1979; Lake, 1980; Lichtenstein, 1984). There is evidence that when hearing children *begin to read*, they shift from visual to phonological processing (Ehri & Wilce, 1985).

With respect to deaf students, it may be that the nature of their internal language is determined, to a certain extent, by the mode of communication to which they have been exposed in infancy and early childhood. Based on error and memory analyses, it has been reported that most students employ a nonspeech-based code, for example, sign (Odom, Blanton, & McIntyre, 1970), visual or graphemic (Blanton, Nunnally, &

Odom, 1967), and dactylic or finger spelling (Locke, 1978). The relationship of nonspeech-based codes to print is not well understood.

Not all deaf students rely on a nonspeech-based code. An extensive study of the use of an internal speech code by deaf students has been undertaken by Conrad (see the review in Conrad, 1979). He showed that internal speech is strongly related to external intelligible speech; however, it was present in some deaf students with unintelligible speech. What is of importance is not necessarily the intelligibility of external speech but the discrimination ability of the internal speech-based code *to the user*.

One of the most important findings of Conrad's work is that the use of internal speech is related to reading ability. This notion was discussed earlier with respect to normally-hearing readers. Conrad found that good deaf readers predominantly employ a speech-based code in mediating print. The superiority of speech recoders over visual or sign recoders is attributed to the more efficient representation of English grammatical structures in working memory capacity. This representation makes it easier to decode nonlinear grammatical structures such as medial relative clauses and the use of the passive voice (Lake, 1980; Lichtenstein, 1984).

It can be inferred from the foregoing discussion that speech recoding is essential to the development of reading for both hearing and deaf students. Yet, the available evidence suggests that the majority of deaf students seem to encode print most effectively either visually and/or in sign. In view of this, it may be that new instructional methods must be developed in order to improve the reading comprehension ability of these students. Or, as Quigley and Paul (1984b) have remarked: "It might also signify that means other than reading should be sought for imparting information to some types of deaf children" (p. 50).

Socioeconomic and Cultural Factors

The effects of socioeconomic and cultural factors on the development of the ability to read and write have been documented for hearing students (e.g., Anderson, 1981) and for deaf students (e.g., Ogden, 1979; Trybus, 1978). A series of investigations by the Center for Assessment and Demographic Studies (discussed previously) uncovered several complex factors significantly related to academic achievement; for example, hearing threshold level and socioeconomic status (Jensema, 1975; Trybus, 1975, 1978). These were found to be inextricably related to others such as speech intelligibility, use of hearing aids, and type of education program. The accumulative benefits of the complex interaction of high SES and other associative factors were highlighted in an extensive study by Ogden (1979). He collected and analyzed demographic information on former students of CID, Clarke School for the Deaf, and St Joseph's Institute for the Deaf. These former deaf students were

found to be highly successful in terms of academic and vocational status.

Written Language

Research on written language and its relationship to reading is attracting the attention of researchers studying normally-hearing children (Tierney & Leys, 1984). Evidence is accruing to suggest that reading and writing are interrelated. Tierney and Leys (1984) have remarked that when students perform one activity, they often engage in the other. In addition, it has been shown that the writing styles of students are affected by the content of their reading materials. For example, reading materials with stilted language tended to engender writing that was also stilted in grammar and format. This is probably true even for deaf students; However, it may be that their stilted, simple written language is influenced also by their limited understanding of complex sentential structures (Quigley et al., 1976) and/or by their educational exposure to stilted, metalinguistic systems (Wilbur, 1977).

Assessment

A variety of procedures have been developed for eliciting and evaluating the writings of deaf students. Typically, the students are exposed to some external, visual stimulus such as a picture, a sequence of pictures, or a film presentation. Then, they are requested to write a short story or a letter regarding the stimulus. Finally, their written productions are analyzed with respect to types of errors produced, types and number of words or structures used, and length and complexity of sentences.

Several criticisms have been made regarding the merits of these techniques (Bloom & Lahey, 1978; Kretschmer & Kretschmer, 1978; Quigley et al., 1976). There is the problem of a lack of standardization in the language-eliciting process mainly due to the issues of validity and reliability. In addition, the contents of the written language samples raise some concerns. Specifically, if the grammatical items under study are not present in the productions, there is difficulty in determining whether this is due to a lack of competency or limitations of the eliciting procedures. It is also extremely difficult to obtain an adequate sample of some of the more complex linguistic constructions (e.g., relative clauses) that would permit an accurate analysis. Even when these complex constructions are produced, they usually appear in sentences which are unintelligible, making it difficult to interpret the construction of the sentence. Despite these shortcomings, it is still possible and useful to depict the typical deaf student's command of written English.

Integration of Research

Since the skills of writing and reading are interrelated, it is not surprising that the research on the written language of deaf students reveals the same low level of achievement as that of their reading comprehension ability. It has been argued that the ability to write is generally contingent on the ability to read which, in turn, depends on the adequate development of a primary language form upon which both reading and writing are based (Quigley & Kretschmer, 1982). While it is possible to use the written language of hearing students to teach them to read (Tierney & Leys, 1984), the same may not be true for most deaf students who do not have an adequate internal representation of English. Thus, it is obvious that correlates of the poor written language skills of deaf students are similar to those of their low reading achievement. The studies included here are discussed in relation to the type of elicitation procedure: free or controlled response; and to type of grammatical analyses: traditional, structural, or generative.

Free Response Studies: Traditional/Structural

In these investigations, a sample of the deaf students' writings is elicited in relation to a visual stimulus, and then analyzed with respect to certain selected aspects, namely, sentence complexity, distribution of form classes, and types of errors. The results are typically compared with those of hearing counterparts. There are no attempts to describe a rule-governed system, if any, under which the deaf students are operating. In general, it is found that the written language productions of most deaf students are stereotypic and on a level similar to young hearing students.

Heider and Heider (1940) found that the proportional use of subordinate clauses, compound, and complex sentences by the 17-year-old deaf student was similar to that of the 10-year-old hearing student. While the deaf students increased their production of complex structures across age, their use of these structures was still limited. This developmental delay pattern was not observed for the total number of words produced; however, the mean sentence length of the 17-year-old deaf student was equivalent to that of the 8-year-old hearing student.

Similar findings were documented by Simmons (1962) and Myklebust (1964). These investigators asserted also that the written productions of deaf students could be classified as rigid or stereotypic. Certain constructions or sentences were found to appear frequently, for example, *They had an idea, I see a ———, and There is a ———*. The prevalence of these phrases has been attributed to the use of formal instructional methods in which deaf students are required to place words in certain categories (van Uden, 1977; Wilbur, 1977).

Free Response Studies: Generative Grammar

The thinking of Chomsky (1957, 1965) had a tremendous impact on the subsequent analyses of language productions. In Chomsky's view, language is generative; that is, the user has an intuitive knowledge of a limited set of rules necessary for producing and comprehending an infinite number of sentences. In other words, language is generated by a set of rules (i.e., grammar) which can be described in developmental stages within the framework of transformational generative grammar. The extensive investigations of Taylor (1969) and Quigley et al. (1976) are representative of the attempts to describe the language productions of deaf students in relation to a specific rule-governed system.

Taylor (1969) analyzed the errors in the written language samples of deaf students, age 10 to 16 years, at four grade levels. The errors can be discussed in relation to four categories: phrase structure, lexical, morphological, and transformational rules. A more detailed description of the categories can be found in Russell, Quigley, and Power (1976).

In relation to phrase structure rules, three general types of errors were found: omissions, redundancy, and order (relatively infrequent). The most frequent omission error was determiners (e.g., *a, an, the, any*), followed by prepositions, direct objects, and verbs. Except for direct object, the frequency of the omissions decreased with age. It was reported also that deaf students tended to use prepositions in a redundant manner more than any other structure, and this type of error did not decrease much with age. More importantly, analyzing all errors in relation to prepositions, Taylor found that the developmental stages of the deaf students resembled those of younger hearing children (e.g., Cazden, 1968).

In analyzing the vocabulary (lexicon) of deaf students, Taylor experienced much difficulty in classifying the errors. She found very few errors which could be clearly identified as, for example, selectional restriction errors. Those that were discernible were related to the count (e.g., *a water*) and plural (e.g., *a pliers*) features. As with the use of prepositions, very little improvement was noted within the age range studied.

The pattern of quantitative reductions and qualitative similarities was also found in the analyses of errors related to morphological rules. Verb morphological inflections proved to be the most difficult with deaf students either omitting, overgeneralizing, or inappropriately using the endings. Next, in order of difficulty, was the plural inflections, and then the possessive inflections which were manifested in redundancy or omission errors.

The application of rules in three major types of transformations was also investigated: conjunctions, nominalization, and relative clauses. The data were limited since very few complex structures appear in the written language of deaf students. The most frequently attempted transformation was conjunction. Taylor reported that deaf students committed errors of omission (*A ant see a tree or bird*) or of location (*The dove got out of the tree and took a leaf threw it down*). The students also experienced difficulty in the application of deletion rules (*The hunter scared the dove and flew away; The ant threw a ball on the ground and put in his room*). These phenomena were documented by the work of Quigley et al. (1976), and are labelled as object-subject and object-object deletions respectively.

With respect to the other two transformations, very limited data were available for error analyses. This was not attributed to deaf students' mastery of the structures, but rather to their infrequent ability to produce them. For nominalization, Taylor found problems with gerunds (*The man began screamed*) and infinitives (*The ant held the thing look like circle*) and copying (*There was a little hole underground which a smart ant lived in it*). Basically, in copying, there is a failure to move the relative pronoun to the beginning of the embedded clause.

Taylor's research is elaborated here mainly because of the attempts to describe the rule violations by deaf students, rather than cataloging them. This procedure represented a major shift from previous investigations. The general results of her investigation revealed that deaf students have mastery over many aspects of the overall simple active declarative sentence structure, particularly in the subject-verb-object format; yet produce many errors in morphology and specific syntactic structures. In addition, very few examples of complex structures were found in the writings of deaf students, and those that did appear were used erroneously.

These findings were also documented in the analyses of written language samples by Quigley and his collaborators (Quigley et al., 1976). Similar to other investigations, only limited examples of the specific structures studied on the Test of Syntactic Abilities (TSA; Quigley, Steinkamp, Power, & Jones, 1978) appeared in the written productions of deaf students. Nevertheless, there was a great deal of similarity between the students' comprehension of the structures on the TSA and their use of them in their written language.

For example, the subtest Negation proved to be the easiest of the structures investigated. Likewise, analyses of the written productions revealed that deaf students appear to have good control over this structure. A similar trend was found for the verb structures which were difficult. On the TSA, the easiest form was the present progressive, followed by perfectives and passives. In the writings, again, the most commonly correctly used structure was the present progressive, then the perfective, and finally, the passive.

Quigley and his associates also conducted additional in-depth analyses of the structures and were able to identify specific problems as well as, in an indirect manner, developmental stages. In general, these stages were similar to those observed for younger hearing students. For example, in relation to the type and position of relative clauses, it was reported that deaf students produced more subject-relative than object-relative pronouns and more final position than medial position relative clauses. Using Question Formation as another example, yes/no questions were more commonly used than Wh-questions (e.g., You ate the cookie, didn't you?) Only one instance of a tag question, produced by a deaf 16-year-old, was located in the entire written language sample. Finally, in relation to the use of complements, it was found that the most commonly written complement was *for-to* (e.g., It is time for John to go) followed by *that* complements (e.g., It is obvious that she is happy), with only a few *POSS-ing* complements (e.g., Harry's driving of the car). A more detailed description of these findings can be found in Quigley et al. (1976).

Controlled Response Studies: Generative Grammar

In controlled response studies the appropriate behavior or response of the subjects is manipulated or controlled by the contents of a test instrument which holds certain variables constant. An example would be to present a pair of sentences which differ on one linguistic unit (e.g., word or structure), and require the subjects to make judgments of grammaticality. These studies are presented with respect to the format used for discussing free response investigations: phrase structure, the lexicon, and transformation.

In relation to phrase structure rules, the work of O'Neill (1973) is illustrative. She constructed a Test of Receptive Language Competence with four categories previously discussed: omission, order, redundancy, and selectional restriction. The deaf students, age 9 to 17 years, were required to judge the grammaticality of sentences generated by correct or incorrect rules in each category. The order of difficulty from easiest to most difficult was: order, omission, redundancy, and selectional restriction. In all categories, the deaf students performed equally as well as the hearing students on selecting the grammatical sentence as 'right'; however, they also labelled the ungrammatical sentence as "right" more than the hearing students. The acceptance of the ungrammatical structures was related to the type of words used in error. The ungrammatical sentences were more likely to be accepted as correct when function words (determiners, prepositions) were incorrectly omitted or used redundantly than when context words (nouns, verbs, adjectives) were similarly used incorrectly. This result is similar to that reported by Taylor (1969) using free response procedures.

In the area of vocabulary development (lexicon), the investigations of O'Neill (1973) and Cooper (1967) are of relevance. As discussed earlier, the most difficult subtest of O'Neill's instrument was the one assessing the students' knowledge of selectional restriction rules. The deaf, as well as hearing, students had difficulty with sentences which violated certain rules; for example, the features of count (*Milk are good for one year*) and animateness (*The desk serenaded Matilda*). Similar to Taylor's results, the scores of the students did not improve much with age.

Cooper (1967) employed Berko's (1958) procedures for assessing deaf students' receptive and productive knowledge of morphological rules. While the scores of the deaf students did improve somewhat with age (up to 19 years), their overall performance was extremely poor. In addition, it was found that the students' knowledge of inflectional morphemes (e.g., verb and noun singular/plural markings) was better than their knowledge of derivational markers (e.g., *-ly* adverb ending, *-ness* noun ending). Again, these findings are in agreement with, and even extend, these reported by Taylor.

The problems of deaf students with transformational rules have been highlighted earlier. The few investigations discussed here also depicted difficulties in certain structures, namely negation and passive voice. Schmitt (1969) assessed deaf students' comprehension and production of negation. In general, as corroborated by Quigley et al. (1976), the students in the 11- to 17-year-old range had little difficulty comprehending the meaning of the negative marker *not* in English sentences. The 8-year-old students, on the other hand, performed so poorly that Schmitt hypothesized they were using a *no negative rule* which meant ignoring the negative marker and treating negative and affirmative sentences as similar.

In another study, Power and Quigley (1973) evaluated deaf students' comprehension and production of three types of passives: reversible, nonreversible (e.g., *The car was washed by the boy*), and agent deleted (e.g., *The man was killed*). Like other investigations, the findings indicated an order of difficulty and a pattern of errors similar to younger hearing children. Power and Quigley concluded, as have others, that most deaf students operate under a rule-governed system which is not standard English.

In a more recent study, Powers and Wilgus (1983) provided additional support for the developmental delay hypothesis. They reported that the use of complex syntactic structures by their deaf students, age 7 to 12 years, increased across age. Contrary to the findings of Quigley et al. (1976), they found more examples of correct usage of relativization and complementation in their oldest students. Powers and Wilgus, however, remarked "that the size of the sample was limited and that the children included in the study were from upper-middle-class environments with excellent parental involvement, which tends to foster language development" (p. 209).

Discourse Analysis

The studies discussed earlier have shown that the written language of deaf students reveals a lack of command over numerous aspects of the standard rules of English grammar. Most of these analyses were conducted on a sentential or intrasentential level. It may be advanced

that the written language problems of deaf students can be viewed in a better light at the intersentential level (Wilbur, 1977, 1979; Kretschmer & Kretschmer, 1978).

Reanalyzing the data of Quigley et al. (1976) in a pragmatic framework (e.g., old versus new information), Wilbur (1977) found that deaf students encountered greater difficulty using correct syntactic structures on a intersentential level than on a sentential level. This resulted in their written language appearing stilted in style. Wilbur argued that difficulty with syntax beyond the sentential level is due to the students' inability to understand "when and how to use them" (p. 87). She concluded that too much instructional emphasis is placed on helping deaf students understand the proper structure of a single sentence and suggested that syntactic development should be considered in a pragmatic context.

Summary

The situation for written language appears to be similar to that for reading although the lack of standard quantitative measures makes longitudinal comparisons more difficult. The findings of several national investigations have been reported here (Heider & Heider, 1940; Myklebust, 1964; Quigley et al., 1976). The quantitative and qualitative comparisons that can be made on these studies, covering a 40-year span, revealed no changes in the mastery of written English by typical, prelingual deaf students during that period.

Research on Instruction

It is safe to conclude that not much is known regarding the effectiveness of instructional practices and materials for teaching deaf students to read and write English (Clarke, Rogers, & Booth, 1982; King, 1984; King & Quigley, 1985). It may be argued that the research presented in this chapter provides an indirect evaluation of current instructional strategies. Nevertheless, while a variety of approaches have been espoused in polemic writings, very little research is being conducted to assess their merits directly. Clarke, Rogers, and Booth (1982) have asserted that "the current state of instructional methodology is one of confused eclecticism" due to "the remarkable lack of empirical data in this critical area" (p. 65).

Instruction and Reading

In discussing instruction and reading, the following topics are briefly highlighted: (a) the extent of preparation and beliefs of instructors, and (b) the use of instructional approaches and materials. As noted by King and Quigley (1985), much of the information regarding these issues has been provided by survey studies. Very little data can be gleaned from other types of studies, for example, observational and experimental. In addition, not much is known concerning the strategies and beliefs of deaf readers. A more extensive treatment of these topics can be found in King and Quigley (1985).

Preparation and Beliefs of Instructors

Information regarding teacher preparation has been reported by Coley and Bockmiller (1980). They reported that approximately 20% of teachers of deaf students had only one or no courses in reading. Since the respondents were those responsible for teaching reading to deaf students, it is possible that higher percentages would have been found if a sample of all teachers of hearing-impaired students was investigated. It is apparent that many teachers of hearing-impaired students are not adequately trained to teach reading.

Data concerning teachers' beliefs about beginning reading instruction can be found in a survey study by Lanfrey (cited in King & Quigley, 1985, chap. 4). It was reported that most teachers preferred meaning-emphasis, rather than code-emphasis, approaches. The teachers were divided on the issue of using top-down or bottom-up approaches to reading. This is also the case for reading teachers of normally-hearing students. Since evidence is accruing to support the notion that reading is a complex, interactive process, it is important to employ both top-down and bottom-up approaches.

Use of Approaches and Materials

LaSasso (1978, 1985) reported on the major instructional approaches and materials used with hearing-impaired students at four instructional levels, that is, primary, intermediate, junior and senior high schools. She examined further whether these approaches were employed in a primary or supplementary manner. It was found that the most common approaches were the language experience approach and basal readers. In the 1985 survey, the language experience approach was reported to be predominantly used at the primary level. Overall, basal readers were used the most and were present in the programs of more than 60% of respondents at the primary, intermediate, and junior high levels.

In relation to basal readers, LaSasso (1985) reported that nearly half of the programs were using *Reading Milestones* (Quigley & King, 1981, 1982, 1983, 1984). This series was used more than the next two basal readers combined (i.e., Houghton-Mifflin and Ginn 360/Ginn 720). It was present in nearly one-third of the programs of those responding at the primary, intermediate, and junior high school levels and in one-fourth of the programs at the senior high level. Furthermore, a large majority of respondents reported to be satisfied (very and moderately) with the series and with its use of the technique of chunking (e.g., *The boy   sat on the wall*). In addition, three-fourths of the respondents stated the major reason for adopting *Reading Milestones* was that it was developed for deaf readers. Nearly half

also remarked that they were not satisfied with other series (respondents could select more than one answer).

The issue of developing and using special reading materials has been discussed in detail by King and Quigley (1985). Typically, special materials are constructed for students with great difficulties in learning to read. Three general approaches have been undertaken: (a) existing materials have been rewritten to a simpler level, (b) instructional strategies used with existing materials have been modified, and (c) special, original materials have been developed. While the use of special materials is surrounded by controversies, it should be remembered that the ultimate goal is to enable the problem reader to utilize eventually the regular, existing materials at some particular stage (Quigley & King, 1981, 1982, 1983, 1984).

The effects of special or adapted materials on the reading comprehension of deaf students have not been extensively investigated (Heine, 1981). A few studies have been conducted in the area of television and film captions (e.g., Braverman, 1981; Braverman, Harrison, Bowker, & Hertzog, 1981), and the results are, at best, equivocal. In relation to special reading materials, Heine (1981) used stories from *Reading Milestones* to explore the effects of higher order and lower order ideas on the reading comprehension ability of deaf students. While no significant differences were found between higher and lower order ideas, Heine did observe that the performances of the deaf students were equal or superior to those of a comparison group of hearing students on comprehension of literal information in the stories. This seems to support the contention that linguistically controlled readers have some beneficial effects on the reading comprehension ability of deaf students.

In sum, much of the information available focused on descriptions of approaches and materials used in teaching reading (King & Quigley, 1985). Not much is known regarding other important issues such as instructional strategies, techniques, organization, time devoted to reading, and the beliefs, strategies, habits, and interests of deaf readers. King and Quigley (1985) analyzed the few studies utilizing instructional techniques and concluded that the merits of these techniques have not been empirically demonstrated.

Instruction and Written Language

Prior to the fairly recent research on communication approaches, much of the research on the language of deaf students was conducted on their written language (Quigley & Paul, 1984b). It is safe to remark that writing and reading are considered major components of the various "how to" materials for teaching language to deaf students (e.g., Anderson, Boren, Caniglia, Howard, & Krohn, 1972; Blackwell, Engen, Fischgrund, & Zarcadoolas, 1978; Groht, 1958; van Uden, 1977). In relation to instruction and written language, the following topics are discussed: (a) the type of language approach and (b) the use of metalinguistic systems.

Type of Language Approach

Traditionally, discussion has focused on the merits of two general language approaches: natural and structural. Briefly, proponents of the natural approach are interested in eliciting and developing various idiomatic and colloquial aspects of the English language. This approach does not use metalinguistic, symbol systems to represent certain structures of English (Groht, 1958; van Uden, 1977). Contrariwise, symbol systems are important to the proponents of structural approaches. They are used to teach the grammar of English in which students are required to place words, phrases, or sentences within certain categories in reading and writing exercises (Anderson et al., 1972; Blackwell et al., 1978). A more detailed description of these may be found in Moores (1982) and in Quigley and Paul (1984b). It should be stressed that no data exist which conclusively demonstrate the superiority of natural or structural approaches.

In a national survey, King (1984) examined the philosophies and language approaches of educational programs for deaf students. Approximately 50% of the respondents indicated the existence of a philosophy concerning language instruction. A little more than half also indicated that a written curriculum (i.e., writing) was employed to teach language. King also found that preschool programs classified their language curricula as natural or combined (natural and structural) whereas those for older students (i.e., primary through high school levels) use the terms combined and eclectic (the discretion of the individual teacher). The natural approach was rarely employed by higher level programs. It was also reported that most respondents believed it is better to combine several methods rather than rely exclusively on one method. Further research is still needed, however, to determine which approach or combination of approaches offers the most benefits in terms of improvement in language development.

Use of Metalinguistic Systems

King (1984) also reported that the majority of the programs used some type of symbol system (i.e., metalinguistic techniques) in the teaching of English, and the percentage of use increased across the instructional levels, from more than 50% at the preschool level to nearly 98% at the high school level. The various systems ranged from traditional/structural approaches (e.g., Anderson et al., 1972; Fitzgerald, 1949) and related aspects (i.e., parts of speech and sentence patterns) to those based on transformational generative grammar (e.g., Blackwell et al., 1978). In addition, many programs employed more than one symbol system. King asserted that research is needed to consider the merits of the various metalinguistic systems.

As previously discussed, the stilted written language of deaf students has been attributed to the use of metalinguistic systems, in which the major focus is on a sentence-by-sentence task of writing. Wilbur (1977), discussed previously, argued that the language problems of deaf students should be viewed and taught on a connected discourse rather than sentential level. It seems that a student will encounter problems in writing on a discourse level if there are immense problems at the sentential level. In essence, it is likely that both levels of writing need to be developed.

Conclusions

Summation

Integration of Research

Since the time of Pintner and his collaborators (1916, 1917), it has been demonstrated that the performance of the average 18- or 19-year-old deaf student in reading and writing English is equivalent to that of the average 8- or 9-year-old hearing student. On achievement batteries, it was noted that advancement in language and reading comprehension abilities proceeded at less than one-half grade level per year. In-depth analyses revealed that the reading difficulties of deaf students are attributed to a multiplicity of problems which were discussed in relation to text-based (e.g., syntax) and reader-based (e.g., memory) variables and their interaction. It is felt that viewing reading in this framework offers the best route to take in conducting research to solve problems.

In relation to written language, deaf students do not have an adequate command of the numerous aspects of the rules of standard English grammar, particularly in the areas of morphology and syntactic structures. It was difficult to collect data on the more complex structures since deaf students rarely produced them in their writings. Even though some of the errors were difficult to catalogue, it was concluded that most deaf students operated under a rule-governed system which was not that of standard English. For example, the use of a subject-verb-object strategy persisted even into the advanced secondary-level age causing problems with some structures which require an hierarchical rather than linear interpretation (e.g., relative clauses, passive voice). The more recent studies in this area are representative of a trend toward describing the errors with respect to some rule system. This should be promising for developing more effective instructional strategies and materials than the previous practice of just listing the errors. There is also a need for a standardized assessment of written language.

It should be emphasized that exceptions to the usual low language and reading achievement levels have been those deaf students in comprehensive, intensively-oriented, private oral programs; those integrated in regular education programs; and those in well-organized Total Communication programs. Some of these students have performed on grade level or better when compared to their hearing counterparts. Most of these deaf students, however, are more select in IQ and SES, and these factors are inextricably related positively to adequate oral communication skills, the exploitation of residual hearing, and well-educated and involved parents. Also of importance are highly-trained, dedicated instructors and administrators, and well-developed educational programs.

Another perspective on the reading and written language difficulties of deaf students has been provided by the research on internal coding strategies. It appears that deaf readers who mediate primarily with a speech-based code to access meaning from print read better than those who rely heavily on nonspeech codes. The advantages of the phonological recoders may be due to their ability to hold in short-term memory certain important, temporal-sequential verbal linguistic units necessary for comprehending hierarchical structures (e.g., relative clauses, passives). This ability may also be necessary for a high level of development in written language. The importance of a speech-based encoding strategy to reading and writing skills seems to emphasize the view that secondary language development is superimposed on the auditory-oral experiences present in the internalized primary language of the student.

Instruction

Owing to meager empirical data, there is not much to conclude regarding the effectiveness of instructional practices and materials in teaching English literacy skills. Despite the preponderance of commercially available materials, little ongoing research is being conducted to assess their merits. It appears that the use of practices and materials has been perpetuated mainly by polemical arguments.

In relation to instruction and reading development, much of what is known has been reported in survey investigations. The results indicated that many instructors of hearing-impaired students have taken few university courses in reading, and thus are not adequately trained in this area. It was also reported that many teachers were divided on the issue of what approaches to use in teaching reading.

The findings of survey studies have indicated also that the two most common instructional programs employed with hearing-impaired students are the language experience approach and basal readers. The most commonly used basal reader was reported to be *Reading Milestones*. Most of the educational programs responding were satisfied with the series and with its use of the chunking technique. One study on the merit of *Reading Milestones* has been conducted, and the results, while limited, still revealed beneficial effects on deaf students' comprehension of literal information in the stories.

There is even less information available regarding instruction and written language development. Historically, there have been two general approaches to language instruction: natural and structural. Some educational programs employed a combination of these approaches whereas others preferred an eclectic approach. In several of these methods, reading and written curricula are used to teach English. Despite their uses, the superiority of either general approach or their combinations has not been empirically demonstrated.

The findings of a national survey revealed that most preschool programs are likely to use natural or combined approaches whereas the others prefer combined and eclectic approaches. In addition, most educational programs combined several methods rather than utilizing one exclusively. It was reported also that a majority of the programs employed some type of metalinguistic symbol system. This use increased across instructional levels, and nearly all high schools responding utilized some aspects of a symbol system in their programs. As with reading approaches and materials, there is a great need for research to assess the merits of the various metalinguistic systems in teaching English.

Implications

In this section, the discussion focuses on two general topics: areas for further research and needs of personnel preparation programs. In the field of deafness, much can be written regarding recommendations for future studies. A synopsis of these recommendations is presented in relation to theory and research concerning basic processes, and research on instruction. Since the authors believe that there is (or should be) a strong inter-relationship among theory, research, and practice, the needs of personnel preparation programs are considered within this conceptual framework.

Areas for Further Research

Much of our knowledge of reading and written language comprehension has come from theory and research concerning the basic processes in these areas. The framework in which these processes are examined have resulted in new theoretical formulations, and subsequently, the reanalyses of reading and written language abilities. It is safe to conclude that most of the research on the language comprehension abilities of deaf students has been conducted on an intrasentential or a sentential level. There is a pressing need to examine these abilities on an intersentential or connected discourse level. It is likely that such endeavors may yield additional information regarding deaf students' difficulties with certain factors discussed in this paper, namely, word knowledge, syntax, and figurative language.

Since reading and writing may be interrelated, it is possible to state that both involve the interaction of bottom-up (text-based) and top-down (reader-based) processes. Research on this interactive process in deaf students is extremely limited. Investigations should focus on, for example, metacognitive or inferencing processes, that is, the manner in which deaf readers use strategies for comprehension or memory. Owing to the importance of prior knowledge to reading comprehension in hearing students, this relationship should be examined also in deaf students to determine the aspects of printed materials that are remembered. In essence, research paradigms may be obtained from those used with hearing students; however, these models may need to be modified or adapted due to the specific characteristics of deaf readers.

Perhaps the most pressing research need is ascertaining the relationship of communication modes and coding strategies to the development of English literacy skills. This is of importance if it is accepted that reading and writing, as secondary language forms, are superimposed on the primary language form via an auditory-oral, recoding process. Indeed, it appears that existing reading techniques assume the presence of an auditory language which is lacking in most deaf students. It has been shown that most deaf students employ nonspeech-based codes which are inextricably related to their exposure to one or more modes of communication. Thus, the manner in which spoken secondary language forms can be superimposed on nonspeech-based, primary language forms needs to be investigated.

Contrary to the increase in knowledge on basic processes, not much is known on how to teach English literacy skills to deaf students, and very little is being done to investigate this matter. In general, survey studies have indicated some of the various instructional approaches and materials that are being utilized in classroom settings. Observational and experimental studies should be conducted to determine their effects on various aspects of reading and writing.

In addition, the amount of time devoted to the various approaches and materials, their organization, and the manner in which they are used should be explored. For example, in relation to metalinguistic symbol systems, deaf students' ability to place words, phrases, and sentences within certain categories should be documented. Obviously, research is necessary to determine what types or combinations of metalinguistic instruction are effective. The merits of utilizing special materials should be investigated.

Finally, as the various areas are being studied, it is imperative for researchers to provide complete descriptions of their samples. At the least, certain important characteristics of subjects discussed previously need to be reported, for example, degree and age at onset of hearing impairments, presence of additional handicaps, communication mode, and possibly the nature of the internal coding strategy. It cannot be overstressed that much of the conflicting data is due to the generalization of findings to dissimilar groups of hearing-impaired students.

Personnel Preparation Programs

It is recommended that teacher training programs receive more theoretically based preparation in English literacy skills. The results of survey investigations indicate that instructors of deaf students are not adequately prepared to teach reading. Given the importance of this skill, it appears that prospective teachers need more training in theory and practice in the area of reading at the university level. A well-balanced program in reading should be complemented by one in language development. If reading is viewed as part of the overall language comprehension process, then it is clear that *part* of deaf students' difficulty with the reading process is attributable to inadequate development in language. It appears superfluous to remark that a good instructor of language and reading needs to know as much about these subjects as, say, a physics teacher knows about physics. This entails, at the very least, a strong background in theory as well as a familiarity with a panorama of instructional strategies.

A familiarity with various instructional practices is the best that can be suggested here in light of limited empirical research. Instructional methods which have been proven successful with normally-hearing students should be explored with deaf students. it is also beneficial for trainee teachers to become aware of those methods, based on current thinking on linguistics and reading, that have been developed for other language-impaired student populations. In addition, owing to the lack of conclusive findings, trainee teachers should not perceive the use of the various approaches as either-or situations; that is, natural *or* structural, bottom-up *or* top-down. Finally, prospective teachers should receive adequate training in assessment and research methodology so that they can participate in evaluating the merits of their practices.

References

Adams, M. (1980). Failures to comprehend and levels of processing in reading. In R. Spiro, B. Bruce, & W. Brewer (Eds.), *Theoretical issues in reading comprehension: Perspectives from cognitive psychology, linguistics, artificial intelligence, and education* (pp. 11–32). Hillsdale, NJ: Erlbaum.

Allen, T. (1986). Patterns of academic achievement among hearing-impaired students: 1974 and 1983. In A. Schildroth & M. Karchmer (Eds.), *Deaf Children in America* (pp. 161–206). San Diego, CA: College-Hill/Little, Brown.

Allen, T., White, C., & Karchmer, M. (1983). Issues in the development of a special edition for hearing-impaired students of the seventh edition of the Stanford Achievement Test. *American Annals of the Deaf, 128*, 34–39.

Anderson, M., Boren, N., Caniglia, J., Howard, W., & Krohn, E. (1972), *Apple Tree: A patterned program for linguistic expansion through reinforced experiences and evaluation.* Beaverton, OR: Dormac.

Anderson, R. (1981). *A proposal to continue a center for the study of reading.* (Tech. Rep. Vols. 1–4). Champaign: University of Illinois, Center for the Study of Reading.

Anderson, R., & Freebody, P. (1979). *Vocabulary knowledge.* (Tech. Rep. No. 136). Champaign: University of Illinois, Center for the Study of Reading. (ERIC Document Reproduction Service No. ED 177 480)

Babb, R. (1979). *A study of the academic achievement and language acquisition levels of deaf children of hearing parents in an educational environment using Signing Exact English as the primary mode of manual communication.* Unpublished doctoral dissertation, University of Illinois, Urbana-Champaign.

Babbini, B., & Quigley, S. (1970). *A study of the growth patterns in language, communication, and educational achievement is six residential schools for deaf students.* Urbana: University of Illinois. (ERIC Document Reproduction Service No. ED 046 208)

Balow, I., & Brill, R. (1975). An evaluation of reading and academic achievement levels of 16 graduating classes of the California School for the Deaf, Riverside. *Volta Review, 77,* 255–266.

Berko, J. (1958). The child's learning of English morphology. *Word, 14,* 150–177.

Blackwell, P., Engen, E., Fischgrund, J., & Zarcadoolas, C. (1978). *Sentences and other systems: A language and learning curriculum for hearing-impaired children.* Washington, DC: Alexander Graham Bell Association for the Deaf.

Blanton, R., Nunnally, J., & Odom, P. (1967). Graphic, phonetic, and associative factors in the verbal behavior of deaf and hearing subjects. *Journal of Speech and Hearing Research, 10,* 225–231.

Bloom, L., & Lahey, M. (1978). *Language development and language disorders.* New York: Wiley.

Boatner, M., & Gates, J. (1969). *A dictionary of idioms for the deaf.* Washington, DC: National Association of the Deaf.

Bornstein, H. (1982). Towards a theory of use for Signed English: From birth through adulthood. *American Annals of the Deaf, 127,* 26–31.

Bornstein, H., & Saulnier, K. (1981). Signed English: A brief follow-up to the first evaluation. *American Annals of the Deaf, 126,* 69–72.

Bornstein, H., Saulnier, K., & Hamilton, L. (1980). Signed English: A first evaluation. *American Annals of the Deaf, 125,* 467–481.

Brasel, K., & Quigley, S. (1977). The influence of certain language and communication environments in early childhood on the development of language in deaf individuals. *Journal of Speech and Hearing Research, 20,* 95–107.

Braverman, B. (1981). Television captioning strategies: A systematic research and development approach. *American Annals of the Deaf, 126,* 1031–1036.

Braverman, B., Harrison, M., Bowker, D., & Hertzog, M. (1981). Effects of language level and visual display on learning from captioned instruction. *Education Communication and Technology, 29,* 147–154.

Brown, R. (1973). *A first language: The early stages.* Cambridge, MA: Harvard University Press.

Cazden, C. (1968). The acquisition of noun and verb inflections. *Child Development, 39,* 433–448.

Chomsky, N. (1957). *Syntactic structures.* The Hague: Mouton.

Chomsky, N. (1965). *Aspects of the theory of syntax.* Cambridge, MA: MIT.

Clarke, B., Rogers, W., & Booth, J. (1982). How hearing-impaired children learn to read: Theoretical and practical issues. In R. E. Kretschmer (Ed.), Reading and the hearing-impaired individual. *Volta Review, 84,* 57–69. [Special Edition].

Coley, J., & Bockmiller, P. (1980). Teaching reading to the deaf: An examination of teacher preparedness and practices. *American Annals of the Deaf, 125,* 909–915.

Conley, J. (1976). Role of idiomatic expressions in the reading of deaf children. *American Annals of the Deaf, 121,* 381–385.

Conrad, R. (1979). *The deaf schoolchild: Language and cognitive function.* London: Harper & Row.

Cooper, R. (1967). The ability of deaf and hearing children to apply morphological rules. *Journal of Speech and Hearing Research, 10,* 77–86.

Cooper, R., & Rosenstein, J. (1966). Language acquisition of deaf children. *Volta Review, 68,* 58–67.

Corson, H. (1973). *Comparing deaf children of oral deaf parents and deaf parents using manual communication with deaf children of hearing parents on academic, social, and communication functioning.* Unpublished doctoral dissertation, University of Cincinnati, OH.

Davis, F. (1944). Fundamental factors of comprehension in reading. *Psychometrika, 9,* 185–197.

Davis, F. (1968). Research in comprehension in reading. *Reading Research Quarterly, 3,* 499–545.

Delaney, M., Stuckless, E. R., & Walter, G. (1984). Total communication effects – A longitudinal study of a school for the deaf in transition. *American Annals of the Deaf, 129,* 481–486.

Di Francesca, S. (1972). *Academic achievement test results of a national testing program for hearing impaired students* (Rep. Series D, No. 9). Washington, DC: Gallaudet College, Office of Demographic Studies.

Dixon, K., Pearson, P. D., & Ortony, A. (1980). *Some reflections on the use of figurative language in children's textbooks.* Paper presented at the annual meeting of the National Reading Conference, San Diego.

Doehring, D., Bonnycastle, D., Ling, A. (1978). Rapid reading skills of integrated hearing impaired children. *Volta Review, 80,* 399–409.

Ehri, L., & Wilce, L. (1985). Movement into reading: Is the first stage of printed word learning visual or phonetic? *Reading Research Quarterly, 20,* 163–179.

Ewoldt, C. (1981). A psycholinguistic description of selected deaf children reading in sign language. *Reading Research Quarterly, 17,* 58–89.

Fitzgerald, E. (1949). *Straight language for the deaf.* Washington, DC: Alexander Graham Bell Association for the Deaf.

Fruchter, A., Wilbur, R., & Fraser, J. (1984). Comprehension of idioms by hearing-impaired students. *Volta Review, 86,* 7–17.

Furth, H. (1966). A comparison of reading test norms of deaf and hearing children. *American Annals of the Deaf, 111,* 461–462.

Gilman, L., Davis, J., & Raffin, M. (1980). Use of common morphemes by hearing impaired children exposed to a system of manual English. *Journal of Auditory Research, 20,* 57–69.

Giorcelli, L. (1982). *The comprehension of some aspects of figurative language by deaf and hearing subjects.* Unpublished doctoral dissertation, University of Illinois, Urbana-Champaign.

Goodman, K. (1967). Reading: A psycholinguistic guessing game. *Journal of the Reading Specialist*, **4**, 126–135.

Groht, M. (1958). *Natural language for deaf children*. Washington, DC: Alexander Graham Bell Association for the Deaf.

Gronlund, N. (1981). *Measurement and evaluation in teaching* (4th ed.). New York: Macmillan.

Gustason, G. (1983). *Teaching and learning signing exact English*. Los Alamitos, CA: Modern Signs Press.

Gustason, G., Pfetzing, D., & Zawolkow, E. (1980). *Signing exact English*. Los Alamitos, CA: Modern Signs Press.

Hatcher, C., & Robbins, N. (1978). *The development of reading skills in hearing-impaired children*. Cedar Falls: University of Northern Iowa. (ERIC Document Reproduction Service No. ED 167 960)

Heider, F., & Heider, G. (1940). A comparison of sentence structure of deaf and hearing children. *Psychological Monographs*, **52**, 52–103.

Heine, M. (1981). *Comprehension of high and low level information in expository passages: A comparison of deaf and hearing readers*. Unpublished doctoral dissertation, University of Pittsburgh, PA.

Iran-Nejad, A., Ortony, A., & Rittenhouse, R. (1981). The comprehension of metaphorical uses of English by deaf children. *Journal of Speech and Hearing Research*, **24**, 551–556.

Jensema, C. (1975). *The relationship between academic achievement and the demographic characteristics of hearing-impaired children and youth* (Series R, No. 2). Washington, DC: Gallaudet College, Office of Demographic Studies.

Jordan, I., Gustason, G., & Rosen, R. (1979). An update on communication trends at programs for the deaf. *American Annals of the Deaf*, **124**, 350–357.

King, C. (1984). National survey of language methods used with hearing-impaired students in the United States. *American Annals of the Deaf*, **129**, 311–316.

King, C., & Quigley, S. (1985). *Reading and deafness*. San Diego, CA: College-Hill.

Kluwin, T. (1981). The grammaticality of manual representations of English in classroom settings. *American Annals of the Deaf*, **126**, 417–421.

Kretschmer, R. E. (1982). Reading and the hearing-impaired individual: Summation and application. In R. E. Kretschmer (Ed.), Reading and the hearing-impaired individual. *Volta Review*, **84**, 107–122. [Special Edition.]

Kretschmer, R. R., & Kretschmer, L. (1978). *Language development and intervention with the hearing impaired*. Baltimore, MD: University Park Press.

Lake, D. (1980). Syntax and sequential memory in hearing impaired children. In H. Reynolds & C. Williams (Eds.), *Proceedings of the Gallaudet conference on reading in relation to deafness* (pp. 193–212). Washington, DC: Gallaudet College, Division of Research.

Lane, H. (1976a). The profoundly deaf: Has oral education succeeded? *Volta Review*, **78**, 329–340.

Lane, H. (1976b). Thoughts on oral advocacy today . . . with memories of the society of oral advocates. *Volta Review*, **78**, 136–140.

Lane, H., & Baker, D. (1974). Reading achievement of the deaf: Another look. *Volta Review*, **76**, 489–499.

Lane, H., & Grosjean, F. (Eds.). (1980). *Recent perspectives on American Sign Language*. Hillsdale, NJ: Erlbaum.

LaSasso, C. (1978). National survey of materials and procedures used to teach reading to hearing-impaired children. *American Annals of the Deaf*, **123**, 22–30.

LaSasso, C. (1985, June). *1984 national survey of materials and procedures used to teach reading to hearing impaired students: Preliminary results*. Paper presented at the 1985 CAID/CEASD National Conference in St. Augustine, FL.

Letourneau, N. (1972). *The effects of multiple meanings of words on the reading comprehension of intermediate grade deaf children: A comparison of two methods of teaching multiple meanings of words and their effects on reading-comprehension*. Unpublished doctoral dissertation, New York University.

Lichtenstein, E. (1984). Deaf working memory processes and English language skills. In D. Martin (Ed.), *International symposium on cognition, education, and deafness: Working papers* (pp. 331–360). Washington, DC: Gallaudet College.

Locke, J. (1978). Phonemic effects in the silent reading of hearing and deaf children. *Cognition*, **6**, 175–187.

Looney, P., & Rose, S. (1979). The acquisition of inflectional suffixes by deaf youngsters using written and fingerspelled modes. *American Annals of the Deaf*, **124**, 765–769.

Makkai, A. (1972). Idiom structure in English. *Janua Linguarum*. The Hague: Mouton.

Marmor, G., & Pettito, L. (1979). Simultaneous communication in the classroom: How well is English grammar represented? *Sign Language Studies*, **23**, 99–136.

Mason, J., Kniseley, E., & Kendall, J. (1979). Effects of polysemous words on sentence comprehension. *Reading Research Quarterly*, **15**, 49–65.

Mason, J., Osborn, J., & Rosenshine, B. (1977). *A consideration of skill hierarchy approaches to the teaching of reading* (Tech. Rep. No. 42). Champaign: University of Illinois, Center for the Study of Reading.

McGill-Franzen, A., & Gormley, K. (1980). The influence of context on deaf readers' understanding of passive sentences. *American Annals of the Deaf*, **125**, 937–942.

Meadow, K. (1968). Early manual communication in relation to the deaf child's intellectual, social, and communicative functioning. *American Annals of the Deaf*, **113**, 29–41.

Messerly, C., & Aram, D. (1980). Academic achievement of hearing-impaired students of hearing parents and of hearing-impaired parents: Another look. *Volta Review*, **82**, 25–32.

Moores, D. (1982). *Educating the deaf: Psychology, principles, and practice* (2nd ed.). Boston, MA: Houghton Mifflin.

Myklebust, H. (1964). *The psychology of deafness* (2nd ed.). New York: Grune & Stratton.

Odom, P., Blanton, R., & McIntyre, C. (1970). Coding medium and word recall by deaf and hearing subjects. *Journal of Speech and Hearing Research*, **13**, 54–58.

Ogden, P. (1979). *Experiences and attitudes of oral deaf adults regarding oralism*. Unpublished doctoral dissertation, University of Illinois, Urbana-Champaign.

O'Neill, M. (1973). *The receptive language competence of deaf children in the use of the base structure rules of transformational generative grammar*. Unpublished doctoral dissertation, University of Pittsburgh, PA.

Paul, P. (1984). *The comprehension of multimeaning words from selected frequency levels by deaf and hearing subjects*. Unpublished doctoral dissertation, University of Illinois, Urbana-Champaign.

Payne, J.-A. (1982). *A study of the comprehension of verb-particle combinations among deaf and hearing subjects.* Unpublished doctoral dissertation, University of Illinois, Urbana-Champaign.

Pearson, P. D. (1985). *The comprehension-revolution: A twenty-year history of process and practice related to reading comprehension* (Reading Education Rep. No. 57). Champaign: University of Illinois, Center for the Study of Reading.

Pearson, P. D., & Gallagher, M. (1983). The instruction of reading comprehension. *Comtemporary Educational Psychology*, **8**, 317–344.

Pflaster, G. (1980). A factor analysis of variables related to academic performance of hearing-impaired children in regular classes. *Volta Review*, **82**, 71–84.

Pintner, R., & Paterson, D. (1916). A measurement of the language ability of deaf children. *Psychological Review*, **23**, 413–436.

Pintner, R., & Paterson, D. (1917). The ability of deaf and hearing children to follow printed directions. *American Annals of the Deaf*, **62**, 448–472.

Power, D., & Quigley, S. (1973). Deaf children's acquisition of the passive voice. *Journal of Speech and Hearing Research*, **16**, 5–11.

Powers, A., & Wilgus, S. (1983). Linguistic complexity in the written language of deaf children. *Volta Review*, **85**, 201–210.

Quigley, S. (1969). *The influence of finger spelling on the development of language, communication, and educational achievement in deaf children.* Urbana: University of Illinois, Institute for Research on Exceptional Children.

Quigley, S., & Frisina, D. (1961). *Institutionalization and psychoeducational development of deaf children.* Council for Exceptional Children Research Monograph (Series A, No. 3).

Quigley, S., & King, C. (Eds.). (1981, 1982, 1983, 1984). *Reading milestones.* Beaverton, OR: Dormac.

Quigley, S., & Kretschmer, R. E. (1982). *The education of deaf children: Issues, theory, and practice.* Baltimore, MD: University Park Press.

Quigley, S., & Paul, P. (1984a). ASL and ESL? *Topics in Early Childhood Special Education*, **3**(4), 17–26.

Quigley, S., & Paul, P. (1984b). *Language and deafness.* San Diego, CA: College-Hill.

Quigley, S., Steinkamp, M., Power, D., & Jones, B. (1978). *Test of Syntactic Abilities: Guide to administration and interpretation.* Beaverton, OR: Dormac.

Quigley, S., Wilbur, R., Power, D., Montanelli, D., & Steinkamp, M. (1976). *Syntactic structures in the language of deaf children* (Final Rep.). Champaign: University of Illinois, Institute for Child Behavior and Development. (ERIC Document Reproduction Service No. ED 119 447)

Raffin, M. (1976). *The acquisition of inflectional morphemes by deaf children using Seeing Essential English.* Unpublished doctoral dissertation, University of Iowa, Iowa City.

Raffin, M., Davis, J., & Gilman, L. (1978). Comprehension of inflectional morphemes by deaf children exposed to a visual English sign system. *Journal of Speech and Hearing Research*, **21**, 387–400.

Reich, C., Hambleton, D., & Houldin, B. (1977). The integration of hearing-impaired children in regular classroom. *American Annals of the Deaf*, **122**, 534–543.

Reich, P., & Bick, M. (1977). How visible is visible English? *Sign Language Studies*, **14**, 59–72.

Robbins, N., & Hatcher, C. (1981). The effects of syntax on the reading comprehension of hearing-impaired children. *Volta Review*, **83**, 105–115.

Rosenshine, B. (1980). Skill hierarchies in reading comprehension. In R. Spiro, B. Bruce, & W. Brewer (Eds.), *Theoretical issues in reading comprehension: Perspective from cognitive psychology, linguistics, artificial intelligence, and education.* (pp. 535–554) Hillsdale, NJ: Erlbaum.

Russell, K., Quigley, S., & Power, D. (1976). *Linguistics and deaf children: Transformational syntax and its applications.* Washington, DC: Alexander Graham Bell Association for the Deaf.

Sadock, J. (1979). Figurative speech and linguistics. In A. Ortony (Ed.), *Metaphor and thought* (pp. 46–63). Cambridge: Cambridge University Press.

Salvia, J., & Ysseldyke, J. (1978). *Assessment in special and remedial education.* Boston, MA: Houghton Mifflin.

Schmitt, P. (1969). *Deaf children's comprehension and production of sentence transformations and verb tenses.* Unpublished doctoral dissertation, University of Illinois, Urbana-Champaign.

Simmons, A. (1962). A comparison of the type-token ratio of spoken and written language of deaf and hearing children. *Volta Review*, **64**, 117–121.

Slobin, D. (1979). *Psycholinguistics* (2nd ed.). Glenview, IL: Scott, Foresman.

Smith, F. (1978). *Understanding reading* (rev. ed.). New York: Holt, Rinehart, & Winston.

Spearritt, D. (1972). Identification of subskills of reading comprehension by maximum likelihood factor analysis. *Reading Research Quarterly*, **8**, 92–111.

Stokoe, W., Jr. (1975). The use of sign language in teaching English. *American Annals of the Deaf*, **120**, 417–421.

Stuckless, E. R., & Birch, J. (1966). The influence of early manual communication on the linguistic development of deaf children. *American Annals of the Deaf*, **111**, 452–460, 499–504.

Stuckless, E. R., & Pollard, G. (1977). Processing of finger spelling and print by deaf students. *American Annals of the Deaf*, **122**, 475–479.

Taylor, L. (1969). *A language analysis of the writing of deaf children.* Unpublished doctoral dissertation, Florida State University, Tallahassee.

Tierney, R., & Leys, M. (1984). *What is the value of connecting reading and writing?* (Reading Education Rep. No. 55). Champaign: University of Illinois, Center for the Study of Reading.

Trybus, R. (1975). Socioeconomic characteristics of hearing impaired students in special educational programs. In C. Williams (Ed.), *Proceedings of the first Gallaudet symposium on research in deafness: The role of research and the cultural and social orientation of the deaf* (pp. 181–188). Washington, DC: Gallaudet College.

Trybus, R. (1978). What the Stanford Achievement Test has to say about the reading abilities of deaf children. In H. Reynolds & C. Williams (Eds.), *Proceedings of the Gallaudet conference on reading in relation to deafness* (pp. 213–221). Washington, DC: Gallaudet College.

Trybus, R., & Karchmer, M. (1977). School achievement scores of hearing impaired children: National data on achievement status and growth patterns. *American Annals of the Deaf*, **122**, 62–69.

van Uden, A. (1977). *A world of language for deaf children, part I: Basic principles.* Amsterdam, Holland: Swets & Zeitlinger.

Vernon, M., & Koh, S. (1970). Early manual communication and deaf children's achievement. *American Annals of the Deaf*, **115**, 527–536.

Walter, G. (1978). Lexical abilities of hearing and hearing impaired children. *American Annals of the Deaf*, **123**, 976–982.

Wilbur, R. (1977). An explanation of deaf children's difficulty with certain syntactic structures in English. *Volta Review*, **79**, 85–92.

Wilbur, R. (1979). *American Sign Language and sign systems*. Baltimore, MD: University Park Press.

Wrightstone, J., Aronow, M., & Moskowitz, S. (1963). Developing reading test norms for deaf children. *American Annals of the Deaf*, **108**, 311–316.

Speech and Hearing in Communication

HARRY LEVITT

City University of New York

Introduction—The sense of hearing plays a crucial role not only in the understanding of speech, but also in providing the cues needed for the acquisition of speech and language in the normal, developing child. This chapter is concerned primarily with the effects of hearing impairment on speech—both speech understanding and speech production—and the methods used to improve communication skills including the use of modern technological aids.

The process of communication by speech involves several distinct stages: the formulation of the message in the mind of the talker, generation of neural signals to control the vocal apparatus, production of the acoustic signal via an appropriate medium (e.g., via air in face-to-face communication), reception of the speech signal at the listener's ear, processing of the received speech signal by the auditory system and, finally, understanding of the message by the listener.

Of the various components of the speech process, the sound transmission stage is most amenable to measurement and control. For example, a hearing aid can be used to amplify the acoustic speech signal. It should be remembered, however, that the acoustic speech transmission path is very frequently supplemented by a visual path (as in face-to-face communication, or while watching television) and that the visual characteristics of speech are not as easy to measure and control as the acoustic characteristics.

A substantial research effort has been devoted to the study of the acoustic characteristics of speech and electronic methods of processing speech signals. Most of this research is applied and is dominated by the needs of the communications and computer industries. There are, nevertheless, important developments in this area which can be utilized to aid the hearing-impaired individuals. There has also been a good deal of research on the production and perception of speech by normal-hearing persons. The body of research on speech production and speech perception by hearing-impaired persons is not as great, but is nevertheless, substantive. In contrast, there has been relatively little research on methods of rehabilitation for hearing-impaired individuals, although considerable effort is expended in providing such services (NIH Panel of Communicative Disorders, 1979).

This chapter is concerned primarily with the effects of hearing impairment on speech perception and production and on methods of intervention. Some understanding of normal speech production and perception is required in order to discuss these issues. The Appendix provides a brief tutorial review for the benefit of readers not familiar with the speech process.

Hearing Impairment and the Audibility of Speech

In order to understand speech it is first necessary to be able to hear the speech signal, or at least a substantial portion of the signal. The most obvious effect of a hearing impairment is that much if not all the speech signal is rendered inaudible. It is possible to alleviate this situation by providing acoustic amplification to raise the level of the received signals. There are, however, limitations to what can be achieved by acoustic amplification. These limitations are dictated largely by the nature and extent of the hearing impairment. A few brief comments on the major types of hearing impairment and the potential for intervention are thus in order.

There are two broad classes of hearing impairment, conductive and sensorineural. A *conductive* hearing loss involves an impairment to the sound-conduction path through the outer and middle ear. Children are particularly prone to a conductive impairment known as otitis media in which the middle ear fills with fluid. Although extremely common, most episodes of otitis media are of short duration with no long-term negative consequences. Recurrent or long-term episodes of otitis media in a young child, however, can result in poorer speech and language development (Friel-Patti, Finitzo-Hieber, Conti, & Brown, 1982).

Otosclerosis is another form of conductive impairment. This disease manifests itself as a bony growth in the cochlea resulting in reduced sensitivity to sound. It is most common in adults, but can also occur in children. Other forms of conductive impairment include perforations of the eardrum, blockage of the outer ear canal, damage to the tiny bones in the middle ear (the ossicles), or to the attached ligaments and membranes.

A *sensorineural* impairment involves damage to, or a congenital defect to, the cochlea (i.e., a *cochlear* or *sensory* impairment) or to the auditory nerve (a *neural* or *retrocochlear* impairment). These two forms of impairment, cochlear and retrocochlear, often show very similar symptons and because of the difficulty in distinguishing between them, it is common practice to categorize these two impairments under the single, broad label, sensorineural. Causes of sensorineural impairment include injury resulting from drugs, excessive exposure to intense sound, disease, and congenital or hereditary factors.

The most common manifestation of a sensorineural hearing impairment is that of a frequency-dependent loss in which the degree of hearing loss increases with increasing freqency. A less common type of loss is that in which the audiogram is relatively flat. U-shaped audiograms have also been obtained in which the hearing loss in the mid frequency range (circa 1000 to 2000Hz range) is greater than that at either low or high frequences. A common characteristic of persons with noise-induced hearing loss is that of a notch in the audiogram in the vicinity of 4000Hz.

Whereas a conductive loss usually involves little more than an attenuation of the acoustic signal, a sensorineural loss is much more serious in that it is almost invariably accompanied by a reduction in the dynamic range of the ear. That is, the increase in the threshold of hearing is not accompanied by a corresponding increase in the level at which sounds become uncomfortably loud. In many cases the loudness discomfort level for the impaired ear is even less than that of a normal ear.

The reduction in dynamic range (from threshold to loudness discomfort level) that typically accompanies a sensorineural impairment is one of the main reasons why simple amplification cannot restore normal hearing to the sensorineurally impaired. If amplification is provided so as to make the most intense components of the speech signal comfortably loud, then the weaker speech sounds will be inaudible. If amplification is provided so as to make the weaker speech sounds audible, then the more intense sounds will be uncomfortably, if not painfully, loud. A major thrust in hearing-aid research is directed towards finding techniques for reducing the dynamic range of speech so as to best match the limited dynamic range of the impaired auditory system.

Figure 1 provides a concise, graphic summary of how several typical sensorineural impairments affect the audibility of the most common speech sounds. The lowest curve shows the normal threshold of hearing as a function of frequency. This curve, as with all the curves in the diagram, is based on measurements obtained with bands of sound that are one-third octave wide. Curves A, B, and C show thresholds of audibility for three typical sensorineural hearing losses. Curve A corresponds to a mild hearing loss, Curve B to a severe hearing loss, and Curve C to a profound hearing loss.

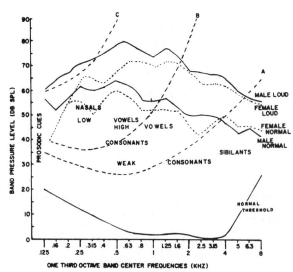

FIGURE 1. Typical Speech Spectrum and Threshold-of-Audibility Curves.

Note. From *The Vanderbilt Hearing Aid Report* (p. 34) by G. A. Studebaker and F. H. Bess (Eds.), Upper Darby, PA, Monographs in Contemporary Audiology.

Four typical speech spectra are shown based on data obtained by Pearsons, Bennett, and Fidel (1976). The highest curve in the diagram shows the average spectrum for a loud male voice at a distance of one meter from the speaker. The dashed curve just below it shows the average spectrum for a loud female voice. The next pair of solid and dashed curves show the average spectra for male and female voices, respectively, at a normal conversation level.

The frequency-intensity regions containing the major cues for various classes of speech sound (at normal conversational level) are also identified in this diagram. Note that the nasals are the most intense sounds and that they are concentrated in the low frequencies. The prosodic cues occupy an even lower frequency region and cover a wider range of relative intensities. The least intense speech sounds are the sibilants and weak consonants (e.g., voiceless consonants terminating a word or phrase). Note that these sounds contain important high-frequency information.

The frequency-intensity regions occupied by each of the sound classes shown in Figure 1 are necessarily approximate. There are important variations in the acoustic structure of speech sounds depending on phonetic context, dialect, interspeaker differences, and other factors. Nevertheless, even as a rough guide, the diagram provides a useful summary of the audibility of the various sounds of speech to hearing-impaired persons.

For the mildly hearing-impaired individual (curve A), only the weak, high-frequency sounds of speech, spoken at a normal conversation level, are audible. Typical examples include sibilants such as /f/ as in *fin*, /θ/ as in *thin*, /s/ as in *sin* and final voiceless stops such as /p/ as in *map*, /t/ as in *mat*, and /k/ as in *make*. For the severely hearing-impaired individual (curve B) almost all of the voiceless consonants and most of the voiced consonents are inaudible. Difficulties are also encountered with vowels having important high-frequency cues, such as the vowel in *feel*. For the profoundly hearing-impaired individual (curve C) only a few of the strong low-frequency vowels and nasal consonants, together with prosodic cues such as the rhythm of speech, are likely to be audible. Even then, some acoustic amplification may be needed to raise these sounds above the threshold of audibility.

Audibility is clearly a basic consideration; it is, however, not the only consideration. Even if a speech is audible it may still be misperceived as a result of reduced auditory resolution and internally generated distortions within the region of audibility. In order for speech to be intelligible, it is necessary not only to hear the sounds of speech, but also to discriminate between them, to recognize them and, most importantly, to understand them in context.

Methods of Intervention

Acoustic Amplification as an Aid to Speech Perception

The most important first step in improving the speech communication skills of the hearing-impaired child is that of improving the audibility of the speech signal. The hearing aid is commonly used for this purpose although, unfortunately, these instruments are not always prescribed properly.

Figure 2 shows the effect of two forms of amplification. In the first all frequences are amplified uniformly. This approach is satisfactory for the mildly hearing-impaired individual in that almost all of the sounds of speech are amplified above the threshold of audibility. The gain shown here is the maximum allowable in that the peak of the speech spectrum is just below the subject's loudness discomfort level (LDL), yet there are many speech sounds that are still inaudible for the severely hearing-impaired individual. Further, even those sounds lying above the threshold of audibility are not easily discriminated because of reduced auditory resolution resulting from the impairment.

For the profoundly hearing-impaired individual, the effect of uniform amplification is to make only the most intense low-frequency sounds audible; for example, the nasals, some of the more powerful vowels, and prosodic cues. Although very limited, this information can be a very useful supplement to speechreading (lipreading).

Because of the limited residual hearing available, particularly for severe or profound hearing impairments, it is essential to utilize the available residual hearing as efficiently as possible. Frequency-dependent

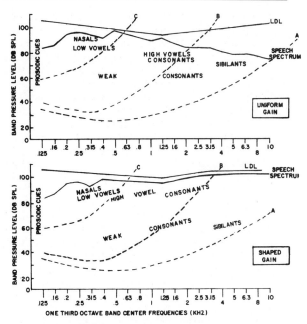

FIGURE 2. Effects of Uniform and Frequency-Selective Amplification on the Speech Spectrum.

Note. From *The Vanderbilt Hearing Aid Report* (p. 34) by G. A. Studebaker and F. H. Bess (Eds.), 1982, Upper Darby, PA, Monographs in Contemporary Audiology.

amplification that is individually prescribed for each hearing loss is a step in this direction.

The second part of Figure 2 shows the effect of individualized shaped-gain amplification such that as much of the speech spectrum as possible is placed in the residual hearing area. This is not necessarily the best approach, in that the amplified speech signal may be too loud. A useful practical compromise is to find that frequency-gain characteristic which places the speech at the most comfortable level at all frequencies (Pascoe, 1978; Skinner, 1979).

The preceding discussion provides a brief overview of the factors limiting speech perception by hearing-impaired persons. Educators and others concerned with the delivery of services to hearing-impaired students need to have quantitative information on how well a hearing-impaired child is likely to perform given appropriate acoustic amplification and a reasonable amount of auditory training. Data obtained by Boothroyd (1984, 1985) on children trained in the oral method provide a concise summary of what can be achieved currently (i.e., with existing hearing-aid technology, methods of hearing-aid prescription, and auditory training).

Figure 3 shows how different speech-pattern contrasts are perceived by children with various degrees of hearing loss. The PTA or Pure Tone Average (i.e., the average loss for tonal stimuli at 500, 1000, and 2000Hz, respectively) is used to specify degree of loss. As is evident from the diagram, children with a mild to moderate loss (PTA < 60dB) only have difficulty in perceiving contrasts involving place of articulation. This difficulty

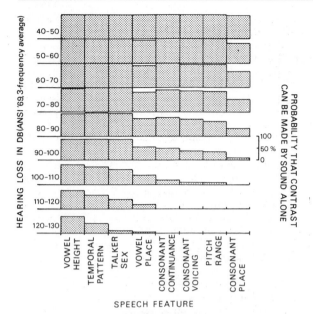

FIGURE 3. The accuracy of perception of speech pattern contrasts along several feature dimensions as a function of degree of sensorineural hearing loss.

Note. These data were obtained by extrapolation and interpolation from the results of experiments reported in "Auditory Perception of speech contrasts by subjects with sensorineural hearing loss" by A. Boothroyd, 1984, *Journal of Speech and Hearing Research* **27**, 134–144.

is experienced primarily with the consonants and, to a lesser extent, with the vowels.

Children with more severe losses (PTA = 60 to 80dB) exhibit difficulty with speech contrasts involving the segmental structure of speech (e.g., vowel place, consonant continuance, consonant voicing, and consonant place) as well as with pitch range. Children with this degree of hearing impairment would typically be integrated into the regular school system (with supporting services) and only a few such children would be placed at a school for deaf students.

Children with severe-to-profound impairments (PTA = 80 to 100dB) have great difficulty with segmental contrasts as well as some difficulty with those contrasts involving suprasegmental cues, such as temporal pattern and talker sex. Many children with this degree of impairment are at schools for deaf students, although a fair proportion have been successfully integrated into the regular school system. In a recent study comparing hearing-impaired children integrated into the regular school system with those at schools for deaf students, it was found that a high proportion of the children who had been successfully integrated also had a fair degree of residual hearing above 4000Hz (Levitt, 1987). This aspect of hearing impairment is not taken into account in the conventional pure-tone average.

The profoundly hearing-impaired child (PTA > 100dB) has great difficulty with all aspects of speech. Only those speech-pattern contrasts involving low-frequency cues are perceived with a moderate degree of success. In the study discussed by Levitt (1987), very few profoundly hearing-impaired children with losses in excess of 100dB had been successfully integrated into the regular school system.

The importance of the data reported here is that they represent actual levels of performance with a fairly typical group of children who have had the benefit of modern methods of intervention. These children should not be regarded as star performers. An analysis of the signals reaching the ear and of the effect of the hearing impairment on the limits of auditory discriminability indicate that much better performance could be obtained. As noted by Boothroyd (1985): The results of experiments on the relationships between speech perception and pure-tone threshold should be taken as lower estimates of auditory potential rather than upper limits. Nevertheless, even these lower estimates show the existence of considerable auditory potential in subjects who only a few decades ago were thought to be beyond the reach of auditorily based training. (Hudgins, 1953.)

In short, using modern methods of intervention, hearing-impaired children are performing at levels better than would have been predicted in the 1950s or 1960s. There is, at the same time, much room for further improvement.

Three avenues of investigation need to be explored in order to improve further the auditory potential of hearing-impaired children. The first is that of identifying the causes of the difference in perceptual performance that have been observed among children with identical degrees of hearing impairment. The second is that of facilitating the learning process. Acoustic amplification may make a sound audible, but the child has to learn to discriminate that sound from other sounds and to recognize sounds in context. The third is to improve the acoustic amplification system. Most previous research on auditory capabilities of hearing-impaired children used hearing aids or other amplification systems which were not ideally matched to each child's needs.

The thrust of much current hearing-aid research is towards finding more efficient ways of matching the dynamic range of the speech signal to the limited dynamic range of the impaired auditory system. Optimization of the frequency-gain characteristic for each user's needs is one approach which has achieved moderately good results (Braida, Durloch, Lippmann, Hicks, Rabinowitz & Reed, 1979). In addition, it is possible to reduce the overall dynamic range of the speech by using amplitude-compression amplification. In this method of amplification, the weaker speech sounds receive additional gain while the stronger speech sounds receive less gain. In this way, the weaker sounds are amplified to lie above the threshold of audibility while the stronger speech sounds are not amplified above the discomfort level.

Placing all of the speech signals within the residual hearing area will not necessarily render speech intelligible, although it is a useful first step. A major problem is the loss of auditory resolution within the residual hearing area. Another potential problem is that of internal noise and auditory distortions generated within the impaired auditory system. There is currently a major, ongoing research effort addressing these issues and, in so doing, determining the most effective method of acoustic amplification.

Auditory Training, Speechreading, and the Intelligent Use of Redundancy

Even with appropriate amplification, not all of the speech signal will be intelligible to the hearing-impaired child. Fortunately, the speech signal is highly redundant and even if many speech cues are missing it is still possible to understand what is said. The thrust of most auditory training programs is to teach the hearing-impaired child to make most effective use of these redundancies.

Redundancy in speech can take many forms. In order to develop effective training programs for improving the speech communication skills of hearing-impaired children it is important to know the nature of these redundancies and how to make use of them. Although general trends can be ascertained, it is important to bear in mind that there are substantial individual differences between children in terms of the nature and degree of the impairment, the effect of the impairment on the perception of the components of speech and, most importantly, in the ability of the hearing-impaired child to integrate different sources of information.

The major sources of information in normal, face-to-face communication are auditory, visual, and contextual. For information received by ear alone, the most common confusions involve the loss of information regarding the place of articulation of speech sounds. Referring back to Figure 1, the sound classes shown in this diagram differ primarily in terms of manner of articulation and voicing. Whereas the acoustic differences between these sound classes are fairly large, for example, nasals have a very different acoustic structure from voiceless fricatives, the sounds within these classes are acoustically very similar. For example, the nasals /m/ and /n/ resemble each other acoustically, as do the fricatives /f/ and /θ/. Note that the sounds making up each pair differ only in the place of articulation.

For the most part, speech sounds that differ solely in terms of their place of articulation are acoustically similar and the most common perceptual confusions are between these sounds. Confusions between sounds that differ in manner of articulation and/or voicing are much less frequent.

In contrast to the above, the most common confusions in speechreading (without auditory input) involve sounds that differ in voicing and/or manner of articulation. Place of articulation cues are relatively easy to see, particularly for sounds produced at or near the front of the mouth (Erber, 1972).

In normal face-to-face communication both auditory and visual cues are available and although we may not be consciously aware of the process, we typically integrate the two sets of cues in order to understand what is said. For the normal-hearing child, these visual cues are useful but not essential for the understanding of speech, except under difficult listening conditions such as a noisy or highly reverberant acoustic environment. For the hearing-impaired child integration of visual and auditory cues is of prime importance.

Another major source of redundancy is that of context. Contextual cues take many forms. These may include cues resulting from phonetic and syntactic constraints, from the statistical characteristics of the language, or from semantic or pragmatic considerations. Many auditory training programs provide the hearing-impaired child with controlled exposure to contextual cues.

Contextual cues at the phonetic level typically involve coarticulatory effects, such as those discussed in the Appendix. As a consequence, severely hearing-impaired children are often able to perceive high-frequency sounds that are nominally beyond the range of their residual hearing by attending to transitional, coarticulatory cues in the lower frequency regions.

Closely related to contextual phonetic cues are statistical cues at the phonetic level. Whereas certain sound sequences typically occur quite frequently, other sequences seldom if ever occur. If only one or two sounds in a commonly occurring sequence are perceived, this may be sufficient for the entire sequence to be identified.

The syntactic rules governing language usage are also an important source of contextual cues. Although the rules of grammar are not strictly adhered to in spoken language, there are violations which simply do not sound right. Sentences containing gross syntactic errors are more likely to be misheard under difficult listening conditions than those that are syntactically correct. Similarly, the statistical characteristics of word sequences influence intelligibility in much the same way as statistical characteristics of phoneme sequences. An improbable word sequence such as *the a the*, for example, would more likely be heard as *the other,* which is statistically much more likely.

Perhaps the most important contextual cues are semantic and/or pragmatic. There is little doubt, for example, that the words *name* and *mane,* although acoustically similar, are unlikely to be mistaken for each other in sentences such as *My name is George*, and *The lion has a golden mane.*

Studies on the relative importance of syntactic and semantic cues in the perception of speech shows that semantic cues dominate. A sentence that makes sense but is syntactically incorrect is more likely to be understood than one that is semantically anomalous but syntactically correct. Semantic cues also often take precedence over conflicting acoustic and/or visual cues. Occasional mis-pronunciations or articulatory errors have only a secondary effect on intelligibility provided these false cues do not alter the meaning of what is said.

The importance of contextual cues for speech intelligibility was recognized some time ago (Miller, Heise, & Lichten, 1951), but it is only recently that standardized test instruments have been developed for assessing the effect of context on speech discrimination ability in normal and hearing-impaired populations. One such test instrument is the SPIN (Speech-in-Noise) test which measures speech discrimination ability in both a high and low context environment (Kalikow, Stevens, & Elliot, 1977). Another important advance has been the development of training and evaluation procedures, such as the method of Continuous Discourse Tracking (De Filippo & Scott, 1978) in which semantic and pragmatic cues play an important role.

Although it is generally recognized that contextual information is crucial for the understanding of speech by hearing-impaired persons there is no general agreement on how best to train hearing-impaired children (or adults) to make maximum use of contextual cues. One school of thought believes that training should focus on teaching hearing-impaired persons to recognize the individual sounds of speech and that, with these improved skills, the understanding of speech in context will be much improved. Training procedures which follow this general thrust are referred to as *analytic*.

The opposing school of thought believes that training should focus on understanding the whole message without attempting to dissect its parts. This general thrust is known variously as the *synthetic* or *cognitive* approach since the focus is on synthesizing the many components of speech into a cognitive whole.

Although the debate as to which approach is more effective has raged since the earliest attempts at systematic speech and auditory training, there have been few attempts at objective, experimental evaluations to resolve the issues.

Of the few experimental studies that have been reported, the evidence appears equally divided. Walden, Prosek, Montgomery, Scherr, and Jones (1977), for example, obtained improvements in lipreading ability after an intensive, highly analytic training regimen. On the other hand, Rubinstein (1985) found no significant different between the improvements obtained with an analytic-and-synthetic versus a synthetic-only method of auditory training. Both of these studies involved adults. Studies with hearing-impaired children have typically concentrated on demonstrating the benefits of speech and auditory training without differentiating between the two approaches. The results have generally been positive with respect to the benefits of auditory training (Wedenburg, 1954; Hudgins, 1953).

A second unresolved issue is whether auditory training should be provided without access to visual (speechreading) cues or whether an integrated approach should be used in which both visual and auditory cues are available. Proponents of the acoustic-only approach argue that:

> The hearing sense, although defective, should be given every opportunity for use (the *unisensory approach*). The child must be taught to think in sound language. In many cases, speechreading may already play an important role for the child and therefore may have to be discouraged, because if the child grows too dependent upon speechreading he will never learn to listen. (Wedenberg, 1981; see also Pollack, 1964, 1970)

It should be noted that proponents of the unisensory approach are not wholly opposed to the use of visual cues but believe rather that auditory training should be "based principally on the auditory sense with the visual sense as a complement, contrary to other methods which are based on the visual sense with the auditory sense as a complement" (Wedenberg, 1981).

There is as yet no clear-cut evidence that one method of training is superior to the other. It is evident, from a number of studies, that overall performance is improved if both visual and auditory cues are combined. The amount of improvement obtained with the addition of visual cues was found to increase with degree of hearing impairment. The speech-reception skills of profoundly deaf children, for example, were found to be primarily dependent on visual speechreading cues, but not wholly so since even profoundly deaf individuals can receive prosodic information through the auditory channel. In cases of total deafness this information will be received tactually with a sufficiently powerful hearing aid. Thus, although there is disagreement as to which is the best method of training for improving speech reception skills, there is strong evidence that overall performance is superior with a multisensory input.

Teachers faced with the task of providing auditory training to deaf children have, for the most part, chosen an eclectic approach. Except for a few institutions where the tenets of a given training philosophy are adhered to rigorously, most auditory training programs appear to have combined elements of the various approaches. Thus, it is not surprising to find the analytic approach being used to some extent followed by work using the synthetic approach. The unisensory approach is often used in auditory training periods assigned for that purpose but with the teaching of speechreading at other times.

The various auditory training programs that have been developed over the years provide educators with a range of possible programs and materials to choose from (see, e.g., Kelly, 1953; Sanders, 1971; Guberina & Asp, 1981; Paterson, 1982; among others). Unfortunately, most of these programs and associated training materials are either aimed at specific subsets of the population or are couched in such general terms that the teacher still needs to develop a large corpus of the material.

There is a need for systematic auditory training systems applicable to a broad range of hearing-impaired children for which the teacher is provided not only with a curriculum and instructional materials, but also whereby to judge relative progress made by each child on the program. One such system is the Auditory Skills Instructional Planning System developed by Thies and Trammell (1983). This system contains three components: a curriculum, a test of auditory comprehension, and a set of training materials. Four areas of ability are covered by the curriculum: discrimination, memory-sequencing, auditory feedback, and figure-ground resolution. The test of auditory comprehension parallels the sequence of objectives in the curriculum and norms are provided for assessing levels of difficulty.

In addition to programs that are geared specifically for auditory training, there are also systematic speech training programs, such as those developed by Haycock (1933); Ewing and Ewing (1964); Magner (1971); Calvert and Silverman (1983, revised edition); Ling (1976), and Osberger, Johnstone, Swarts, and Levitt (1978), in which auditory training is an integral component. A key element in these training programs is the systematic training and testing of auditory ability as the child progresses along the sequential stages of the curriculum.

A new development has been the introduction of computer-assisted instructional procedures. Computer-assisted training and practice is well suited for use by adults and older students, and has been used successfully for this purpose (McGarr, Head, Friedman, Behrman and Youdelman, 1986). Computer-assisted techniques also have great potential for classroom use with younger children (Levitt, 1984). Novel video displays or games can be used to motivate the children, while the tedious tasks of record keeping and objective monitoring of performance can be automated (Braeges and Houde, 1982).

Techniques for teaching speechreading are not very different from those used almost a century ago. One of the earliest training systems of this type was developed by Nitchie (1912) at the New York League for the Hard of Hearing. Initially, Nitchie's system was heavily analytic, but he soon modified his approach to include a substantial synthetic component. Most speechreading training programs in use in the 1980s appear to have this mix, the relative balance between the analytic and synthetic components depending heavily on the clinician's viewpoint (Bruhn, 1949; Jeffers & Barley, 1971; Sanders, 1971; Walden, Erdman, Montgomery, Schwartz, & Prosek, 1981).

Speechreading is taught to both hearing-impaired adults and hearing-impaired children; however, most of the published programs and training materials are designed for hearing-impaired adults or older children with well-developed language skills. Although the same teaching principles can be used with younger children,

such as systematically reducing redundancy in speech-reading exercises, the choice of training material is critical, particularly for the child whose hearing impairment was acquired prelingually.

Studies on the link between language and communication skills show a higher correlation between language and speechreading than between language and any other communication skill (Levitt, 1987). Children with good speechreading skills also have relatively good language and vice versa. It is not clear whether one is the cause of the other, or whether the two sets of skills develop symbiotically. It is important, however, when working with a young hearing-impaired child that the speech-reading materials used be appropriate to that child's level of language functioning. There is a need for the development of systematic speechreading programs for young hearing-impaired children with supporting testing and training materials that will cover a broad range of language abilities. The instructional systems developed for auditory training, as described earlier, could serve as a useful model.

Although there is a considerable diversity of opinion as to which is the best approach to auditory training or speechreading training, there is general agreement as to the importance of early intervention. In order for the hearing-impaired child to learn and benefit from the contextual cues of a language it is necessary for the child to be familiar with the language. Long-term exposure to the sounds of a language in context is an important consideration. As a consequence the hearing-impaired child should be fitted with a properly prescribed hearing aid as early in life as possible and should also be encouraged to use it as much as possible so as to maximize the child's exposure to the sounds of the language. This is particularly important for very young children during their early stages of speech and language development. Wearable tactual aids (in combination with a hearing aid) are also being used increasingly, with favorable results (Friel-Patti & Roeser, 1983; Goldstein & Proctor, 1985).

Speech Production and the Hearing-Impaired Child

The child who is either born with a severe hearing impairment or acquires such an impairment very early in life is faced with a doubly severe handicap. Not only is speech difficult if not impossible to understand, but the lack of exposure to speech during the child's earliest years also serves to impede the normal development of speech and language. This chapter is concerned with speech and hearing and hence issues of language development will not be taken up here.

Patterns of Error in the Speech of Hearing-Impaired Children

There are vast differences between hearing-impaired children in terms of the relative intelligibility of their speech. At the same time, there are common error patterns and characteristics that typify the speech of hearing-impaired individuals. These similarities are quite striking and it has led to the development of a generalized description of deaf speech.

A general theory of speech production in hearing-impaired children by Levitt and Stromberg (1983) takes the position that although there are large individual differences between hearing-impaired children in terms of the overall rate of articulatory errors, once this absolute error rate has been taken into account the pattern of errors is remarkably similar between children. Exceptions occur at either end of the intelligibility scale; that is, children with very good speech intelligibility (close to 100%) make insufficient errors for a pattern to be discernable and children with very poor speech (intelligibility close to zero) often have gross idiosyncratic errors, many of which are not easily defined in conventional phonetic terms.

The vast majority of hearing-impaired children fall well within the above two extremes and most of these children have essentially similar speech characteristics although there are still some significant between group differences, for example, as between prelingually and postlingually deafened children, or children who have had the benefit of superior speech teaching versus those who have not. Most of these between-group differences, however, reflect differences in overall intelligibility and show only secondary differences in error patterns.

At the segmental level, the most common articulatory error in the speech of hearing-impaired children is that of omission of consonants. Consonants produced near the front of the mouth (/p, b, f, v, m/) are much less likely to be omitted than consonants produced in the center or back of the mouth. Similarly, consonants occurring at the start of a word (i.e., the *word-initial* position) are less likely to be omitted than consonants in word-medial or word-final position. Consonants in the word-final position, particularly at the end of a phrase or sentence, are by far the most likely to be omitted.

The next most common set of articulatory errors is that of phoneme substitution. Typically, consonants are substituted for consonants and vowels for vowels. Relatively few substitutions involve consonants for vowels or vice versa. Consonant substitutions typically involve the same place of articulation, particularly for consonants produced at the front of the mouth. Voice-voiceless confusions are extremely frequent, as are errors involving manner of production.

The nasal consonants are frequently substituted by voiced stops with the same place of articulation. The inverse substitution also occurs, but much less frequently. The fricatives show a moderately high rate of substitution by stop consonants with a similar place of articulation, occasionally with an additional voiced/-voiceless substitution (e.g., /b/ for /v/, /t/ for /s/, /d/ for /ʃ/). The corresponding inverse substitution (fricative for stop) also occurs, but less frequently. The affricates are seldom substituted for other consonants, but tend to be substituted by one of their components.

Errors in vowel production differ from consonantal errors in that errors of omission are quite rare. The most common vowel error is that of a lax-tense substitution, such as /I/ for /i/ (e.g., *bit* for *beet*). The reverse substitution, /i/ for /I/, also occurs quite frequently. Another common error type is that of substitution by a more central vowel, such as /I/ by /ɛ/ (*bit* to *beet*) or /ɛ/ by // (*bet* to *but*). A fairly common form of centralization is substitution by the neutral vowel /e/. A third, major class of substitutions is that of a diphthong to one of its components (usually the major component), or to a closely related vowel, for example, /ɛI/ to / /, /aI/ and /aU/ to /a/. Diphthongization of vowels also occurs, but less frequently.

The pattern of segmental errors described above reveals an underlying structure. For the most part, hearing-impaired children tend to place their articulators reasonably accurately; there are relatively few place-of-articulation errors in consonant production and placement errors in vowel production are typically towards a neighbouring more central vowel.

A major source of error is that of improper dynamic control of the articulators and concomitant errors in timing. Stop-nasal substitutions, for example, can be traced to improper timing and control of the velum. Voicing errors are similarly a result of poor timing and control of the voicing mechanism. Fricative to stop substitutions reflect improper control of the articulators in forming the required constriction in the vocal tract. The lax-tense vowel substitutions can also be traced to poor timing and control of the articulators.

By far the most common source of error, however, is that of lack of effort. The most obvious manifestation of this problem is the omission of consonants, particularly at the end of a word or phrase. Other related errors involve partial omissions in the production of diphthongs, affricates and blends. The neutralization of vowels is also a manifestation of lack of effort and should not be regarded simply as improper placement of the articulators.

Suprasegmental errors in the speech of hearing-impaired children also show similar patterns across the range of children, although in this case individual differences and between-group differences are substantially larger. This may be because the most common or most noticeable suprasegmental errors are more amenable to training and correction than the most common segmental errors.

The most common suprasegmental error in the speech of hearing-impaired children is that of excessive prolongation of vowels and other continuant sounds. A related and equally noticeable problem is that of prolonged and inappropriate pauses. A third very common class of errors involves improper control of voice fundamental frequency.

The above patterns are not only perceptually salient, particularly to persons unfamiliar with the speech of hearing-impaired children, they are also especially damaging to intelligibility. Important prosodic cues such as stress juncture and intonation are easily destroyed as a result of changes in stress pattern produced by excessive prolongation, changes in phrasing produced by inappropriate pauses and changes in intonation produced by improper control of voice pitch.

Other suprasegmental problems which do not affect meaning directly, but which contribute to poor speech quality include weak voice, or alternatively, stridency, excessive breathiness, average voice pitch too high or too low, excessive or insufficient nasality, very slow tempo, and either too little (monotonous) or too much (excessive or uncontrolled) variation in voice pitch. Many of the above problems can be traced to improper breathing patterns or to inadequate control of the voicing mechanism (Whitehead, 1983; Stevens, Nickerson, & Rollins, 1983).

The teaching of speech to hearing-impaired children involves many of the same basic issues that occur in auditory training. Whereas it is important that the mechanics of speech production be mastered, at least for the most common sounds of the language, the major concern is that the child be able to combine the sounds of speech into intelligible phrases and sentences. The ability to communicate meaningfully is the key and in order to do this a balance must be reached between teaching the segmental and suprasegmental aspects of speech and the use of speech in communication.

It has been suggested by several researchers that hearing-impaired children have the greatest difficulty in producing those sounds of speech they cannot see (in speechreading) or for which they receive poor proprioceptive feedback (Stark, 1974; Gold, 1978, 1980; Monsen, 1983). This is true to a certain extent that the sounds produced with the least difficulty are those produced at the front of the mouth and which are the most visible. On the other hand, difficulties are also encountered with certain aspects of speech for which adequate feedback cues are usually available to the hearing-impaired child but which, because of their complexity, are not easily recognized. The prosodic features of speech, as well as temporal characters of speech at the segmental level, fall into this category. The symbioses between speech teaching and auditory training is perhaps greatest in this area since the inherent problem appears to be a cognitive one, that of learning patterns where the entity to be recognized (e.g., stress pattern, intonation contour) is the same in both speech reception and speech production.

A related issue is that the hearing-impaired child may have developed a different phonological system since the auditory cues available during the early, crucial stages of speech development are incomplete and hence different from those available to the normal-hearing child. The implications of dealing with children having different phonological systems need to be taken into account in the development and evaluation of speech and auditory training curricula. It is also an important consideration in the development of sensory aids for facilitating speech and language development in prelingually hearing-impaired children.

Several well-organized speech-training programs have been developed over the years (Haycock, 1933; Ewing & Ewing, 1964; Magner, 1971; Calvert & Silverman, 1975). A recent development has been the introduction of a finely detailed sequence of stages through which the child progresses and whose progress at each stage is carefully monitored (Ling, 1976; Osberger et al., 1978). These procedures typically begin with the mechanics of speech production but soon switch to the use of these newly-learned skills in a communicative mode. The sequence of skills that is taught is modelled on normal speech development. A separate problem is that of correcting errors in speech production that have been acquired over the years as a result of either no speech training or improper teaching techniques.

A key element in any effective speech-training program is that of systematic evaluation. The systematic speech-training programs that have recently been developed are thus structurally similar to the recently developed auditory-training programs. The three basic components of these systems are: a structured curriculum, a curriculum-based evaluative instrument (usually a test that can be administered routinely with little difficulty), and teaching materials appropriate to the child's level of language development. One of the dangers inherent in any systematic speech-training program is that too much effort may be spent on the segmental characteristics of speech and too little on the supra-segmental characteristics or on the use of speech as a means of communication. Care should be taken to avoid the attraction of concentrating on those aspects of speech that are easy to teach but which are of only secondary importance in terms of improving overall communication ability.

A practical problem in implementing systematic speech-training programs is that of detailed record keeping. Although some schools have invested in the effort needed to maintain such a system this is not a general practice. The recent introduction of small computers in the classroom offers some hope of alleviating this problem. Research on computer-based techniques for speech training has been in progress for some time (Nickerson & Stevens, 1973; Crichton & Fallside, 1974) and practical systems for classroom use have been developed (McGarr et al., 1986). An important practical benefit is that the task of objectively monitoring each child's progress on the speech-training curriculum is managed effectively and unobtrusively by the computer.

Overall Intelligibility and Factors Influencing the Efficacy of Speech Training

The overall intelligibility of the speech of hearing-impaired individuals is of great practical concern. Although it has been shown on numerous occasions that a well-organized speech-training program can produce improved speech skills (Ling & Milne, 1981; Osberger et al., 1978), can these improved skills translate into significantly more intelligible speech? Ling and Milne (1981) provide data showing that given an appropriate training program beginning early in life, profoundly hearing-impaired children can learn to speak intelligibly. The vast majority of hearing-impaired children, unfortunately, do not come close to this ideal. It is of considerable importance to determine why this is the case and what can be done to ensure that hearing-impaired children are taught to speak intelligibly.

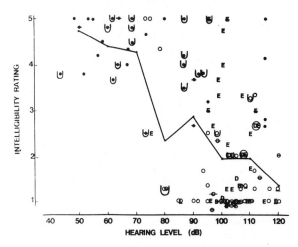

FIGURE 4A. Speech intelligibility as a function of hearing level—"typical" deaf children. The solid curve shows mean intelligibility rating for children averaged over each decade of hearing levels (e.g., mean rating at 60 dB is the average rating for children with hearing levels between 55 and 65 dB).
D = deaf parents.
E = early special education
U = high-frequency hearing (U-shaped audiogram)
O = children at schools for the deaf and neither of above
● = mainstreamed children
bar below symbol = low socioeconomic status
bar through symbol = poor use of hearing aid
A circle enclosed two or more characteristics associated with a single child.

Recent studies by Gold (1978) and Levitt, McGarr, and Geffner (1987) have addressed this issue, and data are available showing the range of speech intelligibility in a large representative sample of hearing-impaired children and the factors that correlate with the achievement of good speech intelligibility. The participants in the study were all ten-year-old children attending state-supported or state-operated schools for deaf students

in New York during a given school year (roughly 120 children). In addition, a smaller sample of 43 hearing-impaired children integrated into the New York City school system were included in the study. For further information on the sampling procedures and other data on these children, see Levitt, McGarr, and Geffner (in press).

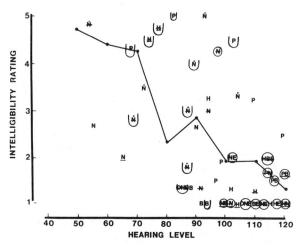

FIGURE 4B. Speech intelligibility as a function of hearing level—special cases. The solid curve shows the average score for "typical" deaf children taken from Figure 4A.
B = severe behavioral/emotional problems
D = deaf parents
E = early special education
H = other handicaps ("minimally brain damaged"; "retarded")
N = non-English-speaking home (not including sign language)
P = postlingually hearing impaired
U = high-frequency hearing (U-shaped audiogram)
● = mainstreamed
bar through symbol = low socioeconomic status
bar below symbol = poor use of hearing aid
A circle encloses two or more characteristics associated with a single child

Note: From *Development of Language and Communication Skills in Hearing-Impaired Children* (pp. 133, 134) by H. Levitt, N. S. McGarr, and D. Geffner (Eds.), 1987, ASHA Monographs. *Number 26*, Rockville, MD: American Speech-Language-Hearing Association.

One of the most important factors affecting speech intelligibility is that of hearing loss. Figure 4 shows ratings of overall intelligibility as a function of hearing level (pure tone average at 500, 1,000, and 2,000Hz). The figure is subdivided into two parts. The upper part (Figure 4A) shows intelligibility ratings for children of the type who have typically been included in studies of speech intelligibility in hearing-impaired children (e.g., prelingually hearing-impaired, no additional handicapping conditions). Figure 4B shows data for children who are special in some way and have traditionally been excluded from studies of this type.

The measure of overall speech intelligibility was a five-point rating scale based on that developed at the National Technical Institute for the Deaf (Johnson, 1975). The lowest rating on the scale (1) corresponds to unintelligible speech whereas the highest rating (5) corresponds to fully intelligible speech. The specific categories of the scale are shown in Table 1. The ratings were obtained by trained listeners familiar with the speech of hearing-impaired individuals.

TABLE 1 5-Point Rating Scale of Speech
Intelligibility

Rating	Category Description
1	Speech cannot be understood
2	Speech is very difficult to understand (only isolated words or phrases are intelligible)
3	Speech is difficult to understand, however the gist of the content can be understood
4	Speech is intelligible with the exception of a few words or phrases
5	Speech is completely intelligible

Note: From "Communication Characteristics of NTID Students" by D. Johnson, 1975, *Journal of the Academy of Rehabilitation Audiology*. **8**, 17–32.

The solid curve in Figure 4A shows the mean intelligibility rating averaged over each decade of hearing level. The same curve is reproduced in Figure 4B to serve as a reference for the special children considered in this diagram.

In addition to the effect of hearing level, other factors of interest were shape of audiogram, use of hearing aid, home language, socioeconomic status, whether the parents of the child were deaf, differences between mainstreamed hearing-impaired children and those at schools for the deaf, impact of early special education, prelingual versus postlingual impairment, and other handicapping conditions. The symbols representing these variables are identified in the legend to Figure 4.

Several factors stand out as being particularly important. On the average, speech intelligibility decreases with increasing hearing loss. The magnitude of the reduction covers the entire range, from intelligible speech at a hearing level of about 50dB to unintelligible speech at a hearing level of 120dB. Individual children show substantial variations about this trend. Children with hearing impairments acquired postlingually have far more intelligible speech than that predicted by the average trend. In contrast, children with behavioral/psychological problems or whose home language is not the language of instruction (English) fell well below the average trend.

Three other factors showed significant correlations with improved speech intelligibility. Children who had the benefit of early special education (intervention beginning prior to three years of age) had significantly more intelligible speech. These children are represented by the symbol E in Figure 4A. Similarly, children with

U-shaped audiograms (therefore having some high-frequency residual hearing that is not measured by the conventional pure tone average) also had more intelligible speech. These children are identified by U-shaped symbols in the diagram. Thirdly, the speech of the mainstreamed children (solid discs) was more intelligible than that of children at schools for the deaf (open circles). Note that, with one or two exceptions, children with hearing levels better than 80dB were mainstreamed and, consequently, the comparison between the mainstreamed children and those at schools for the deaf can only be made for hearing levels in excess of 80dB.

It is important to bear in mind that the data reported here are of a correlational nature and do not demonstrate causal relationships. That is, the speech of mainstreamed children may be more intelligible, but this observation should not be interpreted to mean that mainstreaming, in itself, produces more intelligible speech. The reverse may well be the case, as when children are mainstreamed because they have good speech and language skills. It is relevant to note that a larger proportion of the mainstreamed children had U-shaped audiograms than children at schools for deaf students. Audiogram shape is not a criterion for mainstreaming, but children with U-shaped audiograms are more likely to have intelligible speech and, as such, are more likely to be mainstreamed.

Perhaps the most important finding is that a small proportion of the profoundly hearing-impaired children with losses in excess of 100dB have intelligible speech; that is, their speech intelligibility rating is of the order of 4 or 5. Although few in number, these successful cases as well as those reported by Ling and Milne (1981), serve as an existence proof that it is possible to teach profoundly hearing-impaired children to speak intelligibly.

An important need for the future is to study the children at both extremes of performance in order to identify the factors leading to success and failure, respectively, and to implement more effective speech-teaching programs based on these findings. In this way it should be possible to increase the success rate while reducing substantially the unacceptable high failure rate that now exists.

Technology and the Future

One of the great hopes for the future is that advances in modern technology could be used to develop sensory aids that will allow the hearing-impaired child to communicate effectively and, concomitantly, to allow the prelingually hearing-impaired child to develop normal speech and language. A large number of sensory aids have been developed over the years, ranging from devices that simply amplify the acoustic speech signal, to advanced signal-processing systems that attempt to extract the important information-bearing components of the speech signal and to convey this information using another modality. An alternative approach is to use the impaired auditory system, but to recode the speech cues,

TABLE 2 Types of sensory Aids Available

Degree of Speech Processing	MODALITY			
	Audition	Visual	Tactual	Neuro-Electric Stimulation
Nonspeech-Specific	Early Hearing Aids	Envelope Displays Sign Language*	Single-Channel Displays	Single-Channel Cochlear Prosthesis
Speech-Specific Processing Noise-Stripping	Modern Hearing Aids Compression Amplification Frequency Lowering Aid	Spectrum Displays	Multi-Channel Spectrum Displays	Speech-Matched Single-Channel Prosthesis Vocoder Type Multi-Channel Prosthesis
Speech Feature Extraction	Feature-based Frequency Lowering Feature Coding	Feature-Displays (+RP,W) Lipreading* Cued Speech*	Feature Displays Tadoma*	Feature-Coding Prosthesis
Speech-Recognition Processing	Experimental Phoneme Coding	Speech Captioning Phoneme Coding	Automatic Braille for Deaf-Blind	
Telecommunication Aids	Telephone/ Television Amplification Devices	Electronic Mail Video Transmission of sign language Television Captioning Telecomm. Devices for the Deaf, TDD	Telecomm. Devices for Deaf-Blind	

* Natural method of communication, not necessarily involving use of sensory aid.

Note: From "Hearing Impairment and Sensory Aids: a Tutorial Review" by H. Levitt, 1986, *Journal of Rehabilitation Research and Development* **23**, No.1, 13–18.

for example, by frequency transposition so that these cues lie within the range of residual hearing or, alternatively, by stimulating the auditory nerve electrically using an implanted cochlear prosthesis.

Table 2 provides a summary of the many different types of sensory aids that have been developed. The columns of the table represent the four basic categories of sensory aids subdivided according to sensory modality and mode of stimulation, namely, auditory, visual, tactual, and electrical stimulation of the auditory nerve. Electrical stimulation of the skin (electrocutaneous stimulation) is very similar to tactual stimulation and devices of this type are usually grouped with tactual aids. A second important consideration is the degree of speech processing used in the sensory aid. The first four rows of the table show, in order of increasing complexity, the four major levels of speech processing used in sensory aids. The fifth row of the table corresponds to a special category of aids used for telecommunication. These devices are not sensory aids in the strict sense of the term and typically involve the transmission of signals other than speech.

Sensory aids involving nonspeech-specific processing (Row 1 of Table 2) are usually geared towards matching the incoming signals to the characteristics of the sensory modality being used. These aids do not take into account the special characteristics of speech. Early hearing aids were of this form, the original intent being to restore the threshold of hearing to that of a normal-hearing person. This approch, however, did not work very well for reasons discussed in the section on acoustic amplification. Modern hearing aids take into account the average spectrum shape and statistical characteristics of the speech signal.

Other nonspeech-specific sensory aids include single-channel vibrators or visual displays, as well as early single-channel cochlear prostheses. These devices provide profoundly hearing-impaired individuals with some degree of contact with the world of sound. They are able to provide useful cues identifying different classes of environmental sounds as well as important alerting signals (fire alarms, automobile horns, doorbells). Single-channel sensory aids can also be used to supplement lipreading cues but they are not well suited for this purpose unless special precautions are taken (e.g., speech-only not speech-plus-noise should be transmitted) or some additional processing is included to facilitate the transmission of speech cues.

Speech-specific sensory aids (Row 2 of Table 2) involve some form of signal processing that takes into account the average or statistical characteristics of the speech signal, such as spectrum shape, dynamic range, and typical temporal patterns. Most modern sensory aids are of this type. Conventional hearing aids are designed to take into account the average spectrum of the speech signal. Many new hearing aids also incorporate compression amplification which takes the dynamic and temporal characteristics of the speech signal into account. Experimental speech-processing hearing aids have also been developed that lower the high-frequency components of speech to the low-frequency region, where there is often more residual hearing. These devices, although promising on theoretical grounds, have not yet shown any substantial advantages over conventional amplification (Levitt, Pickett, & Houde, 1980).

A number of visual, tactual, and cochlear prostheses have been developed that are specifically geared to the transmission of speech signals. The simplest of these are single-channel devices which are designed to make the envelope of the speech signal as perceptible as possible given the limitations of single-channel stimulation. Examples include the use of compression amplification for matching the large dynamic range of the speech signal to that available in the mode of stimulation being used (Hochmair-Desoyer & Hochmair, 1983), or some form of noise reduction designed to separate out sounds with nonspeech-like characteristics, such as steady background noise, from the speech signal (Franklin, 1984; Goldstein & Proctor, 1985).

A more sophisticated approach to speech-specific processing is to subdivide the speech signal into several continuous frequency bands and to transmit the signal fluctuations in each band either visually, tactually, or by neuro-electric stimulation in a cochlear prosthesis. This is the so-called *vocoder* approach and there is some controversy as to whether hearing-impaired children (or adults) could ever learn to recognize the complex visual or tactual patterns produced by such a display (Levitt et al., 1980). One school of thought argues that speech signals are extremely complex, that the auditory system serves as a unique decoder for this complex signal and that it is unrealistic to expect the visual or tactual system effectively to decode spectrum displays of speech (Liberman, Cooper, Shankweiler, & Studdert-Kennedy, 1968).

The opposing school of thought argues that spectrum displays of speech contain sufficient information to be intelligible and that the human cognitive system has sufficient plasticity for an intelligent, highly motivated person to learn to recognize spectrum displays given sufficient long-term exposure to displays of sufficient resolution (Houde, 1980). Several recent studies have shown significant advances in the human decoding of visual or tactual spectrum displays (Cole, Rudnicky, Zue, & Reddy, 1980; Brooks, Frost; Mason, & Gibson, 1986). Although these results are promising, the total vocabulary learned or the rate of decoding for unconstrained vocabularies is still too small to be of practical value as a communication aid.

Another, more intense controversy surrrounds the use of multi- or single-channel cochlear prostheses. Proponents of multi-channel prostheses point out that the cochlear is essentially a specctrum analyzer and that for speech to be intelligible several different frequency channels in the cochlear need to be stimulated. Proponents of the single-channel cochlear prosthesis argue that the results obtained with single-channel cochlear prostheses are as good, on the average, as those obtained with the considerably more complex multi-channel systems. (See Parkins & Anderson 1983 for further discussion of these opposing viewpoints.)

An even more pressing controversy revolves around the use of cochlear prostheses with young hearing-impaired children. The cochlea is an exquisitively sensitive organ and insertion of an electrode into the cochlea is likely to damage the remaining sensory structures that are still intact. Consequently, an important criterion for candidacy for a cochlear prosthesis is that the patient be profoundly hearing-impaired. It is extremely difficult to determine reliably whether a very young child is profoundly deaf or has significant residual hearing. It is thus quite possible for a child with significant residual hearing to be implanted with a cochlear prosthesis and for that residual hearing to be lost. Since reliable preoperative information on the child's hearing status may not be available, it may never be known whether or not the hearing loss measured at a later stage in the child's life was due, in part, to the cochlear prosthesis.

On the other hand, it is important to provide the hearing-impaired child with an auditory input as early as possible. As reported by Levitt et al. (1987), early intervention and, in particular, early exposure to speech and language produces substantial improvements in speech and language development. Further, for the profoundly hearing-impaired child even a small increase in the amount of auditory input can have a significant impact. The use of a cochlear prosthesis at an early age is thus very attractive from this perspective, provided the problems noted above can be resolved.

An alternative noninvasive method of neuro-electric stimulation is the extracochlear approach developed by Douek, Fourcin, Moore, & Clarke, (1977). In this case the cochlea is stimulated by an external electrode placed on the round window or on the promontory at the round window. Although surgery is involved, the cochlea is left intact. The operation is also reversible. The electrode can be removed without adverse effects if the prosthesis turns out to be unsuccessful. A disadvantage of the extracochlear approach, however, is that a relatively high stimulating current is needed and for some individuals the range from threshold to discomfort is extremely small.

The next level of signal processing in sensory aids involves speech-feature extraction (Row 3, Table 2).

Most sensory aids of this type are still experimental. These devices offer considerable hope for the future since, as is evident from natural modes of communication such as speechreading, cued speech,* and Tadoma it is possible for people to learn to communicate using a limited set of articulatory or phonetically-based cues.

There appear to be two major problems limiting the success of speech-feature displays. The first is the accuracy with which the speech features can be extracted from the speech signal. An error in speech-feature extraction is particularly damaging to the communication process. No automatic speech-extraction system operates without error and the effects of such errors need to be taken into account. The second problem relates to the perceptual complexity of such displays. Even though the set of features to be displayed is limited, the rate at which these features vary in normal speech is high and research on optimizing the display format for ease of comprehension is needed.

The most successful results obtained thus far with experimental speech-feature displays involve neuro-electric stimulation that approximates crudely to the way in which these features are processed in the normal auditory system. In one such system a 22-electrode multichannel cochlear prosthesis is used (Clark, Black, Forster, Patrick, & Tong, 1978). The speech features transmitted are voice fundamental frequency, second formant frequency,† and whether the speech is voiced or unvoiced. Only one electrode pair at a time is stimulated. The place of stimulation in the cochlea conveys information on formant frequency. Periodic, pulsive stimulation is used to signal voicing, the rate of stimulation being proportional to voice fundamental frequency. Voiceless sounds are transmitted by aperiodic stimulation.

Another speech-feature prosthesis is the single-channel extra-cochlear system developed by Douek et al. (1977). In this case voice fundamental frequency is transmitted using period pulsive stimulation.

Both systems have yielded relatively good results (Clarke, Tong, & Dowell, 1983; Fourcin, Douek, Moore, Rosen, Walliker, Howard, Abberton, & Frampton, 1983). For a few subjects, the cochlear prosthesis has yielded spectacular improvements in communication ability. Several cases have now been

reported (for cochlear implants of various types) in which profoundly hearing-impaired persons are now able to communicate effectively with normal-hearing persons, including conversing over the telephone (Hochmaier-Desoyer & Hochmair, 1983; Levitt, Waltzmann, Shapiro, & Cohen, 1986).

All of the subjects in the above experiments have been profoundly hearing-impaired adults with losses acquired postlingually. It may be some time before comparable experimental devices are developed for hearing-impaired children, depending on the outcome of the controversy noted above.

Good results have also been obtained with visual, tactual, and frequency-transposition speech-feature sensory aids used for speech training. Stark (1972), for example, obtained a significant reduction in the voiced/voiceless substitutions using a visual display of voice-onset time. McGarr et al. (1986) have reported successful results in intonation training using both visual and tactual displays of voice fundamental frequency. Guttman, Levitt, and Bellefleur (1970) obtained improvements in fricative production with an audio frequency transposition system. In each of the above applications, the sensory aid displayed only a small subset of speech features at a time, that is, only those features involved in the speech training. Consequently, the displays were relatively simple and with the exception of very young children (4 years of age or younger), the users of the display had no cognitive difficulties in recognizing the features being displayed.

The most advanced level of speech processing in a sensory aid is that in which some form of automatic speech recognition is used (Row 4, Table 2). These aids offer the greatest hope for the future, provided the problem of automatic speech recognition can be solved. The state of the art, at present, is that automatic recognition of limited vocabularies is possible but that open-ended automatic recognition of unconstrained speech is far from possible. It may be that in the not-too-distant future, a practical compromise will be reached between the size of the vocabulary (or other constraints) and the accuracy and speed of recognition such that the device will be of value as a communication tool for hearing-impaired persons.

Hybrid semi-automatic systems have already been developed (Stuckless, 1981). A shorthand typist transcribes what is said. A special shorthand typewriter is used, the output of which is connected to a computer. The signals received from the typewriter are automatically translated into conventional English text that is then displayed on a television monitor. The system operates in real time, the translated text appearing on the screen within seconds of the speech being produced. This system is currently being evaluated in classrooms for deaf students. The results obtained thus far have been favorable (Stuckless & Hurwitz, 1982).

Other sensory aids involving speech-recognition processing include phoneme displays using either visual, tactual or low-frequency auditory stimulation. The

---

* Cued Speech (Cornett, 1967) involves the use of hand signals to disambiguate sounds that look the same in speech-reading, Tadoma (Alcorn, 1932) is a communication technique whereby a deaf-blind person feels the articulatory movements of the speaker. Signing refers to any system of hand signals used by deaf individuals for communication, such as American Sign Language, Signed English, and fingerspelling. These three modes of communication are referred to as "natural" since they do not require any devices for their use. They have been included in Table 2 since they serve as models for possible sensory aids.

† A modified version of this caption has recently been introduced in which information on both first and second formats is transmitted.

potential value of such systems has been demonstrated in experiments using preprocessed stimuli, that is, displays using previously prepared stimuli not containing any errors. (Goldberg, 1972; Levitt & Weiss, 1982). Automatic systems of this type operating reasonably well in real time have yet to be developed.

A special class of technological aids that is rapidly growing in use is that of telecommunication aids (Row 5, Table 2). The two most common telecommunication aids are teletypewriters (or, more generally, telephone devices for the deaf or TDDs) and television captioning. These depend on the transmission of text and are doubly valuable in that they not only provide an effective means of communication for profoundly hearing-impaired individuals, but long-term use of these devices also facilitates the development of language in hearing-impaired children.

The computer revolution has had an important impact on telecommunication aids for deaf persons. Firstly, computer networks for electronic mail and other computer-based applications of TDDs are growing rapidly. Secondly, the mass production of computers, particularly of personal home computers, has reduced the cost of a TDD dramatically. Whereas in the late 1970s the cost of a TDD was prohibitive for the average deaf individual, it is regarded in the late 1980s as an affordable necessity within the deaf community. These economic factors have had a profound effect on the use of TDDs.

Other types of telecommunication aids include telephone devices for deaf–blind persons, such as teletypewriters for Braille or automatic text-to-Braille displays. Research is also currently under way on low-bandwidth video systems for the transmission of sign language over the telephone (Sperling, 1980). Closed-circuit television can be used for this purpose within a given installation (e.g., a school for deaf students) but the transmission of video signals over long distances for purposes of personal communication is uneconomic. As in the case of TDDs, it is believed that if low-bandwidth and hence low-cost video telephones for deaf persons could be developed, the system would find wide application.

In conclusion, it may be noted that the current state of technology allows us not only to measure the acoustic characteristics of speech with relative ease, but also to modify these characteristics in order to facilitate communication with hearing-impaired individuals. The hearing aid is the device most commonly used for this purpose, but other types of sensory aids are being used to an increasing extent. Devices that modify the visual cues available to a hearing-impaired listener are still in an early stage of development but with further advances in video technology they could become a viable option. Research is still in its infancy (Scheinberg, 1980; Montgomery, 1980; Brooke and Summerfield, 1983). The field of acoustic phonetics has already made significant advances in our understanding of the speech process and in the development of acoustically-based sensory aids. With the technological tools now available,

the time may be ripe to begin serious investigation of the analogous field of "video-phonetics."

Concluding Comments

The teaching of communication skills to hearing-impaired children is a complex task and the results of this endeavor, at present, are far from satisfactory. Although it has been shown that well-organized training programs for audition, speechreading, and speech production can produce significant improvements in these skills, relatively few hearing-impaired children in this country are exposed to effective training programs of this type. There are large individual differences between children in their ability to learn to communicate, and these differences must be taken into account in the planning of any effective communication-training program. Postlingually hearing-impaired children, for example, have far less difficulty in acquiring speech than their prelingually impaired peers. Psychological and related behavioral problems mitigate against the effectiveness of any teaching program and improved methods of dealing with these problems are urgently needed.

Children who have had the benefit of effective special education at an early age are more likely to show superior communication skills at a later age than those who have been neglected. Early intervention is clearly an important factor in the education of hearing-impaired children and much more should be done to identify and provide communication training to the very young hearing-impaired child. The quality of early intervention also needs to be improved. Much more is now known about the nature of hearing impairment and its effect on communication, and better use needs to be made of this information in identifying hearing-impaired children and planning their educational programs. For example, children with some high-frequency residual hearing are more likely to acquire better communication skills, yet testing for high-frequency hearing is not performed routinely at most schools and clinics. Similarly, conventional hearing aids are typically not designed to amplify high-frequency sounds (above about 5,000Hz).

There are several extant philosophical issues that pervade the field of communication training. Should such training be primarily analytic or synthetic? Should an acoustic-only approach be used in auditory training or is the multisensory approach more effective? These are important questions that have remained unresolved since the early days of speech and auditory training. There has been a trend in recent years towards more objective assessment of training programs. These studies are beginning to provide the objective evidence needed to answer the above questions and further research of this type is to be encouraged.

Perhaps the most important and pervasive issue of all is whether or not we should attempt to teach oral communication skills to the profoundly hearing-impaired child. This controversy has deep philosophical roots and may be immune from objective resolution.

There is little doubt that it is very difficult to teach practical oral communication skills to the prelingually, profoundly hearing-impaired child and many schools have effectively given up in this effort. At the same time there are many documented cases in which prelingually, profoundly hearing-impaired children have acquired effective oral communication skills. There are many more with severe to profound hearing losses who are able to communicate effectively in this way. The effort required to achieve useful oral communication skills is great, however, and a commitment must be made in the earliest years of life. Although the path is difficult, the opportunity to learn effective oral communication skills should not be denied to the young hearing-impaired child.

The education of hearing-impaired children is heavily dependent on modern technology. The hearing aid, for example, had a revolutionary impact on educational methods that extended well beyond its obvious application to speech and auditory training. Mainstreaming of hearing-impaired children would not be possible without the effective use of hearing aids. Similarly, modern audio-visual technology is playing an increasingly important role at schools for deaf students (Levitt, 1984).

It is important for educators to keep abreast of modern advances in technology and their potential application in the classroom. Three new developments that are likely to have a substantial effect on the teaching of communication skills are (a) the use of special-purpose microcomputers in the classroom with advanced visual and/or tactual displays for conveying speech information, (b) the growing use of wearable tactual sensory aids, and (c) direct electrical stimulation of the auditory nerve (with due regard given to the potential hazards of this approach). A fourth development that seems likely in the not-too-distant future is that of signal-processing hearing aids in which important parameters of the speech signal are extracted and made more easily recognizable to the hearing-impaired child. (Levitt, 1986, 1987).

The teaching of communication skills to hearing-impaired children is a multidisciplinary activity. Acoustics, audiology, computer science, engineering technology, linguistics, phonetics, psychology, special education and speech and language pathology are all involved in some way. It is unrealistic to expect teachers of communication skills to be specialists in all of these areas. It is important, however, that they have a good understanding of those fundamental aspects of these various disciplines that pertain to the education of hearing-impaired students. For example, a teacher is not expected to know how to repair a hearing aid but every teacher of hearing-impaired children should know how to test if a hearing aid is working and should do so at least once a day for every child in the class. Similarly, speech teachers should have a fundamental understanding of phonetics and linguistics. Knowing how to use a

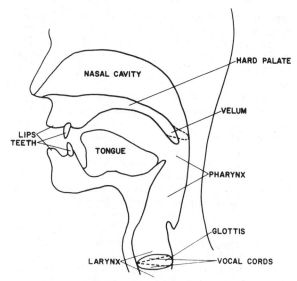

FIGURE A1. Sketch of the human vocal tract during the production of the vowel /i/.

Note: From *Auditory Management of Hearing-Impaired Children* (p. 59) by M. Ross and T. G. Giolas, 1978, Baltimore: University Park Press.

computer in an educational setting is also of great importance.

Given the diverse nature of the field, the preparation of professional personnel for teaching communication skills is arduous. A balance must be maintained between the all-encompassing needs and that which is realistic to expect of a dedicated, intelligent professional. Model preservice and in–service training programs for speech teaching have been developed (Hochberg, Levitt, & Osberger, 1980). These need to be further developed and expanded to take into account recent technological advances. The positive aspects of the few model programs that exist also need to be implemented on a much wider scale so that the skills of all professionals in the field can be upgraded on a continuing basis.

APPENDIX

Normal Speech Production

Figure A1 shows a cross-sectional sketch of the human vocal apparatus. When speech is produced, the lungs produce a flow of air that passes through the vocal tract which consists of the larynx, pharynx, mouth and nasal cavities. Vibrations in this airflow, as modified by constrictions in the vocal tract produced by the articulators (jaw, tongue, teeth, lips, velum), result in the characteristic sounds of speech.

The most important source of sound in speech is the periodic, or almost periodic, vibration generated by the vocal cords. The small opening between the vocal cords is known as the *glottis*. When the vocal cords are pulled tight, the glottis is closed thereby producing a temporary break in the flow of air through the vocal tract. Pressure exerted by the lungs builds up the air pressure below the glottis until a point is reached when the vocal cords can no longer contain this *subglottal* air pressure, causing the vocal cords to fly apart. The glottis is opened momentarily allowing a pulse of air to escape into the vocal tract. With the resulting reduction in subglottal air pressure, the vocal cords once again form an airtight seal and the cycle of events is repeated. The periodic, or almost periodic, train of air pulses produced in this way is heard as a voiced sound. The frequency of vibration of the vocal cords is known as the *voice funda-mental frequency* (Fo) and the associated sound perceived by the listener is known as the *voice pitch*.

Another important source of sound in speech is the random turbulence produced when air is forced to flow through a narrow constriction. Such a constriction may be produced by one or more sets of articulators, for example, by placing the lower lip against the upper row of teeth when an /f/ sound is produced, or by forming a narrow constriction between the tip of the tongue and roof of the mouth when an /s/ sound is produced.

Sounds produced by random turbulence in the air-stream are known as voiceless sounds. Some sounds, such as the voiced fricatives /v/ and /z/, combine both periodic and random sources of vibration.

A third source of sound is that resulting from a transient disturbance in the vocal tract, such as that produced by the release of pressure when a constriction in the vocal tract is suddenly removed. Sounds of this type are known as plosives, or stop consonants. Examples of such sounds are /p, b, t, d, k/ and /g/. Note that stop conson-ants cannot be produced in isolation but must always occur in combination with a vowel or other continuant sound.

The sounds of speech differ not only in terms of the source of acoustic vibration (periodic, random, transi-ent), but also in terms of how these acoustic vibrations are modified by the shape of the vocal tract. Changing the shape of the vocal tract will result in certain sound frequencies being emphasized while other frequencies are de-emphasized or attenuated.

Figure A2 illustrates how the shape of the vocal tract affects the frequency spectrum of vowel sounds. Cross-sectional diagrams are shown for four key vowels, /i/ as in *seen*, /u/ as in *soon*, /a/ as in *father*, and /ae/ as in *sat*. The frequency spectrum of each of these vowels is shown alongside each cross-sectional diagram.

The vowels are typically classified in terms of tongue placement. The /i/ vowel is produced by placing the arch of the tongue high up and forward in the mouth and is thus classified as a *high*, *front* vowel. The /u/ vowel is produced by raising the arch of the tongue toward the back of the mouth, and is classified as a *high*, *back* vowel. The /a/ is a *low*, *back* vowel produced by placing the blade of the tongue low down and toward the back of the mouth. The /ae/ is a *low*, *front* vowel produced by placing the tongue toward the front of the mouth but

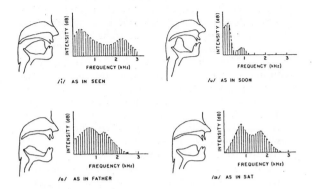

FIGURE A2.   Vocal-tract configurations and approxi-mate power-frequency spectra for four key vowels.

Note: From *Auditory Management of Hearing-Impaired Children* (p. 65) by M. Ross and T. G. Giolas, 1978, Balti-more: University Park Press.

keeping it low behind the lower teeth. These four vowels are important in that they represent extreme positions of tongue placement and serve as useful references for teaching as well as analyzing speech.

Associated with each vowel is a characteristic fre-quency spectrum. Since the vowels are produced by a periodic signal source (the periodic, or nearly periodic, vibrations generated by the vocal cords), the associated frequency spectra are line spectra. As is evident from Figure A2, each frequency spectrum consists of a series of vertical lines. The leftmost line corresponds to the fundamental (Fo), which is the lowest frequency com-ponent of the periodic signal. The remaining lines corre-spond to the harmonic components, the frequency of each harmonic being an integer multiple on the funda-mental frequency. The height of each line represents the relative intensity of that frequency component.

The aspects of the frequency spectrum are particularly important in speech perception. The first is the voiced fundamental frequency, Fo, which is perceived as the *pitch* of the voice. Voice pitch conveys information on prosody and other aspects of intonation. It also helps identify who is talking (e.g., man, woman, child). The second aspect of the spectrum is its envelope, as shown by the dashed line in each of the frequency diagrams of Figure A2. The shape of the spectrum envelope is crucial to the identification of speech sounds.

A major peak in the spectrum envelope is known as a *formant* and is produced by an acoustic resonance in the vocal tract. For purposes of illustration, only the two lowest formants are shown in Figure A2 for each of the vowel spectra. These two formant frequencies are often referred to as F1 and F2, respectively.

The ratio of the formant frequencies F2/F1 is roughly constant for each vowel. For example, F1 = 270Hz and F2 = 2,300Hz for the /i/ vowel shown in Figure A2. These values are typical of a normal male voice. Corre-sponding values for a typical female voice are 310 and

2,800Hz. For a child, typical values are 370 and 3,200Hz, respectively (Peterson & Barney, 1952). Note that although there are large differences in the absolute values of F1 and F2 between men, women, and children (and between speakers, in general) the ratio F2/F1 is roughly constant; that is, F2/F1 = 8.6 Experiments with electronically synthesized speech shown that if a synthesized vowel sound is produced with F2/F1 = 8.6 normal-hearing listeners will typically identify that vowel as an /i/.

It is also important to note that the first formant typically lies below 1,000Hz and that there is relatively little variation between vowels in the frequency of F1. In fact, two of the vowels, /i/ and /u/, have roughly the same first formant frequency, namely, F1 = 300Hz in both cases. In contrast, F2 varies substantially in frequency covering the range from just under 900Hz (for /u/), to well over 2,000Hz (for /i/). For a hearing-impaired child who is unable to hear frequencies above 1,000Hz, only the first formant will be perceived. For this child, /i/ and /u/ will sound much the same, although for other children with a less severe impairment the two vowels will sound distinctly different.

Another important characteristic of a vowel is whether it is *tense* or *lax*. These terms are based on what is loosely believed to be the degree of muscular tension during production of the vowel. A more reliable way to differentiate between tense and lax vowels is whether or not the vowel occurs in word-final position in normal English. A tense vowel can occur with or without a terminating consonant (e.g., the vowel /i/ in *see* or *seed*). A lax vowel does not normally occur in the free form, but is almost invariably terminated (checked) by another sound, usually a consonant (e.g., the vowel /I/ as in *sit*). A tense-lax pair of vowels, such as /i/ and /I/ has essentially the same vocal-tract shape and acoustic spectrum. The two vowels differ primarily in duration, the tense vowel being longer than its lax cognate.

The frequency spectra of the consonantal sounds are, as in the case of the vowels, determined by both the source of sound and the shape of the vocal tract. For the voiceless fricatives, the sound source is random rather than periodic and consequently the frequency spectra of these sounds are continuous and do not have a discrete line structure. Figure A3 shows typical spectra for the fricatives /s/ as in *sin*, /d/ as in *shin*, /f/ as in *fin* and /w/ as in *thin*. The randomness of the sound source is caused by turbulent air flow through a narrow constriction in the vocal tract. The location of this constriction in the vocal tract plays a key role in determining the shape of the resulting frequency spectrum.

The /s/ sound which has almost all of its power in the high frequencies is produced by a narrow constriction towards the center of the mouth between the tip of the tongue and the hard palate. The /d/ sound is produced by a similar, less narrow constriction at a slightly more forward position in the mouth. The /w sound also has most of its power in the high frequencies, but not as high as for /s/.

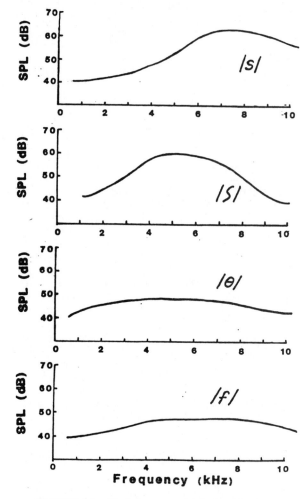

FIGURE A3.   Typical spectra of voiceless fricatives

The /w/ sound is produced by forming a constriction towards the front of the mouth between the tips of the tongue and the upper row of teeth. The constriction for the /f/ sound is produced at the very front of the mouth, between the lower lip and upper teeth. The /f/ and /w/ sounds have similar, relatively flat spectra. They are also relatively weak sounds acoustically. These two sounds are often confused with each other perceptually, even by normal-hearing listeners. Because of their low acoustic power these two sounds are typically rendered inaudible by even a mild hearing impairment.

The voiced fricatives are produced by combining the turbulent air flow produced by a narrow constriction in the vocal tract with the periodic excitation of the vocal tract. The spectra of these sounds have roughly the same envelope structure shown in Figure A3 but, in addition, have superimposed line spectra caused by the periodic vibrations.

The nasal consonants, /m/ as in *sum*, /n/ as in *sun*, and /ŋ/ as in *sung*, are produced by periodic excitation, as in the case of vowels, but unlike the vowels the mouth is blocked forcing the sound to exit through the nose. The nasal consonant /m/ is produced by forming a block at the lips, /n/ is produced by forming a block between the tongue and roof of the mouth, and /ŋ/ is produced by a blockage further back in the mouth.

The nasal consonants are given their distinct quality by a combination of the resonances produced by the nasal cavities with those produced by a blocked oral cavity. Since these resonances interact in a complex way the nasals do not exhibit a simple formant pattern. These resonances are primarily in the low frequency region.

The frequency spectra of the nasal consonants are similar to each other and also to the spectrum of the /u/ vowel. All of these spectra exhibit a distinct line structure with most of the acoustic power in the low-frequency region. As a consequence, the nasal consonants and vowels such as /u/ are often confused with each other perceptually. These confusions occur not only with hearing-impaired persons, but also with normal-hearing persons communicating in noise and by computerized automatic speech recognition systems designed to identify the sounds of speech. The nasal consonants are acoustically very powerful and for hearing-impaired persons typically require less amplification than other sounds of speech.

The stop consonants (also referred to as plosives) are a complex group of sounds that involve dynamic changes in the shape of the vocal tract for their production. Like the nasal consonants they involve a complete blockage of the oral cavity, but this blockage is only temporary. The stop consonant /b/ is produced by temporarily blocking the vocal tract at the lips. The location of this blockage is the same as that for the nasal consonant /m/. For the stop consonant /d/ the blockage occurs more centrally in the mouth in the same location (i.e., place of articulation) as for the nasal consonant /n/. The place of articulation for /g/ is at the back of the mouth, as for the nasal consonant /ŋ/ (as in *sing*). There is typically a break in voicing when a stop is produced.

The voiced stop consonants /b/, /d/, and /g/ are characterized by very short delays between the release from closure and onset of voicing (about 20 ms), whereas the corresponding voiceless stops (/p/, /t/, and /k/, respectively), are characterized by a relatively large delay, of the order of 70 ms, before the onset of voicing. Another cue which signals whether a stop is voiced or voiceless is the relative duration of the preceding vowel. Vowel length is generally longer when preceding a voiced as opposed to a voiceless stop consonant (Raphael, 1972). This cue is particularly important for stop consonants occurring at the end of a word or phrase. Under these conditions, the stop consonant may terminate in closure with no subsequent release and thus no onset-of-voicing cue is available to signal whether the consonant is voiced or voiceless.

The sequence of events from the release to the onset of voicing is quite complex. Since there is movement of the articulators, the shape of the vocal tract is altered resulting in time-varying changes in the formant frequencies. These changes in formant frequency are known as *formant transitions*. The nature and direction of these formant transitions depend on the speech sound following the stop consonant. Generally, these transitions move from initial values corresponding to the acoustic resonances of the blocked vocal tract to those of the following vowel or other continuent sound. The formant transitions are reversed in direction for vowel-stop combinations.

In addition for formant transitions there is also a burst of turbulent air flow that occurs when a stop is released. This short-term turbulence is known as *aspiration*. The voiceless stops typically show more aspiration than their voiced counterparts. It is not uncommon for this burst of aspiration to be perceived as a fricative sound by a hearing-impaired listener.

The spectral shape of a stop consonant changes dramatically during the course of its articulation. This time-varying spectrum is heavily dependent on the spectrum of the adjoining speech sounds, but there is one short period of time when the spectrum of a stop consonant is relatively independent of its neighboring sounds. This is the period immediately following the release from closure. It has been argued that the spectrum shape during this brief period is determined primarily by the place of closure in the vocal tract and is thus characteristic of the specific stop consonant that is produced (Stevens & Blumstein, 1978). If this is the case, it is important that hearing aids with dynamic amplification characteristics, for example, amplitude compression hearing aids, do not alter short-term changes in the shape of the speech spectrum lest they destroy spectral cues that are important for the identification of specific classes of sounds.

Another important class of speech sounds that inherently involves articulatory movement is that of the glides. There are two glides in English, the glide /w/ (as in *we*) in which, initially, the articulators are placed roughly in the position for the vowel /u/. The articulators then move rapidly into position for the following vowel as the glide is produced. The glide /j/ (as in *you*) begins with the articulators placed roughly in position for the vowel /i/. The articulators then move rapidly into position for the following vowel.

The spectrum of a glide, as in the case of stop consonants, is heavily dependent on the spectrum of the following vowel. In some cases, as in words like *we* and *you*, there is substantial articulatory movement and the acoustic cues identifying the glide are quite prominent. In other cases, as in words like *woo* and *ye* where articulatory positions at the start of the glide are similar to those of the following vowel, there is very little articulatory movement and the acoustic cues identifying these glides are extremely subtle. Under these conditions, even normal-hearing listeners have difficulty in identifying the glides.

The *diphthongs* represent a third class of speech sounds that require articulatory movement. Unlike the glides which involve relatively rapid transitional movements (although not as rapid as for a stop consonant), the diphthongs involve the gradual merging of a vowel into another vowel-like sound. It is quite common in normal speech to move the articulators slightly during a vowel sound. If the movement of the articulators is sufficiently large, such that another vowel-like sound is heard, then the vowel if said to be *diphthongized*. For example, the vowel in the word *day* can be produced as /ε/ or as the diphthongized vowel /εI/ where, towards the end of the vowel, the articulators move from the vowel /ε/ position towards that for the vowel /I/.

If as a result of diphthongization there is a change in meaning, for example, a new word is produced, then the diphthongized sound takes on an identity of its own and is known as a *diphthong*. For example, diphthongization of the vowel /U/ in *saw* will result in a new word /sUI/ (*soy*/. The vowel /U/ and the diphthong /UI/ are identified as two separate sounds in English. This is a subtle distinction and hearing-impaired children usually have difficulty in distinguishing between a diphthong and its corresponding vowel components (e.g., between /UI/ and /U/). Severely or profoundly hearing-impaired children also have difficulty in producing diphthongs correctly.

The Sounds of Speech in Context

The sounds of speech are seldom produced in isolation. Speech typically consists of sequences of speech sounds interwoven in such a way that information is conveyed not only by the individual sounds making up the sequence, but also by the way in which these sounds are interlaced.

It is convenient to think of speech as having both a *segmental* and *suprasegmental* structure. The segmental structure relates to the articulatory and acoustic characteristics of individual speech sounds (sometimes referred to as phonemes). The suprasegmental structure of speech takes into account the way in which individual segments of speech interact as well as the way in which sound sequences are modified so as to convey prosodic and other nonsegmental information.

It is important to bear in mind that there is a hierarchy of suprasegmental interactions. At the lowest level (i.e., the level closest to the segmental level), neighboring sounds interact depending on the articulatory maneuvers involved in each sound. That is, the articulation of one sound is dependent on the articulatory mechanisms used in the preceding or following sound. This effect is known as *coarticulation*.

There is as yet no general theory of coarticulation, but several general trends are evident. Coarticulatory effects are greatest with speech sounds requiring movement of the articulators, for example, the stop consonants, glides, and diphthongs. In the case of stops and glides the interdependence between the adjacent sounds is so great that coarticulatory effects may involve combinations of three or even four sounds. In order to demonstrate this effect, the reader should produce the words *pay*, *play*, *ploy*, and *splay* and compare the shape of the lips and position of the tongue tip during the /p/ in each case.

A particularly common form of coarticulation involves anticipatory movements of the articulators. Consider for example, the words *sue* and *see*. There is rounding of the lips during the /s/ in *sue* in preparation for the rounded vowel that follows. The shape of the lips during the /s/ in *see* is quite different. Anticipatory coarticulatory effects involving the lips, teeth, and jaw are particularly important in lipreading since these articulators are the most visible. There are also important, concomitant acoustic interactions. The major peak in the spectrum of /s/ is lower in frequency for *sue* because of the liprounding effect. There is also evidence of secondary spectrum peaks forming towards the end of the /s/ sound in anticipation of the formant structure of the following vowel.

Another common form of coarticulation is that of absorption. This often occurs when adjacent consonants have the same place of articulation. For example, the burst of aspiration during the /t/ in *tar* is absorbed by the frication of the /s/ in *tsar*. This absorption also occurs when the /s/ precedes the /t/ as in *star*. These effects can be both complex and subtle. In many cases, the consonant pair is more easily learned as if it were an independent entity, for example, as if /ts/ were a separate sound in the language.

The *affricates* represent a special class of sounds in which a stop and fricative are absorbed into each other to form a new sound. There are two affricates in English, /tʃ/ as in *church* and /dʒ/ as in *judge*. These two sounds, not surprisingly, are a major source of difficulty for the hearing-impaired child. They are difficult to produce, are often misperceived (usually only the major component of an affricate is heard) and, for a teacher, they are difficult sounds to teach.

Superimposed upon the complex of coarticulatory effects are durational, intensity, and pitch adjustments imposed by the stress pattern appropriate for a given word. For example, the word *refuse* has two distinct meanings depending on which of its two syllables is stressed. If the first syllable is stressed, the word is a noun meaning garbage; if the second syllable is stressed the word is a verb meaning to say no. These effects are, in turn, subjugated to the prosodic requirements of the entire phrase or sentence.

Prosodic information in English is conveyed by three sets of features: stress, intonation, and juncture. Stress is signalled by three physical variables: duration, intensity, and voice fundamental frequency. A stressed syllable is usually of longer duration, of higher intensity, and of higher voice fundamental frequency relative to an unstressed syllable. These three variables do not always act in unison when a syllable is stressed. Intonational cues are transmitted primarily by variations in voice fundamental frequency as well as durational changes. A question, as opposed to a statement, is signalled by raising the voice fundamental frequency at an appropriate location in the sentence. Juncture signals a break in the flow of speech and plays an important role in subdividing speech into phrases and sentences. A common form of juncture is a pause. A pausal juncture is typically accompanied by a prolongation of the preceding syllable and a fall in the voice fundamental frequency just before the pause. Another form of juncture is a sharp change or discontinuity in the voice fundamental frequency.

In addition to prosody, there is yet another overlay of suprasegmental characteristics. These provide non-linguistic information such as who is talking (man, women, or child), the emotional or physical state of the speaker, and other cues that are not indicative of what is said, but rather of how it is said. Cues such as average voice pitch, overall vocal effort, rate of talking, hoarseness, breathiness are very effective indicators in this regard and are often used to convey nonlinguistic information.

A source of great difficulty in describing the suprasegmental characteristics of speech is that the same physical parameter is often used to convey many different cues. For example, a common coarticulatory effect is the lenthening of a vowel before a voiced as opposed to a voiceless consonant. Vowel lengthening is also used to convey stress, as well as to signal the end of a phrase or sentence. At the same time a speaker in a hurry will speak more rapidly by shortening vowel durations.

Speech sounds produced in context can differ quite substantially from the same sounds produced in isolation. A major thrust of current research in speech science is to determine the nature of these differences and how sounds interact in context. Because of the complexity of the suprasegmental characteristics of speech, it is very tempting for teachers to concentrate unduly on the simpler segmental aspects. This temptation should be avoided. Everyday oral communication involves speech in its full complexity rather than the grossly simplified and unnatural production and reception of individual speech sounds.

References

Alcorn, S. (1932). The Tadoma method. *Volta Review*, **34**, 195–198.

Boothroyd, A. (1984). Auditory perception of speech contrasts by subjects with sensorineural hearing loss. *Journal of Speech and Hearing Research*, **27**, 134–144.

Boothroyd, A. (1985). Residual hearing and the problem of carry-over in the speech of the deaf. In J. L. Lauter (Ed.), *Proceedings of the conference on the planning and production of speech in normal and hearing-impaired individuals. ASHA Reports 15*, Rockville, MD: American Speech-Language-Hearing Association.

Braeges, J. L., & Houde, R. A. (1982). Use of speech training aids. In D. G. Sims, G. G. Walter, & R. L. Whitehead. (Eds.), *Deafness and communication*, Baltimore, MD: Williams & Wilkins.

Braida, L. D., Durlach, N. I., Lippmann, R. P., Hicks, B. L., Rabinowitz, W. M., & Reed, C. M. (1979). Hearing Aids—A review of past research on linear amplification, amplitude compression and frequency lowering. *ASHA Monographs Number 19*, Rockville, MD: American Speech-Language-Hearing Association.

Brooke, N. M., & Summerfield, A. Q. (1983). Analysis, synthesis, and perception of visible articulatory movements. *Journal of Phonetics*, **11**, 63–76.

Brooks, P. L., Frost, B. J., Mason, J. L., & Gibson, D. M. (1986). Continuing evaluation of the Queen's University tactile vocoder. I: Identification of open word sets; II: Identification of open set sentences and tracking narrative. *Journal of Rehabilitation Research and Development*, **23**(1), 119–138.

Bruhn, M. E. (1949). *The Mueller-Walle method of lipreading for the hard of hearing*. Washington, DC: A. G. Bell Association for the Deaf.

Calvert, D. R., & Silverman, S. R. (1975). *Speech and deafness*. A. G. Bell Association for the Deaf, Washington DC.

Clark, G. M., Black, R., Forster, I. C., Patrick, J. F., & Tong, Y. C. (1978). Design criteria of a multiple-electrode cochlear implant hearing prosthesis. *Journal of the Acoustical Society of America*, **63**, 631–633.

Clark, G. M., Tong, Y. C., & Dowell, R. C. (1983). Clinical results with a multichannel pseudobipolar system. *Annals of the New York Academy of Sciences*, **405**, 370–376.

Cole, R. A., Rudnicky, A. I., Zue, V. W., & Reddy, D. R. (1979). Speech as patterns on paper. In R. A. Cole (Ed.), *Perception and production of fluent speech*. Hillsdale, New Jersey: Lawrence Erlbaum Associates.

Cornett, R. O. (1967). Cued speech. *American Annals of the Deaf*, **112**, 3–13.

Crichton, R. G., & Fallside, F. (1974). Linear prediction model of speech production with applications to deaf speech training. *Proceedings of the Institution of Electrical Engineers, Control and Science*, **121**, 865–873.

De Fillipo, C. L., & Scott, B. L. (1978). A method for training and evaluating the reception of ongoing speech. *Journal of the Acoustical Society of America*, **63**, 1186–1192.

Douek, E., Fourcin, A. J., Moore, B. C. J., & Clarke, G. P. (1977). A new approach to the cochlear implant. *Proceedings of the Royal Society of Medicine*, **70**, 379–383.

Erber, N. P. (1972). Auditory, visual, and auditory-visual recognition of consonants by children with normal and impaired hearing. *Journal of Speech and Hearing Research*, **15**, 413–422.

Ewing, A., & Ewing, E. C. (1964). *Teaching deaf children to talk*. Manchester: Manchester University Press. Reprinted in the United States of America by A. G. Bell Association for the Deaf, Washington, DC.

Fourcin, A. J., Douek, E. E., Moore, B. C. J., Rosen, S., Walliker, J. R., Howard, D. M., Abberton, E., & Frampton, S. (1983). Speech perception with promontory stimulation. *Annals of the New York Academy of Sciences*, **405**, 280–294.

Franklin, D. (1984). Tactile aids, new help for the profoundly deaf. *The Hearing Journal*, **37**(2), 20–23.

Friel-Patti, S., Finitzo-Hieber, T., Conti, G., & Brown, K. C. (1982). Language delay in infants associated with middle ear disease and mild, fluctuating hearing impairment. *Pediatric Infectious Diseases*, **1**, 104–109.

Friel-Patti, S., & Roeser, R. J. (1983). Evaluating changes in the communication skills of deaf children using vibrotactile stimulation. *Ear and Hearing*, **4**, 31–40.

Gold, T. (1978). *Speech and hearing skills: A comparison between hard-of-hearing and deaf children*. Doctoral Dissertation, City University of New York.

Gold, T. (1980). Speech producuion in hearing-impaired children. *Journal of Communication Disorders*, **13**, 397–418.

Goldberg, A. J. (1972). A visual feature indicator for the severely hard of hearing. *IEEE Transactions on Audio and Electroacoustics, AU-20*, 16–23.

Goldstein, M. H. & Proctor, A. (1985). Tactile aids for profoundly deaf children. *Journal of the Acoustical Society of America*, **77**, 258–265.

Guberina, P., & Asp, C. W. (1981). The verbo-tonal method for rehabilitating people with communication problems. *Monograph 13 International Exchange of Information in Rehabilitation*, New York: World Rehabilitation Fund.

Guttman, N., Levitt, H., & Bellefleur, P. A. (1970). Articulation training of the deaf using low-frequency surrogate fricatives. *Journal of Speech and Hearing Research*, **13**, 19–29.

Haycock, G. S. (1933). *The teaching of speech*. Stoke-on-Trent, England: Hill & Ainsworth. Reprinted in the United States of America by A. G. Bell Association for the Deaf, Washington, D.C.

Hochberg, I., Levitt, H., & Osberger, M. J. (1980). Improving speech services to hearing-impaired children. *ASHA*, **22**(7), 480–486.

Hochmair-Desoyer, E. S., & Hochmair, I. J. (1983). Percepts elicited by different speech-coding strategies. *Annals of the New York Academy of Sciences*, **405**, 295–306.

Houde, R. A. (1980). Visual and tactual aids for speech reception: Spectrum and temporal displays. In H. Levitt, J. M. Pickett, & R. A. Houde (Eds.). *Sensory aids for the hearing impaired*. New York: IEEE Press, Institute of Electrical and Electronic Engineers.

Hudgins, C. V. (1953). The response of profoundly deaf children to auditory training. *Journal of Speech and Hearing Disorders*, **18**, 273–288.

Hultzen, L. S., Allen, Jr., J. H., & Miron, M. S. (1964). *Tables of transitional frequencies of English phonemes*. Urbana, IL: University of Illinois Press.

Jeffers, J., & Barley, M. (1971). *Speechreading, lipreading*, Springfield, IL: Charles C. Thomas.

Johnson, D. (1975). Communication characteristics of NTID students. *Journal of the Academy of Rehabilitation Audiology*, **8**, 17–32.

Kalikow, D. N., Stevens, K. N., & Elliott, L. L. (1977). Development of a test of speech intelligibility in noise using sentence materials with controlled word predictability. *Journal of the Acoustical Society of America*, **61**, 1337–1351.

Kelly, J. C. (1953). *Clinicians handbook for auditory training*. Washington, D.C.: A. G. Bell Association for the Deaf.

Levitt, H. (1978). The acoustics of speech production. In M. Ross & T. G. Giolas (Eds.), *Auditory management of hearing impaired children*. Baltimore, MD: University Park Press.

Levitt, H. (1982). Discrimination ability in the hearing impaired: Spectrum considerations. In G. A. Studebaker & F. Bess (Eds.), *The Vanderbilt hearing aid report*. Upper Darby: Monographs in Contemporary Audiology.

Levitt, H. (1984). Technology and the education of the hearing impaired. In F. Powell, T. Finitzo-Hieber, S. Friel-Patti, & D. Henderson (Eds.), *Education of the hearing impaired child*. San Diego, CA: College Hill Press.

Levitt, H. (1986). Hearing impairment and sensory aids: A tutorial review. *Journal of Rehabilitation Research and Development*, **23**,1No. 1, xiii–xviii.

Levitt, H., (1987), Interrelationships among speech and language measures. In H. Levitt, N. S. McGarr, & D. Geffner, (Eds.), *Development of language and communication skills in hearing-impaired children*. ASHA Monographs Number 26. Rockville, MD: American Speech-Language-Hearing Association.

Levitt, H., McGarr, N. S., & Geffner, D. (1987). Development of language and communication skills in hearing-impaired children. *ASHA Monographs Number 26*. Rockville, MD: American Speech-Language-Hearing Association.

Levitt, H., Pickett, J. M., & Houde, R. A. (1980). *Sensory Aids for the Hearing Impaired*. New York: IEEE Press, Institute of Elecrical and Electronic Engineers.

Levitt, H., & Stromberg, A. (1983). Segmental characteristics of the speech of hearing-impaired children: Factors affecting intelligibility. In I. Hochberg, H. Levitt, & M. J. Osberger (Eds.), *Speech of the hearing impaired, research, training, and personnel preparation*. Baltimore, MD: University Park Press.

Levitt, H., Waltzman, S. B., Shapiro, W. H., & Cohen, N. L. (1986). Evaluation of a cochlear prosthesis using connected discourse tracking. *Journal of Rehabilitation Research and Development*, **23**(1), 147–155.

Levitt, H., & Weiss, M. (1982). Visible speech displays: Feasibility considerations. Annual Convention, American Speech-Language-Hearing Association, Toronto. See also *ASHA, 24*, 767 (abstract).

Liberman, A. M., Cooper, F. S., Shankweiler, D. P., & Studdert-Kennedy, M. (1968). Why are speech spectrograms hard to read? *American Annals of the Deaf*, **113**, 127–133.

Ling, D. (1976). *Speech and the hearing-impaired child: Theory and practice*. Washington, DC. A. G. Bell Association for the Deaf.

Ling, D., & Milne, M. (1981). The development of speech in hearing-impaired children. In F. H. Bess, B. A. Freeman, J. S. Sinclair (Eds.), *Amplification in education*. Washington, D.C.: A. G. Bell Association for the Deaf.

Magner, M. E. (1971). Techniques for teaching. In L. E. Connor (Ed.), *Speech for the deaf child: Knowledge and use*. Washington, D.C.: A. G. Bell Association for the Deaf.

McGarr, N. S., Head, J., Friedman, M., Behrman, A. M., & Youdelman, K. (1986). The use of visual and tactile sensory aids in speech production training: A preliminary report. *Journal of Rehabilitation Research and Development*, **23**(1), 101–110.

Miller, G., Heise, G., & Lichten, W. (1951). The intelligibility of speech as a function of the context of the test materials. *Journal of Experimental Psychology*, **41**, 329–335.

Monsen, R. B. (1983) General effects of deafness on phonation and articulation. In I. Hochberg, H. Levitt, & M. J. Osberger (Eds.), *Speech of the hearing impaired, research, training and personnel preparation*. Baltimore, MD: University Park Press.

Montgomery, A. A. (1980). Development of a model for generating synthetic animated lip shapes. *Journal of the Acoustical Society of America*, **68**, Supplement, page S58 (abstract).

NIH Panel on Communicative Disorders (1979). Report of the panel on communicative disorders to the national advisory neurological and communicative disorders and stroke council. *NIH Publication No. 79–1914*, Washington, D.C.: National Institutes of Health.

Nickerson, R. S., & Stevens, K. N. (1973). Teaching speech to the deaf: Can a computer help? *IEEE Transactions on Audio and Electroacoustics, AU-21*, 445–455.

Nitchie, E. B. (1912). *Lipreading principles and practice*. New York: Frederick A. Stokes Company.

Osberger, M. J., Johnstone, A., Swarts, E., & Levitt, H. (1978). The evaluation of a model speech training program for deaf children. *Journal of Communication Disorders*, **11**, 293–313.

Parkins, C. W., & Anderson, S. W. (Eds.), 1983). Cochlear prostheses, an international symposium, *Annals of the New York Academy of Sciences*, **405**, 1–532.

Pascoe, D. P. (1978). An approach to hearing aid selection. *Hearing Instruments*, **29**, 12–16, 36–37.

Paterson, M. M. (1982). Integration of auditory training with speech and language for severely hearing-impaired children. In D. G. Sims, G. G. Walter, & R. L. Whitehead (Eds.), *Deafness and Communication*, Baltimore, MD: Williams & Wilkins.

Pearsons, K. W., Bennett, R. L., & Fidell, S. (1976). *Speech levels in various environments, Report No. 3281*. Cambridge, MA: Bolt Beranek & Newman.

Peterson, G. E., & Barney, H. L. (1952). Control methods used in a study of the vowels. *Journal of the Acoustical Society of America*, **24**, 175–184.

Pollack, D. (1964). Acoupedics: A unisensory approach to auditory training. *Volta Review*, **66**, 400–409.

Pollack, D. (1970). *Educational audiology for the limited hearing infant*. Washington, D.C.: A. G. Bell Association for the Deaf.

Raphael, L. J. (1972). Preceding vowel duration as a cue to the perception of the voicing characteristic of word final consonants in American English. *Journal of the Acoustical Society of America*, **51**, 1296–1303.

Ross, M., & Giolas, T. G. (1978). *Auditory management of hearing-impaired children*. Baltimore, MD: University Park Press.

Rubenstein, A. (1985). *The effect of synthetic only versus synthetic plus analytic approach to auditory training with adventitiously hearing-impaired adults*. Doctoral dissertation, City University of New York.

Sanders, D. A. (1971). *Aural rehabilitation*. Englewood Cliffs, N.J.: Prentice-Hall, Inc.

Scheinberg, J. S. (1980). Analysis of speechreading cues using an interleaved technique. *Journal of Communication Disorders*, **13**, 484–492.

Skinner, M. W. (1979). Audibility and intelligibility of speech for listeners with sensorineural hearing losses. In P. Yanik (Ed.), *Rehabilitation strategies for sensorineural hearing loss*. New York: Grune & Stratton.

Smith, C. R. (1975). Residual hearing and speech production in deaf children. *Journal of Speech and Hearing Research*, **18**, 795–811.

Sperling, G. (1980). Bandwidth requirements for video transmission of American Sign Language and finger spelling. *Science*, **210**, 797–799.

Stark, R. E. (1972). Teaching /ba/ and /pa/ to deaf children using real-time spectral displays. *Language and Speech*, **15**, 14–29.

Stark, R. E. (Ed.), (1974). *Sensory capabilities of hearing-impaired children*, pp. 35–73, Baltimore, MD: University Park Press.

Stevens, K. N., & Blumstein, S. E. (1978). Invariant cues for place of articulation in stop consonants. *Journal of the Acoustical Society of America*, **64**, 1358–1368.

Stevens, K. N., Nickerson, R. S., & Rollins, A. M. (1983). Suprasegmental and postural aspects of speech production and their effect on articulatory skills and intelligibility. In I. Hochberg, H. Levitt, & M. J. Osberger (Eds,), *Speech of the hearing impaired, Research, training, and personnel preparation*. Baltimore, MD: University Park Press.

Stuckless, R. (1981). Real-time graphic display and language development for the hearing impaired. *Volta Review*, **83**, 291–300.

Stuckless, R., & Hurwitz, A. (1982). Reading speech in real-time print: Dream or reality? *The Deaf American*, **34**(1), 10–15.

Studebaker, G. A., & Bess, F. H., (Eds.) (1982). *The Vanderbilt hearing aid report*. Upper Darby, PA: Monographs in Contemporary Audiology.

Thies, T. L., & Trammell, J. L. (1983). Development and Implementation of the Auditory Skills Instructional Planning System. In I. Hochberg, H. Levitt, & M. J. Osberger (Eds.) *Speech of the hearing impaired, research training and personnel preparation*. Baltimore, MD: University Park Press.

Walden, B. E., Erdman, S. A. Montgomery, A. A., Schwartz, D. M., & Prosek, R. A. (1981). Some effects of training on speech recognition of hearing-impaired adults. *Journal of Speech and Hearing Research*, **24**, 207–216.

Walden, B. E., Prosek, R. A., Montgomery, A. A., Scherr, C. K., & Jones, C. J. (1977). Effects of training on the visual recognition of consonants. *Journal of Speech and Hearing Research*, **20**, 130–145.

Wedenberg, E. (1954). Auditory training of severely hard-of-hearing pre-school children. *Acta Otolaryngologica Supplement*, **110**.

Wedenberg, E. (1981). Auditory training in historical perspective. In F. H. Bess, B. A. Freeman, & J. S. Sinclair, (Eds.), *Amplification in education*. Washington, DC: A. G. Bell Association for the Deaf.

Whitehead, R. L. (1983). Some respiratory and aerodynamic patterns in the speech of the hearing impaired. In I. Hochberg, H. Levitt, & M. J. Osberger (Eds.), *Speech of the hearing impaired, Research, training, and personnel preparation*. Baltimore, MD: University Park Press.

Woodward, M. F., & Barber, C. G. (1960). Phoneme perception in lipreading. *Journal of Speech and Hearing Research*, **3**, 212–222.

Environments and Strategies for Learning and Teaching

SHEILA LOWENBRAUN AND MARIE THOMPSON

University of Washington

Introduction—Educational practices in the field of hearing impairment have changed rapidly and perhaps irrevocably in the 1970s and 1980s. Some of these changes have, at least in part, been the result of educational research efforts; others have taken place because of medical advances, political pressures, legal mandates, and technological breakthroughs. As in many areas of education, massive changes in practice have preceded research activities designed to discover the relative efficacy of the new and old approaches. It is the purpose of this chapter to synthesize the research in four different broad areas directly related to learning environments; to note how each has influenced and been influenced by current practices; and to make recommendations for further research, as well as regulatory and policy changes. The topics to be considered are: (a) changing demographics, (b) total communication, (c) technologies and media, and (d) adoption/adaption of other educational technologies.

Changing Demographics

Because of the development of the rubella vaccine, which has effectively controlled the epidemics that led to periodic increases in the hearing-impaired school population, the percentage of hearing-impaired students in the school-age population has declined. The population has now levelled off at a lower base percentage than 10 years ago, and is expected to rise and fall with the general school-age population. Currently, it is anticipated that there will be a rise in the absolute number of hearing-impaired children because of the expected increase in the population as a whole. Now, however, there is an even lower incidence of hearing impairment, which has always been a low-incidence handicapping condition. At the same time, interpretations of PL 94–142 and other pressures toward mainstreaming may have led to the decentralization of programs, with a trend toward smaller, school district-based programs and away from the larger residential or day schools. Demographic data and studies of the effects

of various placement options on the academic and social development of hearing-impaired children will be examined.

Total Communication

In the 1960s, by far the most commonly officially reported communication method used in teaching hearing-impaired children was the *oral approach*; although in many schools pure oralism existed only as stated policy and some form of sign language was routinely used, or at least tolerated, in both educational and dormitory settings. By the 1980s, a combination of communication modes called *Total Communication* was used in the vast majority of schools and classes for the deaf. Total Communication may be loosely defined as the use of some form of sign language along with the oral approach; however, precise definition of the term for comparison of research studies is elusive.

The studies preceding the widespread adoption of Total Communication will be briefly examined, although these have already been extensively reviewed in the *American Annals of the Deaf* and *Volta Review*. More attention will be focused on studies in the 1970s and 1980s regarding the efficiency of use of Total Communication, that is, how well do simultaneously produced signs and speech coincide, and the effectiveness of Total Communication in improving the language and academic achievement of hearing-impaired children. The sign language component of Total Communication has generally been some variant of Manual English: that is, signs used in English syntactic order, along with invented signs for English syntactic features that are not found in American Sign Language. New areas of research involve the comparison of these English variants with American Sign Language: a distinct and unique language with neither the morphemic nor the syntactic structure of English.

Technologies and Media

Since the 1960s, education of hearing-impaired children has been massively affected by new technological advances. The federal government played an essential role in this regard, through the creation and support of Captioned Films for the Deaf. Since the 1960s, the field has been inundated with the products of educational technology: captioned films and film strips, programmed instruction machines (project LIFE), 8-millimeter loop film cartridges, overhead projectors, closed- and open-captioned television, video tape, laser disc, telecommunication devices for the deaf (TDDs), and, of course, computers. Most of these technological innovations were widely adopted without a sound research base for their efficacy in improving education. Many, like the 8-mm loops were distributed with the aid of extensive federal funding and subsequently became technologically extinct without ever having been carefully evaluated. In this section of the chapter, experimental studies of the effectiveness of various media and technological devices to improve the achievement of hearing-impaired children and youth will be reviewed. No attempt will be made to deal with the vast improvements in amplification devices, which are discussed in Levitt's chapter on "Speech and Hearing in Communication."

Adoption and Adaption of Educational Technologies

The historical roots of education for deaf children are, to a great extent, removed from those of other areas of special education, notably mental retardation, emotional disturbance, and learning disabilities, and from regular education. In the 1960s and before, for example, teachers of hearing-impaired children were often trained in residential-school-based programs rather than in colleges or universities. Even today, in some major universities, teachers of hearing-impaired children are educated through the speech and hearing department rather than the special education department (for example, at San Diego State University, University of South Florida, Adelphi), and local programs for hearing-impaired children are often under the department of speech and hearing rather than special education. This separate development may have made educators of hearing-impaired children less aware of, and less likely to take advantage of, research in other areas of special education. This section will briefly cover the new developments in other areas of special and regular education. Most of these have not yet been evaluated for their utility in promoting educational gains for hearing-impaired students.

Methods of Search and Selection

Two major journals are devoted specifically to education of hearing-impaired children: the *American Annals of the Deaf* and the *Volta Review*. These journals publish the majority of research in the field, along with research reviews, opinion, and policy articles. Both journals were hand searched for the 10-year period of 1974–84.

In addition, the *Journal of Speech and Hearing Research*, the *Journal of Speech and Hearing Disorders*, *Ear and Hearing*, and *Language, Speech, and Hearing Services in the Schools*, publish, from time to time, pertinent education articles. These four were also searched for the 10-year period. For demographic data the publications and resources of the Office of Demographic Studies of Gallaudet College served as a primary source. The journal *Sign Language Studies* provided an important source of research on American Sign Language and other sign systems. It should be noted that the three journals (*Annals*, *Volta Review*, and *Sign Language Studies*) have well-known publication biases in the field; for example, the *Volta Review* is pro-aural/oral-only, the *Annals* is pro-Total Communication, and *Sign Language Studies* is pro-American Sign Language. These biases were kept in mind during research analyses. In addition to the above, ERIC searches were done for each topic for the 10-year period 1974–1984. Both the search for and reporting of the information included in this chapter was limited to the 10-year period because of the cohort problem discussed in Greenberg and Kusché's chapter on "Cognitive, Personal, and Social Development of Deaf Children and Adolescents."

Demographic Data

Absolute Numbers of Hearing-Impaired Children

It is impossible to extract from existing data the absolute number of hearing-impaired children in the population. Data collected by the Office of Special Education vary by state definition. In some states the category of hard of hearing begins at 20 dB; in others a more stringent criterion is maintained. Kirk and Gallagher (1983) quote a 1979 publication of the National Center for Educational Statistics as estimating the prevalence of hearing handicaps as 0.3%–0.5%, or 140,700–230,450 school-age students. The Sixth Annual Report to Congress on the Implementation of Public Law 94–142—The Education for All Handicapped Children Act (1984)—lists 75,337 children between the ages of 3 and 21 served as hard of hearing and deaf during the 1982–83 school year. This is down considerably from the 89,743 so served in school year 1976–77 (p. 6). *The American Annals of the Deaf* (1983) reports 46,257 students being served in those schools and classes responding to their survey of enrollments as of October 1982. It is likely that this lower figure underreports students served in mainstream settings with the resource of itinerant support and those served in smaller day-class programs. By 1985 the figure reported by the *Annals* was 49,552 (p. 132). The apparent growth was probably due to somewhat improved response rather than an actual population increase.

Percent of Special Education Population

Since the estimate of the total number of handicapped children in the population is between 8.2% and 16.2% of the school-age population (3,845,300–7,589,700) (Kirk & Gallagher, 1983), those who are hearing-impaired would seem to make up between 1.8% and 6% of the population of handicapped children. The Sixth Annual Report states that hard-of-hearing and deaf students being served composed 0.18% of the total school enrollment; 10.76% of the school enrollment was identified as handicapped, with by far the largest proportion labelled as learning disabled (p. 3). By these figures deaf and hard-of-hearing students represent 1.6% of the handicapped population currently served in public schools. Hearing-impaired children are a true minority, not only in terms of the general school-age population, but also within the larger special education population.

This low prevalence can, and often does, lead to significant ignorance on the part of special educators about the small subgroup with hearing handicaps. For example, a 1984 special education introductory textbook, which is "non categorical" in organization, deals with the special needs of hearing-impaired children in slightly under one page (of 494), and includes the following definition: "For practical purposes you should simply know that *deafness* means the absence of hearing in both ears." (Ysseldyke & Algozzine, 1984, p. 18). This low prevalence can, and often does, lead to isolation of educators of hearing-impaired children from the special education and regular education academic community.

Number of Special Hearing-Impaired Children

Of the 49,552 hearing-impaired children reported by the *American Annals of the Deaf* (1985) as being served, 10,135 (20.5%) were reported as being multiply handicapped. This included 573 reported as being served in facilities for other handicaps: mainly institutions for blind and mentally retarded children. It is probable that the latter number is an extreme underestimate since it is known, for example, that Down's Syndrome children often have some degree of hearing loss.

Approximately 30% of the multiply handicapped population identified in the *Annals* was labeled as *deaf-learning disabled*, including those with aphasia. An additional 37% were labeled as *deaf-mentally retarded*, and 12% were noted as *deaf-socially/emotionally disturbed*. Other smaller categories were *deaf-blind* and *deaf-blind/mentally retarded*. A significant proportion (19%) was identified only as *deaf/other multiply handicapped*. Presumably this would include orthopedic, neurological, and other health impairments.

The *Annals* does not identify the proportion of hearing-impaired students who come from homes where English is not the primary language. It is known, however, that the Hispanic surnamed portion of the hearing-impaired population is growing proportionally larger (Delgado, 1985) and that these students, as well as Asian and other students who do not receive English or ASL at home, have very special educational needs.

School Demographics

The data in the Sixth Annual Report tell us little about the number of students served as severely hard-of-hearing or deaf, and does not mention the distribution of those served within the "hearing-impaired service system." Hearing-impaired students are served in a variety of placements. Traditionally the majority of such students were educated in relatively large centralized facilities commonly called residential schools. Many students did actually reside at the schools during the term, going home for weekends or, if their residence was far from school, only during major holidays and for summers. Other students, whose homes were near the central schools, commuted daily. Some residential schools were operated by the state (e.g. Washington State School for the Deaf); some were privately operated or church affiliated, but students' tuition was paid by the state (e.g., St Mary's School for the Deaf in New York); and others were private with tuition paid for by parents (e.g., Central Institute for the Deaf in Missouri). In large cities administratively separate day schools served hearing-impaired students. In the 1980s these administrative arrangements still exist, along with a host of relatively new options, including public and private day classes houses in facilities devoted in part to regular education, multidistrict cooperative day class programs, facilities serving other handicapped children, satellite programs of residential schools, itinerant programs, and home-based and center-based parent-infant programs.

The American Annals of the Deaf have published a yearly summary of enrollments in classes and schools for deaf children. Data were gathered through self-reports, with individual programs listed by state. In 1985, school enrollments as of 1 October, 1984 were reported. A total of 793 programs responded. These served 49,552 hearing-impaired students from infant through high school age. In 70 public residential schools 15,517 students were served, and 465 were served in eight private residential schools. In facilities for other handicaps, 1,366 were reported as being served. Thus, of those served in schools and classes for deaf students, 32.25% were served in residential schools. Of the students served by residential schools 60.9% actually lived at the school.

A comparison was made between these data and those reported in the *Annals* for the 1973 school year to see in what way PL 94–142 and various state laws and court decisions influenced the enrollment patterns. In 1973, 51,837 students were listed as served in 827 schools and classes.

The database in the *Annals* may reflect a serious underreporting of smaller day programs, but it is nevertheless interesting to review placement of hearing-impaired students as portrayed in the *Annals* figures.

One precipitous drop from 1973 to 1984 was the number of students enrolled in private residential schools, which fell from 1,387 to 465, a drop of 65%. This might be attributable to the increased availability of public school programs due to PL 94–142. The percentage of enrollment in residential schools now appear to have changed substantially from about 40% of the reporting population to 32%.

Schools that are identified as residential in the self-report may, in fact, have more day students than residential students. The Lexington School for the Deaf in New York was reported as a residential school even though 425 of its 445 students were reported as day students. The distinction between a day and a residential school blurs considerably in cases like this. Such schools might more accurately be called center or centralized schools, which might or might not incorporate a residence for some students.

The 1985 *Annals* reports data on the number of children in each educational setting who are fully or partially mainstreamed. Of the 15,517 reported as attending public residential schools, 299 or 1.9% are fully mainstreamed and 6.2% are partially mainstreamed. Comparable data from students enrolled in public day classes full-time indicate 6,637 of 23,533 (28.2%) as fully mainstreamed and 9,249 (39.28%) as partially mainstreamed. These differences are highly significant. They cannot be fully attributable to either a greater number of multiply handicapped students or a greater severity of hearing loss in residential schools. Although both conditions are present, they would not account for the fact that over 67% of students in day classes experience some integration with normally-hearing peers, while only 8% of residential school students do.

Schildroth (1980) reported on the changes in enrollment in 62 public residential schools for deaf students during the period 1970–78. During this time the population of these schools dropped by 9.8%, according to data reported in the *Annual Survey of Hearing Impaired Children and Youth* of the Office of Demographic Studies. A drop of 8% in the 3 to 17-year-old general student population was noted for the same period. Residential schools in the Northeast and North Central areas experienced sharp losses (22.8% and 18.9%); schools in the West declined at the same rate as the general population; and the schools in the South grew by 4.2% (p. 83). Much of the decline in the Northeast and North Central regions was due to a loss of white students.

An article by Holman (1980) on Due Process Procedures in residential and day schools for deaf students would seem to indicate that the Least Restrictive Environment clause of PL 94–142 has had a mixed impact on self-contained schools for the deaf. Due to PL 94–142, 360 pupils were reported as transferred out of residential schools for deaf students; but during the same time period, 562 pupils were transferred in, with 58.3% of these transfers being by parent request.

During the late 1960s and 1970s a series of national demographic studies on the characteristics of the hearing-impaired child of the United States was undertaken by the Office of Demographic Studies at Gallaudet College. These studies have neither been replicated nor recently updated. Almost all of them reflect data collected prior to the full implementation of PL 94–142 and prior to the widespread adoption of Total Communication. Thus the cohort represented differs significantly from that population currently being served. For this reason, a decision was made by the authors of this chapter not to report studies based on data obtained prior to 1975, since it is of questionable current validity. This is unfortunate since most of the baseline work on extent of loss, identification and testing, etiology, and achievement was done during this period. Two of the later studies do have current relevance and will be briefly discussed.

A study by Karchmer and Peterson (1980) describes the shared characteristics and the differences between students attending the same schools as day and residential pupils in the 1977–78 school year. Both groups of students had virtually identical hearing-loss distributions. The resident group was older than the nonresident group by two years. Day students tended to be from more affluent backgrounds and to be white. They used hearing aids more often and were rated by their teachers as having greater speech intelligibility. The two groups, however, performed similarly on achievement tests. In a related report (Karchmer & Kirwin, 1977), residential status at a residential school was the best predictor of the amount of hearing-aid use in the classroom. "Not living at a residential school is associated with greater amounts of hearing aid use" (p. 16). Other significant variables included year of birth (hearing-aid use declined with age), having a moderate or severe hearing loss, and not having hearing-impaired parents.

MAINSTREAMING AND THE "LEAST RESTRICTIVE ENVIRONMENT"

Introduction

Education of deaf children in the United States has a long history. The first permanent school for deaf students, the American Asylum for the Education of the Deaf and Dumb, was opened in Hartford, Connecticut, in 1817. This residential school is still in existence as the American School for the Deaf. (For a more detailed history see Moores, 1982.) Many of the early schools for deaf students were established by state legislatures to serve all deaf students near major population centers; others were established in relatively rural or remote areas. These state schools, and many of the private ones in the 1800s, were residential. Children lived at the school during the term, sometimes going home at weekends or, more often, if they lived at a distance, only going home on major holidays and during the summer break. Not only were the children educated at residential schools; their teachers also received their training at such schools as Lexington School for the Deaf, and Clarke School. Teachers, too, were segregated: they took little or no coursework in regular education or in "normal schools" or colleges, but rather studied under and were apprenticed to the teachers at their training schools.

Because of the low prevalence of severe hearing impairment in the school-age population, the residential or centralized school offered, and offers, many advantages. Since it can draw from a larger population base, relatively unhampered by commuting distance, sufficient numbers of hearing-impaired children can be gathered to permit appropriately graded classes and, at the secondary level, subject matter specialists and prevocational and vocational teachers who are specifically trained to deal with deaf students. Equally as important is the access that deaf children in schools have to the "unwritten curriculum" described by Garretson (1977). They can interact with a variety of deaf as well as hearing adults since deaf people are often employed as teachers, aids, dormitory counselors, and in other school-related roles. At such a school, students can take part in a variety of extracurricular activities; sports, clubs, and social events are all geared to their special needs. Because of the larger population base, specialists such as speech and language teachers, audiologists, psychologists, and counselors trained to work with the special population are often available. Important too is the availability of a large peer group for socialization.

All these positive factors must be weighed against some important negatives: potential alienation from home and family due to prolonged absences and the inability to communicate, lack of normal peer role models, and an institutional lifestyle that might not be an appropriate preparation for community life as an adult.

Because of the mandates of PL 94–142 and various state laws and court decisions, more and more school districts are operating programs for hearing-impaired children. With a shrinking population base and a larger number of local programs, it is inevitable that the number of students per program will be smaller. Indeed, the smallest program listed in the *Annals* (1985) reported a total of two students; many reported populations of 10 or fewer. The implications for both appropriate educational programming and socialization are obvious.

The Conference of Executives of American Schools for the Deaf in 1976 adopted a position statement on "least restrictive" placements of deaf students (*American Annals of the Deaf*, 1977). This balanced statement indicates that although a goal of education of deaf children is placement in instructional settings that resemble those of hearing children, extreme care must be taken to assess the quality of the educational placement "in terms of both socialization and instruction" (p. 70). The statement emphasizes the point that if a choice must be

made between a "less restrictive environment" and full services, the choice should be toward the full service environment.

With all the controversy over the concept of least restrictive environment, research has not provided either much data or any solutions. The following is a review of studies from 1976 to the present. The studies are of two basic types: those that compare the effects of residential (nonintegrated) placement, and some degrees of less restrictive environment on aspects of the social, emotional, and/or academic growth of hearing-impaired children; and those that analyze predictors of success in integrated environments.

Influence of School Placement on Social, Emotional, and/or Academic Development

Farrugia and Austin (1980) reviewed previous studies on the effect of integrating hearing-impaired students since 1959. Their review of seven studies indicates an overall academic advantage in day-class placement, but a disadvantage in terms of social and emotional growth. In the 1980 study, 200 students aged 10–15 were divided into four groups: deaf public school students (loss of 65 dB or greater), deaf residential school students, hard-of-hearing public school students, and hearing public school students. Students in day classes were considered integrated if they attended a regular public school. No attempt was made to define integration in terms of the extent of time, if any, that the students attended class with hearing peers. The Meadow/Kendal Social-Emotional Assessment Inventory for Deaf Students was used. This instrument asks teachers to rate 69 sentences as descriptors of student behavior in the areas of maturity, social adjustment, emotional adjustment, and self-esteem. Results indicated that deaf students in public schools were ranked lower than the other groups on the scales of maturity, self-esteem, social adjustment, and emotional adjustment. Deaf public school students scored significantly lower than deaf residential school students on each of the four scales. Hard-of-hearing students generally scored as well as hearing students except in the area of self-esteem. The researchers admit the possibility of teacher bias in filling out the questionnaires. We would stress the fact that teachers in residential settings do not have a normally-hearing student population with which to compare their students, and may over-estimate their social abilities.

Antia (1982) analyzed the social interaction of seven classes of hearing-impaired children in five schools, who were partially mainstreamed in Grades 1-6. In four of the five schools the mode of communication was oral; in the fifth, simultaneous communication was used. An observation instrument was used to record four categories of behavior: physical proximity, interaction, mode of communication, and unusual behavior. The hearing-impaired children's behavior in the integrated setting was also compared with their behavior in their special class. Hearing-impaired children were not physically isolated in the regular class, but did interact significantly less often with peers and more often with teachers than did the hearing children. Hearing-impaired children increased their interaction with teachers, increased their use of oral and/or simultaneous communication, and decreased their use of nonverbal communication while in the special class. The authors conclude that physical integration is not sufficient to promote either the use of oral language or social interaction. They do note that some situations in the regular class, such as sharing art materials or working on a cooperative project, increased social interaction.

Reich, Hambleton, and Houldin (1977) report on the academic and social effects of four degrees of mainstreaming from full integration to partial segregation on 195 hearing-impaired children in and around Toronto. Emphasis was on hard-of-hearing rather than severely or profoundly hearing-impaired children. Degree of hearing varied by program type, with more integrated students having considerably better hearing. Using stepwise multiple regression analyses to partial out differences due to hearing loss and other personal and educational background variables, significant differences were found in favor of the more integrated groups at the elementary level. Those in the special hard-of-hearing classes (partial segregation) had significantly lower scores in reading and language than the more integrated groups. Integrated students were also better adjusted socially. No differences were found in language, self-concept, or speech intelligibility. Children in hard-of-hearing classes fell further behind in reading, the longer they remained in these classes. The longer that children were in the itinerant program, the more improvement there was in their language and speech intelligibility. At the high school level fully integrated students declined in self-concept and itinerant students became, with time, somewhat less well-adjusted socially. Thus, for this group of students, integration was seen to have a slight positive effect on achievement and a slight negative effect at the secondary level on self-concept.

Rister (1975) conducted a follow-through study of 88 hearing-impaired children who had received preschool education at the Speech and Hearing Institute of Houston. Questionnaires were sent to parents and to school administrators. Sixty-two percent of the students were enrolled in regular education classes; 38% were in special education. Of the regular education enrollees, 81.9% were reported as achieving adequately for their age or grade level; only 6% of those in special education were so described. Those in regular education had significantly better language on entering the preschool program and gained significantly more before leaving the program than did those in special education. There was greater parental involvement in the regular education group during the preschool years than in the special education group.

Unfortunately, statistical comparisons of the hearing levels of the two groups are not made and Rister concludes that "the degree of hearing impairment does not in itself determine the choice of teaching environment" (p. 287). Although this is unarguably true, it is also interesting to note that 87.3% of the students in special education are reported as having hearing losses of 85 dB or greater, and only 56% of those in regular education are so reported. Of the regular education group, 25.4% have losses of 74 dB or less; only 6.1% of the special education group do, and none of this group is reported as having a loss of 64 dB or less. Thus, one can definitely not dismiss the effect of hearing loss on school placement and academic achievement.

Sarfaty and Katz (1978) administered the Tennessee Self-Concept Scale to 48 eighth- and ninth-grade hearing-impaired students in Israel. This represents the entire hearing-impaired population in the 14 to 15-year-old range in the country. The students were being educated in three different environments: a special school, a special class in a regular school, and in regular schools in integrated programs. The special class group had significantly better hearing than did the other two groups. Results indicated that students in the group integration (special class) setting had the highest scores; the next highest were those of students in individual integration settings; the special school students had by far the lowest scores. The authors note that there was no difference between the three groups on self-acceptance, and all groups scored significantly differently from and worse than a group of normally-hearing peers.

Kennedy, Northcott, McCauley and Williams (1976) report longitudinal data on 11 children with severe to profound hearing losses who were part of a population of 32 graduates of an auditory-oral infant preschool program and were subsequently integrated into regular classes. The procedures by which the 11 were selected is not described so it is not possible to generalize to the population as a whole on the basis of the data provided. The results indicated that children with severe and profound losses were chosen on sociometric instruments significantly more often than were their hearing peers in the first year of the study, at the same rate in the second year, and significantly less frequently in the third year. Hearing-impaired children were not significantly different from their peers in self-perception of status. In achievement, at Grades 2 and 3 the mean scores of the hearing-impaired children were lower than were those of their hearing peers in every area but one: the Peabody Individual Achievement Test spelling subtest. The only significant difference (using a t-test) was in the Metropolitan Achievement Test subtest on word knowledge; on this test the hearing-impaired children's mean was almost two full grades below that of their peers (3.05 vs. 4.96).

Gregory, Shanahan, and Walberg (1984) utilized the data obtained from a large national survey of high school students, the "High School and Beyond" study (1982), and isolated a sample of 514 integrated high school seniors, out of a population of 26,146, who identified themselves as hard-of-hearing or deaf. The hearing-impaired sample was significantly older and had significantly more secondary handicaps (perhaps because many were postrubella) than the group as a whole had. Black students were significantly underrepresented in the hearing-impaired sample, and both Asian and Hispanic groups were overrepresented.

Hearing-impaired students were inferior to their hearing peers in academic achievement in reading, vocabulary, and mathematics; had less school motivation; took fewer academic classes; did less homework; and were less "work orientated." It must be noted that the achievement of these students, although below that of normally-hearing peers, is considerably above the mean for the hearing-impaired population as a whole.

Predictors of Success in Mainstreaming Studies

Brackett and Henninges (1976) investigated the communicative interaction of 13 preschool-age hearing-impaired children educated in an integrated setting with an equivalent number of hearing peers. Results indicated that more interactions in which a hearing-impaired child was the initiator took place in free-play settings than in the structured language group. Hearing-impaired children who could put two words together interacted significantly more often with hearing peers than did children with more limited skills. Children with more limited skills—who by and large also had greater hearing losses—tended to interact more often with hearing-impaired peers and interacted infrequently with hearing students, regardless of the setting.

Pflaster (1980) conducted a factor analysis of the variables related to academic performance of 1,982 hearing-impaired students in mainstreamed settings. Subjects were selected as having a bilateral hearing loss greater than 30 dB and were in regular classes for "almost the entire day" (p. 73); most (90%) received support services from teachers of deaf students or from speech and hearing clinicians. An intercorrelation matrix containing 64 independent variables related to reading scores on the Stanford Achievement Test was obtained. These intercorrelated factors were reduced to 13 orthogonal factors: 3 major and 10 minor. The three major factors were oral communication (factors relating to speech reading and speech), personality (such as motivation, self-concept, frustration tolerance), and linguistic competence. Oral communication factors accounted for 37% of the variance. Minor factors included the intrinsic factors of auditory behavior, self-confidence, artistic ability, and synthetic ability; and the extrinsic factors of sibling constellation (smaller-family children did better); parental acceptance, attitude and expectations; teacher attitude; and administrator attitude. Pflaster does not mention whether her sample students were integrated with or without the support of a manual interpreter; however, one might infer that no manual interpreting services were available. Results, therefore,

might not be applicable to those hearing-impaired students who are provided with interpreting services.

In 1981, Pflaster re-analyzed the data to discover the interrelationships among her previously discussed factors, and 11 oblique (correlated) factors were discovered. The first four of these—suprasegmentals, expressive language, motivation, and receptive language—accounted for 65% of the variance. Other factors were speechreading skills, interpersonal behavior, communicative attitude, personal adjustment, sibling constellation, auditory attitude, and classroom communication. Pflaster concludes that the development of auditory/oral skills is critical to success in the mainstream. Again, no mention of the use of an interpreter is made, and one infers that students were integrated into classes where there was no manual communication available. In neither article does Pflaster talk about absolute magnitudes of achievement difference between students above and below the mean on her predictor variables.

In addition to the Pflaster studies, such authorities as Nix (1976) and Northcott (1973) have edited volumes on the criteria and processes for successfully integrating hearing-impaired children into the mainstream. Both works emphasize approximately the same factors as does Pflaster.

Conclusion

From the foregoing review, it is evident that mixed results and insufficient and perhaps unrepresentative samples preclude definable answers about the effects of various degrees of mainstreaming on hearing-impaired students. It is possible to conclude only very tentatively that exposure to normally-hearing children may yield some degree of academic advantage and some degree of lower self-concept. One might also conclude, less tentatively, that hearing-impaired students on the average do not perform at an academic level near or equal to that of their normally-hearing peers in any setting, and that the absolute magnitude of difference increases with age.

In the preceding studies, it was assumed that the residential school represented a more restrictive educational environment than other placement options. Current demographic data would seem to support this view. Craig and Salem (1975) raise another possibility. These researchers surveyed residential schools for deaf students to determine the extent to which these schools integrated hearing-impaired students with nonhandicapped students. Of 75 responses, 39 indicated some integration. Integration took place most often at the senior high school level and in smaller residential schools. The researchers provide both cumulative data and anecdotal reports based on visits to eight schools. They conclude that "with careful organization, thoughtful selection of the cooperating school, and sensitive encouragement of deaf students, partial integration can serve as a valuable extension of the residential school program for deaf students" (p. 36). No data on the efficacy of the approach are published; however, it would seem to be a fruitful area for research. Neither were any studies found on the effects of mainstreaming using a manual interpreter or interpreter/tutor. The variables cited by Pflaster (1980, 1981), Nix (1976), Northcott (1973), and others as being vital for success in integrated placements may not play the same role if manual communication is available.

TOTAL COMMUNICATION

According to Garretson (1976), Total Communication traces its heritage to the early part of the 16th century when master teachers worked with selected students using a tutorial approach to teach a combination of mimetic gesture, fingerspelling, signs, and speech (p. 88). Classroom instruction, with its incipient controversies between oral and manual methods, began during the 18th century. In the United States, although the use of sign had been introduced by Gallaudet and Clerc, emphasis was placed upon the oral-only approach; and until the late 1960s and early 1970s day schools, day classes, and private residential schools were almost all exclusively oral (Quigley & Paul, 1984). The present-day combined oral, aural, and manual approach to teaching hearing-impaired children, known as Total Communication, was introduced during the late 1960s by Roy Holcomb, a deaf educator and father of a deaf child (Garretson, 1976).

Definition

Total Communication (TC) has been variously described as an approach, a right, a method, and a philosophy. TC, as defined by the Conference of Executives of American Schools for the Deaf, is "a philosophy incorporating appropriate aural, manual, and oral modes of communication in order to ensure effective communication with and among hearing-impaired persons" (Garretson, 1976) p. 88. It depends upon a multidimensional approach which can meet the individual needs of the hearing-impaired child while ensuring that the need for language input is always addressed. It is flexible and includes various modes of communication such as speech, speechreading, writing, and auditory training (using amplification), supported by finger spelling and sign language.

TC allows the child, while learning to use the auditory system and to produce speech, to "interact and experiment with a reliable symbol system, find out for himself how it works and continue to expand it through usage" (Denton, 1972) p. 11. Within this framework, it is anticipated that teaching the use of each modality will receive equal emphasis because each plays a critical part in encouraging a climate of meaningful communication. However, it is also expected that, in order to meet the needs of the individual child, the strengths shown in one mode will be used to supplement the weakness in

another mode (Garretson, 1976). The definition advanced by the National Association of the Deaf (Schlesinger, Meadow, & Yannacone, 1974) differs from the above in that it is referred to as a system, it includes reference to psychological components, and it is more explicit: "TC is a system of human communication which supports the auditory, visual, vocal and psychological components of human communication. It involves the simultaneous use of speech with a manual representation of each spoken word" (p. xx)

Yannacone, in her 1977 speeches elaborates upon the various components of TC as defined above and describes the components as follows:

Auditory:
Early amplification;
Careful selection of an appropriate hearing aid;
Daily monitoring of the hearing aid;
Consistent use of amplification;
Continual training in listening skills, and
Acceptance and understanding of the importance of amplification for speech development.
Speech: Speech intelligibility of the child will be influenced by various factors:
Severity of the hearing loss;
Configuration of the hearing loss;
Age at which amplification is introduced;
Quality of the amplification and auditory training;
Quality of ongoing speech training.
Visual linguistic system: Meaningful symbolic clues based in large part on the vocabulary of American Sign Language. It is augmented by a series of new signs and word endings. The syntax is different from American Sign Language: it reproduces the spoken English syntax. Total Communication also includes attention to the input given through speech reading.
Psychological: Includes the attitudes of the significant people in the deaf child's environment towards the use of Total Communication. Language is not only a system of codified symbols by which people have agreed to abide, it is also invested with a multitude of feelings of great importance. Thus whether the language is accepted, respected, forbidden or despised, whether it is used joyfully and openly or against taboo will be interpreted by the child as acceptance or rejection of himself or herself. If Total Communication is seen as a second class method of presentation, if it is seen as something to be used when all else fails, this will influence the attitudes of the parents and teachers toward learning Total Communication. This in turn will affect how well it is utilized with the child.

The philosophy or system of Total Communication is supported by the National Association of the Deaf (1974), "because it enhances and accelerates language and intellectual development and because its usage implies greater acceptance of the deaf child and his different needs, which in turn promotes greater self-esteem and mastery of the environment" and by psychiatrists who work regularly with hearing-impaired persons because it facilitates communication and provides an environment more conducive to good mental health (e.g., Freeman, 1976; Rainer & Altshuler, 1971; Schlessinger & Meadow, 1972). Garretson (1976), in his summary presentation about TC, specifies elements that should be included in a TC program. His list of elements specifically includes ASL and "gestemic" signs and gestures.

Elements of Total Communication

American Sign Language (Ameslan or ASL)

standard signs	unique grammar
non-English language	unique syntax
some	
fingerspelling	

one sign = one concept

Aural/Oral

amplification	oral gesture (silent mouthing)
lipreading	speech

cued speech (eight hand configurations, four facial positions)

lipsign = one or more phonemes

Fingerspelling

finger rather than hand signs
letters run together as in oral or written production
Rochester method (fingerspelling combined with speech)

hand configuration = one letter

Gestemic

childrenese	natural gestures
esoteric (localisms)	pantomime
international sign	

gesture = one concept

Manual English

Seeing Essential English	fingerspelling
Signed English	standard sign often used as root
Signing Exact English	creation of new signs for
Linguistics of Visual	inflections, ending, tense,
English	affixed, articles

sign = one word or affix

Siglish (Sign English)

Pidgin Sign English	standard sign modified on
fingerspelling	continuum toward English
syntax heavily English-	gear-shifting between
oriented	English and ASL idiom

sign = one concept

From Garretson (1976).

Although proponents of TC advocate some form of sign as a part of the method or philosophy, no single sign system has been identified as the system of choice; instead, individual programs using TC select their own manually coded system. To further complicate matters, there is often frequent borrowing among systems and many programs or communities have developed new signs that are used locally for specific purposes and do not have national recognition or usage (Quigley & Paul, 1984).

An additional complicating factor is reflected in the fact that some professionals equate simultaneous communication (SC) with Total Communication (TC). According to Caccamise, Ayers, Finch, and Mitchell (1978), SC is only one method of communication that might be used within a TC program, and the two are not synonymous. Yet, according to Quigley and Paul, "The combination of signs, fingerspelling, and speech in English word order is known as the simultaneous method" (p. 11).

When the literature discussing the definitions of the various manually coded systems is reviewed, again there is some discrepancy among writers as to what a system is called and what is included within a system. These variable coded systems of English are combined in a variety of ways with oral, oral-aural, speechreading, fingerspelling, and the printed word. These various permutations are taught under the rubric of TC to approximately 65% of the deaf children in the United States (Jordan, Gustason, & Rosen, 1976). The manual systems taught within the TC structure usually follow, to a greater or lesser extent, spoken English. The following are those usually referred to as being used in a TC program.

Manually Coded English

Caccamise et al. (1978) appear to use Manually Coded English as a generic term under which fall three different subsets: Pidgin Sign English, Manual English, and Fingerspelling; whereas Quigley and Paul (1984) refer to Manually Coded English as the use of signs in English order without the use of inflected endings. Finger spelling is used when sign equivalents are not available (p. 8).

Pidgin Sign English (PSE)

Pidgin sign incorporates the use of ASL signs and English word order, but makes limited or no use of the English inflectional system. The proportional use of ASL and English may vary according to who is using it and the purposes and need of that person. According to Caccamise et al. (1978), PSE is "a subset of manually coded English and . . . may include spelling, word-mouthing, fingerspelling, ASL, new signs, body English, facial expression, etc." (p. 898). Other terms that have been applied to this system are Siglish, Ameslish, Sign English, Signed English, and Manual English.

Manual English (ME)

According to Caccamise et al. (1978), this system supplements Pidgin Sign English because new signs are invented as needed to represent new words, inflectional endings, and other structural elements. English word order is preserved and all "little" words as well as endings are used. This system appears to approximate to Quigley and Paul's (1984) Manually Coded English, except that their definition does not include the use of the English inflectional system.

Some Manual English systems attempt to maintain the meaning or concept intact when developing vocabulary so that "*right* answer," "turn *right*," "*write*," and "*rite*" would all have distinct signs. Other systems differ because they vary in the degree of closeness they maintain to the "root" meanings of words and because they build a sign lexicon that involves meaning, pronunciation, and spelling of spoken English. Examples of Manual English systems include Seeing Exact English (SEE I), Signing Exact English (SEE II), Linguistics of Visual English (LOVE), and a Signed English system developed at Galluadet for deaf children between the ages of one and six years.

Fingerspelling

Hand and figure configurations that represent the 26 letters of the English alphabet and the arabic numerals used in English permit a person to "write in the air." "Fingerspelling may or may not be used in conjunction with speech. Visible English and the Rochester Method use fingerspelling and speech exclusively" (Caccamise et al., 1978, p. 898).

The fact that there is inconsistency, disagreement, and no single definition of TC or for the manual systems used within TC affects the knowledge that can be derived from research in this area, since most investigators either do not understand that many sign systems exist or they fail to specify the system when reporting their studies. The problem is exacerbated by the fact that conclusions about deficiencies within "the system" (TC) or success in using it are based on a very limited number of research studies.

Studies of TC

Adoption of TC

In an attempt to discern how many programs were using TC, Garretson (1976) sent questionnaires to 145 educational programs for hearing-impaired students in the United States, each having an enrollment of at least 100 students. He received information about the year the use of TC was officially implemented within the programs of 76 respondents. The data provided in this report indicate that new TC programs increased from zero in 1965–66 to over 75 in 1975–76. Of the programs reporting, 76 (87.7%) were using TC and all of these were using TC from preschool until graduation. Programs which had not adopted a TC approach numbered 15 (12.3%). Although Garretson states that he requested a definition of TC from each program, no information is provided the reader about responses to this question or whether it included a request for type of sign system used.

Jordan, Gustason, and Rosen (1976) surveyed 970 educational programs for hearing-impaired students to find out what type of communication method was being used and what system of sign was being used as a part of TC. Programs responding numbered 796, or 82% of the programs surveyed. In this questionnaire, Jordan et al. defined TC as "the use of manual signs, fingerspelling, speechreading, and amplification" (p. 527). As these authors point out, the data evaluating the use of TC is more clearly viewed when referenced to classrooms rather than programs. Their results showed that "the number of classes reporting the use of TC as the primary mode is far greater than the number of classes reporting the use of all other modes combined" (p. 528); it is the method used in 64% of all classes included in the response. The investigators' attempt to determine what type of manual communication was used within TC programs could only be accomplished by listing books of sign vocabulary and having personnel check those most used. The reason that the investigators were forced to use this type of questionnaire was the variability among programs across the country in terms of definitions and terminology used when discussing TC.

In 1979, Jordan, Gustason, and Rosen again found that the use of TC was increasing, and Trybus (1979) reported that nearly 66% of all special programs subscribe to a TC approach. These reports fail to provide the specific demographic information that is needed in order to begin to look carefully at the area of TC and whether or not it contributes to the education of hearing-impaired children. We still do not have complete information about how many hearing-impaired students are involved in TC programs, how each TC program is defined, how many in TC programs are using a specific manual approach and which one that might be, what additional elements are incorporated into the TC program, what the degree of hearing loss is, and how many use a manual system at school only or at home and at school.

Efficiency of TC: Congruence of Speech and Sign

One of the problems identified in using manually coded systems is the amount of time it takes to transmit information. The use of signs can take up to two and one-half times longer than spoken language (Bellugi & Fisher, 1972), suggesting a lack of congruence between signed and spoken English. Kluwin (1981b) identifies two incongruencies between manually coded and spoken English: (a) a single concept such as *dogs* requires two motions (*dog* plus *s*) in sign, with the two movements being made at different points on the body; thus, the time it takes to *say* "dogs" is far shorter; and (b) it is more difficult to "short-cut" in sign, for example, *gonna* instead of *go-ing to*. It is of interest, however, to note that Montgomery and Mitchell (1981), evaluating British sign systems, found that British Signed English

(BSE) is more rapid than MCE as reported in an examination by Bellugi and Fisher. Mitchell (1982) summarizes the use of MCE within TC: "All available evidence suggests that deaf children can acquire English through the use of MCE systems. What is less clear, however, is whether MCE systems are at present being used to their best advantage" (p. 335).

How Well TC is Taught

There appear to be few studies that address the issue of how well TC is being modeled, either by parents or teachers. The few that are available suggest that most adults are not providing the best model for children to replicate. Marmor and Pettito (1979) assessed two teachers as they communicated with the deaf children in their classes in order to determine how well their communication represented English grammar. The two teachers were selected by the school administrator because they had "an exceptionally good command of Manual English and simultaneous communication . . ." (p. 100). Results of this study showed very clearly that what the students were receiving was far from a perfect reproduction of spoken English. Function words and other important grammatical parts of the linguistic message were missing, as were some key or content words. Declarative sentences and questions were signed incorrectly 90% of the time, pronouns and verb tenses were incorrect about 66% of the time, and "relative clauses were ungrammatical in all instances." Kluwin (1981a) examined three different groups of teachers in the classroom: hearing teachers inexperienced at signing, experienced signing teachers, and deaf teachers. Although he found that practice and experience increased the quality of the communication, he also found that the teachers in the study were more interested in communicating content, as opposed to maintaining form, and that generally the teachers did not conform to the notion that Manual English accurately represents spoken English. The same lack of adherence to English structure was found by Reich and Bick (1977). Ungrammatical signing was found to be used also by hearing mothers who had started learning sign at the time their children were identified as having a hearing loss, had taken numerous sign classes, and had been signing with their children for at least two years. When communication samples of the mothers were evaluated, a mean of only 40.5 utterances was signed completely (Swisher & Thompson, 1985). Thus, one of the variables to be considered when evaluating the effectiveness of TC is how carefully the signed portion of TC is being used and taught by adults who are teaching it to very young children and students.

Effectiveness of TC

IC Studies

Considering the controversy surrounding the use of TC versus the oral-aural approach, there are relatively few experimental studies that carefully define and control the required variables (including identification of the specific sign system) and compare the outcomes of the two methods, TC and oral-aural.

Several studies in the 1960s supported the use of sign and suggested at least improved language and no difference in speech production (e.g., Montgomery, 1966; Stuckless & Birch, 1966). Nix (1975) dismisses these studies because they were not designed to address the question of TC versus oral-aural and because of design flaws. Nix states also that many studies that supported the use of sign were descriptive rather than experimental, but this same thing can be said of support for oral programs (e.g., Reeves, 1977). Because of the cohort problem and because TC did not evolve until the late 1960s, it might be more profitable to review research studies that followed during the 1970s and early 1980s.

The following section reports studies reviewing oral and TC approaches and language development, as well as comparing TC and oral-aural, first for the very young child and then for school-age students.

Early Childhood

Whether supporting a TC or oral-aural approach, it appears that professionals agree that early identification and early education of hearing-impaired children and their families is of the utmost importance. However, although studies have been reported that support comparability of development of language in deaf infants with deaf parents to that of hearing infants with hearing parents (e.g., Bellugi & Klima, 1982; Newport & Ashbrook, 1977) and substantial development in vocabulary and semantic relationships (Schlesinger & Meadow, 1972), few studies make direct comparisons between TC and oral-aural programs. Rather, most hearing-impaired children appear to be examined within an individual set, such as ASL, TC, or oral-aural. For example, Skarakis and Prutting (1977) studied four profoundly deaf children for four weeks. The children, between 35 and 50 months old, were in an oral program. The authors found that the children were following the developmental language steps of normally-hearing children but were severely delayed, functioning between 9 and 18 months. Schlessinger and Meadow (1972) and Collins-Ahlgren (1975) provide detailed longitudinal descriptions of young children reared in environments where signing was used. These investigators found that (a) the emergence of signs generally paralleled the emergence of oral language in normally-hearing children, (b) the children's speech production increased as they became more proficient in using sign, and (c) the communicative interactions between mothers and children showed decreased frustration and stress. Three case studies (Gardner & Zorfass, 1983; Prinz & Prinz, 1979; Thompson & Swisher, 1985) follow the language development of young children with severe to profound hearing loss. These children developed proficiency in use of language through signs and, eventually, used speech to communicate, thus demonstrating that the use of a sign system does not preclude the use of speech.

Comparative Studies of Young Children

TC vs. Oral-Aural. Two recent longitudinal studies describe language acquisition using aural, oral, and TC approaches. Shafer and Lynch (1981) studied for four to seven months the language of six hearing-impaired children 14–30 months old who were divided evenly among oral, aural, or TC groups. Compared to the language development of normal-hearing children, the language of these hearing-impaired children developed more slowly and their lexicons were not as varied. Significantly, at all states of language measured, the TC group had larger vocabularies and longer mean lengths of utterance (MLU) than the oral and aural groups. By the end of the study, two children in the TC group were producing most language orally without signs. Nordèn (1981), reporting preliminary results of a longitudinal study of 23 preschool children in Malmö, Sweden, found that using signs accelerated language development and helped children use their residual hearing because the signs gave meaning to the sounds. Further, TC assisted the children's general adjustment to the classroom and social interaction with peers and adults. The children reared in an oral environment had adjustment problems, evidenced particularly by their pretending to understand when they really did not. The presence in this environment "was an obstacle to their learning and their language development." Finally, much to the researchers' surprise, the TC children developed spontaneous speech.

> The results of our study demonstrate that it is well advised to introduce signs as early as possible in the communication with a hearing-impaired child in order not to lose important years of communication. With children who have functional residual hearing, speech will develop spontaneously in an environment using total communication. (Nordèn, 1981, p. 405).

Greenberg, Calderon, and Kusché (1984) evaluated the effects of two early intervention (3–5 years of age) programs for hearing-impaired children. One delivered systematic services, which included an emphasis on manual input, to families of very young hearing-impaired children. The other program was unsystematic and the earliest intervention focused on oral-aural skills. The experimental group (systematic instruction, including emphasis upon manual skills) showed advanced communication skills and the families provided longer, more relaxed interaction with their children. Communication using intelligible speech was poor for both groups (5.5%). The authors report that the poor speech reflected a criticism by parents in both groups that too little emphasis had been placed on oral skills. These data are supported by an earlier study (Meadow, Greenberg,

Erting, & Carmichael, 1981) that compared interaction and communication between dyads of deaf mothers-deaf children, hearing mothers-hearing children, and oral hearing mothers-deaf children, manual mothers-deaf children. Results indicated that oral-only mothers spent less time interacting with their children than any of the other groups.

Two studies that might be referred to as ex post facto quasi-experiments (Nix, 1975) are those of Brasel and Quigley (1977) and Parasnis (1983). Although the research in these reports was accomplished with older students, they are included in this section because the results are reflective of the early education these students received. Brasel and Quigley studied the effects of different communication modes during early childhood by testing the language of children between the ages of 10 and 18 years. The four groups of students were organized on the basis of hearing or deaf parents and whether Manual English, average Manual English, intensive oral, or average oral communication had been used with them when they were very young. The two manual groups had deaf parents who either possessed above average or average manual skills. Results showed that the Manual English group performed significantly better than the intensive oral group on four of the six language structures tested, significantly better than the average oral group on all language structures tested, but better than the average manual group on only one test measure.

Somewhat different results were obtained by Parasnis (1983), who evaluated cognitive and language skills (spoken, written, and signed) of college-age deaf students, as well as field independence ("the ability to perceive a visual form embedded within a surrounding context," p. 588). The two groups in this study were (a) deaf students of deaf parents who were enveloped in ASL from birth, and (b) deaf students whose hearing parents used oral communication when they were young. This latter group learned to sign between the ages of 6 to 12 years. In general, the two groups performed equally on all tests except those of speech reception and speech intelligibility. On these two tests, the students with hearing parents were superior. Although Parasnis makes the point that therefore early exposure to ASL (or sign) is not necessarily responsible for cognitive and communication development, he fails to point out that both of his groups were essentially manual from *at least* 12 years to college age.

School-Age and Older

Most studies evaluating TC during school-age years have concentrated on TC in relation to language development, communication, or general learning. Few comparative studies are available. Various studies have examined the development of an idiosyncratic sign system by deaf children who were enrolled in oral programs and felt a need to communicate (Goldin-Meadow & Feldman, 1977; Mohay, 1983). Other studies have shown that students whose parents sign consistently have greater comprehension of syntactic structures and more advanced operational skills than most students whose parents do not (Dolman, 1983), or that parents and educators are frustrated when the deaf child does not sign carefully and communication is impaired (Cokely & Gawlik, 1974). Unimodal versus bimodal learning was examined by Brooks, Hudson, and Reisberg (1981), and by Stall and Marshall (1984). Both investigations found that hearing-impaired students learned more quickly and retained information when using fingerspelling and/or lipreading to accompany auditory input as opposed to using auditory methods alone.

Bornstein, Saulnier, and Hamilton (1980) studied twenty 4-year-old deaf children, who were using Signed English (SE), for a period of four years. Annual language testing showed that vocabulary learned by these students was accelerated because it was similar to that reported for other deaf children who were three years older. However, the communications mode of the "other deaf" children is not provided. The rate of growth was reported to be only 45% of that established as normal for hearing peers.

Geers, Moog, and Schick (1984) used the Grammatical Analysis of Elicited Language—Simple Sentence Level (GAEL-S) where children produce a sentence in response to the examiner moving objects to measure differences in grammatical skills between students from oral and TC programs. In this test, if the child's first production is considered to be grammatically incorrect, the examiner produces a corrected model; the student then imitates this corrected model. Using this test, Geers found that oral students performed better than TC students on certain grammatical structures (demonstratives, pronouns, articles, quantifiers, adjectives, possessives, verbs, object noun, and subject noun), whereas TC students performed better on copula, negative, and copula inflection. Both groups performed equally on verb inflections, prepositions, conjunctions, and wh— questions. It is possible that the results of this study could, at least in part, reflect the emphasis placed on certain structures by teachers in the various programs from which the students were selected.

In an attempt to respond to concern about deterioration of speech and speechreading skills if manual communication is used, Conklin, Subtelny, and Walker (1980) evaluated speech, speechreading, and manual skills for 78 deaf students at the National Technical Institute for the Deaf for a period of two years. The results of this study clearly support the premise that speech and speechreading need not deteriorate when manual communication is used. It should be noted, however, that NTID places great emphasis upon learning and/or maintaining these speech and speechreading skills as well as consistent use of hearing aids. Contrary to the results of the above study, Geers, et al. (1984) found that oral production of TC students was significantly

poorer than most students enrolled in oral programs; however, the TC programs are not described.

Comparative Studies of School-Age Children

Visible English (VE) vs. TC. Reportedly, some professionals have felt that VE (fingerspelling) is superior to TC since there is a one-to-one correspondence between VE and spoken English. Such a system could provide full use of function morphemes as well as linguistically important word endings. Comparing VE and TC, Quigley (1969) found that student achievement was higher in schools using VE, but these findings were not supported in the comparative studies of Klopping (1972) and Moores, Weiss, and Goodman (1973). These latter researchers found TC to be superior to VE.

Reich and Bick (1977) attempted to measure specific components of VE that had been identified as contributing to superior learning. They videotaped teachers selected by administrators in both programs (15 TC and 11 VE) and found that the message communicated via VE was not superior to TC. Teachers using either system dropped morphemes about equally, but "degree of inaccuracy or 'mumbling' of function morphemes was significantly greater in fingerspelling than signed English" (p. 577), and the mismatch between fingerspelled items and spoken English was at least as great as that in TC.

TC vs. Oral-Aural. The few studies that attempt to evaluate the outcome of using TC vs. oral-aural do not necessarily specify the type of manual system used; neither do they all specify home involvement or length of time using a given method. Furfey (1974) studied students in Baltimore who had either been enrolled in a TC or oral program consistently. Mean scores were calculated for degree of hearing loss, communication with hearing persons, and communication with deaf persons. The results, although not statistically treated, were definitely in favor of the TC program even though those students had the more severe hearing losses.

Matkin and Matkin (1985) attempted to analyze the effects of TC by distributing questionnaires to parents of children previously enrolled in an oral-aural program for a minimum of two years. They requested information about social, emotional, and educational growth as well as achievements in speech, speechreading, and hearing aid use. Information gathered on 48 students (median age 13 years) showed that oral-aural education was initiated at an average age of 22 months. TC was introduced to 82% of the children at 6 years and at 3 years for the other 8%. The majority of the parents sampled in this study were very positive about educational growth and did not feel that learning to use sign had had a deleterious effect on speech, speechreading, or hearing aid use.

Studies using a more experimental design and communication/language test results as a basis for comparing methods suggest either (a) that TC is superior to oral methods and provides more effective communication (Grove, Sullivan, & Rodda, 1979; Rodda & Grove,

1982); (b) that combined oral and signed productions do not differ significantly from spoken productions (Geers, Moog, & Schick, 1984) except in speech production where TC children were judged to be far less intelligible than oral children; or (c) that there are few differences when comparing the language ability of both hearing-impaired groups and that of their hearing peers (Knell & Klonoff, 1983)

Educationally, at least two studies support the use of TC. Chasen and Zuckerman (1976) studied two groups of third graders exposed to the same curriculum but different teaching methods, either oral or TC. Pre-post-test results showed that the TC group's improvement in comprehending and using math concepts and overall communication skills was significantly better than the oral group's. Increase in reading skills was greater for the TC group but not statistically significant.

Newell (1978) studied 28 students who had attended oral-aural programs prior to entering the secondary program. After rewriting four short stories to delete idiomatic expressions and simplify grammatical structure, the stories were presented to the students under four conditions: oral, manual, simultaneous, and interpreted. The results indicated that deaf adolescents comprehend factual information better when it is presented in an oral-manual fashion. Statistically both the simultaneous method (TC) and the interpreted presentation were significantly better than either the manual or oral alone. The 80% comprehension reported in Newell's study closely resembles the 75% comprehension reported in Klopping (1972) and the 79% comprehension from White and Stevenson's (1975) study, even though Newell's population was quite different; for example, from an oral-aural background, attending public school day classes. Newell concludes that generally the oral-manual method enhances education, especially for those "students who in past educational practices might have been excluded from exposure to sign language because of their general ability and speechreading proficiency" (p. 562)

Finally, one 10-year study evaluated the effects of introducing TC into a previously oral/aural school environment (Delaney, Stuckless, & Walter, 1984) and measured the changes by using results of academic achievement tests and perceived effects of faculty members on student performance and communication. Faculty perceptions were measured at three different times, 1971, 1973, and 1982, for effects TC might have or did have on four aspects of student performance: academic achievement, speech development, speechreading, and reading of writing. According to the 1971 survey, most faculty members had a positive attitude about implementing TC and most were still convinced of the positive effects in 1982, 11 years later. The two areas that were less favorably perceived in 1982 were those of speech and speechreading. The faculty members were unanimous in their opinion that academic achievement and reading and writing were positively affected by the use of TC.

In order to measure academic achievement, students were divided into three groups: pre-TC (oral-aural prior to introduction of TC, mixed (students attending the program from 1972 to 1976), and TC (students attending the program from 1977 through 1981), and tested using the California Achievement Test (CAT) in the areas of reading comprehension, mathematics, and overall academic achievement. Results demonstrated significant differences between groups, with the TC group scoring highest, the mixed group second, and the pre-TC group third. Further, contrary to the faculty's belief, speech-reading scores indicated similar differences, with the TC group scoring significantly better than the mixed group and the mixed group significantly higher than the pre-TC group. Although results demonstrated significant improvement during the 10-year study, both perceived and measured, the researchers provide other circumstances that might have contributed to these changes, such as changes in curriculum, increasing the number of speech therapists, adding to the FM loop amplification systems, greater responsiveness to the needs of the individual student, and greater community involvement.

Conclusions

The controversy between total communication and oralism is still alive, flourishing, and spirited. It appears that the data available lean in the direction of supporting TC as a viable means of teaching hearing-impaired children. However, before definitive statements can be made in support of either a total communication or oral approach, far more carefully designed research must be accomplished, avoiding the problems identified:

1. Data-based studies about students in oral programs must be made available.

2. Authors must clearly define what is meant by TC in their studies: for example, are auditory training and speech emphasized or are they given only token acknowledgement?

3. Exactly what sign system is being used must be clearly described and its use in the classroom, home, and so forth must be validated by the researchers.

4. Information about the length of time students have been involved in a TC program, the degree of hearing loss, and whether TC is used both at home and in school needs to be included in each study.

5. Additional data-based studies are needed that compare results of oral versus TC programs. These studies must match students for all the variables that affect hearing-impaired students: such as time of onset, time of intervention, degree of loss, parental support, and hearing-aid usage, and they must include factual, descriptive information about the educational program.

6. Studies need to be designed to evaluate beyond speech and grammatical structure. Such studies would assess the pragmatic components of language, and therefore how successful students from different programs are at using their language to communicate.

7. Finally, research is needed to evaluate how successful these young people from oral and TC backgrounds are after leaving school. Do oral students, in fact, mix with the hearing society for employment and socialization? Do students from either group receive higher salaries or achieve greater professional success?

Until the time that such data are available, the success or failure of TC as a viable method for teaching/learning cannot be labeled either better or worse than the oral or oral-aural methods.

TECHNOLOGY AND MEDIA

Use of Media in Schools and Classes for Hearing Impaired Students

Since at least the 1960s, educators of hearing-impaired children have had access to a wide variety of media through the distribution and educational programs of Captioned Films for the the Deaf and other federal, state, and local agencies. It is the intent of this section to examine the patterns of adoption and use of media in schools and classes for hearing impaired students and the research support for media use. Discussion of amplification devices is covered in Levitt's chapter on "Speech and Hearing in Communication" and is specifically excluded from the following section.

A report of the Office of Demographic Studies of Gallaudet College (Rawlings & Rubin, 1978) surveyed the media equipment available in 724 programs for hearing-impaired students. Student/equipment ratios are also provided. A checklist of 63 media equipment items was presented to the participating schools, and respondents were asked to indicate any other equipment not on the list. Results indicated that schools and classes had access to a wide variety of equipment, including audio devices, graphics and reproduction, electronic display, photography, and projected and magnified display devices. The 724 programs reported having a total of 6,233 overhead projectors, 6,168 screens, 5,478 silent filmstrip projectors, and 3,486 record players, as well as considerable other media equipment. These data, of course, do not indicate the utilization of the devices, merely their availability.

Harding and Tidball (1982) surveyed microcomputer availability. In 45 states, 120 schools responded to the survey. Of these, 50 reported having one or more microcomputers available; the computer most often cited as available was Apple (28 programs). The number of computers in a school or district ranged from 1 to 50, with 34 schools reporting five or fewer computers. Financial support, lack of suitable software, lack of teacher training and awareness, and insufficient numbers of computers were perceived as the chief barriers to using the microcomputer in the classroom, with funding perceived as the largest problem.

In 1983, a survey by Rose and Waldron (1984) used a different sample with 224 completed survey forms from 45 public and private residential schools, 66 resource rooms, and 113 classrooms in regular school buildings. A total of 979 microcomputers were available in 115 programs, with a mean of 8 per program. The majority (66%) again were Apple. While BASIC was reported as available to 85% of the programs, such "user-friendly" languages as LOGO, Blocks, and PILOT were infrequently reported. Computers were reported as being used most frequently for drill, practice, and tutorials.

The teacher of the hearing-impaired students was most frequently cited as the person primarily responsible for the microcomputer center. Most teachers had been trained through in-service programs. If this sample is comparable with that of Harding and Tidball, there was an approximately 10% increase in programs having microcomputers available between 1982 and 1983.

Evaluation of Media

Most current summaries and meta-analyses of media comparison studies clearly suggest that media do not influence learning under any conditions. The best current evidence is that media are mere vehicles that deliver instruction but do not influence student achievement any more than the truck that delivers our groceries causes changes in our nutrition. (Clark, 1983, p. 445)

Education of hearing-impaired children since the 1960s has been strongly influenced by the influx of "new" media, both hardware, such as that distributed widely by Captioned Films for the Deaf and the software, captioned films, captioned filmstrips, 8-mm and super 8-mm loops, overhead transparencies, programmed instruction sequences, and computer-assisted instructional software distributed by Captioned Films, as well as that produced by state, local, and private funds. Because of the promise of visual media in circumventing the communication handicap imposed by hearing loss, much time and energy has been spent on developing and producing media packages for hearing-impaired students. Much time also has been spent reporting on the use of these devices and materials. There has, however, been a distinct paucity of research on the effectiveness of media in promoting the academic development of hearing-impaired students; the research that does exist is, at best, inconclusive.

Pfau (1969) reported on the success of Project LIFE (Language Improvement to Facilitate Education of Hearing-Impaired Children), a programmed instruction approach to the teaching of language. After five years of product development and testing, the project led to the conclusion that "instruction for the development of true expressive language can be much more effectively accomplished by an average teacher of the deaf than it can by machine" (p. 829). Pfau's presentation was a part of a series of annual symposia on Research and the Utilization of Media for Teaching the Deaf, which took place from 1963 through 1983, with the exception of the period 1975–77. The presentations at these symposia are each contained in a special issue of the *American Annals of the Deaf*. Although the titles of the symposia stress research, a perusal of the symposia issues for the period 1979–83 indicates that a very small proportion of the reports are data-based and almost none have a valid experimental design that compares learner performance using new media or new software with those of a control group taught through more conventional approaches. A special edition of the *Volta Review* (September 1981), on Learning Technology and the Hearing Impaired also contains no data-based experiments or evaluation.

Reading back over the symposia reports is like taking a trip through media history. In 1971, programmed instruction (mostly paper-and-pencil, linear type) for hearing-impaired children was emphasized, with materials like the Sullivan Reading Series being lauded (Murphy, 1971). The beginning of computer-assisted instruction was evident in the presentation by Suppies (1971). He did present evaluative data in support of his Computer Assisted Instruction math program; however, the data were from normally-hearing children used in a previous study. In 1972, the affective domain and how media could influence it was the theme. Among the media, instructional television was praised as a vehicle for allowing growth in the affective areas (Schmitt, 1972). In other years various media hardware and software, including 8-mm single-concept films, closed- and open-caption television, multimedia presentations, and overhead projectors were presented as aids in such areas as career development, language acquisition, and education of gifted and multiply handicapped students. In all these cases, although the tones of the presentations were extremely positive, no data in support of the use of any of the media were presented.

By the 1980s the hot topic was computer-assisted instruction, specifically through the use of microcomputers. The September 1982 symposium was entitled "Microcomputers in Education of the Hearing Impaired," with the lead article entitled "Microcomputers: Macro-Learning for the Hearing Impaired." Microcomputers were reported as being useful in the improvement of reading comprehension (Pollard & Shaw, 1982). teaching lipreading (Hight, 1982), supplementing language instruction (Olsen, 1982), and teaching sign language (Johnson, 1982). One article presented a quantitative evaluation of a microcomputer-based early-reading program (Prinz, Nelson, & Stedt, 1982). In this study, 10 children between the ages of 2 and 6 used the software for 10 weeks. All children between the ages of 3 and 6 "demonstrated significant gains in word recognition and identification when comparing performance over a six-week period" (p. 533). Mean percentage of improvement and percentage correct was provided. No statistical analysis of significance was presented, nor was there a control group.

Stuckless (1983a), in the symposium on Computer Assisted Research and Instruction for the Hearing Impaired (1983) keynote speech, urges caution in the wholesale adoption of microcomputers in educating hearing-impaired students. He states that the movements toward programmed instruction in the late 1950s and 1960s and earlier mainframe computer linkages "did not add appreciably to the quality of education for hearing-impaired students at the time" (p. 516). Stuckless notes that appropriate use of the microcomputer depends on systematic evaluation of software applications, and that the 1982 symposium lacked presentations dealing with such evaluation efforts.

Although most of the presentations at the 1983 symposium were not data-based, some indication of a trend toward evaluation of specific techniques and materials exists. Smaldino, Schloss, Goldsmith, and Selinger (1983) randomly selected 12 hearing-impaired students and 12 normally-hearing controls, all of whom were residents at a developmental center, randomly divided into two experimental and two control groups of six. Students were seen individually by the same teacher for five 5-minute instructional periods. The two computer-assisted groups used the MECC program *Huckle*, a math problem-solving game that involves finding a point on a line or grid. The teacher-directed groups received equivalent information from a script that paralleled the computer presentation. For these students no difference was found under the two conditions in number of responses. Normally-hearing students using the computer made significantly more correct responses than did hearing-impaired students in the teacher-directed condition. The latter also made significantly more errors than either normally-hearing groups. Brawley and Peterson (1983) report on the development of an interactive disc system with software designed to promote language growth. A sophisticated evaluation design is presented; however, no results were yet available on the experimental group.

Stuckless (1983b) presents the results of the first year of research and development of a process to transliterate speech into print for hearing-impaired students in regular classes. He reports on attempts to reduce the error rate and progress from an initial 85% correct to a 95% correct rate. The subjective preferences of students exposed to the written display and sign language interpreters is briefly mentioned, with students about equally divided in their choice. In an earlier study at the National Technical Institute for the Deaf, Caccamise, Blasdel, and Meath-Lang (1977) compared hearing-impaired young adults' comprehension of the same information presented in simultaneous communication under three conditions: live, via closed circuit television, and through rear projection. A control group did not view the lecture. Results indicated that live presentation produced significantly better scores in a true–false test than did either of the other two modes. The control groups achieved significantly lower scores than any of the other groups.

Summary

There has been widespread availability of educational media and technology in schools and classes for hearing-impaired students. Much time, energy, and funds have been expended in developing and adapting software to the needs of hearing-impaired children, and much interest has been generated through symposia and special publications. However, relatively few studies have evaluated the efficacy of a particular medium, or a particular piece of educational software in increasing the academic achievement of the students. These few evaluative studies that do exist do not seem to refute Clark's (1983) contention that research with normally-hearing learners indicates that media utilization per se does not materially increase learning. It is, however, essential to note that access to captioned films and television provides the hearing-impaired child with at least an approximation of the rich sources of audio-visual information available to hearing students. Thus, the importance of media availability can assuredly not be measured only in terms of enhancement of academic achievement. Aesthetic appreciation, availability of alternate means of presenting a repertoire of information, and teacher and student satisfaction must also be considered.

THE STATE OF PRACTICE

Demography/Mainstreaming

Research into the demographic characteristics of the hearing-impaired population, and into the effect of school placements on educational and social characteristics appears to have had little effect on practice to date. Rather, the distribution of hearing-impaired students into various program options is considerably more influenced by geography, economics, legal and legislative mandates, and internal political considerations. That this is so is evidenced by the varied patterns of school placement in different geographic areas. We have seen, for instance, that students residing in the Southeast are statistically considerably more likely to be educated in residential schools than are their peers in the North. Research on the effects of varying degrees of integration on the academic and social development of hearing-impaired children was very limited. We could find no evidence in the literature that any of the studies had been (or indeed could be) replicated. All the studies were post-hoc comparisons of children who had already been placed in various settings. Thus, in the published literature there is no true experimental study of placement effects, and it might be argued that because of the Individualized Education Program process and Human Subject experimental controls, none is possible.

The comparisons that have been made all compare students in residential schools with those in day school or day class options or students receiving varying proportions of their education in regular classes. The residential versus day placement issue is especially politically loaded. There is a lot of vested interest on the part of the deaf community as well as the administrators and staffs of the residential schools in maintaining the residential school as a viable placement option, preferably one that can be freely chosen by parents without the necessity for proving that it is the least restrictive alternative for a particular student. In the state of Washington, for example, parents may apply to have their child educated at the state residential school. If the child is accepted, the school district is not able to negotiate another placement option through the Individualized Education Program process. Even when a student could be adequately served in a local school district program, parental desire is paramount. This type of process effectively removes the residential school from its place on a continuum of service model.

We did not locate studies that evaluated student achievement or social characteristics in programs that differed from each other in variables other than residence, degree of mainstreaming, or communication modality. Specifically lacking were studies of hearing-impaired populations educated in schools or classes exhibiting varying degrees of conformity to those attributes that are known or believed to contribute to success in hearing students.

These variables, which are delineated in the various excellence in education/effective schools publications, include such things as administrative organization, size of program, physical plant characteristics, expectations for achievement, direct instruction, and curriculum organization. Size of program is an especially interesting variable. Program size, as reported in the *Annals* directory issue, ranged from 2 students to over 500. Although there are published guidelines from the Conference of Educational Administrators Serving the Deaf (CEASD) on program size, no empirical data exist. It is possible that many of the effects attributed to residential or day placement could be better attributed to program size variation.

In summary, the placement of hearing-impaired children does not appear to be influenced by research findings; and indeed these findings are too meager and uncertain to provide a good basis for decision making. Pflaster's study (1980, 1981) does provide potentially valuable guidelines for determining which students might be suitable candidates for integration into regular classes without the support of a manual interpreter. The extent to which her findings, and the guidelines suggested by Nix (1976), Northcott (1973), and others, have been utilized by placement teams in decision making is not known. No similar guidelines for integration into regular classes with the support of an interpreter were found.

Total Communication

Total Communication, or at least some variant of manual communication along with oral language, is now reported as used in the majority of programs for hearing-impaired children in the United States. The adoption of TC was influenced by two types of research, the Babbidge Report (1967) and similar studies that severely criticized the achievement levels of hearing-impaired children; and the comparisons of deaf children having deaf parents with deaf children of hearing parents, with the difference being attributed at least in part to the early exposure to manual communication. The invention of a grammatical English form of sign language provided the necessary impetus for the rapid spread of TC throughout the educational system. The state of the art, in this case, was both influenced by research and influenced it.

Research is now dealing with the effects of the widespread adoption of TC. These research efforts are greatly hampered by the absence of a uniform definition of TC, the presence of multiple sign systems, and the inefficient use of Total Communication by teachers and parents. The first generations of teachers who were specifically trained to teach using TC—as opposed to taking in-service training in manual communication as an add-on to the oral approach—are just now making an impact on the field; and college- and university-level instructors, many of whom were themselves educated and subsequently taught in the oral tradition, are still in the process of incorporating TC into their own educational strategies.

It is possible that the true magnitude of the effect of Total Communication on the education of hearing-impaired children will not be known for some time, until a steady state of practice has been achieved. In the interim, some programs are already going beyond TC to teach AMESLAN as a first language and introduce English as a second language in a bilingual-bicultural program.

Technology

The review of research on technology and media stressed the widespread availability of electronic media in programs for hearing-impaired students, including the rapid growth in availability of microcomputers. Also stressed was the amount of effort that has been spent on the production, modification, dissemination, and field testing (by popularity) of media packages. The evaluative research that exists in our field is meager and in general does not support the use of electronic media per se as an effective tool for enhancing the academic skills of hearing-impaired children. This conclusion is in agreement with general research in the use of electronic media to enhance learning. Thus, research data would indicate that no more time and effort should be spent trying to improve the academic performance of students through the wholesale production and distribution of media packages such as captioned educational films and filmstrips. These tools are valuable for other aesthetic reasons, and allow hearing-impaired children access to the benefits enjoyed by other students, but have not

been proven to be effective and efficient purveyors of knowledge. It is unlikely that teachers in the field are aware of this lack of proven effectiveness. They use media to supplement their instruction, provide variety, and motivate students. These, indeed, might easily be sufficient reason to keep on producing media packages.

Perhaps attention should be given to the production of learning packages based on validated instructional techniques (such as direct instruction) and integrated into a valid developmental curriculum designed for hearing-impaired students. The choice of medium seems less important than the content of the packages, although there appears to be more support for paper-and-pencil than for the more elaborate media.

Obviously, results of the use of computerized instructional programs are not yet in. If there is to be further development in this area, it might be wise to adapt to the computer those learning packages and sequences that have already been validated and sequenced into a curriculum.

Summary

With certain exceptions, notably the early manual communication studies, research in the areas of demography, mainstreaming, technology, and Total Communication has been more reactive than pro-active. Often, in these areas, widespread adoption of a practice has precluded attempts to analyze its effectiveness. Thus, instead of leading the field, research follows it. Instead of true experimental studies, post-hoc evaluations predominate.

EFFECTIVE SCHOOLS AND SCHOOL EFFECTS

The search for variables or characteristics that appear to contribute directly to student achievement has received great emphasis within the past 10 to 15 years. Within this broad base of what creates effective schools are two very different philosophical approaches to research: effective schools and school effects.

Effective Schools

The researchers involved in this particular approach have attempted to identify specific schooling practices that lead directly to improved classroom behavior and academic success for students, no matter what their background or home environment. Various studies attempt to (a) identify characteristics of inner-city schools where students achieve high levels of reading when compared to national norms (e.g., Weber, 1974); (b) compare a number of high-achieving schools to the same number of low-achieving schools; or (c) investigate schools where students demonstrated consistent performance improvement or decline (Frazer, Walberg, Welch & Hattie, 1987).

Although the characteristics of these successful schools may vary slightly from investigator to investigator, results of this research have basically produced a five-factor model for effective schooling. The model typically involves some combination of: strong administrative leadership, emphasis on basic educational skills, a safe and orderly school climate, high teacher expectation for all students, and a system for assessing and monitoring school performance (Wendling & Cohen, 1981).

The results of these and other effective school studies have been challenged by Purkey and Smith (1983) and Ralph and Fennesey (1983) as being uneven in terms of quality. Some findings are fairly well-supported while others are speculative. Therefore, at the present time, a complete understanding of effectiveness may not be possible.

School Effects

Research in this area is directed toward investigating the home environment and how it might affect student achievement. Results of this research suggest that home background is the major influence and predictor of school achievement. Frazer, Walberg, Welch, and Hattie (1987), for example, points out that there is relatively little variance in average test scores among schools when socioeconomic and aptitude differences are controlled. Studies range from case studies that evaluate how home environment influences homework (e.g., McDermott, 1984), to developing a partnership between home and school (e.g., Danzberger & Usden, 1984), to the relationship between parents' educational expectations and the students' actual academic achievement (e.g., Seginer, 1983). Results of these studies demonstrate that when parents are involved with their child's education, the academic achievement is greater than the achievement of those students whose parents, for whatever reasons, do not care or are not involved.

The factors influencing the effectiveness of schools have not been addressed in research involving hearing-impaired students. Although dichotomous studies (e.g., residential vs. day, mainstream vs. self-contained) have been done, there has been no work in defining the variables that affect student achievement within different schools of the same basic type. It is recommended that such research be undertaken, using the available knowledge base from regular education.

NEEDS AND RECOMMENDATIONS

A. Problems that exist in conceptualizing and communicating about problems in the field.

1. Lack of current, adequate demographic data. The Office of Demographic Studies (1960s and 1970s) reports on incidence, etiology, secondary handicaps, achievement, and so forth, urgently need to be updated. If they were they could be used as a basis for obtaining representative samples for research studies.

2. Lack of standardized reports of prevalence of varying degrees of hearing loss.

3. Lack of standard definitions of placement options. Currently schools may label themselves as residential even if fewer than 10% of the students live in the school. Mainstreaming covers everything from presence in the same building to full-time education in a regular classroom.

4. Lack of a definition of Total Communication that is accepted and used by everyone in the field. This might include standardized definitions of the different English-based sign systems currently in use.

B. Needed areas of research and development.

1. Characteristics of effective programs for hearing-impaired students. Are there schools or programs that are doing a much better than average job of educating hearing-impaired children as measured by student achievement? What are the characteristics of these programs on such dimensions as: (a) administrative organization, (b) teacher preparation, (c) size and physical plant, (d) expectations for achievement, (e) methods of communication, (f) academic curriculum, (g) instructional techniques?

Along what dimensions must an "average" program be modified to make it "excellent"? Is it possible to set up a true model based on research into maximum effectiveness?

2. Evaluation of the effectiveness of such special education techniques as: (a) behavior modification, (b) precision teaching, (c) direct instruction, in enhancing the language, communication, and academic achievement of hearing-impaired children.

Originally the authors wished to review studies that used these technologies with hearing-impaired children. With the exception of a few studies using behavior modification with severely multiply handicapped students, we could find none.

3. Analysis of the effects of various learning and teaching variables on the academic achievement of hearing-impaired children (e.g., time-on-task, direct teacher instruction, type of feedback).

4. How do the various factors related to mainstreaming and the least restrictive environment influence the development of hearing-impaired children?

It is possible that the Cascade Model, which places residential schools near the bottom of the placement hierarchy as a "more restrictive environment" is not applicable to hearing-impaired students. A model incorporating access to hearing-impaired peers and adults as well as physical, social, and educational integration with hearing peers might be formulated and tested. This type of model might allow the possibility that a large residential school with mainstreaming into nearby community schools and recreational facilities might be a less restrictive environment than a one-room, mixed age-range program located in a public school.

Specific questions that research might answer include:

(a) How is program size (i.e., the availability of a hearing-impaired peer group) related to academic achievement, self-esteem, and social development?

(b) Is the availability of deaf adult role models significantly positively related to academic and/or social growth?

(c) What are the characteristics of those residential schools that have actively promoted mainstreaming programs?

(d) Are there significant differences in the attitudes, social adjustment, and/or academic achievement of hearing-impaired adults who have graduated from various program types?

(e) To what are the differences in enrollment patterns in the various states or regions due? Do the different patterns lead to different results in achievement and/or adjustment?

(f) If integration takes place with the aid of an interpreter, are the characteristics determined by Pflaster still as important in determining success? Are there other characteristics that emerge?

5. What is the effect of Total Communication and other communication options on hearing-impaired students' academic achievement and social development?

(a) Experimental studies of Total Communication versus AMESLAN (bilingual, bicultural) versus aural-oral only. Studies must have adequate experimental control over variables.

(b) Is there a way to improve the efficiency of the use of Total Communication? Are there inherent limitations in the accurate simultaneous use of manual and oral modes?

(c) Is any one form of Manually Coded English superior to another by any objective criterion?

C. Implications for teacher education.

1. New teachers must be trained to work in a variety of educational settings. This implies that all teachers of hearing-impaired students have preparation in regular education, and that teacher preparation programs should be located within departments of education.

2. Teacher educators should have periodic updates on research in education, special education, and education of hearing-impaired children. These updates should go beyond the information usually available at national conventions and should include specific procedures for incorporating the new information into training sequences.

3. Both new and current teachers should be explicitly taught how to use Total Communication without sacrificing or short changing the auditory-oral component. There is currently no text or other resource that deals explicitly with the problems involved in teaching speech or implementing an auditory training program in a TC environment. Generally, the sign system and speech development are taught in separate classes by different individuals, and teachers must figure out on their own how to combine the two.

References

Antia, S. (1982). Social interaction of partially mainstreamed hearing-impaired children. *American Annals of the Deaf,* **127**(1), 18–25.

The Babbidge Report (1967). *Advisory Committee on the Education of the Deaf. A report to the Secretary of Health, Education and Welfare by his advisory committee on the education of the Deaf.* Washington, D.C. U.S. Dept of Health, Educ. and Welfare.

Bellugi, A., & Fisher, S. (1972). A comparison of sign language and spoken language. *Cognition, 1,* 173–200.

Bellugi, U., & Klima, E. (1982). The acquisition of three morphological systems in American Sign Language. *Papers and Reports on Child Language Development, 21,* 135–141.

Bornstein, H., Saulnier, K., & Hamilton, L. (1980). Signed English: A First Evaluation. *American Annals of the Deaf,* **125**(4), 467–481.

Brackett, D., & Henniges, M. (1976). Communicative interaction of preschool hearing-impaired children in an integrated setting. *Volta Review,* **78**(6), 276–285.

Brasel, K., & Quigley, S. (1977). Influence of certain language and communication environments in early childhood on the development of language in deaf individuals. *Journal of Speech and Hearing Research, 20,* 95–107.

Brawley, R., & Peterson, B. (1983) Interactive videodisc: An innovative instruction system. *American Annals of the Deaf,* **128**(5), 685–700.

Brooks, R., Hudson, F., & Reisberg, L. (1981). The effectiveness of unimodal vs. bimodal presentations of material to be learned by hearing-impaired students. *American Annals of the Deaf,* **126**(7), 835–839.

Caccamise, F., Blasdel, R., & Meath-Lang, B. (1977). Hearing impaired persons' simultaneous reception of information under live and two visual motion media conditions. *American Annals of the Deaf,* **122**(3), 339–343.

Caccamise, F., Ayers, R., Finch, S., & Mitchell, M. (1978). Signs and manual communication systems: Selection, standardization, and development. *American Annals of the Deaf,* **123**(7), 887–902.

Chasen, B., & Zuckerman, M. (1976). The effects of total communication and oralism on deaf third-grade "Rubella" students. *American Annals of the Deaf,* **121,** 394–402.

Clark, R. (1983). Reconsidering research on learning from media. *Review of Educational Research,* **53**(4), 445–459.

Cokely, D., & Gawlik, R. (1974). Option two: Childrenese as pidgin. *The Deaf American,* **28**(8), 5–6.

Collins-Ahlgren, M. (1975). Language development of two deaf children. *American Annals of the Deaf,* **120,** 525–539.

Conklin, J., Subtelny, J., & Walker, G. (1980). Analysis of the communication skills of young deaf adults over a two-year interval of technical training. *American Annals of the Deaf,* **125**(3), 388–393.

Craig, W., & Salem, J. (1975). Partial integration of deaf with hearing students: Residential school perspectives. *American Annals of the Deaf,* **120**(1), 28–36.

Danzberger, J., & Usden, M. (1984) Building partnerships: The Atalanta experience. Phi Delta Kappan, **65**(6), 393–396.

Delgado, G. (1985) *Advocate for the Deaf,* **2**(4).

Delaney, M. Stuckless, E., & Walter, G. (1984). Total communication effects—longitudinal study using schools for the deaf in transition. *American Annals of the Deaf,* **129**(6), 481–486.

Denton, D. (1972). A philosophical foundation for total communication. *The Hoosier*, **86,** 1–16.

Dolman, D. (1983). A study of the relationship between syntactic development and concrete operations in deaf children. *American Annals of the Deaf*, **128**(6), 813–819.

Farrugia, D., & Austin, G. (1980). A study of social-emotional adjustment patterns of hearing-impaired students in different educational settings. *American Annals of the Deaf*, **125**(5), 535–541.

Frazer, B., Walberg, H., Welch, W., & Hattie, J. (1987). Synthesis of educational productivity research. *International Journal of Educational Research*, **11**(2), 155–244.

Freeman, R. (1976). Psychosocial problems associated with childhood hearing impairment. In P. Henderson (Ed.), *Hearing and hearing impairment* (pp. 405–415). London: Royal National Institute for the Deaf.

Furfey, P. (1974). Total communication and the Baltimore deaf survey. *American Annals of the Deaf*, **119**(4), 337–382.

Gardner, J., & Zorfass, J. (1983) From sign to speech: The language development of a hearing-impaired child. *American Annals of the Deaf*, **128**(1), 20–24.

Garretson, M. (1976). A bicentennial monograph on hearing impairment. *Volta Review*, **78**(4), 88–95.

Garretson, M. (1977). The residential school. *The Deaf American*, **29,** 19-22.

Geers, A., Moog, J., & Schick, B. (1984). Acquisition of spoken and signed English by profoundly deaf children. *Journal of Speech and Hearing Disorders*, **49,** 378–388.

Goldin-Meadow, S., & Feldman, S. (1977). The development of language-like communication without a language model. *Science*, **197**(4301), 401–403.

Greenberg, M., Calderon, R., & Kusché, C. (1984). Early intervention using simultaneous communication in infants: The effect of communication development. *Child Development*, **55,** 607–616.

Gregory, J., Shanahan, T., & Walberg, H. (1984). Mainstreaming hearing impaired high school seniors: A reanalysis of a national survey. *American Annals of the Deaf*, **129**(1), 11–16.

Grove, C., Sullivan, F., & Rodda, M. (1979). Communication and language in severely deaf adolsecents. *British Journal of Psychology*, **70,** 531–540.

Harding, R., & Tidball, L. (1982). A national microcomputer-software survey of current microcomputer usage in schools for the hearing impaired. *American Annals of the Deaf*, **127**(5), 673–683.

Hight, R. (1982). Lip-reading trainer: Teaching aid for the hearing impaired. *American Annals of the Deaf*, **127**(5), 564–568.

Holman, G. (1980). Due process: A status report on schools for deaf children. *American Annals of the Deaf*, **125**(2), 92–102.

Johnson, D. (1982). DEAFSIGN: A series of computerized instructional programs for the teaching of sign language. *American Annals of the Deaf*, **127**(5), 556–558.

Jordan, I., Gustason, G., & Rosen, R. (1976). Current communication trends in programs for the deaf. *American Annals for the Deaf*, **121**(6), 527–532.

Jordan, I., Gustason, G., & Rosen, R. (1979). An update on communication trends at programs for the deaf. *American Annals of the Deaf*, **124,** 350–357.

Karchmer, M., & Kirwin, L. (1977). *The use of hearing aids by hearing-impaired students in the United States.* Washington, D.C.: Office of Demographic Studies, Gallaudet College, Series S, Number 2.

Karchmer, M. & Peterson, L (1980) *Commuter students at residential schools for the deaf.* Washington, D.C.: Gallaudet College, Office of Demographic Studies. (series R, No. 7).

Kennedy, P., Northcott, W., McCauley, R., & Williams, S. (1976). Longitudinal sociometric and cross-sectional data on mainstreaming hearing impaired children: implications for preschool programming. *Volta Review*, **78**(2), 71–81.

Kirk, S., & Gallagher, J. (1983). *Educating exceptional children* (4th ed.). Boston: Houghton-Mifflin Co.

Klopping, H. (1972). Language understanding of deaf students under three auditory-visual stimulus conditions. *American Annals of the Deaf*, **117**(3), 389–396.

Kluwin, T. (1981a). The grammaticality of manual representations of English in classroom settings. *American Annals of the Deaf*, **126**(4), 417–421.

Kluwin, T. (1981b). A rationale for modifying classroom signing systems. *Sign Language Studies*, **31,** 179–187.

Knell, S., & Klonoff, E. (1983). Language sampling in deaf children: A comparison of oral and signed communication modes. *Journal of Communication Disorders*, **16**(6), 435–447.

Marmor, G., & Pettito, L. (1979). Simultaneous communication in the classroom: How well is English grammar represented? *Sign Language Studies*, **23,** 99–136.

Matkin, A., & Matkin, N. (1985). Benefits of total communication perceived by parents of hearing-impaired children. *Language, Speech, and Hearing Services in Schools*, **16**(1), 64–74.

McDermott, R. (1984). When school goes home: some problems in the organization of homework. *Teachers College Record*, **85**(3), 391–409.

Meadow, K., Greenburg, M., Erting, C., & Carmichael, H. (1981). Interactions of deaf mothers and deaf preschool children: Comparisons with three other groups of deaf and hearing dyads. *American Annals of the Deaf*, **126**(4), 454–468.

Mitchell, G. (1982). Can deaf children acquire English? An evaluation of manually coded English systems in terms of the principles of language acquisition. *American Annals of the Deaf*, **127**(3), 331–336.

Mohay, H. (1983). The effects of cued speech on the language development of three deaf children. *Sign Language Studies*, **38,** 25–47.

Montgomery, G. (1966). The relationship of oral skills to manual communication in profoundly deaf adolescents. *American Annals of the Deaf*, **126**(4), 454–468.

Montgomery, G., & Mitchell, G. (1981) A comparative analysis of video records of Ameslan, British Sign Language, and British Signed English transmissions of varying texts. *Proceedings of the International Symposium on Sign Language Research*, Bristol, England.

Moores, D. (1982). *Educating the deaf; psychology principle and practice.* 2nd ed., Boston: Houghton Mifflin Co.

Moores, D., Weiss, K., & Goodman, M. (1973). Receptive abilities of deaf children across five modes of communication. *Exceptional Children*, September, 22–28.

Murphy, H. (1971). Activities in preprogrammed instruction at the Southwest School for the Deaf. *American Annals of the Deaf*, **116**(5), 480–483.

Newell, W. (1978). A study of the ability of day-class deaf adolescents to comprehend factual information using four communication variables. *American Annals of the Deaf*, 558–562.

Newman, L. (1971). Total communication. *The Deaf American*, **23**(5), 19–20.

Newport, E., & Ashbrook, E. (1977). The emergences of semantic relations in American Sign Language. *Papers and Reports on Child Development*, 13, 16–21.

Nix, G. (1975). Total Communication: A review of studies offered in its support. *Volta Review*, November, 470–494.

Nix, G. (Ed.). (1976). *Mainstream education for hearing-impaired children*. New York: Grune & Stratton.

Nordèn, K. (1981). Learning processes and personality development in deaf children. *American Annals of the Deaf*, 126, 404–410.

Northcott, W. (Ed.). (1973). *The hearing-impaired child in a regular classroom: Preschool, elementary and secondary years*. Washington, D.C.: A. G. Bell Association for the Deaf.

Olsen, J. (1982). Do I have to go to recess? Electronic supplements in language development. *American Annals of the Deaf*, 127(5), 602–608.

Parasnis, I. (1983). Effects of parental deafness and early exposure to manual communication on the cognitive skills, English language skills, and field independence of young deaf adults. *Journal of Speech and Hearing Research*, 26, 588–594.

Pfau, G. (1969). Project LIFE PI Analysis. *Symposium on research and utilization of educational media for teaching the deaf*, Lincoln, Nebraska.

Pflaster, G. (1980). A factor analysis of variables related to academic performance of hearing-impaired children in regular classes. *Volta Review*, 82(2), 71–84.

Pflaster, G. (1981). A second analysis of factors related to the academic performance of hearing-impaired children in the mainstream. *Volta Review*, 82(2), 71–80.

Pollard, G., & Shaw, C. (1982). Microcomputer reading comprehension improvement program for the deaf. *American Annals of the Deaf*, 127, 483–485.

Prinz, P., Nelson, K., & Stadt, J. (1982). Early reading in young deaf children using microcomputer technology. *American Annals of the Deaf*, 127(5), 483–485.

Prinz, P., & Prinz, E. (1979). Simultaneous acquisition of ASL and spoken English. *Sign Language Studies*, 25, 283–296.

Puskey, S., & Smith, M. (1983). Effective Schools: a review. *Elementary School Journal*, 83(4) 427–452.

Quigley, S. (1969). *The influence of finger spelling on the development of language, communication and the educational achievement in deaf children*. Urbana, Illinois: Institute for Research on Exceptional Children.

Quigley, S., & Paul, P. (1984). *Language and deafness*. San Diego: College-Hill.

Ralph, J. & Fennessey, J. (1983) Science or reform: some questions about the effective school model. *Phi Delta Kappan*, 64(10), 689–694.

Rainer, J., & Altshuler, K. (1971). A psychiatric program for the deaf: Experiences and implications. *American Journal of Psychiatry*, 127, 103–108.

Rawlings, B., & Rubin, F. (1978). *A survey of media equipment available in special education programs for hearing impaired students*. Washington, D.C.: Office of Demographic Studies, Gaullaudet College, Series C, Number 3.

Reeves, J. (1977). Scope for oralism. *Volta Review*, 79(1), 43–54.

Reich, P., & Bick, M. (1977). How visible is visible English? *Sign Language Studies*, 14, 59–72.

Reich, C., Hambleton, D., & Houldin, B. (1977). The integration of hearing-impaired children in regular classrooms. *American Annals of the Deaf*, 122(6), 534–543.

Rister, A. (1975). Deaf children in mainstream education. *Volta Review*, 77, 279–290.

Rodda, M., & Grove, C. (1982). A pilot study of language structures in the receptive language of deaf subjects. *Annals of Canadian Educators for the Hearing-Impaired*, 8(3), 168-181.

Rose, S., & Waldron, M. (1984). Microcomputer use in programs for hearing-impaired children. *American Annals of the Deaf*, 130, 338–342.

Sarfaty, L., & Katz, S. (1978). The self-concept and adjustment patterns of hearing-impaired pupils in different school settings. *American Annals of the Deaf*, 123(4), 438–441.

Schildroth, A. (1980). Public residential schools for deaf students in the United States, 1970-1978. *American Annals of the Deaf*, 125(2), 80–91.

Schlesinger, H., & Meadow, K. (1972). *Sound and sign*. Berkeley: University of California Press.

Schlesinger, H., Meadow, K., & Yannacone, C. (1974). *Deaf American*, 32–34.

Schmitt, R. (1972). The affective domain: A challenge to ITV. *American Annals of the Deaf*, 117(5), 439–499.

Seginer, R. (1983). Parents' educational expectations and children's academic achievement: a literature review. *Merrill-Palmer Quarterly*, 29(1), 1–23.

Shafer, D., & Lynch, J. (1981). Emergent language of six prelingually deaf children. *Journal of the British Association of Teachers of the Deaf*, 5, 94–111.

Sixth annual report to Congress on the implementation of Public Law 94–142: The Education for all Handicapped Children Act, U.S. Department of Education, 1984.

Skarakis, E., & Prutting, C. (1977). Early communication: Semantic functions and early communicative intentions in the communication of the preschool child with impaired-hearing. *American Annals of the Deaf*, 122, 382–391.

Smaldino, S., Schloss, P., Goldsmith, L., & Selinger, J. (1983). Analysis of the relative instructional efficiency of microcomputer-based instruction and teacher-directed instruction for hearing impaired and normal hearing youth. *American Annals of the Deaf*, 128(5), 642–647.

Stall, C. H., & Marshall, P. (1984). The role of manual encoding in learning by the prelingually deaf: An initial investigation. *Sign Language Studies*, 42, 31–37.

Statement on "Least Restrictive" placements for deaf students. (1977, April). *American Annals of the Deaf*, 122(2), 70–71.

Stepp, R., Jr. (1982). Microcomputers: Macro-learning for the hearing impaired. *American Annals of the Deaf*, 127(5), 472–475.

Stuckless, E. R. (1983a). The microcomputer in the instruction of hearing-impaired students: Tool or distraction. *American Annals of the Deaf*, 128(5), 515–520.

Stuckless, E. R. (1983b). Real-time transliteration of speech into print for hearing-impaired students in regular classes. *American Annals of the Deaf*, 128(5), 619–624.

Stuckless, E. R., & Birch, J. (1966). The influence of early manual communication on the linguistic development of deaf children. *American Annals of the Deaf*, 111, 452–460.

Suppies, P. (1971). Computer assisted instruction for deaf students. *American Annals of the Deaf*, 116(5), 500–508.

Swisher, M., & Thompson, M. (1985). Mothers learning simultaneous communication: The dimensions of the task. *American Annals of the Deaf*, 130(3), 212–217.

Thompson, M., & Swisher, M. (1985). Acquiring language through total communication. *Ear and Hearing*, 6(1), 29–32.

Trybus, R., (1979). *Overview of psychological and demographic research with hearing-impaired people.* Washington, D.C.: Research Institute, Gallaudet College.

Weber, B. (1974). *State of New York Review*, p.171.

Wendling, W., & Cohen, J. (1981). Education resources and student achievement; good news for the schools. *Journal of Education*, 7(1), 44–63.

White, A., & Stevenson, V. (1975). The effects of total communication, oral communication, and reading on the learning of factual information in residential school deaf children. *American Annals of the Deaf,* **120,** 48–5.

Yannacone, C. (1977). Speech presented at the conference, Mental Health Principles and Deaf Children, made possible by a grant from DHEW, Office of Education, Bureau of Education for the Handicapped (#G007401441), and sponsored by the University of California, San Francisco, Continuing Education in Health Sciences, June 4–5.

Ysseldyke, J., & Algozzine, R. (1984). *Introduction to special education.* Boston: Houghton-Mifflin.

Academic Development and Preparation for Work

HARRY G. LANG

National Technical Institute for the Deaf
Rochester Institute of Technology

Abstract—A review of the literature pertaining to academic subjects such as science, mathematics, and social studies reveals a highly neglected area of research in the education of hearing-impaired students. Educational and communication researchers have traditionally focused their investigations on the hypothetical factors contributing to the educational lags of hearing-impaired students. Empirical research studies examining pedagogical strategies are scarce. There is a serious dearth of research on instructional materials development and on the potential of the contextual bases provided by science, mathematics, and social studies for language, communication, cognitive, social, moral, and career development of hearing-impaired students in various types of school programs.

The absence of such a research base is reflected in the quality of teaching and materials development and the author calls for increased research to ameliorate the problem.

Introduction

In recent years the concerns of professionals in public education regarding the quality of American schooling have been reiterated in numerous ways. Discussions about declines in standardized test scores and reports from the National Commission on Excellence in Education (1983), the National Research Council (1979), and the National Science Foundation (Weiss, 1978, Stake & Easley, 1978) have created a mood for change reminiscent of the post-Sputnik concerns which led to curricular reforms across the country. In retrospect, however, few educators of hearing-impaired students share a *déjà vu* feeling with professionals in public education. The curricular reforms in science, mathematics, and social studies during the 1960s did not have as great an impact on school programs for hearing-impaired students as they did in public school programs. While Public Law 94–142 helped to provide additional educational opportunities, a large proportion of the hearing-impaired school-age population remains in special education environments. Even many "mainstreamed" students are taught in resource rooms and otherwise precluded from reaping the benefits of the science,

mathematics, and social studies curriculum innovations of the past two decades. The quality of schooling in these three content areas remains inadequate in most programs for hearing-impaired students. Numerous research studies and surveys of programmatic offerings provide substantive data which indicate the serious deficiencies in academic development programs which prepare hearing-impaired students for postsecondary education or for direct entrance into the labor force.

The present review of research, including the identification of needs in preparing hearing-impaired students for the work force, and recommendations for the direction research should take in regard to these issues, is both timely and crucial for several reasons. First, in many respects this review is seminal. Few efforts have been taken in the past to assess extensively the state of academic preparation for this population in school science, mathematics, and social studies, particularly within the context of the career development process. Second, along with the National Commission on Excellence in Education report and, more importantly, the national concern regarding scientific literacy which led to the establishment of the Commission, the continued positive effects of Public Law 94–142 have created a general mood among funding agencies and professional organizations conducive to research and development. In addition to the $50 million the National Science Foundation has provided for precollege science and mathematics education, for example, there was at least $200 million more in 1985 for states, local education agencies, and the Department of Education (Aldridge, 1984a).

The learning of mathematics, science, and social studies overlaps the career development process, another current concern generated by rapidly changing technology. Career development is a lifelong process involving maturation and growth. Career education is distinguished from career development in that career education is the accumulation of planned and unplanned experiences, both formal and informal, which promote career development in the school, home, and community environments. From the elementary years when the child first develops a fundamental awareness of the variety of occupational categories and begins to clarify values and interests, to the secondary and postsecondary experiences when certain skills and knowledge are acquired during specialization in chosen areas of interest, the student ideally makes connections between the content of the courses and the *raison d'être* of the curriculum, namely, academic development* and preparation for work.

Unfortunately for many hearing-impaired students (as well as for many hearing students), the process of infusing career development into the academic program has been largely ineffectual. For hearing-impaired students, the reasons are more numerous. Very often the concomitants and effects of deafness, particularly the justifiable concerns about communication skills development (language, speech, use of residual hearing, sign communication, and others) lead toward a heavy emphasis on reducing such obvious lags in development at the expense of the content learning. This is true even in the secondary school programs where science, mathematics, and social studies take a back seat to continued, intensive, (albeit important), emphasis on communication skills.

In science and mathematics and, to a lesser extent, in social studies, trends in policy making and the efforts of public education personnel to assist special educators in effecting change in these areas of the curriculum has been generally encouraging. Yet, there are profound problems confronting professionals in the field of educating hearing-impaired students that have the potential to impede desired changes for some time to come. Research involving curricular adaptations and documented efforts to evaluate science, mathematics, and social studies are practically nonexistent. There has also been very little research on pedagogy. Assessment techniques and outcomes reported in the literature for these content areas have focused primarily on national standardized tests, rather than on teacher-developed instruments. Such standardized tests, whether norm-referenced or criterion-referenced, are not appropriate for program or course evaluation where hearing-impaired students are served.

Integration of Research

Today's world is a scene of rapid change, which places demands on the individual's capability to adapt to societal transformations and to technological progress; and economic change which necessitates sound academic development and preparation for the work force.

---

* For the purpose of this review, *academic development* will be defined as the process of acquiring skills and knowledge in three major content areas: science, mathematics, and social studies. Academic development overlaps and is interwoven with the career development, personal/social/moral development, and communication skills development of the hearing-impaired student.

Disparities in the academic development of hearing-impaired persons are everywhere apparent in the literature, and the data collected on both national and regional levels invariably show the serious lags hearing-impaired students have in comparison to hearing students in educational attainment (Christiansen, 1982). Scores from academic achievement tests of the 1970s and 1980s reveal that hearing-impaired students demonstrate a rate of progress below the average established by hearing students of the same chronological age (DiFrancesca, 1971; Trybus & Karchmer, 1977). This, in itself, is reason enough for further research, development, and policy making. Yet viewed within the global context of general education, the state of academic development of hearing-impaired students in mathematics, science, and social studies is an even more critical concern. Major reports by the National Commission on Excellence in Education (1983) and the National Science Foundation (Weiss, 1978) point out the shortcomings of American schooling for the hearing population. These shortcomings are only exacerbated by a handicapping condition, particularly one like deafness. The determinants, concomitants, and effects of hearing loss and their implications for curriculum development, personnel training, and educational policy making should undergird our research.

Ironically, the bridge between research and practice in the field of educating hearing-impaired students, especially in the areas of academic development, remains not only unbuilt, but without a design. At the most, several needs assessments have been conducted with little adequate follow-up from either professional organizations serving the hearing-impaired population or postsecondary institutions which have traditionally undertaken supportive roles in such issues. On the other hand, independent of the needs assessment, there have been attempts by post-secondary institutions to develop curriculum materials for national use. In the post-Sputnik era, for example, the Bureau of Education for the Handicapped funded a 5-year project at Ball State University in Indiana to produce curriculum materials in such areas as science, mathematics, social studies, vocational education, and social/personal development. Although selected teachers were involved in producing the 30 volumes, the project had relatively low impact on the field because the materials were not successfully marketed. Efforts by other institutions described later in this review have failed mostly because the consumers (i.e., teachers) were not part of the development of the curriculum products. These failed efforts indicate that we should plan carefully in the future, not only to involve teachers in the development of the materials, but also to make sure that the marketing and evaluation stages are funded and implemented.

Academic Development

In August, 1981, U.S. Secretary of Education T. H. Bell created the National Commission on Excellence in

Education and directed it to present a report on the quality of education in the United States. The report, titled *A Nation at Risk: The Imperative for Educational Reform* (National Commission on Excellence in Education, 1983), was submitted to Bell in April, 1983. It described in detail how the gains in student achievement made in the wake of the Sputnik challenge have been squandered and the essential support system dismantled. The "risk" of the title has many indicators. For example, on 19 international comparison tests of student achievement completed in the early 1970's, American students were never first or second. In comparison with other industrialized nations, American students were last seven times.

Over 23 million American adults are functionally illiterate on the simplest tests of everyday reading, writing, and comprehension. Average achievement of high school students on most standardized tests is now lower than when Sputnik was launched. A steady decline in the College Board's Scholastic Aptitude Tests (SAT) from 1963 to 1980 has been observed. Nearly 40% of 17-year-olds cannot draw inferences from written materials. One-fifth can write a persuasive essay. Only one-third can solve a mathematics problem requiring several steps (National Commission on Excellence in Education, 1983). There was a steady decline in science achievement scores of U.S. 17-year-olds as measured by national assessments of science in 1969, 1973, and 1977. Remedial mathematics courses in public 4-year colleges increased by 72% between 1975 and 1980. These courses now make up one-fourth of all mathematics courses taught in those institutions. It would be most informative if we had similar data for comparing hearing-impaired students with these national trends.

Interestingly, the 1982 Gallup Poll of the Public's Attitudes Toward the Public Schools clearly shows the support for education as a major foundation for the future of this country. More than 75% of all those questioned believed that every student planning to go to college should take four years of mathematics, English, history/U.S. government, and science. There appears to be less patience for undemanding and superfluous high school offerings. Among the recommendations in *A Nation at Risk*, one that is particularly relevant to this chapter is that all students seeking a diploma be required to take additional mathematics, science, and social studies courses in high school.

Science Education for Hearing-Impaired Students

National Surveys: State of the Art. In the late 1970s and early 1980s, steps were taken to survey present practices and needs of science teachers working with hearing-impaired students. Sunal and Burch (1982) surveyed elementary science teachers in 47 residential schools and reported that 21% have no established science programs for grades K-6. Fewer than 20% of the schools surveyed

used guidelines for special help, or strategies and activities different from approaches used in regular school curricula. The authors concluded that if this sample is typical of all schools in the population, science teachers in a majority of schools are not providing appropriate science instruction for young hearing-impaired students..

During the 1978-79 school year, a hearing-impaired scientist visited school programs in 20 states in a special role-model project supported by the American Association for the Advancement of Science (Redden, 1979). He interacted with over 4,600 individuals during his travels. The summary paper on this project reports his observation that hearing-impaired students do not seem to realize that their lives depend on science. His interchange with the students focused not only on science but also on their self-image, and his description of the attitudes of teachers, parents, and students, the inadequate facilities and curriculum materials, and the poor preparation of many science teachers, provided a rationale for a major survey in the early 1980s (Lang & Propp, 1982). The study had the following goals: (a) to examine the education and training of those teachers responsible for science classes; (b) to provide a description of the general adequacy of science curricula, instructional resources, and facilities; and (c) to identify major needs in science education for hearing-impaired students.

There were responses from 480 science teachers representing 326 school programs in 45 states and the District of Columbia, with 34.7% of the respondents teaching science to hearing-impaired students in residential schools and 65.3% teaching in mainstream programs (both public day schools and public day classes). The respondents represented a wide range of program sizes and grade levels. Data obtained in this survey indicate that a high proportion of hearing-impaired students are being taught science in classroom facilities that are inadequate. While a creative teacher can rise above a poor teaching environment, very few educators would debate the logic that inadequate facilities constitute a serious constraint on any science curriculum.

A quarter of a century ago, the seminal Woods Hole Conference, 9–18 September, 1959, led to a federally funded national effort to develop new science curriculum materials emphasizing direct manipulative "hands-on" experiences and the inquiry approach. Recently, however, there has been a decline in use of inquiry-based materials due, in part, to new teachers not having taken science methods courses which emphasize these federally funded materials (National Research Council, 1979). This decline is apparent in the data for teachers of hearing-impaired students as well (Lang & Propp, 1982). Only 12.2% of the 480 teachers in this study identified their curriculum materials as primarily process-oriented.

Elementary-Level Science. Hearing-impaired children learn to assimilate knowledge as both the mind and the environment make their contributions to an understanding of the world. Methods founded on activity which promote thinking about cause and effect relationships have often been promoted by experienced teachers. Leitman (1968), for example, wrote that the many hours spent by these children in groups tend to foster passivity, which runs counter to the need to explore the environment. Owsley (1962) emphasized that science, more than any other subject in the curriculum for hearing-impaired students, should teach a scientific approach to problem-solving. This involves asking questions, making careful observations, and being tolerant of new ideas. The elementary school, where children retain flexible minds, is the ideal place to begin. Owsley wrote that even more important than acquiring a substantial body of scientific information, teachers must equip hearing-impaired children with a method of work and a habit of critical thinking.

Little research has been conducted, however, to qualify the perspectives put forth by teachers in these general articles. Such views are most germane to this chapter, however, since they suggest emphases for empirical studies over the next decade. Various aspects of attribution theory, for example, may help to clarify how hearing-impaired students deal with cause and effect relationships. If we are to meet the goal of teaching appropriate problem-solving and critical thinking skills, then it might be beneficial to examine more closely the progress being made in the area of information processing. In addition, it is important to emphasize at this point that a meta-analysis of 160 empirical research studies with hearing students has shown that manipulative techniques have noteworthy effects on achievement, problem-solving, and science knowledge acquisition (Wise & Okey, 1983).

There are several modern programs for other populations focusing on teaching/learning strategies which may prove effective with hearing-impaired children. Science-A Process Approach (S-APA) is a series of over 100 modules built around an activity-oriented curriculum aimed at developing various processes of science. The project utilizes instructional kits, booklets for teachers with objectives, evaluation instruments, and suggested teaching strategies. However, few school programs for hearing-impaired children are presently using the S-APA curriculum (Lang & Propp, 1982).

Dietz and Ridley (1975) describe the application of the Science Curriculum Improvement Study (SCIS), to the education of young hearing-impaired children at the Oralingua School in Whittier, California. Developed at the University of California at Berkeley, SCIS is a sequence of physical and life science modular units using the laboratory investigation approach for Grades K-6. Involvement with SCIS materials encouraged the hearing-impaired children to express their ideas about activities while developing an understanding of the science concepts. Again, few teachers are using SCIS with hearing-impaired students (Lang & Propp, 1982).

There are other curricular projects that focus on a discovery approach which may well prove more successful with hearing-impaired children than traditional lecture methods. The Conceptually Oriented Program in Elementary Science (COPES) is a nonreading project for children with serious verbal problems in Grades K-6. Developed at New York University, the instructional units include materials which assist in evaluating the child's understanding of major conceptual schemes. The United Science and Mathematics for Elementary Schools (USMES) program is an interdisciplinary study of problems from the school and community environment (K-8). The Learning Research and Development Center in Pittsburgh, Pennsylvania has a comprehensive K-6 curriculum with a learning management system available for those interested in individualization. These programs should be evaluated for their effectiveness with hearing-impaired children.

Linn, Hadary, Rosenberg, and Haushalter (1979) describe a special adaptation of SCIS, S-APA, and Elementary Science Study (ESS) materials for hearing-impaired children in a program at American University. The program, which also emphasizes discovery, involves changing auditory observations to visual ones, and makes use of parallel lessons in art which assist in internalizing the science experience. The researchers feel that the use of artistic expression provides the child with a means of communicating feelings, interpretations, and cognitive gains to peers and teachers. These researchers investigated cognitive learning and social integration in resource room and mainstream settings. The cognitive test results for the elementary, hearing-impaired children showed no difference in gains.

Only one effort has been taken to develop a national elementary science curriculum for use with hearing-impaired students. The Kendall Demonstration Elementary School (KDES), located on the campus of Gallaudet College for the Deaf, designed a series of curriculum guides with suggestions for teachers. KDES has distributed 385 of the science guides. The guides were developed by curriculum teams and include objectives, materials, activities, vocabulary lists, and suggestions for evaluation. The original emphasis on Piaget-based materials proved too cumbersome for many teachers, however, and the guides are now being revised to include a spiralling content approach. KDES has an extensive evaluation base for their approach, including student characteristics and achievement data, follow-up surveys on use of the guides, and a criterion-referenced, computer-generated testing system. The school is making efforts to disseminate the program to others and to provide appropriate support and training in its use (M. Hallau, personal communication, December, 1984).

Intermediate-Level Science. Science activities on the junior high level should emphasize discovery of principles and experimental solutions to problems. Constantly verifying anticipated results does not assist the student in thinking critically and discovering relationships. It does not confirm that students understand how they achieved certain results, nor that they are able to apply them to other problems. Anselmini (1967), in describing a junior high school science curriculum for hearing-impaired students in New York City, emphasized the factors of individual laboratory lessons, hands-on experiences, utilization of media, and planning a careful sequence of science topics. The topics should provide not only an understanding of facts and skills, but should give the hearing-impaired student a background for future course work. Anselmini also stressed the importance of correlating science instruction with the development of language, reading, speech, and speechreading skills.

On the junior high level, some research has supported the advocacy of direct, manipulative experiences. Boyd and George (1973), for example, described a study designed to determine if experiences in manipulating physical objects could increase classification abilities of hearing-impaired students 10 to 13 years old. The 26 students were taught using SCIS and SAPA materials. A statistical analysis revealed increased scores for the hearing-impaired students in the experimental group.

Van Wagner (1980) concluded from his investigation with 13 to 17-year-old hearing-impaired students that a multisensory hands-on science approach promotes cognitive growth. The total average increase of subjects in the experimental group was 324% on the science content test used in the study as opposed to 187% for the control group.

Although there is a lack of research literature pertaining to curricula in science for hearing-impaired students above the elementary grades, it is apparent that open-ended experiments which arouse interest in additional discovery can capitalize on the hearing-impaired student's developing mental abilities. Hands-on experiences provide more communicative variety which can also motivate students to learn. Contemporary curricula such as the Intermediate Science Curriculum Study (ISCS) and the Inquiry Development Project (IDP) may prove more effective with hearing-impaired students than traditional, didactic methods of teaching general science.

A program developed by the Biological Sciences Curriculum Study (BSCS) group at the University of Colorado, entitled ME NOW, has also been successfully tested at the Model Secondary School for the Deaf in Washington, D.C. (Grant, 1975: Grant, Rosenstein, & Knight, 1975). Low-verbal, hearing-impaired students of normal intelligence clearly attained cognitive gains and retained portions of these gains when instructed with the innovative science program. The largest amount of retained information was in the highest cognitive category, indicating that additional empirical research studies applying materials developed with careful attention to language dimensions bear further attention. Unfortunately, no follow-up studies have been reported in the literature.

For hearing-impaired students, successful science instruction has demanded either revision of curriculum materials originally developed for hearing students, or starting from scratch with original strategies which an experienced teacher believes will work. Typical revisions of materials for use with 7 to 9-year-old hearing-impaired students at the Texas School for the Deaf were cited in one research study by Borron (1978). Language was carefully structured in all exercises and directional language that was necessary for the performance of the activities was taught before the exercise was begun.

One effort to develop a national curriculum for intermediate-level hearing-impaired science students has been reported in the literature (Szymanski-Sunal & Sunal, 1981). The Science for the Hearing Impaired (SFHI) program was developed as part of a National Science Foundation grant project to adapt two Houghton-Mifflin science programs for use with hearing-impaired students (ages 9–13). This adaptation included reorganization of objectives and content within lessons, deliberate and appropriate teaching of science processes and inquiry skills, multisensory presentation of content through active participation, paraphrasing of text and use of language and identification cards, a selected science vocabulary taught through active experience, a variety of communication techniques, and a placement and evaluation system for science learning designed around the capabilities of hearing-impaired students. Additional assessment of students in this first available program at the national level included cognitive development, prepost unit tests of science learning and language development, and science interests and attitudes. The SFHI program was field tested on 135 students selected from rural, suburban, and urban classes. Teachers reported the program as better than other science programs because SFHI was more complete, experience-oriented, had good in-class and home activities, required less work than developing their own materials or using a text, and was clearly presented and already adapted to hearing-impaired student's needs.

Secondary-Level Science. Many of the science curriculum projects that have been developed for hearing high school pupils have not been extensively used with the hearing-impaired student, in spite of their emphasis on manipulative techniques and use of visual media. Perhaps the lack of use of these federally-funded projects in school programs serving hearing-impaired students is because the materials were originally developed with the science-oriented student in mind. The reading levels are quite challenging in these materials. In summary, no national curriculum is available for hearing-impaired, high school science students. The Gallaudet College curriculum bank includes a number of curriculum guides from school programs for hearing-impaired students. These are teacher-generated outlines of courses which have had little or no research-based assistance in their development.

Research on pedagogy has been equally scarce on this level. In one investigation, Kluwin (1981) studied 23 teachers from secondary programs of three schools on the East Coast, and found no difference in the signing behavior of reading/English and math/science teachers. While subject matter did not seem to make a difference, experience in the use of manual communication was a clear factor in the grammaticality incorporated in communicating the content.

Postsecondary Science. Even on the college level, educators frequently advocate the use of exploratory hands-on experimental work as important to the reinforcement of a concept or theory when teaching hearing-impaired students. Higgins (1971) stressed the primary use of the eye in collecting information, whether it is used to interpret oral or manual language, visual aids, or experimental findings. Bybee (1972) discussed the use of physical exploration as a "powerful motivator" toward learning science and, more importantly, language. Lang (1973) described the success encountered in a curriculum which emphasized direct use of manipulatives in individualized instruction in college physics.

Only a few research studies have been conducted in the areas of curriculum and pedagogy for postsecondary hearing-impaired students in science. In one study, Quinsland and Long (1986) compared the effects of direct experience learning and lecture learning on 50 postsecondary level hearing-impaired learners. The experiential treatment subjects demonstrated superior long-term retention over the lecture subjects. He found that the addition of a short "processing" activity at the conclusion of the instructional activity, where learners are required to reflect upon the recent learning experience, resulted in a significant improvement in retention across both lecture and experiential treatments.

Quinsland, Templeton, and Egelston-Dodd (1980) developed a course based on innovative use of mediation strategies to teach more than 4,000 medical word elements. The multicolored, split-frame slide technique increased comprehension scores and reduced student learning time by one-third. Braverman, Egelston-Dodd, and Egelston (1979) found that the use of verbal and pictorial cues facilitated relearning more than initial learning of terminology in a science course. When learning many vocabulary terms in a short time, the use of cues to label related groups may inhibit rather than facilitate learning by doubling the amount of original information.

Multiply-Handicapped Hearing-Impaired Students in Science. While little research has been conducted on science teaching and curriculum development for hearing-impaired students with additional handicaps, some exciting materials and strategies are available and bear

further investigation. The Science Activities for the Visually Impaired (SAVI) curriculum (DeLucchi, Thier, & Malone, 1980), for example, has found success in the education of visually-impaired students. Based on "hands-on" activities, the SAVI curriculum has a long history of research and development (Struve, Thier, Linn, & Hadary, 1975). Other studies support the premise that direct experience with physical objects can facilitate learning among students with vision impairments (Linn & Peterson, 1973). Van Wagner (1980) used SAVI materials with severely and profoundly hearing-impaired students (having no vision impairments), found improved performance in cognitive growth. Curriculum development and instructional strategies focusing on "multisensory" science experiences (Malone & DeLucchi, 1981) appear to be of benefit to all students, regardless of handicapping conditions(s), and there have been direct attempts to offer integrated laboratory science to visually-impaired, hearing-impaired and emotionally disturbed children (Hadary & Cohen, 1978).

Similarly, research with learning disabled students in science programs provides encouraging findings. These studies should be replicated with students who are hearing-impaired. Esler (1979), for example, used an ESS unit "Sink or Float" with Peabody Individual Achievement Test (PIAT) pretests and posttests and selected Piagetian tasks, finding an appreciable change in the number of children who were judged to be conservers. These learning disabled students also improved their scores in three of the four PIAT subjects: mathematics, reading, and spelling. Successful science teaching approaches with learning disabled and emotionally handicapped students have been described by Slavin (1979) in biology and by Rice (1983) in general science.

The response to PL 94–142 in the field of science education has led to a plethora of literature on teaching handicapped students (Lang, 1982). Books on teaching and curriculum development, including chapters on research-based topics, have been published by the National Education Association (Corrick, 1981) and the National Science Teachers Association (Hofman & Ricker, 1979). A book on classroom testing in science for hearing-impaired, visually-impaired and mobility-impaired/orthopedically-disabled students is also available (Lang, 1983).

Mathematics Education for Hearing-Impaired Students

As in science, the history of teaching mathematics to hearing-impaired students has not been extensively recorded in the literature. Until the early 1970s, few articles and even less research relating to mathematics education in school programs for hearing-impaired students were published. Broadbent and Daniele (1982) wrote in their comprehensive review of the literature on teaching mathematics to hearing-impaired students that the great emphasis placed on the development of language skills is reflected throughout the literature on teaching. Both research and general theoretical writings focusing on other academic areas have suffered accordingly. The dearth of literature on teaching mathematics to hearing-impaired students has also been noted by Suppes (1974), Johnson (1977) and Sinatra (1978). Suppes found practically no work which would shed light on the general traits hearing-impaired children take with them into arithmetic classes.

National Surveys: State of the Art. Johnson (1977) surveyed mathematics programs, materials, and methods in schools for hearing-impaired students, finding many mathematics programs suffering from neglect. He suggested that additional attention be given to increasing instructional time in mathematics and in providing better training to math teachers.

Elementary-Level Mathematics. Ross (1966), in a study of probability concepts in hearing-impaired and hearing children, found slightly poorer performance among the younger hearing-impaired students. The older hearing-impaired students, still language deficient, caught up with the hearing subjects. Springer (1976) found hearing-impaired children to be about three years behind hearing students in the ability to conserve numbers. Pendergrass and Hodges (1976) investigated group problem-solving situations, concluding that hearing-impaired students were not very proficient in question skills, an important aspect of group problem-solving.

Becker (1974) adapted a concept attainment task to study the performance of hearing-impaired and hearing children in problem-solving situations. She found in all of the hearing-impaired pupils a serious lack of a systematic approach. The performance on the logical discovery task was not proportionate to the children's oral ability.

Only one attempt to disseminate a national curriculum in elementary mathematics has been made. The Kendal Demonstration Elementary School in Washington D.C. developed a curriculum guide in 1982, and distributed 338 mathematics guides. As with the science guides, the math series appears to be utilized primarily in mainstream programs. While few programs use the KDES guides as a curriculum, teachers are gleaning objectives, strategies, and evaluation processes from them to meet their needs (L. M. Goldberg, personal communication, December 3, 1984).

Intermediate-Level Mathematics. Rosenstein, Lowenbraun, and Jones (1967) in a survey of programs for hearing-impaired students in New York State reported that 78.9% of 9 to 11-year-old students and 82% of the 12 to 14-year-old students use standard arithmetic textbooks ranging in reading difficulty from reading readiness to a Grade 6 level.

Secondary-Level Mathematics. Hauptman (1980) investigated spatial reasoning ability in order better to understand how these abilities relate to interest and achievement in mathematics. The results of this study suggest that spatial reasoning, orientation, and visualization are significantly correlated with achievement in mathematics, especially where the concepts are essentially spatial in nature.

Jensema (1975) and Karchmer (1977) indicated that the degree of hearing loss did not appear to have as significant an effect on mathematics computation subtests scores on standardized achievement tests as this variable had on areas more dependent on language skills. Austin (1975) examined eight concepts tested by various achievement test items and concluded that hearing-impaired students 18–20 years old closely paralleled levels of performance demonstrated by 14-year-old hearing students.

Fischgrund (1978) identified a hierarchical nature to mathematics word problems. The problems encountered by hearing-impaired students at the secondary school level are syntactically more complex, and the intricate relationships of syntax and cognitive processing appear to present a major stumbling block for student achievement.

Suppes and his colleagues at the Institute for Mathematical Studies in the Social Sciences (IMSSS) at Stanford conducted an ambitious project to investigate the potential of Computer Assisted Instruction (CAI) for hearing-impaired students. The primary emphasis of the Stanford program was on computational skill development (Suppes, 1971, 1974; Suppes, Fletcher, & Zanotti, 1976; Suppes, Fletcher, Zanotti, Lorton, & Searle, 1973). Made up of 14 sequential mathematical strands, the program provided a high degree of individualization. Results of the 3-year program indicated that the greatest gains on tests were achieved by hearing-impaired students receiving the most exposure to the computer sessions. As pointed out by Broadbent and Daniele (1982), it is important to note that among the Texas School for the Deaf students in this study, the group receiving the most mathematics sessions improved an average of 0.96 grade equivalent on mathematics computation scores after a 5 month period (Culbertson, 1974). Suppes (1974) reported that the cognitive performances of hearing-impaired students is as good as hearing students when the cognitive task does not directly involve verbal ability, and that the performance of hearing-impaired students was almost always better than disadvantaged hearing peers. The IMSSS also studied the performance of hearing-impaired and disadvantaged hearing children on arithmetic word problems, finding no difference in the performance measures examined (number of steps used to solve the problems, time needed, and proportion of problems requiring a hint).

In a study of the efficacy of programmed instruction, Bornstein (1964) included four teachers and 150 students divided into experimental and control groups. He found similar performance in first-year algebra and geometry and only slightly more favorable performance in intermediate algebra among students using programmed textbooks.

The Model Secondary School for the Deaf and the National Technical Institute for the Deaf jointly sponsored a project to identify skills which should be emphasized in mathematics and science programs for hearing-impaired students. Nine skills were identified and a brochure *Promoting a Clear Path to Technical Education* (Bone et al., 1984) was disseminated to thousands of educators. The committee based their recomendations on a joint position statement of the National Council of Teachers of Mathematics and the Mathematics Association of America (Recommendations for the Preparation of High School Students for College Mathematical Courses, 1978).

Post secondary Mathematics. Few research studies have been conducted with hearing-impaired students on the post secondary level. Stone and Raman (1979) investigated several instructional settings, finding that personalized systems of instruction (i.e., individualized, self-paced learning environments) are not necessarily superior to group lecture formats in terms of final grades and time needed to complete the course.

Sinatra (1979) studied the effects of multiple, iconic embodiment (images) on the ability of hearing-impaired college students to generalize probability concepts. He concluded that exposure to an increased number of different iconic embodiments did not improve such ability to generalize.

To examine how well hearing-impaired students are being prepared in basic metric skills, Lang (1979) administered a test to 283 high school graduates, concluding that the students lacked sufficient understanding in the areas of estimation, measurement, conversion, and use of metric symbols over four content areas (mass, length, volume and temperature).

Osguthorpe, Long, and Ellsworth (1980) found that repeated review of class notes was much more helpful to hearing-impaired than to hearing college students and that such review affects memory tasks more than higher level processing. The authors conclude that their findings point to the limitations of review as a facilitative learning process in courses emphasizing concept acquisition and problem-solving. In addition, they found evidence of potential problems hearing-impaired students have with recognition items on classroom tests and suggests that teachers do not automatically assume that recognition items are less difficult than recall items.

Multiply-Handicapped Hearing-Impaired Students in Mathematics. Based on the work of research scientists at the American Printing House for the Blind (for example, see Franks, 1970; Franks & Huff, 1977), one textbook has been published with nearly 200 activities focusing on fundamental mathematics operations and schema for students having the double handicap of vision and hearing loss (Franks, Albrecht & Lang, 1984).

Social Studies Education for Hearing-Impaired Students

Athough there is a great diversity of goals and objectives among educators in social studies, there is a general agreement on the central role in educating young people as citizens. Historically, the curriculum has focused on contemporary social problems, their place in the school, and their relationship to history (Hertzberg, 1982). The dominant pattern of elementary social studies (K–6) is the framework of "expanding environments": self, home, school, community, families, neighborhoods, state history and geographic regions, U.S. history and world cultures. In secondary education the dominant pattern remains similar to that described by the Committee on Social Studies in 1916: world history, U.S. history, civics/government, world cultures/history, American government, and sociology/psychology.

Stake and Easley (1978) found articulation of the social studies curriculum weak at all grade levels in public education. More than one-half of social studies teachers of normally-hearing students view this articulation as a problem (Weiss, 1978). One important reason for this problem is that in most cases the elementary and secondary programs occur in separate schools. The articulation problem is not unlike that in mathematics and science (Lengel & Superka, 1982).

A second factor which may be more important to social studies than to mathematics and science is the role and use of textbooks, which are developed separately for the various courses (Patrick & Hawke, 1982). Still another reason, apparently without a rational basis, is the attitude of some educators that social studies does not lend itself well to sequential development (Joyce & Allman-Brooks, 1979; Lengel & Superka, 1982). Unlike many other countries, the United States has no legal or professional authority for dictating the organization of school curriculum. Yet, ironically, the similarity in offerings in social studies has the effect of a central coordinating agency (Lengel & Superka, 1982; Stake & Easley, 1978).

The Educational Products Information Exchange Institute (EPIE, 1977) reported that at all levels of the curriculum, 90% of classroom time involves use of materials with two-thirds of this time spent with printed materials. There is an implication from this finding that hearing-impaired students, with all their difficulties in English, may find such an approach less effectual.

Unfortunately, a comprehensive survey of major publishers revealed that heavy emphasis on printed materials will continue to dominate (Schneider & Van Sickle, 1979).

Sixty percent of secondary social studies teachers in the United States make use of film at least once every two weeks (Fartana, 1980). High school teachers rarely use hands-on materials (Weiss, 1978). Numerous studies have indicated the benefit of materials distinguished by clearly-stated objectives with high correspondence to specific lessons (Martorella, 1977). The extent to which the media and exemplary materials are used in school programs serving hearing-impaired students is not known.

Stake and Easley (1978) provide evidence of the low priority of social studies at the elementary level in both the value systems of the school and of the teachers. Science not only shares this low priority but in a few case studied by these researchers it was even lower.

In high school, teachers appear to be concerned over reading ability, student apathy, and a shortage of individualized instruction materials (Weiss, 1978). The reading ability of the students was a very serious problem with more than 90% of the teachers in Grade 7–9 expressing concern. These teachers consider the difficulty of the materials and the lack of funding critical problems in dealing with the needs of the "slow learner." These perceived problems and needs were similar for both junior and senior high teachers. The latter, however, also emphasized the inadequate articulation across grade levels with nearly two-thirds of these senior high teachers identifying this problem as "serious."

Only one study of significance to this review of research could be found on the subject of curriculum development and teaching in social studies programs for hearing-impaired students. Kluwin and Lindsay (1984) report on an investigation of 20 experienced teachers of hearing-impaired students in academic subject classes, including science, mathematics, and social studies in which a multiple regression analysis of classroom interaction variables indicated that the largest amount of variance was accounted for by the teacher's monitoring of classroom procedures. Positive attitudes toward the instructional environment appear to result from less teacher monitoring rather than from more. The second most important predictor of positive class attitude was the willingness of the teacher to attend to a student's effort until that student comprehended the task.

In addition to the review of the literature, a letter was sent to administrators in more than 75 school programs. No other sources of research in social studies curricula for hearing-impaired students were identified. The Kendal Demonstration Elementary School has disseminated 380 social studies guides which are organized by year and have suggestions for focusing on the development of concepts and thinking skills. As with the maths and science guides, the KDES materials represent a lone, albeit commendable, effort to establish national coordination in a much neglected area.

Other Research in Science, Mathematics, and Social Studies

There are two additional major sources of research which should be closely examined in order to find implications for teaching and curriculum development in school programs serving hearing-impaired students. Neither of these areas have been adequately bridged.

The first source of research is the plethora of studies with normally-hearing students. With the advent of meta-analysis, educators have been galvanized over recent years into synthesizing the research literature. These analyses have yielded significant trends which should provide directional markers for researchers in our field. While a discussion of these findings is beyond the scope of this review, some illustrative examples may serve to reinforce the value of these meta-analyses.

Shymansky, Kyle, and Alport (1983) studied the effects of new approaches to science that have been developed since the 1960s. They compared 105 experimental studies which employed 18 different outcome measures and from which 341 effect sizes were calculated, finding the new science curricula improved students' problem-solving, creativity, use of techniques in science, and understanding of spatial relations. The new advances did not improve factual recall, low-level synthesis, or reading skills.

Willett, Yamashita, and Anderson (1983) examined 130 studies (341 effect sizes) involving instructional systems. The most pronounced effects were found for teaching programs which utilized principles of contract learning, mastery learning, personalized instruction, and computer-simulated experiments. One finding that may be important to teachers of hearing-impaired students is that excessive use of slides and tapes produced negative consequences for cognitive learning.

Wise and Okey (1983) studied the effects of teaching techniques. A total of 400 effect sizes were identified in 160 empirical studies. The effects on cognitive variables (achievement, problem-solving, science knowledge) were noteworthy for focusing (alerting students to objectives), manipulative techniques, questioning (especially wait-time), and material revision. Inquiry teaching had positive effects on learning "process" (use of scientific method), but was not superior to traditional methods for imparting factual knowledge.

Sweitzer and Anderson (1983) summarized 68 studies on teacher training, concluding that the most influential variables were the number of science courses, teaching methods courses, use of teacher-directed concrete modes of instruction, modeling, video technology, and print material.

A meta-analysis of the relationships between student characteristics and student outcomes in science was conducted by Fleming and Malone (1983). After comparing

168 studies, one major conclusion was drawn which is germane to the present review: cognitive achievement in science was predicted most strongly by language ability.

While meta-analyses throughout the area of "academic development" may prove valuable, a second major source of research is comparably so. Numerous studies have been conducted with hearing-impaired students either as "pure" research or "applied" investigations not directly focusing on mathematics, science, or social studies instruction. General research on pedagogy, for example, may provide helpful information to teachers. As an illustration, Wolff (1977) investigated the actual classroom time devoted to communication with cognitive content in preschool, primary, intermediate, and high school classes in three schools serving hearing-impaired students. The study compared several predominant methodologies and found teachers of hearing-impaired students less directive than public school teachers. He suggests that since there is evidence to suggest that the communication methodologies appear to influence the cognitive behavior of teachers, additional research may shed light on the identification of classroom situations which may benefit more from one methodology than another.

In their chapter on "Cognitive, Personal, and Social Development of Deaf Children and Adolescents," Greenberg and Kusché cite numerous "pure" research studies on cognition and perception which have implications for teachers in academic development programs. Science and maths teachers, for example, will benefit from the findings reported by these authors on such relevant areas as color perception; discrimination tasks involving numbers, sequences, and shape recognition; categorization; rule learning; discovery; and problem-solving. The general fields of attribution theory and information processing and their relationship to academic development of hearing-impaired students bear further investigation. Similarly, Quigley and Paul's chapter on language development and Lowenbraun and Thompson's chapter on "Environments and Strategies for Learning and Teaching" provide a wealth of information to enhance instruction and curriculum development efforts. Levitt's chapter provides additional background information for teachers incorporating speech and hearing skills development in the academic classroom.

Language and Academic Development

The continued emphasis on language skills development for many hearing-impaired students may be so intense that it may possibly have detrimental effects on their achievements in other academic areas. Maxwell (1979), in her discussion of a model for curriculum development at the middle and upper levels in school programs for hearing-impaired students, summarizes the feelings of many educators in science, mathematics, and social studies: Teaching language devoid of content has limited effectiveness.

Various studies have shown evidence to support the belief that a lack of linguistic experience has no substantial impact on a child's understanding of concepts (Grant, Rosenstein, & Knight, 1975; Robertson & Youniss, 1969; Watts, 1979). It appeared to Watts, for example, that systems of operations such as spatial understanding form part of a general system of thinking mechanisms directed towards the concrete physical world. The most important generalization made from his investigation is that teachers need to create another perspective in which the ability to think occupies a key role in the classroom. Knowledge is acquired through interaction with the environment. Too much emphasis on discrete language skills may exclude the development of the concepts. The expansion of the hearing-impaired student's expressive language should not be an end in itself, but should be related to the development of the conceptual processes and comprehension. An investigation by McGill-Franzen and Gormley (1980) appears to support this belief. The results of the study indicate that syntax is better understood by hearing-impaired readers when embedded in familiar prose context.

The issue of language development permeates discussions on teaching and learning mathematics. Research in mathematics education for hearing-impaired students has focused primarily on achievement on standardized tests. Broadbent and Daniele (1982) write that most of the articles published in mathematics for the hearing-impaired student are based on professional experience and opinion rather than empirical study. Performance of hearing-impaired students on standardized tests in mathematics appear to show that these students achieve higher scores in arithmetic computation and lower scores in areas which require more verbal skills such as paragraph meaning and word problems (DiFrancesca, 1971; Gentile & DiFrancesca, 1969; Trybus & Karchmer, 1977). Based on early national assessments by the Office of Demographic Studies at Gallaudet College, the Special Edition of the Stanford Achievement Test for Hearing-Impaired Students (SAT-HI) was developed. These tests have been carefully examined for linguistic bias and are normed for the hearing-impaired population of examinees.

DiFrancesca (1971) and Karchmer (1977) provided data which appear to support a trend later described by Broadbent and Daniele (1982). During the first few years of school, hearing-impaired students score higher in reading than in arithmetic on the subtests of the Stanford Achievement Tests. After the third grade, the reverse is true. The greatest gains in arithmetic appear between the ages of 10 and 16. Broadbent and Daniele believe that one explanation may be found in the overwhelming emphasis on language development, vocabulary, and reading skills in the first 3 years. While it is true that such priorities may limit the opportunities for early mathematics learning, the levels of difficulty of the reading and language skills per se are increasing as well. Hence, the reversal may not be explained entirely by time-on-task.

Concern about reading skills in science is not unique to teachers of hearing-impaired students either. In one National Science Teachers Association survey of 360 middle/junior high school science personnel from 39 states and the District of Columbia, a chief concern of junior high school teachers was reading in science classes (Hofman, 1977). Science teachers of hearing students ranked reading skills as the most prevalent problem on a list of potential classroom problems.

In social studies, hearing-impaired students would surely benefit from the excellent use of graphics and the general attractiveness of current textbooks as compared to the texts of past decades. Patrick and Hawke (1982), however, report that modern textbooks tend to be difficult to read. Teachers of hearing students commonly complain about this readability problem. The use of such printed materials may be even more inappropriate for the hearing-impaired student. However, Pricket and Hunt (1977) found that educators considered "academic materials designed specifically for deaf students" very unlikely to be developed (p. 375).

Clearly, more research is needed to determine if the current curricular emphases are the most appropriate. Language development of hearing-impaired students may be facilitated by infusing it as an integral component of mathematics, science, and social studies courses. With a structured approach to a spiral curriculum, both language and the concepts needed to use language in a functional way may be taught together.

Classroom Assessment of Hearing-Impaired Students

When teachers develop their own tests for use in their classrooms, test items must be carefully written in order that all students clearly understand what is being asked. The language of the test items may be the determining factor in whether or not a student demonstrates mastery of the course content. This is especially true for the hearing-impaired student. Testing hearing-impaired students in the classroom is a multidimensional problem. There are no reliable tests which can differentiate reasoning itself from the language needed for the demonstration of reasoning. The intricate and subtle connection between these two has escaped many educators. When developing a test item for an achievement test to be administered to a hearing-impaired student, a number of language considerations should be made. The reader is referred to the chapter by Quigley and Paul which cites research indicating the special precautions needed to be taken in the use of vocabulary and certain syntactic structures of English.

McKee and Hausknect's (1980) review of the literature on the classroom assessment of hearing-impaired students provides us with a discussion of syntax problems. They recommended minimizing the number of compound and complex sentences used in the test items and in the instructions for tests. This includes the

use of relative pronouns, conjunctions, and complementation. Rudner (1978) described several additional linguistic structures that are difficult for hearing-impaired students. These structures include conditionals, comparatives, inferentials and low-information pronouns. The conditionals sometimes present problems in the development and scoring of a science or mathematics test because the students may not realize that a statement in a part of a sentence is dependent on other information for its completion. They may read parts of the sentence in isolation.

The seriousness of the hearing-impaired student's reading comprehension problems has been documented in numerous research studies (e.g., Cooper & Rosenstein, 1966; DiFrancesca, 1971), but most of these investigations do not deal with the relationship of reading ability to testing and test development. The literature is especially lacking in information which would help the classroom teacher with some practical recommendations. Although not focusing specifically on tests, Hargis (1969) discussed how reading difficulties may confound the assessment of problem-solving abilities. The average hearing-impaired child achieves close to normal levels in arithmetic computation, for example, but when the numerical or quantitative problems are expressed as "word" or "thought" problems, the significance of language achievement becomes apparent. Hargis suggests sequentially ordered instruction and a careful grammatical approach to teaching the language aspect of arithmetic.

Deafness as a language handicap presents a formidable challenge to the hearing-impaired reader even during leisure reading. The added pressure of time constraints during a testing situation may increase test anxiety. Although some educators believe that time may be essential for the hearing-impaired student to piece together the complexity and abstraction inherent in the test items, research has not revealed overwhelming support. In a study involving 614 hearing-impaired students, Garrison and Coggiola (1980) investigated the adequacy of time limits in the administration of two subtests of the Differential Aptitude Test battery. No evidence was adduced to indicate that hearing-impaired examinees would profit from an extension of testing time. Further investigation appears necessary to clarify this issue.

In terms of interpreting achievement test scores, one must be cautious when generalizing about the hearing-impaired student's ability and understanding of concepts. The differences between scores of hearing and hearing-impaired students may be a result of the hearing-impaired students' educational experience, including a general lag in basic conceptual perspectives due to limited social opportunities and communicative interaction with family and peers. Austin (1975) linked this lag in conceptual perspectives to language skills. Some of the science concepts tested on the instruments he used appear to include knowledge influenced primarily by practical experience. The learning of these concepts would not necessarily require formal language skills. Austin pointed out, however, that language skills are required to demonstrate this knowledge on written tests.

LaSasso (1979) warned that drawing inferences about a hearing-impaired student's comprehension of a passage from correct or incorrect responses to test questions is not as straightforward as it might appear. It is often difficult to assess whether the student has actually comprehended the test question itself. LaSasso's research provided some evidence that hearing-impaired children found Wh-questions (those beginning with *who*, *what*, *where*, *why*, and *how*) significantly less difficult than questions using an incomplete statement.

Garrison, Tesch, and DeCaro (1978) found that hearing-impaired adolescents tend to agree rather than disagree with test questions written in a true/false format. They also described the difficulties hearing-impaired students have in understanding negatives which are implied by comparisons or inferences. Double negatives also present problems and should be used with great caution.

Little research has been conducted on the performance of hearing-impaired students on true/false, multiple choice, and matching items. Comparative studies may prove valuable to test developers. Which type of test item proves more difficult for hearing-impaired students? What are the linguistic and experiential factors inherent in these items? These questions have ramifications for both classroom, teacher-developed tests, and standardized tests used for placement, college entrance, and/or employment. In one study (McKee & Lang, 1982), no significant differences were found in the performance of hearing-impaired physics students on equivalent true/false and multiple-choice test items. It was hypothesized that the unusual preference for multiple-choice tests expressed by the hearing-impaired students reflected the more abstract nature of true/false items. The data, however, did not support this hypothesis. This study suggested the need for more definitive research on the format and syntax of test items.

Lang (1983) reviewed the above studies and others pertaining to administration of classroom tests, and provided a list of suggestions to teachers for developing tests based on the review of research.

In the mid-1960s, discussion on the misuse of Stanford Achievement Test results for advancing students from one level to another was meant to encourage researchers to develop more appropriate assessment devices for evaluating academic development and preparation for work (Babbidge, 1965). Jensema (1980) more recently reiterated this point. He writes that almost all education programs for hearing-impaired students utilize commercially published achievement tests and because of lack of information, misconceptions, or local tradition, these tests and their results are often incorrectly applied. Efforts have been made to accommodate the special needs of hearing-impaired students taking the Stanford Achievement Test in relation to test item sequencing, communication of instructions, and score interpretation

(Allen, White, & Karchmer, 1983). Jensema (1978) writes, however, that many achievement tests, including the Hearing-Impaired Version of the Stanford Achievement Test (SAT-HI) do not give exact measures of achievement and should not be used to measure academic development over short periods of time. When school programs for hearing-impaired students administer the same achievement test to all its students several times a year in order to observe changes in performance, they are wasting both time and money. Yet even with these concerns, the inadequacy of research on teacher-developed and commercially-produced tests appropriate for use with hearing-impaired students remains serious. One has only to look at the compilation of tests in *Assessment of Hearing-Impaired People* (Zieziula, 1983) to see two major indicators of the absence of research. There are practically no norms for hearing-impaired students for all of the standardized achievement tests listed in science, mathematics, and social studies. Nor are there such norms for the various vocational aptitude tests, vocational interest tests, or work evaluation instruments. Secondly, the number of references related to hearing-impaired persons is so small that the conclusion can be made that these evaluation tools have not been extensively researched with hearing-impaired populations.

Bragman (1982) reviewed the research literature on test instructions for hearing-impaired students, concluding that there is limited information available as to the most appropriate method of conveying test instructions. She writes that since the main purpose of tests is to determine the real needs of the student in order to develop appropriate educational programs, it is crucial that research be conducted to determine methods of giving instructions. Research should also be done on the effects various methods of conveying instructions have on test performance and the validity of the evaluation instrument.

Personnel Preparation

The problem of finding qualified science and mathematics teachers is not unique to special education. Nationwide, the number of new math teachers has decline 77% over the past decade. For science teachers, the drop-off is 65% (*Newsweek*, 14 February, 1983). Of those who are teaching maths and science, 30% are underqualified, including half of those newly certified, and 42 states are officially short-staffed in both math and science.

Feistritzer (1984) collected data from nearly 1,300 teacher training institutions and predicts with supportive data that a severe teacher shortage will occur by 1992. Those teachers available will have been trained in programs lacking stringency. She cites astonishing data indicating that 82% of the institutions ignore SAT and ACT scores in considering applicants.

Although nearly 74% of the 480 science teachers of hearing-impaired students in the Lang and Propp (1982)

study had no degrees in science education, 38% had bachelor's degrees and 49% had master's degrees in the "education of the deaf." Almost half of these teachers stated that they did not even take one science education course. These teachers are in need of assistance and the quality of their teaching is probably reflected somewhat in the quality of the academic development of their students. The status quo for mathematics and social studies teachers is not much different.

The Lang and Propp study also indicated that few science teachers have had formal education leading to degrees in areas of physical science. For example, 30.4% had fewer than six credits in undergraduate science and 81% had completed fewer than six credits of graduate school science courses. Of the teachers responding, 37.8% had a bachelor's degree and 49.2% had a master's degree in the education of hearing-impaired students. Many had had college education in other disciplines besides science education and the education of hearing-impaired students. This includes BA and MA degrees in such disciplines as music, finance, home economics, art history, mathematics, administration, and physical education. A large number of respondents had degrees in general and special education, particularly in speech pathology and audiology.

The problem of teacher training in the field of science education for hearing-impaired students appears to be even more critical than in public education. As in the public schools, teachers are reassigned to teach science and math classes for which they are not qualified. Reassignment of this nature has occurred on such a massive scale in public schools that approximately 30% of all math and science teachers in secondary-school classrooms are now either completely unqualified or severely underqualified to teach those subjects (Aldridge, 1984b). Aldridge laments that even with this crisis, the supply of science and mathematics teachers his declined by a factor of four in the past decade. In school programs for hearing-impaired students, this problem is even more serious. It is no wonder that the curriculum exhibits so many deficiencies. The implications for research and development are formidable.

Although it is understandable that training programs are not accessible to many teachers, the Lang and Propp survey revealed surprising results. Few science teachers (8.4%) are members of the National Science Teachers Association, an organization which publishes periodicals for elementary, secondary, and post-secondary teachers. A wealth of information is available in these publications on pedagogical strategies, curriculum development, and research in science teaching.

Corbett and Jensema (1981) conducted a comprehensive study of nearly 5,000 teachers in school programs for hearing-impaired students. The data from their survey substantiates the need expressed above. The percentage of undergraduate majors recorded by teachers in this study was never greater than 5% for any of the areas in the physical sciences or social studies.

Leading graduate majors did not include any of these areas, indicating that the number of teachers was probably less than 1% for each category. Of the 628 secondary teachers from academic areas responding to the survey, fewer than 17% of the mathematics teachers indicated that they were certified by the Council on Education of the Deaf (CED). The statistics for science, history, and social studies were 15.1%, 10.5%, and 12.7%, respectively. The fact that many teachers are teaching subjects in which they lack training is apparent from the data showing the percentage of the 4,887 teachers who are teaching in each of the categories.

On the postsecondary level the situation is no better. Although there are about 10,000 hearing-impaired students attending college in the United States, attrition remains a serious problem. College faculty, too, have inadequate programmatic opportunities to prepare themselves to teach students with hearing losses (Conner & Lang, 1987).

Preparation for Work

Career Education for Hearing-Impaired Students

In today's highly competitive job market, it is often difficult for disabled persons, such as those who are hearing-impaired, to achieve vocational success (Schein & Delk, 1974). One source of difficulty for hearing-impaired individuals is the variety of erroneous notions, myths, and stereotypes about deafness held by employers. Both unemployment and underemployment of hearing-impaired people today can be partly attributed to these misconceptions. An equally powerful impediment to vocational success may be that hearing-impaired persons too frequently internalize these erroneous notions into their own value systems. The resultant lack of self-confidence may hinder hearing-impaired persons in their efforts to obtain jobs commensurate with skills and training and to advance subsequently in their careers. Although the classroom can play a major role in fostering self-awareness, few school programs serving hearing-impaired students have adequate K-12 career education experiences. For example, many hearing-impaired students in science have little exposure to hearing-impaired adults who have succeeded in various careers and, hence, could serve as role models in directing them toward white-collar jobs (Lang & Propp, 1982). One probable result of this lack of exposure is that many hearing-impaired students receive a rather limited view of career options. Egelston-Dodd (1977), for example, found that high school graduates often believe that their deafness precludes entrance into certain fields of employment.

Infusion is a process of interweaving career development concepts into subject matter classes (as opposed to the "add-on" approach where separate career education classes are offered). The distinct advantage of the infusion method is that it provides a link between the subject matter and the world of work, hence providing more relevance to the learning process. A great deal of research has been done on various aspects of career education and development. However, there is a complete absence of research reported in the literature on the efficacy of the infusion method with hearing-impaired students. The present review on infusion will necessarily focus on those studies conducted with normal-hearing students with the hope that it will stimulate interest in research on infusion techniques with hearing-impaired students.

Bryant (1976) reported statistically significant gains in cognitive growth as measured by a test battery on vocabulary, language, mechanics, and expression for an experimental group receiving career education concepts integrated into the lesson plan. The U.S. Office of Education evaluated a number of studies which addressed the relationship between career education infusion and achievement of basic skills. Of these studies, 19 (50%) were rated as providing strong evidence of the efficacy of infusion, 16 (42%) were moderately supportive, while only three (8%) indicated negligible impact (Bonnett, 1977; Datta, 1976; High, 1977).

Some teachers are concerned that integrating career education may impede growth in the academic subject area: Bhaerman's (1977) review of 38 studies showed no such interference. The infusion method also showed promise through modest but consistent gains in grade-equivalent scores of slow learners and disadvantaged youth. Encouraging results of infusion attempts were reported across school systems, on different levels, and in different subject areas (Bhaerman, 1977). Although the present review is not comprehensive, the reports cited are representative of the literature and provide substantial evidence that the efficacy of the infusion method bears further validation with the unique audience of hearing-impaired students.

Career education proponents make no promises that infusion will promote achievement of the content. The promise made is that basic skill development will not suffer in the process (Wilson, 1977). Hence, the implications for enhanced learning through infusion of both subject matter and career education concepts found in the literature reviews are good.

Lang and Stinson (1982) reported on interviews conducted with hearing-impaired students in a postsecondary technical education program in order to learn about certain aspects of the students' career development. These interviews provided descriptive information concerning the career awareness of hearing-impaired students during their first few weeks in a technical education program. The findings yielded by the interviews suggest that the students had progressed in their career development to a point where most of them felt capable of making an initial selection of a career for themselves. Although the students interviewed appeared to be confident about their choice of a major during the time of the interview, within a year more than

half had changed their major. The interviews revealed certain shortcomings in career development. There were indications that students may not have thought carefully about the skills that they would need in their chosen field or about their chances of obtaining these skills. Many of the students interviewed did not appear confident that they could succeed in college. This last finding is consistent with that of Garrison, Tesch, and DeCaro (1978) who investigated the self-confidence of postsecondary hearing-impaired students and found that the hearing-impaired students were less self-confident than were a group of normally-hearing individuals.

In developing procedures and in interpreting the findings of the Lang and Stinson study, there was little previous empirically-based knowledge to draw upon. In one of the few studies of the career-development processes of postsecondary hearing-impaired students, Kersting (1976) concluded that these students seemed less capable of making responsible vocational decisions than normally-hearing peers. Occupational stereotyping may also interfere with effective career exploration (Egelston-Dodd, 1977). Cook and Rossett (1975) provided additional findings indicating that sex-role attitudes of hearing-impaired adolescent women influence their vocational and lifestyle choices. Meisegeier (1980) studied the extent to which hearing-impaired college students perceived their parents as sources of influence for their occupational aspirations. Both male and female students perceived their fathers and mothers, regardless of their parents' hearing status, as being influential in the development of occupational goals *if they could communicate with their parents*.

Hearing-impaired high school graduates often lack an adequate understanding of their own proficiencies and limitations, the occupational choices available to them, the skills necessary for certain occupations, and the formal training necessary to enter these occupations. As a result, their expectations regarding occupational choice may be highly inappropriate. For some students, expectations are too low and, consequently, failure to realize their full potential may result in occupational status not commensurate with their abilities. For others, career expectations may be too high. Or they may have simply developed an erroneous belief in what a certain career holds for them. Regardless of the reason, time wasted in change-of-majors and further career exploration in postsecondary environments may lead to a sense of frustration (Bishop et al., 1979). For these reasons, it is apparent that many hearing-impaired high school graduates are not adequately prepared to make career decisions even though they are often expected to make such decisions at this critical point in their lives.

Young hearing-impaired adults exhibit certain deficiencies in their career development which career education programs should address. Numerous studies have shown that educators recognize the inadequacy of career education in school programs serving hearing-impaired students. Maruggi (1980), for example, found a strong, positive reaction toward career education goals among administrators and vocational and academic faculty in residential and day programs. Maruggi concludes that while career education has the potential for improving the formal preparation of young hearing-impaired people in our society, the support of educators is necessary in order successfully to implement programs and meet the career development needs of this population. He stresses the importance of well-planned career education programs in the schools. Prickett and Hunt (1977) identified high priority areas in need of attention in the education of hearing-impaired students over the next 10 years. Out of 48 "high-desirability" items, "more attention to career education and career needs of the deaf" ranked eighth. In another study, Curtis (1976) surveyed educators to prioritize the needs for instructional materials. Again, career education ranked as a high priority need. Respondents felt a strong need for instructional materials to assist them with developing in their students a positive view of self and others, positive attitudes toward preparation required for occupation, knowledge of duties and responsibilities involved in various occupations, and knowledge of specific sources of information about careers.

There has been very little research in the area of programmatic efforts focusing on career education for hearing-impaired students. General articles have been published describing the efforts of teachers (Maxwell, Cleary, Lubbers, & Ireland, 1977; Polansky, 1979; Wentling, Butterweck & Zook, 1976). Miller (1978) examined the knowledge of deafness of 146 occupational educators involved in mainstream instruction of hearing-impaired students. He found a relative deficiency in background knowledge about characteristics of mainstreamed students.

It is interesting to see how hearing-impaired students change their attitudes about learning once they have had some actual experience in the world of work. Research has shown, for example, a high correlation between positive attitude toward learning English beyond required courses in school and the amount of work experience students have (Meath-Lang, 1978). Cooperation is needed between the schools and local business and industry in establishing work experiences for hearing-impaired students.

The late 1970s and the 1980s can be characterized as a time of considerable concern for change in school programs serving hearing-impaired students. The National Project on Career Education (Updegraff, Steffan, Bishop, & Egelston-Dodd, 1979), sponsored by both the National Technical Institute for the Deaf and the Gallaudet Pre-College Programs, is one example of the involvement and attention of postsecondary education programs in this change. In 1978, two national working conferences on career development for hearing-impaired students brought together educators from across the United States to identify future priorities in career education. Issues recognized as highly important included inservice training of faculty and staff in the

schools serving hearing-impaired students and a comprehensive plan for implementing career education in these programs. The NPCE was developed as a response to these conferences.

The payoff of research to improve K-12 career education programs would be an increased number of hearing-impaired college graduates entering technical and professional careers. Hearing-impaired persons now have available a number of quality postsecondary technical institutions for further training and career development. With enhanced career education research in the K-12 curriculum, more and more hearing-impaired students should benefit from these programs.

Postsecondary Education

During the decade 1972–82 the number of recognized college programs for deaf students increased fourfold. The April, 1985 issue of the *American Annals of the Deaf* lists 77 postsecondary programs specifically for hearing-impaired students or with support services for mainstreaming. Nearly half of these programs are in the West and South. DiLorenzo and Junco (1984) examined factors which accounted for enrollment trends in postsecondary institutions, finding that as additional postsecondary programs for hearing-impaired students were established, enrollments of students at the National Technical Institute for the Deaf decreased for geographically distant states. By comparing NTID enrollments with the national census data, they were able to identify states with student representation at NTID significantly below or above expected enrollments. The difference between the two groups of states was found to be related to the dominant type of educational environment experiences by the hearing-impaired students in high school. Quigley, Jenne, and Phillips (1968) concluded earlier that goals and values students develop in mainstream and integrated environments predispose them to seek similar postsecondary environments.

Between 20% and 50% of *all* first-year students entering college are not prepared to make a valid career choice (*Education Today*, 1978). DiLorenzo and Welsh (1981) report that 31% of students entering NTID have made career program changes, three-fourths of them during the first year. Murphy and Jacobs (1979) provide data on undecided students at the California State University, Northridge. Twenty-three percent of their hearing-impaired students (as compared to 10% of their hearing students) appear unsure when choosing majors.

It is assumed that the soundness of young hearing-impaired adults' vocational decisions reflects the adequacy of their career education. It is also assumed that individuals who make appropriate decisions are more likely to obtain jobs which are commensurate with their skills and training than are those who make inappropriate decisions. Individuals in the latter group are more likely to be underemployed in relation to their skills and training. These assumptions suggest that career education may play a powerful role in increasing the number of hearing-impaired persons who are employed in positions consistent with their skills and training; that is, holding higher-level positions in the occupational hierarchy. This reasoning points to the critical need for further research to determine: (a) the effect of career education programs upon occupational choice, and (b) the subsequent effect of these choices upon occupational attainment.

The Gallaudet College Alumni Survey (1984) reported that 60% of the graduates are working for agencies or companies primarily serving hearing-impaired persons. Of the 10 most frequently reported occupations, two were technology-related (4% of the alumni in computer programming and 1% in computer systems analysis).

Results of research on NTID graduate follow-up indicate both a low level of unemployment and of underemployment. Employment at the professional level approaches 50% and job satisfaction remains high. Salary increases were found to be in excess of the Consumer Price Index (Welsh & Parker, 1982). These researchers also report that NTID graduates pursue additional education in substantial numbers and are typically independent of government transfer payments.

These findings regarding unemployment and underemployment are not typical, however. Some studies have reported high unemployment rates among hearing-impaired adults (Berger, Holdt, & LaForge, 1972). Others have indicated that the problem may be one of underemployment (Schein & Delk, 1974). Schroedel (1976) discusses the lower socioeconomic status (SES) of hearing-impaired persons as compared to hearing persons. He found that younger hearing-impaired persons in the labor force are better educated than older hearing-impaired persons, and that workers from higher SES families averaged more education than those from low SES backgrounds. Hearing-impaired workers with hearing-impaired parents were approximately a year ahead in average educational attainment compared to hearing-impaired workers with hearing parents. Recent studies by MacLeod, Welsh, and Parker (1982) suggest that both unemployment and underemployment may contribute to the deficits in SES.

Lerman (1976) reviewed evidence indicating that employment conditions of hearing-impaired persons have been chronically depressed. Christiansen (1982) provides a comprehensive review of these problems. In terms of the relationship between educational achievement and occupational status, he describes the position of hearing-impaired people compared to the general population of the United States as less favorable now than it was earlier this century. In the 1930s and early 1940s, for example, studies found little difference in the number of years of schooling between the two populations. By the 1950s, there were clear indications that hearing-impaired persons attended school for a fewer number of years. In the early 1970s the employment

rate appeared to be approaching parity, then may have declined through the decade.

Marron and Egelston-Dodd (1982) reports that the majority of hearing-impaired workers are found in skilled and semiskilled manual occupations. In spite of job satisfaction, hearing-impaired workers generally have not had as many opportunities for advancement and often remain in the same job for extremely long periods of time (Christiansen, 1982). Incomes have not kept up with the income increases of the general population in recent years.

While there has been considerable research conducted in the area of employment mobility for the general population, there exists little evidence on the extent and pattern of mobility among hearing-impaired workers. Marron (1982) found a substantial amount of occupational mobility among hearing-impaired graduates of a postsecondary institution. His finding that race and sex are not significant determinants of the incidence of mobility is consistent with past research on the general population. Degree and calendar year of graduation were found to be important predictors.

Needs and Recommendations

In the mid-1960s a report to the Secretary of Health, Education, and Welfare by his Advisory Committee on the Education of the Deaf, described the need for cohesiveness within the field (Babbidge, 1965). The committee recommended that a panel be convened to develop a proposed program of comprehensive research into the problems of educating hearing-impaired students. The proposed program would hopefully have a major emphasis on programmatic research. While the research efforts of the two decades since the Babbidge report have enriched our knowledge base, they have been far from "programmatic," and the bridge between research and practice remains largely unbuilt. Researchers frequently publish their findings in specialized journals read neither by classroom teachers nor school administrators responsible for policy making. The field of education of hearing-impaired students lacks a range of professional journals that would adequately disseminate research findings in order to meet the needs of the personnel.

On the other hand, teachers in science, mathematics, and social studies are neither subscribing to the teaching journals nor joining professional organizations in the discipline areas they teach. These teachers are also not members of the major professional organizations in the education of hearing-impaired students (Lang & Propp, 1982; Corbett & Jensema, 1981). Hence, there is not only a need for extensive research in the area of academic development and preparation for work, but a concomitant need to find ways effectively to communicate these findings and apply the research to enhance teaching, curriculum development, and policy making. This latter responsibility rests on the shoulders of researchers as well as their colleagues in the field.

Toward a Theory of Academic Development

As stated by Melcher (1972), Kopp (1972), and again by Prickett and Hunt (1977), a major need in the field of educating hearing-impaired students is that of long-range planning. In the case of academic development, this need has been reiterated in the literature (Johnson, 1977; Lang, Egelston-Dodd, & Sachs, 1983; Lang & Propp, 1982). There is a strong need for research on the academic development of students and the quality of teacher training programs for personnel in the elementary, intermediate, and secondary school environments.

Prickett and Hunt (1977) used the Delphi procedure to collect 473 statements from 134 respondents in the field of educating hearing-impaired students. These data were reduced to 76 generic statements which were returned to the respondents for evaluation on both likelihood and desirability of occurrence. This study found that more specialization by teachers of hearing-impaired students is expected to be required in the future. A majority of the items pertaining to changes in academic programs were ranked as both likely and desirable. Yet, of the first 21 items in the table showing desirability-likelihood discrepancies, six deal with the need for more research. The feeling of unlikelihood stems from a pessimism about the lack of research funding.

In 1985, this author mailed a five-item questionnaire to school administrators of 75 residential school programs serving hearing-impaired students. Responses were received from 31 of these, and 41 pertinent recommendations for research were provided. The school personnel were asked if they had available any reports on their own research efforts to adapt or develop curricula in science, mathematics, and social studies. Several schools mentioned that they had curriculum objectives, sections of accreditation reports, outlines, texts, computer-assisted instructional materials, and visual aids. One school mentioned that they had workshops to help teachers adapt materials. None of the schools could offer a research-based approach to curriculum development. The responses indicated that many schools develop their curricula by establishing objectives based either on state requirements or individual decisions. There does not seem to be much effort to correlate achievement to criterion-referenced or norm-referenced standards (i.e., national assessments, school-based domains of skills, etc.). There was no mention of utilizing professional organizations in these three content areas to identify exemplary programs designs or to use evaluation methods to assess the appropriateness of the choice of objectives and goals for a curriculum. Several schools mentioned processes which were "systematic" or "efficient," but had no documentation to describe them. Science, mathematics, and social studies are considered the "weakest" areas of many school programs, with much more energy being expended in developing English language materials.

When asked if they were aware of any masters' theses, doctoral dissertations, or other unpublished research studies pertaining to the development of curriculum materials for mathematics, science, or social studies, only one of the 31 respondents mentioned a reference. The lack of perception of published and unpublished literature relevant to this important area was substantiated by many of the respondents' comments. Ironically, many of the respondents were curriculum coordinators and, ideally, would have attempted to locate such references in the process of their plans of work. The 41 needs statements collected in this brief survey (persons interested in the list of 41 recommended research questions may write to the author) overlapped the findings of this literature review, resulting in three general areas of recommended research for the next decade: curriculum and teaching (including scope, sequence, assessment, language-controlled materials, thinking skills, etc.); career education; and personnel preparation.

Curriculum and Teaching

More attention needs to be focused on the development of materials appropriate to the needs of hearing-impaired students. Professional organizations and post-secondary institutions should assist educators in K-12 programs to prioritize areas for development and revision. As suggested by Johnson (1977) there is a need to develop a field-oriented evaluation of programs identified as successful on the basis of student performance. There needs to be a serious emphasis on teacher expectations of student performance. Operationally, high expectations require consistent exposure of students to a variety of educational experiences presented in an integrated way. In the four other chapters in this section there is a wealth of information which can be gleaned from the empirical research studies on language, cognition, and other parameters of teaching and learning. This information base coupled with a new emphasis on research in pedagogy and curriculum development in the education of hearing-impaired students should lead toward a sound theory of academic development which seriously examines deafness as an educational condition. The various learning characteristics of hearing-impaired students should provide implications for a new generation of materials developed with this solid research base. Educators should develop a national curriculum bank of materials which are versatile and multi-faceted, allowing individual school programs to utilize them in accordance with state or local requirements. While a "standardized national curriculum" may be recommended as the materials bank grows, the individual units should continue to be accessible for independent use, hence allowing the largest possible audience to reap benefits from the research.

Supplementary materials and activities should be made available through research and development to provide challenges to gifted and talented hearing-impaired students in secondary school programs.

Special materials should be developed for hearing-impaired students with learning disabilities and other handicapping conditions.

Research on networking on state, regional, and national levels may result in more effective programs. Collaborative efforts to define a curriculum to satisfy state requirements, for example, may cut down on duplication of efforts when school programs are already understaffed and overworked. The most effective and efficient ways for post-secondary institutions to articulate with K-12 programs in better preparing students also need to be identified through research.

Although it is generally accepted that stronger foundations are laid if the hearing-impaired student's thinking is closely related to concrete perceptual experiences, such an emphasis is not common. Research needs to be conducted on the efficacy of direct, manipulative learning materials and how to articulate their importance in teacher training programs. In schools for hearing-impaired students, the accountability issue involves pressure on teachers to develop communication skills in their students, necessitating attention being given to appropriate division and integration of teaching time allotted to these skills and content courses. Researchers need to provide a database to support the curriculum materials and pedagogical strategies which attempt simultaneously to meet these diverse needs and demands.

Along with research on teaching and learning styles and on the development of exemplary curriculum materials, investigations are needed in the area of assessment, particularly vocabulary comprehension, understanding second and third meanings of words, and the formats of test items. At present we know very little about test-wiseness of hearing-impaired students, for example. Research is also needed to assist those responsible for management with such aspects of the curriculum as class size, time-on-task, tracking, role(s) of supervisors and principals, and organization of school programs into class groups. Such data will facilitate administrative decision-making and improve the quality of the school's offerings.

The issue of language development will always be a high priority in the education of hearing-impaired students. Most of the research being done today follows the tradition of examining and describing the linguistic difficulties. More emphasis is needed on time-on-task investigations which look at language development within the context of academic subjects as well as within the language curriculum per se. The potential of qualitative research, especially in such areas as journals and attitude studies may provide teachers and researchers with exciting, new perspectives. In addition, with millions of English as a Second Language (ESL) students in public education classes today, educators of hearing-impaired students should regard their knowledge about teaching language-impaired students as a special talent which should be of benefit to colleagues. Conversely, ESL practices should be examined more thoroughly for their potential applications to enhancing the education of hearing-impaired students. Most importantly, the school curriculum for hearing-impared students should not be viewed as a set of distinct subjects which displace one another. The need to place higher emphasis on language development should not preclude the study of science, mathematics, and social studies at any grade level. The infusion of language development throughout the school curriculum may result in reducing lags in both academic subjects and in English. The potential of a systematic and comprehensive approach to this time-on-task issue bears further investigation.

Career Education

More emphasis is needed in the curriculum, especially in social studies, on the "deaf experience." Hearing-impaired students need to see their place in the greater society, develop self-advocacy, self-identity, and a sense of culture and heritage. They need to be made aware of their legal rights and ethical responsibilities. As members of a "minority" group, they need a sense of the social justice and equity movements as they have occurred through our history. There is a surprising lack of research on the use of hearing-impaired role models in the school program. Investigations are needed to examine the potential positively to affect motivation and achievement of hearing-impaired students through increased exposure to successful hearing-impaired adults.

The use of hearing-impaired role models is only one aspect of the infusion approach to career education. Research is needed on the efficacy of interweaving subject matter and career development concepts. Studies are needed to identify appropriate areas for intervention strategies such as in the elimination of stereotyping or in meeting the special career development needs of gifted and talented hearing-impaired students.

On the postsecondary level, educators would benefit from investigations on increasing students' persistence and retention in career programs and the extent to which remediation influences the curriculum development efforts in college-level courses. Research toward the development of improved continuing education programs for hearing-impaired adults is also needed.

Personnel Preparation

There are two basic types of personnel preparation programs: (a) those that focus on skills needed to teach hearing-impaired students; and (b) those that prepare teachers in specific subject areas (math, science, social studies). The former need to develop more stringent requirements for trainees to acquire discipline knowledge as well as pedagogical and curriculum development skills in the specialized areas (e.g., discovery learning). The latter type of programs need to offer additional courses in deafness as an educational condition. Traditionally, on the elementary and intermediate levels, teachers have had generic skills without adequate discipline knowledge. Unfortunately, few secondary teachers are well-trained in subject-matter areas either. This trend must be reversed if we are to provide meaningful academic development and preparation for work. Sweitzer and Anderson (1983) summarized 68 research studies on teacher training. One of the most influential variables is the number of discipline-related (content) courses.

Either type of trainee may be employed in various school environments. Regardless of the training, individuals will need to update their skills and knowledge through inservice programs as well. Research needs to be done on the type of offerings which will improve personnel preparation. Without this research the quality of education will continue to suffer.

On the secondary level, it is crucial that teachers be recruited with degrees in the subject areas of science, mathematics, and social studies. Once they have been trained in the theory and methodologies effective for educating hearing-impaired students, they should be well-equipped to accept the challenges of both college-bound students and those who plan immediate entrance into the labor force upon graduation from high school. Research is needed to identify exemplary training programs. The needs of itinerant and resource room personnel should also be investigated. With the growing number of post-secondary programs in the United States, the Council of Education of the Deaf (CED) should give serious thought to conducting research on the inservice and preservice training needs for college-level teachers.

Educational Policies

During the 1960s and 1970s black students were special policy targets. Reading programs and elementary schools were primary beneficiaries of Title I and other monies. Brown (1983) described National Assessment of Educational Progress data that provides strong circumstantial evidence that such focused policy attention and resources may have had measurable positive impact on educational attainment. If this is true, then educators of hearing-impaired students should take a serious look at the focus of these policies and resources. Educational researchers should begin to look at the national assessments and other standardized tests as closely as they have the Hearing-Impaired Version of the Stanford Achievement Test. General policy questions should relate specifically to Public Law 94–142, the Education of All Handicapped Children Act, as well as other relevant legislation. Declines and improvements of test scores should be measured longitudinally and these trends need to be communicated to program directors and classroom teachers in much the same way they are for the general population of current examinees. Appropriate norms need to be developed for the hearing-impaired population as well.

There is a great deal of ambiguity in the research literature regarding the level of literacy of hearing-impaired students. Improved standardized assessments permitting both criterion-referenced and norm-referenced evaluations need to be developed. The implications for policy makng are formidable.

If there is a national crisis mathematics, science, and social studies achievement among hearing-impaired students, how does this crisis compare with that for normally-hearing students? Are the strategies also appropriate for hearing-impaired students? Researchers should examine, for example, if hearing-impaired students whose first language is not English (e.g., American Sign Language, Spanish, etc.) compare favourably with normally-hearing students having non-English backgrounds.

We should determine how best to continue the momentum gained during the last decade with disadvantaged students in helping hearing-impaired students in terms of policies and resources. We are not taking advantage of the National Science Foundation monies currently available for developing precollege science and mathematics materials and strategies. Research in the education of hearing-impaired students is largely uncoordinated. We can learn from the findings on policy-making and national assessments of the general population over the past decade as we prepare to develop new policies in the education of hearing-impaired students. The professional organizations for educators of hearing-impaired students should have an important role in this policy making.

If research on the various components of the school curriculum described in this report could be woven into the fabric of the school program, great strides would be made in enhancing the academic development and preparation of hearing-impaired students for the workforce.

References

Aldridge, W. G. (1984a). Federal Program ALERT, *NSTA Report*, October, Washington, DC: National Science Teachers Association.

Aldridge, W. G. (1984b). Why a crisis in science education? *Education Week*, **iv**(22).

Allen, T. E., White, C. S., & Karchmer, M. A. (1983). Issues on the development of a special edition for hearing-impaired students of the seventh edition of the Stanford Achievement Test. *American Annals of the Deaf*, **128**, 34–39.

Anselmini, A. (1967). A science program in a school for the deaf. *Proceedings of the International Conference on Oral Education of the Hearing-Impaired*. Washington, DC: The Volta Bureau.

Austin, G. F. (1975). Knowledge of selected concepts obtained by an adolescent deaf population. *American Annals of the Deaf*, **120**, 360–370.

Babbidge, H. (1965). *Education of the deaf in the United States*. Washington, DC: U.S. Government Printing Office.

Becker, S. (1974) The performance of deaf and hearing children on a logical discovery task. *Volta Review*, **76**, 537–545.

Berger, D. G., Holdt, T. J., & LaForge, R. A. *Effective vocational guidance of the adult deaf* (Final Rep. of RSA Grant No/RD-2018). Salem: OR State Board of Control, 1972. (ERIC No. ED078 231).

Bhaerman, R. D. (1977). *Career education and basic academic achievement—A descriptive analysis of the research*. Washington, DC: U.S. Department of Health, Education and Welfare. Office of Education.

Bishop, M., Crandall, K., Hinkle, B., Peterson, B., Streim, N., & Vos, S. (1979). *Early stages of career development: A concept paper*. Rochester, NY: Rochester Institute of Technology, National Technical Institute for the Deaf.

Bone, A. A., Carr, J. A., Daniele, V. A., Fisher, R., Fones, N. B., Innes, J. I., Maher, H. P., Osborn, J. G., & Rockwell, D. L. (1984). *Promoting a clear path to technical education*. Washington, DC: Model Secondary School for the Deaf.

Bonnett, D. G. (1977). *What does career education do for kids? A synthesis of 1975-76 results*. Crawfordsville, IN: New Education Directions.

Bornstein, H. (1964) *An evaluation of high school mathematics programmed texts when used with deaf students*. Washington, DC: Gallaudet College. (ERIC Document Reproduction Service No. ED 003 292).

Borron, R. (1978). Modifying science instruction to meet the needs of the hearing impaired. *Journal of Research in Science Teaching*, **15**, 257–262.

Boyd, E., & George, K. (1973). The effect of science inquiry on the abstract categorization behavior of deaf children. *Journal of Research in Science Teaching*, **10**, 91–99.

Bragman, R. (1982). Review of research on test instructions for deaf children. *American Annals of the Deaf*, **127**, 337–346.

Braverman, B. B., Egelston-Dodd, J., & Egelston, R. L. (1979). Cue utilization by deaf students in learning medical terminology. *Journal of Research in Science Teaching*, **16**, 91–103.

Broadbent, F. W., & Daniele, V. A. (1982). A review of research on mathematics and deafness. *Directions*. **3**(11), 1982, 27–36.

Brown, R. (1983). *National assessment findings and educational policy questions*. Report No. SY-CA-50. National Assessment of Educational Progress. Princeton, NJ: Educational Testing Service.

Bryant, R. S. (1976). *The efficacy of career education: Academic achievement*. Washington, DC: National Advisory Council for Career Education.

Bybee, R. W. (1972). A review of literature on science for the deaf. *Science Education*, **56**, 237–242.

Christiansen, J. B. (1982). The socioeconomic status of the deaf population: A review of the literature. In J. B. Christiansen & J. Egelston-Dodd (Eds.), *The socioeconomic status of the deaf population*. Washington, DC: Gallaudet College.

Conner, K., & Lang, H. G. (1987). Teaching the hearing-impaired college student: current perspectives in faculty development. In D. Kurfiss (Ed.) *To improve the academy*. Professional and Organizational Development Network. Stillwater, OK: New Forums Press.

Cook, L., & Rossett, A. (1975). The sex role attitudes of deaf adolescent women and their implications for vocational choice. *American Annals of the Deaf*, **20**, 341–345.

Cooper, R. L., & Rosenstein, J. (1966). Language acquisition of deaf children. *Volta Review*, **68**, 58–67.

Corbett, E. E., Jr., & Jensema, C. J. (1981). *Teachers of the deaf*. Washington, DC: Gallaudet College Press.

Corrick, M. E. (Ed.) (1981). *Teaching handicapped students science*. Washington, DC: National Education Association.

Culberstson, L. (1974). CAI—Beneficial teaching tool at Texas School for the Deaf. *American Annals of the Deaf*, **119**, 34–40.

Curtis, J. (1976). Educators of the hearing impaired prioritize the needs for instructional materials. *American Annals of the Deaf*, **121**, 486–488.

Datta, J. (1976). *Career education: What proof do we have that it works?* Report of Panel Session to the Commissioner, National Conference on Career Education, Houston, Texas, November 8. (ERIC Document Reproduction Service No. CE 014–833).

DeLucchi, L., Thier, H. D., & Malone, L. (1980). Science activities for the visually impaired (SAVI): Developing a model. *Exceptional Children*, **46**, 287–288.

Dietz, J., & Ridley, P. (1975). Helping the deaf hear. *SCIS Newsletter*, **27**, 7.

DiFrancesca, S. (1971). *Academic achievement test results of a national testing program for hearing-impaired students*. Washington, DC: Office of Demographic Studies, Gallaudet College (9, Series D).

DiLorenzo, L., & Junco, V. (1984). *The national representation of the student body of NTID/RIT*. Rochester Institute of Technology, National Technical Institute for the Deaf, Division of Career Opportunities.

DiLorenzo, L., & Welsh, W. (1981). *Concept paper—Follow-up: How long to receive a degree*. Rochester NY: Rochester Institute of Technology, National Technical Institute for the Deaf.

Egelston-Dodd, J. (1977). Overcoming occupational stereotypes related to sex and deafness. *American Annals of the Deaf*, **122**, 489–491.

EPIE (1977). Report on a national study of the nature and the quality of instructional materials most used by teachers and learners. *EPIE Report No. 76*. New York: Educational Products Information Exchange Institute.

Esler, W. K. (1979). Fun and gains with science. *School Science and Mathematics*, **79**, 637–640.

Fartana, L. (1980). *Perspectives on the social studies*. Research Report No. 78. Bloomington, IN: Agency for Instructional Television.

Feistritzer, E. (1984). *The making of a teacher*. Washington, DC: National Center for Education Information.

Fischgrund, J. (1978). *Mixing apples and oranges: Syntactic complexity and math word problems*. Paper presented at Model Secondary School for the Deaf research conference, September, Washington, DC.

Fleming, M. L., & Malone, M. R. (1983). The relationship of student characteristics and student performance in science as viewed by meta-analysis research. *Journal of Research in Science Teaching*, **20**, 481–495.

Franks, F. L. (1970). Measurement in science for blind students. *Teaching Exceptional Children*, **3**, 2–11.

Franks, F. L., & Huff, R. (1977). Educational materials development in primary science: Linear measurement for young blind students. *Education of the Visually Handicapped*, **9**, 23–28.

Franks, F. L., Albrecht, S., & Lang, H. G. (1984). *Focus in mathematics*. (Fundamental operations and concepts:

Underlying Schema). American Printing House for The Blind.

Gallaudet College Alumni Survey (1984). Washington, DC: Gallaudet College Research Institute.

Garrison, W. M., & Coggiola D. C. (1980). *Time limits in standardized testing: Effects on ability estimation*. Rochester, NY: National Technical Institute for the Deaf, Rochester Institute of Technology. (ERIC Document Reproduction Service No. ED 209 905).

Garrison, W., Tesch, S., & DeCaro, P. (1978). An assessment of self-concept levels among postsecondary deaf adolescents. *American Annals of the Deaf*, **123**, 968–975.

Gentile, A., & Di Francesca, S. (1969). *Academic achievement test performance of hearing-impaired students, United States: Spring 1969*. Washington, DC: Gallaudet College, Office of Demographic Studies.

Grant, W. D. (1975). *Me Now* and *Me And My Environment*: Science for the exceptional student. *Science Education*, **59**, 249–254.

Grant, W. D., Rosenstein, J., & Knight, D. L. (1975). A project to determine the feasibility of BSCS'S *Me Now* for hearing-impaired students. *American Annals of the Deaf*, **120**, 63–69.

Hadary, D. E., & Cohen, S. H. (1978). *Laboratory science and art for blind, deaf, and emotionally disturbed children*. Baltimore, MA: University Park Press.

Hargis, C. H. (1969). The grammar of the noun phrase and arithmetic instruction for deaf children. *American Annals of the Deaf*, **114**, 766–769.

Hauptman, A. R. (1980). An investigation of the spatial reasoning abilities of hearing-impaired students. *Directions*, **1**(3), 43–44.

Hertzberg, H. W. (1982). Social studies reform: The lessons of history. In I. Morrissett (Ed.), *Social studies in the 1980s*. Alexandria, VA: Association for Supervision and Curriculum Development.

Higgins, F. (1971). *Teaching science to the deaf*. Paper presented at the Annual Meeting of the National Science Teachers Association, March 1971, Washington, DC.

High, S. C. (1977). *The efficacy of career education: An update*. Washington, DC: Office of Career Education, U.S. Office of Education.

Hofman, H. (1977). Middle school/junior high school survey report. *Science and Children*, **14**, 33–35.

Hofman, H., & Ricker, K. (Eds.) (1979). *Science education and the physically handicapped*. Washington, DC: National Science Teachers Association.

Jensema, C. (1975). *The relationship between academic achievement and the demographic characteristics of hearing-impaired children and youth*. Washington, DC: Gallaudet College, Office of Demographic Studies.

Jensema, C. (1978). A comment on measurement error in achievement tests for the hearing impaired. *American Annals of the Deaf*, **123**, 496–499.

Jensema, C. (1980). Considerations in utilizing achievement tests for the hearing impaired. *American Annals of the Deaf*, **125**, 495–498.

Johnson, K. (1977). A survey of mathematics programs, materials, and methods in schools for the deaf. *American Annals of the Deaf*, **122**, 19–25.

Joyce, W. W., & Allman-Brooks, J. E. (1979). *Teaching social studies in the elementary and middle schools*. New York: Holt, Rinehart & Winston.

Karchmer, M. (1977). *Longitudinal trends in achievement test scores of hearing-impaired students*. Washington, DC: Gallaudet College, Office of Demographic Studies.

Kersting, J. (1976). *Career maturity measurements of NTID students*. Paper presented at the National Technical Institute for the Deaf Mini-Convention.

Kluwin, T. N. (1981). The grammaticality of manual representations of English in classroom settings. *American Annals of the Deaf*, **126**, 417–421.

Kluwin, T. N., & Lindsay, M. (1984). The effects of the teacher's behavior on deaf student's perception of the organizational environment of the classroom. *American Annals of the Deaf*, **129**, 386–391.

Kopp, H. G. (1972). The need for objective evaluation of the states and goals of comprehensive public education programs. In *Report of the Proceedings of the Forty-fifth Meeting of the Convention of American Instructors of the Deaf*, Washington, DC: U.S. Government Printing Office, pp. 350–354.

Lang, H. G. (1973). Teaching physics to the deaf. *The Physics Teacher*, **11**, 527–531.

Lang, H. G. (1979). Metric education for deaf and hard-of-hearing children. *American Annals of the Deaf*, **124**, 358–365.

Lang, H. G. (1982). Preparing science teachers to deal with handicapped students. *Science Education*, **67**, 541–547.

Lang, H. G. (1983). Testing hearing-impaired students in science. In H. Lang (Ed.), *Testing physically handicapped students in science: A resource book for teachers*. Morgantown, WV: Printech.

Lang, H. G., Egelston-Dodd, J., & Sachs, M. C. (1983). Science education for hearing-impaired students in the eighties: Priorities and projections. *American Annals of the Deaf*, **128**, 801–808.

Lang, H. G., & Propp, G. (1982). Science education for hearing-impaired students: State-of-the-art. *American Annals of the Deaf*, **127**, 860–869.

Lang, H. G., & Stinson, M. (1982). Career education and the occupational status of deaf persons: Concepts, research, and implications. In J. B. Christiansen & J. Egelston-Dodd (Eds.), *Socioeconomic status of the deaf population*. Washington, DC: Gallaudet College Press.

LaSasso, C. (1979). The effect of WH question format versus incomplete statement format on deaf students' demonstration of comprehension of text-explicit information. *American Annals of the Deaf*, **124**, 833–837.

Leitman, A. (1968). *Science for deaf children*. Washington, DC: The Volta Bureau.

Lengel, J. G., & Superka, D. P. (1982). Curriculum patterns. In I. Morrissett (Ed.), *Social studies in the 1980s*. Alexandria, VA: Association for Supervision and Curriculum Development.

Lerman, A. (1976). Vocational development. In B. Bolton (Ed.), *Psychology of deafness for rehabilitation counselors*. Baltimore MA: University Park Press.

Linn, M. C., Hadary, D., Rosenberg, R., & Haushalter, R. (1979). Science education for the deaf: Comparison of ideal resource and mainstream settings. *Journal of Research in Science Teaching*, **16**, 305–316.

Linn, M., & Peterson, R. (1973). The effect of direct experience with objects on middle class, culturally diverse, and visually impaired young children. *Journal of Research in Science Teaching*, **10**, 83–90.

MacLeod, J. E., Welsh, W. A., & Parker, C. A. (1982). *Graduate follow-up project of secondary programs for the deaf*. Rochester, NY: Planning and Evaluation Systems, National Technical Institute for the Deaf.

Malone, L., & DeLucchi, L. (1981). Multisensory science experiences—Meeting special needs. In M. E. Corrick (Ed.) *Teaching handicapped student science*. Washington, DC: National Education Association.

Marron, M. (1982). *Determinants of mobility among deaf graduates of the Rochester Institute of Technology*. Rochester, NY: National Technical Institute for the Deaf, Institutional Planning and Research Report No. 48.

Marron, M. & Egelston-Dodd, J. (1982). Social and economic patterns: A context for the career development of deaf students. In J. B. Christiansen & J. Egelston-Dodd (Eds.), *Socioeconomic status of the deaf population*. Washington, DC: Gallaudet College Press.

Martorella, P. H. (1977). Research on social studies learning and instruction: Cognition. In *Review of research in social studies education: 1970–1975*. Boulder, CO: Social Science Education Consortium and ERIC Clearinghouse for Social Studies/Social Science Education: Washington, DC: National Council for the Social Studies.

Maruggi, E. A. (1980). Perceptions of educators of the deaf toward career education goals for secondary level deaf students. In J. Egelston-Dodd (Ed.), *Trainer's manual: Career education/planning skills*: Rochester, NY: National Technical Institute for the Deaf.

Maxwell, M. (1979). A model for curriculum development at the middle and upper school levels in programs for the deaf. *American Annals of the Deaf*, 124, 425–432.

Maxwell, M., Cleary, D., Lubbers, E., & Ireland, A. (1977). Employment and basic skills: A program for low-achieving high school students. *American Annals of the Deaf*, 122, 563–566.

McGill-Franzen, A., & Gormley, K. A. (1980). The influence of context on deaf readers' understanding of passive sentences. *American Annals of the Deaf*, 125, 937–942.

McKee, B. G., & Hausknecht, M. A. (1980). Classroom assessment techniques for hearing-impaired students: A literature review. *Directions*, 1, 9–15.

McKee, B. G., & Lang, H. G. (1982). A comparison of deaf students' performance on true-false and multiple-choice items. *American Annals of the Deaf*, 127, 59–54.

Meath-Lang, B. (1978). A comparative study of experienced and non-experienced groups of deaf college students: Their attitudes toward language learning. *Teaching English to the Deaf*, 5, 9–15.

Meisegeier, R. (1980). The relationship between deaf students and their parents in the development of occupational goals. *Directions*, 1, 9–10.

Melcher, J. W. (1972). Some unmet needs of deaf children. In *Report of the Proceedings of the Forty-fifth Meeting of the Convention of American Instructors of the Deaf*, Washington, DC: U.S. Government Printing Office, pp. 88–93.

Miller, J. K. (1978). *Mainstreaming the deaf in occupational education: Knowledge and attitudes in the school environment*. Paper presented at the annual meeting of the American Educational Research Association, Toronto.

Murphy, H., & Jacobs, J. L. (1979). *A comparison of the majors of deaf and hearing students at California State University, Northridge*. National Center on Deafness, Publication Series No. 3.

National Commission on Excellence in Education (1983). *A nation at risk: The imperative for educational reform*. Washington, DC: Government Printing Office.

National Research Council (1979). *The State of School Science*. Washington, DC: Commission of Human Resources.

Osguthorpe, R. T., Long, G. T., & Ellsworth, R. G. (1980). The effects of reviewing class notes for deaf and hearing students. *American Annals of the Deaf*, 125, 544–558.

Owsley, P. J. (1962). Teaching science to deaf children. *American Annals of the Deaf*, 107, 339–342.

Patrick, J. J., & Hawke, S. D. (1982). Curriculum materials. In I. Morrissett (ed.), *Social studies in the 1980s*. Alexandria, VA: Association for Supervision and Curriculum Development.

Pendergrass, R., & Hodges, M. (1976). Deaf students in group problem solving situations: A study of the interactive process. *American Annals of the Deaf*, 121, 327–330.

Polansky, D. W. (1979). A model summer employment program for deaf youth. *American Annals of the Deaf*, 124, 450–457.

Prickett, H. T. & Hunt, J. T. (1977). Education of the deaf—The next ten years. *American Annals of the Deaf*, 122, 365–381.

Quigley, S., Jenne, W. & Phillips, S. (1968). *Deaf students in colleges and universities*. Ann Arbor, MI: Edwards Brothers.

Quinsland, L. K., & Long, G. (1986). *Experimental learning vs. lecture learning: A comparative study with post-secondary hearing-impaired learners*. Papers presented at the Annual Meeting of the American Educational Research Association, San Francisco, April.

Quinsland, L. K., Templeton, D. C., & Egelston-Dodd, J. (1980). Facilitating the learning of medical terminology through the use of effective mediation strategies: A model for the teaching of technical vocabulary. *American Annals of the Deaf*, 125, 780–785.

Recommendations for the preparation of high school students for college mathematics courses. (1978). *American Mathematics Monthly*, 85, 228–231.

Redden, M. R. (1979). *Summary report for a project titled "A design for utilizing successful disabled scientists as role models."* Washington, DC: American Association for the Advancement of Science.

Rice, J. R. (1983). A special science fair: LD Children—What they can do. *Science and Children*, 20, 15–17.

Robertson, A., & Youniss, J. (1969). Anticipatory visual imagery in deaf and hearing children. *Child Development*, 40, 123–135.

Rosenstein, J., Lowenbraun, S., & Jones, J. (1967). *A survey of educational programs for deaf children with special problems in communication in New York State*. (Project #JH30–67–003A) Title I, State Department of Education.

Ross, B. (1966). Probability concepts in deaf and hearing children. *Child Development*, 37, 917–328.

Rudner, L. M. (1978). Using standard tests with the hearing impaired: The problem of item bias. *Volta Review*, 80, 31–40.

Schein, J. D., & Delk, M. T. (1974). *The deaf population of the United States*. Silver Spring, MD: National Association of the Deaf.

Schneider, D. O., & Van Sickle, R. L. (1979). The status of the social studies: The publishers' perspective. *Social Education*, 43, 461–465.

Schroedel, J. G. (1976). *Variables related to the attainment of occupational status among deaf adults*. Unpublished doctoral dissertation, New York University.

Shymansky, J. A., Kyle, W. C., Jr., & Alport, J. M. (1983). The effects of new science curricula on student performance. *Journal of Research in Science Teaching*, **20**, 387–404.

Sinatra, R. (1978). *Diagnostic mathematics with deaf learners: Some issues and possible solutions*. Paper presented at the Fifth National Conference on Diagnostic and Prescriptive Mathematics, Scottsdale, AR, April.

Sinatra, R. (1979). *The effect of instructional sequences involving iconic embodiments on the attainment of concepts embodied symbolically*. Paper presented at a research meeting on the psychology of deafness, Gallaudet College, Washington, DC, February.

Slavin, L. E. (1979). A viable approach for LD/EH students in a biology course. *American Biology Teacher*, **41**, 164–170.

Springer, S. (1976). *The development of conservation of number in deaf and hearing children*. Paper presented at Canadian Psychological Association, April, 1979.

Stake, R. E., & Easley, J. (1978). *Case studies in science education* (National Science Foundation Report SE 78–74, 2 vols.). Washington, DC: U.S. Government Printing Office.

Stone, J. B., & Raman, M. L. (1979). *Beyond PSI: An investigation of small group instruction*. Paper presented at the Annual Meeting of the American Educational Research Association, San Francisco, California.

Struve, N. L., Thier, H. D., Linn, M., & Hadary, D. E. (1975). The effect of an experimental science curriculum for the visually impaired on course objectives and manipulative skills. *Education of the Visually Handicapped*, **7**, 9.

Sunal, D. W., & Burch, D. (1982). School science programs for hearing-impaired students. *American Annals of the Deaf*, **127**, 411–417.

Suppes, P. (1971). Computer-assisted instruction for deaf students. *American Annals of the Deaf*, **116**, 500–508.

Suppes, P. (1974). A survey of cognition in handicapped children. *Review of Educational Research*, **44**, 145–176.

Suppes, P., Fletcher, J. D., & Zanotti, M. (1976). Models of individual trajectories in computer-assisted instruction for deaf students. *Journal of Educational Psychology*, **68**, 119–127.

Suppes, P., Fletcher, J. D., Zanotti, M., Lorton, P., & Searle, B. (1973). *Evaluations of computer-assisted instruction in elementary mathematics of hearing-impaired students* (Tech. Rep. 200). Stanford, CA: Stanford University, Institute for Mathematical Studies in the Social Sciences. (ERIC Document Reproduction Service No. ED 084–722).

Sweitzer, G. L., & Anderson, R. D. (1983). A meta-analysis of research on science teacher education practices associated with inquiry strategy. *Journal of Research in Science Teaching*, **20**, 453–466.

Szymanski-Sunal, C., & Sunal, D. W. (1981). *Adapting science for hearing-impaired adolescents*. Morgantown, VA: Virginia University, College of Human Resources and Education. (ERIC Document Reproduction Service No. ED 219 267).

Trybus, R., & Karchmer, M. (1977). School achievement scores of hearing impaired children: National data on achievement status and growth patterns. *American Annals of the Deaf*, **122**, 62–69.

Updegraff, D. R., Steffan, R. C., Jr., Bishop, M. E., & Egelston-Dodd, J. (1979). *Career development for the hearing impaired: Proceedings of two working conferences*. Washington, DC: Gallaudet College.

Van Wagner, Jr., B. (1980). *Cognitive growth via hands-on science activities for severe and profound hearing-impaired students in a self-contained classroom*. Doctoral dissertation, University of Northern Colorado.

Watts, W. J. (1979). The influence of language on the development of quantitative, spatial, and social thinking in deaf children. *American Annals of the Deaf*, **124**, 46–56.

Weiss, I. R. (1978). *Report of the 1977 national survey of science, mathematics, and social studies education* (National Science Foundation Report SE 78–72). Washington, DC: U.S. Government Printing Office.

Welsh, W. A. & Parker, C. A. (1982). *The comparative status of deaf graduates of Rochester Institute of Technology, 1978–80*. Institutional Planning and Research. Rochester NY: Rochester Institute of Technology, National Technical Institute for the Deaf, Report No. 42.

Wentling, T. L., Butterweck, T. C., & Zook, G. A. (1976). Career education and evaluation for hearing-impaired adolescents: An example program. *Volta Review*, **78**, 144–151.

Willett, J. B., Yamashita, J. M., & Anderson, R. D. (1983). A metanalysis of instructional systems applied in science teaching. *Journal of Research in Science Teaching*, **20**, 405–417.

Wilson, J. H. (1977). *Career education: What research says to the teacher*. Washington, DC: National Education Association.

Wise, K. C., & Okey, J. R. (1983). A meta-analysis of the effects of various science teaching strategies on achievement. *Journal of Research in Science Teaching*, **20**, 419–435.

Wolff, S. (1977). Cognition and communication in classrooms for deaf students. *American Annals of the Deaf*, **122**, 319–327.

Zieziula, F. R. (Ed.) (1983). *Assessment of hearing-impaired people*. Washington, DC: Gallaudet College Press.

Cognitive, Personal, and Social Development of Deaf Children and Adolescents

MARK T. GREENBERG, Ph.D. AND CAROL A. KUSCHÉ, Ph.D.

Department of Psychology University of Washington

Abstract—The purpose of this chapter is to present an integrated review of the current state of research of the cognitive, intellectual, social, personality, and family development of deaf children. The chapter reviews research in diverse area. The sections on cognitive and intellectual development include reviews of research on intelligence and achievement, cognitive tasks, cognitive style, concept formation, problem solving, hemispheric specialization and the development of perceptual, memory, and motor skills. The section on social development covers research on social competence, social cognition, peer and teacher interaction, and family processes and interaction. The review is followed by comments on the process and structures that support research in deafness. Recommendations are suggested both to improve the state-of-the-art of research as well as its ability to contribute to the practice of educating and supporting deaf children and their families.

INTRODUCTION

The purpose of this chapter is to explore the cognitive/intellectual, social, and personality development of children who have significant hearing impairments. As these domains cover a wide variety of topics and an extremely large number of research projects, this review, of necessity, is selective. Its intention is to cover research in these domains that is of significant importance to current practices; and dilemmas confronting theorists, researchers, and practitioners concerned with deaf children.

Terminology

In order to clarify terminology used in this review, a number of definitional terms require operational citeria. The terms of *deafness* and *hearing-impairment* have been defined from a variety of different perspectives, including audiological, cultural, and behavioral criteria. The term *hearing-impaired* is often used to denote the entire spectrum of hearing loss from mild to profound. In contrast, the term *deaf* has been restricted to the

subgroup of hearing-impaired persons whose hearing loss is profound (greater than approximately 90 decibels across the speech range). This distinction appears to be useful given the findings of much greater use of visually-based language systems and lower speech intelligibility in persons who have hearing losses in the profound range (Karchmer, 1985). As in the chapter by Quigley and Paul, this review will focus primarily on hearing-impaired children with losses in the profound range, with some consideration given to those with severe hearing loss (70 to 89 dB). Thus, the terms deaf and hearing-impaired will both be utilized to denote this limited subgroup of hearing-impaired persons. Further, similar to Quigley and Paul, this review will also focus primarily on prelingually deafened children, that is, those whose hearing losses were sustained prior to 2 years of age.

The third major variable to be defined is *Total Communication*. In this paper, Total Communication (TC) is defined as a philosophy in which appropriate use is made of all possible communication modes (aural, oral, and manual) in order to develop effective communication (Meadow, 1980a). This philosophy does not specify a particular method of instruction (i.e., sign systems, ASL, fingerspelling) or how oral and manual methods should be combined. The term *simultaneous communication* will be used to refer to educational approaches that attempt simultaneously to utilize an English-based sign system with speech (Schlesinger, 1978).

The Revolution in Deaf Education—A Cohort Problem

A major dilemma involved in interpreting research on the hearing-impaired population, and in drawing conclusions regarding its generalizability, concerns the issue of cohort differences which are defined as differences due to year of birth or the experience of specific environmental circumstances (Achenbach, 1978). This cohort difficulty is further compounded because it has seldom been noted to be a problem and past researchers have often failed to provide sufficient information regarding subject characteristics to allow for careful interpretation of their findings. Both Meadow (1978) and Quigley and Kretschmer (1982) have previously discussed the related issues of subject selection criteria and other factors that may impact generalizability of findings. This cohort effect is especially problematic when conclusions are reached on the basis of a limited number of research findings. This fallacy of generalizability may become even more problematic as researchers who are not familiar with the demographics of deafness begin to base conclusions on past research (cf. the section on hemispheric laterality).

There are at least seven important changes that have rapidly altered the educational and social context of deaf children. First, prior to 1970 almost all deaf children were educated by oral-only methods. With the introduction of the TC philosophy, there has been a rapid change in communication techniques. Karchmer (1985) reports that approximately 87% of profoundly deaf children and 75% of severely hearing-impaired children now receive some type of sign language instruction (sign system or ASL) in American schools. Second, there has been a rapid increase in the number of children served and in the quality and range of services provided under the rubric of early intervention, that is, services to deaf children under age 3 (Greenberg & Calderon, 1984). Third, as a result of PL 94-142 and other factors, there has been a significant decrease in the number of children (especially elementary-age) who reside at, or are served by, residential schools and a concomitant rise in the number attending daily classes in local school districts. This has led to both the proliferation of public school programs and increased responsibility for families as primary educators of their children. Fourth, in the past two decades, there has been a growing recognition of the legitimacy of American Sign Language with regard to both its structural features and its strong, positive sociolinguistic impact for deaf persons (Baker & Battison, 1980). Fifth, related to the preceding change there has been a further recognition of the strength, value, and structure of the deaf community and deaf culture (Higgins, 1980; Nash & Nash, 1981; Padden, 1980). Sixth, in the past two decades there have been important technological changes that have led to improvements in hearing amplification both for individuals and in group settings, for example, FM units in classrooms. Seventh, sociological changes have led to greater numbers of deaf children from non-English speaking homes, while medical innovations have resulted in higher survival rates and more multihandicapped children with hearing losses.

Given the "turn-around" time for research and publication, it is fairly safe to state that most American research published prior to 1980 involved one of the following groups of deaf children:

1. Oral-only: those who were educated by oral-only methods with possibly some gesture or sign language used in extraeducational environments. As many of these children lost their hearing after age 2 and selection biases led to only the most successful children remaining in this cohort, these children are not likely to be representative of the hearing-impaired population.

2. Oral failures: those who were first educated in oral-only methods, who were not successful in the early years and who were later exposed to one of a variety of sign systems or ASL. Although these children are often represented as total communicators in the literature, these children lacked consistent, positive, early linguistic input, and so are not representative of the potential effectiveness of TC (Moores, 1982).

3. Deaf of deaf parents: those who had early sign language input because they were born to deaf parents and were exposed to signs in their home (less than 10% of deaf children). For a variety of reasons including the differences in the early home environment, the availability of deaf role models, the high percentage of genetic etiologies for their deafness, and often their primary exposure to ASL rather than an English-based sign system, this group cannot be interpreted as representative of the effects of TC, as has often been done in the literature (Kusché, Greenberg, & Garfield, 1983; Meadow, Greenberg, Erting, & Carmichael, 1981).

Thus, it is apparent that most of the available research provides little information that can be simply applied to the new cohort of deaf children presently being educated, that is, deaf children who have been introduced to TC through early intervention programs and who go to schools that encourage the use of an English-based sign system in the home. What little research exists regarding this population, which educators most need to be informed about, is derived from cohorts of young American deaf children. Studies based on foreign samples of children are even more likely to involve one of the three groups listed above, for example, virtually all research on British samples involves orally-trained children.

The most convincing evidence of this cohort effect is a recently published 10-year study which examined three cohorts of deaf children: those who were enrolled prior to the implementation of TC, those that began with oral methods and experienced the school's shift to TC, and those that began school and received most of their education in TC (Delaney, Stuckless, & Walter, 1984). Results on measures of academic achievement indicated significant differences favoring the most recent cohort. However, the effects cannot be ascribed only to the implementation of TC as a variety of curricular and technological changes also occurred at the school during this time span.

Further cohort differences that also require mention involve changes in the onset of hearing loss (pre- vs. postlingual), etiology (the reduction in deafness caused by rubella and infections due to antibiotics and vaccines), age of diagnosis, school placement and hours in mainstream contexts, familiarity with the deaf community, and the introduction of new educational technology.

This cohort effect is a critical methodologica point. The population we are currently educating is *not* representative of those that have been studied by most researchers in the last 60 years. What follows in the present chapter therefore describes what we know about cognitive growth, information processing, social interaction, family life, personality development, and so forth, of children who do not represent the majority of deaf children in the United States today. This information, while still valuable in clarifying our understanding of deafness, must nevertheless by synthesized and interpreted with caution.

These cohort effects are sometimes quite subtle. In one research project (Greenberg, Kusché, Gustafson & Calderon, 1985), it was found that children with later diagnosis, later intervention, and later introduction to manual communication were performing much better than those who received early diagnosis, intervention, and sign language. However, this was because the former group also included some children who were postlingually deafened quite late in childhood. The implications of these findings are thus much different than they would have appeared with adequate sample specification.

With all of these caveats regarding the interpretation of past research, unless otherwise specified, it can be assumed that publications concerning research prior to 1980 include one of the above three groups. Where it is known and of particular importance, the important characteristics of the populations studied will be noted.

Integration of Research: State of the Art

In the following review of the research, the domain of cognitive and intellectual development will first be covered, followed by a review of the domains of family, social, and personality development. However, it should be recognized that they are only being examined separately for heuristic reasons. It is critical to the educational process to view children holistically and for educational efforts to be directed toward the whole person. This is especially so with many deaf children given the relative impoverishment of their communicative environments. Further, it is clear that for all children there are a variety of direct and indirect influences and feedback loops between the growth process in cognition, communication, social competence, and the developing sense of self (Kegan, 1982).

AN OVERVIEW OF THE HISTORY OF COGNITION AND DEAFNESS

For most of recorded history, the deaf population has been mistakenly and quite unfortunately considered to be "deaf and dumb," in terms of being mute and of having inferior intelligence. As Moores (1982) noted in his historical review of cognition and deafness, scientific perspectives on intelligence over the course of the 20th century have evolved in three major stages: the deaf as inferior, the deaf as concrete, and the deaf as intellectually normal. The inferiority hypothesis was advanced by Pintner, Eisenson, and Stanton (1941), who concluded that deaf individuals evidenced an average retardation of 10 IQ points on nonverbal tests as compared to hearing norms. In 1953, Myklebust concluded that deaf children were quantitatively equal, but qualitatively unequal, to hearing children. Finally, Furth (1964) suggested that, in general, differences between deaf and hearing children could be accounted for by difficulties with test instructions or by a lack of general life experiences. In spite of numerous indications to the contrary, Furth concluded that the "thinking processes of deaf children are similar to those of hearing children and therefore must be explained without recourse to verbal processes" (p 70).

The differences in these perspectives on cognition and deafness are likely multiply determined. Most apparently, improvements both in the quantity and quality of research have certainly allowed for better understanding. In addition, the importance of cohort changes should not be overlooked, as was noted earlier. The improvements observed in cognitive functioning over the past 80 years, which are especially notable since the late 1970s, may well speak positively to the many innovations and changes in the education of deaf students (e.g., the advent of early intervention programs, increases in the use of TC in the schools, etc.). It is unfortunate that educators have received relatively little praise for those improvements, as the literature generally speaks only to "deficits" and "deficiencies."

INTELLIGENCE AND ACHIEVEMENT

It has been repeatedly found that although the nonverbal intelligence scores of deaf children are comparable to those of normal-hearing children, achievement scores in academic subjects are quite poor (Meadow, 1980a). Hirshoren, Hurley, and Kavale (1979) reported that a prediction of school achievement for any given individual deaf child based on his or her individual IQ score would be only 6.3% more accurate than a prediction based on the group average. Given the frequent misunderstandings in this controversial area, it is important to clarify what is measured by nonverbal intelligence tests and tests of scholastic achievement.

Intelligence tests are designed to measure a child's potential for learning at a given point in time. The idea implicit in measuring "potential" is that the child has had a history of more or less average experiences in interacting with the environment. Given that a child has had a "normal" background, an intelligence test is used to evaluate how much the child has been able to profit from his or her lifetime of daily experiences as compared to other children of the same age.

Each individual appears to be born with a genetically determined reaction range for intellectual potential;

during the maturational years, the development of various cognitive capacities can vary widely within these genetically determined limits. Given relatively normal environments, it is estimated that the average reaction range for intelligence is 25 IQ points, but larger deficits are found in hearing children when they have been raised in extremely deprived environments (Scarr-Salapatek, 1975). Environment input thus interacts with biological potential over the course of development to determine intellectual abilities, which appear to become increasingly "set" or "canalized" as the individual matures.

Achievement tests, on the other hand, are used to assess how much the child has learned in the school setting, which is a smaller and particular subset of daily life experiences. It should be noted that children can demonstrate achievement which is below their potential, but cannot achieve beyond that of which they are capable (i.e., the term "underachiever" is valid, but "overachiever" is not).

It should be obvious that most deaf children have not had "normal" backgrounds with regard to language-related areas, and this is one of the major reasons why verbal intelligence tests are considered to be invalid and are rarely used with this group. With regard to nonverbal intelligence tests, it appears that the assumption that the deaf child has been exposed to an "average" nonverbal environment has greater validity, although sequential/verbal memory and language nevertheless appear to play some role in nonverbal intellectual development.

Nonverbal intelligence tests largely evaluate what children have learned from a lifetime of nonverbal experiences and how they process this information, while achievement tests generally assess what children have learned in language-related areas at school; in other words, with deaf children, we generally compare *nonverbal* learning capacity with *verbal* achievement. It should therefore not be surprising to find that the two show very dissimilar rates of development, although it is important to note that they are nevertheless significantly related. Watson, Sullivan, Moeller, and Jensen (1982) reported an average multiple correlation of 0.68 between individual nonverbal intelligence subscales and measures of language performance for deaf children ages 6 to 10, which is only slightly less than that reported for hearing children.

Nonverbal Intelligence

At the present time, there is agreement that on performance subtests of IQ batteries, deaf children as a group obtain scores that fall within the average range for nonverbal intelligence (Meadow, 1980a). Recently, a separate set of performances norms for the Weschler Intelligence Scale for Children-Revised (WISC-R) was established for deaf students (Anderson & Sisco, 1977). Although the performance scores of deaf children are similar to hearing norms, a peculiar subtest profile has

been detected which suggests that experiential deprivation induced by sensory loss affects the overall profile pattern (Ray, 1979). A factor analytic study of the Hiskey-Nebraska Test of Learning Aptitude, another test frequently used with deaf children, suggested that different cognitive abilities were being assessed for deaf and hearing children between the ages of 3 and 10, especially with regard to memory for colors and block design (Bolton, 1978). Hiskey (1956) reported that deaf children excelled slightly on items of the Hiskey-Nebraska Test which required almost exclusive use of visual perception, but that hearing children had a decided advantage on all nonverbal items where vocalization aided retention. He also observed that "a nonverbal response of the immediate recall type is often strengthened through the utilization of supplementary sensory and motor cues" (p. 333). (For a more complete review of the IQ literature, see Vernon 1968.)

With regard to subgroups of deaf students, it has been found that white deaf children score significantly better on the WISC-R performance scale (by approximately 20 IQ points) than do Black deaf children (Hurley, Hirshoren, Hunt, & Kavale, 1979). This finding is consistent with research reported for the hearing population, in that Black hearing children typically score lower on performance IQ, but not on verbal IQ scales, as compared to white hearing children (Eysenck, 1971). It has also been noted in numerous studies that deaf children having a genetic etiology for deafness (and either deaf *or* hearing parents) score significantly higher on nonverbal IQ tests than deaf children with other etiologies and frequently significantly higher than the norms for the hearing population (Conrad, 1979; Kusché, Greenberg, & Garfield, 1983). Across the entire deaf population, degree of hearing loss and nonverbal intelligence scores are not significantly related (Conrad, 1979; Meadow, 1980a).

Academic Achievement

Overall, deaf children as a group generally demonstrate poor academic achievement (Meadow, 1980a). During the first 3 years of school, deaf children obtain their highest achievement scores in reading. After Grade 3, however, achievement scores in arithmetic and spelling are better than those in reading (Gentile & DiFrancesca, 1969; Meadow, 1980a). By late adolescence, the reading ability of the average deaf individual is approximately equivalent to that of a fourth of fifth grade hearing child, both in the U.S. (Furth, 1966) and in Great Britain (Conrad, 1977b, 1979). More comprehensive testing efforts (such as the use of the "cloze" procedure) suggest that reading deficiencies are likely even more pronounced (Moores, 1967; Wolff, 1973).

Longitudinal data indicate that the average increment in reading achievement over time is slightly less than 0.3 grade equivalents per year (Trybus & Karchmer, 1977), and improvement after the age of 9 appears to be minimal (Wrightstone, Aronow, & Muskowitz, 1963). Wilson (1979) has noted that up to the third-grade level, reading tests focus mainly on vocabulary and word analysis skills; reading comprehension and the ability to infer meaning become increasingly important after this level and are the skills which appear to cause the most difficulty for deaf children.

In the area of mathematics, the average deaf adolescent leaves school with a seventh grade mathematical ability, both in the U.S. (Karchmer, 1985) and in Great Britain (Wood, Wood, & Howarth, 1983), thus indicating a 3-year difference in favor of arithmetic as compared to reading over the course of the child's education. Growth in mathematical ability has been found to be about 0.5 grade equivalents per year (Babbini & Quigley, 1970). Computer-assisted learning in mathematics has been shown to result in slightly faster rates of progress for deaf children than for hearing children (Suppes, 1974). Wood et al. (1983) also reported that 15% of the deaf school-leavers studied had mathematical abilities which were at or above their chronological ages.

The average deaf adolescent also leaves school with about a seventh grade spelling ability (Quigley & Kretschmer, 1982), and it should be noted that similar superior spelling compared to reading ability is rarely found in an English-speaking hearing population (Frith, 1983). Matched for *reading age*, deaf adolescents are much better spellers than are younger hearing children (Gaines, Mandler, & Bryant, 1981). Moreover, during the elementary school years, deaf children appear to be much better at spelling than either their hearing (Hoemann, Andrews, Florian, Hoemann, & Jensema, 1976) or hard-of-hearing peers (Templin, 1948). It has also been found that phonetic spelling errors are made far less often by deaf children than by hearing children (Hanson, Shankweiler, & Fischer, 1983).

According to Gates and Chase (1926), a likely explanation for the large discrepancy between spelling and reading is that:

> the deaf owe their remarkable spelling ability primarily to a peculiarly effective type of perceiving, of reacting visually to words . . . normal children fail to develop this precise, accurate and—as far as the effects on spelling are concerned—effective form of word observation because they rely mainly on the easier, perhaps more natural—yet for spelling less productive—device of phonetic translation. (p. 299)

Hearing loss has been found to be significantly associated with reading ability (Conrad, 1979), but is only marginally correlated with mathematics ability (Wood et al., 1983). However, it is important to note that even hard-of-hearing students demonstrate great difficulty with reading comprehension (Karchmer, Milone, & Wolk, 1979). In other words, any hearing loss appears to be very detrimental with regard to reading achievement.

The achievement scores of black and white deaf children are remarkably similar, in spite of the large differences noted in nonverbal intelligence (Hurley et al., 1979). Numerous studies have indicated that genetically deaf children evidence better achievement scores than do deaf children with other etiologies (Meadow, 1968; Stuckless & Birch, 1966). Research has also suggested that genetic factors are strongly related to nonverbal intelligence for these children, while early sign language experience may be more important with regard to achievement (Brasel & Quigley, 1977; Kusché, Greenberg, & Garfield, 1983).

INFORMATION PROCESSING: THE PERSPECTIVE OF THE 1980S

In 1978, Tomlinson-Keasey and Kelly proposed that deaf children's early experience of limited accessibility to linguistic symbols resulted in alterations in the development of their information-processing abilities. This hypothesis, which focuses on differences in information processing, will be further developed in conceptualizing the cognitive development of deaf individuals. However, it is important to emphasize that while many deaf individuals share similar developmental histories, there is much heterogeneity in styles of processing information within the deaf population.

The theory of different modes of thinking or of processing information has been developed by a number of major theorists (e.g., Bruner, Piaget, Werner) and most recently has become popular in the idea of multiple intelligences (Gardner, 1983). A more limited formulation, the tricode theory of information processing (Anderson, 1978), focuses on the ability of human beings to process three different kinds of information: visual-spatial (e.g., "reading" an X-ray, remembering the image of a painting), verbal-sequential (e.g., reading this paragraph, rehearsing lines for a theatrical play), and abstract-propositional (e.g., understanding that all dogs are mammals though all mammals are not dogs, recalling the logic required for the proof of a geometric theorem). The types of information optimal for each of these three areas are frequently different, and to complicate matters further, we often use these modes in combination. Anderson has suggested that there is a strong survival advantage to having three separate codes with the capacity for intercommunication between them. Although the tricode theory does not take other modes of processing into account (e.g., sensorimotor or enactive, sensoriaffective), we nevertheless find it very helpful in organizing and understanding the cognitive development of deaf children.

Unfortunately, it is not always easy to tell which type of processing leads to which specific results for a given task. This is especially important in evaluating "verbal" and "nonverbal" tests. Tasks may appear to be nonverbal when in fact linguistic knowledge or the use of internalized verbal mediation can affect performance. For example, uneducated adults with normal intelligence respond quite differently from their educated counterparts in such diverse "nonverbal" areas as color classification, perception of geometric shapes, reasoning and problem-solving abilities, imagination, and self-awareness, even when reading and writing skills are not involved during testing (Luria, 1976). On the converse side, nonverbal skills (e.g., vision, proprioception) can play important roles in what appear to be verbal tasks, such as reading and spelling.

A large body of research has shown that deaf individuals as a group demonstrate both similarities and differences in the efficiency of processing modes as compared to hearing individuals. In general, deaf individuals perform equal to or better than hearing individuals on tasks where visual strategies or holistic processing (mediated primarily by the right cerebral hemisphere in the hearing population) are optimally adaptive. In contrast, deaf individuals perform differently or more poorly on tasks where verbal-sequential strategies (mediated primarily by the left cerebral hemisphere in the hearing population) or abstract-propositional processing (mediated by the associational areas in the frontal cortex) are most effective. In addition, learning disabled deaf children show patterns of processing information which are different from those of nonlearning disabled deaf children, and it appears that subtypes of learning disabilities can be diagnosed from divergent patterns of processing different types of information.

Information processing has been studied from a Piagetian developmental perspective and as it is reflected in an individual's cognitive style. Different cognitive developmental functions have been studied separately (e.g., perception, motor skills, memory) and in combination with regard to performance on various tasks (e.g., reading, categorization, rule learning, problem-solving). Each of these areas will be addressed separately, but it should be remembered that these divisions are arbitrarily determined in large part by the available research.

Piagetian Tasks

Observations of deaf infants and toddlers suggests that development proceeds normally through the sensorimotor stage, except in the area of vocal imitation (Best & Roberts, 1976). Studies concerning the preoperational years (approximately 2 to 6) are relatively scarce, but the research presently available suggests that nonlinguistic differences between deaf and hearing children first begin to appear near the end of this stage in such areas as seriation and transitivity (Furth, 1964; Youniss & Furth, 1965, 1966a).

After the age of 6, large differences are found in such areas as seriation, multiple seriation, correspondence, reverse correspondence, transitivity, and multiple classification (Youniss, 1967), with deaf children demonstrating performances which are more similar to those of young preoperational hearing children than to those

of their age-matched, concrete-operational hearing peers. Deaf latency-age children lag behind their peers with regard to sequential inferential reasoning, but are equal in performance with regard to simultaneous inferential reasoning (Bradshaw, 1964, cited by Furth, 1964).

Numerous studies have all consistently indicated significant developmental delays with regard to the attainment of conservation of number, quantity, length, weight, area, and volume (Furth, 1964, 1966; Oleron & Herren, 1961). Furthermore, these delays or gaps become increasingly larger with increasing age (ranging from 2 to 8 years) up through the teenage years. The "average" deaf child does not demonstrate a concrete operational understanding of conservation of weight or liquid until he or she is well into adolescence. Although earlier studies may have been confounded by linguistic difficulties in testing instructions, even with extensive modifications and improvements in directions, deaf children continue to show considerable delay (2 to 3 years) in understanding the concept of conservation (Furth, 1973, Rittenhouse, 1977).

On the other hand, school-age deaf children generally perform similarly to hearing peers on concrete operational tasks which involve the ability to visualize physical stimuli, such as in understanding the concept of horizontality, the projection of shadows, or the concept of rotation (Robertson & Youniss, 1969; Youniss & Robertson, 1970). Watts (1979) compared task performance in a group of deaf latency-age children and found that they simultaneously performed at a preoperational level with regard to conservation tasks and at a concrete operational level with regard to understanding horizontality. Deaf children show only a slight developmental delay in making simple probability predictions (Ross, 1966), but demonstrate relatively poor understanding of more complex probability tasks (Ross & Hoeman, 1975). Interestingly, deaf boys evidence significantly better performance in both horizontality (Murphy-Berman, Witters, & Harding, 1984; Watts, 1979) and probability predictions (Ross, 1966; Youniss, 1974) than do deaf girls.

Relatively little research has been undertaken with regard to formal operational thinking in deaf individuals, but the research which is available suggests that deaf adolescents show a marked variability in performance which appears to be both task and person dependent. Furth and Youniss (1969) reported that of seven deaf adolescent boys tested, none succeeded or failed on all of the six formal operational tasks given, but five succeeded on at least one. Combinatorial thinking, probability, and conservation of volume appeared to be more difficult than judgment of space, discovery of factors involved with momentum and an inclined plane, and discovery of factors controlling flexibility. None of the adolescents were completely successful on conservation of volume. In a subsequent study of combinatorial thinking, Furth and Youniss (1971) reported that deaf adolescents (ages 14–20) demonstrated markedly better performances in combining numbers as opposed to colors.

Research has similarly demonstrated variable results for formal operational training; while some deaf adolescents have been trained to show some understanding of formal operational concepts, others do not seem to be able to learn these concepts with the same training (Furth, 1973). Youniss (1974) found that combinatorial thinking was significantly related to schooling with his Costa Rican sample (ages 7 to 14), while classification skills, conservation, transitivity, and probability were not. Probability and combinatorial thinking were marginally nonsignificantly related to age. Youniss also reported a significant relationship between combinatorial thinking and transitive inference.

In summary, research involving Piagetian tasks indicates that in certain areas, deaf children first begin to show developmental delays near the end of the preschool years. With regard to tasks where visual attention and perception lead to correct responses (e.g., seriation tasks, simple probability tasks), developmental delays do not exist or tend to disappear relatively quickly. The ability accurately to perceive horizontality, for example, requires an individual to utilize relevant and disregard irrelevant cues in processing visual-spatial information. On the other hand, when reliance on visual perception leads to incorrect inferences, developmental delays are notable. In demonstrating conservation, for example, an individual cannot be convinced by the illusion of visual perception that one dimension is greater than its counterpart, but must take into account the concepts of reversibility, compensation, and so forth.

Piagetian research suggests that deaf children tend to rely heavily on visual-spatial processing and sometimes have difficulty with the simultaneous processing of multiple perspectives. For the average deaf child, the understanding of conceptual information does not appear to override visual perception until adolescence, while this same transition occurs between the ages of 5 and 7 for the average hearing child. As a result, the elementary school-age deaf child thinks predominantly in a preoperational manner in some areas, but processes information in a concrete operational way in others. However, it should be recalled that we know relatively little about deaf children who have received early, consistent linguistic input through TC; research is needed to compare different types of early language experience (e.g., oral, ASL, English, bilingual) with Piagetian stage development.

Given the research currently available, it appears that language deprivation influences the way information is processed, which in turn results in a type of experiential deprivation (i.e., experiences are mediated primarily through sensorimotor and visual-spatial means, with less input from verbal-sequential or abstract-propositional modes of thinking); processing differences, in turn, appear to affect the development of further concept formation. Although Furth (1964, 1973) has interpreted the literature as evidence that language does not affect

thinking, we believe that language has a strong effect on concrete and formal operational modes of thinking, while it has relatively less influence on sensorimotor and preoperational thought (largely based on visual-spatial processing). With regard to abstract-proportional (or formal operational) thought, it may be that episodic memories which are encoded linguistically and/or symbolically (in speech or in signs) in the hippocampal areas (Kesner & Baker, 1980), perhaps through the use of verbal/sign mediation, are more easily translated into propositional concepts or schemes in the association areas of the cortex (Linton, 1980) than are visually encoded memories or images.

Cognitive Style

With regard to cognitive style, Parasnis and Long (1979) reported that deaf students as a group tend to be more field-dependent (that is, are less able to differentiate objects from their backgrounds) than are their hearing peers. At younger ages (10 to 12), deaf girls appear to be more field-independent than deaf boys (Gibson, 1984), but by adolescence, the reverse is true, with deaf boys significantly more field-independent than deaf girls (Fiebert, 1967). Moreover, increasing field-independency with age (found with hearing children of both sexes) is found for deaf boys, but not for deaf girls, and age is a significant predictor of field-independence for deaf males, but not for deaf females. Spatial abilities are significantly related to the field-independency scores of deaf children, but age of hearing loss onset and degree of hearing loss are not.

Reading and language abilities have been found to be good predictors of field-independence if age and IQ are controlled. Davey and LaSasso (1984) found that cognitive style in deaf adolescents accounted for 7% of the variance in reading comprehension scores; in addition, field-independent deaf students utilized more effective memory strategies during reading and performed better on multiple-choice tests than their field-dependent counterparts.

Perceptual Development
Visual Perception

Tests involving visual perception have generally shown that deaf children score more poorly than hearing children on nonverbal tasks when verbal mediation can facilitate responding, but score equal to or better when verbal mediation interferes with performance. Deaf children perform especially well on tasks requiring visual recognition of target words or letters (Chen, 1976; Gates & Chase, 1926; Locke, 1978), since verbal mediation tends to cause interference with the accuracy of performance on these tasks. However, inferior performance has been frequently noted for visual perceptual tasks which require discriminatory as opposed to holistic processing (Furth & Mendez, 1963), especially with regard to tasks requiring visual discrimination of more complex stimuli (e.g., numbers, sequences, syllables, and words) as opposed to geometric forms or figures (Doehring & Rosenstein, 1969). Speed of visual perception has been found to be more highly correlated with reading vocabulary scores for deaf than for hearing children, but nonverbal intelligence does not appear to be highly related to speed of visual perception (Doehring & Rosenstein, 1969).

Several studies involving the Bender Gestalt Test of Visual-Motor Skills have all indicated that deaf school-age children score significantly worse than hearing children on what is obstensibly a nonverbal drawing task (Clarke & Leslie, 1971; Gilbert & Levee, 1967; Keogh, Vernon, & Smith, 1970). The errors which are most common are those which suggest impulsivity, immaturity, sloppiness, and the lack of verbal mediation (e.g., labeling the figures before drawing them). Age-appropriate planning, organizational abilities, and motivation to work carefully and accurately appear to be problematic areas. A subset of types of errors noted by Keogh et al. (1970) suggested a subgroup of organically-impaired deaf children. These may be the deaf children who are generally diagnosed as having additional learning difficulties, but further research is needed to confirm this hypothesis.

Visual Perception and Receptive Language Abilities

Visual perception is of especial importance for deaf individuals with regard to receptive communication. Because of the similarities of groups of phonemes and the rapidity of speech, it is estimated that the ambiguities in the English visual code require the lipreader to process 40 phonemes through the use of only 16 visemes (Erber, 1974). In comparing the lipreading abilities of deaf and hearing adolescents, Conrad (1977a) found no differences between the two groups and reported significantly better performance for both groups in reading printed test items as compared to lipreading them. The relatively poor lipreading ability of the deaf subjects was therefore not due to linguistic impairment, but more likely to difficulties inherent in the visual perception of oral English.

In studying the receptive communication abilities of deaf children, Grove and Rodda (1984) found that when very simple stimuli were used, reading was most effective, followed by Total Communication, manual communication, and oral communication. White and Stevenson (1975) reported similar results and noted that average and bright deaf children were able to assimilate significantly more information than their low-functioning peers when information was presented through reading, TC, or manual methods, but found no differences between the IQ groups when information was presented orally. Erber (1975) reported that combined auditory-visual perception was superior to perception through either audition or vision alone for deaf and hearing children as well as for deaf and hearing adults. Grove and Rodda (1984) suggested that combining the oral and visual systems creates a more robust short-term memory trace and that oral methods alone result in short-term memory overload and a low signal/noise ratio. However, it should also be noted that printed stimuli can be reread, while repetition is not available in the other modes. This is of great importance in deaf education, since teachers may often assume that deaf children have received their communications, when in fact they have not.

Robbins (1981) compared the reading comprehension of deaf children and adolescents on paragraphs with and without accompanying sign language pictures above the English words and found that reading comprehension was significantly better when signs were included. Gilman, Davis, and Raffin (1980) reported a highly significant effect on deaf children's understanding of morphemes in written language when teachers were consistent (as opposed to inconsistent) in using Seeing Essential English in conjunction with their spoken utterances. Visual perception thus appears to interact with environmental input to significantly affect the English language development of deaf children.

Tactile and Spatial Perception

Schiff and Dytell (1971) found that deaf and hearing children and adolescents showed no differences in ability to utilize their tactile sense to identify letters and that errors in both groups paralleled those found with visually presented letters. Blank and Bridger (1966) similarly found no differences between deaf and hearing preschoolers with regard to utilization of cross-modal transfer (tactile-visual), but they noted that the deaf children were more proficient in using tactual cues. Hauptman (1980) has suggested that because deaf children utilize their visual and tactile senses to a greater degree than hearing children, they may develop a different concept of space.

Kane (1979) reported that young deaf children (ages 8–11) made significantly more location and orientation errors than young hearing children when topographical cues were absent and relied more often on a self-reference system for making spatial judgments, suggesting that young deaf subjects were more egocentric in making hypothetical spatial judgments. No differences were found between older deaf and hearing children (ages 15–18), however, and both older groups were found to be better at spatial judgments than both younger groups.

Motor Development

Compared to their hearing peers, deaf children as a group show deficits in static equilibrium, balance, locomotor coordination, and more complex kinesthetic skills, but show no differences in the area of speed (Boyd, 1967). Deafness due to meningitis is especially likely to result in problems with kinesthesis and balance due to impairment in the functioning of the semicircular canal, until such time as individuals learn to compensate by using the senses of vision, proprioception, and/or touch (Padden, 1959). Deaf children with an endogenous (hereditary) etiology show a somewhat better growth pattern than do deaf children with an exogenous prenatal etiology; this latter group tends to show the poorest level of performance and the slowest rate of development, but differences are small and all etiological groups evidence deficient motor development (Boyd, 1967). Nevertheless, some deaf individuals perform as well as normal children, so that motor problems are not inherently associated with hearing loss.

Grimsley (1972) noted that visual cues aided deaf, but not hearing, adolescents in their ability to balance and further found that deaf adolescents could learn a balance task as well as their hearing counterparts. Pennella (1979) outlined a physical education program aimed at improving kinesthesia, balance, and equilibrium in deaf childen, and noted that many deaf individuals are successful athletes in spite of difficulties with maintaining equilibrium. With regard to fine motor development, deaf children show slight deficits in clerical speed and accuracy (Arnold & Walter, 1979), but are comparable to hearing children with regard to eye-hand coordination (Myklebust, 1964).

Memory Development

Encoding

In general, short-term memory differences between hearing and deaf children are not found when items to be remembered are presented simultaneously (Blair, 1957; Withrow, 1968), and deaf individuals have been found to perform as well as or significantly better than hearing subjects on memory tasks which involve visual tracking, motor recall, or location in space (Blair, 1957; Neville & Bellugi, 1978). Numerous studies, however, have repeatedly shown that deaf children and adults evidence large deficits in the processing of sequentially or temporally presented stimuli of numerous types, such as digits, words, pictures, signs, and so forth (Kusché, 1984a). It should be noted that these deficits are found for both verbal and visual sequential memory tasks. The ability to recall ordered information appears to be related to the meaningfulness of the information for hearing individuals, but not for deaf subjects (Odom & Blanton, 1967). Deficits in delayed recall of designs, word lists, and pictures after various durations (15 secs, 5 min, and 20 min) have also been reported for deaf as compared to hearing children (Bonvillian, 1983; Rozanova, 1966).

Research involving the memory abilities of ASL signers has shown that the surface form of ASL appears to be recalled only briefly, while the semantic content of the sentences can be remembered for a longer period of time (Poizner, Bellugi, & Tweney, 1981). Siple,

Caccamise, and Brewer (1982) found that skilled deaf and hearing signers encoded invented ASL-like signs in terms of linguistic structure (i.e., utilized linguistic abstraction), while unskilled signers encoded signs as visual-pictorial events, thus suggesting that sign language skill affects method of memory encoding.

Lantz and Lenneberg (1966) reported that color *recognition* was significantly poorer for deaf 6-year-olds as compared to their hearing controls, although both groups were similar in color *perception*. Deaf and hearing adults, on the other hand, showed no differences in overall color recognition scores, but demonstrated different patterns of color recognition. The patterns of the deaf children and deaf adults were similar, however, and could be predicted from communication accuracy scores which also showed pattern differences from those of the hearing adults.

> Apparently, sometime before the age of six, the deaf establish a characteristic pattern of memory . . . To a significant extent, this pattern remains in effect in adulthood, but now, with the acquisition of language, a new mnemonic vehicle has become available . . . The deaf when communicating to each other or to themselves apparently make a different use of English than the hearing population. (Lantz & Lenneberg, 1966, pp. 777–778)

The authors also noted that:

> the fact that some of the deaf children in this study possessed the same names for the colors as the hearing children, but were far inferior to them on ability to remember the colors, makes it clear that the mere possession of a verbal label does not necessarily affect cognitive behavior. (p. 779)

Memory, Language, and Reading Achievement

It is known that at least two important factors are related to good reading comprehension in hearing children: (a) short-term memory capacities, which involves phonetic encoding in the hearing population; and (b) processing speed, which includes retrieval from semantic memory, scanning speed of working memory contents, linguistic understanding, and past language experience (Hess & Radtke, 1981). Reading thus appears to be a language-based skill that ultimately depends upon automatic processing and unconscious linguistic awareness (Mattingly, 1972).

Watson et al. (1982) found that subtests on IQ tests which required visual memory (particularly visual sequential memory), consistently entered multiple regression equations as the best predictors of language performance ($r=0.59$—0.76), suggesting that visual memory skills are important in the English language acquisition of signing deaf children. This was particularly notable in that language performance did not increase as a function of age in this group of children (ages 6 to 10). Visual sequential memory skills therefore appear to be highly related to receptive and expressive language achievement, and these linguistic abilities are in turn related to reading ability.

However, visual sequential memory appears to be less than optimal with regard to encoding during the reading process; rather, "phonetic encoding" or "inner speech" appears to be especially important for facilitating the retention of ordered information in working memory (Lichtenstein, 1984). The relationship of different types of memory skills to language and reading is therefore difficult to unravel. It should also be noted that while phonetic encoding does not involve visual memory, high-quality speech is nevertheless not required for "inner speech" to be effective during the encoding process. It may be that sensorimotor memory (involving proprioception associated with tongue and mouth movements) is an important factor involved in the "speech-based" memory encoding process.

Memory encoding strategies differ between deaf and hearing individuals at all developmental levels that have been studied, and research indicates that there is much variability among deaf subjects in the types of encoding strategies that are utilized during reading (Kusché, 1984a, 1985). In addition, it has been found that many deaf individuals rely on more than one encoding strategy (Lichtenstein, 1984). Types of encoding strategies which have been found to be used by deaf individuals include visual (O'Connor & Hermelin, 1973), speech-based (Conrad, 1979), semantic (Moulton & Beasley, 1975), cherological (signs) (Bellugi, Klima, & Siple, 1975), and finger-spelling (Hirsh-Pasek & Treiman, 1982).

Significant correlations between reading skills and short-term memory capacities have been reported for both deaf and hearing children (Blair, 1957; Hartung, 1970). Lichtenstein (1984) reported that working memory processes accounted for approximately 40% of the variance in syntactic skills in his population of signing deaf college students; moreover, word-order errors in writing were made primarily by students with below average working memory capacities. Lake (1981) found that both encoding efficiency and perceptual bias in deaf children's comparisons of arbitrary sequences in short-term memory were related to their syntactic ability; furthermore, time-lag correlations over a year suggested a causal role for short-term memory in the development of syntactical abilities in deaf children.

Hanson, Liberman, and Shankweiler (1984) reported that young TC deaf children (median age = 8.75) who were classiified as good readers appeared to use both speech and fingerspelling codes in short-term recall, while poor deaf readers did not utilize either of these linguistically-based codes in recall. These investigators suggested that beginning reading success for deaf children is related to the ability to utilize linguistically recoded representations of language. Conrad (1979) found that for orally-trained British deaf adolescents, the use of "internal speech" had a larger effect on reading achievement than did hearing loss. He suggested

that without internal speech, children are likely to be below average readers. This argument is further supported by the fact that visual short-term memory has a rapid decay rate as compared to phonetic short-term memory (Sperling, 1960).

Hung, Tzeng, and Warren (1981) reported that "deaf subjects are capable of linguistic coding strategy, but they do not apply it to process printed English sentences" (p. 583) and "deaf children do not have the phonological repertoire upon which English orthography is based" (p. 606). They also noted that deaf children do not generally seem to develop automaticity for such skills as letter decoding and word recognition.

In summary, the encoding strategies utilized by the majority of deaf individuals appear to be less than optimal for maintaining sequential information in working memory, which in turn seems to be of causal importance with regard to poor reading comprehension. Nevertheless, there is a large variation in individual differences. While many researchers emphasize the importance of inner speech or phonetic encoding, the literature suggests that kinesthetic or proprioceptive recoding associated wtih phonetic encoding may be an important factor in the durability of the memory trace (Hintzman, 1967).

Hardyck and Petrinovich (1970) have proposed that an auditory-proprioceptive stimulus complex may be used as a stable mediator during the early process of learning to read. This stimulus complex allows for the development of neural analogues. Once developed, these neural analogues ultimately replace the auditory-proprioceptive process and render it unnecessary; automatic processing is then possible. This distinction is very important for deaf educators and researchers, since fingerspelling and signs allow for proprioceptive recoding, but not for phonetic encoding. In addition, it has been pointed out that the cortical areas controlling hand and vocal movements are adjacent in the brain (Schlesinger & Meadow, 1972).

Long-term semantic memory is also of crucial importance for reading comprehension, because knowledge which is prestored in semantic memory as propositional percepts and schemes will influence the way new information is assimilated, understood, and remembered (Cohen, 1983). Contextual information at the beginning of a piece of writing allows the reader to select the relevant conceptual framework and to map incoming information onto it. Context thus enhances or biases understanding and retention of information.

Without context and a conceptual framework, information is difficult to comprehend, process, and remember. Since this area is covered by Quigley and Paul in their chapter on "English Language Development," it will not be reviewed here, except to note that the conceptual knowledge and semantic long-term memory stores of deaf children are deficient as compared to hearing children, due to linguistic and concomitant environmental deprivation. Because deaf children are generally weak in their automatic processing of the patterns, rules, and strategies for linguistic performance (i.e., in primary linguistic knowledge), they lack the repertoire necessary for easy transference to a new language-based skill. Thus we can see that both of the major factors associated with good reading comprehension, short-term memory and processing speed, are problematic areas for deaf children. Finally, long-term semantic memory is also negatively affected by short-term working memory deficits, because processing in short-term memory is often (though apparently not always) necessary for long-term semantic storage.

Rehearsal Strategies

Recently, researchers have begun to look at the rehearsal strategies (Flavell, 1977) of deaf children. Bebko (1980) studied deaf children ages 5 to 15 and found that the spontaneous use of rehearsal strategies emerged from 3 to 5 years later than the spontaneous use of verbal rehearsal in hearing children, although the pattern of emergence was the same. Oral children used verbal, while TC children used manual rehearsal strategies. Youniss and Furth (1966b) reported that deaf children ages 7 to 10 showed improvement in visual recognition scores with age due to the improved use of effective labeling strategies. Liben (1984) reported that deaf children (9–12) and adults both used semantic clustering during memory tasks; in addition, the children were able to enhance recall after instruction in categorization.

O'Connor (1979) reported that the imposition of verbal labels improved the recall performance of deaf children (age 12), while Swanson and O'Connor (1981) reported similar findings for the use of vocalization, signing, and fingerspelling. Hirsch-Pasek and Treiman (1982) reported that most of the deaf students in their study "had not thought" to use fingerspelling, but raised their sight word identification scores after this strategy was suggested to them by the experimenters. Barmeier (1981) found that rehearsal through fingerspelling and writing were equally effective; both strategies readily led to generalization, especially if practice involved recall rather than looking at the word. Thus, the teaching of memory encoding processes and rehearsal strategies appears to be a highly promising area in deaf education that requires the development and implementation of curricular materials in the early grades.

Strategies and Metacognitions in the Reading Process

Research with preschool-age deaf children indicates that reading material based on a child's own experience helps to facilitate reading achievement, apparently because it is inherently more meaningful to the child (Gormley & Geoffrion, 1981; Söderbergh, 1981; Stauffer, 1979). Parental assistance in learning to read also appears to facilitate the process (Lieding &

Gammel, 1982), probably because the child perceives reading to be a pleasurable activity he or she can share with the parents.

Morrison (1981) found that the primary reading strategies reported by deaf adolescents were to use dictionaries or ask someone for help. These deaf subjects also had inaccurate perceptions of their reading abilities, with most overestimating their abilities and considering themselves good readers. When asked what they remembered about learning to read, below average readers recalled reading many books, average readers recalled learning new words, while above average readers remembered writing or acting out stories. The average and above average readers also reported having had more parental assistance in learning to read.

Dodds (1982) found improvement in the use of reading comprehension strategies when deaf children were appropriately oriented to the task and also reported improvements in the spontaneous use of these strategies with age. Davey, LaSasso, and Macready (1983) reported that deaf students are less efficient than their hearing counterparts at locating answers to reading questions when they are permitted to look back at the reading material. These researchers suggested that the deaf students may utilize an inefficient "visual matching" strategy of locating key words in the text that match the question stems, and they recommended that instruction in both test-taking and study skills would be beneficial for deaf students.

Concepts and Concept Formation

Young deaf children perform similarly to hearing children on categorization tasks when the criterion is based on only one physical salient characteristic such as color or number (Ottem, 1980). However, when multiple classification is possible or simultaneous attention to two or more characteristics is necessary for task performance, deaf children score poorly, demonstrate a strong tendency to remain attached to a single concept, and show a distinct difficulty in shifting from one sorting principle to another (Oleron, 1953; Ottem, 1980). Oleron (1953) concluded that deaf children differ from hearing children "in that they have a tendency to give too much importance to the observed elements . . . the mental processes of the deaf are characterized by an especial concern for observed data" (p. 308).

Furth (1961) reported that young deaf children (ages 7–12) performed similarly or better than same-age hearing peers on tasks involving sameness and symmetry, but performed quite poorly on the concept of opposition and on transferring this concept to new tasks. Continuing with Ottem's observation, it can be noted that the characteristics of sameness and symmetry are much more iconically salient than is the understanding of oppositeness, which requires an underlying propositional scheme or concept.

105

As with classification tasks, deaf children tend to perform similarly to their hearing counterparts when rule-learning tasks are not overly complex and when attention to only one attribute at a time is necessary. Deaf and hearing children demonstrate comparable performances in understanding underlying concepts such as nothing versus something, whole-part, extreme values, temporal discontiguity, reversal shifts, and visual rules. Examples of tasks where deaf children perform more poorly include transfer of concepts, verbally mediated transfer, and subset selection (Furth, 1964, 1971).

With regard to symbol use, Wright (1955) noted that symbols and symbol systems tend to be perceived by the deaf as an "inventory of things" rather than as a hierarchical system or as classes with meaningful relationships. However, Furth (1966) found that after 4 days of teaching logical thinking of symbolized class concepts and connectives to 9, 13, and 16-year-old deaf children and adolescents, even the youngest children were successful in some symbol use. Furth and Youniss (1965) found that deaf adolescents could perform similarly to hearing adults with regard to symbol *use*, but these same adolescents were far behind 10-year-old hearing children on symbol *discovery* (Furth, 1973). Kates (1969) found that deaf and hearing adolescents who gave correct verbal descriptions of symbolic expressions were significantly superior in both symbol use and discovery, suggesting that verbal mediation of rules leads to more successful transfer of learning.

Research regarding hierarchical classification with oral deaf and hearing preschool children has shown no differences in their ability to categorize objects at a perceptual or basic level, but deaf preschool children demonstrate significantly poorer performance at the superordinate level and are significantly inferior in receptive and expressive knowledge of category labels (Friedman, 1984). Furthermore, correlations between superordinate categorization and both receptive and expressive language were found to be significant. Friedman concluded that "basic level concepts may be acquired more quickly because they do not require the sophisticated language skills that are needed for the acquisition of superordinate concepts" (p. 270). However, after the deaf children were given only one nonverbal demonstration of the superordinate construct, they performed similarly to their hearing controls on a second superordinate task. This suggests that language may not be necessary for prototypic representation per se, but may nevertheless be very important for organizing information according to shared attributes so as to allow for the discovery or spontaneous use of superordinate concepts.

With regard to elementary school-age deaf and hearing children, major differences in the developmental acquisition of levels of categorization have been found (Silverman, 1967). Hearing children demonstrated increases in superordinate responding with age, but showed no changes in functional responding. Deaf children, on the other hand, evidenced age-related decreases in superordinate responding and demonstrated concomitant increases in functional responding. In other words, "the deaf child's growth in functional responding parallels the hearing child's growth in superordinate responding" (p. 249). Furthermore, categorizational responding was related to reading achievement levels for deaf children, but not for hearing children, and the high-achieving deaf children resembled the high-achieving hearing children in both functional and superordinate responding.

Silverman (1967) noted that the use of superordinate categorization "reduces the strain of information impinging upon the child and, according to Piaget (1950) and Inhelder (1962), it permits the child to engage in formal reasoning" (p. 248) and commented, "Perhaps in the absence of a superordinate strategy, the deaf child assumes a functional orientation to his environment" (p. 249). Since information in long-term semantic memory is believed to be stored economically in a hierarchical manner in the associational cortex (Linton, 1980), a deficit in hierarchical classification skills would negatively affect efficiency of storage and retrieval of information, which we frequently observe in the linguistic behaviors of deaf children.

Deficient understanding of hierarchical structure may also affect language and reading comprehension. It has been suggested that deaf children may perceive standard English in a linear fashion, rather than as a hierarchical structure, which may account for many of their problems with English (Quigley & King, 1980). Bishop (1982) noted the strikingly similar deviant patterns of language comprehension in deaf children and children with Landau-Kleffner syndrome and concluded that the idiosyncratic patterns of both groups of children were due to their failure to abstract the hierarchical structure of sentences, which resulted as a secondary consequence of their heavy reliance on visual means to learn grammar and master syntax.

Current thinking about concept formation has been strongly influenced by the idea that concepts are represented as prototypes, which are constructs that combine the features of greatest cue validity so as to represent the central tendency of members of a particular category (Cohen, 1983). According to Rosch, Mervis, Gray, Johnson, and Boyes-Braem (1976), basic level categories (e.g., chairs, tables) are easiest to learn because they are most discriminable (i.e., cue validity is highest) and are more easily represented by visual images. Superordinate (e.g., furniture) and subordinate (e.g., coffee table, dining table) categories, on the other hand, are less visually salient and require a greater degree of abstraction. As Cohen (1983) noted, "information that is readily available in a percept may not be recoverable in an image" (p. 51), thus making visual mediation less efficient for encoding many abstract concepts.

Given our present level of knowledge, it is difficult to deduce whether deaf children demonstrate a mediational (lack of knowledge) or production (failure to use the knowledge they have) deficiency with regard to categorization strategies, but it seems likely that both are important factors and may play relatively different roles at different ages. It is apparent, however, that deaf children need and would greatly benefit from classroom instruction involving classification, categorization, and hierarchical thinking.

Finally, Rosch et al. (1976) maintain that with sign languages, basic level concepts tend to predominate, while super- and subordinate labels are sometimes missing. Research designed to investigate this issue would be very beneficial; if indeed this is the case, then missing super- and subordinate signs could be invented to facilitate development of hierarchical thinking. The effects of different types of sign languages on concept formation and categorization is another area of research that is lacking at the present time and which is badly needed.

Reasoning and Problem-Solving

Reasoning and problem-solving tasks require the integration and use of a number of different cognitive skills. Not surprisingly, deaf children demonstrate increasingly worse performance as tasks become more difficult, and complex abstract reasoning ability is deficient with both verbal and nonverbal tasks. Deaf children demonstrate inferior performance in such areas as abstract verbal and nonverbal reasoning, nonverbal reasoning by analogy, nonverbal mechanical reasoning, and reasoning concerning physical causality which involves the concepts of probability, chance, or the personalization of answers (Arnold & Walter, 1979: Templin, 1950). Herrick (1980) found no significant relationships between nonverbal concept formation and either communication skills or prevocational competency with deaf adolescents enrolled in vocational training programs. Interestingly, verbal metaphors appear to be equally difficult for both deaf and hard-of-hearing adolescents (Rittenhouse, Morreau, & Iran-Nejad, 1981).

In tests of simpler nonverbal conceptual problems involving the integration of sensory impressions, on the other hand, orally-trained deaf children and adolescents demonstrate no differences in ability to perceive, abstract, or generalize (Rosenstein, 1960). Kates, Yudin, and Tiffany (1962), however, reported that deaf adolescents showed greater cautiousness or reluctance in taking the initial step in problem-solving. Blanton and Nunnally (1964) found that deaf children demonstrated a more external locus of evaluation than did hearing children; these researchers suggested that deaf children feel inadequate about making meaningful judgments and so tend to rely on others to evaluate environmental situations for them.

With difficult problem-solving tasks, it has been found that deaf and hearing children utilize similar strategies and proceed through the same stages of cognitive development, but the progress of hearing children is more rapid, and it is not clear whether deaf children ever achieve the same final level of understanding. Furthermore, performance by deaf children on problem-solving tasks has been found to be correlated with exposure to language, and correct verbal reasoning tends to accompany accurate performance (Meadow, 1980a). Rittenhouse et al. (1981) reported that verbal metaphor comprehension was highly related to performance on Piagetian conservation tasks ($r=0.88$), and both age and intelligence were found to affect metaphor comprehension in an upward direction.

Templin (1950) reported that deaf adolescents scored poorly on reasoning tasks which were most dependent on specific training. Furthermore, research has shown that both low- and high-achieving deaf children can profit from instructions regarding the rules necessary to solve nonverbal reasoning tasks (Huberty, 1980; Greenberg, Kusché, Gustafson, & Calderon, 1985). Huberty (1980) reported that deaf children showed improved nonverbal reasoning performance when they were given assistance with a task, even if they had not received prior training, but that training effects became apparent when assistance was not provided. This suggests that both mediational and production deficits are important factors in the problem-solving and reasoning deficiencies noted with deaf children.

In summary, the reasoning and problem-solving literature suggests few differences between deaf and hearing children when reasoning can be mediated through visual means. When abstract, analogical, semantic, propositional, or superordinate reasoning is necessary for performance, however, deaf children show developmental delays. Moreover, without intervention, improvements over time appear to be slow, and both mediational and production deficiencies seem to play important roles in the differences which have been observed. However, the small amount of literature currently available suggests that educational intervention can be very beneficial in facilitating improvements in the reasoning and problem-solving abilities of deaf children.

Cognitive Processes in Learning Disabled and Multiple-Handicapped Deaf Children

Few studies currently exist in which deaf children with additional handicaps and/or learning problems have been studied as separate groups. In an exceptional 10-year longitudinal study, Affolter (1984) compared the development of normal deaf children, normal hearing children, deaf children with learning problems, and hearing children with learning problems on a large variety of performance tasks. Affolter found that both the deaf and hearing learning-impaired groups differed from the normal deaf and hearing groups in numerous areas including eye contact, complex motor skills, eye-hand coordination, imitation of gestures, problem-solving skills, symbolic nonverbal play behavior, drawing, picture recognition, and recognition of successive patterns in auditory, visual, and vibro-tactile presentation conditions.

Affolter also found that both the deaf and hearing learning disabled children fell into three different subgroups: (a) children who had difficulty with integrating tactile-kinesthetic information; (b) children who had difficulty with processing simultaneous input from disparate modalities (i.e., intermodal processing deficits), including most of the children diagnosed as autistic; and (c) children who had difficulty with sequencing events or stimuli. Affolter proposed that deferred imitation, symbolic nonverbal processing, and language acquisition require a critical amount of tactile-kinesthetic information processing and modality interconnection, while direct imitation and speech-sound development require a critical amount of sequential integration.

Dinner (1981) reported that the greater the number and/or more severe the behaviors associated with language/learning disability in deaf children ages 7 to 11.5, the poorer the receptive sign language performance. A sign language test battery was also assessed and was found to discriminate between subjects who exhibited behavior characteristics of language/learning disability from those who did not.

Schloss, Smith, Goldsmith, and Selinger (1984) pointed out the impoverished state of the literature with regard to the learning disabled deaf population and emphasized the need for instructional curricula, assessment batteries, intervention prosthetics, educational activities, progress evaluations, and so forth, and provided some recommendations in these areas. A demonstration project involving a social learning curriculum for educating severely multiple-handicapped deaf children showed measurable improvements and progress for this group of children following a year of instruction (Naiman, 1979). The program emphasized perceptual-motor skills, concept formation, and social learning skills.

Hemispheric Specialization/Lateralization

For English-speaking hearing individuals, the left hemisphere appears to be primarily responsible for processing verbal, sequential, and analytical information, while the right hemisphere specializes in the processing of nonverbal, visual-spatial, simultaneous, affective, and holistic material (Geschwind, 1979). Furthermore, hemispheric specialization and lateralization and other aspects of neurological development appear to depend on environmental stimulation for development (Cummins, Livesey, Evans, & Walsh, 1979). It has therefore been hypothesized that linguistic deprivation and the resulting deficiency in linguistic stimulation experienced by many deaf individuals may result in differences in hemispheric development and/or processing abilities (Kusché, 1984a, 1985).

In general, research has indicated that hemispheric differences exist between hearing and deaf groups with regard to processing both linguistic and nonlinguistic stimuli (Ross, 1983). It is not entirely clear, however, whether this represents differences in neurological/brain organization, information-processing strategies, or both. In addition, and of great importance, is the implication from the research presently available that the deaf population is not a homogeneous group with regard to hemispheric specialization; of crucial importance is the suggestion that early educational and linguistic environments, genetic factors, linguistic competency, proficiency in verbal and sign language skills, and primary mode of communication (oral, fingerspelling, ASL, Signed English, etc.) are all important factors in the development of cerebral specialization in deaf individuals.

Significant differences between deaf and hearing groups have been found with regard to reaction times and accuracy of recognition for the left versus right visual fields, left versus right ear advantage, and accuracy of recognition in the left versus right tactile fields (Ling, 1971; Ross, 1983; Vargha-Khadem, 1982). Some of these studies further provide data suggesting processing or specialization differences due to primary communication mode. EEG differences between deaf and hearing adults during verbal and nonverbal activities also suggest processing and/or specialization discrepancies (Sutter, 1982).

Weston and Weinman (1983) reported that deaf children do not appear to be as strongly lateralized with regard to handedness as hearing children, especially when hearing losses are greater than 90 dB. Gottlieb, Doran, and Whitley (1964) reported that hearing boys are more strongly right-sighted than deaf boys, but differences were not found for girls. These researchers also found that right-handed, right-sighted deaf children consistently had high speech grades than did right-handed, left-sighted or right-handed, mixed-sighted deaf children matched for degree of hearing loss. Interestingly, Boyd (1967) reported that in laterality comparisons of speed of manual dexterity, deaf children demonstrating right hand preference showed superior performance with the *left* hand, while the opposite was found for deaf children having a left hand preference. Further research is needed, but if this surprising finding is substantiated, we would need to investigate why deaf children show better performance with their least preferred hand. Hemispheric lateralization thus appears to have important implications for education, but our knowledge of this area is relatively poor; further research regarding hemispheric specialization/lateralization and the cognitive development of deaf children is therefore badly needed.

Summary and Conclusions Regarding Cognition and Deafness

An extensive amount of data suggests that deaf children rely heavily upon visual-spatial perception and processing strategies and show strength in the area of holistic, simultaneous visual processing. Weaknesses, on the other hand, involve areas in which verbal-sequential and/or abstract-propositional processing are necessary for optimal performance. According to the tricode theory of information processing, deaf children as a group are thereby demonstrating satisfactory development for only one of the the three types of information processing possible (although sensorimotor thought also appears to develop normally). There seems to be much variation within the deaf population, however, and as noted earlier, we know little about the current cohort being educated today. Overall, it appears that language deprivation results in specific experiential deficits, which in turn selectively affects cognitive development and information-processing skills and flexibility.

Linguistic skills allow us to mentally manipulate objects and ideas in time and space, to perceive reality from new perspectives, to discover and consider alternative strategies for solving problems, to retain and access material in memory better, to communicate and share with others, and so forth. Labeling and categorizing information linguistically can lead to changes in our visual perception of reality and may contribute to the formation of new schemes, abstract concepts, prototypes, and so forth. Linguistic deficits appear to impact numerous areas of cognition such as academic achievement, conservation, cognitive style, visual perception, short-term working memory, semantic memory, motor skills, concept formation, categorization, symbol discovery, superordinate reasoning, analytic and complex reasoning skills, learning strategies, and problem-solving abilities.

The use of different processing strategies during development may result in different patterns of brain organization and specialization, which in turn may further influence information-processing capacities. It has been found that different patterns of cognitive growth appear to be demonstrated by learning disabled as opposed to normal deaf children, but we need to know more about the specific attributes of these and other subgroups of deaf children (e.g., deaf-blind children, mentally retarded deaf children, minority deaf children). Finally, the literature clearly indicates that various types of specialized training and educational intervention programs specifically designed for deaf children (and various subtypes of deaf children) are needed.

SOCIAL AND PERSONALITY DEVELOPMENT

While no "personality" can be ascribed to all deaf persons, research has shown that a number of characteristics appear frequently and are believed to be the result of communicative and experiential deprivation experienced during infancy and childhood (Altshuler, 1978; Levine, 1981; Liben, 1978). The literature on social competence can be heuristically divided into four domains: (a) prevalence of psychological/behavioral disorders; (b) psychometric assessment of social maturity;

(c) examination of personality traits/characteristics; and (d) the deaf child's social-cognitive skills or understanding.

Research on Social Competence

Psychological/Behavioral Disorders

Meadow (1980a) and Meadow and Trybus (1979) have comprehensively reviewed the extensive literature on behavior problems in deaf children. The prevalence of moderate and severe emotional disorders ranged from 8% in a survey of 44,000 children (Jensema & Trybus, 1975) to 20–30% in smaller, clinical-experimental investigations (Freeman, Malkin, & Hastings, 1975; Meadow, 1980a; Schlesinger & Meadow, 1972; Vernon, 1969). However, the report of lower rates by the Annual Survey of the Hearing-Impaired (Jensema & Trybus, 1975) is probably due to underreporting by the teachers because they did not want to "label" their schools or children for the purposes of a survey research project with no apparent tangible gain. In a representative study, Schlesinger and Meadow (1972) compared teacher ratings of emotional disturbance at a residential school to local prevalence rates for hearing children. Of the deaf students, 11% were severely disturbed, while another 17.6% displayed disruptive problems. Comparatively, the figures for hearing students were 2.4% and 7.3% respectively. Schein (1975) indicates that these figures may even be an underestimate, as he found that 10% of the deaf group studied was not in school, due to behavior problems. Cohen (1980) discusses the lack of standardized measures or diagnostic procedures to assess behavior problems in this population and the need for multitrait, multimethod studies.

In an attempt to examine the types of behavior problems, Reivich and Rothrock (1972) rated deaf children on the Behavior Problem Checklist (BPC) of Quay and Peterson (1967). The results were very similar to the conduct, personality, and immaturity dimensions found in hearing children, but two factors appeared to be specific to the deaf children. These were isolation and communication. However, they only accounted for 9% of the variance, with the first three factors accounting for approximately 70%. Hirshoren and Schaittjer (1979) used the BPC to study 192 children at a day school for the deaf. The first three factors extracted were again identical to those of hearing children. They found one additional factor, passive inferiority, which was unique to the day school children and which might have resulted from having lived in an environment with hearing children. However, Reivich and Rothrock's factors of isolation and communication were not identified in this study. Williams (1970) examined 51 deaf children with a behavior checklist and also noted that the psychiatric disorders encountered were similar to those found in hearing children. However, in none of these reports were associated factors such as age, hearing loss, home environment, etiology, or parental hearing status examined.

Vernon (1969), as well as others, has cautioned that these high figures should not be interpreted as deaf children having a greater proportion of psychotic disturbances. In fact, Rainer, Altshuler, and Kallman (1969) found no greater incidence of psychotic disorders and a lower incidence of depression in the deaf adult population of New York State than was found in the general hearing population. Instead, these figures should alert us to the crucial importance of communicative competence for developing self-control, self-esteem, identification, and an understanding of one's environment. In fact, it is believed that when deaf children gain more language through the use of manual communication and become integrated in their own socio-cultural group and heritage, problems linked to social isolation and low self-esteem may become attenuated. However, because deaf persons both underutilize and are underserved by the existing community mental health systems in most states, there is a paucity of information on the presence of neurotic and character disorders or problems of adjustment in daily living.

In summary, the estimated rate of behavior problems is quite high. Due to the absence of either clear diagnostic criteria or longitudinal investigations, it is difficult to predict which types of childhood emotional problems may have serious long-term consequences. Further, at present there is little research on how these disorders may be remediated by such factors as language growth, maturation, intervention in the classroom or family environment, contact with deaf role models, or individual, family, or group psychotherapy.

Social Maturity

Reviews by Dicarlo and Dolphin (1952) and Meadow (1975) concluded that social maturity of deaf children, as measured by the Vineland Social Maturity Scale (Doll, 1965), is lower than hearing norms. Meadow (1975, 1980a) noted, however, that in most cases, no control groups were used, and the degree of hearing loss, etiology, and other relevant variables were not examined. Greenberg (1980a) criticized the existing literature for its use of the Vineland Scale with deaf children because items supposedly measuring social maturity are confounded with those requiring oral language skills, especially as the age level increases. This bias may partially account for the findings of Myklebust (1964) of declining social maturity with age.

Since educational and treatment programs for deaf students have undergone great changes since the 1960s, past research may provide little predictive validity for the current generation of deaf children. This assumption is born out by three recent studies. Schlesinger and Meadow (1972) found that social competence in a group of profoundly deaf preschoolers was related to their communicative ability. In two independent studies involving profoundly deaf preschoolers, most of whom

had received early intervention, Greenberg (1980a, 1983) found that social age was similar to hearing norms as assessed by the Alpern-Boll Developmental Profile (Alpern & Boll, 1972). Within the sample, children using Total Communication received higher parental estimates of social age than did the oral children.

Meadow (1968) examined how hearing status of parents might affect social maturity by comparing 54 matched pairs of residential deaf children with deaf versus hearing parents. If was found that those with deaf parents received higher ratings on maturity, independence, and ability to take responsibility. Comparing these two groups to a third sample of deaf children living at home with their hearing parents, Schlesinger and Meadow (1972) concluded that day school students with hearing parents received ratings that were lower than residential students with deaf parents, but higher than those of residential students with hearing parents. Quarrington and Solomon (1975) reported that a higher frequency of home visitation was positively related to social maturity in deaf children who attended residential schools. Thus, hearing status of parents, type of school, and other potential variables interact in complex and possibly bidirectional ways to predict social maturity of deaf children.

Meadow (1980b, 1983b) standardized and validated the Social-Emotional Assessment Inventory for Deaf Students (SEAI) which is the first such measure for use with this population. This measure is completed by teachers and was normed on over 2,000 school-age children. Three factors are assessed: self-image, emotional maturity, and social adjustment. On the self-image scale, girls were seen as demonstrating higher self-images, as were students younger than 16 years of age. Meadow and Dyssegaard (1983) compared the SEAI scores completed by Danish and American teachers. Cross-cultural differences indicated that Danish teachers evaluated the children as more reserved and introspective, while the American teachers evaluated the children as more extroverted. Both sets of teachers perceived deaf children as lacking in responsibility, independence, and motivation. Farrugia and Austin (1980) used the SEAI to compare the maturity, self-esteem, and adjustment of 200 deaf and hard-of-hearing 10- to 15-year-olds in residential schools and day schools and hearing controls. Results indicated that deaf students attending residential schools and hearing controls were similar in all areas. Hard-of-hearing and deaf students in public schools had lower levels of social and emotional adjustment and maturity than the other two groups. The authors cited the greater social isolation and rejection experienced by the deaf day students as contributing factors.

Dyssegaard and Meadow (1984) reported that deaf children with learning disabilities showed greater problems on the SEAI. Further, compared to hearing children, deaf children were more accident-prone, destructive, impulsive, and had more difficulty distinguishing fact from fiction. These findings were interpreted as the result of experiential deficits due to communicative deprivation. Meadow (1983a) developed a similar measure for preschoolers (SEAI-P) which was normed on over 800 preschoolers. Four scales emerged: social/communicative, impulsive/dominating, developmental lags, and anxious/compulsive behaviors. Boys scored more poorly than girls on the first three scales. Both the SEAI and SEAI-P have shown adequate test-retest and inter-rater reliability.

Personality Development

Investigations of personality development in the deaf and hard-of-hearing are greatly hampered by impaired reading ability. The fact that the average deaf person reads at approximately the fifth grade level (Karchmer, 1985) makes the use of written inventories very suspect. Titus (1965), Meadow (1969) and Garrison and Tesch (1978) have independently concluded that self-concept tests used with hearing children are inappropriate for deaf children and a number of revised measures have been developed (Garrison, Tesch, & DeCaro, 1978; Koelle & Convey, 1982).

Given the above mentioned problems in methodology of self-concept measurement in deaf persons, a number of studies have used special methodologies to measure self-esteem. Blanton and Nunnally (1964) used a semantic differential to examine attitudes toward the self and reported that deaf children evaluated themselves more poorly and as less well-adjusted than did hearing children. Garrison, Tesch and DeCaro (1978) also report lower self-esteem in late adolescence using a modified version of the Tennessee Self-Concept Scale. Meadow (1969) developed a "cartoon test" with both written adjectives and sign illustrations to compare the self-concepts of residential school students with deaf versus hearing parents. Self-concept was positively related to family climate, school achievement, and communicative ability. Schlesinger and Meadow (1972) compared these samples to day school deaf children with hearing parents and found the latter group to be similar to the residential students with hearing parents. Using ratings of adjustment, Brill (1960) also compared deaf children with deaf versus hearing parents. While no significant differences were found, those with deaf parents and siblings received more ratings at both positive and negative extremes.

Craig (1965) examined differences in self-evaluation and perception between day and residential deaf students and hearing children aged 9 to 12. Using drawings in a sociometric-choice paradigm, Craig reported that deaf children in both settings gave more positive self-evaluations than did the hearing students. One might interpret these results as indicating either high self-esteem, unrealistic, egocentric perceptions or attempts to make a positive impression on the examiner. Craig reports no reliability or validity of the technique.

Kelliher (1976), using a modified version of the Coopersmith Scale reported that deaf adolescents showed lower self-esteem than matched hearing controls. A within-group comparison of oral versus TC users indicated only one difference: among children with profound hearing loss, TC children had higher scores on the school-esteem subscale compared to oral children. Sussman (1973) found a significant negative relationship between self-esteem and the perception by deaf students that others had negative attitudes towards deafness. This study illustrates how the effects of the perception of stigma in the ecological context can directly affect self-esteem. In summary, research on self-esteem has been plagued by linguistic methodological difficulties. However, at least some groups of deaf children appear to have lower self-esteem than their hearing peers, which may result from their environments, as well as the stigma attached to minority or disabled group membership.

In addition to lower self-esteem and social immaturity, three personality characteristics have commonly been described in deaf persons: impulsivity, egocentricity, and rigidity (Levine, 1960, 1976; Myklebust, 1964). A number of recent investigators have examined these characteristics and the antecedent factors accounting for their appearance. Altshuler, Deming, Vollenweider, Rainer, and Tendler (1976) examined impulsivity in 450 profoundly deaf and hearing students from Yugoslavian and American high schools. Using a battery of tests, results indicated that the deaf students were more impulsive on all measures. However, due to the low intercorrelation among measures, Altshuler (1978) concluded that the different measures tapped different manifestations of the construct of impulsivity.

Chess and Fernandez (1980) longitudinally examined behavioral aspects of impulsivity in 171 deaf rubella children and hearing controls. Deaf children who were multihandicapped showed much higher rates of impulsivity than deaf children with no other handicaps. While only 20% of the deaf children with no handicaps were rated as behaviorally impulsive, this was significantly higher than in hearing controls. There was no standardized psychometric measurement of cognitive impulsivity in this study. R. I. Harris (1978) examined impulsivity using the Matching Familiar Figures (MFF) and Draw-A-Picture Test to compare 50 deaf children of deaf parents to 274 deaf children with hearing parents. Controlling for age, IQ, and SES, children with deaf parents had greater impulse control (i.e., were more reflective). No hearing control was utilized. Harris hypothesized that early linguistic (sign) communication of children with deaf parents enables them to gain greater cognitive self-control (cf. Vygotsky, 1972).

Levine (1956) examined personality characteristics of 31 normally-adjusted adolescent deaf girls using the Rorschach. While there were no signs of emotional disturbance, and low scores were obtained for anxiety and depression, the protocols showed many egocentric, impulsive, and suggestive responses. Hess (1960) used the Make-A-Picture Story to compare deaf and hearing 8 to 10-year-olds and described the deaf children as rigid, egocentric, impulsive, and lacking in deep interpersonal relationships. Both Bindon (1957) and Neyhus (1964) reported similar findings using the same projective technique. Levine and Wagner (1974) gave deaf adults the Hand Projective test and found that personality profiles were highly related to language ability. Those with advanced language skills (high school level) were similar to hearing persons, while those with very low skills (second-grade level) showed pathological signs of immaturity, impulsivity, and rigidity that fit the familiar, but over-generalized deaf stereotype.

Social-Cognitive Ability

Emotional Understanding

Two studies examined the ability of deaf children to interpret facial expressions (Odom, Blanton, & Laukhuf 1973; Sugarman, 1969) and concluded that deaf children were less accurate at interpreting emotional states and situations. They ascribed these deficits to poor linguistic socialization. Blanton and Nunnally (1965), in a large study of residential deaf children, reported a poorer understanding of affective vocabulary in these children than in the hearing controls. Kusché (1984b) developed a reliable and valid pictorial measure to assess emotional understanding in 5 to 13-year-old deaf children. Emotional understanding was positively related to nonverbal intelligence, low scores on impulsivity, reading comprehension, and parent and teacher ratings of fewer behavior problems. No relationships were found between emotional understanding and hearing loss or parental social class. White (1981) also reported a positive relationship between understanding of affective vocabularly and personal adjustment.

Role-Taking

Bachara, Raphael, and Phelan (1980) examined the early stages of role-taking ability in 9 and 14-year-old severely deaf children. They found that deaf children showed greater egocentrism, with a 4 to 5-year delay in role-taking ability as compared to hearing norms. Postlingually deaf children did significantly better than those who were prelingually deafened. Blaesing (1978) similarly found that early school-age deaf children showed poorer perspective-taking skills than did hearing controls. However, Johnson (1981) found no differences in level of role-taking between deaf and hearing children. Two further studies appear to explain the above discrepant findings. First, Young and Brown (1981) found that perspective-taking ability was highly correlated with language ability ($r=0.45$) in deaf children. Second, Kusché and Greenberg (1983) found only a slight delay in role-taking ability when a nonverbal, game-like task was utilized, and made the following conclusions:

School-age deaf children have often been referred to as egocentric, and it has been assumed in the literature that they are delayed in the acquisition of role-taking abilities. The present study suggests that this assumption is somewhat misleading. It may be that these deaf children are able to take another's perspective but are often unable to evaluate or interpret correctly the information conveyed by or available to the other. (1983, p. 146)

The findings of deficiencies in role-taking, when the deaf child must accurately predict the feelings of another, correspond with the marked egocentricity found on projective personality measures. Egocentrism is not a unitary construct and thus it is likely to be shown in situations where the cues to another's need are subtle or when the deaf child does not have the social and emotional understanding to evaluate correctly the other's internal state.

A number of studies have examined the deaf child's ability to take the informational perspective of another, that is, referential communication skills. Hoemann (1972) reported a 2 to 4-year lag in referential communication skills between deaf and hearing children. However, more recently Hoemann and Farquharson (1982) reported that these original findings may have underestimated the deaf children's abilities. Using stimuli that are more ordinary and recognizable, a number of investigators (Breslaw, Griffiths, Wood, & Howarth, 1981; Hoemann & Farquharson, 1982; Jordan, 1975) have found little or no differences between deaf and hearing children. In addition, Hoemann and Farquharson (1982) have shown considerable success in improving these skills in deaf children through brief training procedures.

Social Problem-Solving and Decision-Making Skills

While there has been discussion in the literature regarding the importance of problem-solving skills for deaf children (Bullis, 1985), there has been little examination of this domain. Coady (1984) used an adapted version of the Social Problem Solving Assessment Measure (Elias, Larcen, Zlotlow, & Chinsky, 1978) to examine the correlates of social problem-solving skill in TC deaf children ages 6 to 12. The SPSAM is a series of pictorial stories of social dilemmas typically encountered by children. Compared to normative data on hearing children, deaf children demonstrated rudimentary social understanding, that is, sensitivity to the thoughts and feelings of the other. However, they failed to predict accurately the other's feelings, a deficit in psychological insight. While age-related changes were found in the ability to generate alternative solutions, delays were demonstrated in the ability to anticipate consequences and to construct a series of steps in goal-directed planning. The deaf children projected positive expectancies for outcomes of the dilemmas, but showed little personal initiative. Instead they generally indicated that the story characters had little to do with their outcomes. For children below age 9, nonverbal intelligence and reading ability were significant predictors of problem-solving skills; after age 9, impulsivity as measured by the Matching Familiar Figures Test was the most important predictor. Teacher ratings of social competence showed increased frustration in older children as well as significant relationships between problem-solving skills and social competence.

Attributional Processes

Kusché, Garfield, and Greenberg (1983) examined the social attributions of deaf adolescents in a residential school and compared them to hearing controls. They examined understanding of causes (effort, chance, ability, assistance, hindrance), emotions (pride, shame, surprise, confidence, hopelessness, thankfulness, anger), and the linkage between causes and affects. The deaf adolescents (mean age of 17) performed quite poorly, being comparable to first grade hearing children. While no age effects were found in the deaf sample, language ability was positively related to greater understanding for all areas. Moreover, particular attributional errors were made which may be related to academic achievement and self-esteem. For example, with failure situations, lack of ability was poorly understood as a reason and this concept was often confused with effort. Thus, if a child failed because he or she was not good at a particular skill, the deaf children had perceived that the child had not tried hard enough, that is, attribution of lack of effort. The educational implications of this are quite clear:

> If an individual believes that failure is due to lack of effort when in reality it is due to lack of ability, he or she may try harder to succeed. When the increased effort fails to produce positive results, the individual may simply "give up" and show frustration and poor self-esteem characteristic of learned helplessness (Seligman, 1975). (Kusché, Garfield, & Greenberg, 1983, p. 159.)

Kusché and Greenberg (1983) assessed deaf and hearing children's knowledge of the evaluative concepts of good and bad using a picture-choice paradigm. The children-ranged in age from 4 to 10 years, and all of the deaf children were using Total Communication. On the concept of bad, the deaf children were delayed only in the preschool years. However, they showed a less mature understanding of prosocial "good" throughout the age range. This study points to the fact that knowing evaluative or emotional vocabulary words does not necessarily mean that deaf children have the same understanding of them as do hearing children. Furthermore, since moral development is based on such basic distinctions as prosocial intent, the finding reported by DeCaro and Emerton (1978) that most students entering the National

Technical Institute for the Deaf scored at stages 1 and 2 of Kohlberg's model, was not surprising. However, given the importance of language style for scores on this measure, further studies of moral development are necessary before any conclusions can be drawn.

Related to attributional processes is the construct of locus on control. A variety of studies have confirmed that compared to hearing adolescents, deaf adolescents have a higher external locus of control (Blanton & Nunnally, 1964; Bodner & Johns, 1976; Dowaliby, Burke, & McKee, 1983). Further, external locus of control was found to be related to poor study habits and a lack of acceptance of self-responsibility (Dowaliby et al., 1983). Further, both Busby (1983) and Koelle and Convey (1982) reported significant positive relationships among deaf students between external locus of control and poor academic achievement in a variety of domains. In a related study, McCrone (1979) experimentally demonstrated a high degree of learned helplessness in underachieving deaf adolescents. These findings may also be related to those of Farrugia (1982) who found that deaf students reported lower vocational ambition.

In summary, compared to hearing children, deaf children more frequently show deficiencies in social-cognitive abilities such as understanding emotions, problem-solving, and personal and educationally related attributions. Recent research has shown that individual differences in these children appear to be related to communicative ability and academic achievement and attitudes. At present cause and effect are unclear and it is likely that social-cognitive skills are bidirectionally related to skills in other domains.

Teacher and Peer Interaction

Few assessments of teacher-child communication have been conducted, but those which have been reported characterize this communication as didactic and similar to that of parent-child communication. Craig and Collins (1970) reported that 86% of communication was teacher generated and only 3% was initiated spontaneously by students. Similar findings were reported by Wolff (1977). Further, teachers showed a low rate of responsiveness to student initiations.

Wood, Wood, Griffiths, Howarth, and Howarth (1982) extensively examined teacher-student conversations in oral-only classrooms in England. They reported that when teachers showed high proportions of questions, children showed very low rates of conversation. Thus, a very strong effect was found for teacher style. Deaf children appeared quite passive and only elaborated their own answers 14% of the time. Further, they very infrequently asked for clarification or repetition of teacher communications, which appeared to confirm the suspicion that while they were often in doubt about what the teacher had said, they still took a passive linguistic stance. As might be expected in oral-only children, hearing loss was strongly related to the length of child utterances, but intelligence showed no such relationship. There have been no studies reported in the literature on teacher-student communication style in TC classrooms.

Probably as a result of PL 94–142 there has been growing interest in the nature and quality of hearing-deaf child interactions. A variety of studies on oral-only children in integrated settings have indicated that (a) deaf children show more interactions with deaf children and fewer with hearing children, and (b) deaf children show more interactions with teachers than do hearing children (Darbyshire, 1977; Kennedy, Northcott, McCauley & Williams, 1976; McCauley & Bruninks, 1976; Van Lieshout, Leckie, & Van Sonsbeck, 1976). Brackett and Henniges (1976) reported that amount of hearing-deaf interaction was related to good oral communication skills in the deaf children. Antia (1982) examined the social interactional skills of deaf and hearing children in partial mainstream contexts in Grades 1 to 6. Once again the above conclusions were substantiated. Of particular interest, was Antia's comparison between children from oral and TC classrooms. First, there were no differences in the rate of interaction between these two groups. Second, deaf children used less oral communication when in mainstream situations.

Vandell and George (1981) carefully examined the quality of interaction between pairs of deaf and hearing preschoolers. They reported that hearing children were more likely to reject the deaf child's attempts to interact (over 30% of initiations were rejected), while deaf children seldom rejected hearing children's initiations. Hearing children were also unlikely to modify initiations, continuing to talk to deaf children with little use of gestures, touching, signs, or use of combined modalities. Arnold and Trembley (1979) reported similar findings in a classroom context. Following these findings, Vandell, Anderson, Erhardt, and Wilson (1982) attempted to modify the responses of hearing preschoolers through a 15-session intervention program that provided (a) awareness of deafness and its similarities and differences to functional hearing, (b) teaching techniques of communication including some sign language, and (c) providing deaf "buddies" during free play. Extensive pre-, post-, and follow-up testing was conducted on intervention children and controls. Contrary to expectations, results indicated that the intervention did not facilitate the response skills of the intervention children; in fact, control children showed greater improvement at posttest.

Two recent studies have explored the peer relationships of preschool-age deaf children. Lederberg (in press) observed deaf children in free play with their deaf peers, familiar hearing playmates, and unfamiliar hearing children. The most complex and successful interactions were found with deaf peers. Comparisons among the deaf-hearing dyads indicated that familiarity was important to the quality of interaction. Hearing children were more responsive and used more visual communication when communicating with a deaf friend versus an unfamiliar deaf child. Thus, experience in one-to-one situations may improve the quality of interactions between deaf and hearing children. Lederberg, Chapin, Rosenblatt, and Vandell (in press) compared the play preferences of deaf and hearing children. Similarly to hearing children, results indicated that deaf children preferred and were more responsive to peers of the same age, ethnicity, and gender.

While attempts at facilitating interaction in mainstream settings have proven ineffective with young children, Ladd, Munson and Miller (1984) reported encouraging findings in a high school integration program. In this program, 48 secondary level deaf students were integrated over a 3-year period in occupational education courses at local schools. Findings indicated improvement over time in that deaf students engaged in higher rates of social interaction with hearing peers during the 2nd year of participation. Further, deaf students received average ratings on peer sociometric measures. Parent and teacher interviews indicated improved self-confidence in 60% of the cases. However, over one-half of the deaf students still reported difficulty with making hearing friends at school, and little or no out-of-school contact with hearing peers was reported. Unfortunately, no information was provided on the communication and/or speech skills of these deaf students. Taken together, these findings suggest mainstreaming success may be much higher in the secondary grades where child maturity leads to a more conducive interpersonal climate (Ladd et al., 1984). Modifications for programs involving younger children in mainstream situations appear to be necessary to facilitate higher rates of social interaction in the elementary school years.

Familial Adaptation to Deafness

Given the preceding reviews of research on cognitive, social, and personality development, it is quite clear that language and communication ability are critical determinants of outcome. The following review of family development is unanimous in affirming the critical nature of optimal early and continued communication experience for personal development.

The diagnosis of deafness in an infant or young child creates a crisis of tremendous proportions for most hearing parents and other family members. During the ensuing days, months, and years, most parents experience a wide range of feelings including anger, guilt, confusion, helplessness, and sorrow (Mindel & Vernon, 1971). While such feelings are both common and normal, the ability to express and cope with these emotional states is varied and greatly impacts the family environment as well as the deaf child (Freeman et al., 1975; Freeman, Boese & Carbin, 1981; Greenberg, 1980b; Greenberg, Calderon & Kusché, 1984).

Parent-child interaction

A variety of studies have been conducted on early hearing parent-deaf child communication in families receiving both oral-only and Total Communication approaches. Schlesinger and Meadow (1972) observed mother-child interaction in 40 preschool-age deaf children with hearing parents and 20 matched controls. They found that mothers of deaf children were rated as less permissive and flexible, and more didactic and intrusive. The deaf children were divided into two groups by their communicative competence. Those with more advanced communication skills were similar to the hearing children and significantly different than deaf children with less adequate communication on ratings of creativity and positive affect. However, both groups of deaf children had lower ratings of compliance and pride in skill mastery than the controls. Brinich (1974, 1980), in a further microanalyses of this same data set, reported a significant relationship ($r = 0.44$) between the child's ability to state and request information and nonverbal intelligence.

Altman (1973) found that mothers of more linguistically competent oral deaf children showed more warmth, positive affect, and pressure on the child to perform than did those of less competent children. Linguistic competence (oral) was not related to amount of speech therapy, age of intervention, sex, or IQ. Wedell-Monnig and Lumley (1980) observed six orally-trained deaf children and matched controls. They found that mothers of the deaf children were more dominant while their children showed fewer spontaneous attempts to interact and less independent play. Similarly, Goss (1970), Collins (1969), and Cheskin (1982), found that mothers of deaf children gave more directive and controlling communications than did hearing controls. Henggeler and Cooper (1983), in a study of mother-child interaction with oral preschool-age deaf children, found no differences in the frequency of maternal directives compared to those of a group of mothers with hearing children. However, they reported that the deaf children were less compliant and both deaf children and their mothers showed significantly lower rates of responsivity to each other than did the hearing controls.

Schlesinger and Meadow (1976) followed their sample and observed mother-child interaction again at ages 4.5 to 6 and at 7 to 9 years. At both observations, deaf children rated as higher in communicative competence in the preschool years continued to have interactions that were quite similar to the hearing control group. Those children with lower competence continued to show lower ratings of expressive and instrumental behaviors.

Greenberg (1980b) examined the effects of both communicative mode (oral vs. oral + manual, i.e., simultaneous) and level of communicative competence (high vs. low) on the play interaction of profoundly deaf preschool children and their hearing mothers. Mothers and children were matched on audiologic and demographic variables. While there were no differences in communicative ability between the oral and simultaneous dyads, simultaneous dyads had longer, more complex interactions that contained more cooperation and positive affect than those of oral dyads.

Greenberg and Marvin (1979) examined the phase and quality of attachment behavior in the same sample. Dyads were classified into Phase 3 or 4 of Bowlby's model of attachment (Marvin, 1977). The majority of deaf children (age 3 to 5.5) showed little distress upon separation. Level of communicative competence was highly related to display of the Phase 4 partnership pattern. Among Phase 3 children, simultaneous children were more sociable and less avoidant than the oral children.

The free play observations of Greenberg's (1980b) oral and simultaneous children were compared to a sample of deaf children with deaf parents and a sample of hearing dyads (Meadow et al., 1981). On most measures the deaf children of deaf parents were very similar to the hearing dyads, and their interactions were more complex and reciprocal than those of the simultaneous or oral children with hearing parents. The factors of greater acceptance, learning sign language early from competent signers, and having deaf role models, make the deaf child of deaf parents much different than the great majority of deaf children with hearing parents. This further demonstrates that deafness per se does not necessarily lead to qualitatively poorer parent-child interaction.

Stinson (1974, 1978) examined maternal behavior and child task achievement between families with a hearing or hearing-impaired school-age child (ages 8 to 11 years). As expected, no group differences occurred in maternal support or reward on nonverbal tasks. However, mothers of deaf children provided greater nonspecific support and reward on the more difficult task and such support was related to the child's preference for challenging tasks and better performance. For the hearing children a negative relationship was found between maternal support and child achievement. This was likely because the verbal task was relatively easy so that support/reward might have actually interfered with performance.

Parent Attitudes

Tavormina, Boll, Dunn, Luscomb, and Taylor (1981) assessed parent attitudes of 15 mothers and fathers of deaf children using the Hereford Parent Attitude Survey. These parents scored lower than the hearing norms on the scales of trust, confidence, causation, and acceptance. Greenberg (1978) used the same measure in a study of 28 parents of deaf preschoolers and found that they scored in a similar fashion to the standardization sample. Within-group differences indicated that parents and children using Total Communication had more positive attitudes than did those using oral-only communication. Bodner-Johnson (in press) examined the relationship between factors in the family environment and school achievement in a sample of 125 deaf children 10–12 years of age. The family's adaptation to deafness was significantly related to reading achievement, and parental expectations for achievement were related to both reading and mathematics achievement.

In regard to parenting styles, a number of studies have reported that parents of oral deaf children are more likely to rely on physical punishment when disciplining their child as well as make fewer maturity demands, especially in the absence of effective communication (Barsch, 1968; Gregory, 1976; Schlesinger & Meadow, 1972). In hearing children, the lack of verbal explanation for transgressions and negotiation regarding behavior has been repeatedly shown to produce children who are less independent and lower in compliance and creativity (Damon, 1983).

Marital satisfaction

Assessment of marital satisfaction has not been extensively investigated. Freeman, Malkin, and Hastings (1975) found no differences in the divorce rate among families with deaf children compared to normative percentages in British Columbia. Calderon and Greenberg (1983) compared 20 couples with a young deaf child to a matched sample with hearing children. They found no differences between groups in marital satisfaction; in addition, high marital satisfaction in both groups was related to high life satisfaction and low parental stress.

Summary

The personality and cognitive development of deaf children is greatly influenced by their early and continued interactions and relationships with their parents. Further, due to the ubiquity of their communication delays and the limited number of individuals who can communicate with most young deaf children, the family's adaptation to and understanding of deafness is especially critical for their deaf child's growth. As such, both the natural support systems available to the family (Calderon & Greenberg, 1983) and those provided by early intervention programs are critical to family and child adaptation.

As deaf children constantly influence and are influenced by their milieu, their abilities will result from an interaction of constitutional factors, quality of communication in the home, and quality of educational interventions directed toward both the child and family. Given the importance of early communication, there has been a growing interest in demonstrating the effectiveness of early intervention. In a review of his literature, Greenberg and Calderon (1984) demonstrated that TC approaches appear to show significant short-term effects. However, they recommend a more dynamic assessment of the process of intervention which would examine factors both within the family system and in the family-intervenor communication that lead to the differential effects of such intervention. (See the chapter

by Lowenbraum and Thompson for an extensive review of early intervention.)

With the exception of the longitudinal study by Schlesinger and Meadow (1972, 1976), there have been no published reports on the quality of parent-deaf child or family interaction after the preschool years. Thus, there is little knowledge at present of the stresses encountered or types of coping strategies utilized by parents of older deaf children, or how such strategies might be related to differential outcomes in school or family communication during childhood or adolescence. Studies on family functioning have generally focused on one or a few independent and dependent variables with only one time of data collection. Both Harris (1982), using a family life cycle model, and Schlesinger (1978), utilizing an Eriksonian model, have presented models of child and family development, but there is at present little research to verify their formulations.

Communication, Social Competence, and Identity

Understanding the role of communication in social competence is critical to interpreting the findings reported in this chapter. However, communication should not be confused with language or a specific type of linguistic system. For example, in the early years there is no reason to believe that using ASL (American Sign Language) as one's primary communication system would be any better or worse than utilizing spoken English or a version of Signed English, although further research in this domain is highly recommended. In general, we believe that the results of the above studies are due to socialization which involves language deprivation, discouragement of independence and responsibility, and the absence of incidental learning.

A. E. Harris (1978) has cogently described the effects of language deprivation. These effects include reduced ability for self-regulation and reduced ability to make meaning of life experiences which, in turn, results in limited understanding of social dynamics. Generally, deaf children receive limited explanations for feelings, roles, reasons for actions, and consequences of behaviors (Rodda, 1966). As a result, one might expect that deaf children and adolescents would have poor self-esteem and behavior problems as well as limited understanding of both the causes and meanings of many events. That is, their behavior and interpretation of social events would be limited by their less than optimal socialization through language. Language deficits therefore impact deaf children's internal milieu (e.g., self-esteem, verbal-mediational skills, hemispheric processing strategies), as well as their relationships with the external environment (e.g., interactions with parents, teachers, peers).

The studies reported in this chapter underscore the importance of both familial and societal reactions in the personality development of deaf people. For example, a critical factor is the degree to which parents allow their deaf child to have independent experiences during the crucial preschool years (Schlesinger & Meadow, 1972). While the encouragement of independence facilitates the further development of spontaneity, intellectual and social curiosity, and self-motivated action, parental overprotectiveness is often associated with a restriction of experience and concomitant beliefs in the limitations of one's individual competence.

In addition to issues regarding communication, deafness must also be viewed from a cultural perspective. Meadow and Neman (1976) have elaborated the myriad ways in which stigma may affect or "spoil and identity" of deaf persons. As Emerton, Hurwitz, and Bishop (1979) have noted, on an interpersonal level, stigma leads to deaf persons receiving differential (prejudicial) treatment ranging from pity and overconcern to anger and disgust. Additionally, as a result of the differential (lower) expectations by the majority culture, deaf persons may limit their own personal goals, develop negative self-concepts, or internalize cognitive attributions of helplessness, failure, and inferiority.

From a sociological perspective, most deaf adults are members of two interrelated, but different cultural groups, that is, deaf persons form a minority-like group within a majority culture. But most deaf children (over 90%) grow up in hearing families. Thus, it is useful to conceive of the deaf child as a minority child with no other minority family members to provide models for adjustment and individuality. It is obviously of great value for all family members to have contact and involvement with deaf adults and to conceive of deafness as a difference, rather than a deficit (Freeman et al., 1981). Further, being a deaf adult generally includes participation in a thriving subculture with a proud history, language, and set of rules and norms (Baker & Battison, 1980; Higgins, 1980; Nash & Nash, 1981). Thus, communication with one's family during development and positive identification with one's deaf identity (and deaf culture) *both* appear to be critical to a sense of self-confidence, self-control, and social understanding (Seiler, 1982). For these reasons, we believe that deaf children should be exposed to both English (signed and spoken) and ASL from the early years.

At present, it appears that many deaf children and adults do possess unfavourable characteristics such as immaturity, impulsivity, egocentrism, and poor social comprehension. In spite of the fact that some of these findings may result from socio-cultural or linguistic biases (Delgado, 1982), the evidence nevertheless indicates that many deaf children and adolescents possess significant deficits in knowledge skills, and understanding that impede their daily lives in the deaf and hearing worlds.

The fact that deaf samples demonstrate group differences compared to hearing samples, however, should not obscure the fact that there is substantial variation between deaf persons. Approaches that compare deaf persons (as a group) with hearing persons (as a group) are fraught with a value judgments and assessment problems (Altshuler, 1978; Moores, 1982).

Understanding deafness is a very complex issue which involves the interaction of the individual with a variety of developmental environments and various attitudes including those of the family, school, and culture. We recognize that each person, deaf or hearing, is unique and it is understood that different persons in different situations show divergent adjustment and outcomes. Further, we note that there is no such thing as one "deaf personality." However, as with other individuals who share a combination of poor communication (especially in their early family/developmental environments) and minority/subcultural group status, many deaf persons manifest similar competencies and deficits in the social/ affective domain (Greenberg, Kusché, & Smith, 1982). Given the number of obstacles to growth experienced by many deaf persons, their resiliency and determination is often amazing. As Levine (1981) and A. E. Harris, (1978) have noted, most research on deaf persons has taken a "pathological perspective"; there is a need for this approach to be balanced by an understanding of effective coping with deafness in our culture as well as a greater respect for deaf culture itself.

THE STATE OF PRACTICE

This chapter has identified existing differences and potential deficits in the cognitive/academic and social/ personality development of deaf children. Unfortunately, only a small portion of these research findings and their implications have been incorporated into practice. As Moores (1978) states: "The gap between research and application is wider in the field of special education than in general education. And within special education, this gap is broadest in the area of deafness" (p. 173).

Moores applies Gallagher's (1968) five-step framework to conceptualize the span of efforts between basic research and actual teaching practices. These five steps include basic research, development, demonstration, dissemination, and adoption. Due to the different priorities and institutional frameworks of universities and public schools, most educational research is "basic" and is reported in esoteric language in scientific journals which are of little interest to teachers and administrators. Due to the lack of communication between school programs for the deaf and researchers, there is often no translation of such findings even when applicable to practice. Moores cogently discusses the needs of both university researchers and public school personnnel to cooperate as partners in this five-step process.

Thus, at present, we believe there is a wide gap between basic knowledge regarding deaf children and curricular adoption. Global knowledge (e.g., deaf children often show impulsivity or have difficulties with memory) is generally transmitted to practitioners. However, the specifics of why deaf children show such cognitions or behaviors and how interventions might be developed that follow from the research seldom reach "the field." Thus, with the exception of HCEEP (Handicapped Children's Early Education Programs), projects in the area of early intervention, there has been a paucity of demonstration and training projects that have drawn their approach from research findings or that have been adequately evaluated.

While one reason for lack of application of knowledge is the low rate of demonstration/development projects, mechanisms for knowledge dissemination are also inadequate. Teacher training programs in hearing impairment often do not require sufficient coursework in the areas of cognitive or personality/social development and most graduates of such training programs do not have state-of-the-art knowledge on how the theory translates into specific instructional techniques. Inservice training in school programs is often inadequate to teach new skills. This problem has been increased as a result of the implementation of PL 94-142 leading to the development of many smaller, geographically-dispersed programs. Such programs have few teachers and often no administrator, curriculum specialist, or even psychologist who works solely with hearing-impaired students. Thus, the leadership necessary to implement new curricula and attract appropriate inservice programs is lacking.

Due to the small number of qualified and well-trained school psychologists available to work with deaf children, there is a critical missing link in this process. Teacher dissatisfaction with the psychological assessment of individual differences in cognitive and personality development with deaf children is well-known. Further, the frequent lack of usable recommendations which might translate assessment results into practical strategies for remediation is widespread and in large part is due to lack of trained personnel. Furthermore, teachers frequently feel quite frustrated when their requests for therapeutic intervention for their students are met by protestations from overworked and overloaded school psychologists.

Recent Examples of Research into Practice

Psychosocial Interventions

The psychosocial difficulties of deaf children are widely recognized and there have been numerous researchers and practitioners who have called for preventive approaches including affective education (Becker, 1978; Levine, 1981; Schwartzberg, 1976; Streng, 1957), responsibility training (Galwick, 1983), and play-focused interventions (Sisco, Kranz, Lund, & Schwarz, 1979). However, few attempts have been made to evaluate systematically interventions which either prevent or remediate these problems. While there are numerous social-cognitive and cognitive-behavioral programs to increase social competence in hearing children, such programs cannot be directly applied with deaf

children due to linguistic difficulties and experiential differences.

Some of the "delays" in social and personality development evidenced by deaf children involve deficits in problem-solving and prerequisite skills. Rather than conceptualizing defects in their personality structures, these delays can be seen as deficits in social, cognitive, and communicative skills. Such a conceptualization is the basis for the PATHS (Providing Alternative Thinking Strategies) Project (Greenberg, Kusché, Gustafson, & Calderon, 1985) which is a primary prevention program for profoundly deaf children in the elementary school years. The PATHS Curriculum (Greenberg, Kusche, Calderon, Gustafson, & Coady, 1983), developed in Washington State for use with deaf children ages 6 to 13, focuses on teaching social problem-solving skills (35 lessons), emotional understanding and role-taking abilities (30 lessons), and self-control (12 lessons). Moreover, emphasis is placed on the development of component skills necessary for social development and problem-solving skills, with consideration for the special needs of deaf children. The curriculum contains approximately 75 different lessons, but many lessons require 2–4 days for completion.

In an evaluation of PATHS effectiveness, 54 severely and profoundly deaf children in first to sixth grade were randomly assigned to treatment or control groups and tested pre- and postintervention. The "experimental" teachers and their aides attended a 3-day training workshop and received weekly supervision and observation of the teaching of PATHS lessons. The PATHS lessons were given 4–5 days a week for 25 school weeks. Results indicated that the experimental group showed significant increases in problem identification skills, evaluative understanding, and all aspects of problem-solving: understanding feelings, generating alternatives, planning steps, anticipating consequences, and quality of solutions. Further, teacher ratings indicated increased frustration tolerance and better emotional adjustment in the treatment group. Further, such results also transferred to school performance as evidenced by increased reading achievement scores (Greenberg et al., 1985). Kusché (1984b) evaluated the affective portion of the curriculum and found that use of PATHS resulted in significant changes in understanding and labeling of emotion concepts and that these gains were maintained at 3-month follow-up testing.

In two studies, Schloss and his colleagues (Schloss, Smith, & Schloss, 1984; Smith, Schloss & Schloss, 1984) demonstrated the effectiveness of time-limited behavioral social skills training to increase the social responsiveness and appropriateness of emotionally disturbed deaf adolescents. Jones (1984) reviewed the literature on case studies using behavior modification with deaf students and concluded that they have shown considerable success.

Although a number of additional preventative curricula for deaf children are available (Feelings: Keys to Values, 1981; Interpersonal Relations Curriculum,

1981; Mental Health Curriculum, 1981, there has been no evaluation of their effectiveness to date. In addition, while there has been widespread discussion of the need for effective research and intervention projects in the areas of substance abuse (Kapp, Clark, Jones, & Owens, 1985; Steitler, 1985) and sexuality (Fitz-gerald & Fitz-gerald, 1985) in adolescence, there have been no published evaluations of the effectiveness of interventions/curricula in these domains.

Family-Focused Interventions

Early intervention programs are probably the most productive area to date with regard to demonstrating the effective application of research findings (see chapters by Lowenbraun and Thompson). However, few intervention programs have been directed towards families with school-age or adolescent deaf children. Schoenwald-Oberbeck (1984) recently reported the positive effects of a family-based communication training program using four families with 11 to 14-year-old children.

While no formal evaluations have been reported, a number of model programs for family-school communication have been implemented, including innovative family learning vacations (Aldridge, 1983; Freeman et al., 1981). Greenberg and Calderon (in press) have urged the development of (a) intervention programs targeted to fathers of deaf children, (b) programs that would create social linkages between families with deaf children and members of the deaf community (Freeman et al., 1981), (c) school-family programs that continue to provide TC training to families across the school years, and (d) incorporation of hearing siblings in family intervention programs. At present, there have been no evaluations of such programs.

Cognitive Intervention Programs

In studies with slow-learning hearing children, Feuerstein (1980) has described 21 cognitive deficiencies which he believes result from a passive approach to the environment. This passivity is believed to be due to a lack of "mediated experience." In other words, many "retarded" learners have not been given adequate instruction with respect to their everyday interactions with the environment. Too few mediated experiences lead to poor thinking skills, which in turn result in a reduced ability to learn from future experiences and a passive, "helpless" attitude.

Recently a number of researchers have argued for the utility of Feuerstein's model to increase the cognitive skills and academic achievement of deaf children (Jonas & Martin, 1984; Keane, 1984). In a pilot study with preadolescent deaf students, Keane (1984) found that an experimental group exposed to a short-term intervention in mediated learning performed significantly better than controls. In a more extensive project, Jonas and Martin (1984) evaluated the performance of 41 deaf high-school students who had been given Feuerstein's

Instrumental Enrichment curriculum for one year with a matched set of controls. The results indicated significant improvement for the experimental group in logical and deductive reasoning and problem-solving, and in teacher observations of work habits and classroom behavior. Martin (1984) used a similar, but shorter version of Instrumental Enrichment with deaf college students in a teacher training program. Results indicated improvement in comparative thought processes and increases on self-reports of learning style. Katz and Bucholz (1984) provided a case-study utilizing mediational procedures with a mildly delayed deaf adolescent. Using the process-orientated Learning Potential Assessment Device (LPAD) for evaluation, the researchers reported significant increases in skills in cue detection, making appropriate comparisons, and utilizing logical problem-solving skills.

While no other cognitive instructional curricula have been formally evaluated, a number of researchers and practitioners have called for, or developed, curricular strategies to enhance skills in reflective, philosophic thinking (Rembert, 1984), decision-making abilities (Bullis, 1985), and general thinking skills (Abel & Baker, 1983; Furth, 1973).

Closing Reflections on Research in Deafness

While there is obviously a voluminous research literature in a variety of areas concerning deaf children, the authors are quite concerned about both the quality of much of this work and the dearth of funded projects. The basic issues are as follows. First, there are a very high proportion of projects which are "one-shot" univariate studies, including a very high proportion of unpublished dissertations. Second, there are few longitudinal studies that have received federal grant support. Third, there are very few programmatic research laboratories in the United States concerned with basic or applied research in deafness and development, and when laboratories are developed, their work is sometimes not rigorously researched for effectiveness. Finally, the federal grant structure has not been very supportive of funding *basic* research in cognitive, communicative, social, personality, or family development in deafness. NIH (National Institutes of Health), NIMH (National Institute of Mental Health), and NSF (National Science Foundation) rarely fund grants in deafness as these agencies perceive such topics as falling under the aegis of NIDRR (National Institute on Disability and Rehabilitation Research) and OSEP (Office of Special Education Programs). However, with few exceptions, NIDRR and SEP rarely fund grants that are not of an applied nature. Thus, research in deafness tends to fall between the cracks, and there is an alarmingly high proportion of misguided applied and demonstration projects compared to those in basic research. Such a situation will do little to further our knowledge of deafness or assist in the training of high quality researchers in this field.

NEEDS AND RECOMMENDATIONS

Implications for Personal Preparation Programs

1. Development of more extensive coursework in cognitive, social, personality, and family development of deaf children for preservice training programs for teachers of the deaf. This would include training in important developmental theories, that is, those of Piaget, Luria, Vygotsky, Feuerstein, A. Freud, S. Freud, and E. Erikson.

2. Development of speciality training programs for psychologists in training for preparation for work with deaf children and their families.

3. Development of inservice training programs and summer programs on a regional basis in coordination with local school districts and residential schools to present state-of-the-art knowledge, curricula, and techniques that are derived from recent research findings.

4. Development of specialized training modules for teachers of deaf students on the sociology of deafness, deaf culture, and the structure of American Sign Language.

Areas in Need of Research

1. Conducting new integrated research programs on a variety of topics in cognitive, neurological, social, and personality development with the present cohort of deaf children (those who began early education in TC). This research needs to specify clearly the backgrounds and early communication patterns of the cohort. Some of these studies must, by definition, be longitudinal in nature. Importantly, these projects should examine the interrelationships between various aspects of functioning, for example, memory, perception, reading, emotional development, problem-solving, and so forth. Topics of critical importance would include:

(a) The assessment of differential styles of familial coping and adaptation and its relationship to differential outcomes in deaf children and their families. This research is especially needed with school-age and adolescent children and their families (ages which have received relatively little attention in the 1970s and 1980s).

(b) Accurate, in-depth exploration of behavior disorders and their correlates in early development.

(c) Factors that affect the self-concept and adaptation of deaf children and adolescents in mainstream settings (with children using both oral and/or TC/interpreters in these settings).

(d) The psychological and cognitive/academic functioning of deaf children in small local programs with few support staff versus those in large day or residential programs with support services.

2. In-depth examination of teacher/classroom communication styles and their effect on communicative and academic development, that is, contrasting didactic/direct-instructional approaches with more flexible/discovery-orientated teaching styles.

3. The examination of differential predictors of successful outcome from early intervention programs. This would include an assessment of how family coping style, natural support systems, parent personality, and parent-intervenor communication affect child and family outcomes.

4. Accurate assessment of the rates and correlates of teenage behaviors such as sexuality, substance abuse, and delinquency in order to develop programmatic intervention strategies.

5. Assessment of the perceived stresses experienced by deaf children and adolescents (as they relate to their deafness) and ways of coping that appear successful in the face of such stresses.

6. The development of methodologies to assess parent-deaf adolescent communication.

7. Investigation of the relationship of different modes of communication to different types of cognitive processing. At present, we have little information as to what form of communication best facilitates which types of learning.

8. Research in assessment, diagnosis, and intervention programs for learning disabled deaf children. At the present time, we know little about these subgroups of children or what can be done to facilitate their cognitive growth.

Domains in Need of Program/Curriculum Development and Evaluation

1. The development and evaluation of *preventative* intervention programs in the following areas:

(a) Teaching social-cognitive abilities such as role-taking, understanding of emotions, and social problem-solving in the early school years.

(b) Family communication programs (for the entire family) that develop optimal family discussion and discipline/socialization patterns.

(c) Programs that continue to offer manual communication training to families following early and preschool intervention. The purpose of such programs would be to assist parents in developing more advanced communication skills in manual communication.

(d) The development of specialized intervention programs for fathers of deaf children who are usually not targeted by early intervention projects.

(e) Intervention programs at all ages that tie together members of the deaf community with school programs for the deaf in order to facilitate positive perceptions between these groups, and introduce the teaching of ASL and deaf culture in schools.

(f) Intervention programs that develop ties between hearing families with young deaf children and members of the deaf community.

2. The development and evaluation of intervention programs for adolescents on problem-solving as it relates to interpersonal difficulties, peer pressure, drug and alcohol use, and sexuality.

3. The development and evaluation of attributional training/problem-solving programs to attempt to effect motivation, locus of control, and self-confidence of deaf adolescents and young adults.

4. The development of curricular materials on deaf culture, deaf history, and ASL for use in school programs for deaf students.

5. The development of program coordination between vocational rehabilitation counsellors and school personnel to facilitate the transition between the worlds of school and work.

6. The development of curricula to help facilitate (a) the development of specific component skill areas (e.g., short-term memory encoding abilities) and (b) areas of academic achievement which require skill integration (e.g., reading programs).

Suggestions for Improvement in Communication and Dissemination

1. There is a need for programs to stimulate alliances between local and residential school and university and college research programs in order to facilitate the development of research-based interventions.

2. The above recommendation would be facilitated by supporting projects that would translate theoretical research findings into practical knowledge for classroom use. This might be accomplished by supporting communication between researchers, school administrators, and curriculum specialists in deafness.

Changes in Policies Regulation and Funding Practices

1. Greater concentration of funding programmatic basic research projects in cognitive/neurological, and social/personality/family development in deaf children. Basic research in this area has been severely underfunded.

2. Funding of innovative prevention programs in the domains of social and cognitive development.

3. Strengthening of the research evaluation component of OSEP (Office of Special Education Programs) demonstration projects (Handicapped Children's Early Education Programs and others). These projects have generally produced no, or quite poorly designed, evaluations of their activities.

Acknowledgements

We would like to acknowledge the input of the numerous reviewers who took part in the different stages of the extraordinary process of this project. We would especially like to thank Dr. Amy Lederberg for her detailed and cogent critique. Preparation of this article was partially supported by The William T. Grant Foundation. Due to the space limitations of this project, and the wide range of topics covered here, we have necessarily summarized each area without extensive discussion of methodology or theory. The present work will form the kernal of *Cognitive, Emotional, and Social Development of Deaf Children*.

References

Abel, S. K., & Baker, S. C. (1983). *The infusion process of skills and content in curriculum development*. Paper presented at the Convention of American Instructors of the Deaf, Boston.

Achenbach, T. M. (1978). *Research in developmental psychology: Concepts, strategies, methods*. New York: The Free Press.

Affolter, F. (1984). Development of perceptual processes and problem-solving activities in normal, hearing-impaired, and language-disturbed children: A comparison study based on Piaget's conceptual framework. In D. S. Martin (Ed.), *International Symposium on Cognition, Education, and Deafness, Vol. 1*. Washington, DC: Gallaudet College (pp. 19–33).

Aldridge, L. D. (1983). *Resources for effective family-school relations*. Paper presented at the Convention of American Instructors for the Deaf, Rochester, New York.

Alpern, G. D., & Boll, T. J. (1972). *The developmental profile*. Indianapolis: Psychological Development Publications.

Altman, E. (1973). *Some factors in mother-child interaction related to language competence in children with severe congenital deafness*. Paper presented at Eastern Psychological Association, Washington, DC.

Altshuler, K. Z. (1978) Toward a psychology of deafness? *Journal of Communication Disorders*, **11**, 159–169.

Altshuler, K. Z., Deming, W. E., Vollenweider, J., Rainer, J. D., & Tendler, R. (1976). Impulsivity and profound early deafness: A crosscultural inquiry. *American Annals of the Deaf*, **121**, 331–345.

Anderson, J. R. (1978). Arguments concerning representations for mental imagery. *Psychological Review*, **85**, 249–277.

Anderson, R. J., & Sisco, F. Y. (1977) *Standardization of the WISC-R Performance Scale for deaf children*. Washington, DC: Office of Demographic Studies, Gallaudet College.

Antia, S. D. (1982). Social interaction of partially mainstreamed hearing-impaired children. *American Annals of the Deaf*, **127**(1), 18–25.

Arnold, D., & Tremblay, A. (1979) Interaction of deaf and hearing preschool children. *Journal of Communication Disorders*, **12**, 245–251.

Arnold, P., & Walter, G. (1979). Communication and reasoning skills of deaf and hearing signers. *Perceptual and Motor Skills*, **49**, 192–194.

Babbini, B., & Quigley, S. (1970). *A study of the growth patterns in language, communication, and educational achievement in six residential schools for deaf students*. Urbana, IL: Institute for Research on Exceptional Children.

Bachara, G. H., Raphael, J., & Phelan, W. J. III. (1980). Empathy development in deaf pre-adolescents. *American Annals of the Deaf*, **125**, 38–41.

Baker, C., & Battison, R. (Eds.) (1980). *Sign language and the deaf community*. Silver Spring, MD: National Association of the Deaf.

Barmeier, A. A. (1981). *A nonvocal method for teaching reading and spelling to the deaf*. Unpublished doctoral dissertation, Western Michigan University.

Barsch, R. H. (1968). *The parent of the handicapped child*. Springfield, IL: Charles. C. Thomas.

Bebko, J. M. (1980). *Memory and rehearsal characteristics of profoundly deaf children*. Unpublished doctoral dissertation, York University, Canada.

Becker, S. (1978). An approach to developing personal and social maturity. *Volta Review*, **80**, 105–108.

Bellugi, U., Klima, E. S., & Siple, P. (1975). Remembering in signs. *Cognition*, **3**, 93–125.

Best, B., & Roberts, G. (1976). Early cognitive development in hearing impaired children. *American Annals of the Deaf*, **121**, 560–564.

Bindon, O. M. (1957). Personality characteristics of rubella-deaf children: Implications for teaching of the deaf in general. *American Annals of the Deaf*, **102**, 264–270.

Bishop, D. V. M. (1982). Comprehension of spoken, written, and signed sentences in childhood language disorders. *Journal of Child Psychology and Psychiatry*, **23**(1), 1–20.

Blaesing, L. L. (1978). *Perceptual, affective, and cognitive perspective taking in deaf and hearing children*. Unpublished doctoral dissertation, University of North Carolina at Chapel Hill.

Blair, F. X. (1957). A study of the visual memory of deaf and hearing children. *American Annals of the Deaf*, **102**, 254–263.

Blank, M., & Bridger, W. H. (1966). Conceptual cross-modal transfer in deaf and hearing children. *Child Development*, **37**, 29–38.

Blanton, R. L., & Nunnally, J. C. (1964). Semantic habits and cognitive style processes in the deaf. *Journal of Abnormal and Social Psychology*, **68**, 397–402.

Blanton, R. L., & Nunnally, J. C. (1965). *Language habits, cognitive functions, and self-attitudes in the deaf*. Unpublished manuscript, Department of Psychology, Vanderbilt University.

Bodner, B., & Johns, J. (1976). *A study of locus of control and hearing-impaired students*. Paper presented at the A. G. Bell Association for the Deaf, Boston.

Bodner-Johnson, B. (in press). The family environment and achievement of deaf students: A discriminant analysis. *Exceptional Children*.

Bolton, B. (1978). Differential ability structure in deaf and hearing children. *Applied Psychological Measurement*, **2**, 147–149.

Bonvillian, J. D. (1983). Effects of signability and imagery on word recall of deaf and hearing students. *Perceptual and Motor Skills*, **56**, 775–791.

Boyd, J. (1967). Comparison of motor behavior in deaf and hearing boys. *American Annals of the Deaf*, **112**, 598–605.

Brackett, D., & Henniges, M. (1976). Communicative interaction of preschool hearing impaired children in an integrated setting. *Volta Review*, **78**, 276–285.

Bradshaw, D. H. (1964). *A study of inferred size relations using nonverbal methods*. Unpublished doctoral dissertation, Catholic University of America, Washington, DC.

Brasel, K. E., & Quigley, S. P. (1977). Influence of certain language and communication environments in early childhood on the development of language in deaf individuals. *Journal of Speech and Hearing Research*, **20**, 95–107.

Breslaw, P. I., Griffiths, A. J., Wood, D. J., & Howarth, C. I. (1981). The referential communication skills of deaf children from different educational environments. *Journal of Child Psychology and Psychiatry*, **22**(3), 269–282.

Brill, R. G. (1960). A study in adjustment of three groups of deaf children. *Exceptional Children*, **26**, 464–466.

Brinich, P. M. (1974). *Maternal style and cognitive performance in deaf and hearing children*. Unpublished doctoral dissertation, University of Chicago.

Brinich, P. M. (1980). Childhood deafness and maternal control. *Journal of Communication Disorders*, **13**, 75–81.

Bullis, M. (1985). Decision-making: A theoretical frame of reference in the career education of students with deafness. In G. B. Anderson and D. Watson (Eds.), *The habilitation and rehabilitation of deaf adolescents*. Washington, DC: Gallaudet College Press (pp. 304–316).

Busby, H. R. (1983). *Correlation of achievement of deaf adolescents with the engagement style measure*. Unpublished doctoral dissertation, University of Arizona.

Calderon, R., & Greenberg, M. T. (1983). *Social support and stress in hearing parents with deaf vs. hearing children*. Paper presented at the Western Psychological Association, San Francisco.

Chen, K. (1976). Acoustic image in visual detection for deaf and hearing college students. *The Journal of General Psychology*, **94**, 243–246.

Cheskin, A. (1982). The use of language by hearing mothers of deaf children. *Journal of Communication Disorders*, **15**, 145–153.

Chess, S., & Fernandez, P. (1980). Do deaf children have a typical personality? *Journal of the American Academy of Child Psychiatry*, **19**, 654–664.

Clarke, B. R., & Leslie, P. T. (1971). Visual-motor skills and reading ability of deaf children. *Perceptual and Motor Skills*, **33**, 263–268.

Coady, E. A. (1984). *Social problem solving skills and school related social competency of elementary age deaf students: A descriptive study*. Unpublished doctoral dissertation, University of Washington.

Cohen, B. K. (1980). Emotionally disturbed hearing-impaired children: A review of the literature. *American Annals of the Deaf*, **125**(9), 1040–1048.

Cohen, G. (1983). *The psychology of cognition* (2nd Ed.). New York: Academic Press.

Collins, J. L. (1969). *Communication between deaf children of pre-school age and their mothers*. Unpublished doctoral dissertation, University of Pittsburgh.

Conrad, R. (1977a). Lip-reading by deaf and hearing children. *British Journal of Educational Psychology*, **47**, 60–65.

Conrad, R. (1977b). The reading ability of deaf school-leavers. *British Journal of Educational Psychology*, **47**, 138–148.

Conrad, R. (1979). *The deaf schoolchild: Language and cognitive function*. London: Harper & Row.

Craig, H. B. (1965). A sociometric investigation of the self-concept of the deaf child. *American Annals of the Deaf*, **110**, 456–478.

Craig, W. & Collins, J. (1970). Analysis of communicative interaction in classes for deaf children. *American Annals of the Deaf*, **115**, 79–85.

Cummins, R. A., Livesey, P. J., Evans, J. G. M., & Walsh, R. N. (1979). Mechanism of brain growth by environmental stimulation. *Science*, **205**, 522.

Damon, W. (1983). *Social and personality development*. New York: W. W. Norton.

Darbyshire, J. O. (1977). Play patterns in young children with impaired hearing. *Volta Review*, **79**, 19–26.

Davey, B., & LaSasso, C. (1984). Relations of cognitive style to assessment components of reading comprehension for deaf adolescents. In D. S. Martin (Ed.), *International Symposium on Cognition, Education, and Deafness, Vol. 1*. Washington, DC: Gallaudet College (pp. 67–84).

Davey, B., LaSasso, C., & Macready, G. (1983). Comparison of reading comprehension task performance for deaf and hearing readers. *Journal of Speech and Hearing Research*, **26**, 266–628.

DeCaro, P., & Emerton, R. G. (1978). *A cognitive-developmental investigation of moral reasoning in a deaf population*. Rochester, NY: National Training Institute for Deaf.

Delaney, M., Stuckless, E. R., & Walter, G. G. (1984). Total communication effects—a longitudinal study of a school for the deaf in transition. *American Annals of the Deaf*, **129**(6), 481–486.

Delgado, G. L. (1982). Beyond the norm—social maturity and deafness. *American Annals of the Deaf*, **127**(3), 356–360.

Dicarlo, L. M., & Dolphin, J. E. (1952). Social adjustment and personality development of deaf children: A review of the literature. *Exceptional Children*, **18**, 111–128.

Dinner, M. B. (1981). *A proposed sign language test battery for use in the differential diagnosis of language/learning disability in deaf children*. Unpublished doctoral dissertation, University of Colorado at Boulder.

Dodds, R. G. (1982). *Encoding processes used by deaf children when reading print sentences*. Unpublished doctoral dissertation, University of Toronto, Canada.

Doehring, D. G., & Rosenstein, J. (1969). Speed of visual perception in deaf children. *Journal of Speech and Hearing Research*, **12**, 118–125.

Doll, E. A. (1965). *Vineland Social Maturity Scale: A condensed manual of directions*. Circle Pines, MN: American Guidance Service.

Dowaliby, F. J., Burke, N. E., & McKee, B. G. (1983). A comparison of hearing-imparied and normally hearing students on locus of control, people orientation, and study habits and attitudes. *American Annals of the Deaf*, **128**, 53–59.

Dyssegaard, B., & Meadow, K. P. (1984). *Socio-emotional ratings of deaf and hearing children with learning disabilities and behavioral disturbances*. Unpublished manuscript, Gallaudet College, Washington, DC.

Elias, M., Larcen, S. W., Zlotlow, S. P., & Chinsky, J. H. (1978). *An innovative measure of children's cognitions in problematic interpersonal situations*. Paper presented at the American Psychological Association, Toronto, Canada.

Emerton, G., Hurwitz, T. A., & Bishop, M. E. (1979). Development of social maturity in deaf adolescents and adults. In L. J. Bradford and W. G. Hardy (Eds.), *Hearing and hearing impairment*. New York: Grune & Stratton (pp. 451–460).

Erber, N. P. (1974). Visual perception of speech by deaf children: Recent developments and continuing needs. *Journal of Speech and Hearing Disorders*, **39**, 178–185.

Erber, N. P. (1975). Auditory-visual perception of speech. *Journal of Speech and Hearing Disorders*, **40**, 481–492.

Eysenck, H. J. (1971). *The IQ argument: Race, intelligence, and education*. New York: Library Press.

Farrugia, D. L. (1982). Deaf high school students' vocational interests and attitudes. *American Annals of the Deaf*, **127** (6), 753–762.

Farrugia, D., & Austin, G. F. (1980). A study of social-emotional adjustment patterns of hearing-impaired students in different educational settings. *American Annals of the Deaf*, **110**, 456–478.

Feelings: Keys to Values (1981). (Kendall Demonstration School) Washington, DC: Gallaudet College Press.

Feuerstein, R. (1980), *Instrumental enrichment*. Baltimore: University Park Press.

Fiebert, M. (1967). Cognitive styles in the deaf. *Perceptual and Motor Skills*, **24**, 319–329.

Fitz-gerald, D. R., & Fitz-gerald, M. (1985). Adolescent sexuality: Trials, tribulations, and teaming. In G. B. Anderson and D. Watson (Eds.), *The habilitation and rehabilitation of deaf adolescents*. Washington, DC: Gallaudet College Press (pp. 143–158).

Flavell, J. H. (1977). *Cognitive development*. Englewood Cliffs, NJ.: Prentice-Hall.

Freeman, R., Boese, R., & Carbin, C. (1981). *Can't your deaf child hear?* Baltimore: University Park Press.

Freeman, R. D., Malkin, S. F., & Hastings, J. O. (1975). Psycho-social problems of deaf children and their families: A comparative study. *American Annals of the Deaf*, **120**, 391–405.

Friedman, J. (1984). Classification skills in deaf and normally hearing preschoolers: A study in language and conceptual thought. In D. S. Martin (Ed.), *International Symposium on Cognition, Education, and Deafness, Vol. 1*. Washington, DC: Gallaudet College (pp. 257–275).

Frith, U. (1983). The similarities and differences between reading and spelling problems. In M. Rutter (Ed.), *Developmental neuropsychiatry*. New York: Guilford Press.

Furth, H. G. (1961). Influence of language on the development of concept formation in deaf children. *Journal of Abnormal and Social Psychology*, **63**, 386–389.

Furth, H. G. (1964). Research with the deaf: Implications for language and cognition. *Psychological Bulletin*, **62**, 145–164.

Furth, H. G. (1966). *Thinking without language: Psychological implications of deafness*. New York: The Free Press.

Furth, H. G. (1971). Linguistic deficiency and thinking: Research with deaf subjects 1964–1969. *Psychological Bulletin*, **76**, 58–72.

Furth, H. G. (1973). *Deafness and learning*. Belmont, CA: Wadsworth.

Furth, H. G., & Mendez, R. A. (1963). The influence of language on classification: A theoretical model applied to normal, retarded, and deaf children. *Genetic Psychological Monogram*, **72**, 317–351.

Furth, H. G., & Youniss, J. (1965). The influence of language and experience on discovery and use of logical symbols. *British Journal of Psychology*, **56**, 381–390.

Furth, H. G., & Youniss, J. (1969). Thinking in deaf adolescents: Language and formal operations. *Journal of Communication Disorders*, **2**, 195–202.

Furth, H. G., & Youniss, J. (1971). Formal operations and language: A comparison of deaf and hearing adolescents. *International Journal of Psychology*, **6**, 49–64.

Gaines, R., Mandler, J. M., & Bryant, P. (1981). Immediate and delayed story recall by hearing and deaf children. *Journal of Speech and Hearing Research*, **24**, 463–469.

Gallagher, J. (1968). Organization and special education. *Exceptional Children*, **34**, 435–441.

Galwick, R. (1983). *You can't teach responsibility . . . or can you?* Paper presented at the Convention of American Instructors of the Deaf, Rochester, New York.

Gardner, H. (1983). *Frames of mind*. New York: Basic Books.

Garrison, W. M., & Tesch, S. (1978). Self-concept and deafness: A review of the research literature. *Volta Review*, **80**, 457–466.

Garrison, W. M., Tesch, S., & DeCaro, P. (1978). An assessment of self-concept levels among postsecondary students. *American Annals of the Deaf*, **123**, 968–975.

Gates, A. I., & Chase, E. H. (1926). Methods and theories of learning to spell tested by studies of deaf children. *The Journal of Educational Psychology*, **17**(5), 289–300.

Gentile, A., & DiFrancesca, S. (1969). *Academic achievement test performance of hearing impaired students, United States: Spring 1969*. Series D, Number 1. Washington, DC: Office of Demographic Studies, Gallaudet College.

Geschwind, N. (1979). Specialization of the human brain. *Scientific American*, **241**, 180–201.

Gibson, J. (1984). Field dependence of deaf students: Implications for education. In D. S. Martin (Ed.), *International Symposium on Cognition, Education, and Deafness, Vol. 1*. Washington, DC: Gallaudet College (pp. 47–66).

Gilbert, J., & Levee, R. F. (1967). Performances of deaf and normally-hearing children on the Bender Gestalt and the Archimedes Spiral Tests. *Perceptual and Motor Skills*, **24**, 1059–1066.

Gilman, L. A., Davis, J. M., & Raffin, M. J. (1980). Use of common morphemes by hearing-impaired children exposed to a system of manual English. *Journal of Auditory Research*, **20**, 57–69.

Gormley, K. A., & Geoffrion, L. D. (1981). Another view of using language experience to teach reading to deaf and hearing impaired children. *The Reading Teacher*, **34**, February, 519–525.

Goss, R. M. (1970). Language used by mothers of deaf children and mothers of hearing children. *American Annals of the Deaf*, **115**, 93–96.

Gottlieb, G., Doran, C., & Whitley, S. (1964). Cerebral dominance and speech acquisition in deaf children. *Journal of Abnormal Social Psychology*, **69**, 182–189.

Greenberg, M. T. (1978). *Attachment behavior, communicative competence, and parental attitudes in preschool deaf children*. Unpublished doctoral dissertation, University of Virginia.

Greenberg, M. T. (1980a). Hearing families with deaf children: Stress and functioning as related to communication method. *American Annals of the Deaf*, **125**, 1063–1071.

Greenberg, M. T. (1980b). Social interaction between deaf preschoolers and their mothers: The effects of communication method and communication competence. *Developmental Psychology*, **16**, 465–474.

Greenberg, M. T. (1983). Family stress and child competence: The effects of early intervention for families with deaf infants. *American Annals of the Deaf*, **128**, 407–417.

Greenberg, M. T., & Calderon, R. (1984). Early intervention for deaf children: Outcomes and issues. *Topics in Early Childhood Special Education*, **3**, 1–9.

Greenberg, M. T., & Calderon, R. (in press). Parent programs. In J. Van Clevel (Ed.), *Encyclopedia of deaf people and deafness*. New York: Macmillan.

Greenberg, M. T., Calderon, R., & Kusché, C. A. (1984). Early intervention using simultaneous communication with deaf infants: The effect on communication development. *Child Development*, **55**, 607–616.

Greenberg, M. T., Kusché, C. A., Calderon, R., Gustafason, R., & Coady, B. A. (1983). *The PATHS Curriculum* (2nd Ed.), Department of Psychology, University of Washington.

Greenberg, M. T., Kusché, C. A., Gustafson, R., & Calderon, R. (1985). The PATHS Project: A model for the prevention of psychosocial difficulties in deaf children. In G. B. Anderson and D. Watson (Eds.), *The habilitation and rehabilitation of deaf adolescents*. Washington, DC: Gallaudet College Press (pp. 243–263).

Greenberg, M. T., Kusché, C. A., & Smith, M. (1982). A social-cognitive model of psychosocial difficulties and their prevention in deaf children. In B. Calhane and C. M. Williams, *Research monograph series on the sociology of deafness. Vol. 2. Social aspects of educating deaf persons*, Department of Sociology, Gallaudet College, Washington, DC (pp. 93–132).

Greenberg, M. T., & Marvin, R. S. (1979). Attachment patterns in profoundly deaf preschool children. *Merrill-Palmer Quarterly*, **25**, 265–279.

Gregory, S. (1976). *The deaf child and his family*. New York: John Wiley.

Grimsley, J. R. (1972). *The effects of visual cueness and visual deprivation upon the acquisition and rate of learning of a balance skill among deaf individuals*. Doctoral dissertation, Ann Arbor, Michigan: Xerox University Microfilms, Inc. 72–34,078.

Grove, C., & Rodda, M. (1984). Receptive communication skills of hearing-impaired students: A comparison of four methods of communication. *American Annals of the Deaf*, **129**, 378–385.

Hanson, V. L., Liberman, I. Y., & Shankweiler, D. (1984). Linguistic coding by deaf children in relation to beginning reading success. *Journal of Experimental Child Psychology*, **37**, 378–393.

Hanson, V. L., Shankweiler, D., & Fischer, F. W. (1983). Determinants of spelling ability in deaf and hearing adults: Access to linguistic structure. *Cognition*, **14**, 323–344.

Hardyck, C. D., & Petrinovich, L. R. (1970). Subvocal speech and comprehension level as a function of the difficulty level of reading material. *Journal of Verbal Learning & Verbal Behavior*, **9**, 647–652.

Harris, A. E. (1978). The development of the deaf individual and the deaf community. In L. S. Liben (Ed.), *Deaf children: Developmental perspectives*. New York: Academic Press (pp. 217–233).

Harris, R. I. (1978). The relationship of impulse control to parent hearing status, manual communication, and academic achievement in deaf children. *American Annals of the Deaf*, **123**, 52–67.

Harris, R. I. (1982). Early childhood deafness as a stress-producing family experience: A theoretical perspective. In C. Erting and R. W. Meisegeier (Eds.), *Social aspects of deafness. Vol. 1: Deaf children and the socialization process*. Washington DC: Department of Sociology, Gallaudet College (pp. 155–233).

Hartung, J. E. (1970). Visual perceptual skill, reading ability, and the young deaf child. *Exceptional Children*, **37**, 603–608.

Hauptman, A. R. (1980). An investigation of the spatial reasoning abilities of hearing impaired students. *Directions*, **1**, 43–44.

Henggeler, S. W., & Cooper, P. F. (1983). Deaf child–hearing mother interaction: Extensiveness and reciprocity. *Journal of Pediatric Psychology*, **8**(1), 83–95.

Herrick, H. M. (1980). *Concept formation and prevocational competence in deaf students.* Unpublished doctoral dissertation, Boston University.

Hess, D. W. (1960). *The evaluation of personality and adjustment in deaf and hearing children using a non-verbal modification of Make-A-Picture Story (MAPS) Test.* Unpublished doctoral dissertation, University of Rochester, Rochester, New York.

Hess, T. M., & Radtke, R. C. (1981). Processing and memory factors in children's reading comprehension skill. *Child Development, 52,* 479–488.

Higgins, P. C. (1980). *Outsiders in a hearing world.* Beverly Hills, CA: Sage Publications.

Hintzman, D. L. (1967). Articulatory coding in short-term memory. *Journal of Verbal Learning and Verbal Behavior, 6,* 312–316.

Hirshoren, A., Hurley, O. L., & Kavale, K. (1979). Psychometric characteristics of the WISC-R performance scale with deaf children. *Journal of Speech and Hearing Disorders, 44,* 73–79.

Hirshoren, A., & Schaittjer, C. J. (1979). Dimensions of problem behavior in deaf children. *Journal of Abnormal Child Psychology, 7,* 221–228.

Hirsh-Pasek, K., & Treiman, R. (1982). *Recoding in silent reading: Can the deaf child translate print into a more manageable form?* Unpublished manuscript.

Hiskey, M. C. (1956). A study of the intelligence of deaf and hearing children. *American Annals of the Deaf, 101,* 329–339.

Hoemann, H. W. (1972). The development of communication skills in deaf and hearing children. *Child Development, 43,* 990–1003.

Hoemann, H. W., Andrews, C. E., Florian V. A., Hoemann, S. A., & Jensema, C. J. (1976). The spelling proficiency of deaf children. *American Annals of the Deaf, 121,* 489–493.

Hoemann, H. W., & Farquharson, S. E. (1982). Training referential communication skills in hearing and deaf children: A literature review. In H. Hoemann and R. Wilbur (Eds.), *Research monograph series on the sociology of deafness, Vol. 2. Interpersonal communication and deaf people.* Washington, DC: Department of Sociology, Gallaudet College (pp. 1–57).

Huberty, T. J. R. (1980). *Effects of training and input on the performance of high and low achieving hearing and deaf children.* Unpublished doctoral dissertation, University of Missouri-Columbia.

Hung, D. L., Tzeng, O. J. L., & Warren, D. H. (1981). A chronometric study of sentence processing in deaf children. *Cognitive Psychology, 13,* 583–610.

Hurley, O. L., Hirshoren, A., Hunt, J. T., & Kavale, K. (1979). Predictive validity of two mental ability tests with Black deaf children. *The Journal of Negro Education, 48,* 14–19.

Inhelder, B. (1962). Some aspects of Piaget's genetic approach to cognition. In Thought in the young child: Report of a conference on intellectual development with particular attention to the work of Jean Piaget. *Monographs of the Society for Research in Child Development, 27,* Serial No. 83, pp. 19–34.

Interpersonal Relations Curriculum (1981). (American School for the Deaf, W. Hartford, CT.) Washington, DC: Gallaudet College Press.

Jensema, C. J., & Trybus, R. (1975). *Reported emotional/behavioral problems among hearing impaired children in special educational programs: United States 1972–1973.* Series R, Number 1, Washington, DC: Office of Demographic Studies, Gallaudet College.

Johnson, B. F. (1981). *Communicative and egocentric behaviors of deaf and hearing preschool children.* Unpublished doctoral dissertation, Philadelphia, PA: Temple University.

Jonas, B., & Martin, D. S. (1984). Cognitive improvement of hearing-impaired high school students through instruction in instrumental enrichment. In D. S. Martin (Ed.), *International symposium on cognition, education and deafness, Vol. 2.* Washington, DC: Gallaudet College (pp. 539–560).

Jones, T. W. (1984). Behavior modification studies with hearing-impaired students: A review. *American Annals of the Deaf, 129,* 451–458.

Jordan, I. K. (1975). A referential communication study of signers and speakers using realistic referents. *Sign Language Studies, 6,* 65–103.

Kane, M. P. (1979). *Spatial cognition in deaf and normal-hearing subjects.* Unpublished doctoral dissertation, University of Pittsburgh.

Kapp, D. L., Clark, K., Jones, J., & Owens, P. (1985). Drug and alcohol prevention/education for deaf adolescents: A preventive guidance and counseling program. In G. B. Anderson and D. Watson (Eds.), *The habilitation and rehabilitation of deaf adolescents.* Washington, DC: Gallaudet College Press (pp. 177–186).

Karchmer, M. A. (1985). Demographics and deaf adolescence. In G. B. Anderson and D. Watson (Eds.), *The habilitation and rehabilitation of deaf adolescents.* Washington, DC: Gallaudet College Press (pp. 28–47).

Karchmer, M. A., Milone, Jr., M. N., & Wolk, S. (1979). Educational significance of hearing loss at three levels of severity. *American Annals of the Deaf, 124,* 97–109.

Kates, S. L. (1969). Learning and use of logical symbols by deaf and hearing subjects. *Journal of Abnormal Psychology, 74* (6), 699–705.

Kates, S. L., Yudin, L., & Tiffany, R. K. (1962). Concept attainment by deaf and hearing adolescents. *Journal of Educational Psychology, 53,* 119–126.

Katz, M. A., & Bucholz, E. S. (1984). Use of the LPAD for cognitive enrichment of a deaf child. *School Psychology Review, 13,* 99–106.

Keane, K. (1984). Application of Feuerstein's mediated learning construct to deaf persons. In D. S. Martin (Ed.), *International symposium on cognition, education and deafness, Vol. 1.* Washington, DC: Gallaudet College (pp. 207–220).

Kegan, R. (1982). *The evolving self.* Cambridge: Harvard University Press.

Kelliher, M. H. (1976). *The relationship between mode of communication and the development of self-esteem in the deaf child of hearing parents.* Unpublished doctoral dissertation, Loyola University of Chicago.

Kennedy, P., Northcott, W., McCauley, R., & Williams, S. N. (1976). Longitudinal sociometric and cross sectional data on mainstreamed hearing impaired children: Implications for school planning. *Volta Review, 78,* 71–81.

Keogh, B. K., Vernon, M., & Smith, C. E. (1970). Deafness and visuo-motor function. *The Journal of Special Education, 4,* 41–47.

Kesner, R. P., & Baker, T. B. (1980). Neuroanatomical correlates of language and memory: A developmental perspective. In R. L. Ault (Ed.), *Developmental perspectives* Santa Monica, CA: Goodyear (pp. 156–215).

Koelle, W. H., & Convey, J. J. (1982). The prediction of the achievement of deaf adolescents from self-concept and locus of control measures. *American Annals of the Deaf*, **127**(6), 769–779.

Kusché, C. A. (1984a). Linguistic processing, encoding capacities, and reading achievement in deaf children and adolescents. In D. S. Martin (Ed.), *International Symposium on Cognition, Education, and Deafness, Vol. 2.* Washington, DC: Gallaudet College (pp. 115–120).

Kusché, C. A. (1984b). *The understanding of emotion concepts by deaf children: An assessment of an affective education curriculum.* Unpublished doctoral dissertation, University of Washington.

Kusché, C. A. (1985). Information processing and reading achievement in the deaf population: Implications for learning and hemispheric lateralization. In D. S. Martin (Ed.), *Cognition, education, and deafness: Trends in research and instruction.* Washington, DC: Gallaudet College Press.

Kusché, C. A., Garfield, T. S., & Greenberg, M. T. (1983). The understanding of emotional and social attributions in deaf adolescents. *Journal of Clinical Child Psychology*, **12**, 153–160.

Kusché, C. A., & Greenberg, M. T. (1983). The development of evaluative understanding and role-taking in deaf and hearing children. *Child Development*, **54**, 141–147.

Kusché, C. A., Greenberg, M. T., & Garfield, T. S. (1983). Nonverbal intelligence and verbal achievement in deaf adolescents: An examination of heredity and environment. *American Annals of the Deaf*, **128**(4), 458–466.

Ladd, G. W., Munson, H. L., & Miller, J. K. (1984). Social integration of deaf adolescents in secondary-level mainstreamed programs. *Exceptional Children*, **50**(5), 420–428.

Lake, D. (1981). *Syntax and sequential memory in deaf children.* Unpublished doctoral dissertation, University of Waterloo (Canada).

Lantz, D. L., & Lenneberg, E. H. (1966). Verbal communication and color memory in the deaf and hearing. *Child Development*, **37**, 756–779.

Lederberg, A. R. (in press). Peer interaction in young deaf children: The effect of partner hearing status and familiarity. *Developmental Psychology.*

Lederberg, A. R., Chapin, S., Rosenblatt, V., & Vandell, D. L. (in press). Ethnic, gender, and age preferences among deaf and hearing preschool peers. *Child Development.*

Levine, E. S. (1956). *Youth in a soundless world.* New York: New York University Press.

Levine, E. S. (1960). *The psychology of deafness.* New York: Columbia University Press.

Levine, E. S. (1976). Psycho-cultural determinants in personality development. *Volta Review*, **78**, 258–267.

Levine, E. S. (1981). *The ecology of early deafness.* New York: Columbia University Press.

Levine, E. S., & Wagner, G. E. (1974). Personality patterns of deaf persons. *Perceptual and Motor Skills*, (Monograph Supplement 4-V39).

Liben, L. S. (1978). Developmental perspectives on the experiential deficiencies of deaf children. In L. S. Liben (Ed.), *Deaf children: Developmental perspectives.* New York: Academic Press (pp. 3–20).

Liben, L. S. (1984). The development and use of memory strategies by deaf children and adults. In D. S. Martin (Ed.), *International Symposium on Cognition, Education, and Deafness, Vol. 1.* Washington DC: Gallaudet College (pp. 239–256).

Lichtenstein, E. (1984). Deaf working memory processes and English language skills. In D. S. Martin (Ed.), *International Symposium on Cognition, Education, and Deafness, Vol. 2.* Washington, DC: Gallaudet College (pp. 331–360).

Lieding, R. T., & Gammel, C. (1982). Reading in the preschool. *Volta Review*, **84**, April, 166–171.

Ling, A. (1971). Dichotic listening in hearing-impaired children. *Journal of Speech and Hearing Research*, **14**, 793–803.

Linton, M. (1980). Information processing and developmental memory: An overview. In R. L. Ault (Ed.), *Developmental perspectives*, Santa Monica, CA: Goodyear (pp. 104–155).

Locke, J. L. (1978). Phonemic effects in the silent reading of hearing and deaf children. *Cognition*, **6**, 175–187.

Luria, A. R. (1976). *Cognitive development: Its cultural and social foundations.* Cambridge: Harvard University Press.

Martin, D. S. (1984). Enhancing cognitive performance in the hearing-impaired college student: A pilot study. In D. S. Martin (Ed.), *International symposium on cognition, education and deafness, Vol. 2.* Washington, DC: Gallaudet College (pp. 561–577).

Marvin, R. S. (1977). An ethological-cognitive model of the attenuation of mother–child attachment. In T. M. Alloway and L. Krames (Eds.), *Advances in the study of communication, Vol. 3, Development of social attachments.* New York: Plenum Press (pp. 25-60).

Mattingly, I. G. (1972). Reading, the linguistic process, and linguistic awareness. In J. F. Kavanagh and I. G. Mattingly (Eds.), *Language by ear and by eye: The relationship between speech and reading.* Cambridge: The MIT Press (pp. 133–147).

McCauley, R. W., & Bruninks, R. H. (1976). Behavior interaction of hearing impaired children in regular classrooms. *Journal of Special Education*, **10**, 277–284.

McCrone, W. (1979). Learned helplessness and level of underachievement among deaf adolescents. *Psychology in the Schools*, **16**, 430–434.

Meadow, K. P. (1968). Early manual communication in relation to the deaf child's intelligence, social, and communicative functioning. *American Annals of the Deaf*, **113**, 21–41.

Meadow, K. P. (1969). Self-image, family climate, and deafness. *Social Forces*, **47**, 428–438.

Meadow, K. P. (1975). The development of deaf children. In E. M. Hetherington (Ed.), *Review of child development research* (Vol. 5). Chicago: University of Chicago Press.

Meadow, K. P. (1978). The "natural history" of a research project: An illustration of methodological issues in research with deaf children. In L. S. Liben (Ed.), *Deaf children: Developmental perspectives.* New York: Academic Press (pp. 21–42).

Meadow, K. P. (1980a). *Deafness and child development.* Berkeley, CA: University of California Press.

Meadow, K. P. (1986). *Meadow/Kendall social-emotional assessment inventory for deaf students.* Washington, DC: Gallaudet College.

Meadow, K. P. (1983a). An instrument for assessment of social-emotional adjustment in hearing-impaired preschoolers. *American Annals of the Deaf*, **128**. 826–834.

Meadow, K. P. (1983b). *Revised Manual. Meadow/Kendall Social-Emotional Assessment Inventory for Deaf and Hearing-Impaired Children.* Washington, DC: Pre-College Programs, Gallaudet Research Institute.

Meadow, K. P., & Dyssegaard, B. (1983). Social-emotional adjustment of deaf students. Teachers' ratings of deaf children: An American-Danish comparison. *International Journal of Rehabilitation Research, 6*(3), 345–348.

Meadow, K. P., Greenberg, M. T., Erting, C., & Carmichael, H. S. (1981). Interactions of deaf mothers and deaf preschool children: Comparisons with three other groups of deaf and hearing dyads. *American Annals of the Deaf,* **126,** 454–468.

Meadow, K. P., & Neman, A. (1976). Deafness and stigma. *American Rehabilitation, 2,* 7–9; 19–22.

Meadow, K. P., & Trybus, R. J. (1979). Behavioral and emotional problems of deaf children: An overview. In L. J. Bradford & W. G. Hardy (Eds.), *Hearing and hearing impairment.* New York: Grune & Stratton (pp. 395–404).

Mental Health Curriculum (1981). (Arizona School for the Deaf and Blind, Tucson) Washington, DC: Gallaudet College Press.

Mindel, E., & Vernon, M. (1971). *They grow in silence.* Silver Spring, MD: National Association of the Deaf.

Moores, D. (1967). *Applications of "cloze" procedures to the assessment of psycholinguistic abilities of the deaf.* Unpublished doctoral dissertation. University of Illinois, Urbana.

Moores, D. F. (1978). Current research and theory with the deaf: Educational implications. In L. Liben (Ed.), *Deaf children: Developmental perspectives.* New York: Academic Press (pp. 173–194).

Moores, D. F. (1982). *Educating the deaf: psychology, principles, and practices* (2nd Ed.). Boston: Houghton Mifflin.

Morrison, M. M. (1981). *Investigation of variables associated with the reading abilities of eighty-nine secondary deaf students.* Unpublished doctoral dissertion, University of Northern Colorado.

Moulton, R. D., & Beasley, D. S. (1975). Verbal coding strategies used by hearing-impaired individuals. *Journal of Speech and Hearing Research,* **18,** 559–570.

Murphy-Berman, V., Witters, L., & Harding, R. (1984). Hearing-impaired students' performance on a Piagetian horizontality task. In D. S. Martin (Ed.), *International symposium on cognition, education, and deafness, Vol. 1.* Washington, DC: Gallaudet College (pp. 34-46).

Myklebust, H. (1953). Towards a new understanding of the deaf child. *American Annals of the Deaf,* **98,** 345–357.

Myklebust, H. R. (1964). *The psychology of deafness* (2nd Ed.). New York: Grune & Stratton.

Naiman, D. W. (1979). Educating severely handicapped deaf children. *American Annals of the Deaf,* **124,** 381–396.

Nash, J. E., & Nash, A. (1981). *Deafness in society.* Lexington, MA: Lexington.

Neville, H. J., & Bellugi, U. (1978). Patterns of cerebral specialization in congenitally deaf adults. In P. Siple (Ed.), *Understanding language through sign language research.* New York: Academic Press (pp. 239–257).

Neyhus, A. (1964). The social and emotional adjustment of deaf adults. *Volta Review, 66,* 319–325.

O'Connor, L. M. (1979). *Short-term memory and coding strategies in the deaf.* Unpublished doctoral dissertation, University of Northern Colorado.

O'Connor, N., & Hermelin, B. M. (1973). The spatial or temporal organization of short-term memory. *Quarterly Journal of Experimental Psychology, 25,* 335–343.

Odom, P. B., & Blanton, R. L. (1967). Phrase-learning in deaf and hearing subjects. *Journal of Speech and Hearing Research, 10,* 600–605.

Odom, P. B., Blanton, R. L., & Laukhuf, C. (1973). Facial expressions and interpretation of emotion-arousing situations in deaf and hearing children. *Journal of Abnormal Child Psychology, 1,* 139–151.

Oleron, P. (1953). Conceptual thinking of the deaf. *American Annals of the Deaf,* **98,** 304–310.

Oleron, P., & Herren, H. (1961). L'acquisition des conservations et le langage: Etude comparative sur des enfants sourds et entendants. *Enfance, 14,* 203–219.

Ottem, E. (1980). An analysis of cognitive studies with deaf subjects. *American Annals of the Deaf,* **125,** 564–575.

Padden, C. (1980). The deaf community and the culture of deaf people. In C. Baker and R. Battison (Eds.) *Sign language and the deaf community.* Silver Spring, MD: National Association of the Deaf (pp. 89–104).

Padden, D. A. (1959). Ability of deaf swimmers to orient themselves when submerged in water. *Research Quarterly,* **30,** 214–226.

Parasnis, I., & Long, G. I. (1979). Relationships among spatial skills, communication skills, and field dependence in deaf students. *Perceptual and Motor Skills, 49,* 879–887.

Pennella, L. (1979) Motor ability and the deaf: Research implications. *American Annals of the Deaf,* **124,** 366–372.

Piaget, J. (1950). Principal factors determing intellectual evolution from childhood to adult life. In E. L. Hartley, H. G. Birch, & R. E. Hartley (Eds.), *Outside readings in psychology.* New York: Crowell (pp. 80–90).

Pintner, R., Eisenson, J., & Stanton, M. (1941). *The psychology of the physically handicapped.* New York: Crofts.

Poizner, H., Bellugi, U., & Tweney, R. D. (1981). Processing of formational, semantic, and iconic information in American Sign Language. *Journal of Experimental Psychology: Human Perception and Performance, 7,* 1146–1159.

Quarrington, B., & Solomon, B. (1975). A current study of the social maturity of deaf students. *Canadian Journal of Behavioral Science, 7,* 70–77.

Quay, H. C., & Peterson, D. R. (1967). *Manual for the behavior problem checklist.* Champaign, IL: University of Illinois.

Quigley, S. P., & King, C. M. (1980). Syntactic performance of hearing impaired and normal hearing individuals. *Applied Psycholinguistics, 1,* 329–356.

Quigley, S. P., & Kretschmer, R. E. (1982). *The education of deaf children: Issues, theory and practice.* Baltimore: University Park Press.

Rainer, J. D., Altshuler, K. Z., & Kallman, F. J. (1969). *Family and mental health problems in a deaf population* (2nd Ed.). Springfield, IL: Charles C. Thomas.

Ray, S. (1979). *An adaptation of the "Wechsler Intelligence Scales (Performance) for Children-Revised" for the deaf.* Unpublished doctoral dissertation, University of Tennessee.

Reivich, R. S., & Rothrock, I. A. (1972). Behavior problems of deaf children and adolescents: A factor-analytic study. *Journal of Speech and Hearing Research,* **15,** 93–104.

Rembert, R. (1984). Philosophical inquiry among hearing-impaired students: Promoting the development of thinking skills through the use of philosophy for children programs. In D. S. Martin (Ed.), *International symposium on cognition, education, and deafness, Vol. 2.* Washington, DC: Gallaudet College (pp. 517–538).

Rittenhouse, R. (1977). *Horizontal decalage: The development of conservation in deaf students and the effect of the task instructions on their performance.* Unpublished doctoral dissertation. University of Illinois, Urbana.

Rittenhouse, R. K., Morreau, L. E., & Iran-Nejad, A. (1981). Metaphor and conservation in deaf and hard-of-hearing children. *American Annals of the Deaf,* **126,** 450–453.

Robbins, N. L. (1981). *The effects of signed text on the reading comprehension of hearing-impaired children.* Unpublished doctoral dissertation, University of Nebraska-Lincoln.

Robertson, A., & Youniss, J. (1969). Anticipatory visual imagery in deaf and hearing children. *Child Development,* **40,** 123–135.

Rodda, M. (1966). Social adjustment of deaf adolescents. *Proceedings of a Symposium of the Psychological Study of Deafness and Hearing Impairment,* 33–44.

Rosch, E., Mervis, C. B., Gray, W., Johnson, D., & Boyes-Braem, P. (1976). Basic objects in natural categories. *Cognitive Psychology,* **8,** 382–439.

Rosenstein, J. (1960). Cognitive abilities of deaf children. *Journal of Speech and Hearing Research,* **3,** 108–119.

Ross, B. M. (1966). Probability concepts in deaf and hearing children. *Child Development,* **37,** 917–928.

Ross, B. M., & Hoeman, H. (1975). The attainment of formal operations: A comparison of probability concepts in deaf and hearing adolescents. *Genetic Psychology Monographs,* **91,** 61–119.

Ross, P. (1983). Cerebral specialization in deaf individuals. In S. Segalowitz (Ed.), *Language functions and brain organization.* New York: Academic Press (pp. 287–313).

Rozanova, T. V. (1966). Pictorial memory of deaf children. In R. M. Boskis and A. I. Meshcheryakov (Eds.), *Sensory defects and mental development.* Symposium 33, Moscow: International Congress of Psychology.

Scarr-Salapatek, S. (1975). Genetics and development of intelligence. In F. D. Horowitz (Ed.), *Review of child development research,* **4.** Chicago, University of Chicago Press (pp. 1–57).

Schein, J. D. (1975). Deaf students with other disabilities. *American Annals of the Deaf,* **120,** 92–99.

Schiff, W., & Dytell, R. S. (1971). Tactile identification of letters: A comparison of deaf and hearing children's performances. *Journal of Experimental Child Psychology,* **11,** 150–164.

Schlesinger, H. S. (1978). The acquisition of signed and spoken language. In L. S. Liben (Ed.). *Deaf children: Developmental perspectives.* New York: Academic Press (pp. 69–86).

Schlesinger, H. S., & Meadow, K. (1972). *Sound and sign.* Berkeley, CA: University of California Press.

Schlesinger, H. S., & Meadow, K. P. (Eds.), (1976). *Studies of family interaction, language acquisition, and deafness.* San Francisco: University of California, S. F. Final Report, Office of Maternal and Child Health, Bureau of Community Health Services. (pp. 69–86).

Schloss, P. J., Smith, M. A., Goldsmith, L., & Selinger, J. (1984). Identifying current and relevant curricular sequences for multiply involved hearing-impaired learners. *American Annals of the Deaf,* **129,** 370–374.

Schloss, P. J., Smith, M. A., & Schloss, C. N. (1984). Empirical analysis of a card game designed to promote consumer-related competence among hearing-impaired youth. *American Annals of the Deaf,* **129**(5), 417–423.

Schoenwald-Oberbeck, B. (1984). A communication program for enhancing interaction in families with a hearing-impaired child. *American Annals of the Deaf,* **129**(4), 362–369.

Schwartzberg, J. (1976). Affective education: Ways to help a deaf child learn about his own emotions. *Hearing Rehabilitation Quarterly,* **2,** 15–17.

Seiler, P. (1982). Social aspects of educating deaf persons: Perspectives of a deaf professional. *Deafness monograph, No. 2, Social aspects of educating deaf persons.* Washington, DC: Gallaudet College.

Seligman, M. E. P. (1975). *Helplessness.* San Francisco: W. H. Freeman.

Silverman, R. T. (1967). Categorization behavior and achievement in deaf and hearing children. *Exceptional Children,* **34,** 241–250.

Siple, P., Caccamise, F., & Brewer, L. (1982). Signs as pictures and signs as words: Effect of language knowledge on memory for new vocabulary. *Journal of Experimental Psychology: Learning, Memory, and Cognition,* **8**(6), 619–625.

Sisco, F. H., Kranz, P. L., Lund, N. L., & Schwarz, G. C. (1979). Developmental and compensatory play: A means of facilitating social, emotional, cognitive, and linguistic growth in deaf children. *American Annals of the Deaf,* **124** (7), 850–857.

Smith, M. A., Schloss, P. J., & Schloss, C. N. (1984). An empirical analysis of a social skills training program used with hearing impaired youths. *Journal of Rehabilitation of the Deaf,* **18**(2), 7–14.

Söderbergh, R. (1981). Teaching Swedish deaf preschool children to read. In P. S. Dale & D. Ingram (Eds.), *Child language: An international perspective.* Baltimore, MD: University Park Press (pp. 373–386).

Sperling, G. (1960). The information available in brief visual presentations. *Psychological Monographs,* **74,** No. 498.

Stauffer, R. G. (1979). The language experience approach to reading instruction for deaf and hearing-impaired children. *The Reading Teacher,* **33,** October, 21–24.

Steitler, K. (1985). Substance abuse and the deaf adolescent. In G. B. Anderson and D. Watson (Eds.), *The habilitation and rehabilitation of deaf adolescents.* Washington, DC: Gallaudet College Press (pp. 169–176).

Stinson, M. S. (1974). Maternal reinforcement and help and the achievement motive in hearing and hearing-impaired children. *Developmental Psychology,* **10,** 348–353.

Stinson, M. S. (1978). Effects of deafness on maternal expectations about child development. *Journal of Special Education,* **12,** 75–81.

Streng, A. (1957). Curriculum in school for the deaf. *Volta Review,* **59,** 291–296.

Stuckless, E. R., & Birch, J. W. (1966). The influence of early manual communication on the linguistic development of deaf children. *American Annals of the Deaf,* **111,** 452–460.

Sugarman, I. R. (1969). *The perception of facial expressions of affect by deaf and nondeaf high school students.* Unpublished doctoral dissertation.

Suppes, P. (1974). Cognition in handicapped children. *Review of Educational Research,* **44,** 165–176.

Sussman, A. (1973). *An investigation into the relationship between self-concept of deaf adults and their perceived attitudes toward deafness.* Unpublished doctoral dissertation, New York University.

Sutter, S. (1982). Differences between deaf and hearing adults in task-related EEG asymmetries. *Psychophysiology,* **19,** 124–128.

Swanson, L., & O'Connor, L. (1981). Short-term memory in deaf children in relation to verbal and dactylo-kinesthetic encoding. *Journal of Psychology,* **107,** 231–236.

Tavormina, J. B., Boll, T. J., Dunn, N. J., Luscomb, R. L., & Taylor, J. R. (1981). Psychosocial effects on parents of raising a physically handicapped child. *Journal of Abnormal Child Psychology, 9*, 121–131.

Templin, M. C. (1948). A comparison of the spelling achievement of normal and defective hearing subjects. *Journal of Educational Psychology, 39*, 337–346.

Templin, M. (1950). *The development of reasoning in children with normal and defective hearing.* Minneapolis, MN: University of Minnesota Press.

Titus, E. S. (1965). *The self-concept and adjustment of deaf teenagers.* Unpublished doctoral dissertation, University of Missouri.

Tomlinson-Keasey, C., & Kelly, R. R. (1978). The deaf child's symbolic world. *American Annals of the Deaf, 123*, 452–459.

Trybus, R. J., & Karchmer, M. A. (1977). School achievement scores of hearing-impaired children: National data on achievement status and growth patterns. *American Annals of the Deaf, 122*, 62–69.

Vandell, D., & George, L. (1981). Social interaction in hearing and deaf preschoolers: Successes and failures in initiation. *Child Development, 52*, 627–635.

Vandell, D., Anderson, L., Erhardt, G., & Wilson, K. (1982). Integrating hearing and deaf preschoolers: An attempt to enhance hearing children's interaction with deaf peers. *Child Development, 53*, 1354–1363.

Van Lieshout, C., Leckie, G., & Van Sonsbeck, B. (1976). Social perspective-taking training: Empathy and role-taking ability of preschool children. In K. F. Riefel & J. A. Meacham (Eds.), *The developing individual in a changing world.* Chicago: Aldine.

Vargha-Khadem, F. (1982). Hemispheric specialization for the processing of tactile stimuli in congenitally deaf and hearing children. *Cortex, 18*, 277–286.

Vernon, M. (1968). Fifty years of research on the intelligence of deaf and hard of hearing children: A review of literature and discussion of implications. *Journal of Rehabilitation of the Deaf, 1*, 4–7.

Vernon, M. (1969). Sociological and psychological factors associated with hearing loss. *Journal of Speech & Hearing Research, 12*, 541–563.

Vygotsky, L. S. (1972). *Thought and language.* Cambridge: MIT Press.

Watson, B. U., Sullivan, P. M., Moeller, M. P., & Jensen, J. K. (1982). Nonverbal intelligence and English language ability in deaf children. *Journal of Speech and Hearing Disorders, 47*, 99–204.

Watts, W. J. (1979). The influence of language on the development of quantitative, spatial and social thinking in deaf children. *American Annals of the Deaf, 124*, 46–56.

Wedell-Monnig, J., & Lumley, J. M. (1980). Child deafness and mother–child interaction. *Child Development, 51*, 766–774.

Weston, P., & Weinman, J. (1983). The effects of auditory and linguistic deprivation on lateral preference of deaf children. *Developmental Medicine and Child Neurology, 25*, 207–213.

White, A. H., & Stevenson, V. M. (1975). The effects of total communication, manual communication, oral communication and reading on the learning of factual information in residential school deaf children. *American Annals of the Deaf, 120*, 48–57.

White, F. (1981). *Affective vocabulary and personal adjustment of deaf and hearing adolescent populations.* Unpublished doctoral dissertation, East Texas State University.

Williams, C. E. (1970). Some psychiatric observations in a group of maladjusted deaf children. *Journal of Child Psychology and Psychiatry, 11*, 1–18.

Wilson, K. (1979). *Inference and language processing in hearing and deaf children.* Unpublished doctoral dissertation, Boston University.

Withrow, F. B. (1968). Immediate memory span of deaf and normally hearing children. *Exceptional Children, 35*, 33–41.

Wolff, V. G. (1973). *Language, brain, and hearing: An introduction to the psychology of language with a section on deaf children's learning of language.* London: Methuen.

Wolff, S. (1977). Cognitive and communicative patterns in classrooms of deaf students. *American Annals of the Deaf, 122*, 319–327.

Wood, D. J., Wood, H. A., Griffiths, A. J., Howarth, S. P., & Howarth, C. I. (1982). The structure of conversations with 6- to 10-year-old deaf children. *Journal of Child Psychology and Psychiatry, 23*(3), 295–308.

Wood, D., Wood, H., & Howarth, P. (1983). Mathematical abilities of deaf school-leavers. *British Journal of Developmental Psychology, 1*, 67–73.

Wright, R. H. (1955). *The abstract reasoning of deaf college students.* Unpublished doctoral dissertation. Northwestern University.

Wrightstone, J. W., Aranow, M. S., & Muskowitz, S. (1963). Developing test norms for the deaf child. *American Annals of the Deaf, 108*, 311–316.

Young, E. P., & Brown, S. L. (1981). *The development of social-cognition in deaf preschool children: A pilot study.* Paper presented at the Annual Meeting of the Southeastern Psychological Association, Atlanta, Georgia.

Youniss, J. (1967). Psychological evaluation of the deaf child: Observations of a researcher. *The Eye, Ear, & Throat Monthly, 46*, 458–464.

Youniss, J. (1974). Operational development in deaf Costa Rican subjects. *Child Development, 45*, 212–216.

Youniss, J., & Furth, H. G. (1965). The influence of transitivity on learning in hearing and deaf children. *Child Development, 36*, 533–538.

Youniss, J., & Furth, H. G. (1966a). Prediction of causal events as a function of transitivity and perceptual congruency in hearing and deaf children. *Child Development, 37*, 73–82.

Youniss, J., & Furth, H. G. (1966b). *Spatial and temporal factors in learning with deaf children: An experimental investigation of thinking.* (Vocational Rehabilitation Administration Report RD-1305-S) Washington, DC: Catholic University of America.

Youniss, J., & Robertson, A. (1970). Projective visual imagery as a function of age and deafness. *Child Development, 41*, 215–234.

SECTION 2

Education of Visually Handicapped Children and Youth

Introduction

GERALDINE T. SCHOLL

University of Michigan

Among the low prevalence groups being served under PL 94-142 and PL 89-313, the visually handicapped and deaf-blind groups count the least numbers of children and youth in their populations. The diverse characteristics and widely scattered geographical distribution of these populations, coupled with the small number of personnel required to serve them, complicate the conduct of research in this area. These difficulties tend to discourage the study of the visually handicapped and deaf-blind groups, particularly by researchers and scholar practitioners from related disciplines. Further, the small number of professional personnel in the field results in fewer who are interested in and available for conducting research.

In light of the state of the art and the state of practice in the education of visually handicapped children and youth, five areas were identified for the purposes of this review. These areas, which correspond with the topics of chapters in this section, are the definition of who constitutes the visually handicapped population, how many individuals are included, and what are their demographic characteristics; the developmental characteristics of visually handicapped children and youth; the high prevalence of multiple handicaps in this population; assessment needs; and the current status of technological development.

The first chapter, by Corinne Kirchner, is entitled "National Estimates of Prevalence and Demographics of Children With Visual Impairments." For many years, the visually handicapped field was tied to the definition of blindness for legal purposes. This approach has numerous weaknesses, including a general inapplicability to the identification of educational needs and the lack of attention to how an individual uses vision, namely, his or her functional vision. In addition, there is little consistency in the terminology used to label this population. As described by Kirchner, the absence of an accepted definition is coupled with a lack of data on numbers, because statistical sources of data use different definitions. Finally, there is an absence of data on characteristics of the visually handicapped population such as racial and ethnic composition, geographical distribution, and prevalence of other exceptionalities.

In his chapter on "Implications of Visual Impairments for Child Development," David Warren summarizes findings from his extensive review of the current knowledge base concerning the growth and development of young visually handicapped children. Relatively little is known about the developmental characteristics of visually handicapped children and youth and their similarities and differences from nonvisually handicapped populations. It is often assumed that the former are more alike than different, but whether this is an appropriate assumption is not known. Warren's review of what is known about how visually handicapped children differ from, and in what ways they are similar to, nonhandicapped children in cognitive, affective, psychomotor, and visual characteristics has definite implications for practice.

In addition to similarities in developmental characteristics, the visually handicapped population shares with the total population a potentially similar prevalence of other exceptionalities. This topic is explored by Edwin Hammer in his chapter entitled "Research Issues in Educating Visually Handicapped Persons with Multiple Impairments." There have been studies of severe multiple impairments that accompany visual impairments, but these are in general concerned with the prerubella population. Such studies are not relevant for the current population, which is characterized by low birth weight and shortened length of gestation and is alive as a result of recent advances in neonatal care and treatment. Hammer maintains that educational planners need to know who from among this population require educational intervention that will meet the special needs created by their visual impairment in combination with other disabilities. Assessment plays a critical role in determining the broad range of services that are necessary for their education as well as the particular settings in which their educational programs are best conducted.

The role and the requirements of assessment in this area are reviewed by Geraldine Scholl and Erine Theodorou in their chapter on "Assessment of Blind and Visually Handicapped Children and Youth." The authors note that the use of standardized tests to assess certain groups of handicapped children is increasingly questioned in the literature, particularly in light of differences in development and experience compared with the nonhandicapped population. There is an increasing trend toward the use of informal, nontest-based approaches to assessment; assessment directed to the identification of specific educational interventions; and assessment instruments and procedures selected to answer specific questions.

Scholl and Theodorou discuss assessment needs for visually handicapped children and youth as being especially related to the knowledge base on development and multiple impairments (as described in the chapters in this section by Warren & Hammer). Assessment must encompass the broad range of developmental areas, including cognitive (language, mental, and achievement); psychomotor; affective (social, emotional, and self-concept); and visual (medical and functional). Selection of the most appropriate formal and informal instruments and procedures for these areas depends in large measure on the developmental knowledge base. Additionally, when, how, and under what circumstances tests and procedures can and should be modified are determined by what is known about the differences and similarities between the visually handicapped and "normal" populations. Adaptations for special groups, such as the multiply handicapped and infants, are especially needed, as are assessment procedures for facilitating the transition to adulthood, particularly for those with severe multiple impairments.

In the final chapter in this section, Lawrence Scadden addresses "Implications of the Research and Development of Modern Technology for the Education of Blind and Visually Handicapped Students." Recent advances in technology have changed the lives of all persons, including the handicapped. It is essential to insure that the visually handicapped population will not be left behind in future advances. Thus, Scadden's review of currently available technology, both that which is now accessible to visually handicapped children and youth and that which should be in the future, includes a focus on how technology might be utilized to make educational programs for this population more effective.

Answers to some of the questions surrounding technology and the visually handicapped population are dependent on outcomes from the reviews discussed in the first four chapters of this section. For example, the collection of accurate data on the population (see the chapter by Kirchner) is essential to the development of policies related to technological research and development. Not all persons are able to make use of technology in their daily lives; knowledge gained from the chapters on development (Warren), multiple impairments (Hammer), and assessment (Scholl & Theodorou) can assist in identifying the skills an individual should have in order to make maximum use of currently available and future technological advances. Scadden draws from the preceding four reviews the special needs for research and development in technology for the heterogeneous population of visually handicapped children and youth and makes recommendations for programmatic research.

In summary, the expected outcomes of the reviews and syntheses of research in the five areas in this section on the education of visually handicapped children and youth were the identification of research and development needs, the formulation of an action program of research, and the development of procedures to translate research findings into practice. All of the authors were guided by the goal of improving practice in the education of visually handicapped children and youth on the local level.

National Estimates of Prevalence and Demographics of Children with Visual Impairments

CORINNE KIRCHNER, Ph.D.

American Foundation for the Blind

Abstract—Conceptual distinctions are essential to clarify research on demographic statistics about children with visual impairments. *Prevalence* is distinguished from *incidence*. Also *pathology*, *impairment*, *disability*, and *handicap*, are distinguished in terms of special education, formulated as services designed to reduce or eliminate *disabilities* (limitations in performing tasks, e.g., reading) and *handicap* (limitations in performing roles, e.g., student) for children with impairments and "pathologies" (physiological anomalies and their causes).

The findings of national databases on children with vision problems are assessed for educational policy planning. A major conclusion is that the "child count" compiled by the Office of Special Education Programs is inadequate for planning resources needed to serve visually handicapped children. The limited data on demographic characteristics of such children—age, sex, race—are reviewed.

Recommendations include pursuing the aims of a current "Feasibility study" for an improved national register, with data on demographics and causes, for local area as well as national estimates.

AIMS AND OVERVIEW OF THIS CHAPTER

Information on the number and characteristics of children with severe visual problems is important for special education personnel. The data are needed not only to plan educational services, but also to evaluate them. For example, has outreach been effective? Have sufficient resources—staff and materials—been mobilized? To answer, one needs to know how many children are eligible for services, and how many are receiving them. Also, a national demographic profile of these children is needed to help judge whether findings from small, local studies of social, cognitive, or other developmental functioning can be generalized (see Warren's chapter).

Policymakers increasingly rely on population statistics to allocate resources; statistics are thus vitally related to the special educator's ability to accomplish program goals. Social factors enter into how demographic statistics are generated, and used. These connections point to some of the inherently intriguing aspects of this topic. (Kirchner, 1985, chap. 5).

Indeed, the practical importance of such statistics is so great that a danger arises. Administrators and teachers may rely too heavily on data that are inadequate for their purposes, simply because some data are needed. Given the current weak state of research on prevalence of visual impairment, combined with economic and political pressures to cut back on specialized resources for groups with low prevalence characteristics, that danger seems a reality.

Therefore, a major aim of this chapter is to illuminate technical issues in counting and describing the population of children with severe visual loss. The challenge is to maintain the link between technical research issues and the educational practitioner's concerns.

A key to meeting the challenge lies in the fact that conceptual issues in measuring the population are connected to one way of looking at the central aims of special education. Key concepts to be clarified are *pathology*, *impairment*, *disability*, and *handicap*. Using these conceptual distinctions, the aims of special education can be stated as to remove the handicap and reduce the disabilities of children with impairments. The concepts apply broadly to special education but, in the section on "Definitions", they are discussed in relation to vision problems.

The next section, "Types and Sources of Databases", describes the sources for statistics on children with vision problems. The sources will be classified according to whether they collect data mainly for research or as a byproduct of providing special education services.

With the conceptual and operational bases for data collection clarified, findings are reported in the fourth section. National findings on prevalence and incidence of severe visual loss among children are covered first; then evidence is examined on variation according to demographic characteristics. The challenge here is to extract from available data, in spite of acknowledged weaknesses, estimates that can be useful to planners, providers, and evaluators of services for visually handicapped children.

The final section presents recommendations for collecting, reporting, and using data on this population. The aim is to provide realistic rather than idealistic suggestions in an area of research that, at the present time, one might consider "severely handicapped."

DEFINITIONS

Prevalence and Incidence

The terms *prevalence* and *incidence* are often used interchangeably. However, the field of special education could benefit from keeping them distinct, as does the field of epidemiology.

Prevalence is reserved for the meaning usually assigned to both terms, that is, it refers to the extent that a characteristic, for example visual loss, occurs in a population *at a single point in time*. Prevalence figures are usually reported for a given year, but that is a shorthand to indicate either a single date within the year on which the information was collected, or an "average day" estimated within a longer period of actual data collection.

Incidence refers to the number of *new* occurrences or cases in a population, within a defined *time span*, usually a year.

Both prevalence and incidence can be expressed either as the absolute number of individuals in the population of interest, or as a relative number or *rate*, that is, the number per standard base, for example, 100 or 1,000, and so forth.

Prevalence and incidence figures will be similar if they refer to infants 1 year old or younger, or to conditions from which most people either recover or die very quickly. Otherwise, prevalence figures will be larger than incidence figures. Because special education is concerned with long-term conditions, and a rather wide age range, one should expect a sizable difference between statistics of incidence and prevalence. To illustrate, in a given year the prevalence of blindness among children who are, say, 3 years old (or who are in a range of ages, such as 3–5 years old) is expected to be higher than the incidence of blindness for the same age group; that is because incidence is comprised only of the children who first became blind in the study year, whereas prevalence also includes those who became blind at younger ages, including at birth.

Because the search for medical causes can be pursued more effectively by establishing the correlates of new cases, epidemiologists tend to be more interested in data on incidence than prevalence (Susser, 1973). Educators and rehabilitation professionals tend to focus on prevalence data because they describe the population who may need their services at any given time. However, since the services needed by recently impaired children presumably differ from the needs of longer-term cases,

incidence data could also be useful for educational program planning. For example, a child's initial assessment for program placement may use criteria and professional resources that are different from those required for later assessments of social-emotional adjustment and educational progress.

The task of promoting precise use of these terms is hampered by the fact that the term *low incidence population* has gained a toehold in special education, even though, technically, *low prevalence* is usually meant. For some purposes, this misuse should not cause problems, since the targeted categories—mainly children who are visually impaired, hearing-impaired, or orthopedically impaired—are lower both in incidence and in prevalence than the categories with which they are being contrasted. (For example, see 1982 amendments to the California Education Code). But if there were clarity, it would help push the need to collect better data on incidence—data that are virtually nonexistent—as well as on prevalence. (See Algozzine & Korinek, 1985, for a recent example of correct usage as applied to data on special education.)

Pathology, Impairment, Disability, and Handicap

Whether one seeks measures of prevalence or incidence, the first step is to specify the phenomena to be observed. That might seem obvious, but it may be overlooked because conventional use of terms hides some conceptual confusion.

A bit of history highlights the point. In the early 1960s Stevens (1962) argued that special education was seriously hampered in developing both theory and practice because of confusion in the concepts and terminology used by the field to identify its population and its activities. He observed that the confusion stemmed from applying to the educational situation concepts that are based on the medical model.

Stevens tackled the task of formulating a taxonomy and classification system appropriate for special education. He designed the system to retain the necessary linkage to underlying physiological conditions that characterize students served in special education, while specifying a set of concepts geared to educationally-relevant aspects of those conditions. By his own assessment, the fruits of his labor (prepared as a doctoral dissertation) were both abstract and tentative. But it is important to recognize that the effort was not undertaken as a mere "academic" (in the sense of "impractical") exercise. Stevens had worked for many years in special education, and was stimulated to deal with the taxonomy problem by difficulties he had encountered in a curriculum development project for special education teacher training.

Stevens proposed that the three terms *handicap*, *disability*, and *impairment* should refer to distinct concepts, listed here in order from most to least educationally-relevant.

At about the same time as Stevens's effort, but with no apparent mutual awareness, social scientists concerned with programs serving disabled adults were tackling the same type of conceptual problems. The analytic framework that emerged differed only slightly from Stevens's. However, whereas Stevens's proposals seem to have gone unheeded in subsequent development of special education data collection, the alternative frameworks have been operationalized and used in demographic research. That work has been recognized in sources that are influential, at least potentially, with a range of policymakers and practitioners (Office of Technology Assessment, 1982; World Health Organization, 1980). Therefore, the following discussion draws upon the later work and applies it to the field of special education of visually handicapped children.

Conceptual Definitions

By contrast to Stevens's three concepts, several analysts (Haber, 1967; Nagi, 1969, 1977; Wood, 1980) have proposed a set of four broad concepts; unfortunately the latter authors do not all use the same terminology. Peterson, Lowman, and Kirchner (1978) applied these concepts to data on the prevalence of vision loss for all ages, choosing the set of terms adopted by the World Health Organization (1980), as is done here.

Pathology. This concept refers to the active stage of disease or trauma, that is, disruption to the biological structure or functioning of the individual. Relevant examples with possible effects on vision are diabetes, glaucoma, or cataracts. Measurement of this concept depends on the techniques of medical diagnosis, and treatment also falls squarely within the medical/surgical domain.

Impairment. This concept refers to residual defects in an organ or body parts that may remain after the active phase of a pathology (whether the pathology was of short duration or is a chronic illness). Examples in regard to vision include impairment of acuity, field of vision, contrast sensitivity. Ideally, impairment is identified by laboratory-type testing (e.g., visual evoked potential), in order not to confuse it with the social and psychological dimensions involved in the next two concepts.

Disability. This concept, unlike the previous ones, involves the whole person and refers to limitations in functioning in relation to specific *tasks*. Disability is affected by the presence of impairments but also involves social and psychological dimensions of the situation in which tasks are performed. Reading and

mobility are broadly defined types of tasks which may be affected by various types of visual impairment (or by other types of impairments). Clearly, the examples are educationally important tasks whose performance is affected by motivation, training, technology, and other social factors. Measures of disability include self-reports as well as observations by others.

Handicap. This concept differs from the previous one in that it refers to limitations in performance of major social *roles*, such as attending school or being employed. Roles can be viewed as complex combinations of specific types of tasks. Because of the importance of social factors in structuring roles and setting performance requirements, these factors are significant in creating, or removing, handicap. Ideally, measures of handicap would directly reflect the relevant social environment; for example, teachers' and parents' expectations should be studied when the focus is on childrens' ability to carry out the role of student. However, as a practical matter, such complex research designs are not applied to estimating the number of handicapped children.

Complexity and Severity

Consider these four concepts as a group. The order of presentation here reflects increasingly complex levels of organization from the point of view of individuals: starting with biological subsystems or organs, in reference to pathology and impairment; then moving to the "whole" person, functioning in relation to "tasks," in reference to disability; and finally, to the person in relation to "roles," that is, interacting in his or her social setting, in reference to handicap.

The order of the concepts is not intended to indicate increasing severity of health problems; rather, there are degrees of severity *within* each conceptual level of analysis.

Consequently, one cannot assume the degree of severity at one conceptual level directly from the degree of severity at another level. For example, a child may be severely handicapped, but have only minor disabilities, or vice versa. Furthermore, a person may be handicapped but have no disabilities or even significant impairments. That is the situation of people who face societal discrimination because of a stigmatized condition that has been cured or controlled, for example, former mental patients. That also applies to children who are mislabeled as mentally retarded based on cultural differences, as demonstrated by Mercer's (1973) research, and raised as a concern more recently by a U.S. General Accounting Office study of special education programs (1981).

It is especially difficult, in fact generally not possible, to devise measures of mental and emotional *impairment* that can be isolated from the social contexts in which behavior is evaluated (see Nagi, 1977). This problem applies even more pointedly to the special education category of learning disabilities. Those problems are of concern here insofar as there may be misclassification of children between the visual and the mental, emotional, or learning disability categories.

In sum, in order to describe variation among children in terms of severity of their condition, different variables must be considered in connection with each of the four concepts. Educators' work is directed to reducing the severity of disability and of handicap. Impairment is only one of the variables involved in disability, and it is an even smaller part of the variables involved in handicap, as defined here.

"Legal Blindness"

Although operational measures are discussed in a later section, the definition of "legal blindness" (which is such a measure) requires mention here. In federal regulations for Social Security Administration programs, and in most state administrative codes, the definition of legal blindness (slightly paraphrased) is: "visual acuity of 20/200 or worse in the better eye, with best correction, as measured on the Snellen Chart, or a visual field of 20% or less." As an operational definition, it concerns visual *impairment* (but only limited aspects). Interestingly, only in relation to vision has a quantitative measure of severity of impairment achieved legal, that is, administrative, status. It is used to determine eligibility for various public benefits and has also been adopted by many private rehabilitation agencies.

Scott (1969), in a now-classic sociological study, summarized criticisms of legal blindness as a criterion of need for services. The essential point is that legal blindness refers to impairment but is used *as if* it were a measure of disability, that is, of functional limitations in tasks that involve seeing, and of handicap, that is, limitations in performing roles.

In spite of the long-standing criticisms, some programs rely on the legal blindness criterion: notably, the federal mandate for the American Printing House for the Blind to provide adapted materials free of charge to educational programs is limited to legally blind students. Consequently, statistical evidence on the population meeting that definition is examined below. (However, the federal legislation that mandates special education services does not limit the definition of *visually handicapped* to legal blindness. The impact of the two coexisting federal mandates on available databases about blind and visually handicapped children is also discussed below.)

Additional Comments on the Conceptual Framework

Measures of prevalence that rely on self-reports are often criticized for tapping a subjective component. In this conceptual framework, if the aim is to identify disability or handicap, it is appropriate to reflect the subjective component. The criticism is valid when self-reports are used to measure impairment.

The review of operational measures below will show that it is very difficult in fact to reflect the distinctions that are clear when dealing with abstract concepts. Nevertheless, measurement difficulties that the field of disability research currently experiences could be overcome with sufficient methodological work, just as in many areas of social science (and as in the physical sciences). It should be noted that the methodological limitations are a separate matter from political pressures that affect the operational definitions used in carrying out programs. The latter have been analyzed by Stone (1984) for national disability benefits programs, and by Tomlinson (1982) for special education in Britain; a similar analysis is needed for special education in the United States.

In the introductory section above, the aims of special education (and nonmedical rehabilitation) were described in terms of this conceptual framework. That is, the aims are to reduce the severity of disability and handicap, even when no further reduction of the severity of impairment is possible. (By contrast, the aims of medical care focus on treating or preventing the pathology, and on reducing or preventing the impairment.) It should now be clear that measures distinguishing these concepts are essential for evaluating whether special education goals are being met.

Gaining consensus on terminology to reflect these analytic distinctions will not be easy. Not only are these terms used interchangeably in ordinary discourse, but some of them have acquired "official" status in connection with public programs. The major examples are the programs administered by the Office of Special Education and the Social Security Administration. Although the former uses the term *handicapped*, and the latter uses *disabled*, both are concerned, from an analytic point of view, with people who have limitations in role-functioning.

Furthermore, some of these terms have taken on emotion-laden significance in connection with the activist movement to gain civil rights for people with disabilities. Just as the term *crippled* has become unacceptable because of its strong association with stigmatizing processes, some activists feel that *handicapped* is more stigmatizing than *disability* (Zola, 1984). Here, of course, these terms are used in an evaluatively neutral sense.

TYPES AND SOURCES OF DATABASES

How Databases Vary

Databases on children with visual problems differ in many procedural respects besides the concepts they measure (See Table 1).

TABLE 1

Summary of Major Sources of Statistical Data on Children with Vision Problems

Agency/Name of Database	Primary Function of Database	Timing	Population Covered	Method of Data Collection
U.S. National Center for Health Statistics —Health Examination Survey	Research	Multi-year "cycles"	National sample (no state estimates); age groups vary	Standardized examinations
Health Interview Survey	Research	Annual (some measures at longer intervals)	National sample (no state estimates); all ages	Household interviews
U.S. Bureau of the Census —"Survey of Income and Education"	Research	1976	National sample (state estimates); all ages	Household interviews
—"Survey of Institutionalized Persons"	Research	1976	National sample (no state estimates); all ages	Interviews with staff about residents
U.S. Social Security Administration —Supplemental Security Income	Program operation	Monthly	National roster, reported by state and county; all ages	Enrollment data
—Surveys of "Work and Disability"	Research	1966; 1972; 1978	National sample (no state estimates); minimum age ranges from 16–20; maximum 64 years	Household interviews
National Society to Prevent Blindness	Research	1978 estimates up-dated from 1970 "MRA" (see listing below)	National and state estimates; all ages	State Legal Blindness Registers
U.S. Office of Special Education Programs "Child Count"	Program operation	Annual	National and state; ages 0–21 depending on state	Enrollment data
American Printing House for the Blind	Program operation	Annual	National and state; all ages if enrolled in school below college	Enrollment data
State Legal Blindness Registers	Program operation	Ongoing	Certain states	Reports by eye care practitioners
—"Model Reporting Areas" (MRA)	Program/ research	Discontinued in 1971	16 states (see NSPB above)	

Some are of national scope while others are not. Among national databases, some can be used to obtain state or local figures, while others cannot. Some are collected annually, or at other regular intervals, while others were one-time efforts. Databases also differ in the range of social and demographic information that is collected, and in how the information is made available to users.

An important characteristic of databases relates to the purposes of data collection, classified according to whether the method is part of a research effort or part of the process of administering a program of services or income benefits.

Program statistics are the outcome not only of formal eligibility criteria, that is, the "conceptual definition," but also of the social processes that lead some people even to be considered for eligibility while others are not, and of factors that affect how criteria are actually applied to people who are considered. It is here that issues of "assessment," which result in programmatic decisions about individual children (see chapter by Scholl and Theodorou) become relevant to reviewing data on prevalence and characteristics of children served.

Research statistics are usually based on sampling procedures. Thus, it is necessary to know the sampling design and the extent to which it was fulfilled, that is, the response rate and any bias from nonresponse. Other aspects of research methods that may vary include the use of interviews (in person or by mail or telephone) compared to use of trained observers or analysis of documents.

Both program statistics and research statistics need to be evaluated for possible biases. The difference is that usually more information is given that would permit that evaluation in regard to statistics generated for research.

To a large extent, these characteristics of databases are associated with the agencies that produce them. The major sources are described next, to facilitate the later discussion of findings and to assist the reader who wishes to pursue the issues raised in this chapter. Additional details will be taken up as relevent in the section on findings. The databases are classified by purpose, that is, research or program statistics.

Review of Major Sources of Data

Sources of Research Databases

Each of the three federal agencies described below uses state-of-the-art sample survey methodology, and devotes some of its resources to advancing those methods. The fourth listing, a private agency, has published secondary analyses based on state legal blindness registers, and on some federal statistics, and has conducted special studies.

National Center for Health Statistics (NCHS). Two divisions of this federal agency, founded in 1960, produce periodic prevalence estimates of vision loss for the noninstitutionalized population of the U.S.: the Health Examination Survey (HES) and the Health Interview Survey (HIS).

HES conducts actual examinations on its sample, using physicians and other health professionals at various locations around the country, under testing conditions that are standardized as much as possible, including special training of the testers. Although subjects may be interviewed, it is the objective testing that qualifies this database as providing information on visual *impairment*. Because of the practical requirements of transporting subjects and conducting examinations, HES works in "cycles" that span years. Each cycle focuses on a segment of the population, for example, children from 6–11 years, and on certain health measures. The sample size does not permit state or local estimates and limits detailed analysis according to demographic correlates.

HIS uses a much larger sample of households; nevertheless, according to NCHS's sampling design and stringent criteria for reporting statistically reliable estimates, state estimates are not given. Trained interviewers conduct standard interviews in the home, covering all who live there. Representative subsamples are interviewed each week, so that data reported for a given year can be considered an average over the year. Where possible, persons over 16 are interviewed directly; however "proxy respondents," usually the mother, are accepted. The interview covers health conditions and their effects, utilization of health services, and many social and demographic characteristics. In spite of the length of the basic form that is repeated each year, some topics have been covered only at intervals, including measures of visual problems.

HIS publications use the term *impairments* to report about aspects of vision problems, but because of the self-reporting technique, the responses are weak indicators of impairment, while they can be considered more appropriately as measures of disability and of handicap.

Bureau of the Census. Although the decennial censuses of 1970 and 1980 contained questions related to handicaps, no information on vision or other underlying impairments was collected.

One of the Census Bureau's special studies, the 1976 "Survey of Income and Education," represented the noninstitutional population and included some questions on handicapping conditions. It is of interest here because its very large sample covers all ages and permits estimates at the state level. Another one-time study in the same year, the "Survey of Institutionalized Persons," provided a measure of visual loss as reported by staff members for a sample randomly selected in residential schools and other long-term care institutional settings. Some data are reported separately for persons under 18 years old (U.S. Bureau of the Census, 1978).

Social Security Administration (SSA). Unlike the two previous agencies, SSA's primary mission is to administer several programs, including Disability Insurance and Supplemental Security Income (SSI) for "the Blind," that is, legally blind people who meet the test of low income. Statistics on the count of children who receive "SSI-Blind" payments are available, annually and monthly, by state and by county (not discussed herein).

However, SSA also has a research office that has conducted periodic (1966, 1972, and 1978) representative sample surveys of the general noninstitutional population concerned with disability, focusing on work roles. That focus limited the age span covered; the oldest age is 64 whereas the lower boundary varied from 16 to 20 years across studies. Unfortunately, the sample sizes at the younger ages are too small to yield useful descriptions of visually handicapped youth in the "transition years" from school to work or other community situations. This drawback limits the SSA "Work and Disability" surveys' relevance here, but they are important as a model of attempting to operationalize the key concepts and to examine empirical relationships among them.

National Society to Prevent Blindness *(NSPB). This private agency has oriented its research concerns, as appropriate to its mission of prevention, to the concepts identified here as *pathology* and *impairment*. NSPB has been the primary source of estimates of the prevalence, incidence, and causes of legal blindness, which in turn are based on a set of state legal blindness registers (see below).

NSPB is also a source of secondary analysis of data on the prevalence of severe visual impairment, eye injuries, and eye care utilization, collected by the National Center for Health Statistics (NSPB, 1980).

---

* NSPB has developed, and some school districts have adapted, a standard children's eye report form; it also fosters vision screening programs for preschool and school-age children.

Sources of Program Databases

Office of Special Education Programs (OSEP). As part of this agency's responsibility for administering the major federal programs dealing with education of "handicapped children," statistics have been reported annually since 1976–77 on the number of children served under PL 89-313 and PL 94-142, grouped by the type of impairment that the schools have identified as the source of educational handicap. Because this database is used in annual reports to Congress, and therefore is influential in policy planning and evaluation, its limitations merit considerable attention, specifically as they apply to visually handicapped children. (For recent general critiques, see Algozzine & Korinek, 1985; Gerber, 1984; Greenburg, 1984). Some formal aspects of the database are outlined below.

Although the presence of an impairment must be established, the determination of a child's acceptance into the program, by design, depends primarily on the professional judgment of educators that some special services are needed for the child to fulfill role requirements. Analytically, then, the eligibility criterion is intended to identify children who are handicapped, that is, limited in the role of student.

The annual "child count" is intended to follow uniform national reporting standards (taken as of the same date, using standard categories for type of handicapping condition and educational placement), but there is wide variation in definitions for eligibility and actual procedures at the local and state levels. Since children are to be reported in only one impairment-related category, a key question concerns how children are reported if they have visual impairments along with other impairments. One of the reporting categories is "multi-handicapped," with no further breakdown of the combinations of conditions.

Data are reported by handicapping condition and age (in broad age groupings) and by educational placement, but with no other demographic characteristics.

The American Printing House for the Blind (APH)

APH receives federal funds to provide schools with adapted educational materials for blind students, using the legal blindness definition. "Students" includes adults in programs below college level. An annual register is compiled from reports on a standard form submitted by programs that serve eligible students. It is the reporting agency's responsibility to obtain evidence of the students' legal blindness status; APH does not conduct validation studies. Information reported covers grade level, residential school for the blind or other type of program, visual acuity, broad categories of other handicapping conditions, and type of reading method; birthdate was added in 1984, but no other demographic data are obtained.

State Blindness Registers

Some states maintain "registers" of people who are reported by eye care practitioners to be legally blind. Registers obtain information on age and address and therefore, at least in principle, permit analysis in terms of local units that are useful for educational planning (taking into account the limitations of the legal blindness criterion).

A 1985 survey found that about half the states then maintained a register, and that their procedures varied widely (DeSantis & Schein, 1986). Recent studies in New York state (Alfasso & Haggerty, 1984) and New Jersey (1983) raised serious questions about the accuracy of registers they maintain. By contrast, Massachusetts devotes resources to updating its register and has found it useful for conducting needs assessments of its legally blind population, covering all ages and reporting data for geographic localities within the state (Massachusetts Commission, 1983).

Although current registers are not used to obtain national data, an earlier effort to make national estimates by projecting from a small number of states that agreed to follow standards of reporting is still the basis for estimates issued by NSPB. The project, known as the "Model Reporting Area for Statistics on Blindness," is described more fully later in this chapter.

RESULTS

Prevalence and Incidence of Severe Visual Impairment

Findings and Limitations of the Health Examination Survey (HES)

The HES studies offer a tantalizing array of findings based on standardized vision testing, clinical eye examinations, and medical histories. Those techniques are appropriate for measuring visual *impairment*, that is, the physiological aspects of vision. The testing procedures are designed to minimize sociocultural variables, such as familiarity with print materials, even if they cannot avoid such factors completely.

At first glance the HES study cycles appear to be a goldmine for describing the population of children who require special education due to vision problems, in view of the "objective" testing of representative samples of the general population, even though the results are becoming rather dated. (Table 2 shows the study years and age groups covered by HES cycles with published results on vision. More recent HES cycles have not included measures of vision).

TABLE 2.

Years and Age Groups in HES Cycles
With Tests of Vision

Cycle	Study Years	Age Span	NCHS Publications[a]
1	1960–62	18–79 years	June 1964; April 1968; Aug. 1973
2	1963–65	6–11 years	Feb. 1970; Feb. 1972; June 1972; Aug. 1972
3	1966–70	12–17 years	May 1973; Nov. 1973; Jan. 1974; Dec. 1974; Nov. 1975
4	1971–72	1–74 years	March 1977; Aug. 1978

[a]Some of the later publications include analyses from earlier cycles.

Some of the findings will be summarized here, anticipating that on balance they have limited applicability for special education. They illustrate the general point that measures of impairment reveal little about educationally-relevant disabilities. Specific caveats are pointed out along with the discussion of findings.

Note that these data refer only to prevalence; incidence data are particularly difficult to gather reliably and are rarely reported.

Of the many aspects of impairment tested by HES, binocular acuity is most pertinent here. (Other tests, depending on the study cycle, included: monocular acuity, near and distant, in each eye; motility; pinhole test; retinoscopy; lateral phoria at distance and near; and clinical observations, e.g., of the condition of the lids, scleras, pupils, irises.)

Among 6 to 11-year-olds (Cycle 2), 6% tested at 20/70 or less for distance, the cut-off point sometimes used to identify visual impairment likely to lead to educationally-relevant disabilities. (But see Hatfield, 1975, who suggested 20/50 or less, after correction, as the relevant cut-off. Most states in fact do not use an acuity cut-off to determine visual handicap for special education eligibility, nor is any cut-off specified in PL 94-142.)

Among 12 to 17-year-olds (Cycle 3), many more, 17%, tested at 20/70 or less for distance vision. (Tests at near, and for monocular acuity, yielded slightly higher rates.)

Although the 6 to 17-year-old span was also included in the next cycle, 1971–72, only monocular acuity was tested, and the sample size and response rates were much lower, so that comparison is not warranted. It is noteworthy that the ophthalmological examination portion of that cycle was discontinued after a subsample was completed, due to difficulty in obtaining ophthalmologists around the country to conduct the tests under National Eye Institute supervision (NCHS, Aug., 1978).

The rates just reported, it is essential to realize, if applied to the current population of children in those ages, would yield numbers that are very much larger than any count of visually handicapped children in special education programs. Given the strength of HES methods, can the rates be used to estimate the eligible unserved population? The answer is "no," for two major reasons.

First, they refer to *uncorrected* acuity. NCHS reports that few 6 to 11-year-old children used glasses (or contact lenses); therefore uncorrected vision was close to what would have been found with "usual" correction, but the study did not test "best" correction.

Among 12 to 17-year-old children, one-third did use glasses and most brought them to the study site. When the latter were retested, only 1% were at 20/70 or less. Overall, including children who wore glasses and those who did not, 0.8% tested at 20/70 or worse with usual correction. (NCHS, May, 1973). In this cycle, refraction potential, that is, "best" correction, was tested: most children could be improved to 20/20. From the tables shown, one cannot deduce how many children could be corrected to no better than 20/70 for binocular vision, but clearly it is fewer than the 0.8% found with usual correction (NCHS, Dec., 1974).

Second, these estimates do not distinguish between temporary and long-term impairments. Some children had conditions that might improve in a brief period, such as minor infections or injuries, or even if more serious, might respond to medical treatment. NCHS's analyses address this issue only partially and indirectly, by suggesting that some of the differences in impairment rates between socioeconomic groups might be explained by differences in access to medical care.

These issues also apply, of course, to lower acuity levels. Children who tested at 20/200 or less are of special interest because of the legal blindness definition. Here the data present an additional problem, since the smaller numbers have high sampling variability and therefore are less reliable. The results for uncorrected binocular acuity at that level were 0.8% among children 6–11 years (NCHS, Feb., 1972). Among children 12 to 17 years old, the estimate of 4% with no correction dropped to 0.1% with usual correction (NCHS, May, 1973) and lower with "best" correction (NCHS, Dec., 1974). To this number should be added those with a visual field of 20° or less, but testing of field was not included in the studies.

The last point has more general implications. Although it has been emphasized that the HES could lead to overestimates of special education needs based on poor acuity, other types of visual impairment must be considered. In fact, there is no way to determine from the HES reports how many children had none of the tested impairments, and how many had combinations of impairments at specified levels of severity (not to mention aspects of visual impairment that were not tested). However, data are given to show that children were likely to have more than one type of tested visual impairment.

The HES findings on impairments are perhaps best viewed as indicators of what might be found in a typical school or community vision screening (taking into account the age and socioeconomic characteristics of the local population). Even if children are referred for screening *because* they are viewed by school nurses, parents, or teachers as potentially in need of special education services due to visual impairment, a substantial portion of them may be found to have conditions that can be treated medically or with corrective aids, or to have impairments that were misinterpreted by the referrer as visual.

For example, Roessing (1980) found that about half of a referred group of 138 (in a school district of 31,000 that had been serving only 60 children as visually handicapped) did not require special education services related to vision. Equally significant, of course, the other half, a large portion of whom were already being served in other special education categories, was found to need such services.

Another limitation of HES findings for the purpose of estimating the prevalence of visual impairment, which partially counteracts the factors leading to an overestimate, is that estimates are not available (or considered reliable) for the youngest ages.

Finally, one must consider possible trends over time, since the various cycles span 15–20 years. Although the HES cycles cannot be compared for the same age groups on binocular vision, NCHS did compare findings on monocular acuity for the 12 to 17-year-olds in 1966–70 with those studied in 1971–72, and detected some improvement. The report speculates that this may reflect "improvement in eye care and in socioeconomic conditions [but also may be due to] differences in testing methods and examiners" (NCHS, March, 1977). Among children 6–11, for whom the acuity tests were not comparable between the 1963–65 and 1971–72 studies, there was a slight increase in the percentage who wore glasses, from 10% to 12%.

It does seem likely that the passage of Medicaid in 1965 and other "Great Society" antipoverty programs led to improved access to care in that period, which may have continued. However, poverty indicators suggest that sharp early gains soon stabilized and are beginning to reverse. Between 1959 and 1969, the percentage of children under 18 years old who were living in families below the federally-defined poverty level dropped from 27% to 14%; it rose to 16% by 1979 and to 18% in 1980 (Statistical Abstract, 1982–83).

Before leaving the HES studies on prevalence of visual impairment, it is interesting to consider what the projected number of children would be nationally, if the rates for visual acuity of 20/70 or less from the HES studies were applied to more recent population base data. This must be done with great caution, requiring broad assumptions to try to correct for the facts that temporary pathologies were included, that the testing was done with "usual" rather than "best" correction,

and that not all children who had glasses took them to the test sites.

If the rates reported earlier are arbitrarily cut in half to make that correction, the figures would be 3% of 6 to 11-year-old children and 0.4% of the 12 to 17-year-old group. Using 1981 population data yields approximately 700,000. As will be seen, this is much larger than the figures projected by any of the other databases, using different concepts and measures of visual loss. Possibly, the 3% rate is an unreliably high estimate from a small sample size, or cutting the observed rate in half was too conservative. But it is also useful to consider that the standardized clinical testing may in fact detect much higher prevalence of impairments of that severity than the numbers found when one focuses on measures of disabilities or handicaps that have significant educational consequence.

Findings and Limitations of NSPB Legal Blindness Estimates

Turning next to estimates of legal blindness among children, data have been projected by NSPB (1980) for the age groups "under 5 years" and "5-19 years." The national figures reported for 1978 in fact are projections from much earlier data collected on legal blindness registers in only 16 states, which covered about one-third of the U.S. population, and were not selected to be demographically representative.

Known as "the Model Reporting Area" (or MRA), those states cooperated with the National Institute of Neurological Diseases and Blindness (the predecessor agency to the National Eye Institute), in attempting to maintain uniform procedures, although some variation is recognized (Kahn & Moorhead, 1973). The MRA was discontinued by the National Eye Institute in 1971.

NSPB's techniques for making state and national projections from MRA data are explained in Hatfield (1973), but some details, notably a correction for a presumed undercount, are left unclear. Hatfield built on earlier work by Hurlin (1961) to create an estimating formula which assigns weights to three characteristics of each state's population that were significantly related to the prevalence rate of legal blindness in states considered to have maintained adequate registers. These characteristics or indicators are: the percentage who are nonwhite, the percentage who are age 65 or older, and the infant mortality rate (as an indicator of general morbidity status). It seems clear that the approach, while ingenious, is unsatisfactorily indirect. (The next step of projecting 1970 data to 1978 was a straightforward application of age-stratified rates to the later population base.)

Register data contain social biases that, unlike probability sampling error, are unmeasurable. Kahn and Moorhead (1973), for example, speculated that among all people who would qualify by the legal blindness definition, those who are of lower socioeconomic status

143

are more likely to be placed on legal blindness registers than middle- or upper-class people, and therefore that the count for nonwhites is more complete than for whites. Their reasoning was that poor people are more likely to be in contact with public health and welfare agencies, which would make the report to the register. However, Berkowitz et al.'s (1979) national sample survey, using telephone interviews, does not support this conclusion. That study found that, among persons self-identified as "unable to see to read ordinary newsprint," a higher rate of certified legal blindness was reported by those in upper income groups than in lower income groups.

There continues to be heavy reliance on the original MRA data and the NSPB projections, simply because no other sources exist to estimate prevalence, incidence, causes, and demographics according to the official definition of legal blindness.

Using the NSPB rates, in 1980 the estimated number of legally blind children under 20 years was about 41,500: 6,900 of those were under 5 years old (rate of 0.00042 or 42 per 100,000), and 34,600 were 5–19 years old (61.6 per 100,000). Evidence that these estimates are too low is presented later, in connection with the APH current count.

NSPB explains the additional weakness of its "incidence" estimates, which actually reflect the number of cases added to MRA registers during the year. There may be considderable delay between onset of a visual problem and addition to a register, either because onset was gradual, or because social factors, such as starting school, first bring individuals to attention.

Although the reported rates are open to serious question, when they are applied to the 1980 population, results show about 5,250 new cases of legal blindness under 20 years old: of those 1,600 would have been under 5 years old (9.8 per 100,000) and 3,650 would have been 5 to 19 years old (6.5 per 100,000).

Finally, the NSPB data provide the only basis for estimating the number of children who are "totally blind," a category of special educational concern. (This group was not identified in HES reports, presumably because of small sample size.) There are definitional issues even at this extreme end of the acuity spectrum, depending on whether one chooses to add to the group labeled "totally blind," those with no measurable acuity but with "light perception" (aware of light), and the nnext higher level, "light projection" (can tell the direction from which light is coming). These categories are often grouped as "functional blindness" (Genensky, 1978), or "no useful vision" (although some blind individuals contend that even light perception can be useful for mobility).

The data suggest that a much higher proportion of legally blind children under 5 years old are "functionally blind" than is found among children 5 to 19 years old, and the latter in turrn have higher proportions than succeeding age groups (this comparison also holds for the

"totally blind" subgroup). Nearly 50% of the under-5-year-old group, and 40% of those 5 to 19 years old, had "no useful vision," compared to just over 20% of older persons.

This result must be qualified by the fact that for a very large portion (nearly 40%) of the under-5-year-old group, visual acuity is reported as "unknown." When acuity *was* rated on the eye reports for this youngest group, as Genensky (1978) has speculated plausibly, physicians were likely simply to write "blind," since testing may not have been possible. It is also likely, however, that the causes of blindness among children do yield a higher proportion with no useful vision than is found among older adults. That would have been especially true in the historical period that produced these percentages, which include children of the RLF (retrolental fibroplasia) epidemic of the 1940s–50s. The latter point is supported by Hatfield's (1975) studies of legally blind schoolchildreen, conducted in 1958–59 and 1968–69.

The Rand Corporation study of costs of special education (Kakalik, Furry, Thomas, & Carney, 1981) distinguished between "functionally blind" and "partially sighted" children. The former were reported to have the highest cost per child compared to all of the other handicapping conditions. That conclusion has been criticized, among other reasons, because of possibly distorted calculations based on the presumed small number (which was not actually reported) of functionally blind children in the study (Kirchner, 1983).

Pathology (Causes) of Visual Impairment

Turning next to *causes* of severe visual impairment (referrred to as *pathology* in the conceptual framework outlined earlier), information is very limited. Although pathology occurs prior to impairment, it would have been misleading to start this discussion with a report of the various diseases or injuries that may produce long-term severe visual impairment because diagnostic categories have such a wide range of long-term effeects.

Educators' needs for information on causes of visual impairment are varied, but generally differ from those of health researchers, requiring that different aspects of diagnostic categories be emphasized (see, e.g., Jessop & Stein, 1985). For educators, such variables as sudden or gradual onset, visibility and related social stigma, type and degree of impairing effects (visual and other), variation over short and long time periods leading to uncertainty in management of daily activities, among others, are most relevant for planning services. For health professionals, main interest lies in, among other aspects, the specific etiology and the parts of the eye(s) that are affected, for planning prevention and treatment.

Current information on the nature and distribution of causes is grossly inadequate to meet the needs of either educational or health professionals; what little exists is collected and analyzed almost entirely from the medical point of view. There is, of course, some overlap in the types of information needed; for example, on causes that result from injuries or aggravated impairment associated with school activities.

Collaboration between educators and public health researchers in designing data collection efforts could improve the situation. Schools have the opportunity and authority to obtain diagnostic data but, as Hatfield's (1975) research has shown, even for legally blind children, medical eye reports in school records are often missing or incomplete. This may be because the information is not seen to be of practical use educationally. (However, the MRA registers which were "models" and were designed largely for epidemiological purposes, also had considerable missing information on diagnostic variables.)

The source for the following brief review of data on causes is the NSPB (1980) report based on 1970 MRA data, projected to 1978. According to etiology (not reported for 13% of children under 5 years, and 21% of those 5–19 years), "prenatal influence" was the majority category for both age groups, consisting mainly of hereditary conditions. "Infectious disease" (mainly rubella) was the next largest category for the under-5-year-old group (14%). For both age groups, "injuries/poisonings" (mainly "excess oxygen," i.e., retrolental fibroplasia) accounted for about 10%. "Neoplasms" accounted for about 5% in each age group, followed by "general diseases" (with no single disease accounting for as many as 1%).

When causes are classified by "site and type of affection," conditions affecting the optic nerve and optic pathway were of nearly equal prevalence with those affecting the eyeball, each about 25% for both age groups. Within these broad categories, the main types were optic nerve atrophy and glaucoma, respectively. Next, the broad categories of conditions affecting the retina and the lens were of almost equal prevalence (about 17%), consisting mainly of RLF followed by cataracts.

Considering etiology and type together, the three leading causes for both age groups were found to be, in declining order, prenatal cataract, optic nerve atrophy, and RLF. Not surprisingly, the leading causes for new cases (incidence) were the same as for prevalence in the under-5 group. For the 5 to 19-year-olds, other causes assumed more importance; specifically, albinism, myopia, and macular degeneration tied for third place, replacing RLF.

Prevalence and Incidence of Visual Disability

Educators typically are dissatisfied with measures of visual impairment, pointing out that levels of acuity, for example, may be poor predictors of how children use their vision to accomplish various types of tasks in realistic situations (Roessing, 1980; Weber, 1980). They seek measures of "functional vision," recognizing that both physiological and psychological factors enter into performance. Such measures for representative national samples do not currently exist. That problem is directly related to the state of practice in conducting educational assessments, which is discussed in Scholl and Theodorou's chapter.

NCHS's Health Interview Survey for some years included a question that may be considered an approximation to a functional measure, albeit reported rather than observed, in regard to reading (the question was dropped as of the 1981 HIS). Respondents were asked if they, or the household member for whom they were answering, are "able to see to read ordinary newsprint (even with glasses on, if applicable)." Those who answered they were unable to do so, or who earlier in the interview reported no useful vision in either eye, and who reported the condition was chronic or permanent, were classified as "severely visually impaired." (For children under 6 years old, the proxy respondent's report of "no useful vision" replaced the reading question.) This is more precisely a measure of visual disability than of impairment, because it deals with task-related performance.

For 1977, HIS estimated that about 37,000 noninstitutionalized children under 17 years old met this definition. Earlier, in 1971, the same measure had produced an estimate of about 29,000 (reported in NSPB, 1980). In NCHS's published reports (NCHS, May 1975) of this measure, the youngest category is "under 45". Since the base population of that age declined between those years, the rate rose notably from about 42 per 100,000 to about 56 per 100,000. That trend apparently goes counter to the findings given above for visual *impairment*. There are many possible interpretations for this difference, including the fact that the latter trend was measured only up to 1971–72 which is the earlier year available for the current comparison.

It is nevertheless intriguing to speculate that there are in fact countertrends occurring that reflect the difference in implications of measuring impairment and disability. It is possible that with better access to medical care, fewer children have impaired acuity, but that a greater emphasis in the schools on identifying disabilities (stimulated by the implementation of PL 94-142 during that period), or generally greater emphasis on reading at younger ages, has led to more children whose reading limitations are observed and reported by the parent-respondents to HIS.

Newacheck, Budetti, and McManus (1984) explore a number of possible interpretations of findings from the HIS that there has been a near doubling from 1960 to 1981 of reported handicap (not classified by type of underlying impairments) among children under 17 years old.

Comparing the prevalence rate (or number) estimated from the "reading disability" measure, with the estimates ventured above on the basis of the impairment measure, there is a massive difference, which also is subject to many possible interpretations. Of greatest concern is whether the survey situation is likely to lead to underreporting, that is, is there a motivational factor in reporting about disability which is not the same as the motivational factor in the actual reading task?

Although NCHS has conducted methodological studies on the general questions of proxy reporting, and both proxy and self-reporting of "stigmatized" conditions, they have not dealt specifically with the items on vision. In general, there is underreporting of stigmatizing conditions; however it is greater with self- than proxy reporting.

Probably more important than motivated underreporting is lack of awareness. For example, the latter seems to account for Roessing's (1980) finding that parents were much less likely than school nurses to be a source of referral for vision screening of children who seemed to demonstrate problems with seeing. Parents, however, were equally as likely as classroom teachers to make referrals, and more likely than several other categories of school personnel who presumably had less opportunity to observe the child's visual performance.

There is reason to expect that the prevalence of visual disability in reading is much lower than the prevalence of impairment, using standard acuity testing. Survey measures of disability reflect the fact that people adapt in various ways to task requirements; for example, children adapt to the reading task by holding the materials close to their eyes. Also, although the "newsprint" question is probably a good indicator of standard print size for older children and adults, children in younger grades usually use larger print, so that in practice, a given level of impairment is less disabling (and parents may not be able to answer this question as meaningfully).

This point illustrates that incidence figures require careful interpretation when they refer to disability. The emergence of "new cases" depends not only on the number of people who experience onset of impairment, but on the emergence of newly-relevant tasks. Thus, reading disability is not relevant at very young ages, and there may be age-related spurts in incidence as print size is reduced for older children. (Incidence figures are reported for this HIS measure by NSPB, 1980, but not separately for children.)

The HIS measure of reading disability may be a fairly good indicator of disability in various near-vision tasks, but provides an underestimate for educational purposes because it does not deal with mobility or other tasks that involve distance vision (including visual field). (In 1971, some questions were included on such tasks, but they were not analyzed by age.)

NCHS's estimate of the number of people with "other visual impairments" (even when wearing glasses) is sometimes added to the "severe visual impairment" figure, for a total estimate of the visually impaired population. For example, NSPB (1988) reports 641,000 children under 17 years with "other visual impairments" in 1977 (notably higher than in 1971). But most children in this category probably do not experience substantial limitations in educationally-relevant tasks (e.g., children who are blind in one eye but with good vision in

the other, about one-third of the category, and those who are "color blind.") It seems misleading to use these numbers to estimate need for special education services.

Mention should be made of APH data on the reading medium used by children on its register, considered here from the point of view, specifically, of seeking measures of disability in reading print. Kirchner, Peterson, and Suhr (1979) analyzed the trends from 1963–1978 in the rates of use of braille and/or large type and suggested several interpretations for the patterns found. There is a large and growing group who are reported to use neither braille nor large print but who, unfortunately, are not further classified according to whether they can use regular print, rely on aural methods, or are nonreaders. Thus the APH data do not permit one to determine how much of the declining rate of braille usage is explained by: (a) growth of a group who have *less* disability in reading print (i.e., partially sighted legally blind children who receive training or technology that gives them access to print); or (b) growth of a group who, because of multiple impairments including mental retardation, are *more* disabled in reading; or (c) by other factors such as an inadequate supply of braille teachers or materials.

To conclude this section, there is a great need for research tools that permit estimates of disabilities related to visual impairment. Ideally such measures would specify not only the nature of the tasks, but the conditions and techniques used to accomplish them, including special technologies that provide alternatives to usual visual techniques. This kind of information seems crucial for planning in the area of technology (see Scadden's chapter).

Prevalence of Visual Handicap

Measures that are most appropriately discussed from the point of view of the concept of visual handicap include program statistics, as well as population-based sample surveys which have tried to operationalize the conceptual definition given above.

In HIS, this measure is called "limitation of activity," referring to social roles appropriate to age groups: for children under 6 years, the major role is defined as engaging in "ordinary play with other children"; for 6 to 17-year-olds, it is attending school. People for whom a long-term impairment has been reported are asked about its effects on role participation, using four degrees of severity: (a) not limited; (b) limited, but not in *major* role; (c) limited in amount or kind of participation in major role; and (d) unable to carry on major role.

Peterson et al. (1978) analyzed this measure for people identified as having visual impairments, "severe" compared with "other," from the 1971 HIS. The analysis is merely suggestive for present purposes, because the under-17-year-old group was not analyzed separately. For all ages, it was found that only a minority (38%) of tthose with "severe visual impairment" were "handicapped," nearly half of whom reported they were *unable* to carry on their major role, and most of the rest reported they were *limited* in their major role. (As expected, much smaller proportions of people with "other visual impairments" indicated any limitations in their roles). It is likely that the proportion with reported limitations is higher among school-age children in part because of severity of visual impairment, but more significantly, because of the nature of role requirements in the school situation (compared to the situation of elderly people in retirement, who make up the majority of the severely visually impaired group).

The 1976 "Survey of Income and Education" yielded a much larger estimate of the number of children, ages 5–17, who were limited in major activity due to "serious difficulty seeing or blind"; the estimate was 190,000 (Bureau of Census, unpublished tables, reported in Kirchner et al., 1979). However, one is unable to derive from that study any estimates of severity, either of the visual impairment or of the handicapping effects; presumably, therefore, many children are included in the estimate who would not fit the criteria for special education programming.

In fact, the number of children reported as visually handicapped receiving services in special education programs is much smaller than the SIE estimate, but more in line with the HIS estimates. Theoretically, *if* all children were assessed according to functionally relevant measures of visual disability; *if* uniform criteria were used to define the need for special services and services were actually provided based on those criteria; and *if* visual impairments were always identified even when other types of impairments also required services, the resulting program statistics would offer a good measure of the conceptual definition of handicap. That is, they would reflect the requirements of role performance in the educational setting.

In practice, there are many reasons to question the uniformity and appropriateness of assessment, placement, and reporting practices of these programs, and therefore of the statistics they produce. The basic questions apply to all disability groups in the "child count" annually issued by the Office of Special Education Programs (OSEP), and are discussed in many sources (e.g., most recently, Greenburg, 1984). Analyses that focus on problems with the count of visually handicapped children have been made by Vaughn and Scholl (1980), Kirchner et al. (1979), and Kirchner (1983).

The strategy of these critiques in part was to compare OSEP and APH data, assuming that OSEP figures should be much larger since they include children who are legally blind as well as those with other degrees of severe visual impairment. Before expanding on that analysis, it is necessary to focus on the APH data.

The APH register has been growing continuously: from about 17,100 in 1963 to about 29,400 in 1978 (Kirchner et al., 1979), and has had yearly gains since then, to about 38,000 in 1983–84. (The latter number excludes adults, i.e., over 21 years, who are in educational programs below college level, a small but also growing part of the register.)

Since these are "program" statistics, they must be considered from that point of view. The total number is smaller than the estimated number of legally blind persons under 20 years based on NSPB rates, given above as 41,500. The discrepancy is plausible since older children who are not enrolled in school (i.e., highschool dropouts) are not in the APH count; also, although infant stimulation materials are available from APH, it is likely that many infants are not yet served by educational programs. Furthermore, although the APH roster includes children who are multihandicapped, one must assume that many such children are not reported because theirr educational needs based on the visual impairment are not being sserved, partly because some programs serving multihandicapped children are not aware of APH as a resource.

In terms of "incentives," schools are probably willing to report all eligible children who can use the educational materials provided by APH, since they are free. APH does not conduct validation studies, and it seems a small amount of "over reporting" occurs: Hatfield's (1975) study of a sample of the APH roster in 1969 found that about 5% of the children for whom eye reports were available did not actually meet the legal blindness definition. On the positive side, the APH reporting procedure has a long history supported with consistent efforts to maintain and upgrade awareness at local levels.

Turning to OSEP figures, in each year there has been little difference between the number it reported as "visually handicapped" and the APH roster. In fact, in 1981–82, the APH figure became slightly *larger* than OSEP's, and that discrepancy has grown (Packer & Kirchner, 1985). Furthermore, whereas APH's figure has grown each year, OSEP's has either declined or remained essentially the same between years, from 1977 through the latest data available.

In 1977–78, the number of visually handicapped children was just under 1% of the OSEP total; the overall total has grown, and children reported as visually handicapped (including the deaf-blind category) has declined, thus inching down to an even smaller percentage (Vaughn & Scholl, 1980). (In 1983–84, the visually handicapped count was 31,549; deaf-blind was 2,497, for a total of 34,046 or 0.7% of all children in OSEP statistics. These figures exclude children in territories outside the 50 states and Washington, D.C.) That, in turn, was only 0.07% of all children in the U.S.

Expressing the continuing concern about inaccurate OSEP statistics, Packer and Kirchner (1985) reported an analysis of a telephone survey of state vision consultants or their counterparts conducted by the American Foundation for the Blind and NSPB in 1984–85. The results, considered highly tentative because of partial response, suggested that perhaps 40% of visually handicapped children in the respondents' states were reported in OSEP's "multihandicapped" category (in addition to those who were separately reported as "deaf-blind").

OSEP had introduced the multihandicapped and deaf-blind reporting categories in the second year of the child count. At the time of the change, a decline in the visually handicapped number of about 600 suggested that that was the number of visually handicapped children included in either the multihandicapped or deaf-blind categories; substantial yearly growth of the multi-handicapped category in subsequent years suggests that the number who are visually handicapped within that group is much larger now.

Another source of suspected undercount includes classification of multihandicapped children into another category whether or not the visual problem is known. For example, in some states, there is a clear administrative instruction to report all children who are mentally retarded in that category, even if another impairment is also present. Other evidence comes from Roessing's (1980) study cited above, in which an intensive special visual screening effort doubled the number of children identified for special education services related to vision, compared to the "normal course of events"; one-third of those newly identified were already being served in other special education categories (mostly, it is interesting to note, "orthopedic").

Finally, there is anecdotal evidence, obviously difficult to substantiate, that school districts knowingly place some children in other categories even when vision is the only source of educational disability, because of the actual or suspected high cost of providing appropriate services to only one or two children in a school system.

Although one can only speculate, it is important to consider whether these problems are equally likely to exist in regard to other types of handicapping conditions. Problems of identification may occur for all types of conditions, but we suspect that an undercount, of relatively substantial size, is more likely for conditions that in fact have low prevalence. In part this is because per capita costs of serving such children are larger, while federal reimbursement to schools is based on head counts regardless of actual costs, creating a disincentive. Also, precisely because of low prevalence, professionals in the school systems may be less able to recognize visually-based problems or to make appropriate assessments (see Scholl and Theodorou's chapter).

The state of Nebraska has demonstrated that considerable improvement in finding and reporting visually handicapped children, along with systematic demographic data, is possible. In the early 1980s, that state contracted with Gallaudet College, which has conducted annual state surveys of hearing-impaired children for about 20 years, to design and process a similar study for visually-handicapped children. The number of visually handicapped children reported in Nebraska's schools has risen in each of the early years of the study, clearly a result of concerted effort to optimize reporting, although there may also have been some real increase in the number of eligible children.

To conclude this section, there is reason to stress the critically serious practical consequences of the apparent undercount of visually handicapped children in the OSEP prevalence data. These data are relied upon in federal planning for resource allocation; underestimates are most serious in regard to support for personnel preparation, since specialized teachers are a resource that takes a long time to develop. Discussion with OSEP staff reveals that the child count numbers for visually handicapped children have displaced the formerly used formula estimate of 1 per 1,000 that was based on a survey of school systems in 1962–63 by Jones and Collins (1966). That formula in the 1980s would yield about 25% more than the number reported as visually handicapped by OSEP.

Table 3 summarizes the findings that have been reviewed; it shows the estimated prevalence rates per 1,000 children in the specified study years and age groups of the general population, for the various concepts and measures of vision problems.

Demographic Characteristics—Prevalence Rates and Distribution

Available data permit only the most fragmentary picture of the demographic characteristics of the nation's population of children with visual problems. The small size and geographic dispersion of the population mean that small numbers are included even in the large national sample surveys; while the numbers may be sufficient for reliable estimates of overall prevalence, they definitely are too small to permit estimating demographic subgroups. This is particularly frustrating because those studies generally do collect a rich variety of data on social characteristics. By contrast, the program sources of statistics, for which concern about sampling variation does not apply, do not collect information on social characteristics.

Although this section therefore must be brief, it is worthwhile to indicate the framework that would be desirable to apply. Ideally, data would be presented on a variety of demographic characteristics such as ethnicity, gender, and socioeconomic status. Such information is educationally-relevant in various ways; it would, for example, aid in the development and distribution of career education materials that contain successful role models with whom the children can identify because they share both demographic and visual status characteristics.

Also, ideally, data on demographic variables would be shown in two ways: (a) their distribution in the population of children with visual loss, that is, providing a profile; and (b) as bases for comparing prevalence rates. To illustrate, in terms of the first measure, nonwhite children are a small percentage of the total population of visually handicapped children, even though the second measure would show that the prevalence of visual handicap seems to be higher among nonwhites than whites (Kirchner & Peterson, 1981a).

TABLE 3

Estimated Prevalence Rates of Visual Problems among U.S. Children Using Different Concepts and Measures for Specific Age Groups

Database Name[a]	Year	Ages/Institutional[b]	Measure (and concept)[c]	Prevalence Rate/per 1000	See Text Page for Comment
Jones & Collins (1966)	1962–63	School ages (no further specifics)/ includes inst.	Reports by school districts of children served in programs for the visually handicapped (VH)	1	page 148
NCHS—HES	1963–65	6–11 years/noninst.	Binocular acuity of 20/70 or less (distance)—no correction (VI)	60	page 142
NCHS—HES	1966–70	12–17 years/noninst.	Binocular acuity of 20/70 or less (distance)—no correction (VI)	170	page 142
NCHS—HES	1966–70	12–17 years/noninst.	Subgroup of previous group, tested with "usual" correction (VI)	10	page 142
NCHS—HES	1963–65	6–11 years/noninst.	Binocular acuity of 20/200 or less (distance)—no correction (VI)	8	page 142
NCHS—HES	1966–70	12–17 years/noninst.	Binocular acuity of 20/200 or less (distance)—no correction (VI)	40	page 142
NCHS—HES	1966–70	12–17 years/noninst.	Subgroup of previous group, tested with "usual" correction (VI)	1	page 142
NSPB	1970	under 5 years/ includes inst.	"Legally blind" (projections from MRA registers) (VI)	0.42	page 143
NSPB	1970	5–19 years/includes inst.	"Legally blind" (see previous item) (VI)	0.61	page 143
NCHS—HIS	1971	Birth–17 years/ noninst.	Reported inability "to see to read ordinary newsprint even with glasses." (For ages under 6, report of no useful vision.) (Disability)	0.42	page 145
NCHS—HIS	1977	Birth–17 years/ nonist.	Same as previous item	0.56	page 145
S.I.E.	1976	5–17 years/noninst.	Reported limitation in major role due to "serious difficulty seeing or blindness" (VH)	4	page 147
OSEP	1983–84	Birth–21 years/ includes inst.	Enrolled in special education programs under PL 94–142 or PL 89–313 and classified as "visually handicapped or deaf/blind." (VH)	0.77	page 147
APH	1983–84	Birth–24 years/ includes inst.	Legally blind enrolled in education programs below college level and registered for adapted educational materials. (VI)	0.86	page 147

a)—See text for full names; b)—"Includes institutionalized (inst.)" or "noninstitutionalized (noninst.)" refers to whether or not the database includes any children in residential schools for the blind or other long-term care institutions; c)—"Concept" refers to the conceptual distinctions discussed in the text. "VH" = visually handicapped and "VI" = visually impaired.

Each of these types of statistics is useful for different purposes. The first might be used, for example, to help evaluate how effectively the special education system is achieving the societal goal of diminishing historical differences between racial and sex groups in educational preparation for occupational choices. The second measure might be applied to assessing whether local areas are actually identifying the expected numbers of visually handicapped children, taking into account the demographic composition of their communities.

Finally, it would be important to be able to compare demographic findings according to the distinctions among impairment, disability, and handicap. Demographic profiles and subgroup rates probably differ for these concepts precisely because social selection processes—that is, statuses and roles assigned on the basis of demographic characteristics—enter into the definitions of disability and handicap.

For example, it is likely that children from lower social status groups have higher rates of impairment than their more privileged peers, because of poorer living conditions including access to medical care, but that the rates of handicap are even higher, because of fewer resources to compensate for disabling effects. These expectations have some support from research concerned with work disability among adults (e.g., Luft, 1978), but cannot be tested with available data for school children with visual impairments. Most of the available data comes from the HES cycles, or from the MRA, and therefore is limited to the concept of impairment.

1 Age

Results of the various eye tests and examinations in the HES cycles were analyzed for year-by-year age groups. The patterns are extremely complex, especially if all levels of impairment are included.

A clearer pattern emerges when only *severe* levels of impairment are considered: rates consistently increase with age, especially for distance acuity. But even this finding must be qualified, in part because of possible testing effects (NCHS points out that the tests used with very young children may have been "easier"). Secondly, as is true with all studies of age differences that come from cross-sectional research, it is impossible to know whether the results reflect aging or cohort effects. Since these data are from the 1960s–1970s, suspected increase in the rates of visual impairment at birth, along with other possible historical changes in access to eye care for young school-age children, could lead to different age patterns in today's population.

The MRA data from legal blindness registers in 1970 found much higher prevalence rates for the 5 to 19-year-old groups than for the under-5-year-old group. But as noted earlier, it is likely that underreporting was greater for the youngest age group.

OSEP reports data on visually handicapped children by age, but the data are not very meaningful, especially after taking into account other limitations of that database. The age groups 3–5, 6–17, and 18–21 are shown for children served under PL 94–142, but those served under PL 89–313 are grouped only as 0–20 years. Since states vary in their policies of counting children between the two programs, the age profile from PL 94–142 may distort the actual picture of children served in special education programs. (For a striking example, in Connecticut a state bureau had been designated to have responsibility for education of visually handicapped children even if they are placed in local schools; thus all visually handicapped children there were counted in the PL 89–313 statistics, a practice which has now been changed).

APH has started to collect birthdate information (mainly to aid in tracking children who have moved, rather than for descriptive purposes), but results have not yet been reported.

2 Sex

In general, on the various HES tests, boys had lower rates of visual impairment than girls, although the differences were quite small for some tests and for some age subgroups. (NCHS, Feb., 1970, May, 1973, Dec., 1974). However, based on ophthalmologists' examinations on youths 12–17 years, boys were substantially more likely than girls to have pathologies judged as "medically significant." These findings raise many questions: did sex-role expectations affect the physicians' judgments, or were eye pathologies less likely to result in impairment for teenage boys than for girls of that age?

NSPB's (1980) analysis of MRA legal blindness register data seems to go counter to the HES impairment findings by showing higher numbers, and rates, for boys than girls, especially in the 5 to 19-year-old group but also in the group under 5 years old.

Although APH does not report data by sex, Hatfield's (1975) analysis of a representative sample of the APH roster in 1968–69 also found a slight preponderance of boys in each of the 5-year groups from ages 5–19.

The contrasting patterns for boys and girls that emerge from the HES findings and from the legal blindness registers are not readily explained. Since none of the differences is large, it seems fair to conclude that they reflect artifacts of the methods rather than real sex differences in severe visual impairment at those ages.

It is plausible to hypothesize that there are sex differences in national rates of visual disability and handicap deriving from sex-role socialization even though the long-term social trend is toward diminishing sex differences in task and role expectations. No data exist to examine this hypothesis with children. (For analyses involving adult men and women with visual loss, see Peterson et al., 1978 and Kirchner & Peterson, 1981b).

3 Race

For educational purposes, ethnicity (i.e., the culture to which a child belongs, including language heritage, belief systems concerning blindness and achievement, etc.) is a more educationally-relevant demographic variable than race, to which it is related. The aim would be to understand the various subcultural contexts within which visually handicapped children function.

The 1976 "Survey of Income and Education" did gather useful information on ethnicity, including the language spoken at home, and might merit the considerable effort to analyze the data (which are on "public use tapes") for visually handicapped children. Apart from that possibility, limited data do exist by race, specifically Blacks compared to "all others." Because of the history of racial discrimination in our society, comparisons by race closely reflect socioeconomic differences, for example, levels of family income and education.

Kirchner and Peterson (1981a) examined several data sets across all ages for racial differences in prevalence rates of visual problems. For children, the main sources were the HES and MRA data. Overall it seems clear that prevalence rates of severe visual impairment are higher among nonwhites, explained mainly by their lower socioeconomic status. As noted earlier, even with higher rates, nonwhites are a minority among visually impaired children as they are in the general population.

CONCLUSIONS AND RECOMMENDATIONS FOR RESEARCH

Conclusions

The most remarkable conclusion from this review is how little is reliably known on either a national or local basis about the children who are being served by, or who could benefit from, special education geared to minimizing visual disabilities. Rather than propose a Utopian program of research to provide all the information that would be desirable, some early steps toward that eventual goal are suggested below.

But first, it is well to consider the rationale for *any* investment in this type of research, in view of limited financial resources that are available for practitioners, and for researchers in other areas of expertise that are clearly relevant to improving special education (e.g., research on child development). What might be the concrete uses of improved prevalence and demographic data? One way to deal with that issue is to consider what are the current uses of existing (and generally deficient) data. It is tempting to call for research on that question itself; in fact, a recent doctoral research project sheds some light by its in-depth examination of policy-making for special education for visually handicapped students in the state of Michigan (McIntire, 1987).

It seems clear that prevalence data *are* used by those who decide on the allocation of public monies to special education. The data may be considered directly, as in the tables included in OSEP's annual report to Congress. Or they may have an indirect impact, as in studies of special education costs by handicapping condition (Kirchner, 1983). Informed observers consider it a current crisis for education of visually handicapped children that teacher preparation programs are losing federal funding in part because of the OSEP data; as analyzed above, those data seem to be erroneous.

Another area in which current prevalence data (along with some demographic breakdowns) are called upon is in the decision making for market development of new technologies.

Apparently rare, but potentially productive, is the usage illustrated above (Roessing, 1980), in which an educator used expected numbers based on estimated prevalence rates to justify an outreach effort, and subsequently confirmed that a substantial number of visually handicapped children had not been identified for needed services.

Other uses that have been suggested in the preceding sections appear highly desirable, but perhaps are less pressing in the current climate of scarcity. Those uses include (a) the ability to assess generalizability of small-scale studies of visually handicapped childrens' development according to the demographic characteristics of the national population of such children, and (b) the ability to evaluate whether the goal of minimizing race and sex differences in educational outcomes, including occupational plans, is being met.

To an important extent, progress on these research goals is dependent on first meeting the needs identified in Scholl and Theodorou's chapter on improving educational assessment; it is only through work in that area that adequate measures for determining the prevalence of children with educational *handicap* can be devised.

Recommendations for Research

1. There should be more collaborative planning among federal agencies that collect data on children with visual impairments. A mechanism already exists for this purpose, the "Sub-Committee on Vision" within the Federal Interagency Committee on Handicapped Research under the aegis of the National Institute of Disability and Rehabilitation Research (NIDRR). The Committee does not have funding authority but can serve in a significant advisory capacity for its component agencies which do have funding authority.

Relevant here is the promising fact that NIDRR recently funded a feasibility study conducted in one state (Virginia) toward the long-range aim of mounting an ongoing national census of visually handicapped children. (The study was conducted by AFB and NSPB).

Major objectives of the study were: to identify visually handicapped children who also have other types of impairments, wherever they may be reported in the OSEP system; for each child included, to obtain data on visual impairment and causes (from eye reports available to schools), on basic demographic characteristics, and on certain aspects of educational placement and program (the latter serving as measures of disability and handicap); and to perform validation studies on a sample. If those objectives can be achieved nationally, it would go a long way toward meeting the needs identified in this review. In particular, such a database would be ideally suited to local area analyses (school districts, regions, or states).

Federal and/or foundation funding will be sought for the initial phases of the study, with the issue of long-range funding a matter for attention. The review of problems faced by prior efforts to describe the nation's population of children with visual problems makes clear that only a substantial effort, over several years, can hope to yield significant improvement in the database. Once such a continuing database is underway, it could serve as a sampling frame to facilitate meeting many of the research needs identified in other chapters of this volume.

Even if the proposed annual study gets underway, other steps should be taken to improve knowledge of prevalence, incidence, and demographics in the population of interest. No single study can meet all the informational needs, in part because independent efforts can serve as validation, and in part to expand the range of variables under study. Therefore, other suggestions are made.

2. Methodological studies of three broad types are needed: (a) to improve measurement of the concepts of visual impairment, disability, and handicap; and (b) to expand work on innovative methods of sampling "rare populations," that is, those with low prevalence. Two methods that seem promising are "multiplicity sampling" (Tourangeau & Smith, 1985), and "lists plus probability sampling" (Schein & Delk, 1974). Both are variants of standard probability sampling that identify larger numbers of the target population more economically than could be achieved by simply expanding the size of a probability sample.

The third type of study (c) would be to explore the effects of, and alternatives to, "proxy reporting" in interview surveys, specifically in relation to visually handicapped children.

These types of studies could be conducted on local rather than national samples, or could be added on to national methodological studies conducted for related purposes, for example, by NCHS, SSA, or the Bureau of the Census.

3. Efforts should be made to include one or two general questions in the nation's decennial Census that encompass handicapped people of all ages. (In 1980, the "disability" questions were asked only about people aged 16 years or older.) Recognizing that there is great competition for questions asked in decennial census, even in the longer version given to a sample, these questions cannot be expected to go into detail. The purpose of such questions would be to provide an efficient sampling frame for a postcensus disability survey, as was planned and even pretested in connection with the 1980 census but not carried out due to federal funding cutbacks. Such a postcensus study would provide much-needed detail on the nature of visual impairments, and especially of disabilities and handicap among children in the United States.

References

Alfasso, H., & Haggerty, M. (1984). *Assessment of services to the New York State blind population.* Albany, NY: New York State Department of Social Services.

Algozzine, B., & Korinek, L. (1985). Where is special education for students with high prevalence handicaps going? *Exceptional Children, 51,* 388–394.

Berkowitz, M., Hiatt, L., de Toledo, P., Shapiro, J., & Lurie, M. (1979). *Characteristics, activities and needs of people with limitations in reading print,* v. 2. New York: American Foundation for the Blind.

DeSantis, V. & Schein, J. Blindness Registers (Part 2): Blindness Registers in the United States, *Journal of Visual Impairment and Blindness, 80,* 570–572.

Genensky, S. (1978). Data concerning the partially sighted and the functionally blind. *Journal of Visual Impairment and Blindness, 72,* 177–180.

Gerber, M. (1984). Is congress getting the full story? *Exceptional Children, 51,* 209–244.

Greenburg, D. (1984). The 1984 annual report to Congress: Are we better off? *Exceptional Children, 51,* 203–207.

Haber, L. (December 1967). Identifying the disabled: Concepts and methods in the measurement of disability. *Social Security Survey of the Disabled* (1966 Report No. 1. Washington, DC: Social Security Administration.

Hatfield, E. (1975). Why are they blind? *Sightsaving Review, 45,* 3–22.

Hurlin, R. G. (1962). Estimated prevalence of blindness in the United States, 1960. *Sightsaving Review, 32,* 4–12.

Jessop, D., & Stein, R. (1985). Uncertainty and its relation to the psychological and social correlates of chronic illness in children. *Social Science and Medicine, 20,* 993–999.

Jones, J. W., & Collins, A. P. (1966). *Educational programs for visually handicapped children.* Washington, DC.: Government Printing Office, Office of Education (Bulletin No. 6).

Kahn, H. A., & Moorhead, H. B. (1973). *Statistics on Blindness in the Model Reporting Area, 1969–1970.* (DHEW) publication No. (NIH) 73–427). Washington, DC.: U.S. Government Printing Office.

Kakalik, J. S., Furry, W. S., Thomas, M. A., & Carney, M. F. (1981). *The cost of special education.* (No. N–1792–ED). Santa Monica, CA: The Rand Corporation.

Kirchner, C. (1983). Special education for visually handicapped children: A critique of data on numbers served and costs. *Journal of Visual Impairment and Blindness, 77,* 219–223.

Kirchner, C. (1985). *Data on blindness and visual impairment in the U.S.: A resource manual on characteristics, education, employment and service delivery.* New York, NY: American Foundation for the Blind.

Kirchner, C., & Peterson, R. (1981a). Estimates of race-ethnic groups in the U.S. visually impaired and blind population. *Journal of Visual Impairment and Blindness, 75,* 73–76.

Kirchner, C., & Peterson, R. (1981b). Men, women and blindness: A demographic view. *Journal of Visual Impairment and Blindness, 75,* 26–70.

Kirchner, C., Peterson, R., & Suhr, C. (1979). Trends in school enrollment and reading methods among legally blind school children, 1963–1978. *Journal of Visual Impairment and Blindness, 73,* 373–379.

Luft, H. (1978). *Poverty and health: Economic causes and consequences of health problems.* Cambridge, MA: Ballinger.

Massachusetts Commission for the Blind. (1983). *Directions for the 80's: A Needs Assessment of the Blind.* Boston, MA: Author.

McIntire, J. (1987). *State special education policymaking: The Michigan School for the Blind experience,* Ann Arbor, MI: The University of Michigan, unpublished doctoral dissertation.

Mercer, J. (1973). *Labeling the mentally retarded: Clinical and social system perspectives on mental retardation.* Berkeley, CA: University of California Press.

Nagi, S. (1969). Disability and Rehabilitation: Legal, clinical, and self-concepts and measurement. Columbus, OH: Ohio State University Press, 1969.

Nagi, S. (1977). *Disability in the United States: A plan for an informational system*. Washington, DC.: Office for Handicapped Individuals.

National Center for Health Statistics. (February 1970). Visual acuity of children—United States. *Vital and health statistics* (Series 11 No. 101). Washington DC.: U.S. Department of Health, Education, and Welfare.

National Center for Health Statistics. (February 1972). Binocular visual acuity of children: Demographic and socioeconomic characteristics—United States. *Vital and Health Statistics*, (Series 11, No 112. DHEW Publication No. HSM–72–1031). Rockville, MD: Author.

National Center for Health Statistics. (June 1972). Eye examination and health history findings among children. *Vital and Health Statistics*, (Series 11, No. 115. DHEW Publication No. HSM–72–10557). Rockville, MD: Author.

National Center for Health Statistics. (August 1972). Color vision dificiencies in children. *Vital and health statistics* (Series 11 No. 118 DHW Publication No. HSM–73–1600). Rockville, MD: Author.

National Center for Health Statistics. (May 1973). Visual Acuity of youths 12–17 years. *Vital and Health Statistics* (Series 11, No. 127. DHEW Publication No HSM 73–1609). Rockville, MD: Author.

National Center for Health Statistics. (November 1973). Examination and health history findings among children and youths, 6–17 years. *Vital and health statistics* (Series 11, No. 129. DHEW Publication No. HRA 74–1611). Rockville, MD: Author.

National Center for Health Statistics. (January 1974). Color vision deficiencies in youths 12–17 years of age. *Vital and health statistics* (Series 11, No. 134. DHEW Publication No. HRA–74–16160). Rockville, MD: Author.

National Center for Health Statistics. (December 1974). Refraction status of youths 12–17 years. *Vital and health statistics* (Series 11, No. 148. DHEW Publication No. HRA–75–1630). Rockville, MD: Author.

National Center for Health Statistics. (May 1975). Prevalence of selected impairments—United States—1971. *Vital and health statistics* (Series No. 10, No. 99. DHEW Publication No. HRA–75–1526). Rockville, MD: Author.

National Center for Health Statistics. (November 1975). Eye examination findings among youths aged 12–17 years. *Vital and health statistics* (Series 11, No. 155. DHEW Publication No. HRA–76–1637). Rockville, MD: Author.

National Center for Health Statistics. (March 1977). Monocular visual acuity of persons 4–74 years: United States—1971–1972. *Vital and health statistics* (Series 11, No. 201. DHEW Publication No. HRA–77–1646). Rockville, MD: Author.

National Center for Health Statistics (August 1978). Refraction status and motility defects of persons 4–74 years: United States, 1971–1972. *Vital and health statistics* (Series 11, No. 206), Hyattsville, MD.

National Society to Prevent Blindness. (1980). *Vision problems in the U.S.* New York, NY: Author.

Newachek, P., Budetti, P., & McManus, P. (1984). Trends in childhood disability. *American Journal of Public Health*, **74**, 232–236.

New Jersey Commission for the Blind and Visually Impaired. (1983). *Corrective action plan for needs identified in needs assessment*. Newark, NJ: Author.

Office of Technology Assessment. (May 1982). *Technology and Handicapped People*. Washington, DC.: U.S. Government Printing Office.

Packer, J., & Kirchner, C. (1985). State-level counts of blind and visually handicapped school children. *Journal of Visual Impairment and Blindness*, **79**, 357–261.

Peterson, R., Lowman, C., & Kirchner, C. (1978). Visual handicap: Statistical data on a social process. *Journal of Visual Impairment and Blindness*, **72**, 419–421.

Roessing, L. (1980). Identifying visually impaired children in a California school district. *Journal of Visual Impairment and Blindness*, **74**, 369–372.

Schein, J., & Delk, M. (1974). *The deaf population of the United States*. Silver Springs, MD: National Association of the Deaf.

Scott, R. (1969). *The making of blind men*. New York, NY: Russell Sage.

Statistical Abstract of the United States, 1982–83 (1982). 103rd edition, Washington, DC.: U.S. Bureau of the Census.

Stevens, G. D. (1962). *Taxonomy in special education for children with body disorder: The problem and a proposal*. Unpublished Ed. D. dissertation, Teachers College, Columbia University.

Stone, D. A. (1984). *The disabled state*. Philadelphia, PA.: Temple University Press.

Susser, M. (1973). *Causal thinking in the health sciences*. New York, NY: Oxford University Press.

Tomlinson, S. (1982). *A sociology of special education*. London: Routledge & Kegan Paul.

Tourangeau, R., & Smith, A. W. (1985). Finding subgroups for surveys. *Public Opinion Quarterly*, **49**(3), 351–365.

U.S. Bureau of the Census. (1978). *1976 Survey of institutionalized persons: A study of persons receiving long-term care*. (Current Population Reports, Special Studies, Series P–23, No. 69). Washington, DC.: Government Printing Office.

U.S. General Accounting Office. (September 1981). *Disparities still exist in who gets special education*. Washington, DC.: Government Printing Office.

Vaughn, M., & Scholl, G. (1980). Where have all the children gone? *DVH Newsletter*, **25**(2), 6–7. (Also see paper presented at meeting of Institute for State Education Consultants for the Visually Handicapped, Denver, CO., 1980.)

Weber, G. (1980). Visual disabilities—Their identification and relationship with academic achievement. *Journal of Learning Disabilities*, **13**, 301–305.

Wood, P. H. N. (1980). Appreciating the consequences of disease: The international classification of impairments, disabilities, and handicaps. *WHO Chronicle*, **34**, 376–380.

World Health Organization. (1980). *International classification of impairments, disabilities, and handicaps: A manual of classification relating to the consequences of disease*. Geneva, Switzerland: Author.

Zola, I. (1984). Does it matter what you call us? *Disability and Chronic Disease Quarterly*, **4** (3), 1–2.

Implications of Visual Impairments for Child Development

DAVID H. WARREN

University of California, Riverside

Abstract—A brief overview of the research literature on the effects of visual impairments on child development is presented, concentrating on perceptual and motor development, perceptual-cognitive development, language development, and socialization. A complete treatment of the state of the practice is not possible in such a work: instead, several examples are presented in which research findings have been either directly or indirectly translated into applied programs. The concluding section addresses critical research needs as well as needs for changes in the general context for research and dissemination of research findings.

Introduction

The purpose of this chapter is to review the state of research on the visually handicapped child, and to assess the relationship of the state of practice to the state of research. Before beginning the review of research, it is useful to make several introductory observations.

First, the continuous nature of development should be stressed. A child's success in school and elsewhere is significantly predictable from the child's preschool characteristics, which in turn are heavily related to his or her experiences during infancy. It follows that researchers must be aware of these developmental continuities and take them into account in designing their research; equally importantly, parents and teachers must be aware of the continuous nature of development, and assess the child's current characteristics and potentials in relation to his or her developmental history.

Second, the seemingly simple term *visual handicap* covers a wide range of children (see chapter by Kirchner for demographic considerations). Included are those who have never had any visual function, those who had normal vision for some years before becoming gradually or suddenly partially or totally blind, those with handicaps in addition to the visual loss (see chapter by Hammer), those with selective impairments of parts of the visual field, and those with a general degradation of acuity across the visual field. Thus it is misleading to think of visually handicapped children as being all alike, with the implication that they may all be treated alike with uniform success in educational or other settings.

In fact, this is an extremely heterogeneous population, and one which places correspondingly mixed demands on the people and agencies which deal with it. There are least three major sources of heterogeneity in this population, with their varying implications for treatment of visually handicapped children. The first source results from other handicapping conditions, either minor ones or ones that are major to the extent that the individual is considered to be multiply handicapped. Second, there are several important status variables related to the visual handicap itself. These include the degree of handicap, the age of its onset, the etiology of the handicap, and so on. It should be noted that these variables are not under the control of the individual or those who work with the child, and so while their effects should be understood, they cannot be changed by intervention. The third category, by contrast, consists of variables which can potentially be influenced. These include the vast array of environmental circumstances in which visually handicapped children are raised and educated. They are such factors as the nature of the physical environment, the sensory and learning environment, and particularly the social setting, including patterns of family interaction. It is imperative that these effects be understood by researchers as well as by those who have occasion to work with visually handicapped children.

Foremost among these environmental factors is the nature of the educational setting. Increasingly in recent years it has become prevailing practice to educate visually handicapped children in the public school setting rather than in residential schools for blind students. There is unfortunately little research that has addressed the relative advantages and disadvantages of these educational settings.

State of Current Research

The main goal of this section is a review of the implications of visual handicaps for the development of the child, especially for those areas of development that are related to educational needs or goals. There is far too much research literature to be reviewed comprehensively in a chapter of this length. Thus the approach here will be to identify major themes and to cite representative research findings. Where there are disagreements in the literature, they will generally be identified, with their various sources of evidence. The treatment will thus be exemplary rather than exhaustive. The reader is referred to Warren (1984) for a fuller treatment of the literature on the effects of visual handicaps on infancy and childhood development.

Sensory, Perceptual, and Motor Capabilities

Sensory Compensation

Sensory compensation is the notion that because of the lack or impairment of vision, visually handicapped children are somehow endowed with greater capacities in the remaining sensory modalities. In examining this question, it is important to separate the question of discriminative abilities from the question of attention to sensory information. On the first question, the evidence clearly does not support the compensation notion. Most studies have failed to find differences between visually handicapped groups and sighted groups or among various visually handicapped groups in sensory discrimination capabilities. Examples are Axelrod (1959), who found no differences between visually handicapped and sighted children in tactile light-touch and two-point thresholds, and Hare, Hammill, and Crandell (1970), who found no differences in discrimination of phonemic stimuli. On the other hand, there is some evidence that capacities for focal and sustained attention may be better developed among some visually handicapped individuals than is the case for the sighted population in general. This point holds particularly for auditory attention. A good example is a study by Witkin, Oltman, Chase, and Friedman (1971), who administered, among other tests, a test of perception of auditory imbedded figures. Totally congenitally blind subjects, age 12 to 19, were better able to recognize a simple tonal sequence in a larger auditory complex than a group of sighted control subjects.

In general, though, the sensory compensation notion, which has been advanced with mystical awe in the past, cannot be supported: the visually handicapped child (or adult) does not have keener senses than the sighted, but the visually handicapped child may have developed attentive capabilities to a greater degree than the sighted, although not to a degree that the sighted could not develop, given appropriate conditions.

Audition

For school-age children, the weight of the research evidence supports the conclusion that basic auditory discriminative capabilities are neither better nor worse in visually handicapped children than they are in sighted children, and there are no significant differences among most subgroups of visually handicapped children (excepting, of course, for hearing-impaired children).

For example, Hare et al. (1970) used a sound-discrimination test involving phonemic differences between pairs of words and found no differences between groups of children with varying degrees of vision. A general improvement in auditory discrimination over the age range of 6 to 10 years was found.

On the other hand, there is evidence that auditory attentive capabilities may become better developed in the visually handicapped child than in the sighted, as discussed above (Witkin et al., 1971).

Given the importance of audition as a substitute for vision in the acquisition of information, interest in the possibility of accelerated presentation of auditory textual material is not surprising. A "natural" speaking rate is about 175 words per minute (wpm). To date, the most effective means of providing acceleration beyond this rate is not the simple speeding up of a tape recording, which produces a Donald Duck-like jabber, but rather speech compression, in which very brief segments of the recording are excised at random. The potential usefulness of compressed speech depends on the comprehensibility of the material so delivered. Foulke, Amster, Nolan, and Bixler (1962) tested blind sixth- to eighth-grade Braille readers, with no previous experience with compressed speech, at rates of 175, 225, 275, and 325 wpm. Comprehension for the 175 and 225 wpm rates did not differ from that for Braille, although comprehension began to fall off for some material at faster rates. (The Braille reading rates for these subjects ranged from 57 to 70 wpm.) Gore (1969) compared the comprehension and one-week recall of material presented at 175 wpm with that for 270 wpm compressed speech and found no differences in recall or comprehension, although accelerated speech produced worse performance on both measures.

There are numerous studies with adults that document the specific role of auditory discriminative abilities in mobility performance. There is much less such information for children. An exception is the study by Worchel, Mauney, and Andrew (1950) on the "obstacle sense" in children. The subjects had become totally blind at ages ranging from birth to 11 years, and were 8 to 23 years of age at the time of testing. Of the 34 subjects, 27 could successfully avoid collisions with large objects placed in the travel path, and it was clearly demonstrated that their success was based on the use of auditory echo cues.

There is interesting evidence about variations among visually handicapped children in the ability to localize auditory targets. Spiegelman (1976) compared the auditory localization performance of early and later totally blind (and also sighted) children. The later blind group was significantly better than the congenitally blind group at localizing the targets. Spiegelman suggested that the auditory localization of later blind children was facilitated by a visual framework that was built up during the early years when vision was intact.

Touch

For visually handicapped children, the sense of touch is even more important than it is for sighted children, since it must be relied upon to mediate aspects of perception that vision would ordinarily perform. In addition to its general role as an important avenue of information about the world, touch is particularly important for certain specific functional behaviors, such as the acquisition of textual material via Braille and the perception of pictorial or other representative educational material, such as maps of the spatial environment.

The discrimination of texture by various groups of visually handicapped children is like that of sighted children, and visually handicapped children in particular show a significant improvement in texture discrimination over the early school years, with a leveling off of improvement by about the third grade (Nolan, 1959; Nolan & Morris, 1960). Berla' has conducted important research on the fundamentals of tactile discrimination, particularly those functions that are important for the perception of maps and other graphic displays. For example, variations in raised line width are more easily discriminable with wider than with narrower lines (Berla' & Murr, 1975). Increasing the overall size of a tactile stimulus from 1 to 4 inches produced slower, although not necessarily less accurate, discrimination, and increasing stimulus complexity also led to an increase in discrimination time (Berla', 1972). Morris and Nolan (1963) also studied the effect of size of tactile stimuli and found that stimuli smaller than 0.75 inches were judged less accurately than those larger than 1 inch in diameter. Interestingly, Nolan and Morris (1960) found a positive correlation between roughness discrimination ability and Braille reading scores at the end of the first-grade year. In a study of the Haptic discrimination of length, Duran and Tufenkjian (1970) found no change in the accuracy of length discrimination over the age range of 5 to 14 years, but they found interesting variations in the methods used by the children for the judgment of length, such as juxtaposing the two stimuli to be compared, using a palm span, referring to another body part, timing the finger's movement along the length of the stimulus, and listening to pitch differences between stimuli when they were banged against the table.

This finding is important in calling attention to the wide variation in strategies that visually handicapped children may bring to tactual as well as other perceptual and cognitive tasks. Berla's work is of particular note with respect to tactual strategies in map reading. For example, Berla' and Murr (1974) found that a vertical scan of a graphic map using the two hands together is more effective than the various horizontal scanning strategies. Different children spontaneously used different kinds of strategies, and Berla' and Murr found that in the early grades visually handicapped children benefited from training in the vertical scan strategy. Older children did not improve. In a related study, Berla',

Butterfield, and Murr (1976) found that children who scanned tactual shapes on a map with organized movements were better at discriminating those shapes, especially if they also searched for particular distinctive features of the various shapes. Thus it is clear that attempts to use tactile graphic displays in educational settings with visually handicapped children must be appropriately sensitive to spontaneous differences among children in strategies of processing tactile information, and should consider the possibility that training children, especially younger ones, in the use of the more effective strategies may be productive.

There are also interesting findings relating the successful reading of Braille to various tactual discrimination abilities. For example, Weiner (1963) found that good Braille readers (reading at or above their actual grade placement) were better than poor Braille readers (reading at least one grade below actual grade placement) on several tactual discrimination tasks, including judging differences among similar shapes and sorting blocks into sets on the basis of characteristics such as shape, texture, and thickness. It is not clear whether the better tactual perception by the better Braille readers was a cause or a result of their more effective Braille reading.

In general, there are not consistent patterns of difference in tactual perception between sighted and blind children. However, tasks involving more complex or integrative tasks do show some superiority of sighted children. Gottesman (1971), for example, used a relatively simple form-matching task in which the subject was given a stimulus form and was then asked to choose a matching form from a set of four alternatives. There were not significant differences in performance between the children who were severely visually handicapped from birth and blindfolded sighted children. But in a task involving more integrative demands, Worchel (1951) found significantly better performance in a blindfolded sighted group than in a severely visually handicapped group. In this task, the subject felt the two parts of a form, one part with each hand, then attempted to choose one form from a set of four that corresponded to the spatial combination of the two separate forms. With somewhat older children (age range 12 to 19), Witkin, Birnbaum, Lomonaco, Lehr, and Herman (1968) found that children totally blind since birth were worse than blindfolded sighted children on a tactile embedded figures test, which involved having the subject find a simple raised-line figure that was embedded in a complex figure.

Tactile tasks may also become more complex when memory is involved. If a form has to be remembered to be compared with another, additional demands are involved. Working with textual materials, Millar (1975) established that tactual features are encoded in memory separately from their corresponding phonological features. In a related study, Millar (1978) examined the nature of the tactile Braille features that are, in learning

Braille, associated with the letter names. She determined that young visually handicapped children tend to process Braille patterns as a set of related dots, rather than as a single unified configuration. Presumably, exercises designed to induce the child to process the dot pattern as an integrated shape rather than as a series of dots would simplify the associative learning process.

Spatial Relations

It was noted above that Spiegelman (1976) found better auditory localization performance by later blind children than by those blind from birth, and suggested the involvement of a visual framework in the former, developed as a result of early visual experience. In his study of tactual form perception, Worchel (1951) found better performance by the later blind than the early blind subjects when spatial integration was involved, such as reporting what the result of combining two forms would be. These are both examples of spatial relations performance, and the finding that a period of early vision or some partial vision is facilitative of the perception of spatial relations is typical.

The term *spatial relations* covers a wide range of perceptual tasks, however, and it is oversimplified to conclude that early vision is the only factor determining the quality of performance. Warren, Anooshian, and Bollinger (1973) reviewed the literature on this topic and concluded that there are two major variables that contribute to spatial relations performance, in addition to the factor of early vision. One variable is whether the task is in near space, within arm's reach of the body, or in more extended space. Later blind individuals tend to perform better on those tasks that involve activity close to the body, while there are fewer differences when the task involves locomotion in the extended environment. Second, the complexity of the spatial relations task is important: children who have been visually handicapped from birth tend to perform worse than later blind children on tasks that are relatively complex in their spatial relations demands, while there are fewer differences for simple tasks.

Warren et al. (1973) concluded that the availability of vision during the early years of life may allow the establishment of a spatial perceptual system that is more effectively integrated than would be the case without vision. Young children with useful vision can cross-reference stimuli coming to the different sensory modalities: they can see that the dog that they are touching is the same creature that makes a panting noise, and can see that when the dog moves around, it takes the panting noise with it. Warren et al. suggested that the integration of modes of perceptual stimulation made possible by vision during the early years does not cease if the visual system later becomes impaired: the later blind child retains the spatial relations advantage.

Juurmaa (1973) countered the argument about the role of a visually-based frame of reference, suggesting instead that the research findings may be interpreted largely with reference to the factors of complexity and familiarity. Tasks with familiar stimuli are easier, like tasks with simpler stimuli, and they do not differentiate the early and later blind child. When more complex or unfamiliar stimuli are involved, the later blind child has had more experience with them and therefore does better.

Jones (1975) suggested an alternative to the visual frame of reference explanation of Warren et al. (1973). Jones argued that it is motor behavior, rather than vision, that serves as the bridging link among the spatial modalities. The differences between early and later blind children on spatial relations tasks, according to this hypothesis, are a direct result of the relative lack of motor experience in the early blind child, a lack which is in turn at least in part attributable to the absence or severe impairment of vision during the early years. The relative lack of motor experience, though, is the key, according to Jones. This issue remains an unresolved one but is of considerable theoretical and practical significance. If the key is motor experience, then motor experience can presumably be encouraged. If the key is early vision, then an effective means of substituting for the visual role in integrating the other sensory modalities can be sought by providing experiences that link auditory with tactual stimuli directly.

In any case, spatial relations abilities vary dramatically among visually handicapped children, and since the effective perception and conception of spatial relations is important for other abilities such as mobility, these are important issues for study. There has been renewed interest in the relationship between the study of spatial relations concepts and mobility in the past few years: this area is referred to as *spatial cognition* and has recently been summarized by Warren (1984), who defined spatial cognition as the process of "getting to know a life-sized space." Much of the concern is thus with the learning of novel spatial environments. A study by Fletcher (1980) is a good example.

Fletcher studied the child's understanding of a spatial array, presented either as a life-sized room or as a model of the room, with various items of furniture distributed around it. The exposure of the child to the array was guided by the experimenter or was at the child's own initiative. Two types of question were asked: route questions assessed the child's knowledge of the sequence of items in the room, whereas map questions required a synthesis of the room's overall layout. Sighted blindfolded children did better than blind children, and the latter did relatively better on the route questions than they did on the map questions, suggesting that they were less able than the sighted children to generate a synthesis of the layout.

Many important questions remain to be explored in this new area of research that represents an intersection of perceptual and cognitive issues as they bear on spatial understanding and effective mobility.

Mobility

Mobility refers to the ability to get around in the physical environment. Foulke (1971) defined mobility as "the ability to travel safely, comfortably, gracefully, and independently" (p. 1). Effective mobility involves a complex constellation of skills, and many who work in this area, particularly in the research setting, concur that it is not well understood. However, it is clear that effective mobility depends on several categories of factors. The major factors are discussed below.

Physical fitness and motor skills. Buell (1950) documented various areas of motor performance in which visually handicapped high school children fell well behind sighted norms. Buell attributed these lags to the child's failure to engage in sufficient physical activity before entering school. In turn, he attributed the limited physical activity to the syndrome of parental overprotection that is often mentioned in case histories of visual impairment. Buell's conclusions have more recently been supplemented by Jankowski and Evans (1981), who reported that even in a "progressive" school for blind students with excellent physical facilities, most of the children were overweight and generally poor in their physical fitness. A daily program of structured exercise was urged.

The suggestion that lags in developing motor skills are attributable to an overprotection syndrome may be only part of the picture, however. Fraiberg (e.g., Adelson & Fraiberg, 1974; Fraiberg & Freedman, 1964) reported substantial delays among congenitally and severely visually handicapped infants in the onset of crawling and walking, and attributed these delays to the lag in reaching outward to auditory stimuli. Norris, Spaulding, and Brodie (1957) similarly concluded that visually handicapped infants lag significantly in gross motor skills while not lagging so much in fine motor skills. Burlingham (1965), presenting a contrasting interpretation of the same phenomena, argued that the motor passivity that is seen in many visually handicapped children is due to inhibitions of normal tendencies for movement, simply as a matter of self-protection.

More recently, Hart (1983) has provided a somewhat more optimistic view, suggesting that in the early months of life the visually handicapped infant resists the prone position in favor of the supine, and that attempts to encourage experience in the prone position (with the attendant opportunities for exercising the upper body and arms) may be successful in encouraging crawling, and perhaps the subsequent stages of locomotion, at earlier ages.

Body image and posture. If children do not have a reasonably veridical concept or image of their own bodies, or if they cannot maintain a suitable posture, then they will be disadvantaged in their attempts to control their bodies within the external environment and will have poor mobility. Cratty and Sams (1968) presented strong arguments for the importance of body image as a basis from which the child can learn to structure external space, placing special emphasis on the development of laterality. They pointed out that it is important to encourage children to think as a part of their body image training: it is through the building of "cognitive bridges" that body image can become an effective basis for the development of mature spatial relations abilities. Cratty and Sams identified a series of phases of body image development and described exercises designed to produce adequate progress through these phases. Their program stressed verbal mediation of multimodality experience, and emphasized the importance of a gradual externalization of body image concepts to provide a basis for the conceptualization of external space.

Others have stressed the relationship between posture and mobility. While sighted children have vision to mediate their perception of the vertical, severely visually handicapped children must rely on proprioceptive and vestibular cues (though even a small degree of residual vision may be of considerable benefit, as may a period of early vision before the onset of blindness). Poor posture effectively removes the stable correspondence between body and environment and thus makes mobility more difficult. Siegel and Murphy (1970) provided a detailed analysis of the role that posture plays in orientation and mobility, as well as discussing various training procedures for correcting postural difficulties. Although their work was oriented to older adolescents and adults, the arguments are equally applicable to younger children. In their evaluation study, Siegel and Murphy found a positive correlation between improvements in posture, as a result of the training program, and improvements in mobility.

Perception and conception of space. The sighted person, viewing a spatial environment, enjoys an immediate, detailed, and holistic picture of that space. Furthermore, when the sighted person closes his or her eyes, both immediate and longer-term memories of the visually-perceived spatial structure endure. From such memories, cumulated from one experience to another, a conception of space emerges. Two aspects of this conception should be distinguished. One has to do with the knowledge of familiar places, where repeated visual (and other sensory) exposure to the setting build up a conception of that space such that it can be imaged, such that it can guide locomotor behavior in the dark, and so on. The other has to do with the derivation of "rules of spatial structure" in general: houses tend to be rectilinearly constructed, tend to have ceilings above the walls, tend to have doorways in predictable places. Outside, walkways lead to steps and to doors, sidewalks parallel streets, and so on. In short, there is a regularity about the space that human beings have had an influence on, and this regularity, stored and available as a conception of space, is a valuable aid to mobility in the spatial environment.

An articulated conception of spatial structure is vital to effective mobility in specific spatial settings, and even more so to mobility in novel settings which have not been previously encountered and learned. Body image, posture, and motor maturity and control are important factors in mobility, but no matter how good these may be, visual impairment forces a greater dependence on an effective conceptualization of space, both specific and general, than is the case for the sighted person.

There is evidence in the literature that the conceptualization of space and spatial structure is less effective in early than in later blind persons, and there is less concrete, though even more convincing, evidence that sighted people functioning with vision are better off than visually handicapped people regardless of early visual experience. What is lacking in the research literature, however, is an understanding of the process by which the visually handicapped child constructs a concept of a familiar space over time, and how the child generalizes concepts of familiar spaces into an overall conception of spatial structure in general. In order for maximally effective progress on the mobility issue to be made, this question of the process of construction of spatial understanding will have to be addressed and answered. Linking this issue and the preceding ones is the question of the relationship among the conceptualization of space, motor and locomotor control, and body image and posture. It is not sufficient simply to perceive the surrounding space accurately, or to have a good generalized conception of spatial structure, or to have good posture or motor control: any subset of these abilities without the others will not lead to effective mobility performance. Research on the interrelationships among these areas is critically needed.

Motivation and social support. Not only is the interrelationship among perceptual, cognitive, and motor factors in mobility difficult to unravel, but these factors interact within a larger setting yet. The social support system created by the family and other significant people, such as teachers and rehabilitation specialists, can have a very important impact on the child's desire to become effectively mobile. The social and motivation factors in mobility were discussed by Warren and Kocon (1974), and again in expanded manner by Welsh (1980). No matter how good the perceptual information or the cognitive integration of the world may be, the child must have an adequately strong measure of personal security and self-confidence to venture into it and use those perceptual and cognitive abilities.

What produces this personal security and self-confidence? Two themes appear in the literature. First, the child must establish an adequate "security base," which in turn depends on successful establishment of a solid social attachment. Sandler (1965) noted that warm maternal care tends to be associated with cases of active, mobile children. It seems reasonable to argue that the establishment of strong, early, social interpersonal ties in visually handicapped infants and young children may provide them with adequate emotional security, which may in turn serve as a strong base for their active exploration of the external world, leading to the effective establishment of a basis for acquisition of the spatial relations concepts vital to mobility.

Second, overprotection of the child can certainly interfere with the development of self-confidence (Bauman, 1964; Burlingham, 1964; Thompson, 1969). If parents, older siblings, or others repeatedly do things for the visually handicapped child that children would ordinarily be expected to do for themselves, habit patterns of reliance on others will develop and prevent the emergence of appropriate independence.

Thus, close social ties with significant others set the stage for effective exploration of the physical environment and the resulting development of spatial relations concepts, and appropriate encouragement of visually handicapped children to do things for themselves can prevent them from developing a dysfunctional dependence on others and can foster a sense of self-help capability and motivation that lead to effective mobility.

Mobility aids. No matter how effective a visually handicapped child's conceptualization of space may be, how efficient his or her nonvisual senses may become in mediating the perception of space, how good his or her motor skills may be, or how supportive the social structure, there remains the reasonable expectation that providing a substitute channel for the reception of visual-type spatial information will substantially enhance the child's capacity for effective mobility. The long cane, introduced systematically and effectively after the Second World War, was the first popular "mobility aid": it enabled the user to acquire information about spatial circumstances that lay beyond the range of the feet or the fingertips. Aside from the sighted guide, the long cane, for better or worse, remains the most accepted means of acquiring such information for many visually handicapped travelers, and it remains the principle focus of most mobility training programs.

Almost simultaneously with the popular success of the long cane, though, thoughts emerged that the perception of space could be enhanced by the use of more technologically advanced means. Primary among such devices are the Lasercane, the Russell Pathsounder, and the Sonicguide. Most of the work with these devices has been with adults, although in the past few years some work has appeared, primarily using children, with the Sonicguide. Several examples will be cited: a thorough review appears in Muir, Humphrey, Dodwell, and Humphrey (1985).

Newcomer (1977) studied four children of various ages from kindergarten to high school, and addressed the question of the value of the Sonicguide to the children and in particular the question what they could do with it that they could not have done without it. His conclusion was guardedly positive with respect to the utility of the device in the educational setting.

Strelow, Kay, and Kay (1978) reported two cases, one a developmentally delayed 2.5-year-old and the other a bright 6-year-old. The former had good physical development but serious motor and language delays and social development problems, showing the typical autistic syndrome. Over a 6-month period of work with the Sonicguide, he became able to stand up, take several steps, and eventually follow his mother for several minutes at a time. In addition to the locomotor advances, he showed increased reponsiveness to people and sounds. The second subject, who was verbally precocious but without independent locomotion, showed regular advances in independent mobility with intensive Sonicguide use.

Ferrell (1980) studied four Retinopathy of Prematurity (ROP) infants ranging from 6 to 26 months and found mixed success with a Sonicguide program. The oldest subject showed ready acceptance and understanding of the aid's signals, and the youngest gained effective reaching behavior within two months of use. The two middle children, aged 10 and 14 months, showed much slower progress but did, interestingly, show a reduced incidence of stereotypic behaviors while the aid was in use.

Strelow (1983) reported work with four cases. Two infants, ages 10 and 21 months at the outset of study, showed considerable advances. Two somewhat older children, ages 24 and 26 months at the outset, showed less than satisfactory progress, apparently in part because of the existence of established behaviors that caused a decrease in their responsiveness to the aid signals.

Kay has developed a further adaptation of the Sonicguide, called the Trisensor. In essence, this device adds to the Sonicguide's binaural field a central foveal field of greater resolution, the function of which is to increase central resolution and therefore make spatial tasks requiring finer discrimination more feasible. Kay and Kay (1983) reported very briefly an apparently successful pilot program with school-age children in a school setting.

Many important questions remain to be answered about the use of sensory aids in educational and other settings. For example, there is some evidence that infants may be more adaptable to aids such as the Sonicguide than children of 1 to 3 years (Aitken & Bower, 1982; Strelow, 1983; Strelow et al., 1978), and the suggestion that competing habits developed by 1- to 3-year-olds are interfering (Strelow, 1983) is intriguing. However, success has been better at age 4 and above. The question of this interaction with age, and of the determinants of the interaction, is a key one. So, too, is the question whether a sensory aid such as the Trisensor, whose initial purpose was to facilitate the perception of

spatial relationships, may be an effective educational tool for the introduction of spatial cognitive concepts, as suggested by Kay and Kay (1983).

In any case, the use of electronic sensory aids with children, for a variety of purposes, is clearly in its infancy, and there is much progress to be made in this area. At very least, it is clear that significant advances will depend, at least as much as on the development of technological applications, on the effective understanding of the perceptual and cognitive needs of visually handicapped children.

Perceptual-Cognitive Abilities

The lines of distinction between sensation and perception, between perception and cognition, and between cognition and language are difficult to draw, and it is unrewarding and to some extent a violation of the subject matter to attempt to do so. The distinctions used here are no more than organizational conveniences: they are not intended to reflect an inherent distinction among human abilities. As it was impossible in the preceding section to discuss spatial perception and mobility without reference to cognitive processes, so it is impossible to discuss cognitive development without reference to perception. The term *cognition* is generally used to refer to thought processes which may occur without immediate perceptual experience; particularly with a perceptually handicapped population such as blind persons, it is impossible to discuss cognitive development adequately without reference to the perceptual factors which may impede it.

The principle of developmental continuity is especially important in cognition: aspects of irregular cognitive progress in school-age children may well have their roots in infancy. In the early stages of sensorimotor development, in which infants' actions are largely directed toward themselves rather than outward to objects and events in the world, the scanty evidence suggests that there is little difference between blind and sighted infants. However, in the Piagetian substage of secondary circular reactions, roughly from 4 to 8 months of age, the infant's activities begin to be directed outward, and intentionality of action with respect to the world emerges. Logically, it is at this stage that emergent differences between blind and sighted infants would be expected, since it is in large part the perception of the result of such action that leads to its repetition. Indeed, Sandler (1965) and Fraiberg (1968) reported comparable development in blind and sighted infants through at least 4 months of age, after which developmental divergences began to appear. Fraiberg noted that the achievement of the object concept is delayed in blind children until 3 to 5 years of age, in contrast to the typical estimate of 2 years for the sighted child. While the sighted child searches actively for hidden objects during much of the second year, Fraiberg reported that "we have seen only one blind child between the ages of 16 months and three years who will conduct such a search" (p. 287).

Cognitive development can be considered as a gradual progression from overt actions, to internalized representation of actions and their consequences, to fully representational thought that does not depend on immediate perception or action. Thus internalization is a key process in development. Gradually the child acquires a more refined and appropriate set of classification skills and moves toward a refined understanding of the important properties of the world and objects in it, and toward the ability to deal with the world in representational terms.

Although cognitive skills have implications for virtually every area of human behavior, the relationship of cognitive abilities to the educational experience is especially important. Cognitive capabilities serve as the basis for the assimilation of information and concepts that are taught, and in turn, the individual's cognitive abilities are influenced by the nature of the education that he or she receives.

Vision is ordinarily a very important source of information about the world, the "stuff" on which cognition comes to operate. The totally blind child must build concepts of the world on the basis of other than visual information. Foulke (1962) noted that the nature of the concepts that individuals acquire depends on the nature of their experiences, and that it may thus be expected that the concepts of the visually handicapped child are in some ways more restricted than those of the sighted child. Even a limited amount of visual capability helps in understanding the properties of the world, and the advantages increase as the degree of useful vision increases. The educational implications are very clear: as Barraga (1976) and others have argued, any residual visual ability should be exploited and trained to its highest possible level of functioning. On the other hand, even the fullest exploitation of residual vision may not effectively substitute for similarly full use of the other available sensory modalities, and appropriate provision of experience to the other modalities must not be neglected.

Much of the cognitive research on preschool and school-age children concerns the various conservation concepts, which generally have to do with understanding the physical properties of the world. For example, conservation of substance refers to the concept that matter retains its properties despite perceptually-mediated variations in its immediate form: two smaller balls of clay made out of a single larger ball still contain the same total amount of substance as the larger ball. Many studies have found that severely visually handicapped children show developmental lags in the acquisition of mature conservation concepts. For example, lags in the conservation of substance were found by Tobin (1972) and by Gottesman (1973), in the conservation of liquid volume by Canning (1957), and in the conservation of weight and length, as well as other properties, by Stephens and Simpkins (1974). The latter study is the

broadest in scope, and also the most pessimistic in finding that the lags in conservation abilities do not disappear completely with increasing age. In fact, Stephens and Simpkins found that their group of 14- to 18-year-old visually handicapped children performed much like their group of 6- to 10-year-old sighted subjects on several tests of conservation abilities.

Other researchers are not so pessimistic about the cognitive developmental course of visually handicapped children. Gottesman (1973), for example, found that the proportions of severely visually handicapped children showing successful conservation performance were smaller than those of sighted children during the early elementary years, but that most visually handicapped children in the 8- to 11-year-old range had attained appropriate conservation of weight and substance.

Classification of objects and events based on reasonable criteria is a critical ability underlying the growing cognitive sophistication that occurs with age. Higgins (1973) found that children who had been severely visually handicapped since birth scored considerably worse on concepts involving abstract content than they did on the concepts involving concrete content. There was no corresponding difference for sighted children. Hartlage (1968, 1969) found relative deficits in classification abilities in visually handicapped children for spatial concepts, but not for concepts that did not involve spatial relations.

There are clearly areas of cognitive development in which visually handicapped children lag developmentally behind sighted children. Two major hypotheses are offered to account for these lags. One possibility is that lags in the development of the cognitive capabilities of early and middle childhood, such as classification and conservation, are the result of carryover lags from the earlier sensorimotor period. There is unfortunately little direct data on the progress of the visually handicapped infant through the sensorimotor period, but Stephens (1972) noted a number of areas where the restricted experience of the visually handicapped infant might well have retarding effects. It is reasonable to expect sensorimotor delays to carry over into later aspects of cognitive development. In addition, though, it seems likely that a visual impairment during the preschool and early school-age years, during which time the conservation abilities are normally developing, creates a continuing situation in which the visually handicapped child is not acquiring the kinds of information and experience which normally lead to the differentiation of cognitive abilities.

A second view was offered by Gottesman (1976), who suggested that the observed delays in cognitive development in early school-age blind children are partly the result of the child's reliance on "less sophisticated sensory discrimination abilities" (p. 99). To the extent that vision is needed to provide an effective integration of the information received by the other sensory modalities, as was suggested earlier, the perceptual information available to the visually handicapped child may indeed be less sophisticated and thus may serve cognitive skills less well than in the sighted child. Gottesman found significant lags in the acquisition of various conservation concepts, but these lags tended to decrease with increasing age, with many visually handicapped children in the 8- to 11-year age range showing appropriate conservation of weight and substance. Gottesman suggested that although the lags occur initially, visually handicapped children gradually become able to perform conservation tasks because of their "increased reliance on integrative processes of cognitive functioning, rather than a reliance on the less sophisticated sensory discrimination abilities" (p. 99).

A number of attempts have been made to design training programs for the acquisition of cognitive abilities, in an effort to provide remediation where visually handicapped children show developmental lags as compared with sighted children, or to avoid such delays in the first place. Hill (1970, 1971) reported the results of a study designed to assess the effectivenss of a training program for spatial concepts. Congenitally visually handicapped children, age 7 to 9 and varying in intelligence and degree of vision, were trained several times a week for 3 months, with work on verbalization, identification, manipulation, and recognition of changing spatial relationships. The training group showed significantly greater gains over the course of the study than a control group.

An excellent study of training of classification skills was reported by Friedman and Pasnak (1973), who examined the feasibility of accelerating the acquisition of classification skills in visually handicapped children. Types of classification tasks included verbal and tactual discovery of class problems, and form, orientation, texture, and size classification problems. The classification training group showed a significant improvement from pre- to posttest, while a control group did not. Furthermore, the mean posttest performance of the training group was not different from the performance of a group of sighted children of similar ages. Friedman and Pasnak noted that their study did not attempt to train a cognitive skill at an earlier age than that at which it would normally occur in sighted children: "Rather, children who are chronologically mature were aided in acquiring a concept that they had failed to master because of a sensory handicap" (p. 337).

Stephens, Grube, and Fitzgerald (1977) and Stephens and Grube (1982) reported the results of an intensive and long-term training program for the development of conservation and other cognitive skills in visually handicapped children. The training program was based on the results of investigation of cognitive skills by Stephens and Simpkins (1974), in which the developmental levels of comparably-aged visually handicapped and sighted children were compared. Children in the training group were visually impaired (light perception at most) from birth or within the first 4 years of life, and were in the 90 to 110 IQ range. Compared to a group of visually handicapped children who did not receive training, the training group showed significantly greater gains over

the 17-month period of the training program. The training group showed posttraining scores that were quite similar to those of a sighted control group in conservation tasks, in classification tasks, and in formal operations tasks, while the nontrained visually handicapped group showed significant lags compared to both the training group and the sighted control group, both at the outset of the program and at the end. On the mental imagery and spatial relations tasks, however, the training group did not show such impressive gains. Thus the program of Stephens and her colleagues showed a significant impact on the abilities of visually handicapped children to perform to sighted levels on various cognitive developmental tasks.

It is difficult to summarize this vast literature on cognitive development. Several points recur, however. First, much of the literature is pessimistic in finding that visually handicapped children exhibit distinct developmental lags when compared to sighted children. However, it is rather more optimistic to note that there are many visually handicapped children whose cognitive skills are impressive indeed, whether or not they fall onto the sighted timetable. Further, there seem to be several significant ways in which the cognitive abilities of visually handicapped children can be developmentally enhanced. One of these is the potential for training the child with partial vision to use it effectively. Second, it is likely that intensive research on the experiential dimensions that lead to the development of effective cognitive skills will reveal ways in which visually handicapped children can be encouraged to optimize their cognitive development. Several of the attempts at training present optimistic views. Ideally, however, the greater emphasis should be on the longer-term arrangement of the child's learning environment to foster optimal cognitive growth.

Cognitive-Language Abilities

There has been a continuing argument as to whether language shapes thought, or thought shapes language. No doubt both influences occur. In any case it is clear that language and cognitive development are closely tied together.

This is particularly true of visually handicapped persons. Cutsforth (1932) discussed the tendency of visually handicapped children to use visual vocabulary, and called this tendency "verbalism." He reasoned that since visually handicapped children could not have a first-hand sensory basis for such vocabulary, the use of verbalisms must lead to "incoherent and loose thinking" (p. 89). Therefore, he cautioned, the visually handicapped child should be discouraged from the use of verbalisms. There has been a continuing debate over this issue, and Cutsforth's view is not maintained by many today. Nolan (1960) assessed the incidence of verbalism, using Cutsforth's definition, and found a lower incidence than had been reported by Cutsforth. Nolan suggested that one of the reasons for this change may have been the policy in many educational programs to discourage the use of verbalisms, based on Cutsforth's advice.

One research approach to verbalism is to ask the child to define a set of words, and to identify the objects corresponding to those words. A verbalism is said to occur when a word is defined appropriately but the corresponding object cannot be identified. The notion is that the child has a concept but not the appropriate underlying sensory base. Harley (1963) studied early blind children with at most light perception and found the incidence of verbalism higher among young children, among lower IQ children, and among children with less reported experience with the objects used for experimental stimuli. Based particularly on this last point, Harley suggested that "the key to the reduction of verbalism among blind children is the increasing of interaction with their environments" (p. 32).

More important than the incidence of visually related vocabulary, however, is the meaningfulness of the vocabulary that the child does use, and whether the vocabulary is useful and effective, both as a mediator of internal thought and as a vehicle for interpersonal communication. There is inadequate information to answer this question completely, and in fact the available evidence is somewhat contradictory. DeMott (1972) found no differences in affective meaning of 15 stimulus words between groups of visually handicapped children with less than light perception, visually handicapped children whose vision ranged from movement perception to 20/200, and a sighted group. Dokecki (1966) suggested that "It still remains to be demonstrated that associative and word-thing meanings are functionally different for the blind or any other group" (p. 528).

On the other hand, recent evidence using a more microanalytic approach to linguistic analysis is not so positive. Word meaning in the cognitive sense refers not just to the ability to define a word, but to the word and its relationship to other words. In this, there is evidence that visually handicapped children may have less elaborated meaning networks than sighted children (Andersen, Dunlea, & Kekelis, 1984; Dunlea, 1982). Other differences also emerged: visually handicapped children's use of action words was highly self-directed rather than directed to external objects. Further, their use of relational terms such as *more* was largely centered on themselves rather than on external events.

While there are some differences in language usage and word meaning, most of these have clear explanations in the experiential base of visually handicapped children. The answer, then, to the use of visual words is the same as that to the use of any words. Visually handicapped children should be exposed to a full range of age-appropriate vocabulary, and should be provided with concrete physical experience as well as verbal explanation of referents for the development of meaning. Children from more limited experiential backgrounds need even more special attention to this kind of structured experience. The goal should be to bring the visually handicapped child to the point of maximal use of the language used by the surrounding culture, so that language can aid in meaningful and useful social interaction both within the educational setting and in more general settings.

Social Development

The term social development covers a wide range of topics, from the development of appropriate social relationships with individuals and groups to the development of independent living habits. Vision is clearly very useful to the sighted child in these areas, and the role of the parent or other family member in providing substitute information for the visually handicapped child is important. Thus, the nature of the child's relationships with family members is critical: as much as for the sighted child, it is important that there is an accepting and trusting familial relationship.

Parents or other family members may often be disadvantaged in fulfilling their roles by virtue of their own adverse emotional reactions to the impairment. Sommers (1944) identified several clusters of parental attitudes toward their children's visual handicaps, including feeling personally disgraced, feeling guilty of negligence or of having violated some moral or social code, and viewing the handicap as some kind of punishment of the parent. Sommers also catalogued types of parental adjustment, ranging from genuine, objective, and realistic acceptance of the handicap and its consequences to overt rejection, where the parent resents the child and attributes blame unreasonably for the handicap. Sommers did not explore the impact of these variations on the child, but Endress (1968) found significant (although not necessarily causal) relationships between maternal attitudes toward their visually handicapped preschool children and various characteristics of the children, including social developmental level.

There is a large body of literature about the social maturity and social competence of visually handicapped children. Various measures of social maturity have been developed, including several variations of the Vineland Social Maturity Scale such as the Maxfield-Fjeld and the Maxfield-Buchholz tests (Maxfield and Buchholz, 1957). The Overbrook Social Competency Scale is similar and is described by Bauman (1973). There are also several social adjustment scales which are commonly derived from various personality tests that have been used with visually handicapped children.

The general conclusion from many studies using these scales is that the social competence of visually handicapped children develops differently from that of sighted children. Several factors are undoubtedly involved in this pattern. Vision itself is an important variable. Since vision serves as a very useful source of detailed information, it is not surprising to find that children with partial vision often show less severe social developmental lags than totally blind children. For example, Maxfield and Fjeld (1942) found that a group of partially sighted children exceeded the development of an age-matched group of totally blind children. The pattern of differences was interesting: "The results suggest that the [totally] blind children in this study tend to be more docile, have less initiative, are less active and outgoing, are more introverted, and possibly more cooperative than the partially seeing children" (p. 13). Lairy and Harrison-Covello (1973) also found a disproportionately high number of partially sighted children in their group whose developmental patterns were most nearly like sighted children. The highly competent partially sighted children tended to make more use of their residual vision than less competent children with equivalent vision. Finally, Bauman (1973), using the Overbrook Social Competency Scale, found that children with some useful vision developed many skills significantly earlier than totally blind children. Thus partial vision is an important factor in the development of social skills. At the same time, it is only a potential positive factor whose use must be encouraged in order for the advantages to occur.

The social environment to which the child is exposed is another important factor. McGuinness (1970) used the Vineland scale to compare the social maturity of visually handicapped children in various educational situations, including itinerant teacher, integrated school, and special school settings. The subjects were fourth through sixth graders with at most light perception, most of whom had been visually handicapped since birth. All three groups showed scores somewhat lower than sighted norms. The children in itinerant teacher and integrated school settings showed higher social maturity scores than those from the special school setting. McGuinness suggested that this result was due to the relative lack of contact by children in the special school setting with age-appropriate behavior, and of the greater attention and availability of special help in the special school setting: presumably this places less requirement on the children to solve their own problems.

Schindele (1974) used the Self Concept Adjustment Score to compare the social adjustment of fifth- and sixth-grade visually handicapped and sighted children. The visually handicapped children were from residential or integrated schools. No significant differences emerged between any pair of groups. However, in the residential school group there was an age relationship showing the older children to be relatively less well-adjusted, whereas in the integrated school group the age relationship showed the older children to be better adjusted, as would ordinarily be expected. Schindele suggested that:

> while the social adjustment of visually handicapped students in regular (integrated) schools has developed in a realistic surrounding, the social development of the visually handicapped in a residential school is mainly the result of being brought up in a sheltered and unrealistic environment. In this case

the good social adjustment of these children might be seriously affected as they grow older and especially when they have to leave the residential school. (p. 14.)

Further, for the integrated school group there was a strong positive correlation between social adjustment and intelligence. Schindele suggested that the brighter children are more able to adapt to the greater demands placed on them in the integrated school setting.

Nevertheless, it should be noted that teachers of mainstreamed visually handicapped children frequently report problems with social skills. It is clear that whatever the educational setting, special attention to the development of appropriate social skills is important.

Another important factor in the social development of visually handicapped children is the nature of the parents' own emotional adjustment. Hallenbeck (1954) noted that one of the significant factors related to the absence of emotional disturbance among residential school children is "whether the child had established a good relationship with some person prior to entering the school" (p. 308). Barry and Marshall (1953) found a strong negative relationship between the social competence of 5- to 7-year-old visually handicapped children and the degree of rejection of the child by the mother. The parents' own emotional makeup, both generally and specifically in relation to the fact of the child's handicap, may set broad constraints on the adequacy of the social environment in the home and thus indirectly influence the course of social development by the child. Since these relationships are frequently stated in negative terms, it should be stressed that positive parental factors have a positive effect on the child's social development, no less so for visually handicapped than for sighted children.

Scott (1969) analyzed social development in terms of social role, suggesting that the child's self-concept is acquired in large part through interactions with other people and depends on the expectations that others have for the child. If they expect the child to behave with limitations that they believe to be characteristic of visually handicapped children, then these limitations will come to be part of the child's self-concept and will tend to be expressed in the child's behavior.

A characteristic sometimes attributed to visually handicapped children is a relative dependence on other people, as opposed to a personal independence, and the related characteristic of passivity, as opposed to active interaction with the environment and other people. Some writers (e.g., Burlingham, 1961) attribute these characteristics to the parents' tendency to overprotect the child, a situation which encourages dependency and discourages independence. Such an outcome is avoidable, according to Burlingham. By contrast, Sandler (1965) saw the pattern of passivity as a necessary result of the impairment of vision:

The ego deformation resulting from the blindness occurs in its own right, and is linked with a path of development which basically cannot be reversed by the environment, although its outcome can be modified to a large extent by suitable mothering. (Sandler, 1965, p. 346.)

There is also evidence from several studies using personality measures (e.g., Imamura, 1965; Petrucci, 1953; Wilson, 1967) that visually handicapped adolescents tend to be more dependent and less assertive than their sighted counterparts.

Such results are often presented in the context of the notion that they are undesirable. Some perspective is needed, however. Appropriate dependency behavior is quite suitable for visually handicapped children (as it is for sighted children as well) in certain situations. Such behaviors must be carefully evaluated in the context of the adaptive significance that they have for the individual. It may be quite appropriate, and indeed adaptive in the true survival sense, for visually handicapped children to behave more dependently than sighted children would in the same situation.

Locus of control has to do with people's implicit perception of whether they are in command of the events that affect their lives. Locus of control is thus related to self-concept, passivity, dependency, and other such variables. Internal locus of control describes those who see themselves as exercising substantial control over the events in their lives, whereas external locus of control describes those who see themselves as being highly controlled by other people or events. Land and Vineberg (1965) used a locus of control scale with children over a wide age range, drawn from residential and integrated school settings. No difference appeared between the two groups, but both showed significantly more external locus of control than a comparison group of sighted children. The visually handicapped and sighted groups showed the same relationship of locus of control with age: control became more internal as age increased. There were also some visually handicapped children whose internalized locus of control was as highly developed as that of sighted children. Thus there is substantial variation in this factor in visually handicapped children, and study of the developmental dynamics would be valuable, as would study of the implications of internal versus external locus of control for visually handicapped children.

In sum, the social development of visually handicapped children is different in several ways from that of sighted children, and the factors that produce these differences, as well as the substantial variations among visually handicapped children, are complex. Of particular note is the fact that the social setting itself is heavily involved, and that the characteristics of the social setting are heavily influenced by the reactions of the significant other people who interact with the visually handicapped child. This applies as well to teachers as it does to family members.

Throughout this section on research findings, various studies have been cited which demonstrate a relationship between environmental factors, broadly construed, and development of visually handicapped children. While the importance of environmental factors for development is clear from these studies, more research attention must be devoted to the dynamics of these relationships. In general, the research question should be posed: What are the environmental factors that lead to optimal development, and how do these factors operate to affect development?

STATE OF THE PRACTICE

Much of the research reviewed in the preceding sections has been concerned with the acquisition of basic knowledge about the development of visually handicapped children, and not directly to issues of practical applications of the knowledge so gained. This characteristic is not to be taken as a shortfall in the research; a basis of fundamental knowledge is necessary before effective applications can be developed, and this is particularly so for the questions of the overall developmental progress of visually handicapped children to which this chapter is largely oriented.

There is an additional reason for the difficulty in presenting a representative summary of the "state of the practice," or said another way, the extent to which the findings of research have become embodied in educational programs. Personnel in the area of education of visually handicapped students, like those in other applied areas, generally do not have time in their work week to write for the professional audience, and thus the fruits of their applications, no matter how successful or how solidly grounded in the research-generated knowledge, tend not to find their way into print. Further, it is, unfortunately, a relatively rare applied work setting that materially rewards or even particularly encourages writing for the professional audience. This is not necessarily due to any shortsightedness on the part of the administrators of these programs, but can be attributed to the general insufficiency of funding for education of the visually handicapped students and other special education groups. There is, beyond any doubt, an immense fund of knowledge among personnel working with visually handicapped students that represents attempts, both successful and unsuccessful, to put the fruits of research to work in the applied setting. It is unfortunate that there is insufficient opportunity and reward for this collective knowledge to appear in print.

This landscape is not by any means entirely bleak, however. There are numerous examples in the research already discussed where results have been analyzed with respect to their potential applicability in educational settings, and where programmatic implementation has occurred. Significant examples include the following.

Barraga's (1964) early work on the use of residual vision led to the construction of a 2-month training program of daily lessons. Performance on the Visual Discrimination Test improved as a result of the training. The test was subsequently refined and published as the Visual Efficiency Test (Barraga, 1970). The test has undergone field testing by several researchers, and its modified successor, the Diagnostic Assessment Procedure, has been developed and further tested. As significant as the development of the assessment instruments, though, has been the development and dissemination of the training procedures, called the Program to Develop Efficiency in Visual Functioning. Barraga and her colleagues have devoted years to the dissemination of this program, and their efforts have resulted in a widespread use of the material. It is fair to say that many visually handicapped children are currently functioning at higher levels of visual efficiency than would be the case without the Barraga work, and the model of research, program development and modification, assesssment, and dissemination is a valuable one.

Another program that represents the transition from research to application is that of Stephens and her colleagues. Based on the original research of Stephens and Simpkins (1974) that showed visually handicapped children to be significantly delayed in their development of conservation and classification abilities, Stephens and her colleagues developed a training program for administration to visually handicapped school children. The purpose of the program was to provide a structured set of experiences which would lead to the earlier acquisition of cognitive skills. As reported by Stephens and Grube (1982), the program had significant positive impact in preventing the serious delays that occur spontaneously without intervention. The Stephens program has not, however, had the widespread dissemination that Barraga's work has achieved.

The early promotion and use of the Optacon, a device which converts normal print to tactile display, provides a useful model for development and dissemination. Upon the successful development and evaluation of the Optacon, a dissemination grant was provided to ensure that teachers of visually handicapped children would have an appropriate background in teaching the use of the device. The notion was that every visually handicapped child should have an Optacon available and be able to use it (Spungin, 1985). The model for dissemination, whereby teachers are provided with teaching techniques and materials, is a large-scale venture which could only occur with significant external funding, and needless to say the administration of such a project is a difficult undertaking. However, it is an effective model for the dissemination of crucial knowledge, and may be emulated in other areas.

There are excellent examples of evaluative research whose results have clear implications for educational practice, but which have not had significant adoption reported in the literature. Berla's work on individual differences and strategies of tactile map reading is such an example, and the work in cognitive development of Friedman and Pasnak is another. It may well be that many teachers have adopted the results of these studies into their curriculum strategies, but the literature does not reflect this, and so the extent to which the state of the research knowledge is represented in the state of practice is difficult to determine.

Hill and Blasch (1980) provide an excellent summary of concept development in visually handicapped children, especially with reference to orientation and mobility. In addition to describing the major assessment instruments, they go on to draw the implications of this literature for educational practice.

There are several instances of curricular development and dissemination which exemplify the translation of research into practice. *Project Vision-Up* is an assessment system for visually handicapped children from birth to about 8 years of age, together with a set of curricular materials. Another relatively recent development is the *Reach Out And Teach* project developed at the American Foundation for the Blind under the direction of Dr Kay Ferrell. This set of materials, developed in an attractive audio-visual format, is an impressive accomplishment in its translation of research-generated knowledge into a format that is readily accessible to parents and teachers of visually handicapped children.

There are also examples of materials that have been developed specifically for the school setting. Caton and Pester (1979) describe the development, evaluation, and dissemination of a Braille reading series, under the auspices of the American Printing House for the Blind. The Braille materials, oriented to the prereading and beginning reading stages, were developed with reference to children's readiness in areas such as perceptual development, vocabulary, and conceptual development. More along topical lines, Project MAVIS (Materials Adaptation for Visually Impaired in the Social Studies) and the SAVI/SELPH (Science Activities for the Visually Impaired/Science Enrichment for Learners with Physical Handicaps) program represent social studies and science curricular materials for visually handicapped children through the elementary grades and beyond. The SAVI/SELPH program, developed at the University of California at Berkeley, is a science program with opportunities for hands-on involvement. Project MAVIS, sponsored by the Social Science Education Consortium, provides social studies materials for use with visually handicapped children. Both of these projects represent the combination of pedagogical principles in specific subject areas with consideration of the needs of visually handicapped pupils. The translation of curricular materials into a format suitable for use by teachers with mainstreaming requirements not only makes the teachers' job more feasible, but significantly improves the chances of securing a viable educational outcome.

Despite these examples of projects which are relatively well-known and which have enjoyed considerable dissemination, it is difficult to know the full extent to which research has been translated into educational practice. Reports in the literature are unfortunately rare, for the reasons offered earlier in this section. Generally, it is clear that those who work with visually handicapped children in applied settings are extremely conscious of the special nature of their clientele, and undoubtedly bring much of what they read in the professional literature to bear in their week-to-week dealing with the visually handicapped children for whom they have responsibility. The lack of a vigorous literature on this is, however, unfortunate.

NEEDS AND RECOMMENDATIONS

Topical Issues

A number of issues that are specific to topical areas may be singled out as needing additional concentrated research. Among these are the following.

1. Mobility and its many facets need continuing research effort. Concentration should be on not only the specific perceptual, motor, cognitive, and social factors, but on the interrelations among these factors within an integrated framework.

2. Considering the importance of audition for the visually handicapped child, continuing research on auditory skills, and particularly on auditory selective attention, is vital.

3. Given the visually handicapped child's altered perceptual base for the acquisition of information about the world, continuing study of the relationship of concept development to perception is needed.

4. Visually handicapped children, as sighted children, vary in their abilities to process and organize multiple sources of sensory information, to analyze and synthesize, and to attend selectively to important sources of information while ignoring irrelevant ones. Collectively, these points are referred to as cognitive style. If our goal is to optimize the visually handicapped child's development, attention to cognitive style is imperative.

5. In the language area, issues of meaning are not sufficiently understood. Recent evidence shows that there is experience-based variation in the acquisition of appropriate word meaning, and continuing research attention is needed in this area.

6 Socialization factors, including the roles of family and peer influences, need ongoing research attention. Of particular importance is the influence of the educational setting and its many factors on social development. This topic includes the impact of the school setting on the child's educational achievement but extends well beyond the specific educational setting as well.

General Issues

Additionally, there are a number of important needs that are not specific to topical areas within development, but which extend broadly across these areas. Primary among these are the following.

1. It was noted at the beginning of this chapter that a most important characteristic of the population of visually handicapped children is its heterogeneity. Visually handicapped children vary not only in the range of characteristics related to their visual condition, but also in their experiences, and of course in their educational characteristics and achievements. Research models that do not take appropriate account of variability in causes as well as in effects will not produce knowledge that is theoretically or practically useful. Research models that incorporate the analysis of variability of both independent and dependent variables, on the other hand, hold great promise for the acquisition of useful knowledge about the visually handicapped child. It is an ironic, yet very real, consequence of PL 94–142 that useful research on the visually handicapped child has become more difficult than ever to conduct. The population is now dispersed into a variety of educational settings, whereas before it was relatively more concentrated in special schools. This makes it more difficult to acquire suitable research samples, with the increased costs of research that this produces. The dispersion also increases the variety of environmental factors that produce variability in outcome measures. Appropriate research designs and adequate research funding can overcome these difficulties and in fact turn them to advantage, but both researchers and their funding sources must rise to the occasion.

2. The age at onset of visual loss is one of these important individual differences variables. In some areas, age of onset is a determining variable, and its effects must be understood so that they may be taken into account in designing educational and other experimental programs for the visually handicapped child.

3. The availability of any partial visual function is a similarly important factor. Partial vision is important both as a determining factor in the level of ability and as a source of potential information to assist in the development of a variety of capabilities. Its effects must be continually recognized in order to make the research literature maximally useful. Barraga's (1976) work is of particular note on this point, and it serves as an excellent example of bringing research findings to bear on practice. On the other hand, the goal of making the visually handicapped child function like a sighted child in every respect is not a realistic or reasonable one. A visual handicap carries inherent disadvantages, and it is unrealistic to expect that a small degree of partial vision can be exploited so thoroughly that the partially sighted child will not need special educational services.

4. If the heterogeneity implicit in the visually handicapped population were not enough of a complicating factor, the issue is still further complicated by the fact

that a visual impairment is often, and increasingly, accompanied by another handicap, often more than just one. This creates problems as much for the practitioner as for the researcher, and both must be continuously aware of the implications of multiple handicaps.

5. It is unfortunate that the vast majority of research on visually handicapped children that addresses developmental issues is conducted with a cross-sectional rather than a longitudinal research design. The vast importance of experiential factors in determining characteristics and abilities of visually handicapped children makes it desirable to study visually handicapped children over extended periods of time, even years, so that their development can be viewed continuously and so that appropriate referencing of developmental indicators to experiential variables can be accomplished. Longitudinal research is difficult and expensive to conduct, and assurance of multiyear funding is imperative before such research can be begun. Despite these difficulties, the rewards of longitudinal research make the effort necessary and worthwhile.

6. An issue with as much need for policy as research attention is that of competency goals. Within the educational framework, PL 94–142 requires individualized achievement expectations for each visually handicapped child. Whose responsibility should these be? The school, wishing to be on the safe side, may have the tendency to set goals low so that their achievement can be assured. The parents, wishing to optimize the development of their visually handicapped child, may want to set the goals unrealistically high. Not only is insightful research necessary to resolve this dilemma, but those responsible for policy must be equally inspired to walk this tightrope. Fully objective research on the longer-term effects of mainstreaming is clearly needed, but it is not enough to have this research; it is vital that research findings be put into effect in ways that are independent of the political process, broadly construed.

7. The review of literature contained in the section on the State of Current Research makes it very clear that the experiences of a given visually handicapped child influence to a very large extent his or her potential for adapting to educational demands as well as to the general demands of life. For the present treatment, the educational demands are of particular importance. How can the child's experiential setting be structured in a way that will optimize his or her educational success? The broad implications of this question cannot be overstated. Specific experiences in regard to language development, cognitive development, personal independence, socialization, and virtually every other aspect of development must be continually studied, until the knowledge base is sufficient to allow the effective structuring of the experience of each visually handicapped child, on an individual basis. This is an ambitious goal, but one which if compromised will in turn compromise the prospects of each visually handicapped child for optimal fulfillment of potential.

8. A related point has to do with classroom size. Those whose responsibilities include fiscal management, from legislators to school administrators, will want to minimize the potential drain of visually handicapped or other handicapped children on the resources of the educational system, and this in general means handling more children by fewer teachers and other educational specialists. However, fiscal constraints should not be allowed to dictate resource allocations for visually or otherwise handicapped children. Logically, it seems clear that visually handicapped children need the resources provided by specially trained professionals. But advocates of special services for visually handicapped children must be able to rest their arguments on a solid research base, and this research base is not currently available. It must be made available.

9. I have elsewhere (Warren, 1978) made the point that research on visually handicapped children should have a functional emphasis. It is certainly valuable and important to have "basic" research on the implications of visual impairments for the construction of a knowledge base. However, given the multitude of constraints on research possibilities with visually handicapped children, and given the needs for practical outcomes of such research, it is imperative that any piece of research have maximally useful outcomes. It is not sufficient to study "indicator variables," such as IQ scores, without regard to what these indicators mean for the functional abilities and behaviors of visually handicapped children. Rather, researchers must have a sustained regard for the potential of their efforts to bear on applied issues. Not least of these are educational issues. If indicators of cognitive capabilities are to be assessed, then these should be studied in relation to their education or other implications. The same point holds for indicators of social factors, as well as those in virtually any other area of research.

10. In order for personnel in the field of visual impairment to conduct the research that is needed, there must be adequate funding available. Too often, a research proposal is bounced from one agency to another because it is too "applied" for one, too "basic" for another, or too "preliminary" for any. Effective research on the visually handicapped population is not easy or cheap to conduct. Often external funding is needed even for pilot work toward a larger project, but funding agencies are often hesitant to provide such seed funds. There is no easy solution to these problems; indeed, although it would help, the simple availability of much more research funds does not address the entire problem, for example that of a research proposal that is neither purely applied nor purely basic and is therefore not attractive to any single agency. Perhaps a single clearing house for all research on the visually handicapped population would be feasible, whose function would be to integrate the necessary interactions among agencies and between researchers and agencies.

11. Finally, there is need for a coordinated effort to disseminate the results of research findings and their implications for practice. The published professional

literature is sparse indeed in representing the extend to which research findings have been adopted and embodied in programs of education. There is no doubt that many educational personnel, from teachers to administrators, are abreast of the research literature and make every possible attempt to translate the knowledge that they acquire into practice. However, the results of their efforts are generally not available to the field, except in the relatively rare instances in which they in turn add to the professional literature. Professional personnel must be encouraged to publish the results of their efforts, and they must be rewarded appropriately for their contributions. Concentrated and sustained efforts must be made to make their collective wisdom readily available to their colleagues who work in applied settings with visually handicapped children.

References

Adelson, E., & Fraiberg, S. (1974). Gross motor development in infants blind from birth. *Child Development, 45,* 114–126.

Aitken, S., & Bower, T. G. R. (1982). Intersensory substitution in the blind. *Journal of Experimental Child Psychology, 33,* 309–323.

Andersen, E. S., Dunlea, A., & Kekelis, L. S. (1984). Blind children's language: Resolving some differences. *Journal of Child Language, 11,* 646–665.

Axelrod, S. (1959). *Effects of early blindness.* New York: American Foundation for the Blind (Research Series, No. 7).

Barraga, N. C. (1964). *Increased visual behavior in low vision children.* New York: American Foundation for the Blind (Research Series, No. 13).

Barraga, N. C. (Ed.). (1970). *Visual efficiency scale.* Louisville, KY: American Printing House for the Blind.

Barraga, N. C. (1976). *Visual handicaps and learning: A developmental approach.* Belmont, CA: Wadsworth.

Barry, H., Jr., & Marshall, F. E. (1953). Maladjustment and maternal rejection in retrolental fibroplasia. *Mental Hygiene, 37,* 570–580.

Bauman, M. K. (1964). Group differences disclosed by inventory items. *International Journal for the Education of the Blind, 13,* 101–106.

Bauman, M. K. (1973). *The social competency of visually handicapped children.* Paper presented at conference on The Blind Child in Social Interaction: Developing Relationships with Peers and Adults, New York.

Berla', E. P. (1972). Effects of physical size and complexity on tactual discrimination of blind children. *Exceptional Children, 39,* 120–124.

Berla', E. P., Butterfield, L. H., Jr., & Murr, M. J. (1976). Tactual reading of political maps by blind students: A videomatic behavioral analysis. *Journal of Special Education, 10,* 265–276.

Berla', E. P., & Murr, M. J. (1974). Searching tactual space. *Education of the Visually Handicapped, 6,* 49–58.

Berla', E. P., & Murr, M. J. (1975). Psychophysical functions for active tactual discrimination of line width by blind children. *Perception & Psychophysics, 17,* 607–612.

Buell, C. (1950). Motor performance of visually handicapped children. *Exceptional Children, 17,* 69–72.

Burlingham, D. (1961). Some notes on the development of the blind. *Psychoanalytic Study of the Child, 16,* 121–145.

Burlingham, D. (1964). Hearing and its role in the development of the blind. *Psychoanalytic Study of the Child, 19,* 95–112.

Burlingham, D. (1965). Some problems of ego development in blind children. *Psychoanalytic Study of the Child, 20,* 194–208.

Canning, M. (1957). *Exploring the number concept in blind children.* Unpublished manuscript, University of Birmingham, U.K.

Caton, H., & Pester, E. (1979). *Development of a beginning braille reading series. Final report.* New York: Educational Resources Information Center.

Cratty, B. J., & Sams, T. A. (1968). *The body-image of blind children.* New York: American Foundation for the Blind.

Cutsforth, T. D. (1932). The unreality of words to the blind. *Teachers Forum, 4,* 86–89.

DeMott, R. M. (1972). Verbalism and affective meaning for blind, severely visually impaired, and normally sighted children. *New Outlook for the Blind, 66,* 1–8.

Dokecki, P. C. (1966). Verbalism and the blind: A critical review of the concept and the literature. *Exceptional Children, 32,* 525–530.

Dunlea, A. (1982). *The role of visual information in the emergence of meaning: A comparison of blind and sighted children.* Unpublished doctoral dissertation, University of Southern California.

Duran, P., & Tufenkjian, S. (1970). The measurement of length by congenitally blind children and a quasiformal approach for spatial concepts. *American Foundation for the Blind Research Bulletin, 22,* 47–70.

Endress, D. T. (1968). *Development levels and parental attitudes of preschool blind children in Colorado.* Unpublished doctoral dissertation, Colorado State College.

Ferrell, K. A. (1980). Can infants use the Sonicguide? Two years experience of project VIEW. *Journal of Visual Impairment & Blindness, 74,* 209–220.

Fletcher, J. F. (1980). Spatial representation in blind children. 1: Development compared to sighted children. *Journal of Visual Impairment & Blindness, 74,* 381–385.

Foulke, E. (1962). The role of experience in the formation of concepts. *International Journal for the Education of the Blind, 12,* 1–6.

Foulke, E. (1971). The perceptual basis for mobility. *American Foundation for the Blind Research Bulletin, 23,* 1–8.

Foulke, E., Amster, C. H., Nolan, C. Y., & Bixler, R. H. (1962). The comprehension of rapid speech by the blind. *Exceptional Children, 29,* 134–141.

Fraiberg, S. (1968). Parallel and divergent patterns in blind and sighted infants. *Psychoanalytic Study of the Child, 23,* 264–300.

Fraiberg, S., & Freedman, D. A. (1964). Studies in the ego development of the congenitally blind child. *Psychoanalytic Study of the Child, 19,* 113–169.

Friedman, J., & Pasnak, R. (1973). Accelerated acquisition of classification skills by blind children. *Developmental Psychology, 9,* 333–337.

Gore, G. V. (1969). A comparison of two methods of speeded speech. *Education of the Visually Handicapped, 1,* 69–76.

Gottesman, M. (1971). A comparative study of Piaget's developmental schema of sighted children with that of a group of blind children. *Child Development, 42,* 573–580.

Gottesman, M. (1973). Conservation development in blind children. *Child Development, 44,* 824–827.

Gottesman, M. (1976). Stage development of blind children: A Piagetian view. *New Outlook for the Blind,* **70,** 94–100.

Hallenbeck, J. (1954). Two essential factors in the development of young blind children. *New Outlook for the Blind,* **48,** 308–315.

Hare, B. A., Hammill, D. D., & Crandell, J. M. (1970). Auditory discrimination ability of visually limited children. *New Outlook for the Blind,* **64,** 287–292.

Harley, R. K. (1963). *Verbalism among blind children.* New York: American Foundation for the Blind (Research Series, No. 10).

Hart, V. (1983). *Characteristics of young blind children.* Paper presented at the Second International Symposium on Visually Handicapped Infants and Young Children: Birth to 7. May, Aruba.

Hartlage, L. C. (1968). Deficit in space concepts associated with visual deprivation. *Journal of Learning Disabilities,* **1,** 21–23.

Hartlage, L. C. (1969). Verbal tests of spatial conceptualization. *Journal of Experimental Psychology,* **80,** 180–182.

Higgins, L. C. (1973). *Classification in congenitally blind children.* New York: American Foundation for the Blind (Research Series, No. 25).

Hill, E. W. (1970). The formation of concepts involved in body position in space. *Education of the Visually Handicapped,* **2,** 112–115.

Hill, E. W. (1971). The formation of concepts involved in body position in space. *Education of the Visually Handicapped,* **3,** 21–25.

Hill, E. W., & Blasch, B. B. (1980). Concept development. In R. L. Welsh & B. B. Blasch (Eds.), *Foundations of orientation and mobility,* pp. 265–290. New York: American Foundation for the Blind.

Imamura, S. (1965). *Mother and blind child.* New York: American Foundation for the Blind (Research Series, No. 14).

Jankowski, L. W., & Evans, J. K. (1981). The exercise capacity of blind children. *Journal of Visual Impairment & Blindness,* **75,** 248–251.

Jones, B. (1975). Spatial perception in the blind. *British Journal of Psychology,* **66,** 461–472.

Juurmaa, J. (1973). Transposition in mental spatial manipulation: A theoretical analysis. *American Foundation for the Blind Research Bulletin,* **26,** 87–134.

Kay, L., & Kay, N. (1983). An ultrasonic spatial sensor's role as a developmental aid for blind children. *Transactions of the Ophthalmological Society of New Zealand,* **35,** 38–42.

Lairy, G. C., & Harrison-Covello, A. (1973). The blind child and his parents: Congenital visual defect and the repercussion of family attitudes on the early development of the child. *American Foundation for the Blind Research Bulletin,* **25,** 1–24.

Land, S. L., & Vineberg, S. E. (1965). Locus of control in blind children. *Exceptional Children,* **31,** 257–260.

Maxfield, K. E., & Buchholz, S. (1957). *A social maturity scale for blind preschool children: A guide to its use.* New York: American Foundation for the Blind.

Maxfield, K. E., & Fjeld, H. A. (1942). The social maturity of the visually handicapped preschool child. *Child Development,* **13,** 1–27.

McGuinness, R. M. (1970). A descriptive study of blind children educated in the itinerant teacher, resource room, and special school setting. *American Foundation for the Blind Research Bulletin,* **20,** 1–56.

Millar, S. (1975). Spatial memory by blind and sighted children. *British Journal of Psychology,* **66,** 449–459.

Millar, S. (1978). Tactual shapes. *Occasional Papers of the British Psychological Society,* **2,** 55–59.

Morris, J. E., & Nolan, C. Y. (1963). Minimum sizes for areal type tactual symbols. *International Journal for the Education of the Blind,* **13,** 48–51.

Muir, D. W., Humphrey, G. K., Dodwell, P. C., & Humphrey, D. E. (1985). Use of sonar sensors with human infants. In D. H. Warren & E. R. Strelow (Eds.), *Electronic spatial sensing for the blind: Contributions from perception, rehabilitation, and computer vision,* pp. 299–324. Dordrecht, Netherlands: Martinus-Nijhoff.

Newcomer, J. (1977). Sonicguide: Its use with public school children. *Journal of Visual Impairment & Blindness,* **71,** 268–271.

Nolan, C. Y. (1960). On the unreality of words to the blind. *New Outlook for the Blind,* **54,** 100–102.

Nolan, C. Y. (1959). Roughness discrimination among blind children in the primary grades. *International Journal for the Education of the Blind,* **9,** 97–100.

Nolan, C. Y., & Morris, J. E. (1960). Further results in the development of a test of roughness discrimination. *International Journal for the Education of the Blind,* **10,** 48–50.

Norris, M., Spaulding, P. J., & Brodie, F. H. (1957). *Blindness in children.* Chicago: University of Chicago Press.

Petrucci, D. (1953). The blind child and his adjustment. *New Outlook for the Blind,* **47,** 240–246.

Sandler, A. M. (1965). Aspects of passivity and ego development in the blind infant. *Psychoanalytic Study of the Child,* **18,** 343–361.

Schindele, R. (1974). The social adjustment of visually handicapped children in different educational settings. *American Foundation for the Blind Research Bulletin,* **28,** 125–144.

Scott, R. A. (1969). The socialization of blind children. In D. Goslin (Ed.), *Handbook of socialization theory and research,* pp. 1025–1045. Chicago: Rand McNally.

Siegel, I. M., & Murphy, T. J. (1970). *Postural determinants in the blind.* Final Project Report, Grant RD–3512–SB–700C2. Department of Children and Family Services, Illinois Visually Handicapped Institute, Chicago, Il.

Sommers, V. S. (1944). *The influence of parental attitudes and social environment on the personality development of the adolescent blind.* New York: American Foundation for the Blind.

Spiegelman, M. N. (1976). A comparative study of the effects of early blindness on the development of auditory-spatial learning. In Z. S. Jastrzembska (Ed.), *The effects of blindness and other impairments on early development,* pp. 29–50. New York: American Foundation for the Blind.

Spungin, S. J. (1985). Technology and the blind person: Corridors of insensitivity. In D. H. Warren & E. R. Strelow (Eds.), *Electronic spatial sensing for the blind: Contributions from perception, rehabilitation, and computer vision,* pp. 375–386. Dordrecht, Netherlands: Martinus–Nijhoff.

Stephens, B. (1972). Cognitive processes in the visually impaired. *Education of the Visually Handicapped,* **4,** 106–111.

Stephens, B. & Grube, C. (1982). Development of Piagetian reasoning in congenitally blind children. *Journal of Visual Impairment & Blindness,* **76,** 133–143.

Stephens, B., Grube, C., & Fitzgerald, J. (1977). *Cognitive remediation of blind students.* Final report, Project No.

443CH50410, Grant No. GOO–74–07445. U.S. Office of Education, Bureau of Education for the Handicapped.

Stephens, B., & Simpkins, K. (1974). *The reasoning, moral judgment, and moral conduct of the congenitally blind* (Report No. H23–3197). Office of Education, Bureau of Education for the Handicapped.

Strelow, E. R. (1983). Use of the Binaural Sensory Aid by young children. *Journal of Visual Impairment & Blindness, 77,* 429–438.

Strelow, E. R., Kay, N., & Kay, L. (1978). Binaural Sensory Aid: Case studies of its use by two children. *Journal of Visual Impairment & Blindness, 72,* 1–9.

Thompson, R. P. (1969). Parent-child relationships and visual loss. In M. H. Goldberg & J. R. Swinton (Eds.), *Blindness research: The expanding frontiers. A liberal studies perspective,* pp. 54–66. State College, PA: Pennsylvania State University Press.

Tobin, M. J. (1972). Conservation of substance in the blind and partially sighted. *British Journal of Educational Psychology, 42,* 192–197.

Warren, D. H. (1978). Childhood visual impairment: Sources and uses of knowledge. *Journal of Visual Impairment & Blindness, 72,* 404–411.

Warren, D. H. (1984). *Blindness and early childhood development* (2nd ed.). New York: American Foundation for the Blind.

Warren, D. H., Anooshian, L. J., & Bollinger, J. G. (1973). Early vs. late blindness: The role of early vision in spatial behavior. *American Foundation for the Blind Research Bulletin, 26,* 151–170.

Warren, D. H., & Kocon, J. A. (1974). Factors in the successful mobility of the blind: A review. *American Foundation for the Blind Research Bulletin, 28,* 191–218.

Weiner, L. H. (1963). The performance of good and poor Braille readers on certain tests involving tactual perception. *International Journal for the Education of the Blind, 12,* 72–77.

Welsh, R. L. (1980). Psychosocial dimensions. In R. L. Welsh & B. B. Blasch (Eds.), *Foundations of Orientation and Mobility,* pp. 225–264. New York: American Foundation for the Blind.

Wilson, E. L. (1967). A developmental approach to psychological factors which may inhibit mobility in the visually handicapped person. *New Outlook for the Blind, 61,* 283–289, 308.

Witkin, H. A., Birnbaum, J., Lomonaco, S., Lehr, S., & Herman, J. L. (1968). Cognitive patterning in congenitally totally blind children. *Child Development, 39,* 767–786.

Witkin, H. A., Oltman, P. K., Chase, J. B., & Friedman, F. (1971). Cognitive patterning in the blind. In J. Hellmuth (Ed.), *Cognitive studies* (Vol. 2). pp. 16–46. New York: Brunner/Mazel.

Worchel, P. (1951). Space perception and orientation in the blind. *Psychological Monographs, 65,* 1–28.

Worchel, P., Mauney, J., & Andrew, J. G. (1950). The perception of obstacles by the blind. *Journal of Experimental Psychology, 40,* 746–751.

Research Issues in Educating Visually Handicapped Persons with Multiple Impairments

EDWIN K. HAMMER, Ph.D.

University of Texas at Dallas

INTRODUCTION

The fact that there is not a complete listing or census of the number of visually handicapped persons with multiple impairments is a significant research issue. Such a list does not seem to exist. Why have persons who have visual loss and multiple impairments been overlooked? It would be tempting to complain of ignorance on the part of service providers, or to cast blame on officials, or to hint of conspiracy among those who serve the visually impaired population. However, the causes, more than likely, are simply traditions of the field. It has been traditional to consider those who are visually impaired only from one perspective: lack of visual acuity. If a person had other problems, too often, that person was not included in the delivery of services to visually impaired persons. These individuals were left to the services of other programs to provide education and habilitation.

It is also important to acknowledge that there is not one uniform group of persons who are visually handicapped and multiply impaired. The range of problems is extensive. There are too many levels of function and too many variances in behavior found in persons with multiple handicaps to try to place all of them in one category. There are too many unknown influences that contribute to a person's attainment. It is not possible to assume that any one method or theory describes all. It is an important research issue to explore how services to persons who are visually impaired and multiply-handicapped can be provided. It is an even more pressing issue to identify how this population can be accurately identified.

This chapter will attempt to outline these major issues in developing services to persons who are visually handicapped and have multiple impairments. Four strands will be woven into the discussion as an underlying theme of this exploration. These will be used to propose recommendations for research into the development of services to persons who are multiply handicapped and have visual impairments. These four themes are summarized below:

1. There is no definite count of the number of multiply-handicapped, visually impaired persons among the population of handicapped persons in the United States.

2. There is a need to develop a multiaxial diagnostic system similar to the DSM-3 (Diagnostic and Statistical Manual—Third Edition) of the American Psychiatric Association that may be used to provide standard diagnostic, clinical, and research data on this diverse population.

3. This chapter proposes a new type of teacher of visually impaired students. This person would be an advocate within schools for vision services for all children, including the wide range of services needed by multiply-impaired children who have visual loss. The model for this new professional may be found in the American Speech, Language and Hearing Association professionals in speech pathology and audiology.

4. Denial is a major issue in developing awareness of multihandicapped, visually impaired persons. Too often, professionals discount the role of vision in learning and the effect of visual loss in regard to program considerations.

STATE OF THE ART

Reasons for Lack of Data

Kirchner, in her chapter in this volume on prevalence and demographics, addresses the issues in identifying persons with visual impairment who have additional problems. Factors that seem to contribute to the lack of figures that describe this population include the system of reporting cases through official channels, such as government report forms, cautions against "unduplicated counts" of persons, and continuation of single category designation being the basis for funding from state and federal sources. Until there are accurate figures on the numbers of cases, and the types of problems are identified, there will be little progress made to acknowledge the population of persons who are visually impaired and have multiple handicaps.

The lack of data regarding the numbers of visually impaired, multiply-handicapped persons seems to be directly related to the way that educational service has evolved over time for children who are visually impaired. Selection and placement of children with visual impairments seems to follow historical precedents as well as professional traditions. For many years, educational services to children who were visually impaired were limited to residential schools. These residential schools were first established as boarding schools, similar to other private, residential boarding schools for non-impaired students. As state-supported residential facilities were built, they were based on the model of the boarding school also. These school carried a selectivity for enrollment. Children who attended state-supported residential schools were expected to be ready for academic learning. Emphasis was placed on learning Braille or listening skills as the means of information gathering. Strong emphasis was placed on learning to live within socially acceptable roles as defined for persons who were blind. It was not until after the Second World War that enrollment of visually impaired children in day school programs in local communities became equal to the enrollment in residential schools (Jones, 1961). The key issue at that time was whether the student would learn to read print or to read Braille. Students who did not have academic potential were not continued in school.

Those persons who did not benefit from academic instruction were usually grouped into a category called the "retarded blind" meaning that they were not capable of academic achievement to the degree that permitted them to remain in the traditional school for blind students. It must be remembered that, at that time, there were no assurances that any child could be enrolled in a public school. Certain criteria had to be met for school entrance. The major one was that there was an IQ score that predicted that the child would benefit from academic instruction. It was not unheard of to have children excluded from school because of an indicated lack of potential as measured on a single test. It was not until 1975 that this changed. States were mandated to offer an appropriate education for every child residing in the school district through Public Law 94-142. In some communities, that law is only now being accepted. Until 94-142 went into effect, the IQ score was the major criterion of estimation of educability and in most states "mental retardation takes precedence" meant that if a person did not have an IQ score above 70, it was very doubtful that the individual would be enrolled in a school program. This was true for visually impaired children who were multiply impaired as well as children with other multiple conditions. Often, multiply-impaired children would be tested with instruments that were totally inappropriate for use with multiply-handicapped children. As a result, children with multiple impairments were excluded from school as a general rule.

The tradition that mental retardation took primacy over other functions is still to be found among certain professionals. It may be an unconscious attitude among professionals that "low-functioning" blind persons are limited in learning potential. This may be concluded by certain professionals even without ever having an opportunity to find out how much a "low-functioning" blind person may learn. Often, "low-functioning" has been used to cover a bias that mental retardation takes primacy over visual loss and that persons with mental retardation are hopeless and uneducable. This attitude is slowly being replaced, but it is still to be found.

A second factor in the lack of data regarding multiple-handicapped, visually impaired children is the lack of any assertive policy to see that practices from the field of education of visually impaired students are applied to multiply-handicapped, visually impaired children. Usually, the curriculum followed for this population comes from the curriculum used with children who are mentally retarded. There is no active program to see that aids and devices used with visually impaired students are available routinely for multiply-handicapped, visually impaired students. Often, lenses are not provided to low-functioning visually impaired students. Teachers in classrooms serving multiply-handicapped, visually impaired students do not have information regarding why it is necessary for these students to wear lenses. Until recently, there were few instructional programs for the use of residual vision for visually impaired, multiply-handicapped students. Technology that is routinely used in programs for visually impaired students has not been available for multiply-handicapped, visually impaired students in any organized program. The reason for this is another research issue.

A third factor in the lack of data regarding multiply-handicapped, visually impaired students is the lack of assessment devices that detail the strengths of the learner. Most assessment instruments come from a background of highlighting disability. With the emphasis on appropriate education for each child, there has been a movement toward assessments that identify abilities rather than disabilities. This movement has not reached full impact in the area of multiply-handicapped, visually impaired children's educational programming. The particular shift is from using testing to predict outcome (estimating educability) to using testing to describe behavior (estimating strengths and needs).

A final issue that seems to deter collection of data about the number of multiply-handicapped, visually impaired students may be found in teacher preparation programs. The teacher of visually impaired students may be viewed by other school professionals and medical professionals as an academic tutor for blind children. There is a pressing need for research to identify the skills and processes required by teachers of multiply-handicapped, visually impaired students. Results of these studies would permit the establishment of training programs that prepare personnel to learn the necessary skills to be effective teachers of visually impaired, multiply-handicapped children.

What seems to be needed is a variety of trained personnel. Some may work as advocates for better vision services in *all* educational settings. Others may work in specialty settings with multiply-handicapped, visually impaired students, while still others may be trained to evaluate best practices as related to vision and visually impaired students. There seem to be many possible products of training, but the research to identify these possibilities is missing. Most importantly, there is a need for formalize a training system for teachers of visually impaired students to be prepared to work with multiply-handicapped students. At the present time, there is a limited system of dissemination of information where teachers trade with each other. The established journals and professional literature are not used by teachers to gain information. It is often who you know that makes the difference in how you teach.

The trends in the area of education of the multiply-handicapped, visually impaired individual seem to show that old systems are breaking down and that new systems are slow to take up the slack. For example, the deaf-blind delivery system was started as a national network in 1968, and spread throughout the nation. By 1974, it was possible for deaf-blind children to receive a program in their local community. The minimum program was the home correspondence course from the John Tracy Clinic in Los Angeles. In some states, there were traveling consultants or itinerant teachers who came into the child's home and home town to find local agencies willing to provide ongoing services to the deaf-blind child with support from state and regional centers. A maximum program was a full day school program or a residential program for deaf-blind children that included related services, family services, diagnostic and evaluative services, as well as educational programming. The deaf-blind network has been discontinued. Federal funding has been changed to other priorities and the trend is to place deaf-blind children in programs for severely handicapped students. One of the major charges to service providers to children who are multiply-handicapped and visually impaired is to follow visually impaired children into placements in programs for severely handicapped students to assure that appropriate vision services are a standard part of the program.

The DSM-3 Model

Even with the difficulties of finding out how many children have visual impairment and multiple handicaps, there seems to be a second dilemma that arises. What if these children were found? How would they be described so that there were uniform ways to classify their needs? One of the reasons that multiply-handicapped, visually impaired children are not counted is that reporting forms do not have a place for them to be listed and there are strong admonitions to restrict "unduplicated counts" of children.

The answer to this problem may be found in reporting systems such as the model used by the American Psychiatric Association's system of reporting published under the title *Diagnostic and Statistical Manual of Mental Disorders* (3rd Edition) (American Psychiatric Association, 1980). The DSM-3 is a manual that permits data to be collected on a diverse population in such a manner that it is possible to use these data for clinical application as well as for research purposes, funding qualifications, and diagnostic criteria. In the DSM-3 system, the multiaxial evaluation provides a way to assess every case of mental disorder on each of several "axes." Each of the five axes used in the DSM-3 refers to a different class of information. In order to maintain consistency in reporting (and avoid unduplicated counts) the DSM-3 uses the first three categories for diagnostic assessment. Axis I establishes clinical data that describe the client. Axis 2 codes the specific disorder that is the focus of treatment or attention. The use of Axis 3 provides a way to indicate any physical disorder or condition that is relative to the understanding and management of the individual. These first three axes comprise a basic set of evaluation criteria. All may be used, but it is not always necessary to use each of these axes in describing the client. The goal is to develop accurate descriptors of the current functioning and needs of the client.

Axis 4 is used to code stress in the overall severity of conditions that contribute to the current situation of the client. These stressors reflect the amount of change in a person's life caused by the current situation. The degree to which the event is desired and under the individual's control is coded. The multiplicity of stress factors found in the clinical observations of the client is included. This axis notes external stress factors, not internal stress (these would be noted in Axis 1 or Axis 2). This information is collected in order to develop a treatment plan that addresses all possible factors in the client's life.

Axis 5 of the DSM-3 indicates the highest level of adaptive functioning in the past year. This is divided into three components: social relations, occupational functioning, and use of leisure time.

The rationale for the use of DSM-3 as a source of data collection is that there is a standard framework to address a complex set of problems found in persons exhibiting mental disorders. The clinician is permitted to use combinations of observations, but these fit into specific categories so that the reporting of these clinical observations may be used in many ways: diagnostic, demographic, descriptive, or research data.

There can be little disagreement that the DSM-3 serves as a needed model for the description of persons who are multiply handicapped, including those who are visually impaired and have multiple handicaps. Using such a model, it might be possible to develop the following framework:

1. Axis 1: *Presenting Problems*. This would describe the ways in which a student gathers, processes, and

uses information. It would describe effects rather than causes.

2. Axis 2: *Disorders*. This would be diagnostic. It might be helpful to use classifications of syndromes, although the value of such information is questioned in development of intervention strategies.

3. Axis 3: *Identified Barriers*. This axis would observe the effects of the problem on success for the client. It would outline an ecosystem in which the client was to function. Axis 1 would be client centered while Axis 3 would be environmentally sensitive.

4. Axis 4: *Stress Factors*. This axis is similar to the one used in DSM-3 in that it identifies those factors that keep the client from stabilizing so that learning is effective. Family needs, transportation, after-school care, or medication are some examples. It is important to address Axis 4 issues in the planning and management of a case if success is to be assured.

5. Axis 5: *Adaptive Potential*. This axis combines some of the more traditional aspects of diagnostic practices, mainly prediction. It gives the highest level of functioning observed in the child over the past 12 months. The data may be standardized tests, case notes, or parent or teacher report. The goal of this axis would be to set expectations for a time based upon past performance and future attainment.

The first three axes would be used to establish the personal needs, effects of problems, and the setting in which the client was expected to function. The interaction of these variables could serve as the basis for programming, as well as a basis for describing the client, client problems, and educational needs for research purposes, demographic information, and funding allocations. The format would be much more realistic than a single category form that expects all data to be reduced to a checkmark. These data could be used for a variety of reports and not enter into "duplication" of counts. The use of Axis 4 could clarify some of the environmental issues that continue to play dominant roles in the way a child receives services and the way a child is able to accept services.

To establish a classification reporting system for use with multiply-handicapped persons would require a major, nationally coordinated research study. The American Psychiatric Association worked for many years, through several editions of their diagnostic manual. There is still criticism that it is only used for the purpose of applying for third party insurance payment; however, the reality is that there is increased communication among professionals who rely on the DSM-3 in the transfer of data, the reporting of data, and in the collection of data. It might be possible to include or utilize formats developed by other professions in identifying and tracking clients, services, needs, and intervention strategies. A cost accounting system that has identified cost-points in a manufacturing process would be another example of a way to identify multiply-handicapped children and youth. The point is that there is not a current format that is acceptable, and a new one could advance services by having a multiaxial framework in which to operate.

Variables that would seem to be important for the first three axes would include the vision system, the auditory system, the tactile system, the ability to move in space through types of ambulation, self-care skills, the use of a range of speech, language and gestures, and some measure of sensory integrative development. There would also be a need to identify intellectual function, problem-solving skills, academic achievement, and social-emotional functioning. Each of these variables would need to be broken into points along the variables that served as items on the multiaxial system.

Diagnostic Conditions

The interaction of each of these traits to visual loss is what is found in the multiply-handicapped, visually impaired child. Some of the diagnostic conditions where these traits are found in visually impaired students include prematurity of the retina (previously called retrolental fibroplasia). This condition served as the major crisis population in the visually impaired population from the 1940s to the present. Prematurity of the retina occurs when a child is placed in an incubator and the oxygen is too pure. When moisture is added to pure oxygen, the prematurity of the retina is minimized for new born infants. In this visual condition, it is possible to find motor problems, learning problems, and other problems related to prematurity.

A second condition that demonstrates the interaction of traits of behavior is in a syndrome that includes retinitis pigmentosa. When retinitis pigmentosa occurs with deafness in Usher's syndrome there is a progression of traumatic events in the life of the multihandicapped person (English, 1978). In this condition, the visual loss is first noticed when the young child experiences night blindness. This may be brought to attention by complaints of fear of the dark, clumsiness, or reports that lights have a halo around them. In the multiply-handicapped person, this may be encountered through increased isolation, feelings of being left alone, and increased concern over where others are in spatial relationship. While Usher's syndrome may be diagnosed as early as 5 years of age, in many cases, late diagnosis is made in adolescence or early adult years.

There continues to be a population of children and youth with head injuries that are part of the multihandicapped, visually impaired population. These cases often arise from child abuse or from auto accidents. Often, children with severe brain damage are considered mentally retarded without ever considering the loss of vision and its effects on cognitive potential in children with severe brain injury. In these cases, children may have remission of learned behavior. There may be confusion over what happened to them, or there may be massive brain trauma that extinguishes major cross-modal functions, such as partial sight associated with hemiplegia.

Viral infections also continue to contribute to the population of children with visual handicaps and multiple impairments. These viruses include, but are not limited to toxoplasmosis, hepatitis, cytomegalic inclusion virus, and rubella. These seem to feed on sensory tissue in utero. In small children, there are continual reports of cases of meningitis and encephalitis that cause blindness and other impairment. In the past few years, many of these children were diagnosed as being deaf-blind. The Rand Corporation studied the population called deaf-blind and concluded:

> Of approximately 683,000 youth in the United States who have either hearing or vision handicap, some not reliably known faction are multiply handicapped, i.e., are also mentally retarded, emotionally disturbed, learning disabled, crippled or other health impaired, or have more than one sensory handicap. A very few thousand are both hearing and visually handicapped; while labeled 'deaf-blind' a great diversity of sensory ability exists in that small population, few of whom are both profoundly deaf and totally blind (Kakalik et al., 1974, 7).

It is true that there is confusion over the population that is called "deaf-blind." This stems mainly from the way that the programs to serve that population developed. The rubella epidemic of 1963–65 called specific attention to the increased numbers of children born with congenital rubella syndrome. In 1968, it was estimated (Dantona, 1977) that there were 275 children who were deaf-blind in school programs in the United States. By 1975, that number had increased to 6,148 children. These cases were certified by programs in each state and the controversy that arose was whether these children could benefit from services for "deaf-blind" or whether they were severely and profoundly retarded to the extent that sensory function in vision and hearing was also severely impaired. The major increase in the numbers of children who were classified as being deaf-blind came from the congenital rubella syndrome population. This population did have multiple handicaps, including visual loss and hearing loss; it did not fit into the traditional concept of deaf-blind persons, which usually meant people who were of average intelligence and who had lost their vision and hearing after having acquired language. A few persons existed who were deaf-blind as the result of visual loss in conjunction with congenital hearing loss or an acquired hearing loss found with congenital blindness.

There are two interesting aspects of the emergence of the deaf-blind population. One is that there have always been deaf-blind persons but the primary diagnosis of mental retardation precluded this population from being identified as deaf-blind. The other aspect is that as medical practice improves, more persons are living with more severely involved disabilities. Wolf, Delk, and Schein (1982) surveyed services to deaf persons and services to blind persons and produced an estimate of the number of deaf-blind persons in the United States. Their figure of 13,182 deaf-blind persons of all ages in the United States was translated into a figure of 754 per 100,000 persons as the incidence of deaf-blind.

One of the major needs, therefore, in researching the population of multiply-handicapped, visually impaired persons is an accurate count of the population. This means that some systematic method must be devised to identify this population. Once identified through a screening program, there is a need to describe this population through appropriate assessment.

Assessment Issues

Because of the complexity of conditions presented by multiply-handicapped, visually impaired children, one of the major areas of research and development has been in the assessment of functions of this population. Hammer (1985) reviewed these trends and noted the increase in instruments that are sensitive to describing the needs of multiply-handicapped. Visually impaired persons. One of the earliest studies of the issue of assessment was carried out by Guldager (1970). She postulated that the reticular formation was defective in congenital rubella syndrome children and used a Piagetian approach to assess multihandicapped, visually impaired individuals. In this small sample ($N = 7$), Guldager concluded that there were both psychological and neurological causes due to an isolation that happened because:

1. Sensory deprivation from birth resulted in a lack of development of body image and possible consequent distortion of perceptual, cognitive, and motor development.
2. Isolation from the family, because of the child's failure to respond, caused family members to ignore the child and not to handle the child in the usual care-giver ways, thus creating monotonous environment.
3. Central nervous system was damaged due to the early effects of the rubella virus on neurological growth.
4. Frequent surgery and hospitalization resulted in motor inactivity as well as reduced sensory stimuli (Guldager, 1970).

This study, although limited in sample size, was pioneering in describing characteristics. It also defined key issues in the development of services to young children with multiple problems, including visusl loss, due to rubella. Guilager stated that children who did not advance to a stage of imitation in the sensorimotor period were at risk for learning. Therefore, she proposed intervention strategies for young multihandicapped, visually impaired children focusing on a progression based on the work of Piaget.

This approach had previously been suggested in the work of Van Dijk (1965) in the study of the relationship of motor competence to language development that led

FIGURE 1

PRESYMBOLIC LEVEL

1. EGO CONSCIOUSNESS (ME AND NOT ME DELINEATED)
2. MOTOR PATTERNS FOR EXPERIENCES: RANGESAND CONNECTIONS
3. DEVELOPMENT OF BODY SCHEMA:
      A. SUBSTAGE—CO-ACTIVE MOVEMENT
      B. SUBSTAGE—IMITATION
4. NATURAL GESTURE
      A. SUBSTAGE—DECONTEXTUALIZATION—ANTICIPATION
      B. SUBSTAGE—DENATURALIZATION—HOLOPHRASTIC GESTURE

Note: From Development of Language in the Deaf-Blind Multihandicapped Child: Progression of Instruction. (p.123) by E. K. Hammer (1978). In E. H. Shroyer and D. Tweedie (eds.) *The Multihandicapped Hearing Impaired Child*. Washington, D.C.: Gallaudet College

to cognitive efficiency. Van Dijk has been a major influence in the development of better understanding of the effects of visual loss in multiply-handicapped children.

Van Dijk's approach (see Hammer, 1978; Sternberg, Battle, & Hill, 1980) used the body as the base of communicative behavior in multiply – handicapped, visually impaired children. The relationship of the adult to the child was carefully defined and the use of the adult's body to serve as a model to the child's motor actions was specifically defined. There was a progression that Van Dijk was able to identify and to validate through repeated application that led to his approach to language development. This approach delineated the steps in language development in multiply-impaired children. These steps are outlined in Figure 1

This progression opened the way to interact with multiply-handicapped children to develop language, cognitive abilities, and social skills. It allowed for a systematic method of instruction to be used with this severely impaired population. Van Dijk's methods served as a basis for test instruments used with multiply-handicapped, visually impaired children.

An assessment instrument was developed by Ficociello-Gage (1978): the Assessment of Prevocational and Daily Living Skills. It was based on the work of Guldager, Piaget, and Van Dijk. It proposed a way to look at skills necessary for adolescents who were multiply-handicapped and visually impaired. The construct was to have observations of the child made over time, comparing the child to self on a series of criterion measures. Emphasis was placed on lower-functioning persons who were visually impaired and the outcome was to determine the potential of the individual for independent living.

A similar instrument was developed by Mithaug, Mar, and Stewart (1979) with the Prevocational Assessment

and Curriculum Guide. The PACG was used to rate functions in severely impaired, deaf-blind multihandicapped or visually impaired persons. The results were related to immediate goals that could be used for programming.

Another instrument was developed at the Texas School for the Blind by Wade and Stone (1980) that undertook to evaluate work skills. This test, the Austin Work Skills Evaluation, compared blind, hearing-impaired children on vocational tasks found in work environments. This test compared the person to others with similar disabilities such as deafness or blindness associated with mental retardation. it assessed social skills in a work setting among blind, multihandicapped persons as well as mobility skills, self-help skills, and motor skills development. The scale was also used to compare the individual to self over time so that behaviors and functions were identified in the context of the person's environment rather than in a single testing setting or a simulated work station.

Another instrument, the Behavioral Rating Instrument for Atypical Children (BRIAC), by Ruttenberg et al. attempted to permit observation of integrative functions (ego formation, cognitive attainment, independent functioning). As such, it served as a way to compare the individual to self over time to detect small increments of self-directed behavior in severely impaired individuals. This instrument required that the trainer be instructed in the administration of the test items so that there was reliability of results and internal consistency of administration. This scale was sensitive to picking up small steps of behavior change in multiply-handicapped, visually impaired persons.

The Callier Azusa Scale (Stillman 1978) grew out of the teacher-generated assessment developed by the East San Gabriel Valley program for multihandicapped children in the Los Angeles County School District. The Callier Azusa Scale was one of the original scales that focused on the person functioning below 24 months of age regardless of chronological age. It was specifically designed for low-functioning persons who were visually impaired. It has been reported to have particular strength in motor skills assessment (Day, 1978). The uniqueness of this scale was that it included parents in the assessment team as observers. The multidisciplinary team served as a panel to observe the multiply-handicapped child's behavior. It was required that the panel have at least 2 weeks experience with the child before any formal observations were recorded. Thus, this was also a test that compared the child to self over time and used many observations in order to complete the assessment.

In Michigan, Rudolph and Collins (1978) developed the Manual for Assessment of Deaf-Blind Multihandicapped Children. This instrument was influenced by the work at St Michelgestel, The Netherlands (where Van Dijk worked) through the involvement of Lieka de Leuw, who was in residence at the Michigan School for the Blind as a teacher when this test was developed. This instrument basically compared the child to self over time by making repeated sampling of behaviors. Specific attention was given to the development of language and communicative behaviors in multiply-handicapped, visually impaired children. The scales were normatively developed on the population of multiply-handicapped visually impaired children in the midwestern states of the United States. The test also has a strength in the within-group comparison and listed norms of behavior for multiply-impaired children. A particular strength beyond the important strategies for language development is in the structure provided to observe the child's interaction with the environment. Special attention was given to responses in sign language, use of speech, tactile communication, and the use of communication devices (i.e., communication boards).

The Los Lunas Curriculum System (Everington. 1982) is an outstanding approach that also provided curricular suggestions for visually impaired, multiply-handicapped, mentally retarded children and youth. It focuses on children in the severely impaired range of behavioral performance. The Los Lunas Curriculum System was developed for teaching personnel to use on site to observe functions and then to use the guide as a way to construct an intervention program. The instrument compared the individual to self over time as well as comparing the individual to others at the Los Lunas Hospital and Training Center in New Mexico. The items of the scale are functionally oriented to what the residents of state schools for mentally retarded persons would need in order to progress in such a setting. It has an excellent method of showing how an item may be answered another way for some other set of disabling conditions and still show what could be done for that client in the educational setting. The training component parallels the philosophy of the school program. The teaching staff receives specific instruction in how to be flexible in their approach to instruction. The system also assures that there are ways to have relevent content in the teaching setting that is related to the guide. Specific emphasis was placed on documentation of assessment, of teaching strategies, and of child change.

A widely used approach may be found in the Vision-Up Curriculum (Robinson, 1980). The Vision-Up Kit is a Q-sort technique to be used with parents and teachers to answer questions about the multiply-handicapped, visually impaired child's behavior. An initial screening is completed by the parents using the Q-sort method. Then a more in-depth assessment compares the child to age-mates and to self over time. The Vision-Up program then suggests ways to increase certain behaviors using a Piagetian framework supplemented by activities that increase visual efficiency. The Vision-Up Kit is used with higher-functioning deaf-blind persons or blind multihandicapped children as well as with multiply-handicapped, visually impaired children. Particular emphasis was placed on home-centered programming with preschool-age children in mind as the target population. Cards for home activities for each item on the

assessment profile have been made available for use with parents.

The Developmental Assessment Screening Inventory (DASI) (DuBose and Langley, 1979) started as the Non-verbal Developmental Screening Inventory in 1974 at the Kennedy Center of George Peabody College of Vanderbilt University. It has since been expanded and standardized on a population of severely impaired children with special notation for use with multiply-handicapped, visually impaired children. The DASI is interesting in the way it is organized. Perceptual and perceptual motor items are related to naming by signing, object matching, counting, and following commands so that a continuum is presented in communicative behavioral responses. This is probably the strongest test to be made available for use with multiply-handicapped, visually impaired children who function at or near age level.

A recent instrument has added a new dimension to the assessment issue in identifying the needs of multiply-handicapped, visually impaired persons. This instrument is the Functional Skills Screening Inventory (Becker, Schur, Pacletti, & Hammer, 1984). It is a checklist for setting priorities along two variables: the degree to which a person would be expected to work, and the degree to which a person would be expected to live in the community. The checklist sets priorities in three areas: basic skills, skills needed for sheltered living and work, and skills needed for independent living and work. A unique feature of this instrument is that it is available on the IBM-PC microcomputer for electronic administration, scoring and monitoring of individual progress. The FSSI is to be used in natural settings to assess critical living and working skills in multiply-handicapped, visually impaired populations. While it may be used with children as young as 6 years of age, the true application is to be found in assessing adolescents and young adults for their current level of functioning in eight areas (basic skills and concepts, personal care, community living, social awareness, communication, homemaking, work skills and concepts, and in the level of severity of problem behaviors). There are 343 items on the Functional Skills Screening Inventory. The results of the observations are summarized in three ways:

Priority 1: these skills are the basic elements of life and work skills that are required for the person to live as an adult in any setting or in any work or possible work area. Priority 2: contains skills that are required for successful participation in a supervised living (group home) or in a sheltered work setting where other adults participate. Priority 3: provides a profile of skills that facilitate independent living and competitive work placement in the community.

The computer sets up a database on each person assessed so that the person may be compared to self over time. A profile is generated on each priority and is printed from the computer with successive assessments

FIGURE 2

Pearson Product Moment Correlation Between FSSI and other Tests of Functional Skills: Texas School for the Blind Sample

FSSI SCALE (N = 24)	CALLIER SOCIAL	CALLIER LANG.	CALLIER LIVING SK.	CALLIER MOT/PERC.
SOCIAL TOTAL	.7369			
SOCIAL I	.7946			
SOCIAL II	.6501			
SOCIAL III	.6505			
LANGUAGE TOTAL		.8889		
LANGUAGE I		.8926		
LANGUAGE II		.8476		
LANGUAGE III		.8312		
PERSONAL TOTAL			.9396	
PERSONAL I			.9300	
PERSONAL II			.9347	
PERSONAL III			.5477	
BASIC SKILLS TOTAL				.9080
BASIC SKILLS I				.8930
BASIC SKILLS II				.8801
BASIC SKILLS III				.8555

FSSI SCALE	VINELAND SOCIAL AGE
ADAPTIVE SKILLS	.7193

Note: From Correlation Studies of the Functional Skills Screening Inventory, by H. Becker, 1985, Austin, TX: Functional Resources.

compared on the same graph. The efficiency of the computer enhances the summary of data and the comparison of group data from individual programs. This could be very helpful to administrators in decision making and in monitoring program goals. The computer also increase the possibility of inter- and intraprogram communication by transmitting the results of a person's profile from one terminal to another. This means that the program could also be used by supervisory personnel, administrative personnel, and other decision makers, as well as teaching personnel. It would be possible to use the data on individuals to allocate staff time, analyze trends in programs in terms of gaps of services, monitor child performance, and ascertain needs of staff based upon data from children and youth in the program.

Becker (1983) reported a Cronbach alpha reliability of 0.90 on the preliminary data. Correlation studies (Becker, 1985) also indicate agreement between the FSSI and other measures, as shown in Figure 2.

Other instruments have been developed for use with deaf-blind or visually impaired, multiply-handicapped persons. The American Assocation on Mental Deficiency permitted the staff of the Ellisville State School in Mississippi to adapt the Adaptive Behavior Scales to the population of deaf-blind, multiply-handicapped students residing in that school. This instrument proved to be so helpful in assessing the population that other state have used it also. This is typical of the emergence of assessment instruments developed to assess multiply-handicapped, visually impaired persons. They are strong in describing behaviors, defining strengths, and delineating needs of this most difficult to assess population. Perhaps the most exhaustive review of this issue

is to be found in an article by Robbins (1977). In summarizing, she wrote:

Prior to 1976, educational assessment of deaf-blind children offered only a few tentative beginnings of data collection in an attempt to build norms appropriate to the population and offered valuable but subjective intuitions and observations to guide efforts in differentiating educational needs among the total group . . . during the past years . . . the results is a true recognition of the range of influence the child's learning, including home, community influences, physical and biological effects, temperament, a variety of learning differences and rates of growth among children . . . in the educational assessment of multihandicapped children (Robbins, 1977, p. 133–134).

The importance of the emergence of these tests in the 1970s and early 1980s may be found in the shift that has taken place in assessment. Originally, testing was done in order to predict. With Binet's original test, it was to predict who would not complete the first year of school successfully. Later, this prediction was extended both statistically and professionally so that by the 1950s there was great reliance on standard measures to determine placement and content of educational programs. With changes in service delivery, there were changes in testing. The shift seemed to be away from prediction to description. New tests define behaviors, list age-appropriate functions, and determine the level of ability rather than reporting on the disability or what the person can not do.

Once bahaviors were described by testing, the emphasis shifted to increasing the content in the classroom based upon the potentials and abilities of the multihandicapped. 94-142 impacted that shift to description in testing and that, in turn, created new issues in educating handicapped persons. Hammer (1980) listed some of the areas where research was needed (see Figure 3 below).

Medical Issues

There have been longitudinal studies of children born with congenital rubella syndrome. These studies have tracked the largest group of multiply-handicapped, visually impaired children and youth in the current national population. Desmond (1985) completed her 20-year study of congenital rubella syndrome cases by reviewing their health status. Of the first 100 cases referred to the Baylor Medical Center project in 1963, 53 cases were reviewed at 16–18 years of age. Findings were compared to the evaluations made of the sample cases at 18 months to determine the effects of the rubella virus on development and learning. It was noted that 77% of the children in the sample were diagnosed as multiply handicapped. The death rate among those selected for study indicated that at age 16–18 years the known death rate was 25%.

FIGURE 3

	Medical (Growth)	Educational (Development)	Psycho-social (Maturational)
INFANT TODDLER	Prevention Early Diagnosis Surgeries Medication Genetic Counseling Immunization Issues Epidemiology	Infant Stimulation Neonatal Learning Sensory Training Parent Training Home Programming Community Awareness Neighborhood Day Homes	Mother/Child Bond Sensorimotor Learning Trust V. Mistrust Autonomy v. Doubt Temperament Neurobiological Issues Motor Efficiency Self Esteem
PRESCHOOL ELEMENTARY AGE	Screening (Retinitis Pigmentosa) Otitis Media Neurological Issues Health Care	Visual Efficiency Language Development Motor Development Imitation Symbol Use Anticipation	Adaptive Behavior Preoperational Stage Socialization Group Activities Memory Play
ADOLESCENT AND YOUTH	Progressive Losses Pubescence Corrective Prosthesis Health Maintenance	Prevocational Career Options Home Management Work Placement Continuing Education	Sex Education Individuation Group Living Community Living Family Networking Guardianship Aging

From Issues Related to Diagnosis and Evaluation of Deaf-Blind Persons by E. K. Hammer, 1980. In E. Wolf (ed.) *The 1980s Partnership for Planning For Progress*. Prodeedings of the Helen Keller Centennial on June 21–23, 1980, in Boston. New York: New York Institute for the Education of the Blind.

Of the 53 cases used in the study, 36 were Caucasian, 16 were Black, and 1 was Hispanic. The mean socioeconomic rating, using the Hollingshead Two Factor Index of Social Position, indicated that the families were in a moderate to low socioeconomic level. Sixty-six percent of the sample lived at home while 34% lived in residential settings away from the biological families.

As pertains to visual loss, 30 of the 53 adolescents had impaired vision. The main cause of visual loss was surgical treatment of cataracts in the early years of life. Rubella retinopathy was noted in all subjects in terms of visual problems. Glaucoma was present in 2 of the 30 cases and two had myopia in the severe range. One was considered legally blind (postcataract) with normal hearing. Eight of the sample of 53 cases were considered deaf-blind. At birth, 30 children of the sample of 53 cases were known to be congenital rubella syndrome, and late confirmation of congenital rubella syndrome was made in all cases. Of the 53 infants in 1963. 15 had cataracts bilaterally while 9 had unilateral cataracts. One had glaucoma diagnosed in infancy. Fifteen were diagnosed as having chorioretinitis (viral attack of the retina and choroid membrane of the eye). By age 18, there had been a 2% increase in visual problems in the sample. This was attributed to additional loss due to myopia (two cases) and glaucoma (two cases). Desmond stated that the dominant characteristic of the postcongenital rubella syndrome group was the diversity and multiplicity of handicaps. Multihandicaps occurred in 46% (13 of 25) children who had normal intelligence, in 10 of 13 (77%) of the adolescents who had below average intelligence and in all children functioning in the retarded range (100%).

The educational outcome for this sample was reported. Desmond listed that 15 of the 26 adolescents with average intelligence (or above average intelligence) planned formal education beyond the 12th grade. Three of these had normal hearing and one was blind and had a hearing loss, and 12 had hearing losses only. Desmond took the opportunity in the summation of her 20 years of work with congenital rubella syndrome clients to note the changes that had taken place in the educational system as she, a physician, observed from outside the field. She was moved to note the change in communication systems from a dichotomous oral/manual argument among professionals to the use of manual communication for this population. She also noted that there appeared to be progressively increasing hearing losses in the sample of the population she followed. It would be appropriate to see if there are any progressive visual losses to be found in the larger population of the post-congenital rubella syndrome adolescents.

These results call attention to the medical research that has directly affected the prevalence of multiple handicaps in visually impaired populations since the 1960s. Better seriological tests are available to establish the presence of dangerous components that place a fetus at risk. Vaccine is available to extinguish rubella virus, and other similar viral preventatives are available. There seems to be an ever increasing store of information regarding genetic factors related to visual loss and secondary disabilities. There remains a need for epidemiological surveys of causes of blindness and visual loss in multiply-handicapped populations. In the 1940s and 1950s, there were the crisis populations of prematurity of the retina (RLF). In the 1960s the congenital rubella syndrome children were born. In the 1970s, there were increased casefindings of children who were brain damaged at birth with related visual loss. Reporting systems are needed to alert the field to new or crisis populations of children who have visual losses and who have a high risk for other disabilities. For example, closed head injury cases are surviving due to better trauma care in hospitals. How many of these include visual loss in patients? How many abused children have visual loss from head injuries? It seems that there is a need to monitor casefinding in populations where visual loss may be indicated.

Educational Issues

In the educational area, there is a need to study the impact of Public Law 94-142. In the decade since that law was implemented in the public schools of the United States, there have been many new programs for visually impaired children, including those who have multiple handicaps. It is time to ask if these programs are effective. Special study must be given to the identification of children with visual losses, especially in populations that have other disabilities such as mental retardation, emotional disturbance, severe brain damage, or hearing impairment.

Also in the education area, there is a need to evaluate the curricula that are available for educational intervention with multiply-handicapped, visually impaired children. A new program has been developed called Reach Out and Teach (Ferrell, 1985). This series was based upon the premise of using parents as teachers in meeting the needs of young children who are multiply-handicapped and visually impaired. The Reach Out and Teach program is based upon a survey of persons active in the field of habilitation of children with visual losses. The panel included parents of multihandicapped, visually impaired children as well as parents of blind and partially sighted children, teachers, blind adults, and persons who train teachers. Priorities were listed from this group and then materials were developed over a 3-year period. Only materials that were evaluated as being effective were kept in the project. Included in the materials is initial information about children and about the effects of visual loss on development. Encouragement to start to assist the blind infant or partially sighted, multihandicapped infant was presented with specific materials included; motor activities to increase movement, exploration, and sensory experiences, daily living skills, and communication techniques were included for parents to use to assist in critical developmental interventions in the home. Explanations of sensory development were given so that parents might know how to relate to the child's needs to exhibit curiosity manipulation, and simple schema in order to obtain information about objects in the environment. Along with sensory experiences, there are activities that enhance cognitive skills of thinking, processing information, and use of memory to act on the world to get what is wanted. Materials also raise the prospect of the future for the parents to use in order to better understand the need for services to the child who is multiply-handicapped and visually impaired. This study of ways to involve parents in the initial delivery system is one that needs further research as to its impact on families, on child change, and on alerting the delivery system of the needs of children who are visually impaired and have multiple handicaps beyond visual loss.

There is a need to clarify the role of the parent in the education and habilitation of children who are multiply handicapped. Too often, the program for habilitation is considered to be the total responsibility of the school with minimal parent input. The parent's role in education goes on throughout the child's life and this needs to be recognized as an active portion of the program. Parents need options regarding the degree of involvement they want and can handle at that particular time. There needs to be an understanding that there are varying degrees of involvement that parents can undertake, depending upon the energy available at that time. Sometimes parents may have more emotional energy to use to participate in a decision-making process. At other time, parents may not have any strength to put into active participation in their child's program. This needs to be recognized without placing blame or doubt on the parent. The parents' role in the program for their child may be affiliational role if professionals are trained to understand ways to work with the parents, ways to help parents participate to the degree of their current availability, and ways to learn to communicate to parents so that joint efforts are routine interactions.

Psycho-Social Issues

Research is needed to study the role of adult services in the development of children's services. The gap between educational and rehabilitation services is unnecessary. Yet the client suffers because the delivery system is not effective in the development of intervention strategies for young children. For the multiply-handicapped, visually impaired child there is little doubt that the child will eventually become a client of the rehabilitation services. If these rehabilitation services were started earlier, in middle childhood or even younger, then cost of services might not be as great and the human benefits would have a longer time to flow to the client and society. At this time, there is no data that describes what happens to a multiply-handicapped, visually impaired person as that person grows up and grows older. This must be addressed and the system must become more aligned to outcome and long-term goals for the multihandicapped person.

In viewing the research conducted to help understand the needs of multihandicapped, visually impaired individuals, the knowledge base seems to be increasing. Some of these sources of information come directly from the field of visually impaired children's education; other knowledge comes from experiences of having more multiply-handicapped children in schools so that teachers are facing the daily issues of educating a child with many problems. Some examples of the needs for research are listed below.

Use of Residual Vision with Multiply-Handicapped Infants and Preschool-Age Children

Barraga's work (1964, 1979) has been incorporated into practive with multiply-handicapped, visually impaired children. However, there have not been replication studies of Barraga's work that have addressed multihandicapped, preschool populations in terms of visual efficiency. There needs to be replication studies of this very important concept of visual efficiency that investigates best practice of use of residual vision in multi-handicapped infant and preschool populations. Efron and DuBoff (1975) helped translate the theory of vision efficiency into practice. The results of increased visual behavior were so applicable to multihandicapped, visually impaired children that vision stimulation strategies to increase use of residual vision, and instruction of children in use of their vision in learning were readily incorporated into instruction. What is missing is the documentation that this is working and the degree to which vision stimulation is effective with multihandicapped children.

The Role of Motor Development in Language Development for Multiply-Handicapped, Visually Impaired Children

Van Dijk's study of language development in multiply handicapped, visually impaired children has had a profound impact in programs for deaf-blind persons. Studies have attempted to investigate how well Van Dijk's methods work (Sternberg et al., 1980). There is a need for studies of the effects of a motor-based program for multiply-handicapped children who have visual loss. The Van Dijk approach seems to help visually impaired children in communication skills development, but to what degree does it work and in what instances does it not work? These questions need to be addressed so that the best of this practice is formalized into teacher training, curricula, and the knowledge base.

Need for Greater Knowledge of Teaching Methods

What seems to be critical is that there are not parallel research efforts to the increased methods that have emerged in teaching multiply-handicapped, visually impaired children. The instructional programs for multi-handicapped, visually impaired students are based upon practices that are clinical in nature. Often these are based upon the personality of the teacher or the person who trained the teacher. The old attitude of "it works because I say it works" leaves much to be desired. How may an effective program be transported to other sites? How can the new program avoid reinventing the wheel when it comes to developing assessments, curricula, and evaluation strategies? There has been a low priority on research of methods, except for single subject studies that tend to investigate reward schedules used with multiply-handicaped, visually impaired children. There needs to be more research conducted in terms of best practices, efficient instruction, and child progress.

Reliability and Consistency of Programs

How reliable are instructional strategies from one child to the next and from one program to another? How may replication identify best practices? There is a need to disseminate best practices. This is required from a cost effectiveness standpoint as well as from the standpoint of upgrading services. There are critical issues in terms of teacher variables, setting variables, learner variables, and interactional variables that are not easily researched. The focus of such studies must be to improve the opportunities for learners who are multiply impaired, including visual loss. At the present time, there are minimal quality assurances in programs serving multiply-handicapped, visually impaired children. The variables seem to be based upon personality. When a teacher or teaching personnel are effective, the program becomes effective. When the staff leaves, the program changes also. It is this variance that leads to classrooms within individual schools having wide discrepancies in the quality of education provided multiply-handicapped, visually impaired children. How could research increase internal consistency in the field? This seems to be a pressing issue to be investigated.

STATE OF PRACTICE

Personnel Training

The possibilities of having quality-instruction for multiply-handicapped, visually impaired students is greater than at any other time. The problem is one of whether the teacher has had the opportunity to benefit from certain results and experiences such as training in pinpointing behaviors, instruction in Bobath techniques (Bobath & Bobath, 1974), experience in language development as it applies to multihandicapped, visually impaired children, and understanding of the interaction of visual loss on development. The major discrepancy is that teachers who are newly trained are not trained in the techniques "necessary" to teach the children who will be in their classroom in the public schools. Too many teachers of visually impaired students are without knowledge of the numbers of visually impaired children who are multiply handicapped. Thus, teachers must train themselves or avoid the multiply-handicapped, visually impaired child. This gap in training and actual practice is the most discrepant aspect of educating the child who is visually impaired and multiply handicapped.

A companion need for research in best practices is the need to investigate teacher preparation. Traditionally, university faculty have led the way by being the premier researchers and decision makers about best practices. The advent of PL 94-142 catapulted practices over university input. Immediate application in the public schools put the pressure on local programs to change. Now, there are teachers in classrooms who have best practices and there is no way to give them back into the training program. There simply are not studies of the impact of new training techniques on child change. There are not the studies underway that would show the effects of a Van Dijk approach compared to the delays Fraiberg (1975) points out in the relationship of motor competence and ego formation in visually impaired children. There do not seem to be organized approaches to explore new techniques or ideas that are not currently being used with visually impaired students (for example the work of Feuerstein (1979) or the model of thinking by Guilford (1967)). The few studies that are underway have set out to prove a preselected method (Piagetian reasoning, operant conditioning, functional attainment, etc.) instead of asking the question and comparing the possibilities. It is only through honest inquiry that knowledge will be solidified into a state of better practices. Too often, inquiry is tied to the easy and accessible rather than the needed and unpopular. Studies tend to be tied to funding cycles and thus longitudinal studies are nonexistent. In a situation where the long-term product is the most important finding, there is not funding for long-term study.

Visual Learning

On a more positive note, the research on visual efficiency has been accepted into practice with multiply-handicapped, visually impaired children. This comes from a two-decade effort to establish materials, plan curricula, and train personnel in helping children learn to use residual vision. Key components in this emergence have been the work of Barraga and the translation of Piagetian theory into infant assessment concepts (Uzgiris & Hunt, 1975; Dunst, 1980). This trend offers an exciting prospect in the role of the vision teacher in the public schools. It may be that the new role of the vision teacher is to be trained as a vision specialist who

becomes an advocate and resource for every child receiving educational intervention when that child needs better visual functioning and visual efficiency.

Certainly, infant stimulation programs that focus on visual learning have been accepted into practice. The funding is still not available in many areas of the country, but the practice of working with low vision infants is well incorporated into programs for visually impaired persons. Such practices are not readily available from other professionals or other programs that serve impaired infants. Too often, it seems, the focus of these other programs is to view cognition as a mental act that is separate from any sensory function. Thus, the distant senses are not observed for functional use in some programs for impaired infants. Much of the practice that comes from the visually impaired field of educational practice has been or can easily be transferred over into other programs if there is an understanding of the concepts of visual learning, stimulation, and efficiency.

However, there does not seem to be any group that is translating practice in the area of visually impairment and multiple handicap into other areas. There is not an advocacy group of professionals who go into programs for mentally retarded children to find visually impaired children and to provide services to teachers, parents, and children regarding best practices in increasing visual use, visual learning, and visual efficiency.

Case Reporting

That brings up the issue of casefinding and reporting. There are major discrepancies in the reporting of cases of multiply-handicapped, visually impaired children by state agencies, federal agencies and local shools. It goes back to the old "mental retardation takes precedence" concept or to some form that does not have a place for multiply-handicapped, visually impaired students to be listed. Therefore, there is no one to ask why visually impaired, multiply-handicapped children are not noted on reporting forms. Too many visually impaired children are being lost in counts of children with "severe" mental retardation when the lack of vision is not considered a factor. It is true that these children have serious impairments. It is also true that they function in the mental retardation range and may be so severely impaired that it is difficult to predict potential. Until children are recognized as being blind or severely visually limited, the labels used are not telling the true picture. Once intense visual stimulation, one-to-one instruction and sensory integrative instruction have begun, many positive behaviors start to emerge. This is the lesson learned from the deaf-blind programs. Children who had been held to be hopeless started to function on a higher level once they were recognized as being visually impaired and multiply handicapped. They did not gain full intellectual status or overcome their disabilities; however, many of these children moved from being totally custodial to having self-help skills, and some became productive workers in homes or sheltered work settings. Some moved from being totally passive to being in direction of their own behavior. A few moved from being low functioning in all areas to being able to interact with others and to learn work skills and living skills to a high degree of independence.

Dissemination Networks

There is a formal dissemination network and an informal network that passes information along. The "grapevine" is an informal network usually based around former connections such as training programs, methodological affiliations, or former employment. This network is based upon personalities. Individuals keep in touch with each other to share tips, viewpoints, regulations and rules, and other practices. Generally, information travels quickly across the nation on the grapevine. The more important a piece of information, the faster it travels. Thus, a decision made in Washington regarding funding will find its way across the nation in a matter of days while the official network using the Federal Register, Request for Proposals, or agency policy regulations may take months and even then may not reach consumers who are actually working with the clients. Official announcements from federal agencies go through state guidelines and local regulations so that the original intent may be changed by the time it reaches the consumer.

The formal network consists of organizations set up to disseminate information. The American Foundation for the Blind is a prime dissemination point for most information. Through publications of journals and pamphlets, the Foundation keeps information flowing. Special research seminars are held in selected parts of the country that detail the results of special studies or research findings. Often, these special seminars produce publications that the American Foundation for the Blind disseminates to universities, state agencies, and local agencies.

The formal network also includes the American Printing House for the Blind, a quasi-governmental agency responsible for materials development, dissemination of best practices, and research leadership. The Printing House does an efficient job of networking for support throughout the delivery system, such as its fall meeting that gives providers and decision makers a chance to exchange ideas and get a perspective on what is happening in the field. The American Printing House for the Blind also has a major research component that is dedicated to the study of methods and materials used with blind and visually impaired persons.

Also in the formal network may be found the private facilities that have a long history in the delivery of services to persons with visual loss. The Perkins School for the Blind has served as a major force in service delivery, training, and in identifying best practices. The Howe Press, a division of the Perkins School for the Blind, provides a constant flow of information about the field not only in the United States but also throughout the world. The New York Institute (formerly the New York Institute for the Education of the Blind) has also influenced the field in terms of training and service delivery. This facility made a major contribution to the area of multiply-handicapped, visually impaired children's education and habilitation. Similarly, the Oak Hill School has been a leader.

The Industrial Home for the Blind in New York provided major leadership in the development of services to deaf-blind persons in this country. Their study of rehabilitation services for deaf-blind (Rusalem, 1959) served as the base for all planning for the network of services to deaf-blind persons for educational services as well as for vocational services. The Industrial Home for the Blind sponsored the Helen Keller National Center in its initial phase and was instrumental in forging federal support to build and maintain the Helen Keller Center on Long Island; New York.

State schools for blind students also form a vital component of the dissemination of information. Usually, the information provided through the state school for blind students sets the tone for services for blind and visually impaired persons in that state.

Two other components of the formal network also influence the informal network. These two sources of dissemination form a bridge between the formal and informal ways of dissemination of information to the field. The university training system is one such component. The other is the federal government, represented by the Office of Special Education and Rehabilitation Services. University training programs are usually tied to the needs of local schools or particular interests of the faculty of the university. Research in the university systems is active, but more confined by funding and external influences over the type of research, length of investigation, and priority given to a particular study. There are a few universities that continually turn out researchers in the field of visual impairment and many of these researchers have excellent backgrounds in working with multiply-handicapped, visually impaired persons.

The federal government is the dominant presence in the flow of research efforts. In the area of multiple handicap and visual impairment, the Office of Special Education has a section devoted to the study of practices in educating visually impaired, multiply-handicapped children. Specific priority has been given to severely handicapped children's services so that many studies of the visually impaired, multiply-handicapped population are being handled through severe handicap components in universities and research centers.

In both the formal and informal network, dissemination of information about multiply-handicapped, visually impaired children varies. If there is a federal priority given to investigating visually impaired children who are multiply-handicapped, then there is a flurry of activity. As funding subsides, interests and activity also diminish.

The effect of research findings on the local school district classrooms is not predictable. One of the problems is that many administrators in local school districts still consider the teacher of visually impaired students a person who teaches Braille and is an academic tutor to the blind child. There is little movement to use the teacher of visually impaired students as a member of the multidisciplinary assessment team, even though children who are seen by these teams may have major visual problems along with other disabilities. It may also be said that the teacher of visually impaired students, at the local level, does not serve as an advocate for better visual services to children in the school system. Few teachers of visually impaired students actively seek out students who are visually impaired by demonstrating technology that may be used by such students, by showing teachers how to observe visual functioning in low vision students, or by modeling techniques of visual stimulation to teachers of multiply-handicapped children even when those students are visually impaired. There are many classrooms that have vision stimulation kits that were intended to be used with visually impaired children. If the children are multiply-handicapped and visually impaired, teachers in the classroom may not have any training in teaching visually impaired students and may approach the use of materials as if they were developed primarily for children with mental retardation.

Needs and Recommendations

The primary need in the area of multiply-handicapped, visually impaired children's education is for casefinding to be done on a consistent basis with aggressive policy regarding identification of children who are visually impaired and multiply handicapped. It is not enough that each child be identified; each visually impaired child must receive the vision services that are necessary to promote learning and development, regardless of ancillary conditions. The key change that must be made is in the reporting forms used at the local, state, and federal levels of government. These forms must reflect the lack of vision or degree of visual functions in children without penalizing the child by having one disability take precedence over another. The fear, of course, is in duplicate counting since funding is figured on enrollment forms that require the establishment of a disability to qualify for services. The duplication of head count does not have to be a problem. There must be a place to describe visual function so that services will not be lost to the multiply-handicapped child. In schools, there needs to be some procedure that shows that every child has had a vision screening to establish whether that child is capable of learning through the visual mode. There are machines that can tell the degree to which the most severely impaired child is seeing. These passive readings of visual process could be used by schools to attest visual function in severely impaired children.

In the casefinding area, special projects must be undertaken to identify multiply-handicapped children who have visual or other problems. These special projects must receive support from major components of the formal network: the federal government, the American Foundation for the Blind, the American Printing House for the Blind, and private and state schools. The American Foundation for the Blind has attempted to support casefinding of multiply-handicapped, visually impaired children for decades and at one time kept a registry to focus attention on the number of children and youth in this group. Now is the time to build upon those components to have a major casefinding effort nationally.

Of equal importance to casefinding, there is a pressing need to have training programs that address the needs of multiply-handicapped, visually impaired children and youth. Most training programs for teacher preparation in the area of vision focus on achieving state certification. Usually, state certification requires the teacher of visually impaired students to be a teacher of Braille skills. Other courses generally required besides Braille are courses in the anatomy and physiology of the eye and vision system and methods of teaching the blind child. None of the courses routinely bring in the multiply-handicapped child as a potential student.

There seems to be a pressing need to have a variety of teachers for the visually impaired. One new professional would be a vision specialist who would be an advocate for all children in special education to be reviewed for visual functioning and visual competence. The vision specialist would know about multiple disabilities and would be able to work on the diagnostic team as a resource professional in vision. This would mean that the vision specialist would know about medical aspects of vision, educational aspects of visual function, and the effects of visual loss on developmental attainment. Every child entering a special education class would be seen by the vision specialist so as to have a complete record of how the child sees and what instructional modifications would be needed for that particular child. The model for this type of professional may be found in the speech pathologist and in the audiologist who have national certification and who have professional status to assess, intervene, monitor, and provide therapy as well as prescribe for children in their care. The vision specialist would be responsible for bringing techniques of teaching visually impaired children into classrooms where severly impaired children are located. The vision specialist would also be responsible for the fitting of technological aids and devices for visually impaired children in the school setting.

In developing training programs for an array of teachers of the visually impaired students, it would become necessary to branch into training for teachers of multiply-handicapped, visually impaired children. Topics that would need to be included in such training would be in Bobath techniques, Ayres sensory integrative techniques (Ayres, 1972), Van Dijk techniques, and greater understanding of the role of motor development to vision use. There is a need for training programs to address issues in positioning, normal patterns of motor development, modification of classrooms for motorially impaired children and visually disabled children, and in documentation of the effects of therapy on multiply-handicapped, visually impaired children.

Central to the training of teachers of multiply-handicapped, visually impaired children would be the need to prepare teachers to be problem solvers. No multiply-handicapped child is like any other child. In the area of multiply-handicapped, visually impaired children's education, the differences among children form the basis of programming. Teachers need to be able to use analysis, synthesis, and evaluative thinking skills to address the unique needs of children who are multihandicapped. Thus, the core of training must be in problem-solving, thinking skills for teachers, and in development of the skills to document what has happened, what was present at the beginning, and what outcome was achieved.

Teachers of visually impaired, multiply-handicapped children must have a realistic expectation for each student. What will this child be able to do when he or she becomes an adult and is living in a community? This question must be foremost in the minds of teachers of multihandicapped, visually impaired students. The use of "readiness" skills throughout the child's academic placement is not productive in achieving adult working and living competence. The multiply-handicapped person must be able to live in a home and community and contribute to the maintenance of that living environment. The contribution may be limited to self-feeding, but that is an important contribution for the multiply-handicapped person to achieve.

The major problem that exists in addressing training issues in preparing teachers of multiply-handicapped, visually impaired students is that time is a major factor. Too many training programs are still using semester hours to measure competence. Teachers of multiply-handicapped, visually impaired children must be trained so that they have direct experiences laced with their lectures. Once the trainee has experienced the responsibility of a child who is multiply-handicapped and visually impaired, questions begin to emerge. What has been an abstract memorization becomes real information necessary in order to work with a handicapped student.

There must also be ways to involve university faculty in direct training of multiply-handicapped, visually impaired children. It would be an interesting form of accountability to build faculty performance directly into child progress in classrooms where the faculty's former students are teachers. This would mean that a certain number of students from the university would be assigned to the faculty member for a period of experience that would lead to competence on the part of the trainee. The faculty person would go through the process of training each trainee teacher with placement and eventual follow-up for competent performance as the evaluation of the faculty person's effort.

There are many possibilities for improving the research quality and quantity regarding multihandicapped-visually impaired services. The risk is in change and, whether it is planned or not, change will occur.

References

American Psychiatric Assocation (1980). *Diagnostic and statistical manual of mental disorders* (3rd ed.). Washington, DC: American Psychiatric Association.

Ayres, A. J. (1972) Sensory integrative processes: implications for the deaf-blind from research with learning disabled children, in William Blea (Ed.). *Proceedings of the National Symposium for the Deaf-Blind, Asilomur, California, July, 1972.* Sacramento, CA: Southwestern Regional Deaf-Blind Center.

Barraga, N. C. (1964). *Increased visual behavior in low vision children.* New York: American Foundation for the Blind.

Barraga, N. C. (1979). *Visual handicaps and learning.* Austin, TX: Exceptional Resources.

Becker, H. (1983). *Preliminary effort on internal consistency of the basic life skills screening inventory.* Dallas: South Central Regional Center for Deaf-blind.

Becker, H. (1985). *Correlation studies of the functional skills screening inventory.* Austin TX: Functional Resources Enterprises.

Becker, H., Schur, S., Pacletti, M., & Hammer, E. (1984). *Functional skills screening inventory.* Austin TX: Functional Resource Enterprises.

Bobath, B., & Bobath, K. (1974). *Positioning and moving of hemiplegic patients for nurses and therapists.* London: Western Cerebral Palsy Centre.

Dantona, B. (1977). A History of centers and services for deaf-blind children. In E. L. Lowell & C. C. Rouin (eds.) *State of the art: Perspectives on serving deaf-blind children* (p.18). Sacramento: California State Department of Education.

Day, P. (1978). *Inter-rater reliability studies of the Callier-Azusa Scale.* Unpublished report. Dallas, South-Central Regional Center for Deaf-blind.

Desmond, M. (1985). *Health and educational status of adolescents with congenital rubella syndrome.* Houston: Baylor Medical Center.

DuBose, R., & Langley, B. (1979). *Developmental activities screening inventory.* Boston: Teaching Resources.

Dunst, C. (1980). *A clinical and educational manual for use with the Uzgiris-Hunt Scales of infant psychological development.* Baltimore: University Park Press.

Efron, M., & DuBoff, B. (1975). *A vision guide for teachers of deaf-blind children.* Raleigh, NC: North Carolina Department of Public Instruction.

English, J. (1978). Usher's syndrome: personal, social and emotional implications. *American Annals of the Deaf,* **3**, 357–422.

Everington, C. (1982). *Los Lunas curricular system: a criterion referenced assessment for the severely handicapped.* (4th ed.). Los Lunas, NM: Los Lunas Hospital and Training School.

Ferrell, K. (1985). *Reach out and teach.* New York: American Foundation for the Blind.

Feuerstein, R. (1979). *The dynamic assessment of retarded performers.* Baltimore: University Park Press.

Ficociello-Gage, C. (1978). *Assessment of prevocational and daily living skills.* Denver: Mountain Plains Regional Center for Services to Deaf-Blind.

Fraiberg, S. (1975). The development of human attachments in infants blind from birth. *Merrill-Palmer Quarterly*, **21**, 264–334.

Guilford, J. (1967). *The nature of human intelligence*. New York: McGraw-Hill.

Guldager, V. (1970). *Body image and the severely handicapped rubella child*. Boston: Perkins School for the Blind, (publication #27).

Hammer, E. (1978). Development of language in the deaf-blind multi-handicapped child: Progression of instruction. In E. D. Shroyer & D. L. Tweedie (Eds.), *The multi-handicapped hearing impaired child*. Washington, DC: Gallaudet College Press.

Hammer, E. (1980). Issues related to diagnosis and evaluation of deaf-blind persons. In E. Wolf (ed.), *The 1980s partnership for planning for progress: Proceedings of the Helen Keller Centennial on June 21–23, 1980 in Boston* (p.40). New York: New York Institute for the Education of the Blind.

Hammer, E. (1985). *Assessment of deaf-blind persons*. Unpublished paper presented at the Nordic Training Center, Dronningland, Denmark.

Jones, J. (1961). *Blind children—decree of vision, mode of reading*. Washington, DC: US Government Printing Office.

Kakalik, J., Brewer, G., Dougharty, L., Fleischauer, P., Genesky, S., & Wallen, L. (1977). *Improving services to handicapped children*. Santa Monic CA: The Rand Corporation.

Mithaug, D., Mar, D., & Stewart, J. (1979). *Prevocational assessment and curriculum guide*. Seattle: Exceptional Education.

Robbins, J. (1977). Education assessment of deaf-blind and auditorily-visually impaired children: a survey. In E. L. Lowell & C. C. Rouin (Eds.), *State of the art: Perspectives on serving deaf-blind children* (p.133–134). Sacramento: California State Department of Education.

Robinson, K. (1980) *The vision–up curriculum and guide*. Austin, TX: National Association of Parents of Visually Impaired and Blind.

Rudolph, J., & Collins, M. (1978). *Manual for assessment of deaf-blind multihandicapped children*. Lansing, Michigan: Mid-West Regional Center For Deaf-Blind.

Rusalem, H. (ed.) (1959). *Rehabilitation of deaf-blind persons, I–VII*. New York: Industrial Home for the Blind.

Ruttenberg, B., Kalish, B., Wenar, C., & Wolf, E. (1978). *Behavior rating instrument for autistic and other atypical children*. Chicago: Stoelting.

Sternberg, L., Battle, C., & Hill, J. (1980). Prelanguage communication programming for the severely and profoundly handicapped. *Journal of the Association for the Severely Handicapped*, **5**(3), 224–233.

Stillman, R. (ed.) (1978). *The Callier Azusa Scale*. Reston, VA: Council for Exceptional Children.

Uzgiris, I., & Hunt, J.Mcv. (1975). *Assessment in infancy*. Urbana: University of Illinois Press.

Van Dijk, J. (1965). *Language development in deaf-blind children*. Paper presented at the International Congress on Deaf-Blind, Refenes, Denmark. Boston: Perkins School for the Blind.

Wade, A., & Stone, G. (1980). *Austin work skills evaluation*. Austin: Texas School for the Blind.

Wolf, E., Delk, M., & Schein, J. (1982). *Needs assessment of services to deaf-blind individuals*. Silver Springs MD: Rehabilitation and Education Experts.

Assessment of Blind and Visually Handicapped Children and Youth

GERALDINE T. SCHOLL
ERINE THEODOROU

The University of Michigan, Ann Arbor, Michigan

Abstract—In this chapter the historical background and current assessment practices with visually handicapped pupils are reviewed and related to trends in the field of assessment of handicapped pupils. The state of knowledge is contrasted with procedures, use of available instruments, and dissemination. Needs and recommendations growing out of the identified discrepancy between the state of the art and the state of practice are included for personnel preparation, research, and communication.

INTRODUCTION

Section 121a.532 evaluation procedures and Section 121a.533 placement procedures for PL 94–142 (Department of Health, Education, and Welfare, 1977), require that the use of "tests and other evaluation materials . . . [that] have been validated for the specific purpose for which they are used . . . [are] tailored to assess specific areas of educational need . . . [that] no single procedure is used as the sole criterion . . ." and an evaluation by a multidisciplinary team "including at least one teacher or other specialist with knowledge in the area of suspected disability" be made prior to placement and educational planning for all handicapped children. Because the "suspected disability" for blind and visually handicapped pupils is the visual impairment, assessment procedures used by some school districts for placement and educational planning may include only a visual assessment, usually an eye examination by an ophthalmologist or optometrist. Some teachers of visually handicapped pupils and some state education consultants for visually handicapped pupils report that a comprehensive assessment in all areas of educational need related to the visual impairment is not routinely required for placement.

The reasons for these limited assessment practices are many. Reports from the field suggest that there is little understanding on the part of administrators of the comprehensive educational needs of this low prevalence group. Additionally, there are a limited number of tests and other evaluation instruments and procedures appropriate for visually handicapped pupils (Bauman & Knopf, 1979; Hart, 1983; Warren, 1984); the use of tests adapted and modified for this population is questioned by some psychologists in the field (Bauman, 1973, 1974; Bauman & Knopf, 1979; Fewell, 1983; Warren, 1984); there is a lack of consensus about what instruments should be included in a comprehensive assessment for these pupils (Bauman & Knopf, 1979); psychologists typically have limited knowledge and training in assessing handicapped pupils (Bennett, 1981; Meyers, Sundstrom, & Yoshida, 1974; Sullivan & McDaniel, 1982) and particularly low prevalence categorical groups (Goldwasser, Meyers, Christenson, & Graden, 1983; Morse, 1975; Schoenwald, 1980; Ward, 1982).

Added to these problems are the limited production and dissemination of research related to all aspects in the education of blind and visually handicapped children and youth and the difficulties encountered in conducting well-designed and controlled studies on this population who are heterogeneous in educationally relevant ways, small in number, and widely separated geographically (Scholl, 1985). By extension, these difficulties also apply to the development, standardization, and determination of validity and reliability of assessment instruments, both formal and informal. Further, there is a tendency on the part of some professionals, including many school psychologists, to view pupils with visual impairments as so "different" that typical assessment strategies cannot be applied (Bauman & Knopf, 1979; Morse, 1975). This attitude is reinforced by the nature of the specialized instructional materials and teaching techniques necessary in the educational program but which further contributes to this emphasis on difference.

Assessment is a complex process that involves the attempt to understand the overall developmental status of the individual within his or her environment. An assessment is incomplete when the individual is not considered within the context of the environment, with its support systems, stresses, and the interaction between the individual and the environment.

Assessment is not synonymous with testing. Psychometrics is only one aspect in assessment that focuses on the administration of tests or formal instruments, typically standardized. Assessment includes formal and informal observations, taking developmental and medical histories, conducting interviews with significant others, and reviewing cumulative records and files (Ysseldyke, 1979). Ysseldyke views assessment "as the process of collecting data for the purpose of making decisions for or about students" (p. 87). Such decisions are made in the educational setting for one or more of the following purposes: (a) screening/identification, (b) classification/placement, (c) instructional planning, (d) pupil evaluation, and (e) program evaluation (Salvia & Ysseldyke, 1981).

The first part of this review focuses on the historical background and current trends in assessment of visually handicapped pupils. Selected instruments available to arrive at critical decisions in the education of visually handicapped pupils are used to illustrate these current trends. Strategies and procedures for comprehensive assessment beginning with screening and identification are basic to the issues of definition, determination of the numbers and characteristics of the population known as blind and visually handicapped (see Kirchner's chapter on prevalence and demographics); are critical for a comprehensive assessment of educational needs for handicapped children with other disabilities (see Hammer's chapter on this topic); and in the formulation and continuing evaluation of the individualized education program. Current developments in program evaluation are also summarized.

The second part reviews the current literature on the state of practice in the comprehensive assessment of individual pupils and identifies discrepancies between the current state of practice and the state of the art as included in the first part.

The third part draws on the content of the two preceding parts to summarize needs and formulate recommendations so that more effective educational programs based on improved practices in assessment may be developed.

The review included literature searches of ERIC; Special Education Program (SEP) funded research projects; *Psychological Abstracts; Child Development Abstracts*; and the annual listing of current literature in blindness, visual impairment, and deaf-blindness, which includes *Dissertation Abstracts*, the *Journal of Visual Impairment and Blindness* and *Education of the Visually Handicapped*. The latter are the two chief journals in the field.

STATE OF THE ART

The discussion on the state of the art in the assessment of visually handicapped children and youth begins with a historical background on the development of assessment instruments for use with visually handicapped persons. This will form the backdrop for the review of more recent issues and concerns that have helped to create the current state of the art.

Historical Background

The early history of testing visually handicapped children involved primarily the adaptation of intelligence and achievement tests originally designed for use with sighted persons (Bauman, 1973; Davis, 1970; Gutterman, Ward, & Genshaft, 1985; Malikin & Freedman, 1970). A major impetus for this work arose out of the concern educators had that visually handicapped persons were intellectually inferior to sighted persons (Hayes, 1941).

In the early 1900s R. B. Irwin, a supervisor of programs for visually handicapped children in Cleveland, took his concern over the high number of mentally retarded children in classes for visually handicapped children to Dr H. H. Goddard of the Vineland Training School. A collaboration between Irwin and others at the school resulted in attempts to adapt the Simon-Binet Intelligence Scales into a format that could be used for blind children. In 1914 the initial form of the test was produced by Irwin and Goddard (Davis, 1970).

The leader in the early days of testing was an experimental psychologist from Mt Holyoke College: Dr Samuel P. Hayes. Dr Hayes had long been associated with the Perkins School for the Blind in Watertown, Massachusetts, where he obtained subjects for his interest in the mental and cognitive development of blind children. On his retirement in 1940, he worked full time at Perkins as a clinical psychologist and head of the teacher training program. His work at Perkins and later at Overbrook led to an adaptation of the standard revision of the Binet-Simon Tests in 1915 and then to further adaptations of the Stanford-Binet in 1923 and 1930 called the Condensed Guide for the Standard Revision of the Binet-Simon Tests, popularly known as the Hayes-Binet (Davis, 1970). In 1942 he completed what he hoped would be a bridge between his earlier work and a more refined instrument, the Interim Hayes-Binet (e.g., Gutterman et al., 1985). It has been standardized for blind children and was considered to be reliable for children as young as age 6 (Warren, 1984). Most tasks were introduced verbally, except for the vocabulary words and dissected sentences which were available in braille. Minkus completions and plan of search drawings are made available in braille.

The subsequent head of the Perkins Department of Psychology and Guidance, Carl Davis, following in the footsteps of his predecessor began to work on improving instruments for assessing intellectual potential in visually handicapped children. This culminated in the publication of the Perkins-Binet Tests of Intelligence for the Blind in 1980 (e.g., Gutterman et al., 1985). Performance items and verbal items were available in two forms: one for children who have useful vision, and one for those who do not (Scholl & Schnur, 1976). The Perkins-Binet was withdrawn for further evaluation and development (Gutterman et al., 1985; Teare & Thompson, 1982). In addition to the modifications made to the Stanford-Binet tests, other tests became available for use.

In the late 1940s, Hayes suggested the use of the verbal scale of the Wechsler-Bellevue Intelligence Tests as an alternative method of assessing the intellectual abilities of blind persons (Davis, 1970). With the development of the later Wechsler scales, the use of these verbal scales with the visually handicapped population became a widespread and popular practice (Bauman, 1968, 1974; Bauman & Knopf, 1979; Scholl, 1953).

Assessment of academic achievement in visually handicapped children shares a history with intelligence testing and goes almost as far back in time. Some of the earliest achievement tests adapted for use with visually handicapped pupils occurred as early as 1918 with the adaptation of the Gray Oral Reading Check Tests, the Metropolitan Achievement Tests, the Myers-Ruch High School Progress Test, the Wide Range Achievement (Genshaft, Dare, & O'Malley, 1980) and many editions of the Stanford Achievement Tests (Bauman, 1974). Most of this work on these tests was undertaken at the American Printing House for the Blind.

Many felt that the sole use of verbal tests provided inadequate and incomplete measure of the abilities of visually handicapped persons in general (e.g., Bauman 1973, 1974; Chase, 1972; Newland, 1979; Vander Kolk, 1977; Warren, 1984). One solution was to develop special tests for visually handicapped persons. Bauman (1974) developed the Non-Language Learning Test for use with blind persons. It consists of a form board containing various shapes. The test requires that the shapes be correctly replaced on to the board. Shurrager and Shurrager (1964) developed the Haptic Intelligence Scale (HIS), a test noted for its similarity to the Wechsler performance scale, although it was not intended as an adaptation of the Wechsler scales (Bauman 1974). The Blind Learning Aptitude Test (BLAT) was developed by Newland (1969) in an attempt to measure visually handicapped children's aptitude for learning ("process") as opposed to the evaluation of acquired academic learning or "product" (e.g., Newland, 1977). Newland felt that the Hayes-Binet and, to a lesser extent, the Wechsler scales measured primarily the products of learning experiences. The BLAT involves use of embossed form problems designed to assess the ability to make same/-different discriminations and to extrapolate relationships among series of items (Newland, 1977, 1979; Vander Kolk, 1981). Other tests that were developed or modified for use with visually handicapped persons not requiring verbal responses include a tactile form of the Ravens Progressive Matrices (Rich & Anderson, 1965); an adaptation of the Kohs Block Design Test (Suinn & Dauterman, 1966); and the Tactile Test of Basic Concepts, a tactile analog of the criterion-referenced Boehm Test of Basic Concepts.

Current Trends in Assessment

The purpose of providing this brief historical review is to highlight the fact that the earliest work in assessment of visually handicapped children was somewhat narrow in focus both in terms of the areas which were assessed and in the methodology used to assess these areas. This paralleled the general assessment practices of the day. Tests were developed with the intent "to sort, to predict, and to select with a view to identifying and rewarding a chosen few who are most likely to succeed" (Gordon & Terrell, 1981, p.1168). Assessment was approached from a psychometric orientation with a major emphasis on cognitive development as defined by the intelligence and achievement tests of the time. While there was some social criticism of testing in the 1920s (Haney, 1981) the 1930s were noted for the proliferation of standardized tests for a variety of purposes and in a wide range of subjects (Haney, 1981). Trends in assessment of visually handicapped persons followed suit. The development and use of tests for visually handicapped persons continued with the popularity of vocational guidance in the 1930s and 1940s. With the need to provide rehabilitation to blinded soldiers in the 1940s and 1950s, measures in other areas, such as vocational interest, aptitude, personality, and dexterity were developed (Bauman & Knopf, 1979).

Criticism of standardized tests at large has waxed and waned over the years (Haney, 1981; Gordon & Terrell, 1981). However, criticism reached a peak most recently surrounding the use of intelligence tests for purposes of classification and placement of students into special classes. The concern over testing practices in education occurred in the early 1970s surrounding the IQ controversy and the fairness of intelligence tests for minority students. It was observed that there was a disproportionate classification/placement of minority students in special education classes as a result of use of single IQ scores (e.g., Haney, 1981; Reschly, 1981). These concerns created the call to reform the traditional psychometric approach in use (e.g., Reschly, 1981; Ysseldyke, 1979). Assessment was to involve the gathering of information from numerous sources, rather than a reliance on only a single test score. Furthermore, this information was to be nonbiased and culture-fair (e.g., Reschly, 1981). Legislative mandates supporting these reforms prompted the development of instruments to measure a wide range of behavior in addition to intelligence as measured by traditional intelligence tests, such as adaptive behavior, language development, and sociocultural status (Reschly, 1981). There was a more extensive use of nonstandardized achievement tests, such as criterion-referenced tests. Also, progress in the development of behavioral, developmental, and environmental assessments provided alternative instruments.

The mainstreaming of handicapped children into regular classrooms, the passage of PL 94-142, the need to provide early intervention services for handicapped infants and preschoolers, the trend to deinstitutionalize and consequently serve multiply-handicapped persons, are some of the current educational forces contributing to the shift away from a strictly psychometric approach for making educational decisions. An additional trend impacting on assessment is the push for minimum competency testing in schools across the country (e.g., Amos, 1980; Grise, 1980; Haney, 1981; McCarthy, 1980; Olsen, 1980). As was the case since the earliest days of assessment of visually handicapped children, the test practices and policy at large influenced the development and use of tests for visually handicapped persons. Currently, there is a consensus that the use of norm-referenced, standardized tests with visually handicapped children and youth must be part of a broader, more comprehensive assessment process involving a variety of instruments and procedures (e.g., Genshaft et al., 1980; Scholl & Schnur, 1975; Spungin & Swallow, 1975; Swallow, 1981; Vander Kolk, 1977, 1981; Warren, 1984).

In addition to the current trends and issues in education that have influenced the state of the art in the assessment of visually handicapped children, there are assessment issues unique to the visually handicapped population that also form an important backdrop to the current state of the art of assessment. These unique issues warrant further discussion.

Special Concerns in Assessment of Visually Handicapped Pupils

Use of tests originally designed for sighted persons involve making modifications so that the visually handicapped person responds to and receives information through the remaining senses. Extensive discussions on how to modify and administer specific tests to visually handicapped persons exist in the literature (Bauman, 1973, 1974; Nolan, 1962; Scholl and Schnur, 1975; Vander Kolk, 1981; Warren, 1984). More generally, modifications involve changing the stimulus items and/or the response modes (Swallow, 1981). Swallow (1981) notes that general types of stimulus modifications include: substitution of concrete objects for symbolic words or pictures, transcribing into braille or large print, enlarging print with closed circuit television or magnification, or reading aloud the test items. The response modifications include: the presentation of items in multiple choice or yes/no fashion, use of gestures or pointing; oral responses, typing or brailling answers, or increasing the response time. From a strictly psychometric standpoint, any deviations from the standardized method results in the invalidation of the standardized instrument. However, it is noted that such instruments are not strictly valid or reliable for visually handicapped persons to begin with, given that the instruments were more than likely normed on a sighted population (e.g., Warren, 1984). Norms standardized on visually handicapped persons do exist for some tests, such as the Haptic Intelligence Scale, the Visual Efficiency Scale

(Barraga, 1970), and the Perkins-Binet. However, there is disagreement on whether separate norms are valid, necessary, or desirable (Vander Kolk, 1981; Warren, 1978, 1984).

Some argue that if visually handicapped children are to compete successfully with sighted persons in educational and work settings, it is necessary for comparison to be made between sighted persons and visually handicapped persons in various abilities. Separate norms would not allow for such comparisons to be made. Vander Kolk (1981) suggests that under such circumstances separate norms are not useful. Also, Vander Kolk generally finds separate norms less useful for intelligence and achievement tests provided the test is adequately constructed and the person can understand and respond to the test items. He believes that the Wechsler verbal scales and large print and braille editions available for achievement tests meet many of the needs of visually handicapped persons. In other areas, such as vocational interest and aptitude, he notes that separate norms are desirable since it has been documented that visually handicapped persons respond differently than sighted persons due to the differences in life experiences and social expectancies.

Others take a deeper look at the issue of separate norms and question the validity of using such normative data with visually handicapped children (e.g., Chase, 1975; Warren, 1978, 1984). Warren (1978, 1984) criticizes the use of normative and standardized intelligence and achievement tests modified for use with visually handicapped persons, with or without separate norms, on several grounds. He begins his cogent and elegant critique by noting that there are some basic assumptions and conditions that logically follow when one uses such normative standardized tests that may not hold. The use of a normative approach to assessment of visually handicapped children assumes that cognitive development follows the same progression as with sighted children. While one might identify points where delays occur, and determine whether or not they can be remediated, the progression is assumed to follow the same pattern. Given that this assumption holds true, it follows that the same measures and tests can be used for both sighted and visually handicapped persons, with minor modifications to allow for the visual handicap. It is also assumed that any differences observed between the test performance is attributable to the absence of vision. Warren suggests that these basic assumptions may not hold, given the unique impact the visual loss may have on the course of development. He states that it is not clear that cognitive development is the same for both populations. The visual loss impacts development in ways that are not completely understood and documented. Therefore, a test developed for sighted children may be measuring different behaviors in visually handicapped children. Furthermore, the visual loss may influence test results in an indirect manner due to experiential deprivation, perhaps the result of an overprotective parent or of deficient life or academic experiences. With traditional psychometric tests it is difficult to discriminate between failure due to environmental factors and failure due to deficiencies in aptitude.

Malikin and Freedman (1970) reiterate the concerns raised by Warren when they write:

For the sighted, vision serves as the integrative sense, and much of the learning process is centered about it: "A picture is worth a thousand words." Can it be assumed that the cognitive functions of the blind are the same as those of the sighted? Is it possible that the tests used for the sighted overlook the function of other senses in the learning process? Or that there may be compensatory mechanisms being used? Similar questions can be raised about the concept of intelligence. Some definitions indicate that intelligence is revealed in the way an individual copes with his environment. Does a blind individual interact with his environment as a sighted person does? Does it matter that the early life experience of the blind is so different in important ways from that of the sighted? Are the tasks of the standard intelligence tests now in use appropriate for learning how the blind deal with their environment? Even when the tasks are adapted for use with the blind, one might question whether other test stimuli might not prove more revealing. For example, in using the verbal part of the Wechsler Adult Intelligence Scale, is it forgotten that even verbal cues are related to the images they conjure up? Can we assume that these images are similar for both the sighted and the blind? (Malikin & Freedman, 1970, p.8).

One apparent solution has been to develop special tests for the visually handicapped person. Bauman and Knopf (1979) and others (e.g., Warren, 1978) note that this involves the need to develop normative data using subgroups of visually handicapped children due to the heterogeneity of the population. Visually handicapped persons vary on factors that are known to influence test results, such as onset of blindness (totally blind from birth vs. recently blinded), degree of blindness (totally blind vs. varying levels of vision), and the presence of additional handicaps. Bauman and Knopf (1979) support Warren (1978) and once again raise the issue of validity when they write:

It is very difficult to establish validity with blind subjects. Indeed, validity is often hard to defend with normal subjects, but we simply do not know enough of the mental operations of blind subjects, do not know the sequence of learning, do not know the combination of factors which affects their abstract thinking (1979, p.259).

Current Trends in Assessment of Visually Handicapped Pupils

The documented technical inadequacy of standardized, norm-referenced tests originally designed for use with sighted persons, and the difficulty of developing valid, standardized, normative special tests for visually handicapped children, has produced a disenchantment with traditional psychometric approaches. However, criticism of psychometric testing has stemmed from still other sources.

The need to develop appropriate individualized educational goals for all handicapped children, including visually handicapped children, along with the increasing need to provide services to handicapped infants, preschoolers and multiply-handicapped persons has revealed the limited usefulness of isolated inferred measures of abilities, such as intelligence test scores, stemming from norm-referenced, standardized tests for sighted children (Bagnato 1983; Brown et al. 1980; Duffy & Fedner, 1978; Fewell, 1983, 1984; Hart, 1983; Horowitz, 1981; Strain, Sainato, & Maheady, 1984; Taylor, 1982; Ysseldyke, 1979; Ysseldyke & Thurlow, 1984; Zigmond & Silverman, 1984); and for visually handicapped children (Bourgeault, Harley, Dubose, & Langley, 1977; Chase, 1975; Langley, 1978; Vander Kolk, 1981; Warren, 1978, 1984).

The more recent developments in assessment of visually handicapped children and youth include the proliferation of a variety of behavioral checklists and criterion-referenced tests and other informal measures that directly measure skills across a wide range of subjects including functional vision, academics, orientation and mobility, adaptive and vocational skills (e.g., Swallow, Mangold, & Mangold, 1978). Developmental instruments have been developed or modified for use with visually handicapped infants and children and multiply-handicapped, visually handicapped persons, such as the Developmental Activities Screening Inventory (DuBose & Langley, 1977), and the Haeussermann Scale of Developmental Potential of Preschool Children (Haeussermann, 1958). Many instruments have assessment items that directly lead to curriculum development, such as Growing Up: A Developmental Curriculum (Croft & Robinson, 1984), Program to Develop Efficiency in Visual Functioning (Barraga & Morris, 1980), and the Oregon Project for Visually Impaired and Blind Preschool Children (Brown, Simmons, & Methvin, 1979). This is considered to be an important function of assessment and reflects the trend at large for there to be a clear linkage between assessment and intervention (e.g., Ysseldyke, 1979). There is an additional emphasis on the development of age-appropriate, functional skills that will prepare the handicapped student for independent living in the community. Traditionally, this has not received a strong emphasis within education and consequently within the field of assessment. However, the trends to deinstitutionalize and normalize the handicapped person's quality of life has created a need to begin to teach handicapped young adults functionally useful skills that will allow them to live in the community and to hold jobs. The direct observation of the individual in his or her natural environment, documenting what skills the individual can and cannot do at the present time, is seen as critical in the development of ecologically valid, functional life skills (e.g., Brown et al. 1979; Falvey, Rosenberg, & Grenot-Scheyer, 1983). Use of such an approach with multiply-handicapped, visually handicapped children and youth, is considered to be an important component to the assessment process (e.g., Hammer, in this volume; Langley, 1981).

There is a consensus that the methods and instruments used for the assessment should be a function of the purpose of the assessment, the child's age, onset of the visual handicap, the diagnosis and extent of the visual handicap, the current placement of the child, the presence of other handicaps and the persons available who can provide accurate information (e.g., Vander Kolk, 1981). The possible range of methods include: observations of the child in various settings, interviews, standardized formal tests, informal behavioral and developmental checklists and inventories (e.g., Scholl & Schnur, 1976). The range of subject areas necessary to assess include: vision and visual efficiency, cognitive abilities, academic achievement, perceptual-motor, physical, behavioral, social development, language skills, vocational skills/interests, braille readiness, orientation/mobility skills, and adaptive functioning (e.g., Genshaft et al., 1980; Scholl & Schnur, 1976; Swallow, 1981; Vander Kolk, 1981). Norm-referenced, standardized tests and informal, nonstandardized instruments are available for most subject areas. Some instruments have been specially created for visually handicapped children. Others are borrowed from the literature on assessment of handicapped populations found in the fields of clinical, developmental, and community psychology; special education; and rehabilitation, and modified for use with visually handicapped children.

With the passage of PL 94-142, professionals with little background and/or experience with the low prevalence population of visually handicapped persons have had to make important decisions for and about visually handicapped children and youth. This has prompted the need for those from within the field of visual impairments to compile and disseminate information about available assessment instruments and the use of appropriate procedures to outside groups, such as school psychologists and parents. Agencies such as American Foundation for the Blind and American Printing House for the Blind have served as clearing houses for information on assessment instruments and practices. Additional resources for information can be found throughout the literature through the journals specific to the disability group, such as the *Journal of Visual Impairment and Blindness* and *Education of the Visually Handicapped*.

The following have compiled and described in some detail the available instruments, their purpose, and their appropriateness for use with a visually handicapped population:

1. Bauman (1973, 1974), Clark and Jastrzembska (1970), Genshaft et al. (1980), Scholl and Schnur (1976), Swallow (1981), and Vander Kolk (1981) provide information on general assessment practices and issues including descriptions of available instruments across various subject areas (cognitive, personality, vision, orientation, and mobility) with different subgroups of the visually handicapped population (e.g., infants, children, multiply-handicapped persons etc.).

2. Swallow et al. (1978) and Swallow (1977) provide a compilation of informal assessment checklist or inventories developed by teachers of visually handicapped students to serve as a guide for the assessment of visually handicapped children.

3. Bullard and Barraga (1971), Chase (1975), and Fewell (1983, 1984) provide information on assessment trends, approaches and specific instruments useful in the assessment of visually handicapped infants and young children.

4. Bourgeault et al. (1977), Langley (1978), and Hammer, in his chapter in this volume, provide information on assessment procedures and instruments appropriate for multiply-handicapped, visually handicapped children and youth across various subject areas, including visual screening and assessment. Further information on visual screening and assessment with this population can be found in Barraga and Collins (1979), Cote and Smith (1983), Jose, Smith, and Shane (1980), Langley (1980), Langley and Dubose (1976), Smith and Cote (1982).

5. Jastrzembska (1984) has compiled a list of material resources, including assessment instruments, available for parents and professionals working for visually handicapped preschoolers. A valuable addition to this bibliography is the Reach Out and Teach package of materials (Ferrell, 1985) that compiles training materials for use by parents of visually handicapped and multihandicapped, visually handicapped infants and preschool children.

The extent to which the various available instruments are useful or adequate to meet the various purposes of assessment and the extent to which professionals are aware of or use the available appropriate assessment instruments are discussed in the following part.

THE STATE OF PRACTICE

Overview

The preceding section summarized results from the literature search related to assessment of visually handicapped children and youth, including tests or other instruments and adapted procedures. This part discusses the research and development activity in assessment, problems with adapted instruments, use of available instruments, and dissemination.

Research and Development Activity

While there were reports of some new instruments, these appeared to be developed for a specific research undertaking and lacked normative data. Few incorporated known findings about the growth and development of visually handicapped children, particularly those behaviors and characteristics related to the identification of developmental delays in infants (Hall, Kekelis, & Bailey, 1984). Also lacking are assessments that examine the interrelationships between different areas of development.

With one notable exception, standardization data that were available included small numbers of pupils producing only limited validity and reliability data. The exception is the Visual Efficiency Scale developed following the initial research of Barraga (1964), demonstrating that training could increase visual efficiency. The Visual Efficiency Scale grew out of several years of development, field testing, and standardization (Barraga & Collins, 1979; Barraga, Collins, & Hollis, 1977).

The question might be asked: Why is research related to assessment so limited. There are undoubtedly several reasons. As noted in the preceding part, Bauman and Knopf (1979) and Warren (1978, 1984, and this volume) point out the paucity of basic research on growth and development of blind and visually handicapped children, especially in the cognitive areas. It is difficult to design and standardize valid assessment instruments when little is known about the characteristics of the population for whom the test is intended. A related issue is the difficulty in conducting research on this population, namely, their diverse characteristics in all aspects of growth and development but more specifically in the characteristics related to their visual impairment; their wide geographical separation; the high prevalence of other disabilities within the population; and the heterogeneity of their characteristics, which parallel those in the general population but which become more significant when the total number is small (Scholl, 1985; Vander Kolk, 1977). In addition, the implementation of PL 94-142 has further dispersed the available subject pool through the increase in local district programs that results in greater variability in educational characteristics and also further disperses the population geographically.

These factors make the development of technically adequate instruments a costly process (Warren, 1978, 1984) and lead to the question of whether there is a sufficiently large homogeneous population, even nationwide, to make such assessment research feasible or whether this is a futile approach and different strategies should be explored to describe and characterize the heterogeneity of the population. Such an approach might yield data which will be more useful for describing the

population and thereby lead to more effective assessment strategies. Some efforts are being directed toward implementing this approach but it is too early to determine the long-range impact on assessment practices (Hall et al., 1984; Langley, 1978).

Adapted Instruments and Procedures

The previous part noted reports in the literature of the application of already existing instruments in whole or in part with visually handicapped pupils, such as the verbal subtests of the Wechsler series. Such tests do give information on comparisons with the nonhandicapped population but may not provide information relevant for arriving at decisions regarding identification, placement, and the development or appropriate intervention strategies particularly in light of differences noted in the performance of visually handicapped pupils on the verbal subtests of the Wechsler (Smits & Mommers, 1976; Vander Kolk, 1977). In order to make comparisons and arrive at appropriate decisions, there is a need to know to what standard are comparisons being made and for what purpose is the test administered (Salvia & Ysseldyke, 1981).

In some instances test content and procedures, including instructions and time limits, are modified. Such modifications may restrict the use of the instruments and make generalizations and comparisons with standard norms a questionable procedure. The increasing trend toward competency testing noted in the preceding part calls attention to this practice. Reports from one state with mandatory competency testing reported that with modifications (braille, large print, audio cassette, and extended time) visually handicapped pupils compared favorably with the nonhandicapped school population (McKinney, 1983). The question might be asked about the validity of such comparisons in light of the modifications. Again, the purpose of the assessment will assist in deciding when modifications are useful in the decision-making process and when they are not appropriate.

The trend in assessment of other handicapped groups appears to be away from standardized approaches and toward nonstandardized and less formal approaches that view the child in relationship with the environment or the ecology (Oakland, 1981; Oka & Scholl, 1985; Ross & Holvert, 1985; Smith, 1980; Tucker, 1981). The literature search reported some studies employing such alternatives with visually handicapped school-age pupils (Swallow, 1977; Swallow et al., 1978); with multiply-handicapped pupils (Bourgeault et al. 1977; Hammer, in this volume; Langley, 1978); and with preschool pupils (Bullard & Barraga, 1971; Chase, 1975; Fewell, 1983, 1984). This informal assessment approach, which can focus more directly on the child's environment (school, home, and community) might be more productive particularly in identifying appropriate strategies to assist these pupils in mainstreamed programs to become truly integrated.

TABLE 1

Sales of Test by APH in Braille
and Large Type
1983–85

	1983		1984		1985	
Test	Braille	L.T.	Braille	L.T.	Braille	L.T.
Durrell Listening-Reading Series	84	96	38	155	39	73
Gilmore Oral Reading	52	65	10	13	5	35
Key Math Diagnostic Arithmetic	56		48		19	
Stanford Achievement Tests	150	56	514	1477	630	1686
Academic Skills	98	15	364	738	237	649
Stanford Diagnostic Reading	53	134	66	265	94	218
Wide Range Achievement	361	541	142	524	93	255
Wide Range Vocabulary		61		29		11
Total	854	968	1182	3201	1117	2927
Roughness Discrimination	79		63		80	
Tactile Tests of Basic Concepts	201		177		180	
Total by Year	2102		4623		4304	

These techniques also provide a mechanism for assessing the functional abilities of older visually handicapped youth, especially related to their social skills, daily living skills, orientation and mobility, and potential vocational skills. Finally, such procedures might in the future yield more valid information about developmental characteristics which are unique to subgroups among visually handicapped children and youth. The major criticism of this approach is that it is time consuming and therefore costly because of staff time (Langley, 1981; Oka & Scholl, 1985).

Use of Available Instruments

One critical question is to what extent are the available instruments being used in local school districts. Comprehensive assessment of educational need for identification and placement of visually handicapped pupils, as reported by teachers of visually handicapped pupils, particularly those from suburban and rural areas, appears to be limited to the medical examination by the ophthalmologist or optometrist. Teachers further report that they do a follow-up functional vision assessment to determine the educational limitations of the visual impairment. Anecdotal reports from teachers seem to indicate limited use of other assessment instruments either by themselves or by a school psychologist.

In personal communication, August 23, 1985, Nolan supplied data reported in Table 1 concerning the sales histories for educational tests, both braille and large type, published by the American Printing House for the Blind (APH). These tests typically would be used by teachers as part of their ongoing evaluation of student progress. It should be noted that in addition to these tests, APH prints a number of tests in large type usually ordered in small quantities by particular states or school districts. These are not included in Table 1.

More tests in large type than braille are used, which is a reflection of the increasing numbers of print readers

reported as being enrolled in both residential and day school programs (see Kirchner's chapter on prevalence and demographics). The total number of tests ordered per year appears to be very limited for the approximately 35,000 legally blind and deaf-blind pupils reported to APH. It is not known whether teachers do not know about the availability of these tests or whether they choose not to use them.

Reports from teachers of visually handicapped pupils seem to indicate that school psychologists in their districts are reluctant to assess their pupils. The training of school psychologists is limited in their preparation for assessing handicapped children in general (Bennett, 1981; Meyers et al., 1974; Sullivan & McDaniel, 1982) and more specifically those with low prevalence handicapping conditions (Morse, 1975; Schoenwald, 1980; Ward, 1982). An introductory course in special education or pertaining to exceptional children is required for the accreditation of preparation programs for school psychologists (American Psychological Association, 1980). Sullivan and McDaniel (1982) in a survey of 303 colleges and universities with training programs for school psychologists, found that one-fourth required no courses in handicapping conditions. Even one course could scarcely prepare the school psychologist for the diverse population of handicapped children in the local schools. Additionally, while the intent of PL 94-142 was to move assessment away from the psychometric approach, it would appear that this has not happened (Goldwasser et al., 1983).

Even among psychologists with experience in assessing visually handicapped persons, there is little agreement on the most appropriate tests that can be used with this population nor in evaluation of the usefulness of the tests (Bauman & Knopf, 1979).

In light of these facts, it is little wonder that teachers report limited services from school psychologists for their visually handicapped pupils.

Dissemination

The blindness system tends to talk only to itself. Journals in general special education and related areas publish few articles about the visually handicapped population (Scholl, 1985). It is not known whether there are few submissions or whether the submissions are not of sufficiently high quality to warrant publication. There needs to be a reaching out on the part of educators and other professionals concerned with the education of visually handicapped children and youth to the entire field of special education, as well as general education and related fields so that there can be greater sharing of information.

In the literature search, the majority of assessment-related articles appeared in journals specific to the field of blindness, namely, the *Journal of Visual Impairment and Blindness* and *Education of the Visually Handicapped*. These journals are probably neither widely known nor read by practicing school psychologists and other school personnel. A review of the content of journals specifically for school psychologists was made for the years 1982–84 to determine the number of articles on assessment of visually handicapped persons that appeared in those journals. The journals included the *School Psychology Digest*, *Psychology in the Schools*, *School Psychology Monograph*, and the *School Psychology Review*. One book was reviewed (Vander Kolk, 1977) and one article pertaining to behavior problems in blind children (Hirshoren & Schnittjer, 1983) was included. During this same period of time, "one in brief" article specific to assessment of visually handicapped pupils (Ward & Genshaft, 1983) appeared in *Exceptional Children*. There were none in *Teaching Exceptional Children* nor in the *Journal of Special Education*. It would appear that there is little opportunity for school psychologists to learn about assessment of visually handicapped pupils from their own journals.

The state of practice in inservice training for school psychologists is equally limited. An effort to close the gap between the state of the art and the state of practice in assessment was made by the American Foundation for the Blind in a project partially funded by the federal government. The purpose was to provide inservice training to school psychologists on characteristics, educational needs, and assessment of visually handicapped pupils (Jastrzembska, 1982). This project adopted the trainer of trainers model in which school psychologists from each state in a region were selected to participate in an intensive training period with the expectation that they would return to their respective states to train other school psychologists (Jastrzembska, 1982). The full impact of this project is not actually known; however, with the mobility of professional personnel in the field, it is doubtful whether the results permeated a significant portion of the population of school psychologists in any state or region. The short-term funding (3 years) did not allow for further follow-up.

There have been several activities related to program development. In 1968, the National Accreditation Council of Agencies Serving the Blind and Visually Handicapped (NAC) published the *Self-Study and Evaluation Guide for Residential Schools*, which was designed to precede an on-site review and accreditation. The Guide was revised in 1979 and two supplementary guides were included: Preschool Services (From Birth to Six) and Programs for Multihandicapped Students (National Accreditation Council 1979). As of 1984, 24 residential schools had achieved accreditation through NAC. This represents slightly under one half the eligible schools. It is not known how many have used the materials but have not sought accreditation.

Similar efforts in program evaluation were made for day school programs with the publication of *Guidelines for Public School Programs* (Spungin, 1978) and *Self-Study and Evaluation Guide for Day Programs* (Scholl, 1980). There are no data available to determine the extent to which these documents have been used.

Some states, such as California (California State Department of Education, 1987) and Massachusetts (Stager, 1981), have developed guidelines for instructional programs and services for visually handicapped pupils which include components necessary for a comprehensive assessment of visually handicapped pupils. However, the state consultants for visually handicapped students report that the extent to which these assessment guidelines are actually implemented by the local school districts in these states is not known since guidelines are not mandates and thus are not monitored.

It should be noted that the situation in the area of visually handicapped persons is not unique. It is true for other low prevalence groups, such as the hearing-impaired, physically handicapped, and multiply-handicapped populations.

NEEDS AND RECOMMENDATIONS

This part presents recommendations for action in three areas that may assist in closing the gap between research and practice identified from the content of the preceding sections: personnel preparation, communication of research results particularly to practitioners, and stimulating research and development activity.

Personnel Preparation

Target groups for improving personnel preparation relative to assessment issues include school psychologists, teachers of visually handicapped students, regular and special education teachers, parents, administrators, and other support personnel.

School Psychologists

A major target group for improving assessment practices for visually handicapped pupils are school psychologists. As noted in the preceding sections, their training programs and opportunities for professional development are limited in this categorical area. Ideally, preparation programs should include a specific course and accompanying practice in the assessment of children with low prevalence impairments. However, there would appear to be little likelihood that additional courses could be incorporated into an already crowded academic preparation program. In addition, there are difficulties in creating subspeciality areas within the generic field (Trachtman, 1981). Thus, the first recommendation is:

1. Modules designed to sensitize students to the characteristics and needs of visually handicapped children and youth should be developed and disseminated to school psychology personnel preparation programs. Such modules could also be used for professional development activities for practicing school psychologists. Modules produced on cassettes may increase their usefulness.

Teacher Preparation

The unknown number of pupils enrolled in other special education programs who may also have a visual impairment that may be educationally handicapping calls for an expansion of the role of the multidisciplinary team to include teachers and other professionals in the area of visual handicaps. Instead of being reactive, these personnel should become proactive in advocacy for the rights of all children to effective programs of vision screening. Thus, the second and third recommendations are:

2. The preparation of teachers for visually handicapped pupils should include theory and practice about children with disabilities in addition to their visual impairment so they can function as members of the multidisciplinary team for those handicapped pupils who may also have mild to moderate visual impairments.

3. Teachers and other professionals in the field for visually handicapped students should be trained in advocacy methods and should become advocates for universal vision screening efforts in all schools. Since advocacy efforts are typically directed toward other disciplines, such training should include theory and practice related to strategies for implementing a team approach.

Teachers in special education are typically required to elect a course related to assessment as part of their preparation programs. The content of selected textbooks was examined to determine the extent of inclusion of information regarding assessment of low prevalence and particularly visually handicapped pupils. Table 2 reports the total number of pages of text in each book, the number of pages devoted to all low prevalence groups, and the number of those pages devoted to visual impairments.

Since textbooks frequently mirror the content of a course, it is obvious that prospective special education teachers have limited exposure to the assessment needs of all low prevalence categorical groups including visually handicapped pupils. The number of pupils with visual impairments who have other handicapping conditions and who are enrolled in classes and programs for other impairment is not known (see chapters by Hammer and Kirchner). Available data seem to indicate that many legally blind children must be enrolled in classes and programs for other disability groups and may be served by teachers with little or no knowledge about educating children with a visual impairment, much less about appropriate assessment procedures for them. Therefore, the fourth recommendation is:

4. Teacher preparation programs for all categories of handicapped children should include in their introductory courses and their courses on assessment, content related to the education of children with the low prevalence handicapping conditions and reasonable coverage pertaining to assessment of low prevalence pupils, since the likelihood of having a low prevalence impairment in combination with other impairments appears to be significant.

Parental Involvement

With other handicapped groups, parents have been the strongest advocates for quality programs for their children. This group may hold the key to advocating better assessment practices for their children. To be effective in this arena parents must be provided with information on what constitutes quality programming. Parents of visually impaired children have only recently been organized. There are three national groups, all with small numbers of members: National Association of Parents of the Visually Impaired (NAPVI); Parents of Blind Children, a division of the National Federation of the Blind; and a special interest group for parents within the American Council of the Blind. The fifth recommendation is:

5. Parent groups should be given information and advocacy training so that they will know what assessment procedures should be included in a comprehensive assessment for their children and can advocate on their behalf in cooperation with educators of visually handicapped pupils to insure implementation of such procedures.

Administrators

Administrators are the key to providing quality programs for handicapped pupils. There is some evidence that placement decisions for handicapped pupils are frequently made on the basis of the availability of programs and that administrators do not often understand the role of the assessment in the process of placement (Meyers et al., 1974). The sixth recommendation is:

TABLE 2

Treatment of Low Prevalence and Visually Handicapped
Populations in Selected Assessment Texts

Text	Total	Number of Pages	
		Low Prevalence	Visually Handicapped
Goldman, Stein, & Guerry (1983)	384	28	1
Hargrove & Potect (1984)	328	40	4
McLoughlin & Lewis (1981)	613	None	None
Salvia & Ysseldyke (1981)	548	54	11
Swanson & Watson (1982)	392	3	1
Taylor (1984)	340	20	12
Wallace & Larsen (1978)	486	None	None
Zigmond, Vallecorsa, & Silverman (1983)	346	None	None

6. Inservice and preservice personnel preparation programs for administrators should include information about the role that assessment should play in the placement and educational planning for low prevalence categorical groups. For these and for all handicapped pupils administrators should seek to provide a comprehensive assessment program.

Other Support Personnel

An appropriate assessment for visually handicapped children and youth requires the participation of other support personnel, including ophthalmologists, optometrists, school social workers, guidance personnel, and regular teachers. The medical personnel are especially in need of information about educational programs so that they might deal with parents in a more knowledgeable way since they are usually the first to identify the visual impairment. The seventh recommendation addresses the needs of this group:

7. Funds for projects that address the needs of support personnel for information about educational programs and their appropriate cooperative role in the assessment process should be made available. Special communication linkages between special education professional organizations and organizations specific to these groups should be encouraged.

Communication

There is a lack of information about visual impairments among professionals tangentially related to education and more specifically to assessment. These groups include psychologists, social workers, administrators, physical therapists, occupational therapists, speech and hearing specialists, and other professional personnel, both those working in schools and in the community. Communication links need to be established between the blindness field and other related disciplines. A recommendation regarding this area is:

8. Professionals, particularly researchers, should insure that the dissemination of their studies related to

assessment of visually handicapped children and youth, with implications noted, should be submitted to journals outside the blindness field.

There is limited communication between and among teachers, many of whom have informal assessment instruments which they have developed and which might be useful to others. Reports from the American Foundation for the Blind indicate that there is considerable demand for teacher-oriented materials, such as Swallow (1977) and Swallow et al. (1978). There is a need for teachers to have a mechanism for sharing assessment practices which they have developed and refined. A recommendation for such sharing is:

9. A central clearinghouse should be established for teachers to share their informal assessment instruments. With the increasing availability and use of the telecommunication network, SpecialNet, teachers may be able to set up a communication link for this purpose. In addition, publication of a compilation of such instruments might also be considered.

Research

There is a serious shortage of researchers in assessment since the work of Hayes and Bauman. Professionals from education and from psychology who will work with and study assessment issues related to this low prevalence population on a long-term basis should be recruited. A long-term commitment to programmatic research would be necessary. Researchers with interest in and knowledge of qualitative research strategies are particularly needed for research on small N groups, such as visually handicapped pupils. Qualititative research requires more intensive efforts on the part of researchers in planning, implementing, and interpreting results. Such long-term studies are often not reviewed favorably when submitted for funding. Therefore, the final recommendation is:

10. A national research plan should be developed to seek answers to the questions, problems, and issues regarding assessment posed in this chapter. Funding must be sought on a long-term basis.

CONCLUSIONS

Visually handicapped students are a low prevalence category: there are small numbers of pupils, small numbers of teachers and other professional personnel, and little opportunity for other school personnel to know of the special needs of this group. Administrators tend to look at the few pupils who are visually impaired and to seek ways of accommodating them in other educational settings at a lesser cost rather than providing a placement that will serve all their educational needs appropriately. Comprehensive assessment of these pupils is basic to planning and implementing appropriate educational programs.

Dissemination of knowledge is the responsibility of professional workers in this field together with concerted efforts on the part of other special educators to see that this group of pupils and professional personnel are not neglected by the system. Special funding is essential to insure that what is currently known from research findings is translated into practice. This may require a greater expenditure of funds per capita than may be required for the high prevalence categorical groups.

References

American Psychological Association (1980). *Criteria for accreditation of doctoral training programs and internships in professional psychology.* Washington DC: Author.

Amos, K. A. (1980). Competency testing: Will the LD student be included? *Exceptional Children,* **47**(3), 194–197.

Bagnato, S. J. (1983). Psychological and educational assessment of exceptionality. In R. M. Smith, J. T. Neisworth, & F. M. Hunt (Eds.), *The exceptional child: A functional approach* (pp. 100–121). New York: McGraw-Hill.

Barraga, N. C. (1964). *Increased visual behavior in low vision children.* New York: American Foundation for the Blind.

Barraga, N. C. (Ed.). (1970). *Visual efficiency scale.* Louisville, KY: American Printing House for the Blind.

Barraga, N. C., & Collins, M. E. (1979). Development of efficiency in visual functioning: Rationale for a comprehensive program. *Journal of Visual Impairment and Blindness,* **74**(3), 121–126.

Barraga, N. C., Collins, M., & Hollis, J. (1977). Development of efficiency in visual functioning: A literature analysis. *Journal of Visual Impairment and Blindness,* **71**(9), 387–391.

Barraga, N. C., & Morris, J. E. (1980). *Program to develop efficiency in visual functioning.* Louisville, KY: American Printing House for the Blind.

Bauman, M. K. (1968). *A report and a reprint: Tests used in the pyschological evaluation of blind and visually handicapped persons and a manual of norms for tests used in counseling blind persons.* Washington: American Association of Workers for the Blind.

Bauman, M. K. (1973). Psychological and educational assessment. In B. Lowenfeld (Ed.), *The visually handicapped child in school.* (pp. 93–115) New York: John Day.

Bauman, M. K. (1974). Blind and partially sighted. In M. V. Wisland (Ed.), *Psychoeducational diagnosis of exceptional children.* (pp. 159–89) Springfield, MA: Charles C Thomas.

Bauman, M. K. & Knopf, C. A. (1979). Psychological tests used with blind and visually handicapped persons. *School Psychology Digest,* **8**(3), 257–270.

Bennet, R. E. (1981). Professional competence and the assessment of exceptional children in special education. *School Psychology Monograph,* **2**(1), 3–57.

Bourgeault, S. E., Harley, R. K., Dubose, R. F., Langley, M. B., (1977). Assessment and programming for blind children with severely handicapping conditions. *Journal of Visual Impairment and Blindness,* **71**(2), 49–53.

Brown, L., Branston, M. B., Hamre-Nietupski, S., Pumpian, I., Certo, N., & Grunewald, L. (1979). A strategy for developing chronological age appropriate and functional curricular content for severely handicapped adolescents and young adults. *Journal of Special Education,* **3**(1), 81–90.

Brown, L., Falvey, M., Vincent, L., Kaye, N., Johnson, F. Ferrara-Parrish, P., & Grunewald, L. (1980). Strategies for generating comprehensive, longitudinal and chronological age appropriate individual educational plans for adolescent and young adult severely handicapped students. *Journal of Special Education,* **14**(2), 199–215.

Brown, D., Simmons, V., & Methvin, J. (1979). *The Oregon project for visually impaired and blind preschool children.* Medford, OR: Jackson County Education Service.

Bullard, B. M. & Barraga, N. (1971) Subtests of evaluative instruments applicable for use with preschool visually handicapped children. *Education of the visually handicapped,* **3**(4), 116–122.

California State Department of Education (1987). *Program Guidelines for visually impaired individuals.* Revised edition. Sacramento, Ca: California State Department of Education.

Chase, J. B. (1972). Evaluation of blind and severely visually impaired persons. In M. D. Graham (Ed.), *Science and blindness: Retrospective and prospective* (pp. 53–58). New York: American Foundation for the Blind.

Chase, J. B. (1975). Developmental assessment of handicapped infants and young children: with special attention to the visually impaired. *New Outlook for the Blind,* **69**, 73–82.

Clark, L. L., & Jastrzembska, Z. Z. (1970). *Proceedings of the Conference on New Approaches to the Evaluation of Blind Persons.* New York: American Foundation for the Blind.

Cote, K. S., & Smith, A. (1983). Assessment of the multiply handicapped. In T. Jose (Ed.), *Understanding low vision* (pp. 379–402). New York: American Foundation for the Blind.

Croft, N. B., & Robinson, L. B. (1984). *Growing up: A developmental curriculum.* Austin, TX: Now: Parent Consultants.

Davis, C. J. (1970). New developments in the intelligence testing of blind children. In L. L. Clark & Z. Z. Jastrzembska (Eds.), *Proceedings of the Conference on New Approaches to the Evaluation of Blind Persons* (pp. 83–92). New York: American Foundation for the Blind.

Department of Health, Education, and Welfare (1977). Education of handicapped children: Implementation of Part B of the Education of the Handicapped Act. *Federal register,* Part II, August 23, 1977. Washington: Author.

DuBose, R. F., & Langley, M. B. (1977). Developmental activities screening inventory. Boston: Teaching Resources.

Duffy, J. B., & Fedner, M. L. (1978). Educational diagnosis with instructional use. *Exceptional Children*, **44**(4), 246–251.

Falvey, M. A., Rosenberg, R. L., & Grenot-Scheyer, M. (1983). Strategies for assessing students with multiply handicapping conditions. In S. Ray, M. J. O'Neill, & N. T. Morris (Eds.), *Low incidence children: A guide to psychoeducational assessment* (pp. 245–273). Natchitoches, LA: Steven Ray.

Ferrell, K. A. (1985). *Reach out and teach: Meeting the training needs of parents of visually handicapped/multihandicapped young children*. New York: American Foundation for the Blind.

Fewell, R. R. (1983). New directions in the assessment of young handicapped children. In C. R. Reynolds & J. H. Clark (Eds.)., *Assessment and programming for young children with low-incidence handicaps* (pp. 1–41). New York: Plenum Press.

Fewell, R. R. (1984). Assessment of preschool handicapped children. *Educational Psychologist*, **19** (3), 172–179.

Genshaft, J. L., Dare, N. L., & O'Malley, P. L. (1980). Assessing the visually impaired child: A school psychology view. *Journal of Visual Impairment and Blindness*, **74**, 344–350.

Goldman, J., Stein, C., Guerry, S. (1983). *Psychological methods of child assessment*. New York: Brunner/Mazel.

Goldwasser, E., Meyers, J., Christenson, S., & Graden, J. (1983). The impact of PL 94–142 on the practice of school psychology: A national survey. *Psychology in the Schools*, **20**, 153–165.

Gordon, E. W., & Terrell, M. D. (1981). The changed social context of testing. *American Psychologist*, **36**(10), 1167–1171.

Grise, P. J. (1980) Florida's minimum competency testing program for handicapped students. *Exceptional Children*, **47**(3), 186–191.

Gutterman, J., Ward, M., & Genshaft, J. (1985). Correlations of scores of low vision children on the Perkins-Binet tests of intelligence for the blind, the WISC-R and the WRAT. *Journal of Visual Impairment and Blindness*, **79**(2), 55–58.

Haeussermann, E. (1958). Developmental potential for preschool children. New York: Grune & Stratton.

Hall, A., Kekelis, L., & Bailey, I. (1984). *Review of research pertaining to the assessment of infants with visual impairment*. Unpublished manuscript.

Haney, W. (1981). Validity, vaudeville, and values: A short history of social concerns over standardized testing. *American Psychologist*, **36**(10), 1021–1033.

Hargrove, L. J., & Potect, J. A. (1984). *Assessment in special education: The education evaluation*. Englewood Cliffs, N. J.: Prentice-Hall.

Hart, V. (1983). Assessment of visually handicapped preschoolers. In C. R. Reynolds & J. H. Clark (Eds.), *Assessment and programming for young children with low-incidence handicaps* (pp. 201–221). New York: Plenum Press.

Hayes, S. P. (1941). *Contributions to a psychology of blindness*. New York: American Foundation for the Blind.

Hirshoren, A., Schnittjer, C. J. (1983). Behavior problems in blind children and youth: A prevalence study. *Psychology in the Schools*, **20**, 197–201.

Horowitz, F. D. (1981). Toward a model of early infant development. In C. C. Brown (Ed.), *Infants at risk: Assessment and intervention—an update for health care professionals and parents* (pp. 31–48). Palm Beach, FL: Johnson & Johnson Product Co.

Jastrzembska, Z. (1982). *Model for a workshop on assessment of blind and visually impaired students*. New York: American Foundation for the Blind.

Jastrzembska, Z. (1984). Resources for parents and professionals working with visually handicapped preschoolers. *Education of the Visually Handicapped*, **16**(3), 115–134.

Jose, R., Smith, A., & Shane, K. (1980). Evaluating and stimulating vision in the multiply impaired. *Journal of Visual Impairment and Blindness*, **10**(4), 97–114.

Langley, B. (1978). Psychoeducational assessment of the multiply handicapped blind child: Issues and methods. *Education of the Visually Handicapped*, **10**(4), 97–114.

Langley, B. (1980). *Functional vision inventory for the multiply and severely handicapped*. Chicago: Stoelting.

Langley, B. (1986). Psychoeducational assessment of visually impaired students with additional handicaps. In D. Ellis (Ed.), *Sensory impairments in the mentally handicapped people* (pp. 253–296). San Diego: College Hill Press.

Langley, B., & DuBose, R. F. (1976). Functional vision screening for severely handicapped children. *New Outlook for the Blind*, **70**, 346–350.

Malikin, D., & Freedman, S. (1970). Test construction or adaptation for use with blind persons. In L. L. Clark and Z. Z. Jastrzembska (Eds.), *Proceedings of the Conference on New Approaches to the Evaluation of Blind Persons* (pp. 7–18). New York: American Foundation for the Blind.

McCarthy, M. M. (1980) Minimum competency testing and handicapped students. *Exceptional Children*, **47**(3), 166–173.

McKinney, J. D. (1983). Performance of handicapped students on the North Carolina minimum competency test. *Exceptional Children*, **49**(6), 547–550.

McLoughlin, J. A. & Lewis, R. B. (1981). *Assessing special students: Strategies and procedures*. Columbus: C. E. Merrill.

Meyers, C. E., Sundstrom, P. E., & Yoshida, R. K. (1974). The school psychologist and assessment in special education. *School Psychology Monograph*, **2**(1), 3–57.

Morse, J. L. (1975). Answering the questions of the psychologist assessing the visually handicapped child. *New Outlook for the Blind*, **69**(8), 350–353.

National Accreditation Council for Agencies Serving the Blind and Visually Handicapped (1979). *Self-study and evaluation guide for residential schools*. New York City: Author.

Newland, T. E. (1969). *The blind learning aptitude test*. Urbana, Illinois: University of Illinois.

Newland, T. E. (1977). Tested "intelligence" in children. *School Psychology Monograph*, **3**, 1–44.

Newland, T. E. (1979). The Blind Learning Aptitude Test. *Journal of Visual Impairment and Blindness*, **73**(4), 134–139.

Nolan, C. Y. (1962). Evaluating the scholastic achievement of visually handicapped children. *Exceptional Children*, **28**, 493–496.

Oakland, T. (1981). *Nonbiased assessment*. Minneapolis: University of Minnesota National School Psychology Inservice Training Network.

Oka, E., & Scholl, G. T. (1985). Non-test-based approaches to assessment. In G. T. Scholl (Ed.), *The school psychologist and the exceptional child*, (pp. 39–59). Reston, VA: The Council for Exceptional Children.

Olsen, K. R. (1980) Minimum competency testing and the IECP process. *Exceptional children*, **47**(3), 176–183.

Reschly, D. J. (1981). Psychological testing in educational classification and placement. *American Psychologist*, **36** (10), 1094–1102.

Rich, C. R., & Anderson, R. P. (1965). A tactual form of the progressive matrices for use with blind children. *Personnel and Guidance Journal*, **43**(9), 912–919.

Ross, R., & Holvert, J. (1985). *Strategies for educating students with severe handicaps*. Boston: Little, Brown.

Salvia, J., & Ysseldyke, J. E. (1981). *Assessment in special and remedial education* (2nd ed.). Boston: Houghton Mifflin.

Schoenwald, B. (1980). The great training default. *Directive Teacher*, **2**, 19–30.

Scholl, G. T. (1953). Intelligence tests for visually handicapped children. *Exceptional Children*, **20**, 116–120, 122–123.

Scholl, G. T. (1980). *Self study and evaluation guide for day school programs for visually handicapped pupils: A guide for program improvement*. Reston, VA: Council for Exceptional Children.

Scholl, G. T. (1985). Education of visually handicapped children and youth: Issues.

Scholl, G. T. & Schnur, R. (1975). Measures of psychological, vocational and educational functioning in the blind and visually handicapped: Introductory remarks: *New Outlook for the Blind*, **69**(8), 365–370.

Scholl, G. T., & Schnur, R. (1976). *Measures of psychological, vocational, and educational functioning in the blind and visually handicapped*. New York: American Foundation for the Blind.

Shurrager, H. C., & Shurrager, P. S. (1964). *Manual for the Haptic Intelligence Scale for the Blind*. Chicago: Psychology Research Technology Center, Illinois Institute of Technology.

Smith, C. R. (1980). Assessment alternatives: Non-standardized procedures. *The School Psychology Review*, **9**(1), 46–57.

Smith, A. J., & Cote, K. S. (1982). *Look at me: A resource manual for the development of residual vision in multiply impaired children*. Philadelphia, PA: Pennsylvania College of Optometry Press.

Smits, B. W., & Mommers, M. J. (1976). Differences between blind and sighted children on WISC Verbal subtests. *New Outlook for the Blind*, **70**, 240–246.

Spungin, S. J. & Swallow, R. M. (1975). Psychoeducational assessment: Role of psychologist to teacher of the visually handicapped. *Education of the visually handicapped*, **7**(3), 67–76.

Spungin, S. J. (1978). *Guidelines for public school programs serving visually handicapped children*. New York: American Foundation for the Blind.

Stager, J. D. (1981). *Program assessment guide for public school special education services to visually handicapped students*. Springfield, MA: Massachusetts Department of Education.

Strain, P. R., Sainato, D. M., & Maheady, L. (1984). Toward a functional assessment of severely handicapped learners. *Educational Psychologist*, **19**(3), 180–187.

Suinn, R. M. & Dauterman, W. L. (1966). *A manual for the Stanford-Kohs Block Design Test for the Blind*. Washington: Vocational Rehabilitation Administration.

Sullivan, P. D., & McDaniel, E. A. (1982). Survey of special education coursework in school psychology training programs. *Exceptional Children*, **46**, 541–543.

Swallow, R. M. (1977). *Assessment of visually handicapped children and youth*. New York: American Foundation for the Blind.

Swallow, R. M. (1981). Fifty assessment instruments commonly used with blind and partially seeing individuals. *Journal of Visual Impairment and Blindness*, **75**(2), 65–72.

Swallow, R. M., Mangold, S., & Mangold, P. (1978). *Informal assessment of developmental skills for visually handicaped students*. New York: American Foundation for the Blind.

Swanson, H. L., & Watson, B. L. (1982). *Educational and psychological assessment of exceptional children*. St. Louis: C. V. Mosby.

Taylor, R. L. (1982). Assessment. In L. Sternberg & G. L. Adams (Eds.), *Educating severely and profoundly handicapped students* (pp. 47–93). Rockville, M.D.: Aspen Systems.

Taylor, R. L. (1984). *Assessment of exceptional students: Educational and psychological procedures*. Englewood Cliffs, N.J.: Prentice-Hall.

Teare, J., & Thompson, R. (1982). Concurrent validity of the Perkins-Binet Tests of Intelligence for the Blind. *Journal of Visual Impairment and Blindness*, **76**(7), 279–280.

Trachtman, G. M. (1981). On such a full sea. *School Psychology Review*, **10**(2), 138–181.

Tucker, J. A. (1981). *Non test-based assessment: A training module*. Minneapolis: National School Psychology Inservice Training Network, University of Minnesota.

Vander Kolk, C. J. (1977). Intelligence testing for visually impaired persons. *Journal of Visual Impairment and Blindness*, **71**(4), 158–163.

Vander Kolk, C. J. (1981). *Assessment and planning with the visually impaired*. Baltimore: University Park Press.

Wallace, G. & Larsen, S. C. (1978). *Educational assessment of learning problems: Testing for teaching*. Boston: Allyn and Bacon.

Ward, M. F. (1982) Attitudes and concerns of school psychologists toward assessment of visually handicapped children. *DVH Newsletter*, **27**, 29–43.

Ward, M., & Genshaft, J. (1983). The Perkins-Binet test: A critique and recommendations for administration. *Exceptional Children*, **49**(5), 450–452.

Warren, D. (1978). Cognitive development, assessment and the I.E.P. *DVH Newsletter*, **22**(1), 1–6.

Warren, D. (1984). *Blindness and early childhood development* (2nd ed.), New York: American Foundation for the Blind.

Ysseldyke, J. E. (1979). Issues in psychoeducational assessment. In G. Phye & D. J. Reschly (Eds.), *School psychology: Perspectives and issues* (pp. 87–121). New York: Academic Press.

Ysseldyke, J. E., & Thurlow, M. L. (1984). Assessment practices in special education: adequacy and appropriateness. *Educational Psychologist*, **19**(3), 121–136.

Zigmond, N., & Silverman, R. (1984). Informal assessment for program planning and evaluation in special education. *Educational Psychologist*, **19**(3), 163–171.

Zigmond, N., Vallecorsa, A., & Silverman, R. (1983). *Assessment for instructional planning in special education*. Englewood Cliffs, N.J.: Prentice-Hall.

Implications of the Research and Development of Modern Technology on the Education of Blind and Visually Handicapped Students

LAWRENCE A. SCADDEN, Ph.D.

Electronic Industries Foundation

Abstract—Modern technology is enhancing the educational opportunities of blind and visually handicapped students. Innovative instrumentation can assist in the teaching of orientation and mobility skills, activities of daily living, and academic disciplines. The most significant improvements appear in areas related to the acquisition and creation of written information. Microcomputers and special access technology—composed of Braille, synthetic speech, and large-character displays—can provide these students with newfound independence in the manipulation of printed information. There is, however, an apparent gap between the state of the art in educational technology for this population and the state of educational practice. Future utilization of these technologies will require the development of appropriate instruction provided for these students by trained special education professionals. Research and development efforts are also needed to perfect the technology and its applications.

INTRODUCTION

Technology is affecting modern society as people seek time- and effort-saving means to perform common daily functions. The impact of technology can be seen in education, employment, recreation, and household activities. The electronic component which is having the greatest impact today is the microprocessor, the "computer on a chip." The microprocessor is the "brain" which is being used to control home appliances, manufacturing instruments, automobile fuel injection and exhaust emission systems, video games, and, of course, computers. Most economists and social scientists anticipate that society as a whole will continue to be altered as the technology revolution evolves. This impact will be especially noticeable as people and businesses alike utilize computers more and more for the creation, processing, and distribution of written information.

Implications of Technology for People with Visual Impairment

Eventually, no single group may benefit from the proliferation of technology in modern society more than will that comprised of people who are blind or visually impaired. The consideration of the two areas in daily life which are most adversely affected by restricted vision—namely independent, safe travel and access to printed information—should provide the basis for supporting this hypothesis.

The information normally used by sighted individuals for accomplishing the tasks associated with these endeavors typically is obtained visually. The sighted pedestrian or driver uses visual information for the identification of familiar landmarks which serve for orientation to the environment and for detection of obstacles, stairs, and other changes in the traveled surface which may prove to be hazardous. Similarly, information presented on printed pages, dials, and meters contained in home and work instruments and appliances, and that presented on cathode ray tube and video projection screens, can typically be discriminated solely through the use of vision. The inability to access these multitudinous visual media can severely restrict the independence and the educational and employment opportunities of those individuals living with visual impairments. Thus, blindness and visual impairment will become a handicap for those people seeking educational and employment opportunities within the environments which emphasize independent access to and manipulation of visually presented information.

Sensory aid technology can significantly reduce the effects of visual impairment by providing the user with information regarding the environment and objects contained within it, information normally obtained visually. Sensory aids are devices which either increase the usability of information presented to a sensory system:

sensory enhancement, or present information customarily associated with one sensory modality through another intact system: *sensory substitution*. Common examples of sensory enhancement aids are spectacles, magnifying lenses, and closed-circuit television magnifiers which enhance the usability of visual information by providing increased magnification, illumination, and/or contrast. (Hearing aids and other amplification systems serve similar sensory enhancement functions for people with hearing impairments.) Sensory substitution aids include canes, Braille, tape recorders, and high technology devices such as the Optacon. In each case, information typically obtained visually is presented and secured through another modality.

Sensory aids are used in both of the major areas previously listed as producing restricted functioning for blind and visually impaired people, namely travel and access to printed information. Technology exists which assists users in obtaining information regarding the presence of obstacles in a pathway, the spatial layout of one's environment, the output of a calculator or measurement tool, or the contents of an alphanumeric display.

The curricula in special education programs serving blind and visually handicapped students should encompass training in orientation and mobility, independent living skills, and the more traditional academic disciplines which emphasize literacy and computational skills. The vast majority of modern technological devices which can positively contribute to the education of blind and visually handicapped students relate to addressing these latter literacy and computational needs. Thus, more attention will be focused on these devices in the following pages, although a brief review of sensory aid technology relating to orientation and mobility and to activities of daily living will be presented.

Electronic Information and the Microcomputer

The rapid proliferation in our society of the microcomputer and other microprocessor-based informational display instruments is producing an increasing use of electronic information. In an era which has been characterized as experiencing an "information explosion," there is increased reliance upon the creation, processing, and transmission of information in electronic form. This growing use of technology has strong implications for blind and visually impaired individuals because equality in access to electronically stored information can be provided by specially designed display devices. As many writers have suggested (e.g., Ashcroft, 1984; Scadden, 1984a), this technology may have more positive implications for blind and visually impaired individuals than for any other group of people because new, innovative devices can provide independent access to the creation and retrieval of electronically stored information for this group. The importance of electronic information—and

the computer, the primary tool used for its manipulation—is becoming more pervasive almost daily. In education, employment, and daily living, the computer is becoming almost ubiquitous although it is often invisible as it exists as the controller of appliances and automobile equipment.

More importantly for this discussion, the computer is being used increasingly on all levels of education. Ashcroft (1984) quoted Don Senese of the Government Printing Office as saying:

> Today we no longer ask, "Will computers be used in schools." We know they are and that they are being purchased by schools faster than we can keep count. Indeed, surveys of computers in schools are outdated by the time they are published. (p. 109)

Despite this admonition, some data regarding educational utilization of computers are in order here although care must be taken in extrapolating these numbers to present or future dates.

The *Journal of Visual Impairment and Blindness*, in its November 1984 special issue on microcomputer technology, reported in its "Random Access" column that results of one study indicated that 86% of public school districts already have microcomputers for use by students in at least one school. The study also reported that the number of microcomputers in public elementary schools tripled between the year 1982 and 1983. The proportion of visually impaired students with access to computers is apparently far below that of their sighted peers. One study conducted by Kapperman and quoted by Ashcroft (1984) indicated that 42 out of 46 residential schools for visually handicapped students responded to a survey regarding computer usage. These schools reported that only 55% have computers and that only 40% are using them with students in some kind of instructional capacity. An earlier study conducted in the year 1980 and reported by Ashcroft (1984) indicated that only 3% of visually impaired students were learning about computers in school, but a year later, the number had risen to 23%.

This discrepancy may not be surprising, but its implications present an irony. Blind and visually impaired students have typically been dependent upon sighted assistance in educational and employment settings in the past. Today, with students and workers interacting with information contained electronically within the domain of a computer, the blind and visually impaired student could have equal and independent access to the vast majority of these activities if appropriate sensory aid access technology and training were provided. The microcomputer operates on the manipulation of electrical signals, digitized information which can be presented by a video display terminal (VDT), voice synthesizer, or Braille display.

Technology Utilization

The longstanding gap between sighted and visually impaired students may actually be increased rather than nearly eliminated unless appropriate technology and training are provided visually handicapped students. The apparent gap between the state of the art and the reality of current practice (i.e., distribution and utilization of existing sensory aid technology) is an issue which must be addressed both by researchers and policy makers. Three elements appear to contribute significantly to inadequate technology utilization: economic considerations, adequacy of evaluative data dissemination, and availability of quality relevant instructor training.

Economic Considerations

High technology sensory aids are typically expensive. The relatively small market eliminates the use of "economy of scale" production techniques normally employed by large manufacturers, a primary principle in unit price reduction. Marketing personnel costs, which also must be reflected in product prices, are relatively constant regardless of the size of the potential market, thus increasing the per unit marketing costs when small sales volumes are concerned. Additionally, maintenance service contracts are often prohibitive, a fact which again reflects actual cost of serving this volume. Finally, over time, the rapidly changing world of modern technology can have a negative impact upon the economics of providing up-to-date technology for any group, whether in education or business. This fact has been most noteworthy in the field of sensory aids as it relates to the availability of replacement parts for older devices. As electronic component suppliers terminate production of out-of-date components, repair may become impossible for the manufacturer, a situation which can be overcome only by the added expense of replacement of the entire instrument. (Repair of early models of the Optacon is a good example of this problem.)

The history of talking calculators provides an example of the economics of sensory aids from a different perspective. The first talking calculators were priced at approximately $400, similar to that of the first pocket calculators introduced about two years earlier for the sighted public. As the technology for calculators proliferated generally, the price of standard calculators dropped rapidly to below $10.00. At the same time, speech output calculators were introduced on the general market as a novelty which might have wide appeal. This broad marketing strategy had special benefit for blind and visually impaired individuals who then could obtain a talking calculator for under $60.00. Shortly, it became evident that the general public did not have strong interest in this product, and it is becoming more and more difficult to obtain such systems. If it becomes necessary again to reply upon specialized production of such units for the blind and visually impaired market, prices can be expected to rise.

Adequacy of Evaluative Data Dissemination

Both users and purchasers should have adequate performance data regarding sensory aids, both hardware and software, in order to make appropriate selection. Such data are often unavailable because systematic evaluations are rarely conducted and because even anecdotal reports of personal experience with the aids and devices are not regularly collected and disseminated. One factor which contributes to the lack of systematic evaluations again relates to the rapid change in the state of the art of modern technology. A systematic evaluation may take up to two years to plan, fund, conduct, analyze, and report. Such a time frame would often be completed after the model or version originally evaluated is obsolete. A second factor contributing to the lack of adequate evaluative informational data relates to the fact that no single clearinghouse for evaluation data currently exists. The American Foundation for the Blind has proposed the creation of a touchtone telephone-activated and interrogated database which would provide up-to-date evaluative information on new and innovative hardware and software sensory aid technology. Until this type of evaluative information service is established and appropriately managed, the gap in adequate information will continue to exist.

Availability of Quality Relevant Instructor Training Programs

Some professional special educators have hypothesized that sensory aid technology often goes unused because adequate instruction is unavailable. It is essential that training in use of new technology accompany its purchase. Techniques for insuring that visually handicapped students are exposed to the necessary technology training must be designed and implemented. Expanded use of locally-based inservice training of special education professionals is needed, but more attention must be given to the development of quality "teacher friendly" training packages which can enable the instructor to be self-trained.

Review of technical literature

Two professional journals—*Education of the Visually Handicapped* and the *Journal of Visual Impairment and Blindness*—regularly feature articles relating to sensory aid technology. Frequently, these articles are directly relevant to special education. Both journals published special issues concerned with microcomputer technology and visually impaired people in 1984. These two issues—namely the Winter 1984 issue of *Education of the Visually Handicapped* and the November 1984 issue of the *Journal of Visual Impairment and Blindness*—

provide an excellent review of current technology and practices related to technology utilization in special education and rehabilitation of blind and visually impaired individuals.

Three other specialized periodicals must be mentioned as having provided material related to technology and its potential in special education. In the past, the *Aids and Appliances Review* (AAR), formerly published by the Carroll Center for the Blind in Newton, Massachusetts, provided a quarterly detailed review of some category of sensory aid technology. Two issues of this periodical were devoted exclusively to computer access technology for blind and visually impaired microcomputer users. The combined issue containing Numbers 9 and 10 of *AAR*, published in the fall of 1983, and issue Number 11, published in the winter of 1984, were devoted to voice and Braille output displays for microcomputers respectively. *Sensory Aids Technology Update* published monthly by the Sensory Aids Foundation in Palo Alto, California is another valuable resource. In addition, the quarterly newsletter from The Hadley School for the Blind in Winnetka, Illinois, *The Orbit*, is a periodical which often contains a feature article on the use of modern technology in special education.

Four books also provide valuable discussions of the role of technology in the present and future. Perhaps the best known, Naisbitt's *Megatrends*, (1982) provides a detailed description of economic and social changes forecasted for the future. Two others, namely Toffler's *The Third Wave* (1980) and Deken's *The Electronic Cottage* (1981), include specific references to the use of modern technology by blind and other disabled people for enhancing the quality of life. Finally, Bowe's *Personal Computers and Special Needs* (1984) is devoted exclusively to the use of microcomputers for meeting the special needs of disabled and elderly individuals.

The resources listed above were used as the primary sources of the state of the art reviews presented in the following section of this chapter. With a few exceptions, these journals and books contain the most recent, relevant, and objective information concerning modern technology and its current and potential application for blind and visually impaired students. An attempt was made to select sources which have research and/or evaluation data to support claims; however, adequate research is often lacking regarding the efficacy of innovative technology as it might be used in a special education setting. When cited, anecdotal reports will be identified.

Information concerning the state of the art in special education professional personnel preparation, as it relates to the role of technology, was obtained chiefly through personal communication with other professionals in the relevant educational disciplines. Precious little information is available within the formal corpus of recorded experience and practice, but that dearth apparently reflects adequately the current state of the art, as will become clear in both the State of the Art and the State of Practice sections which follow. It will also receive attention in the recommendations section at the end of the chapter, although perhaps not receiving the priority it deserves because it is much more a policy and practice issue than it is a research question.

STATE OF THE ART

The primary emphasis in this chapter is placed upon electronic sensory aids which provide access to information for blind and visually handicapped students. Following a brief review of sensory aids which have been used in orientation and mobility tasks and in activities of daily living, an extensive state of the art review is presented relating to the access of printed and electronic information. A discussion of computers and the sensory aid technology which provides access to them for blind and visually impaired people will follow.

Orientation and Mobility

Numerous efforts have been made to design and build electronic travel aids for blind pedestrians. The goal has been to develop a device which can either replace the long cane or the dog guide or, at least, augment the information provided by them. To date, these electronic travel aids have provided blind travelers with little more than a modicum of additional obstacle detection. The majority of the devices which have appeared on the market use ultrasonic beams which electronically sweep the environment in front of the pedestrian. Sound reflected by nearby objects is detected by the system and translated into audible or tactile signals which typically give coded information as to the distance of the object. Direction of the detected surface can normally be judged by knowledge of the direction in which the device is pointed. Other devices have been built into long canes or designed to attach to a standard long cane. In these cases, the resulting long cane is normally judged to be too heavy for normal long cane techniques.

Electronic travel aids have been rejected by most blind travelers for four major reasons: high cost, minimal supplemental environmental information, masking of normal environmental sounds used for orientation and mobility, and negative cosmetic considerations. The primary positive features of commercial electronic travel aids have been the ability of the traveler to detect overhanging obstacles normally not discernable with a cane. Extensive reviews of the electronic travel aids which have been developed over the past 25 years can be found in the writings of Clark (1963) and Brabyn (1985).

Recent research conducted in New Zealand, Canada, and the United States with the Trisensor, an experimental environmental scanning system, however, suggests that future environmental sensors may assist congenitally blind infants develop exploratory behavior earlier than previously observed and thus provide needed intervention in the eradication of commonly discerned delays in development (Easton, 1985). The Trisensor can be worn by infants or young toddlers as the unit emits an ultrasonic beam which reflects off objects and is translated into distinctive audible patterns of sound and presented by small earphones worn near the ears. These sounds give information as to the distance, position, and texture of the surfaces detected. Studies suggest that these devices may enhance the development of exploratory behavior in young blind infants and encourage increased mobile activity at an age when spatial concepts are normally learned. Systematic research will be required to determine the efficacy of these devices and the concomitant intervention strategies needed to facilitate the development of spatial concepts and appropriate orientation and mobility skills.

Activities of Daily Living

Informational displays provided by measurement instruments are commonplace for sighted individuals in employment, activities of daily living, and education. Thermometers, scales, pressure gauges, and other tools are used without regard to the importance of the visual markings. Recent introduction of similar devices with the addition of speech displays are now providing blind and visually impaired individuals with important and independent access to desired measurements within their environment including body temperature, blood pressure, and blood glucose levels. The proliferation of other speech output technology to be used in activities of daily living—such as the calculator, clocks, and scales—are already widely accepted and used. The introduction of these tools for activities of daily living within special education curricula of the future should significantly increase the independence of blind and visually impaired people as they advance into adulthood.

Computer Access Technology

The class of sensory aid technology used by blind and visually impaired individuals to access computers had been termed "access technology." According to Ashcroft (1984, p. 110), access technology is defined as, "the equipment, equipment interfacing, software, and instruction and instructional materials enabling independent use of microcomputers by visually impaired students." This technology may provide the computer user with tactile, auditory, or enlarged visual displays. Despite this emphasis, other computer-based technology to be used in the education of blind and visually impaired students will be discussed in the following pages.

Futurists predict an ever increasing use of electronically stored reading materials for all of society in the years to come, and this evolution will have special benefits for visually impaired and other "print handicapped" readers (Deken, 1981; Scadden, 1984a). Storage

media and display technology require attention if visually impaired students are to benefit fully from the capacity of modern technology in the meeting of their literacy needs. The transition to electronically stored written information, however, will not be immediate or complete. Thus, the reading of normal print materials by visually impaired individuals through the use of computer-based technology will also be addressed.

Finally, much of the information generated within scientific laboratories is displayed by special instrumentation. Access to these scientific instruments within the educational setting cannot be ignored when considering the accelerating significance of these disciplines in the nation's economy.

The remaining pages in this state of the art review section will be divided into four topic areas: sensory aid information display technology in special education, the use of sensory aid technology in meeting general education curricular requirements, career education and vocational training, and special education professional personnel preparation. Subsequently, these four topic areas will be the basis for discussions related to current implementation practices and recommendations for future research activities.

Sensory Aid Information Display Technology in Special Education

A number of reviews have been published which describe the various types of sensory aid technology that are being used by blind and visually impaired people (Goodrich, 1984; Ruconich, 1984; Scadden, 1982–1983). The primary emphasis of these reviews relates to technology used to store and retrieve written material and to "access technology," instrumentation utilized to display the output of computers in a readable form. The review by Scadden, however, does review the status of reading machines as well. A comparative review of optical character recognition (OCR) systems used for the preparation of reading material for translation into Braille or synthesized speech has yet to appear. The relatively new use of such equipment for this purpose has undoubtedly contributed to this gap in the published body of knowledge. An effort will be made here to describe work currently being done in this area.

Sensory aid display technology can be divided into three categories based upon the sensory modality selected for the informational display: tactile, auditory, and visual. Each of these three categories typically can be subdivided even further based upon the method of producing the information. These forms of information display are relevant to later discussions of reading machines, microcomputer utilization, and specialized measurement instrumentation.

Tactile Displays

Braille remains the primary tactile means for displaying information to blind people. Attempts have been made to provide tactile analogs of visual images. The Optacon is, of course, the one example of such a device becoming widely accepted. It will be discussed more fully later.

Although Braille is reported by the National Library Service for the Blind and Physically Handicapped and by the American Printing House for the Blind as being used by less than 20% of the legally blind population, it remains a viable reading medium for many readers. The American Foundation for the Blind (Kirchner, Peterson, & Suhr, 1979) reported that approximately 40% of the functionally totally blind population regularly use Braille. It must be recognized that the vast proportion of those classified as blind have enough residual vision to make reading through the visual medium possible. Further, the reduced need to use the tactual sense for environmental exploration by those with residual vision decreases the likelihood that they will develop the tactual sensitivity needed for fluent Braille reading. In addition, diabetic and many older blind individuals experience various degrees of peripheral neuropathy which also restricts their capability of mastering the Braille code. Despite the limited number of Braille readers, Braille remains the preferred reading medium for many blind and deaf-blind people. The production and display of Braille is divided into two categories, paper and electronic Braille.

Paper Braille. Paper Braille is that produced by a press or embosser. In most situations, the Braille today is embossed on full pages although paper tape was used in the past in early models of Braille embossers. In fact, Evans and Simpkins (1972) reported the first experiments with computer-aided instruction with blind students using a paper-tape embosser. This early study demonstrated potential, but its limitations were caused by the slowness and awkwardness of reading and reviewing this linear and continuous Braille display.

Within the last three years, Braille embossers have become commercially available which provide hardcopy, paper Braille output for computers, for a relatively affordable price, around $3,000. Previously, most Braille embossers were priced in the $15,000 range. Of course, speed of embossing is sacrificed with the lower cost embossers; but for many individuals, these systems are proving valuable.

Ruconich (1984) reviewed the primary advantages and disadvantages of paper Braille. The primary advantage for many Braille readers relates to the capability of reviewing an entire page of material at a time, comparing lines, randomly searching for specific information, or reading columnar material. A second advantage relates to its portability. The hard copy can be taken and read without use of an electronic device. A third advantage relates to the capacity of some Braille embossers to produce tactile graphics (drawings composed of dots or other symbols). Thus, simple graphs,

maps, or diagrams can be reproduced for tactual examination. Often these tactile graphics must be rescaled to permit discriminability by the Braille readers through eliminating otherwise cluttered displays.

The primary disadvantages of paper Braille relate to its bulk, difficulty in storage, and expense in producing large quantities of material. These disadvantages are heightened when the embosser is being used as an output system for a computer program. In many cases today, computer information is displayed for the convenience and pleasure of the sighted user. Lines are often skipped, only a few words may appear centered on each line, and other lines may contain only asterisks or other visually compelling symbols. The result of such formatting is that even more Braille paper is used. Further, the material will appear in "computer Braille" (comprised of uncontracted Braille and special punctuation) rather than Grade Two, thus increasing the amount of paper required. For these reasons, paper Braille displays for computer programs must be carefully selected to meet the specific requirements of the blind user. Individualized programs, straight text, or tactile graphics may be appropriate and cost effective uses of a paper Braille computer display.

Electronic Braille. Electronic Braille, or paperless Braille, is becoming a popular substitute for paper Braille, especially when used in conjunction with a computer. The electronic Braille system is characterized by having each Braille cell comprised of six or eight electromechanically operated pins arranged in the standard Braille configuration. The typical system is limited to a single line of Braille cells. Electrical signals will present a line of Braille which is replaced by the next line upon the touch of a command switch. Commercially available electronic Braille devices have lines which vary from 20 to 40 cells in length.

Four additional features of the electronic Braille devices warrant description here. First, most of these systems contain a storage medium for mass storage of information. This storage system is either an audio cassette or a computer disk. In either case, electrical signals stored on the storage system can equal several hundred Braille pages that can be read or manipulated. Usually, these devices also contain sufficient "random access" computer memory permitting the user to review material directly held in this temporary medium before storing it permanently on tape or disk. Second, most devices have a Braille keyboard which allows users to enter data into the device for their own use. Third, the systems normally have a standardized computer connector allowing the user to obtain information sent from another electronic communication system. This connector permits use of the device as a display for a computer as well as for storing material for subsequent reading. Fourth, many of these devices contain computer logic which permits the user to operate the unit as a Braille word processor.

The obvious advantage of the electronic Braille devices over paper Braille is the storage capacity of the electronic media, whether tape or disk. When used as a computer display device, the electronic Braille system eliminates the waste of great quantities of paper while searching through a computer data bank for desired information. Most of the commercially available electronic Braille systems are also battery operated, providing portability.

The chief disadvantages of these systems relate to the limited amount of material which can be displayed at a time. A single line does not permit easy scanning of formatted material such as columns or graphs. Although the electronics within the system normally allow the user to search for specific words or phrases and to advance over blocks of material at will, the user does not have the same random scanning capability provided by paper Braille. Another limitation to date of electronic Braille devices relates to the lack of standardization of techniques used to store material on cassettes. No two companies use the same coding technique. Eventually, as digital disk storage replaces the audio tape medium for the electronic Braille devices, this problem should be eliminated. Finally, these devices are expensive, $5,000 to $10,000.

The Optacon. The third tactile display device in the Optacon, an "optical-to-tactile converter." This well-known, portable system can be used by blind people to read normal print. A small camera is moved across a line of print, and each character is converted into a two-dimensional vibrating facsimile displayed on a finger. The regular lens of the Optacon can be used to read normal computer printouts. An optional CRT lens has been designed to allow the user to read many computer video display screens.

The single most important advantage of the Optacon is that it provides immediate, independent access to printed materials, including computer displays. This versatility allows the user to read many kinds of material including graphs and columnar material. Its primary disadvantage is the slow rates of reading speeds that can be achieved with this unit. Few Optacon readers achieve reading speeds of over 60 words per minute, with the average being considerably lower. Many users do not advance beyond 30 to 40 words per minute with the system. The Optacon also costs about $4,200, a fact which must be considered a disadvantage for most individuals.

Auditory Displays

Speech has long been the preferred medium of many blind people to obtain information. Human readers, disc recordings, and finally open-reel and cassette tape have increased the availability of reading material. Compressed speech—electronic systems which allow a recording to be accelerated without increasing the pitch of the speaker's voice is used by many blind people for rapid reading by listening.

Synthetic speech. Speech is also the most frequently used computer display system for blind and visually impaired computer users, but economics may be as important as preference. Speech synthesizers are becoming less expensive while the quality is being improved. A speech synthesizer is an electronic device that enunciates sounds which mimic vocal phonemes. Rules of speech stored within a computer or the synthesizer itself will string phonemes together to generate speech paralleling the strings of letters sent to the system from an electronic communications device. Most individuals learn to understand voice synthesizers within two hours of practice (Goodrich, 1984). Synthetic speech is not as practical with some forms of information. For instance, the reading materials contained within the diverse subjects of poetry and mathematics can best be mastered by occasional character by character examination, a process which does not lend itself to continuous presentation by a speech synthesizer.

Another form of synthetic speech can be produced by digitizing words spoken by a human speaker and then storing this information on a solid-state chip. This technique provides high-quality speech but a limited vocabulary. This approach is very useful for providing the output for an instrument which will not require an unlimited vocabulary. Measurement devices, calculators, and clocks are common examples of systems which use this form of synthetic speech.

Three major advantages can be presented for synthetic speech as it relates to other information displays for blind and visually impaired readers. First, it can be used by a wide variety of individuals. Virtually all blind and visually impaired people—except for those people with severe hearing impairments—can successfully use synthetic speech. Braille readers and large print readers alike can benefit from voice displays. Second, in many cases, good speech synthesizers are relatively inexpensive, under $400. Third, reading rates are often faster with auditory displays than with either Braille or large print.

The primary disadvantage of synthetic speech displays relates to the difficulty of independently reviewing the format of the material or rereading a word or phrase. This control over scanning and rescanning can be provided by devices which are equipped with special computer control software. Without this capability, the information is transient, heard once and then lost. Finally, synthetic speech displays cannot be used to present pictorial information.

Tonal displays. Another form of auditory display is that which is made up of nonverbal sounds: beeps, tones, or chords and patterns of sounds. Early reading machines attempted to use such information coding.

Today, virtually all computers present a variety of different sounds signalling prompts and warnings. These signal tones were included for the general sighted market, but they are especially helpful for the visually impaired user. Light-probes are another common device which have proved valuable to many students and professionals (See *Aids and Appliances Review*, Number 7). A more sophisticated use of patterned tonal output is being used by scientists at East Carolina University for providing an output for chemical and geological analysis. A more detailed description of work by these scientists will be reviewed later in this chapter based upon their most recent publication (Morrison & Lunney, 1984).

Visual Displays

Since the vast majority of people who fall within the generally accepted legal definition of blindness have some functional residual vision, it is essential that appropriate large character displays be provided them. Large print (generally defined as being 18-point type or larger, compared to 8- or 10-point type for normal print) can be generated through a variety of technological approaches.

Closed-circuit television magnifiers. The most widely known magnification technique, other than that provided by optical aids, is that of the use of closed-circuit television (CCTV) magnification devices. A closed-circuit television camera is focused upon a printed page, computer screen, drawing, or other informational display of interest. The output of the camera is displayed on a television screen in an enlarged form. Letter sizes of as much as 60 times normal size have been known to be used, although such magnification is rarely considered to be useful for most visually impaired readers. These systems are used most successfully with printed material. Placing a camera in front of an electronic display, such as a computer monitor, often results in blurring caused by incompatible scanning sequences of the camera and the screen.

Large character computer displays. For a computer display, the capability of generating large-character displays can be built directly into the permanent memory of the system. Several specially developed computer terminals with this capability are commercially available (Morrissette, 1984). These large character computer terminals permit the user to vary the print size, the polarity of the character (light on dark or dark on light), the contrast, and occasionally the color of the display.

A second technique for generating large print on a computer screen is through the use of specially developed software. These programs automatically display large characters on the television-like monitor. An alternative method, which is currently the most popular, utilizes specialized hardware attached to a computer which enlarges the print and allows the user to scan the full screen with manual controls.

Large print ink-printers. Finally, it must be mentioned that a number of large print ink-printers have been introduced commercially over the last several years. Few have remained on the market, but today there are software packages available which permit a user to create large character print on the rapidly proliferating dot-matrix printers.

The chief advantage of using large print displays for individuals with low vision relates to the use of a common and familiar medium for a large number of visually impaired people. Disadvantages relate to the relatively slow speeds which are normally obtained and to the fact that graphic information is laborious and difficult, although possible for some people, to trace out. Fatigue and eyestrain are also common for many visually impaired individuals requiring this medium to be used as a supplement to auditory displays.

Sensory Aid Technology in the General Education Curricula

Electronic technology has been steadily increasing in its use and its effectiveness within the classroom for all students. Longstanding utilization of audio-visual equipment was supplemented by the electronic calculator and later the microcomputer. Although computer-aided instruction (CAI) has been around the educational arena for over 20 years, it was the introduction of the microcomputer since the mid-1970s which began to revolutionize traditional educational processes through augmentation with technology. As indicated earlier in this chapter, the vast majority of school districts in this country have some microcomputers for use by students, and the number is growing faster than anyone can count (Ashcroft, 1984).

Sanford (1984) reported the traditional educational uses of computers which included the following: computer-aided instruction, information storage and management, and computer-managed instruction. Sanford continued by presenting the more innovative reasons for using computers within educational settings. These are as follows: individualization of instruction; instant and nonjudgemental feedback; enhanced normalization, motivation, and reinforcement; and self-paced repetitive drill and practice.

Each of the reasons cited by Sanford for the expanding use of computer technology in education appears to be valid for all students—able-bodied and disabled alike—but they are perhaps most pertinent to the education of blind and visually handicapped students in light of emerging educational trends. As Kessler (1984) pointed out, we not only have a legal obligation to these students, but we can provide the best education for them and meet their educational needs by insuring access to educational technology required for various instructional curricula. Finally, although Sanford (1984) did not specifically refer to independence as a reason for utilizing computers in the classroom, and it may be subsumed under the category of "enhanced normalization," it merits special attention when discussing the special education needs of blind and visually handicapped students. The following discussion should underscore this important result of the educational use of sensory aid technology.

The following paragraphs will attempt to document many changes in an evolving educational community which involve technology, and to describe efforts to meet the special educational needs of blind and visually handicapped students. Observations made by some of the innovators regarding successes and drawbacks will be cited.

The Microcomputer in Evolving Educational Practices

The years between the mid-1960s and mid-1980s have seen innumerable public reports concerning negative aspects of public education: declining reading, math, and science scores; and increased school vandalism and campus violence. Government reports and public concern have resulted in many changes, including greater attention to science and technology. Many states now are mandating computer literacy as an academic requirement for high school graduation. Many elementary schools are beginning this training as early as the primary years. Some colleges are requiring—even providing—college freshmen ownership of personal computers (Kessler, 1984). With the increase of the proliferation of computers within public school settings, a large, new industry of educational software is growing to meet and to create a demand for commercially available, educational program packages.

Scadden (1984a) documented three additional results to the public outcries caused by declining discipline and grades within the public school systems. First, alternative schools are springing up throughout the country, and an increasing number of parents are petitioning their states to permit them to engage in home teaching of their children. Secondly, commercial home study, or distance education, is on the rise. Correspondence schools which were formerly almost exlusively for the provision of remedial education now offer a wide variety of degree and certificate alternatives. Thirdly, the rapidly growing educational software industry includes a large number of tutorial programs which permit individuals within their homes to study many academic and hobby-related subjects. The microcomputer is playing an important role in each of these three alternatives to traditional educational programs. The computer can be used to interact with an instructor located at a remote location or to provide instantaneous feedback or reinforcement to a concept being learned.

Implications of the Microcomputer in the Education of Visually Handicapped Students

The implications for blind and visually handicapped students of each of the trends in education listed above are clear. If these students are to have the same advantages and alternatives as their sighted peers, they must have access to computer programs. Many programs have been initiated to fill this potentially serious gap in equal educational opportunity. One must be discussed here because of its interesting and important findings. Others will be cited later.

Brunken (1984) described an extensive demonstration program conducted at the Nebraska School for the Blind in the use of microcomputers by blind and visually handicapped students. Most importantly, this study showed that these students could learn to operate microcomputers and access technology for some school-related work. Student success in the microcomputer program was affected by several factors: prior knowledge of the keyboard, development of listening skills, ability to follow directions, level of cognitive development, and general level of literacy. Related to the topic of literacy, the Nebraska researchers found that a background in reading with either Braille or print provided an increased understanding of the format of written material, including paragraphing, spelling, and punctuation. Finally, this study resulted in a 10% increase in school grades by students who used microcomputers as a word processor for the preparation and editing of school materials.

The studies conducted in Nebraska should be replicated elsewhere to determine whether these findings can be generalized to other populations of blind and visually handicapped students. Nevertheless, the reports emanating from Nebraska and from other model programs present research and evaluation findings which should have broad implications for the specialized training provided blind and visually handicapped students: (a) Keyboard skills, or basic typing, must be taught; (b) the ability to listen and to follow directions must be taught; (c) print or Braille reading should be emphasized whenever possible; (d) word processing should be the first skill taught with microcomputers, while database access may be the second skill taught to enable students to avail themselves of remote literature research capabilities; (e) specialized computer-aided instructional materials should be developed with speech output software to be used with blind and visually handicapped students.

The issue of placing emphasis upon Braille reading by totally blind students, whenever possible, has been a controversial topic in recent years. Mack (1984) forcefully advocated more emphasis upon the teaching of listening skills even if it reduced the amount of training given in Braille reading. Her conclusions were based upon the findings that blind adults do not use Braille as much as they do audio for obtaining information and entertainment. The results from the Nebraska School for the Blind, however, would suggest that the use of Braille during the educational process may contribute an important dimension to mastery of basic skills of literacy which will subsequently transfer to the broader activity of interacting with a computer. This conclusion would support the position taken by Foulke (1981) who promoted the use of Braille for the teaching of mathematics and science. Further, Michaelis and Wiggins, quoted by Goodrich (1984), stated that Braille and speech together provide the most effective means of reading some computer output displays, such as accounting spreadsheets.

Reading Technology

The preceding discussion of the relative merits of Braille and speech reading media used by blind people leads directly to consideration of the current state of the art of reading technology and expectations for the near future.

Audio cassette recordings will apparently remain the primary medium for the presentation of educational reading material for many blind and visually handicapped students for the foreseeable future. The technology underlying the recording and playback of this material is not changing dramatically, although it is improving and the costs are declining. Speech compressors are not widely available but can be expected to continue to be of interest to many aural readers (Scadden, 1982–1983). More dramatic enhancements are being realized in the production of alternative forms of producing and presenting Braille material and digitized information which can be assimilated through the sensory modality of choice.

The introduction in the late 1970s of electronic, or paperless Braille, equipment provided a viable option for the storage and retrieval of Braille material as well as providing a Braille display for computers. As described earlier in this chapter, these devices can store up to several hundred Braille pages on a single cassette or diskette. Techniques for production books or periodicals in this medium have been developed and are leading to increased use of electronic Braille as an alternative to paper Braille (Raeder, 1984).

Electronic Braille, as now commonly used, relies upon the recording of specialized codes of auditory tones on the cassette. This technique has led to a wide variety of auditory coding approaches. Paperless Braille tapes made for one machine are incompatible for reading on machines made by other manufacturers. The increasing use of digitized information should lead to the capability of personal selection of the device and medium by which information is read (Deken, 1981). High density storage of digitized, electronic information can be produced by laser technology on video discs and other emerging media. The user can then chose to have this information displayed on a print screen, speech output system, paper Braille, or electronic Braille display. The future of reading material is changing for all of our society, and the change should provide more educational equality for blind and visually handicapped students.

Accessing printed material

Although it is essential to plan for the future, it is important to understand and to utilize the capabilities present today. Raeder (1984) described a variety of techniques which can currently be used to produce reading materials for blind and visually impaired readers. The basis for modern alternatives rests again on the fact that literary information is commonly produced and stored electronically. This information, typically prepared for transmission to an ink-printer for use by sighted readers, can be used to create reading material for blind or visually impaired readers by utilizing a different output or storage system rather than the standard printer. Again, the information could be sent to an electronic Braille device or alternatively to an affordable Braille embosser. It could be sent to a printer which generates large print; or finally, it could be stored on microcomputer diskettes to be used by the visually handicapped student with whatever display device is preferred.

Alternative media for storing this electronic information also exist. For example, material can be obtained from publishers on compositor or computer tapes through special permission arrangements. Although many of the printer control commands existing on these tapes must be removed prior to use with other storage or display equipment, this process provides the educational institution with a viable option for producing reading materials for special education students. A second alternative relates to the proliferation of commercial data banks which house a multitude of literary material: journals, encyclopedias, and current events furnished by the large wire services. These can be accessed with microcomputers for storage and personal use. Third, material can be entered manually by a typist into a computer, stored, translated into Grade Two by the computer if necessary, and then transmitted to the desired sensory aid system for use by the student.

Another data entry technique which has only recently begun to be accepted as a viable and potentially extremely useful technique is that provided by the use of automatic scanning and optical character recognition (OCR) systems (Raeder, 1984). Print material can be placed on one of the commercially available OCR systems to be "read" by the computer. The material is digitized and either stored on a disk or sent to some other display device. The well-known Kurzweil Reading Machine, which presents the output of the OCR system as synthetic speech, is one form of such an instrument. This approach has much wider application in the field of special education, in that printed material can be produced for use in a variety of display modes. The Kurzweil Data Entry System, the DEST system, and the TOTEC are three well-known OCR devices on the commercial market, and each system continues to improve in performance and flexibility.

The publicly accessible data banks described earlier provide a valuable resource for blind and visually handicapped students for independent literature research. Scadden (1984b) described the use of NEXIS, one large data service, by chemistry students for the independent access to professional journals concerned with chemistry, a subject for which it is difficult to obtain qualified readers. With microcomputers, these students have been able to obtain and read a wide range of relevant scientific material independently. Similar examples from other disciplines were cited by the author in the same paper. Blind and visually handicapped students in special education programs should be taught the techniques of accessing relevant data banks for the purpose of obtaining reading material of interest. Such independent skills will be of value within the educational setting and later in activities of daily living. Thus, word processing and data bank access are two very important reasons why blind and visually handicapped students should be taught the use of microcomputers (Scadden, 1983a, 1983b).

Scientific Laboratory Sensory Aids

In a later section of this chapter concerned with vocational education, the importance of the growing number of career opportunities in the sciences will be discussed, with an emphasis upon the need for enhanced scientific educational possibilities for blind and visually handicapped students. Morrison and Lunney (1984) extensively documented the history of increased laboratory opportunities for blind and visually handicapped students. They stressed the need for improved technology for all laboratory sciences giving special attention to their discipline of chemistry. In this review, the researchers described in detail instrumentation which will provide blind and visually impaired science students independence and flexibility within a science curriculum. In the past, such students have fared adequately within classroom activities, but they have not had the independence within the laboratory environment necessary to provide them with the experiences required for the mastery of competitive scientific skills. Now that the majority of scientific laboratory observations and measurements are being made with the aid of sophisticated instruments, the independence and competitiveness of blind and visually handicapped students can be developed if the appropriate output displays can be provided for the measurement instruments. Morrison and Lunney (1984) summarize this advocacy position: "Indeed, if a visually handicapped student plans to do laboratory work as a scientist, technician, or engineer, he or she will have to operate apparatus independently,

so why should the student not start early with the right tools?" (p. 418).

Morrison and Lunney (1984) described the development of scientific measurement equipment for visually impaired science students which has been named the ULTRA (the Universal Laboratory Training and Research Aid). The ULTRA has been designed to provide blind or visually handicapped students with a self-contained microcomputer that can be used for computational and word-processing activities, as well as to provide them input from a wide variety of laboratory measurement devices commonly used in chemistry, physics, geology, and other sciences. The output for this system could be synthetic speech, Braille, large print, or a series of tonal patterns, depending upon the availability of display technology and upon the specific application. Further research and evaluation of this system is needed, but the ULTRA appears to provide an enriched future for blind and visually impaired individuals desiring to enter scientific disciplines. The ULTRA has also been designed in a modular fashion so that it can be updated expeditiously and relatively inexpensively.

Career Education and Vocational Training

Special education professionals concerned with providing guidance and/or training to blind and visually handicapped students for future employment activities must be cognizant of the trends in the national labor market. Technology—especially the microcomputer and its peripheral sensory aids—will be extremely important in achieving competitive job readiness skills for individuals with visual impairment. A number of citations can be given which review the current use of technology by blind and visually impaired workers and which describe the trends observed today and forecasted for the remainder of this century (Goodrich, 1984; Scadden, 1982–83, 1983b, 1984a). The following paragraphs will highlight the major observations of these reviews which are relevant for career education and vocational training of professionals in the special education of blind and visually handicapped students.

The Information Economy

Most economists and futurists state that our society is changing from one based upon industrial manufacturing to one based upon the creation and distribution of information. Naisbitt (1982) presented a series of statistics documenting the change in the labor force. In 1950, only 17% of the labor force worked primarily with written information: materials such as correspondence, reports, invoices, receipts, forms, diagrams, and specifications. In today's labor force, over 60% of the workers are so employed. Simultaneously, fewer individuals are engaged in the direct manufacturing of goods. Perhaps the most important aspect of these changes in career activities, as they relate to the blind and visually impaired worker, is the fact that there is an ever increasing use of electronics in the creation, processing, and distribution of this information. The importance of the computer in these activities is accelerating. Predictions differ widely regarding the magnitude and timing of the computer's impact upon the labor force, but most futurists agree that over 60% of the work-stations in the United States by the year 1990 will be electronically based. In other words, there will be a computer or microprocessor involved in the processing and display of information of some kind with which the worker must interact. It is clear that people who cannot successfully interact with these displays will be at a severe disadvantage in the labor market. Scadden (1984a) stated that these data must impact the special education and rehabilitation professions:

> Thus, it is essential that all necessary provisions and training be made available to blind and visually impaired individuals. It requires that appropriate, high quality speech and tactile computer displays and support software be developed and distributed and that blind and visually impaired individuals have access to educational and training programs that will prepare them for the employment world of tomorrow. (p. 395)

Scientific Careers

Toffler (1980) identified four clusters of industry which will experience rapid growth in the coming decades, and which—along with the existing three largest industries: steel, automobiles, and chemicals—will dominate the industrial economy in the future. These four industrial clusters are the following: electronics and computers, space, oceanographics, and the biological sciences. All of these industrial clusters—along with chemicals—emphasize the sciences. Even the remaining two large industries—steel and automobiles—employ a large number of engineers and scientists. The remainder of the overall economy will be dominated by government and service industries which again are comprised mainly of workers who are engaged in the manipulation of information.

The "Knowledge Worker"

The term "knowledge worker" has been coined to refer to the large number of individuals who work with ideas, concepts, and information. The review of the industries and businesses which will serve as the backbone of the future's economy results in the unequivocal realization that career education and vocational training must emphasize the significance of preparing for employment as a "knowledge" worker whenever possible and appropriate.

Blind and visually impaired individuals have the opportunity to compete fully in the primary activities of the "knowledge" worker in the creation, transmission,

and monitoring of symbolic information given the appropriate information display and adequate educational training.

Decentralization of employment

With the wide dissemination of computer and telecommunication technology, millions of jobs could be performed from home or other remote locations because the nature of the work involves the creation and distribution of symbolic information. This fact is leading to a decentralization of the national labor force, according to economists and other social scientists (Toffler, 1980; Deken, 1981). A microcomputer and a telephone link will be sufficient to tie many workers and small business establishments to more centralized facilities.

Two kinds of workers are emerging in the decentralized work force: the telecommuter and the "electronic cottage industry" worker. The telecommuter is the employee of a firm who conducts assigned tasks from a remote site and interacts with the central facility by way of a computer and telecommunication equipment. The "electronic cottage industry" worker is the individual who is self-employed or who works for a small business engaged in the creation, processing, and/or transmission of electronic information. Such small businesses sell their services to other individuals, larger firms, or organizations. Small electronic firms are springing up across the country selling such services as the design of new products and software, the handling of paper-work and files for larger institutions, scheduling for local transportation services, data processing and accounting services, word processing and payrolling, and marketing. Other small entrepreneurs are providing management services for other small businesses.

The decentralization of employment must be considered a viable career option for blind and visually impaired individuals, although it cannot be permitted to become a stereotyped solution to the vocational rehabilitation needs of this population. As home-based employment can create isolation from the rest of society, this employment option must be retained only for those without other feasible opportunities and for those who chose it. Nevertheless, with appropriate training and technology, telecommuting and small electronic entrepreneurial activities serve as innovative alternatives.

Employment Opportunities for Multihandicapped Visually Impaired Individuals

Even the "nonknowledge" worker of the future will often require access to computerized information. Manufacturing is already becoming computerized with the advent and increased use of processes known as "computer assisted design" and "computer assisted manufacturing," CAD-CAM. In these processes, there will, for a long time in the future, still be human workers employed to monitor computer activity. The computer information will be displayed visually, auditorally, or even tactually. Toffler (1980) proposed that many of these repetitive, monitoring tasks could be performed by individuals with lower intellectual capabilities because the information could be presented through voice synthesis with detailed instructions of step-by-step actions to be undertaken. Scadden (1984a) carried this principle a step further by suggesting that many of these tasks were within the capabilities of numerous multihandicapped blind and other disabled individuals given the appropriate displays, training, and response systems. Considering the large number of multihandicapped blind and severely visually handicapped students present today within the special education programs in the country, these options must be systematically investigated. In many situations, the multihandicapped blind worker will require alternative input techniques because neither the standard keyboard nor the visually mediated keyboard emulators commonly used with sighted orthopedically handicapped computer users are appropriate. Speech recognition systems or aurally mediated keyboard emulators must be developed and tested for these individuals.

Synopsis of Career Education Needs

In conclusion, it is clear that career education and vocational training must take into consideration societal and economic changes. A report of the U.S. Office of Technology Assessment (1982) stated that:

> Modern society is undergoing profound technological and social changes brought about by what has been the information revolution. . . . A key element of all of these educational needs is that they will constantly change. In a rapidly advancing technological society, it is unlikely that the skills and information base needed for initial employment will be those needed for the same job as a few years later. Lifelong retraining is expected to become the norm for many people. (p. 1)

Special Education Professional Personnel Preparation

Since the completion of the Bureau of Education for the Handicapped's national Optacon Dissemination Program, and its concurrent special educator Optacon training program conducted by the University of Pittsburgh, there has not been a strong or systematic national effort relating to the preparation of special education personnel in the field of technology for blind or visually handicapped students. Of course, many pockets of inservice teacher training related to technology exist within individual teacher preparation programs, such as at Peabody College, Vanderbilt University; Teachers

College, Columbia University; Northern Colorado University; San Francisco State University; and California State University, Los Angeles. These latter programs deserve credit for their attempts and their successes, but to date they have not had the resources to provide either the breadth or depth of training necessary to impact the needs of the vast majority of the nation's blind and visually impaired elementary and secondary level students.

The Optacon Dissemination Program was unique in that the personnel training which was provided was related directly to the provision of an Optacon to a specific school district. In this case, the specific technology "drove" the personnel preparation activity. There is no reason to anticipate that similar sensory aid dissemination programs will emerge in the foreseeable future; thus the successes of the University of Pittsburgh in training over 1,000 special educators in the use of educational technology (Heubner, 1980) may not be generalizable to future situations. The majority of the activities prevailing within the university-based special education personnel preparation programs which relate to technology for the blind and visually handicapped student are conducted as inservice, summer programs. The one exception has been the Peabody graduate program which accepts applications from special educators interested in pursuing advanced degree studies related to the application of sensory aid technology to the needs of blind and visually handicapped students. Although only a few individuals have received this advanced training, the program has succeeded in increasing the body of knowledge regarding this field through the conduct of research and demonstration programs. (For example, the entire special issue of *Education of the Visually Handicapped* which was devoted to microcomputer technology was based upon activities of individuals connected with the Peabody program.)

STATE OF PRACTICE

Gaps between the emergence of new technology for the blind and visually handicapped student and its utilization must be anticipated on economic grounds if on no other. Sensory aid devices are commonly expensive, a problem which is virtually impossible for the manufacturers and distributors to remedy based upon the low prevalance population being served. Economy of scale production permitted by increased quantities can never be realized as the means to reduce the unit cost of these aids. Thus, school districts, institutions, organizations, agencies, and individuals alike, must budget in advance to acquire the funds necessary to procure needed instrumentation.

An additional problem often confronting users of sensory aids has been produced by the fact that technology in general in our society is changing so rapidly that sensory aids designed to provide suitable output for some device, such as a computer, may not be appropriate for the next generation of the device. This problem has not

215

as yet been acute within special education because educational facilities are not able to upgrade rapidly to advanced technological systems. However, this has been a problem in many institutions and agencies engaged in vocational training. An example of this gap caused by timing may be in order. IBM released in 1980 the Audio Typing Unit, a system designed to provide blind word processor operators full vocabulary screen review capability when using the IBM MagCard word processor product line. Unfortunately, this speech system had been under development for several years, and by the time it was ready for the marketplace, the word processors for which it was intended were not commonly being used. A number of vocational training facilities adequately trained students on this system only to find that competitive jobs were not available. Fortunately for many students, word processing skills can readily be transferred from one machine to another. For those who could find adequate output displays for newer machines, the training was valuable. For many others, it did not lead to productive employment.

Data collected regarding the number of microcomputers in school districts in the nation cannot be fairly compared to data regarding the percentage of visually handicapped students receiving microcomputer training. Anecdotal data, however, from many special educators and sensory aid distributors suggest that a gap between knowledge and practice probably exists. It is clear that blind and visually handicapped students can profit as much, and probably more, from the use of microcomputers in schools than their fully sighted peers. Many blind and visually handicapped students are not able to participate in "computer literacy" courses in mainstream programs because appropriate sensory aid display technology is not available. Despite this discrepancy between research results and educational practice, there are numerous exemplary programs which illustrate that modern technology is being used and research findings are being implemented in many locations. Some examples will be briefly described.

The Peabody College Program

The Peabody College microcomputer program, entitled "Research on Multimedia Access to Microcomputers for Visually Impaired Youth" (Ashcroft, 1984), supported by the U.S. Department of Education, has investigated techniques for providing access to microcomputers for this population of students. Several residential and public school programs have participated in this research and demonstration effort. Results have demonstrated that blind and visually handicapped students can learn to operate microcomputers and sensory aid access technology, and perform school assignments more independently and with higher grades (Brunken, 1984).

The Peabody program had several objectives, including the following: to study microcomputer systems which would be made accessible to visually handicapped

students through touch, voice, and large print; to develop and evaluate instructional programs for teaching visually handicapped students to use these multimedia microcomputer systems through access technology; and to develop and evaluate instructional material for inservice and preservice training of educational personnel. Documentation of the program successes and curricular materials including software packages are available from the institution. These materials should be of value to professional personnel training programs initiating their own curriculum relating to the use of technology for the education of blind and visually handicapped students.

The Nebraska School Program

One of the institutions participating in the Peabody project was the Nebraska School for the Visually Handicapped. Brunken (1984) described the Nebraska program and its findings. This demonstration project developed eight levels of microcomputer utilization for the participating visually handicapped students. These activities were the following: tutorial activities related to repetitive tasks encountered in such courses as spelling, typing, math, science, social studies, and language arts; (b) computer literacy; (c) prevocational training related to skills required in careers which utilize computer technology; (d) personal applications of microcomputer and sensory aid technology; (e) computer programming; (f) career planning through the exploration of different careers described in specially developed computerized materials; (g) word processing; and (h) the administration of files.

The Sensory Aids Foundation Program

The Sensory Aids Foundation (SAF) studied the effectiveness of using Apple computers with blind and visually handicapped elementary students in the San Francisco Bay Area. This study (Sensory Aids Foundation, 1984) found that Apple microcomputers could be operated successfully using speech synthesizers, but many commercially available educational software packages were inaccessible to blind students using speech output because the programs were protected from transmission to peripheral devices. Similar limitations have been noted by Brunken (1984) and Young (1984). Brunken (1984) stated that visually handicapped students, using large print displays, had greater access to these programs because they could frequently use the video screen rather than an audio display. Special software is available from SAF.

Software Evaluation

Ashcroft (1984) emphasized that any practitioner interested in utilizing commercial software must carefully evaluate the programs first. He presented criteria that could be used in this evaluation process which include: determining its effectiveness, insuring that it can be used with the desired access technology, avoiding programs in which time of response is significant, and identifying software in which pictorial or graphic information is minimal.

Summer Training Programs

A number of summer programs have been held to provide microcomputer experience to blind and visually handicapped students. One summer camp devoted to this activity has been described by Farrera and Murray (1984). This program, conducted in Houston, was for teenagers who differed widely in background and intellectual capability. The "computer camp" concept appears to warrant replication in other locations.

An additional approach to providing an introduction to microcomputers for blind and visually handicapped students is that offered through a home study correspondence course from The Hadley School for the Blind (Scadden, 1983a). Blind and visually handicapped students can enroll in a four part course on microcomputer and sensory aid access technology. Some augmentation is offered through hands-on experience provided by collaborating rehabilitation and educational facilities.

The summer training program concept has also been used successfully for inservice training of special educators in the area of the application of microcomputer and sensory aid access technology. Professional personnel training programs as those offered at Teachers College, Columbia University; the University of Northern Colorado, San Francisco State University; and California State University at Los Angeles, are four examples of such programs.

An additional summer program, conducted for teachers by a private rehabilitation agency, merits special attention. The Carroll Center for the Blind has conducted summer programs for teachers of blind and visually handicapped students in the use of microcomputers and sensory aid technology. Instructional materials were developed under a grant from the Rehabilitation Services Administration and have been made available to interested individuals. These Carroll Center programs have received positive evaluations from participants.

Availability of Sensory Aids in Institutions of Higher Learning

On the college and university level, blind and visually handicapped students have begun to receive the technology necessary for increased independence and competitive productivity. Kessler (1964) described needs of the visually impaired college student and the attempts of one institution, the University of North Carolina, to meet these needs. Morrison and Lunney (1984) described the research at East Carolina University which should increase the ability of blind and visually

handicapped students at all levels to compete successfully in scientific disciplines. Finally, an example of a state-wide effort to make computer technology accessible to blind and visually handicapped students is provided by the current activities by the State of Virginia. With a grant from the U.S. Department of Education, the Virginia Department for the Visually Handicapped is investigating the computer needs of blind and visually handicapped students on each of the State's college and university campuses. Appropriate hardware and software will be purchased and installed on selected campuses as demonstration projects. To date, the Department has determined that computer usage is required in virtually all curricula in the mid 1980s: business, education, law, the humanities, and science and engineering.

The Xerox Corporation awarded 100 colleges and universities Kurzweil Reading Machines for use by blind and visually handicapped students. Although many of these machines have not received adequate usage, an increasing number of institutions are finding innovative ways of utilizing the optical character recognition capability of these systems for the production of reading materials in paper Braille, on electronic Braille cassettes, or on microcomputer disks. Information regarding these applications should be disseminated more widely so that other students can benefit from similar capability of machines which are currently idle.

Literacy Training

Another area in which there appears to be discrepancy between knowledge and practice relates to the universal instruction of basic skills of literacy to blind and visually handicapped students. The observations of Brunken (1984) presented earlier concerning the fact that students who have basic language skills progress more rapidly in microcomputer training is supplemented by many acecdotal reports from computer training programs which express alarm over the number of blind and visually impaired high school graduates who are not proficient in language or writing skills.

In a paper presented at a National Conference on Literacy and Disabled People, Scadden (1984b) said that this problem has arisen partially from inadequate instruction and from a lack of rigorous demand for independent demonstration of individual competencies. Further, he stated that:

> Partial blame can also be placed at the doorstep of technology which has led many educational systems to encourage blind students to learn reading and writing skills solely through auditory techniques. Many blind students never master Braille reading and writing skills. Critics of Braille correctly state that recordings are less expensive than Braille, readily obtained, and easily stored. . . . However, . . . the mechanics of spelling and grammar are mastered more rapidly by blind people by reading tactually

and through practice in the creation of written passages. In a culture and an economy which emphasize written communication, to be fully competitive in information related careers, disabled and nondisabled people alike will have to be proficient in language arts.

At this national literacy conference, U.S. Secretary of Education T. H. Bell stated that one objective of the national education program should be to help students learn to help themselves. Assistant Secretary Madeleine Will embellished this theme in direct reference to disabled students by saying that, "We must work to decrease their dependency." She continued by saying, "We should encourage all students to perform at the boundaries of their personal limitations." Educational practices may not be fully in line with these objectives considering the performance of many visually impaired high school graduates. In the final section of this chapter, research is recommended to investigate techniques to reduce the gap between the objective of increased independence and the observation of possible increased dependency.

Dissemination of information concerning research and demonstration activities must be enhanced. The normal means of using publication and public presentations at professional conferences must be continued, but the number of inservice training programs must be increased. Funds for providing educator stipends are needed to promote participation in these training programs. The use of telecommunication networks, such as SpecialNet, and utilization of teleconferencing techniques, must also be promoted, both for dissemination of information by the innovators, and by special educators desiring new ideas, concepts, and practices.

NEEDS AND RECOMMENDATIONS

The preceding sections have identified a number of areas in which specific research, evaluation, and demonstration projects are needed if blind and visually handicapped students are to realize the full benefits accruing from the utilization of modern computer and sensory aid technology. The following pages will briefly list major priorities in the following five areas: technology research and development, technology evaluation, application of technology in the general educational curricula, career education and vocational training, and special education professional personnel preparation.

Technology Research and Development

1. Research and development efforts are needed to provide an inexpensive means of producing paperless Braille displays. The piezoelectric and solenoid technologies used today are inappropriate for production of affordable electromechanical Braille or tactile graphic displays.

2. Full-page electromechanical tactile graphic displays are required for the presentation of two-dimensionally formatted materials—graph and columnar material—for the tactual review of computer generated information. Simultaneously, symbology appropriate for tactile graphs displays must be developed, tested, and standardized.

3. The development of techniques for preparing and storing reading materials of the future must have the participation of educators knowledgeable in the needs of blind and visually impaired individuals. Laser technology, used with video disk and other storage media, will be developed; and these technologies must be appropriate for access by blind and visually impaired individuals for information display in visual, auditory, and tactile forms.

4. Special education and rehabilitation specialists must work closely with computer manufacturers to guarantee that future generations of personal computers will be accessible by blind and visually impaired individuals using sensory aid technology.

5. Attempts should be made to standardize the audio technique used for encoding electronic Braille information on paperless Braille cassettes.

6. Demonstration projects are required that will perfect the means by which blind and visually impaired computer users can access write-protected disks with sensory aid display technology without jeopardizing copyright privileges of the software developers. These efforts will require cooperation of researchers, application program software developers, and disk operating system producers.

7. Specialized application software must be developed to allow blind and visually impaired individuals to have access to the less expensive microcomputers and access technology for needed applications such as word processing, information storage and retrieval, data-base access, and recreational activities.

8. Further development of optical character recognition (OCR) system-based reading and data entry systems is needed to improve the performance and to reduce the unit cost.

9. Research and demonstration projects are needed for the implementation of techniques to enhance the dissemination of reading materials through telecommunication instrumentation for use by blind and visually impaired readers. Both telephone line-based databanks and satellite communication systems must be investigated and tested. Appropriate training programs will then be needed.

Technology Evaluation

1. Evaluation programs must be designed, funded, and implemented which will systematically investigate the efficacy of utilizing environmental sensing devices with congenitally blind infants for the purpose of promoting exploratory behavior and thus reducing the

developmental delays frequently observed in these children.

2. Instruments of measurement which can provide increased personal independence in activities of daily living should be evaluated and introduced into special education curricula.

Application of Technology in General Education Curricula

1. A demonstration project is needed which engages special education professionals and science curriculum specialists in a cooperative venture which will result in innovative efforts designed to enhance the training of blind and visually handicapped students in scientific disciplines. Advanced science education for these students will be required if they are to be able to compete for employment in the growing scientifically-based industries. Guidance from both groups of professionals will be required so that appropriate instruments and techniques for blind and visually handicapped students can be developed.

2. Evaluation of the ULTRA scientific measurement device is needed on all levels of science education to determine its effectiveness and value for different populations of blind and visually handicapped students. Science teachers from mainstream programs must be provided inservice training in the use of the device and in general orientation to the needs of blind and visually handicapped students.

3. Research and demonstration projects are needed to investigate optimal methods of teaching Braille reading and listening skills to students with varied intellectual capabilities. These projects should investigate the use of auditory feedback during Braille learning—as with the experimental Texas Instruments Wand being tested at the Veterans Administration Central Blind Rehabilitation Center by Dr John Trimble, and methodology to enhance the intelligibility and acceptance of speech synthesizers.

4. Evaluation of the newly emerging Braille computer code for use by Braille transcribers and computer users must be thoroughly conducted and be followed by systematic refinement.

5. The development of improved techniques of teaching microcomputer-based word processing skills for all blind and visually handicapped students on the elementary school level is needed.

6. The development and evaluation of curricula are needed that will maximize literacy skills for blind students who must use auditory information displays because of their tactual limitations. These curricula must emphasize skills which include writing, spelling, and punctuation.

Career Education and Vocational Training

1. Demonstration projects must be established which bring together professionals from industry, special education and rehabilitation to design and test career education and vocational training programs which will prepare multihandicapped blind students for appropriate tasks within a computerized manufacturing world, one based upon "CAD-CAM." These programs must include examination of appropriate speech output displays and, often for motor impaired individuals, alternative input techniques for data entry. These input techniques may require development of new approaches other than the common "mouthsticks" and "eyeblink" switching techniques commonly used with sighted motor impaired individuals.

2. Demonstration vocational training programs are needed to test the feasibility of training blind and visually handicapped students in a variety of electronically-based entrepreneurial careers. These projects would emphasize the management and conduct of activities which are currently in demand within the employment marketplace. Today, these activities would include: word processing, accounting, database management, marketing, and software development.

3. Development and demonstration projects are needed in the area of expanding realistic career education and vocational training for blind and visually handicapped students in the scientific disciplines.

Special Education Professional Personnel Preparation

1. Demonstration programs are needed immediately to provide inservice training to special educators who serve blind and visually handicapped students to familiarize them with the use of computer and sensory aid technology. These professionals must be presented with the realities of a changing world and become computer literate themselves so that they can assist their students maximally.

2. Development and demonstration of innovative information dissemination within the field of special education of blind and visually handicapped students is needed. SpecialNet should be expanded, and educators should be encouraged to utilize its services. Teleconferencing and other telecommunication techniques, including by satellite, should be investigated. Innovative approaches must be developed to enhance the flow of information from researchers to the practitioners in order to increase utilization of new technologies.

References

American Foundation for the Blind (1984). *Journal of Visual Impairment and Blindness*, **78**, 393–472.

Ashcroft, S. C. (1984). Research on multimedia access to microcomputers for visually impaired youth. *Education of the Visually Handicapped*, **15**, 108–118.

Bowe, F. G. (1984). *Personal computers and special needs.* Berkeley: Sybex.

Brabyn, J. (1985). A review of mobility aids and means of assessment. In D. H. Warren & E. R. Strelow (Eds.), *Electronic spatial sensing for the blind*, 13–27. Dordrecht, Netherlands: Martinus-Nijhoff.

Brunken, P. (1984). Independence for the visually handicapped through technology. *Education of the Visually Handicapped*, **15**, 127–133.

The Carroll Center for the Blind (1982). *Aids and Appliances Review*, **7**, 1–28.

The Carroll Center for the Blind (1983). *Aids and Appliances Review*, **9–10**, 1–60.

The Carroll Center for the Blind (1984). *Aids and Appliances Review*, **11**, 1–67.

Clark, L. L. (1963). *Proceedings of the Conference on Technology and Blindness*, New York: American Foundation for the Blind.

Deken, J. (1981). *The electronic cottage.* New York: Morrow.

Easton, R. D. (1985). Sonar sensory aid and children's spatial cognition. In D. H. Warren & E. R. Strelow (Eds.), *Electronic spatial sensing for the blind*, 239–256. Dordrecht, Netherlands: Martinus-Nijhoff.

Evans, R., & Simpkins, K. (1972). Computer assisted instruction for the blind. *Education of the Visually Handicapped*, **4**, 83–85.

Farrera, E. O., & Murray, J. G. (1984). Summer computer camp for blind and visually impaired teenagers. *Journal of Visual Impairment and Blindness*, **78**, 441–443.

Foulke, E. (1981). Impact of science and technology on the early years. *Journal of Visual Impairment and Blindness*, **75**, 101–108.

Goodrich, G. L. (1984). Applications of microcomputers by visually impaired persons. *Journal of Visual Impairment & Blindness*, **78**, 408–414.

Heldref Publications (1984). *Education of the Visually Handicapped*, **15**, 106–144.

Heubner, K. (1980). *An Optacon dissemination project follow-through: A national evaluation study.* Unpublished doctoral dissertation, University of Pittsburgh.

Kessler, J. (1984). Accessible computers in the university. *Journal of Visual Impairment and Blindness*, **78**, 414–417.

Kirchner, C., Peterson, R., & Suhr, C. (1979). Trends in school enrollment and reading methods among legally blind school children, 1963–1978. *Journal of Visual Impairment and Blindness*, **73**, 373–379.

Mack, C. (1984). How useful is braille? Reports of blind adults. *Journal of Visual Impairment and Blindness*, **78**, 311–313.

Morrison, R. C., & Lunney, D. (1984). The microcomputer as a laboratory aid for visually impaired science students. *Journal of Visual Impairment and Blindness*, **78**, 418–425.

Morrissette, D. L. (1984). Large-print computers: An evaluation of their features. *Journal of Visual Impairment and Blindness*, **78**, 427–433.

Naisbitt, J. (1982). *Megatrends.* New York: Warner Books.

Office of Technology Assessment (1982). *Informational Technology and Its Impact on American Education.* Washington: Government Printing Office (TPO Stock No. 052-003-00888-2).

Raeder, W. M. (1984). Electronically controlled Braille machines. *Aids and Appliances Review*, **11**, 55–60.

Ruconich, S. (1984). Evaluating microcomputer access technology for use by visually impaired students. *Education of the Visually Handicapped*, **15**, 119–125.

Sanford, L. (1984). A formative evaluation of an instructional program designed to teach visually impaired students to use microcomputers. *Education of the Visually Handicapped*, **15**, 135–144.

Scadden, L. A. (1982–1983). Technology and the labor market, Implications for blind and visually impaired persons. *Blindness Annual*, 17–24.

Scadden, L. A. (1983a). Independence through computer use. *The Orbit*, **8**, 1–5.

Scadden, L. A. (1983b). Microcomputers in the lives of blind people. *Aids and Appliances Review*, **9–10**, 5–6.

Scadden, L. A. (1984a). Blindness in the information age: Equality or irony? *Journal of Visual Impairment and Blindness*, **78**, 394–400.

Scadden, L. A. (1984b). The use of technology in literacy instruction for special populations. The promise and the problems. (Unpublished proceedings.) *Conference on Literacy and Disabled People.* Washington, June 1984.

Scadden, L. A. (1984c). Microcomputers in education and employment of disabled people. (Unpublished proceedings.) *The Second International Symposium on Design for Disabled People.* Tel Aviv: November 1984.

Sensory Aids Foundation. (1984). *A project to make Apple computers accessible to blind children.* U.S. Department of Education Grant Number: G00-83-00349 (final report).

Toffler, A. (1980). *The Third Wave.* New York: Morrow.

Young, M. F. (1984). Constraints on microcomputer access for visually impaired persons. *Journal of Visual Impairment and Blindness*, **78**, 426–427.

SECTION 3

Handicapped Infants

Introduction

VERNA HART

University of Pittsburgh

Early intervention with handicapped infants is itself in its infancy. Although some studies have been carried out with various types of babies, little effort has been expended on a broad-based, well-conceived, systematic approach with the very young handicapped population.

Various factors have contributed to the lack of well-planned and well-implemented services for handicapped infants. Among these has been the absence, in most of the 50 states, of permissive or mandatory legislation enabling individual school districts to use state educational monies for handicapped infants. Because of the lack of state funding for their programs, many school districts have relied on federal funds. Much of this money is awarded for a limited time span, and handicapped infant programs are thus subject to cuts or termination. Even the incentive grants of PL 94-142 have been of little help, for the original legislation designated use of federal funds for children 3 years and older. Until the legislation was recently amended, there was no stipulation that federal funds could be used with younger children.

Because numerous school districts have taken no responsibility for early intervention services, this task, if undertaken at all, has been assumed by nonprofit United Fund organizations and other private groups, such as the Association for Retarded Citizens, Easter Seal, and United Cerebral Palsy, or by public agencies such as departments of health, welfare, human services, and mental health/mental retardation. In any given community, handicapped infants may be served by a number of individual agencies. Some infants are provided for by several agencies, causing duplication of sparse resources. Many of the programs are very small and have high administrative costs, and personnel with little expertise. Much of the success of these programs depends on the availability and predictability of funding, as well as on the commitment and knowledge of the administration and staff.

Another factor contributing to deficient services has been the lack of leadership in planning and administering the services. Because there has been no mandate, there remains the question of who serves the children. Leadership, in most instances, has been assumed by interested parties rather than through legal delegation of responsibilities. Interagency cooperation has been encouraged, but much has been on a voluntary basis. Again, much of the initiative has been assumed by interested parties rather than through a carefully conceived plan for the most efficacious administration.

A third factor responsible for lack of services is the insufficiency of funds for screening and follow-up programs. Although some funds may be available to serve handicapped infants, no clear means have been identified for knowing which children are most in need of the services. It is known that some babies who are definitely identified as handicapped are in need of such services, but most handicaps do not appear during an infant's initial hospital stay. Most visual problems are not identifiable in those first early days. Similarly, hearing problems can be overlooked, and unless there is sophisticated equipment for testing, such as with the auditory-evoked potentials, most hospitals don't even attempt to screen babies. Many less sophisticated newborn auditory screening programs have been abandoned when their cost has been considered in light of the numbers of false positives, false negatives, and those truly in need.

Unless a child is physically involved or presents stigmata, retardation is difficult to identify in a newborn. Some children present reflex or tone abnormalities, but whether these are indications of a later neurological problem is uncertain. Seizures are common in many newborns, but there are no clear-cut indications of which particular children will later develop epilepsy. Not all children who have abnormal crying, who are hyperactive, who resist cuddling, or who are fussy and difficult infants will develop behavioral or learning disorders. Most premature babies will grow and attain normal developmental milestones. Some of these infants, however, will need intervention from the earliest time possible. Professionals also know from previous experience that sending children into some households puts them in great jeopardy for depressed future development and that early intervention for such children is critical. However, current knowledge is unable to help identify which specific children are most at risk in which households, and the present level of funding prohibits a follow-up of all the children who have been deemed to be at high risk for handicapping conditions.

Because there are so many problems that may be missed in the initial hospital stay, there is a great need for screening programs to identify those children in need of intervention. There are large numbers of children who are at risk for various types of developmental and learning problems. To serve all the children who are labeled at risk because of medical, environmental, or hereditary problems would be extremely costly. Therefore, a well-conceived and well-funded program is needed to identify predictors for those children who will need services and those who will not, and leadership is required in the design and implementation of such large-scale screening. It is also important to remember that, because many children will not be brought to screening or medical centers following their release from the hospital, innovative methods must be identified for reaching those most in need.

Lack of research is another problem that inhibits maximum services to handicapped infants. Although the literature is full of short-term studies of newborns at risk for developmental delays, there have been few longitudinal studies that have controlled enough variables to indicate clearly which factors are critical in identifying and serving handicapped infants. Much information is needed regarding the most appropriate intervention for those who are identified. Who should follow up children who have left the hospital labeled as at risk? Who should serve them? What training should providers of services have? What interventions work best with what types of children? What is the best way to involve the children's parents? What are the critical early indicators? What are the best ways to assess the children and measure their gains? What other indicators should be measured to determine the efficacy of interventions? In these days of declining resources, where should energy and money be targeted?

There is a definite lapse between the identification of problems by medical personnel and the provision of services by educators. Nationally, there are also definite discrepancies between the little that has been learned from experience and research, the state of the art, and the state of practice for the young handicapped population. In most states that have passed legislation allowing use of state educational funds for handicapped infants, there has been little attempt to apply current research regarding the most appropriate types of program delivery and intervention for infants. Subsequently, most of the models in operation today are those which have been used in demonstration programs with older preschool handicapped children. Because there is a definite body of information showing that infants are quite distinct from older handicapped preschool chidlren, closer ties between the state of the art and the state of practice are needed.

The Handicapped Children's Early Education Program of the United States Department of Education has done much to aid the cause of early intervention for handicapped children. Originally designed to serve the then-neglected age span of birth to 9 years, the program, after passage of PL 94-142, began to focus on the preschool age. Recently, its major emphasis has been on serving the birth-to-2-years population. Personnel supported through this program have been very innovative in finding the resources to continue services after federal funds have been terminated. As a result, thousands of children have been and continue to be served. However, because the program was originally designed to support demonstration programs, it has contributed little in the way of controlled research data regarding the best ways to educate the types of children who have been served.

Due to these and other factors, the state of practice in handicapped infant education presents many unanswered questions. It is our hope that the five chapters comprising this section on handicapped infants will serve to clarify the issues surrounding some of the questions noted below and provide directions for answering them.

Infant education is still at a beginning level of sophistication in most areas of the country. Although increasing numbers of young children are being identified as high risk of effective early identification and there is a growing belief in the efficacy of early intervention, there is little information for determining which infants will most probably require intervention services. How can the identification process be refined to locate handicapped children effectively; to avoid erroneously identifying children as needing services, and to avoid letting other needy children slip through the early identification system, only to be picked up years later? Scott and Carran address such questions in their chapter entitled "Identification and Referral of Handicapped Infants." Reviewing the work of medical and behavioral scientists, these authors examine current identification procedures, screening efforts, and methods of diagnosis and evaluation. Noting the rapid advances in neonatal medicine that have resulted in the survival of many low and very low birthweight infants who require follow-up care and special services, Scott and Carran examine the concept of being at risk for handicapping conditions. In addition, they discuss how risk factors may be considered in identifying, treating, and preventing handicapping conditions in young children.

Closely related to the issue of identification and referral is the lack of comprehensive assessment instruments for handicapped infants and the need for predictive devices. Could such devices aid in determining which infants are most in need of intervention? Is the developmental sequence for infants with various types of handicapping conditions specific to each designated handicapping condition? Are techniques used with nonhandicapped infants viable for those with handicaps? What is the most efficacious period for intervention with the population? There is a problem with the validity, reliability, and standardization of most of the current instrumentation as far as handicapped infants are concerned. There is also difficulty in using present tests with the broad spectrum of children in need of testing. Are the instruments equally effective with high-risk, developmentally delayed infants as with infants who have different types of identified handicapping conditions? The population is known for its variance. Do we need distinct tests for the various types of infants?

In their chapter on the topic "Infant Assessment," Sheehan and Klein note the relationships between approaches to assessment and current and historical conceptions of the nature of intelligence, the role of psychoeducational intervention, and handicapped infants themselves. In this context, the authors review issues central to a critique of infant assessment, particularly in five different areas of development. They stress the importance of clarifying the purposes served by assessment and ensuring the match between assessment tools and the use of resulting data.

An additional area of concern in handicapped infant education is that of the efficacy of early intervention. Although there is an increasing amount of literature available, there are few hard data to support the premises as to the most effective age for intervention, the kinds of interventions to be used with the various types of handicapping conditions, the most effective programs for parents, and the types of children most in need of services. What is the best procedure for determining this information? Major issues within the field relate not only to the identification of those truly in need of early intervention and the best ways to deliver the services, but also to the plasticity of the brain and its ability sometimes to overcome conditions that many professionals have felt certain would result in severe handicaps. Although studies continue in the medical field regarding this matter, the role of early intervention has yet to be determined.

In their chapter on "Efficacy of Early Intervention," Dunst, Snyder, and Mankinen review and critique, from a causal analysis perspective, more than 100 studies in the efficacy literature. They also pose a number of questions for consideration by program administrators and direct service staff in determining the degree to which their own programs operate from an information base that reflects state-of-the-art knowledge.

In addition to the areas discussed above, there are a number of other important, unresolved issues related to handicapped infants. These include questions concerning the families of such children. What is the impact of a handicapped child on his or her family? What are the roles expected of the family members living with such a child? How effective are the various parent intervention programs currently in force? This section's chapter by Gallagher and Bristol, entitled "Families of Young Handicapped Children," addresses these and other questions, giving special emphasis to the roles of fathers and single parents in adapting to their handicapped children.

A final issue of concern is the types of personnel needed to serve the handicapped infant population. Nurses, physical therapists, child development majors, social workers, occupational therapists, developmental psychologists, early educators, and special educators are currently working in the field. What types of preparation should these professionals have in order maximally to serve the population? What types of curriculum should be used with infants? At the present time, interventionists seem to be using techniques from their fields that have been implemented effectively with older preschool children and borrowing from various other disciplines to create a more comprehensive multidisciplinary approach. Is this the most effective means of serving infants? Because of the multiplicity of problems that many infants currently display, interventionists must be familiar with a wide variety of handicaps, as well as with medical and ecological conditions. Handicapped infants, for the most part, do not present just one problem; interventionists must be familiar with problems that can occur in the physical, sensory, affective, and social domains.

In the final chapter of this section, entitled "Personnel Preparation: Handicapped Infants," Bricker and Slentz review literature pertaining to the preparation of educational personnel to work with handicapped infants and their families. In addition, these authors present the results of a national survey of training programs in early childhood/special education, and they offer a number of research and policy recommendations prompted by their work.

Because of the myriad of largely unresolved issues discussed above, a review of research on handicapped infants does not result in a large amount of data with specific answers. Instead, it points out that the field is at a state where specific guidance is needed for future work. If more direction is not forthcoming, there will be a tendency to continue using random measures that have not proven to be the most effective for serving handicapped infants.

Identification and Referral of Handicapped Infants

KEITH G. SCOTT AND DEBORAH T. CARRAN

University of Miami

INTRODUCTION

The identification and referral of handicapped infants is a topic that has undergone profound changes since the mid-1970s. There are two major and related reasons for these changes. First, the concept of who should receive educational services has been extended to include both the most severely handicapped infants and those who may only be at risk for becoming handicapped but who do not yet manifest a designated categorical disorder. Many of these children were previously denied a free public education due to the severity of the handicap or the lack of explicit categorization given to potential educational disorders; in an attempt to resolve such problems PL 94-142 was enacted. Secondly, there have been profound changes in the population of infants who survive birth due to advances in neonatal medicine (Budetti, Barrand, McManus, & Heiner, 1981). In the authors' opinion, these factors have led to an almost total but generally unstated revolution in thought about handicapped and at-risk infants and the services they require. This chapter attempts to define the field and clarify the underlying conceptions, assumptions, and state of knowledge.

Sources of information and literature for this chapter have been generally limited to medical and behaviorally-oriented sources. The reason for this is that obvious handicapping conditions generally have a genetic, familial or physical etiology. Disorders such as Down's syndrome, phenylketonuria (PKU), and cerebral palsy are identified early in their course and treatment is quickely initiated. Because of this, these conditions are identified as part of medical care. Other handicapping conditions, usually of a milder severity like learning disabilities, psychosocial retardation, and emotional problems are often not identified until the child is in school. For this reason, such conditions are not detected early in their course. This has often limited these conditions to educational and behavioral research. Recently, however, medical research has become more concerned with these milder conditions, often looking for a biological agent as a source of the disorder. The traditional segregation of research in such fields as retardation into either biological or environmental causes (Stein & Susser, 1963), is clearly inappropriate.

Much of the critical information presented represents the combined efforts of medical and behavioral scientists. The medical sources have specified identification methodologies, referral networks, and prevention strategies which have recently been viewed as applicable to handicapped infants. Educational and behavioral scientists have followed the outcome of high risk handicapped infants using standard infant tests and behavioral outcome measures. The interdisciplinary effort of medical and behavioral scientists has provided an abundance of literature in recent years, but the topics are restrictive in terms of disorders and sampling methods. As an example, recent follow-up studies with psychoeducational outcomes are restricted to small samples from teaching hospital clinics. Data available, concerning the association between perinatal events and later developmental outcome, are controversial. Studies have shown little association if any (Cohen & Parmelee, 1983; Cohen, Sigman, Parmelee, & Beckwith, 1982), while other studies do identify some important predictor variables (Ramey, Stedman, Bonders-Patterson, & Mengel, 1978; Siegel et al., 1982). Ramey et al. have shown that information available from birth certificates may be important in predicting later psychoeducational status. This may have an implication in terms of identification, referral, and tracking which will be discussed later in this chapter.

The chapter divides itself into five major sections that stem directly from the reasons for change outlined above. In the first section populations are identified who need to be detected and the trends in infant mortality and morbidity are reviewed. Aside from infants with obvious handicapping conditions, many infants are at risk of developing a handicap because they were born at a low birthweight (LBW), weighing between 1,501 and 2,500 grams, or a very low birthweight (VLBW), less than 1,501 grams. These LBW and VLBW infants are cared for in a neonatal intensive care unit (NICU) until their release from the hospital. It has been the rapid advance in the medical technology of NICUs which has lead to a dramatic increase in the survival of these LBW and VLBW infants. (Budetti et al., 1981). This surviving population has created a need for follow-up care and special services.

The second section of the chapter deals with existing methods of identification and referral of handicapped infants. Identification procedures, screening efforts, and diagnosis and evaluation are reviewed. This is followed by the third section which discusses the concept of risk, or the probability of developing a handicapping condition. The risk of handicaps is discussed within an epidemiological framework which facilitates the description of a specific population and details methodology for research. One important issue discussed is comprehensive computerized tracking of high risk and handicapped infants. Tracking enables children to be followed over periods of time to determine their progress and/or medical condition. Degrees of prevention are then briefly discussed in the fourth section as they apply to handicapping conditions.

The fifth part of the chapter presents an epidemiological perspective of handicapping conditions. A Multiple Risk Factor model is put forth which incorporates these perspectives into a theoretical framework. The Multiple Risk Factor model is concerned with the identification of contributing risk factors: that is, characteristics of the individual or their environment which increase the chances of contracting a disorder. Risk factors may be treated or controlled in an attempt to prevent the disorder.

Recommendations for future research and social policy implications conclude the chapter.

THE POPULATION OF HANDICAPPED AND HIGH RISK INFANTS

One way to conceptualize the children who may potentially need identification and referral is to consider the populations of infants who receive care at birth. In the most basic analysis there are two major infant populations. The first are apparently healthy babies who are born without complications. These infants have a normal gestational course and weigh within normal limits. The second population of concern are those infants who are not healthy, due to a variety of reasons. They are born too soon, have varying degrees of interuterine growth retardation or, due to maternal factors, are delivered with medical complications. To the learned reader this may appear to be an over-simplification of the identification process. However, when dealing with neonates, nonobvious medical developmental problems are difficult, if not impossible, to detect. Longitudinal research done with these populations of infants has indicated the later group as at-risk candidates for a variety of developmental problems (Nobel-Jamieson, Lukeman, Silverman, & Davies,

1982; Siegel, 1982). It is, therefore, important to understand the difference between these two groups of infants and the resulting prognosis and changing birth patterns which are occurring due to medical technological advances.

Infants from the Normal Nursery

These children generally have healthy parents, normal gestation, uncomplicated delivery, and are of a normal birth weight. Furthermore, they have no detectable physical, metabolic, or neurological deficits. In recent years, such children account for approximately 94% of all births, according to the National Center for Health Statistics. Smith and Simons (1975) suggest that about 0.1% of these infants will have severe developmental problems usually detected during a medical examination before their first birthday. The majority of children who eventually receive special education services in school will come from these normal apparently healthy infants. They will suffer from mild and moderate psychoeducational handicaps that either cannot at present be measured in infancy or will develop later due to experiential factors.

Infants from Neonatal Intensive Care Units

Infants from these special newborn nurseries have a number of distinct problems which are commonly present. The majority (90%) are of low birthweight, weighing less than 2,500 grams. The rate of such births has fallen for almost two decades. It appears to have leveled off at approximately 6% of all births (National Center for Health Statistics, September, 1984). They may also be critically ill and/or suffer from respiratory distress. Some will be separated from their mothers for prolonged periods of time in isolettes and be deprived of most normal interaction, handling, and vestibular stimulation. The mother will see the infant only on hospital visits. For the purposes of this chapter, there are at least four notable subgroups from the NICU.

1. Infants who have identifiable, typically severe, illnesses or disorders that are most likely to require medical and educational interventions throughout their developmental period and beyond. Such infants are identified by the neonatologist during the initial hospital stay. Examples are children with genetic disorders, cranial facial anomalies, spina bifida, and severe hearing loss. They constitute approximately 0.2% of all births and are candidates for birth defect registers (Smith & Simons, 1975).

2. Infants who are born weighing less than 1,000 grams (2.2 lbs). Sometimes called fetal infants, the neonatal survival rate of these children is now 40%, having doubled since the mid-1970s (Ross, 1983). They typically receive prolonged hospitalization and may begin to receive developmental interventions before discharge. The mortality rate for fetal infants has dropped

very rapidly in the last few years. As a result, the prevalence of handicaps among the survivors has not been established. This is particularly true for handicaps such as moderate levels of retardation, sensory problems and specific learning disabilities.

3. Infants who are of 1,000–1,500 grams birthweight. Together with those described immediately above, these infants have been called Very Low Birthweight infants (VLBW). The survival rate is approximately 85% for this weight group, having improved since the mid-1970s (Ross, 1983). Again, due to the rapid changes in care and survival, long-term outcome is unclear.

4. Infants who are 1,500–2,500 grams birthweight. These infants have been typically called Low Birthweight (LBW) infants. LBW infants appear to recover more quickly than they did in the mid-1970s as a result of advances in treatment and care. Data from the Collaborative Perinatal Study (Broman, Nichols, & Kennedy, 1975), and other major studies (Wiener, 1968) suggest that special education services are required perhaps 2.5 times more frequently by this group of children when compared to a group of normal birthweight children. It should be noted that these data pertain to children born in the 1950s, long before the rapid development of modern intensive care nurseries. More recent comprehensive data are not available, as the majority of recent studies are based on survivors of individual nurseries. Such populations prohibit explicit incidence determination.

These various subpopulations include both infants who will develop normally and infants who may have a handicapping condition. Infants with deformities and handicaps are, based on our experience, fewer than 20% of all infants from NICUs. The remaining 80% are termed high risk. The literature is clear (Siegel, 1982; Scott & Masi, 1979) that they are more than normally likely to develop psychoeducational problems that will require special education. Our ability to predict later developmental outcome from infant assessments is very poor (see Sheehan & Klein's chapter in this volume), thereby limiting the ability of professionals to identify and refer children during infancy who have, or may have, mild to moderate psychoeducational problems. The alternatives for referral are to (a) wait until a problem becomes manifest through either follow up evaluations, caregiver reports, or school progress, or (b) recommend a preventive intervention in an "undesignated at risk" category.

Trends in Infant Morbidity and Mortality

Infants weighing 2,500 grams (5.5 lb) or less at birth are designated as low birthweight infants. Since the mid-1950s there have been numerous studies relating LBW to developmental outcome in an attempt to determine the prevalence, or number of existing cases, of such disorders. Most infants born who weigh less than 2,500 grams develop normally (Cohen et al., 1982; Yu, Orgill,

Bajuk, & Astbury, 1984). However, many investigations have shown a much higher prevalence, of approximately 20%, for later neurological, intellectual, or behavioral problems in LBW children when compared to infants who weighed more than 2,500 grams at birth (Arias & Tomich, 1982; Drillien, Thompson, & Burgoyne, 1980; Fitzhardinge & Steven, 1972; Lubchenco, Delivoria-Papadopoulos, & Searls, 1972; Lubchenco et al. 1963). Broad development problems, which range from a mild to moderate severity, will be referred to as morbidity. Due to a heightened risk of morbidity, these neonates are called high risk infants.

In order better to understand the birth trends of the United States, it is necessary to understand the three basic measures that describe the population of births: the absolute number, rate, and proportion. A description of each will follow. A failure to recognize the difference between these measures has led to widespread misunderstanding of natality data. For example, the nation's attention has, in the past few years, been concerned with the purported teenage pregnancy epidemic. The cause for concern was attributed to an increase in the absolute percentage of teenage births which occurred. This is accurate, but the reason is not due to an increase in the absolute number of teenage births. Rather, the proportional increase is due to the decline in absolute number of births to women in other age groups. In reality the birth rate for teenagers has been declining, but at a much slower rate than the birth rates for older women (especially women 20–29 years of age). It is important to understand the terminology.

The first is the absolute number. This is all the recorded number of births in the U.S. during a specific time period. It is the absolute number from which the other two measures, rate and proportion, are derived.

The measure of proportion is more commonly referred to as the percentage. The percentage value reflects the proportional distribution of births for various categories within the population. Similar to this measure is rate.

Rate is a descriptive term which expresses the proportion of people who have or develop a disease among all those in the total group who are determined to be at risk of having or developing the disorder. Rate summarizes how frequently an event occurs independent of absolute size. It is usually expressed as a number per thousand persons (e.g., 4/1,000).

TABLE 1

Incidence of Low Birth Weight*

Birth Weight	1972	1982	Decade Change
< 1000 g	17,895	20,528	+ 13%
1001–1500	20,467	22,383	+ 9%
1501–2500	210,967	203,144	− 4%

*Data from National Center for Health Statistics, Final Natality Statistics, 1972 and Advance Final Natality Statistics, 1982.

The number of all births weighing less than 2,500 grams, or incidence of low birthweight, declined 15% between 1966 and 1981 (Budetti et al., 1981). However, nearly 250,000 infants are born annually in the United States weighing less than 2,500 grams. This is a relatively small proportion of all newborns, but these LBW and VLBW infants account for more than half of all infant deaths under one year and nearly three-quarters of all infant deaths, less than 28 days old. As startling as these mortality figures seem, there has been a significant increase in the average percentage of survivors since 1972, as above in Table 1. This information, from the National Center for Health Statistics, reflects the increase in survivorship evident since the early 1970s.

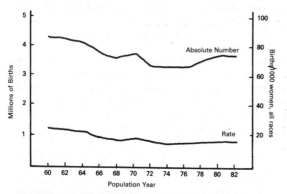

FIGURE 1. The absolute number of births and birth rate/1,000 women of all races for various years. Data from the National Center for Health Statistics.

Using the final statistics available from the National Center for Health Statistics (NCHS), the major birth trends of the U.S. may be considered. Between 1960 and 1982 the absolute number of births fell from 4,257,805 to 3,680,537. The birth rates have also decreased over the same years from 23.7/1,000 women of all races in 1960 to 15.9/1,000 women of all races in 1982. Figure 1 gives a much clearer picture of this data, especially for the intermediate years between 1960 and 1982. The absolute number of births and birth rate/1,000 is on the rise since a low in 1973. Therefore, with an increase in the absolute number and a moderate rise in the rate of births since 1973, a concomitant change may have occurred with regard to LBW and VLBW births.

Figure 2, depicting LBW trends since 1970, is similar to Figure 1. The absolute number of LBW births fell between 1970 and 1976, but has consistently been rising since 1976. This probably results from the increased number of births to U.S. women since the mid-1970s. A constant rate of low-weight births will result in a higher absolute number of LBW babies in years when more babies are born. The proportion of LBW births from all live births is also presented in Figure 2. This measure has remained fairly constant since 1970, dropping only about one percentage point by 1982. That is, the proportion of LBW births is remaining fairly stable. However, the absolute number of LBW births is increasing.

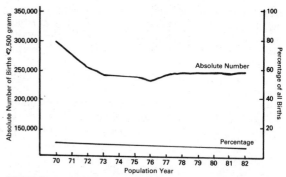

FIGURE 2. The absolute number of births weighing less than 2500 grams and the percentage of all live births. Data from National Center for Health Statistics.

When the incidence figures of LBW are considered in conjunction with the mortality (death) values for LBW infants, a pattern of increased survivorship emerges. Determination of mortality figures was accomplished using Final Mortality Statistics from NCHS for various years. Deaths attributed to immaturity unqualified, short gestation, or unspecified low birth-weight were the categories referenced. Because many states do not report infant death by birthweight, we believe these values to be very conservative and are in the process of finding other sources.

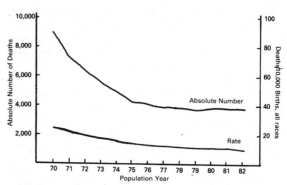

FIGURE 3. The absolute number of infant deaths and death rate/10,000 births, all races, attributed to immaturity unqualified, short gestation, or unspecified low birthweight. Data from National Center for Health Statistics.

The NCHS data do show a dramatic reduction in the absolute number of infant deaths due to unspecified low birthweight. (See Figure 3.) The rate for the same death category has also fallen from 23/10,000 death in 1970 to only 9.3/10,000 by 1982. This substantiates what the literature reports as the dramatic reduction in infant deaths. (Horwood, Boyle, Torrance, & Sinclair, 1982; Lee, Paneth, Gartner, Pearlman, & Gruss, 1980; Ross, 1983).

A comprehensive literature review of follow-up studies since 1960 of VLBW infants has been presented by Ross (1983). In terms of mortality, survival rates for infants 1,000 to 1,500 grams has increased by 15%. During this same period, the survival rate for infants less than 1,000 grams has doubled from 20% to 40%. These increased survival rates demonstrate the success of neonatal intensive care units and related services. Yet, caution must be used when the morbidity of this VLBW population is considered.

Variability in the estimates of morbidity of LBW and VLBW populations result from an absence of appropriately designed follow-up studies. The recent data, rather than being collected on a representative sample, consists largely of follow-up from individual clinics in teaching hospitals. The populations from these clinics are often samples selected on medical criteria reflecting concerns about health rather than psychoeducational concerns. The clinics provide diagnostic rather than primary health care service and drop-out rates are extremely high, especially for those infants perceived as developing normally (Budetti et al., 1981; National Institute of Child Health and Human Development Task Force on Epidemiology, 1984). Consequently, many of the psychoeducationally at risk infants are not identified as such until they are experiencing problems in the school system.

Prospective cohort studies of low birthweight including VLBW infants vary in regard to the exact proportion of handicapped survivors. Since 1960 there have been many studies published reporting various figures of morbidity in the VLBW population. Studies from the early 1970s, reporting the results of a decade of birth cohort outcomes, list the morbidity of high risk infants as ranging from a low of 7% to as high as 30% (Horwood et al., 1982). When other reports are considered with the previously mentioned one, an average of 15% to 20% morbidity for this VLBW population has been postulated (Kitchen et al., 1982; Ross, 1983).

When the relatively constant estimated morbidity figure of 20% is considered in relation to the increasing survivorship of the VLBW population, it is clear that a growing number of handicapped infants, who previously would not have survived, are now living. Ross (1983) stresses the point, "Even if morbidity rates for all infants less than 1,500 grams had not increased during the past 20 years, the mere increase in survival rates for this group suggests that the number of children with handicaps has risen" (p. 38). Due to these increasing numbers and for both economic and social reasons, increased attention should be directed toward the prevention of low-weight births.

Theoretical Perspectives of Handicapped Infants

Five major models have been advanced in favor of early identification and referral of children who are handicapped. For different reasons, it has been postulated that the benefits of early identification will manifest themselves through the positive effects of early intervention.

The first model is a standard one in medicine from the perspective of treating an acute disease. This position is that a disease, caused by a pathogen, is more easily remediated early in its course before the destructive agent is well-established or has had the time to spread. This is based on an acute infectious disease model of a disorder. In its original application it is so self-evident as to be beyond debate. As this medical model applies to developmental disorders, it has not been generally appropriate. Handicaps in children are typically due to multiple causes that gradually manifest themselves in the form of developmental delays. The failure of appropriate behavior to develop, rather than the occurrence of inappropriate behavior, constitutes an early sign.

The second model is that there are early critical or sensitive developmental periods during which environmental stimuli have an unusually marked effect on behavior. Said behaviors are persistently retained throughout the individual's life span and are emitted on presentation of the original training stimuli. This is an ethological model based on the classical studies of Tinbergen (1948) and others, and served as a theoretical basis for Headstart (Bloom, 1964; Hunt, 1961).

The third model is related theoretically to the second. This position first argues that there is considerable plasticity in development (Sigman, 1982; Bloom, 1964). That is, the organism can be modified by the environment and, therefore, by intervention. Further, the argument is made that the plasticity is greater in younger than in older organisms such that recovery from physiological insult such as brain damage (Geshwind, 1974; Hecaen, 1976) occurs more readily in the young. Models to relate these two mechanisms, early critical periods and early plasticity, have been put forward in terms of physiological mechanisms. It should be pointed out that the major data for these theoretical positions are restricted to information about nonhuman organisms.

The fourth model has been presented elsewhere by Scott (1978). According to this position, the failure to identify problems early results in an accumulated developmental lag. Intervention, to be successful, requires the delayed infant to acquire new behaviors at a faster than normal rate in order to catch up. The delayed infant's normal peers will continue to learn at an accelerated rate during this developmental period. This argument is self-evident and makes a simple straightforward case for early identification and intervention of delayed infants. In the case of children with permanent disabilities, the model argues for early intervention so that secondary delays can be minimized through the use of alternative modalities and response systems.

Recently a fifth model has come into currency. It has been adopted largely due to the impact of the markedly increased survival rates of LBW infants and the potential for psychoeducational disorders and other mild

231

handicaps these infants represent. The "risk" model of developmental delay derives from the modern medical paradigm developed by epidemiologists to account for chronic disorders such as heart disease and cancer. The central idea is that the multiple causes of a disorder are associated with individual characteristics or histories (risk factors). These risk factors may be themselves inconsequential or even undetected (silent), but make an individual more than normally susceptible to a disorder. This model is particularly applicable to prevention planning (Scott & Carran, 1987).

We have presented the model in greater detail elsewhere (Scott & Carran, 1985) and as it applies to the problems of LBW in some detail (Carran & Scott, 1985). The term "high risk infant" has become very pervasive in the infancy literature but an underlying etiological model has not been stated explicitly. In view of the simplicity and potential a risk model possesses, we will apply it later in this paper to the risk of low-weight births.

IDENTIFICATION FOR REFERRAL PROCESSES

The referral process may only occur after an infant has been identified as potentially handicapped. There are a number or combination of identification methods available, but the three basic stages in the process are location, screening, and diagnosis/evaluation. Diagnosis and evaluation are the eventual consequences of identification but will not be considered here. (For a thorough and in-depth discussion of diagnosis and evaluation see the chapter by Sheehan and Klein in this volume.)

Location of Handicapped Children

Two major methods of locating children in need of services have been risk or disability registers and Child Find. Disability registers have typically been the product of state health authorities for specific conditions such as genetic and metabolic diseases, birth defects, cranial facial anomalies, and hearing impairment. So far as a literature search revealed, there are few comprehensive nonmedical handicapping condition registers as do exist in other countries. Medical registers are commonly computerized. The counterpart in education is Child Find. Health registers and Child Find have not been electronically linked, which has led to duplicated services. Commonly, Child Find locates children for the educational system who had initially received medical care but had been "lost" or never referred.

Identification is neither simple nor straightforward. This is a major concern for interventionists. Too often children who do not have an obvious handicap are looked upon as "normal" and skirt identification. These apparently "normal" children with mild handicapping conditions such as mild retardation, learning disabilities, or emotional handicaps are often in normal elementary classrooms for some time before their problem is noticed.

The implementation of a Child Find program, for the purpose of identifying children up to 21 years of age who may be in need of special educational services, was the first step in alerting the public to the needs of handicapped children. Prior to this time, these children identified as handicapped had generally been discriminated against and not given the opportunity of a free, public education. With the passage of PL 94–142, the Education for All Handicapped Children Act, *all* children were legally given the right to an education. Therefore, as many of these children as possible had to be located, informed, and enrolled.

Child Find, like any identification process, is not a single service. It is one part of a network. However, the following points are specific to this identification process and should be kept in mind (Bradley, 1977; National Association of State Directors of Special Education, 1976):

1. Federal and state legislative requirements must be observed.
2. The Child Find planning process must be followed according to the national standards.
3. Interagency cooperation must be maintained. This is especially critical for children who, once identified, must be referred for further testing, evaluation and placement.
4. Proper collection and utilization of data must be maintained to permit periodic program evaluation and provide a reference for future programs concerned with identification.
5. All records must be kept strictly confidential.

Child Find proved to be an enormous success as measured by the number of handicapped and potentially handicapped children who have been found and referred (Hoffman, 1977). However, referral patterns need to become more systematic during the developmental period and better coordinated with the medical community if the prevalence of handicapping conditions is to be reduced.

Screening

Screening requires taking a brief sampling of behaviors and is a key step in the early identification of particular mild and moderate handicapping conditions. The alternative is to give complete clinical assessments on all children referred. This is prohibitively expensive in both time and money, as many or most children assessed will turn out to be functioning within a normal range.

The advantages of screening are evident. A screen ideally is easy to administer, takes very little time to administer, and is quickly scored or evaluated. As a result of these advantages a screen is considered inexpensive in both professional time and money compared to the administration of an entire test battery. Another and perhaps the best credit given to screens is that large numbers of individuals may be served. As a result, and depending upon the prevalence of the disorder of interest, more potentially afflicted individuals may be detected.

A screen operates on the assumption that the symptoms of a handicapping condition can be detected and measured. The essence of screening is to apply relatively quick tests that will sort out those who probably have a handicap from those who do not. The children identified as probably handicapped by the screening test are "screened in" and then referred for a complete diagnosis and evaluation. This is essential both to confirm the results of the screening and to arrive at an appropriate preventive educational plan. Screening is thus a systematic tool in a plan of secondary prevention that aims at identifying handicaps early, then promptly intervenes to minimize any long-term undesirable consequences.

A general consideration of criteria for pediatric screening is presented by Frankenburg and Camp (1975). In the case of screening for psychoeducational disorders, a number of criteria are of particular importance for identifying and referring high risk/handicapped infants.

1. The handicapping condition should be well-described and specific enough so that a set of characteristics can be presented. That is, it should be sufficiently specific so that a defined service program should be available for children who are identified.

2. Tests or measures of demonstrated reliability and predictive power must be available. Their lack is a critical flaw in most screening programs.

3. There should be an intervention available that is validated by research and demonstration programs.

4. Procedures must be adequate in the follow-up phases of a program so that handicapped children will receive services. This means more than just advising on availability of services. Parents must be made aware of the advantages of the program and encouraged to participate.

5. The use of categorical labels and any other potential stigmatizations should be avoided if possible.

6. The screening and detection must be socially acceptable in the community where they are employed.

7. The programmatic cost of screening must be kept in balance with the cost of service delivery following identification.

In a review of six programs for very young children, Trohanis, Meyer, and Prestridge (1982) offered some pertinent observations which have importance for planning, expanding, or implementing screening services. They noted that many terms are used interchangeably. When words such as screening, assessment, evaluation, and diagnosis are not precisely defined, program development and implementation may be adversely affected. Likewise, diverse instruments are often used which may not be appropriate screening devices when used outside of their designed context. Appropriate instrumentation and definition of screening is needed.

Perhaps the most important point that Trohanis, Meyer, and Prestridge make is the lack of assessment of program implementation and of outcome. A screening program should include these assessments as integral components. Modifications and changes can be implemented in a very short time to benefit both the time and cost effectiveness of the program. This is one of the attractive benefits of screening versus a complete evaluation.

Unfortunately, screening devices are not 100% effective. Two main classes of error occur, false positives and false negatives. False positives are individuals referred as handicapped but who are normal. They are determined, after a full diagnostic evaluation, to be free of the disorder. False positives should be minimized since the children and their families are placed in a stressful situation and the post-screening diagnostic procedures are expensive.

The second class of error are false negatives. These are children who actually have a disorder but are not detected by the screening device. The problem here lies in what Mulliken and Buckley (1983) state as a family's experience of "false security." That is the sense that they believe their child is developing normally while necessary services are not being provided at critical times. When the child is finally diagnosed as having the disorder, considerable time has elapsed and the prognosis is often not as favorable as with an earlier detection.

Screening is both cost and time effective when the alternative of doing a full diagnostic evaluation on all children is considered. It is also relatively easy to evaluate large numbers of individuals in a brief period of time. Screening should be an integral part of a systematic approach to identification, referral and placement. A fuller review of preschool screening is available in a recent article (Scott & Hogan, 1982).

THE RISK OF HANDICAPPING CONDITIONS

Risk

Through epidemiology, the concept of risk has been successfully developed and refined. The descriptive concept of risk implies an elevated potential for an individual to contract a disorder, or in some situations not to contract the disorder, when compared to an individual not at risk. The analytic concept of risk differs from the descriptive aspect by assigning a numerical value to an individual's risk potential. The relative risk represents the strength of an association between a factor (or exposure) and a condition.

Risk as a descriptive concept indicates an association between some personal characteristic, event, or behavior and a handicapping condition. The term is not used to denote a necessary or definitive outcome; instead it specifies a potential or possibility that an individual, with a specific characteristic, will acquire the outcome of concern. Often risk is stated in relative terms. Thus a "high risk" infant is at much greater than normal risk for becoming handicapped. It has been shown (Scott & Masi, 1979) that most high risk infants, defined by birthweight, have normal outcomes and that they account for only a minority of the children who are eventually diagnosed as handicapped. An attempt will be made to spell out the utility and limits of risk designations and registers.

Risk Register

The strategy of screening or identifying a small group of infants so that the majority of children with "invisible" handicaps could be detected has long been advocated. The concept goes back at least to Lindon (1961) and was advanced by Sheridan (1962). The idea of local authorities maintaining "At Risk" registers was promoted by the Sheldon Committee Report of the British Ministry of Health (1967) and also by a working group of the World Health Organization (1967).

The risk register is based on a model where it is supposed that some generally "invisible" condition places the infant at highly inflated levels of risk for a handicap. This factor could have three major sources: (a) congenital or family history of specific disorders, such as deafness (genetic risk), (b) events that include complications during pregnancy or delivery that might produce latent or manifest birth defects (neonatal risk), and (c) psychosocial problems, such as environmental deprivation, neglect, or abuse (social risk).

On the basis of such factors, the ambition is to create a "register of risk" and thus, by screening or following a subsection of the population, to detect a major proportion of children who may later have handicapping conditions. Thus the model defines the risk factor as a latent or invisible handicap in some large percentage of children who are included in a register.

Risk registers have proven useful, but they are insufficiently powerful to lead to the identification of most children with handicaps. In general, as the risk factors become better specified, the proportion of listed children who are likely to have a handicap increases sharply. However, this highly selected at-risk population becomes a smaller segment of the total population and represents only a minority of all handicapped children.

In the case of neonatal risk, the primary function of a register of risk is to detect a high percentage of handicapping conditions among a low percentage of the population. Lindon (1961) suggested that an optimal risk register would contain 10% to 20% of live births among whom a majority of handicaps would be detected. However, this concept has so far not proven successful; Oppe (1967) described many of the difficulties encountered in the utilization of the concept by country and Greater London Borough authorities. Alberman and Goldstein (1970) reviewed the British experience and considered the statistical properties of risk registers, using data from the Perinatal Mortality Survey (Butler & Bonham, 1963; Butler & Alberman, 1969) that included 98% of all births ($N = 17{,}418$) for one week of March, 1958 in England, Wales, and Scotland; their analysis suggests that a register could not hope to detect a majority of handicaps.

The statistical and theoretical difficulty associated with detecting a large number of handicaps in a small proportion of the population is discussed in detail elsewhere (Scott & Masi, 1979). It can be clarified by constructing a chart (see Figure 4) demonstrating the distribution of outcome for 10,000 births. This diagram is based on Wiener's (1968) study following the developmental progression of 500 low birthweight (< 2,500 grams) and 492 matched normal birthweight children. While the estimates of the more severe conditions were less stable than those for the mild conditions due to a smaller number of severe cases, cross-checks with other data suggest they were reasonably representative. For the present purpose, the use of this single database minimizes confounding due to age of the sample at measurement, socioeconomic factors, and demographic variables. The data were also simple in that they are restricted to a single handicap-mental retardation—defined in terms of IQ. A similar overall pattern was obtained when results of multiple classifications and multiple databases were employed.

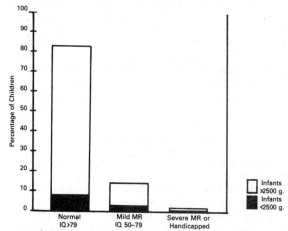

FIGURE 4. Prevalence of handicaps at 8–10 years of age in a population of 10,000 children.

Figure 4, which is based on data from children born in 1958 (see Scott & Masi, 1979) shows a register of risk defined by low birthweight which produces a markedly higher prevalence of handicaps when compared to a matched sample of offspring born of a normal birthweight. However, these risk registers fail to detect the majority of children with handicaps. The diagram demonstrates that for this specific cohort of infants weighing under 2,500 grams, almost 30% are handicapped. However, since this LBW cohort only represents 10% of the entire population, only approximately 3% of the total handicapped population (15%) is found among this group. Of infants over 2,500 grams at birth, only about 13% are handicapped, that is, will be referred for special educational services at some time during the school years. However, because this group is nine times as large as the risk group, the majority of handicapped children are found in the non-risk group. Of the total handicapped population (15% of all births in this cohort), 3% are found in the high-risk group and 12% are found in the low-risk group. If the criterion for being on a risk register is made narrower, (e.g., < 1,500 grams birthweight), or multiple criteria are employed, the prevalence rate in the risk group rises, but such registers tend to include an even smaller proportion of the total handicapped population. At the other extreme, when the register is enlarged, the prevalence in the risk group will decrease. Data presented by Rogers (1968) show that even when the proportion in the risk group is 25% of the population, it will include less than half of the children who are handicapped. Other data on hearing impairment show that less than half the children can be detected as neonates by the use of a risk register (Pappas, 1983).

The risk register is valuable as an indicator of infants and children who need longitudinal follow-up and periodic development evaluations. Programs of preventive intervention may enroll children who are at risk in the full knowledge that for only some of them will the services be essential in preventing later problems. if research in the future produces techniques of measurement that allow latent invisible risk factors to become manifest and directly measurable, risk registers will be more effective. Until that time however, we must rely on available instruments to determine whether once the children at risk are identified, they are developing normally. The easiest and most efficient way to do this is screening.

Computerized Tracking

Health registers are generally restricted to a group or type of health disorders such as cancer, and genetic or birth defects that have been used in a number of states as well as other countries. These registers, besides providing an epidemiological database for studying regional causes and patterns of disease, allow clients to be tracked so that they can be made aware of services available to them. For example Children's Medical Services of the State of Florida supports an Infant Hearing Screening Program and maintains a register of infants who have severe binaural hearing loss. Children located by this program are referred by phone or letter to the local educational agency for follow-up. The systematic nature of such follow-up relies on the skill and contacts of the professionals involved. Low birthweight infants, on the other hand, are only referred when there is a clear categorical handicap present. Such patterns of patchwork referral appear to be common, with the exception of a very few states including Maryland and New Jersey.

In many instances, children referred to Child Find have already received medical services but have not been referred to a local educational agency. Child Find

specialists are often efficient with programs of community liaison and include health care providers such as pediatricians and nurses as well as social agencies. However, this is an inefficient system and needs to be supplemented by an effective computerized child tracking system.

In a check at the Mailman Center for Child Development for Child Find referrals to the Florida Diagnostic Learning Resources System (FDLRS) regional center in the local public schools, 29% of the children were found to have previously received an evaluation. The records provided by parent recall rarely included such reports. As a result, children were frequently evaluated at FDLRS with very incomplete clinical case histories. The situation is further complicated by children dropping out of the system when they make the transition from medical to educational settings. Further research is needed to document the optimal methodology and effectiveness of computerized tracking that would bridge this transition. Unfortunately there is a lack of information on this topic. Tracking children with handicaps through computerized networks is a new approach and one that has been born out of technological advances. For this reason, history is in the making; history which both demands acceptance and rigid analysis.

A tracking system would simplify follow-up within and between the medical system or the educational system. With such systematic tracking, high-tech improved case management would facilitate precursors of educational handicaps.

POPULATIONS IN NEED OF TRACKING

Assessing the Risk of Handicaps

The characteristics by which risks may be defined are those involving the natural and medical history of the individual, or variables reflecting an individual's socioeconomic status, or environmental history. Risks then include both the endogenous (biological) and exogenous (environmental) factors identified in traditional etiologies of handicapping conditions such as mental retardation.

Endogenous factors, or natural history risks, include such variables as poor maternal health, low birthweight, inadequate prenatal care, and perinatal complication. These roughly cover any factor which may be identified as contributing to some physiological state which elevates an individual's relative risk for a handicapping condition. In contrast, extrinsic environmental risks include poor maternal child interactions, poor maternal caretaking, malnutrition, lack of appropriate stimulation, substandard living condition, and poor hygiene.

Some handicapping conditions, such as mental retardation, have been thought of as being caused by either biological events or psychosocial/environmental events. The biological origin of this handicap entails genetic defects, birth defects, or a pattern of symptoms which fit a known syndrome. In contrast, handicaps of a psychosocial nature generally refer to a condition which has no known medically related cause. In this case, many mild handicaps are viewed as environmental in nature.

Medical and behavioral science research has recently been concerned with the development of risk factor models. When these models are applied to chronic diseases, such as coronary heart disease or cancer, the biological, familial, psychological, social, and environmental risks are all seen to combine in facilitating the development of the disorder. This represents a new concept of combined multiple risks. Due to the combined effects of these risk factors, an individual is postulated to be at a heightened relative risk resulting from the interactive nature of these risks. With this new insight into the complexity of etiologies, methodology has necessarily been broadened to deal with a large set of interrelated risks (Scott & Carran, 1985).

Behavioral medicine is a prime example of this recent trend. Risk of hypertension has been shown to be influenced by a number of contributing risk factors. These contributing risks include a person's salt intake, stress level, smoking habits, personality type, and obesity. Someone whose lifestyle involves one of these contributing risk factors, such as smoking, is more at risk for developing heart disease than a matched control subject who does not smoke. However, as individuals incorporate more of the contributing risks associated with hypertension into their life, their chance of developing coronary heart disease increases further. Results of the Framingham Project have revealed that if an individual is at risk due to a combination of risks, the result is more than simply additive. In a famous study using a multivariate scale of combined risks, Truett, Cornfield and Kannel (1967) cited the combined risk factors of cholesterol, cigarette smoking, abnormal ECG and blood pressure as major contributing risk factors to coronary heart disease. The combined effect of all risk factors was shown to produce a difference in the incidence of coronary heart disease, between the highest and lowest deciles, of thirty-fold for men and seventy-fold for women.

TABLE 2

Contributing Risk Factors

Risk Factors for LBW	Risk Factors for Psycho-educational Handicaps
Maternal Age	Maternal Education
Maternal Education	Nutrition
Prenatal Care	Ethnicity
Nutrition	Socioeconomic Status
Nativity of Mother	Low Birthweight
Ethnicity	Medical Condition

Parallels may be shown to exist in the causation of handicapping conditions (Scott & Carran, 1985). For example, teenage mothers from Black urban minorities are at greatly increased risk of having a low birthweight infant, as can be seen in the left portion of Table 2. This LBW infant, as a result, is medically at risk because of the biological conditions associated with his or her birth status. However, as shown in the right side of Table 2, this medical risk can combine with other environmental factors listed which are contributing risk factors for psychoeducational handicaps.

From this premise it may be argued that the identification of these various risk factors and determination of their potential combinations would be invaluable. With this information, early identification, assessment, and intervention of "at risk" or potentially handicapped infants could be refined. The first step in this process however, is the identification of the risk factors which are believed to contribute to a handicapping condition such as the contributing risk factors associated with low birthweight listed in Table 2. Many of these contributing risk factors are used as the "noncategorical" basis for high risk identification.

Noncategorical labeling appropriates funds on the basis of services needed in lieu of categories of deviant development. Hobbs (1975) recommended this type of noncategorical labeling and suggests that services could be rendered on a more flexible and integrated basis while at the same time children are not saddled with a categorical label that they must endure for the rest of their lives. Some intervention programs already reflect these concepts while other programs maintain specific categories.

The next step in this epidemiological enterprise is the quantification of relative risk ratios for the informed utilization of resources. This latter process has barely begun, as will be discussed later.

The major implication of risk models for identification and referral is that children should be served *before* a handicapping condition becomes manifest. Therefore, a general prevention model should be an integral structure of the guidelines of any program instituted for the purposes of identification and referral.

Prevention of Handicapping Conditions

Identification presents two simultaneous goals. The first logically seeks to locate handicapped infants for the purpose of referral. The second goal of identification is prevention. Future prevention results from analyses of previous or ongoing identification procedures. Common etiological characteristics or events associated with the condition of interest represent the contributing risk factors upon which prevention strategies are based.

Prevention is narrowly defined as inhibiting the development of a disorder before it occurs. More broadly defined, prevention includes measures or interventions that interrupt or slow the progression of a disorder. Thus, different levels of prevention are said to exist.

A general prevention model approaches any handicapping condition in a hierarchical manner. It provides the tools to facilitate the development and implementation of a prevention plan, while at the same time conceptualizing the relations among the various causes. In this way incidence, or the number of new cases of the condition, may be reduced in subpopulations purported to be at an elevated risk.

The general prevention model approaches any particular handicapping condition through one of three preventive levels each targeted at a particular stage of the disorder: *primary, secondary,* and *tertiary* (Mausner & Kramer, 1985). Each step will be discussed as it is seen to pertain to handicapping conditions.

In *primary prevention*, one promotes health and adjustment by minimizing or totally eliminating risks. Maternal prenatal health care, proper infant nutrition, and regular medical visits are but a few of the examples of primary prevention. Generally, well baby care can be viewed as primary prevention in that it aims to promote normal developmental progress and prevent delays.

Under the stage of *secondary prevention* a risk factor or a disorder once present may be reduced, eliminated, or "cured." Working examples are the High-Risk Clinics, Headstart and the Abecedarian Daycare Program (Ramey, MacPhee, & Yeates, 1982). Any early childhood special education program that aims to correct a delay and discharge its graduates to regular education classes is a form of secondary prevention.

With *tertiary prevention*, management of the preexisting disorder is the aim so that the individual may lead as nearly a normal life as possible by being brought to his or her maximum potential. There as been a concerted effort in this country to improve the lives of severe and profoundly retarded citizens beginning with PL 94-142, the Education for all Handicapped Children Act, by achieving habilitation in the least restrictive environment.

It is apparent how neatly these concepts map on to the majority of handicapping conditions, especially in the case of normalization and services for the severe and profoundly handicapped population.

THE MULTIPLE RISK FACTOR MODEL

In the previous discussion of populations in need of tracking, the discussion centered primarily on the high risk, LBW infant. The reason for this strategy was to highlight handicaps which are not apparent from birth and which need the services of identification and referral the most. For the reasons of latency of identification and the resulting risk of morbidity in this population, the aforementioned Multiple Risk Factor Model (MRF) gives, in the authors' views, the most salient, well-rounded, and applicable perspective of handicapping conditions. Consideration of individual characteristics facilitates the application of an appropriate prevention strategy or level.

It is important to note the commonly interactive nature of risk factors. Independently, each may increase the probability of an infant being born of a low birthweight, but the effect of the interaction of two or more of these risk factor variables increases the risk of a handicapping condition even more. This fact serves as the premise upon which a Multiple Risk Factor Model (MRF) for handicapping conditions has been structured.

Handicaps in children are typically due to multiple causes which are manifest through developmental delays. Theories which have viewed handicapping conditions as being caused by a single agent have proven unsatisfactory. A MRF theory has been postulated which takes into account an individual's endogenous (biological) and exogenous (environmental) circumstances. These circumstances are termed risks. The MRF model considers biological and environmental risks as sources in all etiologies of handicapping conditions.

Psychosocial retardation, for example, has a high prevalence among urban, minority, and low income groups (Grossman, 1983; Mercer, 1970; Vogt, 1973). These psychosocial conditions have been demonstrated to be highly associated with LBW (Taffel, 1980). There are many seemingly normal births to this population where there are prevalent subclinical neurological conditions (associated with malnutrition, for example), which when associated with poor environmental stimulation lead to subnormal intellectual performance (President's Committee on Mental Retardation, 1980). Such combinations of causes are likely to be much more deleterious than would be either effect alone. Psychosocial causes of handicaps are a complex set of etiologies which must include biological factors if they are to be fully understood. This type of multiple-agent conceptualization is required as the predominant theoretical basis of a prevention model.

While in principle there is considerable information to suggest the appropriateness of such multiple causation models, the specific details require much further research. Crucial to such research endeavors is the ability to track longitudinally, or in a historical retrospective fashion, the case histories of relatively large numbers of children with different categorical handicaps. However, in the absence of longitudinal systematic tracking data beginning in infancy and extending through the middle school years, the relative contributions of social, medical, and environmental risk factors, as causes of particular categorical handicaps, remains theoretical.

NEEDS AND RECOMMENDATIONS

At this stage these particular needs are considered to be of particularly high importance.

Personnel Preparation

It is essential that both medical personnel and educational personnel be trained so that the links between medical care and early childhood special education are seen as essentially the same. The major point is that early child health and educational services cannot be separated. Computerized tracking systems and risk registers may be the solution to this problem. This topic is fully addressed in the chapter by Bricker and Slentz.

Parents

The issues and concerns of the parents of a handicapped child are generally the last thought on the minds of researchers, educationists, and practitioners. This is unfortunate, but it is reality. Parents complain of poor communication and a lack of dissemination of information, while practitioners, educationists, and researchers forge ahead looking for answers to alleviate the problems the handicapped child presents. These two groups have a common goal of helping the handicapped child. Therefore, they should logically join forces.

The strength of parent groups has been seen with the implementation of PL 94-142. Parent advocacy groups, armed with a series of the state court decisions and state legislation, played a major role in the passage of this important piece of Federal legislation. The strength of this group rests in its dedication.

The professionals concerned with handicapped children have their strength in information. Equipped with research results and theories, the professionals need to be closer to the legislative process. This will enable relevant research to be more easily translated into legislation.

These two groups must work together. Parents must be better informed and social policy must reflect the work of oustanding research. United, these two groups will be a formidable litigant for handicapped infants.

Research

There is a major conceptual problem in that risk is viewed commonly as either biological or psychocultural in origin. In many, if not most instances, *multiple risks are involved* in the etiology of early childhood handicaps. Social and behavioral factors are involved in the etiology of many "biological" handicaps and again become important in intervention. From this theoretical perspective, new directions in research will evolve.

Major research efforts are needed in a number of areas that include the following suggestions:

1. Studies on efficacy of computerized tracking should be undertaken so that infants at risk receive follow-up services and do not drop out of the care system to be "found" in middle childhood when they encounter school difficulties.

2. Longitudinal studies of infants who are at risk and who are handicapped should be mounted to study the pattern(s) of antecedent risks.

3. Wherever records will allow, historical retrospective studies should be made of handicapped children and normal controls to document the patterns of antecedent

risks. In epidemiology these studies are called case-control studies and their well-worked-out rigorous methodology (Schlesselman, 1982) has been almost totally ignored by behavioral scientists and educators. Case-control studies have been a major tool in understanding heart disease in the last 20 years and have also been used with great success in the study of cancer.

4. Research needs to concentrate on multiple causes or risks and how they combine. It is necessary to study representative groups of infants who are handicapped and infants who are at risk for handicapping conditions, rather than arbitrary samples from tracking hospitals. This implies a real need for disability-specific longitudinal studies.

Policy Implications

Policy in the area of infant needs and services follows the same dark path as does most child legislation. Everyone wants to do something but they cannot determine what is best, how to regulate the choice, nor how to fund it. For these reasons, and as this chapter has evidenced, much more research in the areas of infancy and childhood developmental outcome are needed if early identification and referral of handicapped infants is to become universally available.

The identification of infants who do not have obvious handicaps is extremely difficult. The process is only facilitated as the child ages. However, through risk registers, computerized tracking, and the development of infant screening devices, some headway may be achieved. The success of computerized tracking will be achieved, but it must occur through an interdisciplinary effort with the medical community. Medicine has had good results in the area of identification research and has much to offer. Educational professionals and behavioral scientists must take a more active role if co-investigation with the medical domain is to be accomplished. Both disciplines have the same goal of improving the quality of life for the handicapped or at-risk individual. An interdisciplinary effort should produce results of a greater magnitude. With this joint approach in mind, funding of future research should be provided to projects which offer diverse methodologies through interdisciplinary endeavors. University Affiliated Facilities (UAFs) were founded upon such a premise and serve as major centers for community service and social programs. Likewise, the Mental Retardation Research Centers were established to conduct research in this manner. These programs should be used to their fullest potential.

There are a wide variety of service and social programs which exist for handicapped infants at the state level. For example, the state of Florida, through Health and Rehabilitative Services, supports programs for infants with severe and profound handicaps. These intervention programs are community-based in target neighborhoods. However, the availability of such programs does not exist for at-risk infants. There is no comprehensive service delivery system for the infant who is at risk for mild to moderate handicaps. The mandate for well baby care services would be one method of accomplishing appropriate health care for these infants.

State-supported well baby care services are available in most western countries. The United States, without this service, may be regarded as neglecting its future generations. The link between psychosocial retardation with associated development delays and medical problems is a strong one. It is strongly believed that proper regular medical attention, in the form of well baby care, to target populations of infants may be viewed as a national prevention strategy.

An important issue at the heart of policy making, for both the state and national levels, is the categorization of infants. The basic difference between the noncategorically at-risk infant and the infant who is eligible for compensatory education is very narrow. The risk factors for both categories of infants overlap. These infants are generally from the same socioeconomic environment, and their mothers share similar demographic characteristics. The categories are separated by medical risk weighing less than 2,500 grams and experienced some type of medical problem. The infant eligible for compensatory education will generally not have had perinatal medical complications and have been born weighing more than 2,500 grams. Yet the stimulation and developmental needs of these two groups of children are similar. The implications of categorization demands further investigation.

Research must necessarily become more diverse, interdisciplinary-oriented, and ecologically valid if it is to serve as a significant determinant of future social policy. Without a qualified base upon which legislation may be structured, we, as advisors to the lawmakers, will be viewed as squanderers of the tax payer's dollars. The projects we support will be seen as meeting the ephemeral needs of the few. The needs of the handicapped infant are not ephemeral, but are forever with the child unless appropriate and successful intervention strategies are instituted, funded, and regulated.

Throughout the process of policy making, more than just the individual must be considered. With agency involvement, the family, community, and society at large will become involved. Just as PL 94-142 made America aware of the educational access problems that handicapped individuals face, similar legislation will make America aware of the pain and frustration parents of handicapped infants must live with.

Issues such as home care versus hospital care, access to community service programs, respite care for caretakers of severely handicapped children, and availability of alternative financial sources for parents of infants with severe medical problems are but a few of the issues facing parents and funding agencies when the infant has an obvious handicap. What of the infant with the nonobvious handicap? The parents of a nonobviously handicapped infant often live with a false feeling of security that their child is developing normally. These parents must confront problems similar to those previously mentioned, but at a later point in time. This often creates untold stress as parents realize their normal child is handicapped.

Through the early identification of risk factors, which research may show to be strongly correlated with handicapping conditions, intervention services may be initiated at an early date to prevent developmental problems. Social policies are drastically needed in this area beginning with mandatory sensory screening during infancy, and continuous developmental screening into the preschool ages. Programs initiated to mandate services for infants at risk for developmental delay and those obviously handicapped would be a credit to our nation.

References

Alberman, E. A., & Goldstein, H. (1970). The 'At Risk' register: A statistical evaluation. *British Journal of Preventive and Social Medicine*, **24**, 129–135.

Arias, F., & Tomich, P. (1982). Etiology and outcome of low birth weight & preterm infants. *Obstetrics and Gynecology*, **60**(3), 277–281.

Bloom, B. S. (1964). *Stability and change in human characteristics*. New York: Wiley.

Bradley, R. A. (1977). *Child Find Manual*. (Contract No. OEC-0-74-7895). Washington: Bureau of Education for the Handicapped.

British Ministry of Health (1967). Child Welfare Centers, Report of the Subcommittee, Standing Medical Advisory Committee (The Sheldon Report). London: Her Majesties Stationery Office.

Broman, S. H., Nichols, P. L., & Kennedy, W. A. (1975). *Preschool IQ: Prenatal and early developmental correlates*. New York: Wiley.

Budetti, P., Barrand, N., McManus, P., & Heiner, L. (1981). *The implications of cost-effectiveness analysis of medical technology*. (Library of Congress Catalog Number 80-600161). Washington: U.S. Government Printing Office.

Butler, N. R., & Alberman, E. D. (Eds.) (1969). *Perinatal problems: The second report of the 1958 British perinatal mortality survey*. Livingstone: Edinburgh, and London.

Butler, N. R., & Bonham, D. G. (1963). *Perinatal mortality: The first report of the 1958 British perinatal mortality survey*. Livingstone: Edinburgh & London.

Carran, D. T., & Scott, K. G. (1985). *Relative effects of maternal age and education on the incidence of low birthweight*. Manuscripts submitted for publication.

Cohen, S. E., & Parmelee, A. H. (1983). Prediction of five-year Stanford-Binet series in preterm infants. *Child Development*, **54**, 1242-1253.

Cohen, S. E., Sigman, M., Parmelee, A. H., & Beckwith, L. (1982). Perinatal risk and developmental outcome in preterm infants. *Seminars in Perinatology*, **6**(4), 334–339.

Drillien, C. M., Thompson, A. J. M., & Burgoyne, K. (1980). Low birth weight children at early school age. A longitudinal study. *Developmental Medicine and Child Neurology*, **22**, 26–47.

Escalona, S. K., & Moriarity, A. (1961). Prediction of school-age intelligence from infant tests. *Child Development*, **32**, 597–605.

Fitzhardinge, P. M., & Steven, E. M. (1972). The small for date infant II: Neurological and intellectual sequelae. *Pediatrics*, **50**(1).

Frankenburg, W. K., & Camp, B. W. (1975). *Pediatric screening test*. Springfield, IL: Charles C. Thomas.

Geshwind, N. (1974). Late changes in the nervous system: An overview. In D. G. Stein, J. J. Rosen, & N. Butters (Eds.), *Plasticity and recovery of function in the central nervous system*. New York: Academic Press.

Grossman, H. J. (Ed.) (1983). *Classification in mental retardation* (8th ed). Washington: American Association on Mental Deficiency.

Hecaen, H. (1976). Acquired aphasia in children and the onto-genesis of hemispherical functional specialization. *Brain and Language*, **3**, 114–134.

Hobbs, N. (Ed.). (1975). *Issues in the classification of children* (2 vols.). San Francisco: Jossey-Bass.

Hoffman, D. (1977). *Familiarity with Child Find*. Paper presented at the Annual International Convention, the Council for Exceptional Children, Atlanta, Georgia.

Horwood, S. P., Boyle, M. H., Torrance, G. W., & Sinclair, J. C. (1982). Mortality and morbidity of 500 to 1,499 gram birthweight infants live-born to residents of a defined geographic region before and after neonatal intensive care. *Pediatrics*, **69**(5), 613–620.

Hunt, J. McV. (1961). *Intelligence and experience*. New York: Ronald Press.

Kitchen, W. H., Yu, V.Y.H., Orgill, A., Ford, G. W., Richards, A., Astbury, J., Ryan, M. M., Russo, W., Lissenden, J. V., Bajuk, B., Keith C. G., & Nave, J. R. M. (1982). Collaborative study of very-low-birthweight infants: Outcome of two-year-old survivors. *Lancet*, **1**, 1457–1460.

Lee, K. S., Paneth, N., Gartner, L. M., Pearlman, M. A., & Gruss, L. (1980). Neonatal mortality: An analysis of the recent improvement in the U.S. *American Journal of Public Health*, **70**, 14–21.

Lindon, R. L. (1961). Risk register. *Cerebral Palsy Bulletin*, **3**, 481.

Lubchenco, L. O., Delivoria-Papadopoulos, M., & Searls, D. (1972). Long-term follow up studies of prematurely born infants II: Influence of birthweight and gestational age on sequelae. *Journal of Pediatrics*, **80**, 509.

Lubchenco. L. O., Horner, F. A., Reid, L. H., Hix, I. E., Metcalf, D., Cohig, R., Elliot, H. C., & Boung, M. (1963). Sequelae of premature birth. Evaluation of premature infants of low birthweights at ten years of age. *American Journal of Diseases of Children*, **106**, 101–115.

Mausner, J. S., & Kramer, S. (1985). *Epidemiology: An introductory text*. Philadelphia: W. B. Saunders.

Mercer, J. R. (1970). Sociological perspectives on mild mental retardation. In M. C. Haywood (Ed.), *Socio-cultural aspects of mental retardation*. New York: Appleton-Century-Crofts.

Mercer, J. R. (1973). *Labeling the mentally retarded*. Berkeley: University of California Press.

Mulliken, R. K., & Buckley, J. J. (1983). *Assessment of multi-handicapped and developmentally disabled children*. Rockville, MD: Aspen-Systems Corporation.

National Association of State Directors of Special Education. (1976). *Child identification: A handbook for implementation*. Washington: Office of Education, Mid-East Regional Resource Center.

National Center for Health Statistics. Selected vital and health statistics in poverty and nonpoverty areas of 19 large cities—U.S., 1969–1971., by S. J. Ventura, et al. *Vital and Health Statistics*. (Series 21, No. 26. DHEW Pub. No. HRA 76–1904). Health Resources Administration. Washington: U.S. Government Printing Office, No. 1975.

National Center for Health Statistics (September 1984). Advanced report of final natality statistics, 1982. *Monthly Vital Statistics Report*. Vol. 33, No. 6 Supp. DHHS Pub. No. (PHS) 84–1120. Public Health Service. Hyattsville, MD: National Centre for Health.

Nobel-Jamieson, C. M., Lukeman, D., Silverman, M., & Davies, P. A. (1982). Low birthweight children at school age: Neurological, psychological, and pulmonary function. *Seminars in Perinatology*, **6**(4), 266–273.

Oppe, T. E. (1967). Risk register for babies. *Developmental Medicine and Child Neurology*, **9**, 13.

Pappas, D. G. (1983). A study of high-risk registry for sensori-neural hearing impairment. *Otolaryngology and Head and Neck Surgery*, **91**(1), 41–44.

President's Committee on Mental Retardation (1980). *Mental retardation: Prevention strategies that work*. (DHHS Publication No. OHDS 80–21029). Washington: U.S. Government Printing Office.

Ramey, C. T., MacPhee, D., & Yeates, K. O. (1982). Preventing developmental retardation: A general systems model. In L. Bond & J. Jolffee (Eds.), *Facilitating infant and early childhood development* (pp. 363–401). Hanover, NH: University Press of New England.

Ramey, C. T., Stedman, D. J., Bordens-Patterson, A., & Mengel, W. (1978). Predicting school failure from information at birth. *American Journal of Mental Deficiency*, **82**(6), 525–534.

Rogers, M. G. (1968). Risk registers for early detection of handicaps. *Developmental Medicine and Child Neurology*, **10**, 651–661.

Ross, G. (1983) Mortality and morbidity in very low birthweight infants. *Pediatric Annals*, **12**, 32–44.

Schlesselman, J. J. (1982). *Case-control studies. Design, conduct analysis*. New York: Oxford University Press.

Scott, K. G. (1978). The rationale and methodological considerations underlying early cognitive and behavioral assessments. In F. D. Minifie & L. L. Lloyd (Eds.), *Communication and cognitive abilities—Early behavioral assessment* (pp. 3–20). Baltimore, MD: University Park Press.

Scott, K. G., & Carran, D. T. (1985). *Multiple risk factor model of mental retardation*. Manuscript submitted for publication.

Scott, K. G., & Carran, D. T. (1987). The epidemiology of Mental Retardation. *American Psychologist*.

Scott, K. G., & Hogan, A. E. (1982). Methods for identification of high-risk and handicapped infants. In C. T. Ramey & P. L. Trohanis (Eds.), *Finding and educating high-risk and handicapped infants* (pp. 69–82). Baltimore, MD: University Park Press.

Scott, K. G., & Masi, W. (1979). The outcome from and utility of registers of risk. In T. M. Field, A. M. Sostek, S. Goldberg, & H. H. Shuman (Eds.), *Infants born at risk* (pp. 485–496). New York: Spectrum Publications.

Sheridan, M. D. (1962). Infants at risk of handicapping conditions. *Monthly Bulletin of the Ministry of Health Laboratory Services*, **21**, 238.

Siegel, L. (1982). The prediction of possible learning disabilities in preterm and full-term children. In T. Field & A. Sostek (Eds.). *Psychological, perceptual, and cognitive processes* (p. 295–315). New York: Grune & Stratton.

Siegel, L. S., Saigal, S., Rosenbaum, P., Morton, R. A., Young, A., Berenbaum, S., & Stoskopf, B. (1982). Predictions of development in preterm and full-term infants. A model for detecting the at-risk child. *Journal of Pediatric Psychology*, **7**(2), 135–148.

Sigman, M. (1982). Plasticity in development. Implications for intervention. In L. A. Bond & J. M. Joffee (Eds.), *Facilitating infant and early childhood development* (pp. 98–116). Hanover, NH: University Press of New England.

Smith, D. W., & Simons, F. E. R. (1975). Rational diagnostic evaluation of the child with mental deficiency. *American Journal of Diseases of Childhood*, **129**, 1285–1290.

Stein, Z., & Susser, M. (1963). The social distribution of mental retardation. *American Journal of Mental Deficiency*, **68**, 811–821.

Taffel, S. (1980). *Factors associated with low birthweight, United States, 1976*. (DHEW Publication No. 80–1915). National Center for Health Statistics. (Vital and Health Statistics-Series 21, No. 37). Washington: U.S. Government Printing Office.

Tinbergen, N. (1948). Social releases and the experimental method required for their study. *Wilson Bulletin*, **60**, 6–52.

Trohanis, P. L., Meyer, R. A., & Prestridge, S. (1982). A report on selected screening programs for high-risk and handicapped infants. In C. T. Ramey and P. L. Trohanis (Eds.), *Finding and educating high-risk and handicapped infants*. Baltimore, MD: University Park Press.

Truett, J., Cornfield, J., & Kannel, W. (1967). A multivariate analysis of the risk of coronary heart disease in Framingham. *Journal of Chronic Diseases*, **20**, 511–524.

Vogt, D. K. (1973). *Literacy among youths 12–17 years*. U.S. DHEW Publication No. (HRA) 74–1613. Washington: U.S. Government Printing Office.

Wiener, G. (1968). *Long-term study of prematures: Summary of published findings*. ERIC Report No. ED043389, PS003651. Washington: Office of Education, Department of Health, Education, and Welfare.

World Health Organization. (1967). *The early detection and treatment of handicapping defects in young children*. Report in a working group. Regional Office of Europe, World Health Organization, Copenhagen, Denmark.

Yu, V. Y. H., Orgill, A. A., Bajuk, B., & Astbury, J. (1984). Survival and 2-year outcome of extremely preterm infants. *British Journal of Obstetrics and Gynaecology*, **91**, 640–646.

Infant Assessment

ROBERT SHEEHAN, Ph.D. AND NANCY KLEIN, Ph.d.

Cleveland State University

Abstract—The role of infant assessment has grown rather than diminished in the several years of preparing this Volume. The 1986 passage of Public Law 99-457, with federal support for intervention with handicapped, developmentally delayed and at-risk infant and toddlers insures the pivotal role that infant assessment will play in early intervention efforts. Lead agencies that will be working with infants and toddlers have been identified in every state in the country. These agencies are now establishing statewide interagency plans, and sponsoring demonstration programs to provide psychoeducational intervention to infants and toddlers who are handicapped, developmentally delayed, or at-risk.

The existing body of infant assessment measures may be of use in identifying handicapped and developmentally delayed infants and toddlers, but these measures are of much less utility in planning psychoeducational intervention with such children and their families. Reasons for this limited utility are numerous. Infant measures were not originally designed to guide intervention efforts. Infant development occurs as a function of a variety of maturational and environmental factors, factors that result in limited predictive validity for assessment results with many infants and toddlers.

In this review, the authors state a need for more instruments that document the powerful influence of the dynamic interactions between infants and caregivers. Interactional measures hold great promise as useful tools for psychoeducational intervention. The authors also advocate for continued recognition of the importance of clinical skill for those professional who are assessing young children. The perfect assessment battery is limited by the skill and sensitivity of its user.

INTRODUCTION

In preparing this chapter we are confronted with a dual task. We must describe the state of the art of infant assessment in such a way that common themes are identified. Areas of divergence must also be clarified. We must also chart a course into the next century. What must be done to prepare our assessment efforts for the year 2000? Can we make any comment that will highlight future directions in the area of infant assessment?

As we reviewed the history of intelligence testing and the emergence of infant assessment tools we perceived several close relationships: those that exist between our approach to testing and assessment and our beliefs about the nature of intelligence; the role of psychoeducational intervention; and even our conceptions of the economic contributions of citizens in this country. We cannot review infant assessment independent of these other current and historical forces, or our contribution would only be a description of current practice, and of limited use in planning for the next century.

In this chapter we acknowledge our growing acceptance of Gould's (1981) thesis that quantitative data are "as subject to cultural constraint as any other aspect of science" (p. 27). Clearly, our culture's conception of infants, particularly handicapped infants and infants born at risk, has influenced the way in which the infants have been assessed. We optimistically assert that a new cultural conception of these infants can emerge, and will emerge, through the next century. We hope that those of us who assess infants, and develop assessment measures, take an active role in this change process.

Five preliminary comments regarding this chapter will provide a context for this material. First: The chapter is illustrative and provocative rather than exhaustive. A complete review of the infant assessment area would necessitate much more than a single chapter. It would require an in-depth analysis of psychometric issues, clinical issues, and research issues related to systematic data collection.

The second comment: Discussion of infant assessment is at the issues level rather than the nuts and bolts level. This is to place infant assessment in a particular perspective. The present chapter reviews several issues central to a critique of infant assessment. It discusses particular strengths and weaknesses of infant assessment in five areas of development.

Our third preliminary comment: A primary belief influencing our perceptions is that the choice of a specific instrument is determined by the degree to which it measures what an assessor is seeking to measure. Said differently, thought is given to the match between the intended purpose of the assessment tool and the use that is made of the obtained assessment data. Thought is also given to the cultural and historical factors that might be influencing one's initial belief about the purpose of assessment. We are all too familiar with the infrequency with which we challenge our own beliefs about the purpose for infant assessment.

Clarifying the purpose of assessment should receive the primary emphasis in any discussion of infant measures. Otherwise, one will put the proverbial cart before the horse and will create a situation in which selection of measures preceeds determination of purposes for assessment data (a situation that unfortunately exists all too often in intervention programs with handicapped and at-risk infants).

The fourth point we wish to make by way of introduction: We discuss infant assessment tools in different domains of infant performance. We are, however, aware that the interrelations between these domains of performance are at times strong and at other times disconnected. This is partially because two major achievements of the sensorimotor period are the coordination of schemes and the differentiation of responses. Although we discuss assessment measures in one or another area of infant development, performance on these areas frequently reflects other domains as well.

One final point also serves as a foundation for this chapter: We find cultural diversity in the differing emphasis placed by parents on one set of behaviors as compared to another. These factors are of critical importance in designing and implementing early intervention programs. Sociologists, anthropologists, psychologists, and educators have made us aware of the influences of cultural differences in developmental patterns. The thoughtful incorporation of varying cultural preferences in the assessment process depends on the program administrators and the sensitivity of program staff.

Earlier Reviews of Infant Measures

A challenge facing educators working with infants is to locate instruments relevant to the complex components of psychoeducational intervention and research. Reviews of infant assessment tools have been growing steadily since 1976. They have been uniformly pessimistic regarding the utility of existing instrumentation procedures (Sheehan, 1982).

These reviews point out the consistently poor predictive validity of the existing early childhood measures. Pearson Product Moment Correlations of infant test performance (24 months or younger) with later childhood performance rarely exceed 0.3 even when coupled with additional indices. This means that infant test performance rarely accounts for more than 10% of the variation we see in later childhood performance. Obviously the relationship between infant performance and later childhood performance is stronger for children who are severely impaired at birth but the necessity of assessment data to confirm handicapped status is dramatically lessened.

Another consistent conclusion of these reviews is that most infant assessment tools fail to provide clear guidance with regard to the specific nature of psychoeducational intervention (Lewis & Fox, 1980). The three infant assessment tools that have received the most psychometric scrutiny (Bayley Scales, Gesell Schedules, Cattell) prove to be of little use in designing specific intervention programs for children, just as a standardized intelligence test for older children (i.e., Stanford-Binet) is of little use in planning an Individualized Educational Program (IEP).

Although such pessimism is justified, a number of factors continue to promote the use of existing assessment tools. This occurs while new instrumentation, and less traditionally structured instrumentation, is being developed. Several of these factors include:

1. Need for common languages of communication among researches regarding assessment of infant performance and development. In this case, the common data might be thought of as common language.

2. Need for standardized measures for use in psychoeducational intervention programs.

3. Pressure from funding agencies for accountability as documented by standardized yardsticks.

The present chapter goes beyond past reviews of infant assessment. It does so by clarifying the context in which infant assessment is occurring. A critique of the adequacy of existing measures will not contribute to planning for the next century's assessment unless the critique recognizes the context that determines assessment activity.

Sources for this Review

Researchers interested in the instruments used in infant assessment have at their disposal a vast and diverse literature about infant behavior and development. This literature includes the research published in journals about child development, mental retardation, developmental psychology, psychobiology, medicine, and infant development. It also includes the large number of texts, edited volumes, technical reports, and unpublished research reports.

One source used extensively in this review is a recent volume (Bricker, 1982) published as a result of an invited working conference held in the Asilomar Conference Center, Pacific Grove, California. The title of this volume, *Intervention with At-Risk and Handicapped Infants: From Research to Application* describes infant intervention as the central focus of the conference. Seventeen researchers presented their views on infant intervention and reacted to the views of others. Among the many topics addressed at that conference was the subject of infant assessment.

Another source used extensively in preparing this review were the draft chapters submitted to Wachs and Sheehan for an edited volume. This volume, *Assessment of Developmentally Disabled Children* (Wachs & Sheehan, 1988), includes a number of chapters addressing the issue of assessment of developmentally disabled children. In addition this chapter presents research from current literature, including journals and books on specific developmental issues.

Relevance of this Review

The relevance of this review is clear to educators dealing with fundamental knowledge of the performance and development of handicapped and at-risk infants. One major source of knowledge concerning the development of these infants is derived from our assessment tools.

As clinicians and researchers attempted to generalize from one infant to another, formal standardized assessment tools were developed. For example, the naturalistic observations of Piaget regarding his own infants' cognitive psychomotor development led to the development of several scales of psychomotor intelligence (Casati & Lezine, 1968; Uzgiris & Hunt, 1975). The accuracy of such generalizations regarding infant behavior and development is a direct function of the adequacy of our instrumentation.

Our society demands a scientific approach to psychoeducational intervention. This is an era of federal deficits, shrinking state and local budgets, and increased competition for decreasing resources. Psychoeducational intervention must be constantly justified upon the basis of valid assessment data. The adequacy of these data, and the degree to which they reflect treatment efforts, directly influence the continued availability of such services.

Reviews of assessment issues are also necessary to insure that educators do not oversell the utility of infant measures. Educators need tools to enhance their own ability to measure and monitor infant progress in their programs. Few legislators, however, understand that a program might be quite effective with little documentary outcome data. Conversely, any intervention program using an entire battery of measures is likely to find one or more significant outcomes by chance.

Educators who are aware of the limitations of current data collection tools can help insure that reasonable expectations are communicated for intervention with handicapped and at-risk infants. A "truth in advertising" perspective may place early intervention into a more realistic context for advocates, parents, and enlightened policy makers.

The external pressures for accountability are unlikely to abate in the near future. We must, however, caution against the misuse of quantitative data and point out the limitations of normative assessment. Normative assessment reveals little about a specific infant's capabilities. Such assessment provides only one estimate (and possibly an inaccurate estimate) of each child's subsequent performance. Intervention programs serve such a wide range of infants that averaging normative assessment data across an entire group may clarify little and obscure a great deal of the true child performance occurring in an intervention program.

Definition of Terms

Handicapped infants are those children, aged birth to 3 years, who are developmentally disabled or at risk by virtue of environmental, biological, and diagnosed factors (Tjossem, 1976). In this definition, toddlers (2-3 years) are considered to be infants. Most infant intervention programs include toddlers, and one frequent consequence of developmental disability for toddlers is a pattern of development that more closely resembles younger infants. Also of note is that this definition includes neonates (newborns from birth to 28 days).

Assessment is purposeful data collection related to an infant's developmental performance level in one or more areas. Clearly one may engage in purposeful data collection for a broad range of reasons. One achievement of the past several years is the articulation of the various purposes of infant assessment (Cross & Goin, 1977; Sheehan, 1982). Infant assessment may occur for the following purposes:

1. *Description:* describing patterns of infant development and behavior (e.g., Gesell, 1940; Piaget, 1952). Measures useful for description must include many items. They must be useable in a variety of settings and allow for strong clinical judgment. They should reflect a number of philosophical and theoretical belief systems.

2. *Screening:* identifying infants in need of further, more extensive assessment (e.g., Brooks-Gunn & Lewis, 1983; Frankenburg, van Doornick, Liddell, & Dick, 1976). Measures useful for screening should be able to be administered quickly, in a cost efficient fashion. They should have a demonstrated ability to avoid false negatives (thereby resulting in developmental disabilities of infants being undetected).

3. *Program referral:* identifying infants developmentally disabled or at risk for developmental disability and candidates for intervention (e.g., Bricker, 1982). Data collection tools used in this fashion should have a demonstrated ability to avoid false positives (thereby resulting in few false identifications). They should be culturally fair, and broad in scope.

4. *Prediction:* determining predicted future developmental status of infants (McCall, Eichorn, & Hogarty, 1977). Data collection tools used for this purpose should have demonstrated predictive validity. They should be summarizeable in such a concise fashion that any obtained predictions are easily understood.

5. *Theory development and validation:* development, refinement, or validation of theory regarding infant development or refinement (e.g., Kopp, Sigman, & Parmelee, 1974; Uzgiris & Hunt, 1975). The link between theory and instrumentation is important with measures used for this purpose.

6. *Instructional planning:* gathering data for purposes of determining individual short-term and long-term goals for psychoeducational intervention (e.g., Bagnato & Neisworth, 1982). Clearly data collection tools useful for instructional planning should contain a number of items. They should be useful in a variety of settings,

and be able to be administered by teachers. They must include items that are of instructional relevance (i.e., be targets for psychoeducational intervention).

7. *Program evaluation:* gathering infant progress data to determine whether psychoeducational intervention has been effective (e.g., Sheehan & Krakow, 1981). Measures used for this purpose must be of demonstrated credibility. They must be broad enough to capture the many goals of psychoeducational intervention. They also must be administered quickly enough and easily enough so that they do not significantly detract from intervention.

8. *Environmental description:* describing the home and/or educational setting of an infant (e.g., Wachs, Francis, & McQueston, 1979). Measures useful for describing home and educational environments must capture the salient characteristics of extremely complex settings without being negatively influenced by cultural and subcultural considerations. These measures must also be manageable enough to be used in a wide variety of uncontrolled settings, and they must yield data that can be clustered into meaningful units.

Intervenors must begin any assessment effort with a cautious analysis of whether an instrument is useful for its intended purpose. In many cases, the persons conducting the assessment will also have direct service responsibilities. Those persons' efforts will be redirected from intervention to assessment. The information gained from assessment must be worth enough to compensate for this redirection. Similarly, infants' time during the assessment process may be being redirected from direct services. Fortunately, much direct service involves activities that are similar to infant assessment; however, this is not always the case.

State of the Art of Infant Assessment Role of Theory and Cultural Context in Infant Assessment

The role of theory as a guide to psychoeducational intervention is evident in the field of early childhood education. Examples of theoretically-guided intervention models include the Montessori preschools, the High Scope Cognitively Oriented Curriculum developed by Weikart and colleagues (Weikart, Epstein, Schweinhart, & Bond, 1978), and the behavioral preschool programs developed for handicapped preschoolers by Alice Hayden and her associates (Hayden & Haring, 1976).

Theory has been used as a guide to psychoeducational assessment much more sporadically. For example, three commonly used assessment tools are: the Gesell Schedules (Knoblock & Pasamanick, 1974), the Cattell (Cattell, 1940), and the Bayley Scales of Infant Development (Bayley, 1969).

The first of these measures, the Gesell, provides normative data on infant behavior. High frequency behaviors were identified in developing items for this test. Selection of items for this measure does not reflect any particular structure of intelligence. Rather the Gesell is designed to yield descriptive data of the maturationist view of child development.

The second measure, the Cattell, provided an assessment of infant intelligence in a way that resembled the already existing Stanford-Binet tests for older children. The starting point for the Cattell, however, was to arrange the items of the Gesell in an age scale similar to that of the Binet. Items that involved reliance on gross motor behavior were deleted. Other items were added to the new measure.

The intent of the Cattell was similar to that of the Binet, to devise a nonmotorically-based predictive tool to assess later functioning. The structure of intelligence that is evident in the development of the Cattell is a strong belief in a single (*G*-factor) intelligence.

The third measure, the Bayley Scales, was developed as a method to study the growth changes in mental and motor abilities in infants. The Bayley Scales relied heavily upon the Gesell test items, clustering them in a different fashion, adding and deleting items, but including the bulk of those items.

The Bayley Scales, the Cattell, and the Gesell contain 274 items, 95 items, and 366 items respectively. The Bayley Scales divide the items into mental development, psychomotor development, and infant behavior.

The Cattell items are designed to assess cognitive function, while the Gesell Developmental Schedules subdivide items into seven different categories (gross motor, fine motor, receptive and expressive language, cognitive, self-help, personal-social). Cohen, Gross, and Haring (1976) identify the overlap in items and predicted developmental ages for these three instruments (and 21 additional instruments). They document the enormous similarities of the data collection tools.

The period of time in which these three infant assessment measures were developed and refined spanned more than 50 years. Yet, their similarities are far more evident than their differences. This is in spite of the rapid changes that have occurred in child development theory, and despite the differing purposes for developing each measure.

In the light of the dramatic changes occurring in the growth of theories of the development of intelligence during those 50 years, such similarity of measures is remarkable. This may be because "The press to move from behavioristic definitions of molecular phenomena toward more abstract psychological processes was least felt by those studying infancy" (Yang, 1979, p. 176).

Yang (1979) further offers two possible reasons for the communality in the three measures. He suggests that the raw data for infant assessment failed to change because of the conservatism on the part of most scale developers. This was a conservativism directed primarily at achieving and maintaining psychometric stability. The scale properties of the measures were enhanced by using the same bulk of items. Changes were then directed primarily at the arrangement of items.

The second reason for this overlap of the measures is the presumption that infant intelligence, compared to adult intelligence, is relatively simple (Yang, 1979). If this is so, creativity with regard to test development focuses on arrangement of items, and analysis of existing items, rather than at qualitatively different items.

We suggest yet another reason why these three measures are so similar. Each measure reflects an attitude in our culture that distinctions can and should be made between infants functioning at various levels of performance. The measures reflect an attempt to assess performance independent of environmental effects (an hereditarian perspective), and enshrine performance on a podium called intelligence.

One revision of the Gesell that did occur in the construction of the Cattell was the deletion of items influenced by home training (Cattell, 1940). (Considering that much intervention with infants is directed at home stimulation, it is little wonder that we question the utility of these measures with handicapped and at-risk infants.)

The primary utility of an intelligence test is to rank order individuals based upon their performance, a commitment evident in many aspects of our society. Tests such as the Bayley, the Cattell, and the Gesell are of more use in answering "Who to teach?" than in answering "What to teach?" or "How to teach?" This reflects an orientation evident in the intelligence testing occurring with older children, an orientation ultimately reflecting our society's values.

The maturational theory proposed by Gesell, the predictive attempts of Cattell, and items found on the Bayley Scales run counter to the goals of early intervention. Do behavioral changes occurring in response to intervention with handicapped infants appear in the same sequence as maturational theory would suggest? If not, do we have an alternative theory to explain such changes?

Our concern in this area is not only with regard to the assessment efforts of Gesell, Cattell, and Bayley. In spite of our fascination with Piaget's theory of sensorimotor development, what aspects of the theory provide guidelines for responses to intervention?

The most widely used of the Piagetian scales, the Uzgiris-Hunt Ordinal Scales of Development (Uzgiris & Hunt, 1975) represent various domains of sensorimotor development. The use of eliciting situations rather than prescribed material is a particular strength of these scales. They are amenable to training efforts across disparate populations and contexts. While the Uzgiris-Hunt Scales (and other Piaget-inspired scales) are based upon developmental theory, they share several problems with other assessment measures. Little is known about the following: (a) The *expected effect of intervention* with handicapped infants; (b) the *necessity or relevance of sensorimotor training* with atypical infants; or (c) the *need for modifications* of testing procedures for many handicapped infants. Theoretical formulations are essential for the development of appropriate and useful assessment tools for at-risk and handicapped infants. Appropriate scales must include qualitative and quantitative developmental targets for assessment.

Why must theory provide the basis for instruments? Why must theory determine the expected effect of intervention? Kopp (1982) argues that the lack of explicit, well-articulated, theoretical formulations have contributed to an exceedingly fragmented research literature in the infancy area.

The authors have spent the decade from the mid-1970s observing the efforts of clinicians and researchers to assess effectiveness of early intervention with handicapped and at-risk infants. Equivocal findings are yielded by most standardized developmental instruments.

The use of many instruments for purposes for which they are ill-suited results in findings which are fragmented, confusing, and of limited generalizability or predictive validity. Absence of theory in our instruments limits our ability to put the representative skills and subskills into a cohesive conceptual context.

We urge reviewers to avoid a narrow monolithic perspective in analyzing the theoretical formulations and culturally-driven biases of infant assessment tools. Theory is needed which is sufficiently comprehensive to address the following areas:

1. Theory regarding the normal course of development and divergent developmental patterns (Hanson, 1984).

2. Theory regarding handicapped and at-risk infants' response to psychoeducational intervention (Bricker, 1982).

3. Theory regarding the functioning of the family systems of handicapped and at-risk infants (Foster, Berger, & McLean, 1981; Sheehan, 1984).

4. Theory accounting for quantitative aspects of development (milestones) and broad enough to integrate factors that are qualitative, interactive, and highly influential in nature (Bromwich, 1981; Kaye, 1982, Sameroff and Chandler, 1975).

Theoretically-derived formulations of infant development are rarely described by educators as the foundation for newly developed nonstandardized infant data collection tools. We acknowledge the existence of pressures to assess and intervene with handicapped and at-risk infants. Coupled with the existence of instruments that are largely a collection of descriptive statements about infant development, it is no wonder that many educators have chosen to mix and match items to suit their purposes.

If the Cattell appears to have too few psychomotor items, and motor development is the target areas, many professionals have selected items from the Bayley Scales, and put them together with the Cattell into a new scale (without any subsequent psychometric validation). They have used the new scale, and disseminated that scale to others. This results in an atheoretical nonstandardized tool. In light of the Federal government's push during the 1970s and 1980s for disseminable materials, new scales found ready vehicles for dissemination.

A variety of additional pressures have influenced the development of assessment tools. The existence of a well-established network of infant intervention efforts operates in concert with the belief, in regular and special education, that intervention should be data-based. This puts enormous pressure on the educational community to use readily available and familiar infant assessment tools. Similarly, although there is a strong belief among educators that intervention with handicapped and at-risk infants is useful, the pressure to document the cost effectiveness of such intervention is also quite strong (e.g., Casto, White, & Taylor, 1983).

This pressure to demonstrate cost effectiveness imposes a requirement that both sustains the use of currently available tools, despite their limitations, and also mitigates construction of more valid instruments.

These pressures have resulted in a proliferation of infant data collection tools. Johnson and Kopp (1979) describe the characteristics of 67 such instruments. We estimate that no fewer than 300 infant assessment instruments have been developed and at least partially disseminated since the mid-1970s. Careful examination of these instruments reveals that despite their obvious quantity, their psychometric quality and construct validity are highly variable, if not suspect. A final note on this subject: Despite the large number of infant instruments, careful analysis of these tools reveals such enormous commonalities that the number of uniquely designed tools is likely fewer than five!

Context of Infant Development

Mother–Infant Interaction

Before we discuss the assessment of infants, we will argue for the inclusion of mother-infant interaction variables as criteria for identification, program planning, and program evaluation. Parent-infant interactions clearly influence development. Issues presented in this section provide a context for reviewing infants' development. So important is dyadic interaction to the growth and development of infants that to neglect their inclusion in the assessment process may result in unidimensional data.

Since the mid-1960s, mother-infant interaction has received significant attention in the research literature. This body of knowledge includes the effect of the infant on the caregiver (e.g., Lewis & Rosenblum, 1984). It also includes the effect of the infant on maternal caregiving patterns (Brazelton, Koslowski, & Main, 1974; Osofsky & Connors, 1979). Differing maternal responsivity to their infants has been studied as a function of age, birth order, and gender (Clarke-Stewart, 1973; Lewis & Weinraub, 1974; Moss, 1967).

The handicapped infant, whether deaf, blind, or severely retarded, presents unique caretaking problems.

These are compounded by the emotional responses of parents to the unexpected and painful news that their child is handicapped. This difficult reality will most certainly influence maternal-infant interactions.

The work of Goldberg, Brachfeld, and Divitto (1980) and Field (1977) with preterm children indicates the influence of at-risk, in this case preterm, status on maternal behavior and interaction. Field (1983) found that high risk infants have less fun during early interactions. Other work (Eheart, 1982; Kogan & Tyler, 1973; Vietze, Abernathy, Ashe & Faulstich, 1974) has focused on mothers. These studies identified specific maternal responses which differentiated handicapped infants and their mothers from nonhandicapped dyads.

The findings generated by the study of parental influences on infant functioning have been remarkably similar. Beckwith, Cohen, Kopp, Parmelee, and Marci (1976), Clarke-Stewart (1973), have identified the positive role played by attentive, warm, stimulating, responsive, and nonrestrictive mothers in fostering intellectual development.

Ainsworth (1973) has found that infants with mothers who are nurturant, responsive to their needs, and accepting of their limits as immature organisms tend to develop secure as opposed to resistant or avoidant attachments. Securely attached infants are more competent in play (Belsky, Garduque, & Hrncir, 1984) and more competent and autonomous as toddlers (Sroufe, 1978).

While interaction variables have not traditionally been targets of assessment for handicapped and at-risk infants, such data are of critical importance because of the unusual problems encountered by these populations. As example we cite those infants who we characterize as an environmentally at-risk population. These infants experience environmental stresses including teenage pregnancy, substance abuse, and disrupted households. Each of these factors could potentially interfere with the development of a secure mother-child attachment.

In a comprehensive review of early human experience, Belsky (1971) presents several studies exploring familial variables which influence early development. He proposes that in addition to parent-infant interaction, the larger family unit should be a unit of analysis in our attempts to decipher the complexities of development. Such information has application to the assessment and identification of infants at risk of developmental delay. Ramey, Farran, and Campbell (1979) found that information about infants (age 6 to 20 months) and their mothers is highly predictive of later intelligence.

One social interaction model for intervention recently reported (McCollum, 1984; McCollum & Stayton, 1985) is the Social Interaction Assessment/Intervention (SIAI) model. This model assumes that social interaction is complex. Intervention must be based on the assessment of typical interactive patterns. "The fit between infant and caregiver is the ultimate focus of intervention; however, it is the adult member of the dyad who can consciously alter different aspects of his or her own interactive behavior" (McCollum & Stayton, 1985, p. 126).

Caring for an infant with a handicapping condition imposes both physical and emotional strain on the caretaking process of their parents. Attachment theory maintains that sensory input, hearing, seeing, and touching as well as ambulation (as reflected in proximity seeking) are elements which lead to the development of attachment. This thinking guides our concern about the ability of congenitally blind, deaf, and physically handicapped children to form secure attachments with their mothers.

We caution educators that assessment of mother-infant interaction requires a high degree of assessor sensitivity. The cultural implications of mother-infant assessment are only dimly perceived. Differing cultural experiences may result in differing interaction patterns. Assessment must reflect our cultural context. We have encountered many programs in which the majority of families are culturally different from the entire program staff.

Bell (1977) suggests that the study of interaction between parents and their children with congenital defects may help to isolate long-term parent and child effects. Bell (1977) describes a model of parent-child interaction to guide both assessment and intervention. This model could also provide the basis for development of a new outcome measure. Bell's model, which he labeled "lower-limit behavior," is briefly described as follows:

> . . . a feedback system encompassing both parental behavior and expectations. When the child's behavior deviates from expectations, the parent responds with classes of behavior aimed at bringing the child behavior into an "acceptable" range. When the child shows "low activity, inhibited behavior, low assertiveness, slow development and lack of competence, . . . behaviors such as drawing attention to stimuli, positively reinforcing increases in activity, urging, prompting, and demanding increased performance emerge from the parent repertoire. (p. 60)

Developmentally-based programs for infants and toddlers who are handicapped or at risk of developmental delay do not traditionally assess interactive variables. The transactional theory proposed by Sameroff and Chandler (1975) and the importance of mother-infant interaction provide a sound rationale for including this area as a component in intervention programs.

Kaye (1982) maintains that infants take time to become part of the family system and that three factors influence this integration: parents' attitudes, organized baby cycles, and managing the baby's affect. Kaye cautions against intervention related to mother-infant communication, which "comes naturally." Despite this

caution, the confounding of a handicapping condition in dyadic communication cannot be overlooked. As example, mother-infant interaction does not come naturally with blind infants. Intervention in these cases is clearly warranted and can be highly successful (Fraiberg, 1971).

We also recognize that our suggestion is not original. Others have argued for the importance of such data at all stages of the identification and intervention process. Our experience, however, has shown that interveners are afraid to highlight interaction data and reluctant to collect such data as they are viewed as "soft data" by our culture. However, data gathered from coding video taped sessions of maternal-child interactions can be highly reliable. Research employing this methodology holds potential to counter arguments regarding the "softness" of these data.

There is an attitude pervasive in our culture that interaction data reflect process but are not focused enough to identify or evaluate. We challenge that attitude and identify its origins as deriving from our 19th century view of fixed, single factor intelligence. To prepare for the 21st century we must admit to the utility of interaction data. We must continue revising our conceptions of intelligence to encompass a broader, more fluid perspective.

Evaluation of the Home Environment

Thus far in our discussion we have maintained the importance of environment in influencing healthy optimal growth and development. While the quality of mother-infant interaction is one aspect of the environment, several other dimensions are described by scholars (Yarrow, Rubenstein, & Pedersen, 1975). The most widely cited instrument in this area is the Home Observation for the Measurement of the Environment (HOME) (Caldwell & Bradley, 1981). It contains 45 items clustered into six subscales: (a) emotional and verbal responsivity of the mother, (b) avoidance of restriction and punishment, (c) organization of the physical and temporal environment, (d) provision of appropriate play materials, (e) maternal involvement with children, (f) opportunity for variety in daily routine. Bradley and Caldwell (1976, 1980) found a strong relationship between home environment scores in the first year of life and IQ at 36 and 54 months. The HOME does have has a number of cultural biases that have not been fully acknowledged and remediated.

The Purdue Home Stimulation Inventory (PHSI) (Wachs, Francis, & McQueston, 1979) measures similar aspects of the environment. The researchers found a clear relationship between physical environmental parameters and early cognitive development.

The growing literature documenting the relationship of environmental variables to later intellectual function and the availability of tools to assess these variables provides an opportunity to use research data for intervention purposes. Assessment of environmental characteristics for at-risk infants is another potential source of information for identification of infants for intervention.

Assessment of Neuromotor Development

Motor development is clearly of major relevance for all interactions that an infant may have with the environment. From control of primitive reflexes to mastery of upright mobility, the developmental progression of motor skills is complex and arduous.

The Apgar scale (Apgar, 1953) is still the most widely used assessment tool administered at birth. As a screening tool, the Apgar yields mixed results (Broman, Nichols, & Kennedy, 1975). Argument could be made, however, that administration of the Apgar at birth and 5 minutes after birth provides a clinically useful structured examination for medical staff.

Several neonatal assessment tools exist that are useful for screening and identifying infants at risk for continued developmental disabilities. The most widely cited current tool is the Neonatal Behavioral Assessment Scale (Tronick & Brazelton, 1975). One advantage of the Neonatal Behavioral Assessment Scale is that it examines neurological responses and general responses to the environment, in contrast with Prechtl's neurological examination of full-term infants (Prechtl & Beintema, 1977) which addresses only neurological status. Tronick and Brazelton (1975) found strong predictive validity of their behavioral assessment (i.e., 87% correct diagnosis of abnormality in 53 neonates) with less overidentification than was yielded by only neurological examination.

Once neuromotor development progresses beyond the neonatal period, there is almost a quantum leap toward assessment tools that assess motor development at a much more general level. The most widely used of these tools is the motor subscale of the Bayley Scales of Infant Development (Bayley, 1969). The progression from the first item of this scale (lifts head when held at shoulder) to the last 12-month item (walks alone) takes only 42 steps! Included in these 42 items are such divergent items as "retains red ring" and "head balanced." The gross motor and fine motor subscales of the Gesell Developmental Schedules (Gesell & Amatruda, 1982) are similar in their enormous range of items.

In examining the motor scales of standardized developmental measures, one is forced to conclude that their relevance is directed primarily at screening. This is because of the different value associated with success or failure on the items and the fact that failure on one of these items may be accounted for by a variety of causes including muscle tone, strength, tonicity, or any one of a number of other related and unrelated factors.

A number of variables related to motoric performance are not a part of a normal developmental sequence, but are present at birth (or shortly thereafter). These variables include muscle tone, muscle strength, postural reactions, structural mobility, and structural integrity.

These variables are typically examined in a clinical fashion by the physical therapist/occupational therapist who is conducting the motoric examination. They should also play an important role in a screening or programmatic referral assessment conducted by an educator with little specific training in motor development. Assessing the quality of tone is especially important in working with certain populations of handicapped children (e.g., children with Down's syndrome or cerebral palsy).

Recently, Cech, Josephs, Pearl, and Gallagher (1985) attempted to include these nondevelopmental motoric variables in an assessment tool, the Chicago Infant Neuromotor Assessment (CINMA). The CINMA includes a discrete score of each of the following motor domains: (a) passive muscle tone, (b) active muscle tone, (c) development of balance reactions, (d) hemispheric asymmetries, and (e) motor skills.

Motoric assessment of handicapped and at-risk infants will not advance if the only focus is on broad developmental milestones evident in so many developmental measures (e.g., psychomotor index of the Bayley). Infant motoric assessment must include a combination of age-related and nonage-related items, reflecting both motoric behavior and neuromotor developmental processes and "quality" of tone.

Assessment of Perceptual Development

Assessment of Vision and Visual Perception

There has been a small, but significant, revolution during the past several decades regarding the visual competence of infants. We have moved from the previously held view of the infant as "blind at birth" to a substantial literature documenting visual competence (Banks & Salapatek, 1983).

Much of our current understanding of visual perception is an outgrowth of work with animals (Lamb & Campos, 1982). Building on the animal literature, the work of behavioral researchers indicated that infants could see, and Fantz (1961, 1963) provided clear evidence of form perception in infants. In his studies, infants were shown two different figures and an observer looking at the infant's eyes recorded which figure the infant looked at and for how long. Using a variety of visual stimuli that varied in color, intensity, and pattern, Fantz found that infants preferred checkerboard patterns to uniform gray patterns and preferred a real face to a distorted face.

The goal of many visual assessment procedures is to document that infants can discriminate among various stimuli. Assessment paradigms of this type might be classified into one of four approaches. The first approach, an approach exemplified by the work of Fantz (1961, 1963) and Kagan (1970), uses attention and memory as an outcome variable being measured in response to systematic changes in stimuli. Testing procedures typically require a structured setting, an ability to track infant eye movements, and a quantity of data over repeated exposures to stimuli. Although much work has been done in the area of visual recognition memory, there have been no theoretical formulations presented which link early visual processing to late intellectual development.

A second approach to assessment of visual perception is more affective in tone, measuring infant's startle or laughter in response to novel stimuli. The work of Stroufe and Waters (1976), Cicchetti and Sroufe (1976), Zelazo (1979), and Kagan (1979) typify this approach. In one of Zelazo's paradigms, a toy car or ball is released from a resting position to roll down a ramp. Infants are presented with the object rolling as one would expect, and they are also exposed to the ball or car exhibiting an unexpected event (i.e., the car taps an object that does not fall over, or the ball disappears). Infant behaviors being assessed include anticipatory fixation, clapping, waving, twisting, leg kicking, and so forth.

Yet a third variation on assessment procedures is to expose infants to stimuli (or unexpected events) and record physiological reactions. Bower's (1974) examinations of infant object permanence and constancy are classic examples of such a paradigm. Outcome variables in procedures such as this type include cardiac acceleration and deceleration, tensing of muscles, and so forth.

A fourth approach to assessing visual perception is to measure an infant's neurological responses to visual stimuli. The most common approach to this is to measure the electroencephalographic recordings (EEG) of the infant. A number of studies of this type have been conducted by Courchesne (1977, 1978a, 1978b) with mixed results. Several of these studies provided fairly reliable measure of visual discrimination (with infants older than 6 months). At other times the studies failed to yield a consistent EEG recording in response to visual discrimination tasks (with infants less than 6 months). A neurological outcome measure that holds great promise is the visual evoked potential (VEP). This test procedure identifies cortical or brain stem responses to varying visual (or auditory) stimuli. Such testing is still in its infancy. Researchers are currently working to explore the utility of such data for intervention efforts with handicapped and at-risk infants.

Once again, the assessment procedures discussed have clear implications for research and may have implications for identification of children with visual perception problems. The predictive validity of these measures has been documented in some studies (Fagan & McGarth, 1981; Fagan & Singer, 1982; Rose & Wallace, 1985). However, the implications for psychoeducational programming have not been presented. This may be due in part to an absence of a theoretical framework for visual recognition memory.

Assessment of Audition and Auditory Perception

There is much less information available regarding auditory perception than visual perception during the infancy period. Aslin, Pisoni, and Jusczyk (1983) have presented a comprehensive review of auditory perception research and conclude the following: (a) basic auditory function begins several weeks before the 40th postconceptual month; (b) the quality of this function is unknown; (c) the precise role of experience on auditory perception remains unknown as are basic underlying processes. In light of these conclusions, it is no wonder that the relevance of assessment procedures in the auditory perception area is unclear.

The same general classes of assessment procedures exist in the auditory area as in the visual area. These include elicited motor responses, startle and laughter in response to auditory stimuli, cardiac acceleration and deceleration, and auditory brainstem response (ABR). One exception to our comparison with the status of visual perception must be noted. The work of Stein and associates (Stein, Ozdamar, Kraus & Paton, 1983; Stein, Ozdamar & Schabel, 1981; Stein, Palmer & Weinberg, 1982) and others have been consistently demonstrating the value of auditory brainstem responses to the early identification of deaf and hard of hearing infants. These procedures have potential for early identification of auditory perception problems.

Assessment of Cognitive Development

Researchers in the field agree that infant intelligence tests have poor predictive validity with regard to later measured cognitive functioning (Brooks & Weinraub, 1976; McCall, 1979). The exception to this conclusion is assessment of severely retarded children (and these children are usually also identifiable through clinical observation).

Before we can begin discussion of the assessment of infant intelligence we must again raise the issue of the purpose of assessment. If one's purpose is to use cognitive assessment tools for screening or program referral, measures such as the Cattell, the Bayley Scales, or the Gesell Developmental Schedules will likely serve an immediate need. This will be accomplished, however, with a high degree of error for moderately and mildly delayed children, and a high number of false positive decisions. If one's purpose in assessment is to obtain data that are predictive or are of use for psychoeducational programming, then infant intelligence measures are unreliable predictors and inadequate guides.

In an attempt to explain the lack of predictive power of the infant intelligence measures, Harris (1983) suggests three possible explanations:

1. IQ scores at early ages may be inherently unreliable.

2. The very nature of infant intelligence and childhood intelligence is different from the intelligence of older individuals.

3. Infant IQ tests have been devised for ease and reliability of administration which led to the inclusion of codable motor and vocal behaviors. Perhaps the inclusion of items "that depend on more subtle observations of attention, habituation, concept formation, and so forth . . . might show a stronger link to later intelligence" (Harris, 1983, p. 752).

A useful assessment tool is a tool based upon a theoretical formulation. In the area of infant intelligence, we turn away from the standard developmental measures (because of the problems noted above) and turn toward the measures of sensorimotor intelligence that reflect Piaget's writings.

The Piagetian tool referenced most widely is the Uzgiris-Hunt Scales. Research with normal children using the Uzgiris-Hunt Scales has raised questions regarding congruence of performance across the six content areas included in the Scales. Erratic test performance including regression has been noted in the course of repeated testing (Kopp, Sigman, & Parmelee, 1974). This lack of congruence was also noted by King and Seegmuller (1973) who found insignificant intercorrelations among the seven scales. Kopp, Sigman, and Parmelee (1974), found that less than 1% of the normal infants exhibited concordant performance across all seven tests. They concluded: "it is clear from these data that sensorimotor development is characterized by unevenness and the capabilities exhibited in one area of performance have little relationship to abilities measured in another aspect of performance at a given age" (p. 692).

The work of Robinson and Robinson (1978) and Dunst (1980, 1981) describes the use of the Uzgiris-Hunt Scales for Clinical Assessment and intervention with a handicapped and at-risk infant population. Dunst (1980) describes a clinical procedure utilizing the Scales that is designed to determine several issues: (a) Is a child showing delayed or non-delayed sensorimotor performance; (b) is a child showing normal or atypical patterns of sensorimotor development; (c) the extent to which deviations in a child's patterns of development are present; (d) the specific nature of any deviations; (e) what types of interventions are indicated. In addition, Dunst (1980) has constructed a Profile of Abilities form for the landmarks on the Uzgiris-Hunt Scale as the basis for describing the patterns of development.

After presenting several case studies in which the ordinal scales were used to describe levels of development, Dunst (1983) concluded:

> Despite possible shortcomings and limitations, ordinal scales offer an alternative set of procedures for assessing the early acquisition of cognitive competencies . . . Perhaps their strongest asset is that

they lend themselves readily to the design of interventions and the evaluation of the impacts of different environmental influences. (p. 60)

Clearly, this is an assessment procedure that begs further study, particularly with infants with sensory and multiple impairments. Furthermore, we strongly urge the continued study of environmental correlates related to landmarks on the ordinal scales, particularly as they have implications for intervention with at-risk populations.

Harris summarized the data from several studies using sensorimotor assessments by concluding that it is not only difficult to predict later development from infant intelligence but it is difficult to predict performance from one domain in the sensorimotor area to another. Our analysis of infant intelligence measures is not optimistic. For the most part, we see the utility of the data collection tools as being largely confirmatory of clinical judgment. In our own practice, when clinical judgment and intelligence data conflict, we are more inclined to trust clinical judgment. Such a response, though likely an accurate perception of the limitations of current data collection tools, will have to become reversed in response to stronger instruments.

Assessment of Temperament

Temperament is defined as an infant's constitutionally-based patterns of reaction to stimuli and the infant's capacity for self-regulation (Rothbart, 1984). In this definition, the reference to constitutionally-based patterns, present at birth, implies an expected continuity of this construct across time. It also suggests some implications of temperament for performance in other areas. Further, a defining characteristic of temperament is that it is independent of situational influences. Keogh and Pullis (1980) refer to temperament as behavioral individuality, a term that captures many of the points noted above.

Major constructs assessed by temperament data collection tools include: mood, distractibility, activity rate, rhythmicity, approach/withdrawal, intensity, persistence, and so forth. Data on each of these dimensions are clustered to yield temperament categories for infants and young children.

The single most accurate generalization to make regarding assessment of infant temperament is that it rarely occurs with reference to psychoeducational intervention. When such assessment does occur, it is almost always for purpose of theory development and application.

The infant assessment tool used most often in the temperament area is the questionnaire developed by Carey (1970) and revised by Carey and McDevitt (1978). The 1970 Carey tool and the revision are based upon the interview tool developed and reported by Thomas and Chess over a 15-year time period (Thomas & Chess, 1977).

Criticisms of the Carey have been raised in the literature. For example, several authors (Greenberg & Field, 1982) question the construct validity of the Carey Temperament Questionnaire. This questioning is because the instrument is completed by an infant's parent(s) rather than by an objective observer. The critics have questioned whether this rating procedure yields valid and reliable data.

Second, the Carey Infant Temperament Questionnaire was developed with a population of nonhandicapped infants. Greenberg and Field (1982) offer several excellent suggestions for modifying the Carey Infant Temperament Questionnaire. Among their proposals is the addition of more specific information regarding handicapped populations, including a widening of the scoring method to include a neutral dimension. This is a dimension which would reflect the lack of any given activity or response. This neutral or flat response is one which sometimes differentiates between a typical and atypical infant population. Furthermore, in addition to a neutral response, they suggest the inclusion of a response that would indicate passivity, and lack of active play.

Bates (1980) and his colleagues have been studying temperament using the Infant Characteristics Questionnaire (ICQ). Infant temperament has shown considerable stability from one assessment point to another. Clearly, this is a line of research that begs further study, particularly in terms of implications for intervention.

Assessment of temperament has primarily focused on research questions and has rarely been used for purposes of screening, program referral, prediction, or program evaluation. While few practitioners would argue that temperament does not influence intervention efforts, too little is known about infant temperament to make placement decisions based upon temperament. Similarly we cannot yet design and evaluate psychoeducational intervention directed to modification of infant temperament.

Carey (1985) argues that temperament data can aid the clinician in fostering parent-child relationships when individual infant temperaments interfere with those relationships. He also suggests that such data can educate parents about normal growth and development so as better to understand their children's behavior. This issue is particularly true in light of our previous comments on the importance of parent-infant interaction data. One goal of researchers in this area should be to determine the relevance of temperament data for psychoeducational intervention.

Assessment of Communication

A major contribution of the past 15 years, and a fact overlooked by the many preceding decades of descriptive assessment of infants, is that infants and caregivers engage in meaningful communication. This begins long before the infants begin to use formal language (Vietz, Abernathy, Ashe, & Faulstich, 1978). This should come as no surprise to us when we realize that infants recognize and prefer their mother's voice to the voice of an unfamiliar woman in the first weeks of life. Neonates respond to that voice within cyclical patterns of excitement and habituation, initiation and responding, gazing and aversion, and upset and contentment. Such patterns of regulation provide the basis for infant-adult communication (Cross, 1977, 1978).

Initiation of communication is largely the domain of the parent during the first 4 or 5 months of life (Kaye, 1982). Communication assessment during this early period is directed primarily at parental communicative activities. From the 5th month, the infant begins to play a more reciprocal role in initiating and responding to communication with adults. The dyadic nature of communication insures that the role of the adult in infant-adult communication is still quite important. The responsivity of adults to infant communicative attempts is especially important.

One assessment tool that meets the need for assessing reciprocal communication activities is the Parent Behavior Progression (Bromwich, 1981). This instrument yields data describing the interaction between an infant and a parent or child care provider in a variety of common situations. In this scale responsivity of mother to infant and infant to mother are integral to the assessment process. The following example of one item from the Parent Behavior Progression is illustrative:

> Sequences or chains of pleasurable interactions between parent and infant suggest mutuality in the relationship. Examples: Baby coos, mother nuzzles baby, baby coos back, etc. . . , or mother moves her head side to side, baby follows visually and smiles, mother moves head to other side, etc. (p. 346)

A major strength of this instrument is that it reflects a theoretical formulation of dyadic interaction as a catalyst for developmental progress. Thus evaluative criteria include interaction variables related to theory. The instrument was an outgrowth of ongoing intervention with handicapped and at-risk infants and their parents; therefore it also reflects a strong theoretical base pertaining to a systems approach to early intervention (Sheehan, 1984).

Briefly stated, a systems approach to intervention is one emphasizing the pattern of transactional communications rather than any one particular communicative attempt. Intervention is based upon interrupting dysfunctional cycles of behavior, making use of the reactions of persons in the system to those interruptions. (See Auerswald, 1972, for a discussion of applications of systems theory to family therapy.)

The drawback of the Parent Behavior Progression is the paucity of psychometric data supporting the tool. While the instrument was used in several published studies (Hanson, 1984; Sheehan & Krakow, 1981) there are insufficient data to validate its psychometric properties.

As with motor development, more than one mode of infant assessment tools exist in the communication area. A number of "developmental measures" are available which contain communication items throughout the infancy period. These tools measure infant communication in either a report fashion or in a structured, static test session. For example, the Bayley Scales of Infant Development (Bayley, 1969) describe "vocalizes once or twice" by the 3rd month. By the 5th month, the infant is to vocalize two different sounds. By the 14th month the infant is to listen selectively to familiar words. In these instances verbal performance of the infant in response to the tester is assessed.

The degree to which such a procedure is an accurate assessment for infants (perhaps the infant doesn't want to utter a sound) is questionable. Similarly, the generalizability of data gathered from an infant in this fashion to the functioning of the infant in a familiar environment such as home must also be questioned.

Another instrument developed by recording high-frequency behaviors and arranging them into an ordinal sequence is the Receptive Expressive Emergent Language Scale, or REEL (Bzoch & League 1970). The REEL is a questionnaire which supplements observed speech and language skills with reports from someone who knows the child. Although it delineates speech and language acquisition by small age increments, it does so in the absence of a coordinating theory.

One measure of communication skills that has a broadly-based view of language development is the Sequenced Inventory of Communication Development, SICD (Hedrick, Prather, & Tobin, 1975). This instrument contains many more communication items than on the typical language measure. It yields data in 4-month increments in the following areas of communication: awareness of environmental sounds and speech sounds, discrimination of environmental sounds and speech sounds, understanding, initiating of communication, imitating communication, and responding to communication. Additionally, the SICD also includes a 50-response language sample, an invaluable tool for clinicians and researchers alike.

In addition to the traditional developmental measures that include assessment of communication performance, a number of alternative assessment procedures tap this important area of functioning. Kagan, Kearsley, and Zelazo (1978) have developed assessment measures examining infants' processing of visual and auditory information (Zelazo, 1982). One component of these procedures is an assessment of laugh and startle response of infants to discrepant events.

Similarly, Bridges and Cicchetti (1982) have examined differences in vocal activity, smiling, and laughter between various groups of typical and atypical infants. These non-traditional and somewhat naturalistic testing procedures offer an intriguing and ecologically relevant assessment of early infant communication. To date, the relevance of these data for psychoeducational intervention is uncertain. Are they data that have only descriptive utility (and possibly predictive utility)? Or are they data with broader implications?

Summary and Recommendations

The pessimism which characterizes this review of infant assessment tools echoes that of Brooks and Weinraub (1976), Honzik (1976), Sheehan (1982), and Brooks-Gunn and Lewis (1983). An important difference in the current review is the acknowledgement that assessment of handicapped and at-risk infants which standard developmental measures occurs in response to a variety of pressures and in a strong cultural context. These pressures are not likely to diminish. In fact, the current Federal budget debate insures sustained pressures. We do recognize, however, that the emphasis on intelligence testing is at least being questioned in our society, albeit on a grade school level. Perhaps this awareness that testing should answer questions of true instructional relevance will also become evident at the infancy level.

A second important difference in the current review is the plea for more comprehensive theoretical formulations that explain infant growth and development especially related to intervention. Such foundations can then serve as a basis for infant evaluation and intervention effects. Increasing the theoretical strength of new measures will likely yield data collection tools that have much more relevance for intervention. Existence of such instructionally relevant measures might hasten our society's willingness to assure a free public education to all children (and infants) irrespective of their developmental status.

We are concerned that, despite explication of several of the varying purposes of assessment, the intervention community and the research community persist in their search for instruments that are "reliable" and "valid" without consistently addressing the issue of "reliable for what?" and "valid for what purpose?" We are also concerned that training issues with regard to assessment are not fully understood or acknowledged.

How can researchers and interveners best proceed with regard to infant assessment? First, we must continue our efforts to identify assessment procedures that do have validity for one or more of the specified purposes of infant intervention. Early identification of at-risk and handicapped infants for purposes of instruction still lack strong empirical data collection procedures. In this respect, the work of Fagan (1978), Bridges and Cicchetti (1982), and Zelazo (1979) hold great promise.

Second, we must recognize the pressures that are at work insuring that standard developmental instruments will likely continue to be used in psychoeducational intervention settings, despite their inadequacy for specific psychoeducational programming or program evaluation. Perhaps an improved way to view this situation is that the standard developmental instruments are one (small) part of the clinical component of intervention. Sheehan (1982) has argued that use of such instruments may not be harmful, provided that their limitations are acknowledged, though they may be of questionable utility. Again, the issue of purposes of assessment must provide the context for justification of continued use.

Third, we must continue to advocate for more sophisticated instruments that reflect new knowledge of infant growth and development generated since the mid-1970s. Central to these research efforts have been findings which document the powerful influence of the dynamic interactions between infants and caregivers. How are these data being reflected in intervention with handicapped and at-risk infants? These instruments must reflect an awareness of the complexities of intervention with children and families, and the dyadic relationship that exists between infants and primary care providers. This will represent a startling departure from our reliance on the standardized lists of high-frequency infant behaviors.

Given that we have limited resources that can be directed toward instrument development, the time has come further to differentiate the purposes of assessment. We urge the development of assessment tools that have specific relevance for culturally divergent target populations whose developmental difficulties require participation in individually designed psychoeducational intervention.

Lastly, we remind the reader that the knowledge, skills, and sensitivity of the intervener(s) may, in reality, transcend all other issues. By that we mean that even the perfect assessment battery is counterproductive in the hands of an unskilled or insensitive user. Alternatively, sensitive intervenors have substantively contributed to the development of infants even within the limits present in our existing instruments.

Early intervention is primarily a transaction between people who need help and those who have requisite skills to provide the help. Those who need the help are often vulnerable and worried. Assessment efforts should reflect our sensitivity to these needs of the handicapped and at-risk infants and their families whom we are serving.

References

Ainsworth, M. (1973). The development of infant-mother interaction. In B. Caldwell and H. Riciutti (Eds.), *Review of child development research* (Vol. 3). Chicago: University of Chicago Press.

Apgar, V. (1953). A proposal for a new method of resolution of the newborn infant. *Current Researches in Anesthesia and Analgesia*, **32**, 260–267.

Aslin, R., Pisoni, D., & Jusczyk, P. (1983). Auditory development and speech perception in infancy. In P. Musson (Ed.), *Handbook of child psychology* (4th ed., Vol. 2). New York: Wiley.

Auerswald, E. (1972). Families, change, and the ecological perspective. In A. Ferber, M. Mendelsohn, & A. Napier (Eds.), *The book of family therapy*. Boston: Houghton, Mifflin.

Bagnato, S., & Neisworth, J. (1982). *Linking developmental assessment and curriculum: Prescriptions for early information*. Rockville, MD: Aspen Systems.

Banks, M., & Salapatek, P. (1983). Infant visual perception. In P. Musson (Ed.), *Handbook of child psychology* (Vol. 2). New York: Wiley.

Bates, J. (1980). The concepts of difficult temperament. *Merrill Palmer Quarterly*, **26**, 299–319.

Bayley, M. (1969). *Manual for the Bayley scales of infant development*. New York: Psychological Corporation.

Beckwith, L., Cohen, S., Kopp. C., Parmelee, A., & Marci, T. (1976). Caregiver-infant interaction and early cognitive development in preterm infants. *Child Development*, **47**, 579–587.

Bell, R. (1977). Socialization findings examined. In R. Q. Bell and L. V. Harper (Eds.), *Child effects on adults* (pp. 53–84). Hillsdale, NJ: Erlbaum.

Belsky, J. (1971). Early human experience: a family perspective. *Developmental Psychology*, **17** (1), 3–23.

Belsky, J., Garduque, L., & Hrncir, W. (1984) Assessing performance, competence, and executive capacity in infant play: Relations to home environment and security of attachment. *Developmental Psychology*, **20** (3), 406–417.

Bower T. (1974) *Development in infancy*. San Francisco: W. H. Freeman.

Bradley, R., & Caldwell, B. (1976). The relation of infants' home environments to mental test performance at fifty-four months: a follow-up study. *Child Development*, **47**, 1172–1174.

Bradley, R., & Caldwell, B. (1980). The relationship of home environment, cognitive competence, and IQ among males and females. *Child Development*, **51**, 1140–1148.

Brazelton, T., Koslowski, B., & Main, M. (1974). The origin of reciprocity: The early mother-infant interaction. In M. Lewis & L. Rosenblum (Eds.), *The effect of the infant on its caregiver: The origins of behavior* (Vol. 1). New York: Wiley.

Bricker, D. (Ed.). (1982). *Intervention with at-risk and handicapped infants: From research to application*. Baltimore, MD: University Park Press.

Bridges, F., & Cicchetti, D. (1982). Mother ratings of temperament characteristics of Down syndrome infants. *Developmental Psychology*, **18**, 238–244.

Broman, S., Nichols, P., & Kennedy, W. (1975). *Preschool IQ: Pre natal and early developmental correlates*. Hillsdale, NJ: Erlbaum.

Bromwich, R. (1981). *Working with parents and infants: An interactional approach*. Baltimore, MD: University Park Press.

Brooks, J., & Weinraub, M. (1976). A history of infant intelligence testing. In M. Lewis (Ed.), *Origins of intelligence*. New York: Plenum.

Brooks-Gunn, J. & Lewis, M. (1983). Screening and diagnosing handicapped infants. *Topics in Early Childhood Special Education*, **3** (1), 14–28.

Bzoch, K. R., & League, R. (1970). *Receptive-expressive emergent language scale*. Gainesville, FL: Antinga.

Caldwell, B., & Bradley, R. (1981). *Home observation for measurement of the environment*. New York: Dorsey.

Carey, W. (1970). A simplified method for measuring infant temperament. *Journal of Pediatrics*, **77** (2), 188–194.

Carey, W. (1985). Clinical use of temperament data in pediatrics. *Journal of Developmental and Behavioral Pediatrics*, **6** (3), 128–131.

Carey, W., McDevitt, S. (1978). A revision of the infant temperament questionnaire. *Pediatrics*, **61**, 735.

Casati, L., & Lezine, I. (1968). *Les Etapes de L'Intelligence Sensorinotrice*, Les Edition du Centre Psychologie Applique, Paris.

Casto, G., White, K., & Taylor, C. (1983). An early intervention research institute: Studies of the efficacy and cost effectiveness of early intervention at Utah State. *Journal of the Division of Early Childhood*, **7**, 5–17.

Cattell, P. (1940). *The measurement of intelligence of infants and young children*. New York: Psychological Corporation.

Cech, D., Josephs, A., Pearl, O., & Gallagher, R. (1985). *The Chicago infant neuromotor assessment*, Chicago, IL: Illinois Institute for Developmental Disabilities.

Cicchetti, D., & Sroufe, A. (1976). The relationship between affective and cognitive development in Down's syndrome infants. *Child Development*, **47**, 920–929.

Clarke-Stewart K. (1973). Interactions between mothers and their young children: Characteristics and consequences. *Monographs of the Society for Research in Child Development*, **38**, (6–7, Serial No. 153).

Cohen, M., Gross, P., & Haring, N. (1976). Developmental pinpoints. In N. Haring and L. Brown (Eds.), *Teaching the severely handicapped* (Vol. I). New York: Grune & Stratton.

Courchesne, E. (1977). Event-related brain potentials: A comparison between children and adults. *Science*, **197**, 589–592.

Courchesne, E. (1978a). Neurophysiological correlates of cognitive development: Changes in long-latency event-related potentials from childhood to adulthood. *Electroencephalography and Clinical Neurophysiology*, **45**, 468–482.

Courchesne, E. (1978b). Changes in P3 waves with event repetition: Long term effects on scalp distribution and amplitude. *Electroencephalography and Clinical Neurophysiology*, **45**, 754–766.

Cross, T. (1977). Mothers' speech adjustments: The selection of child listener variables. In C. E. Snow & C. A. Ferguson (Eds.), *Talking to children*. Cambridge, MA: Cambridge University Press.

Cross, T. (1978). Mothers' speech and its association with rate of linquistic development in young children. In N. Waterson & C. Anon (Eds.), *The development of communication*. New York: Wiley.

Cross L., & Goin, K. (1977). *Identifying handicapped children: A guide to casefinding, screening, diagnosis, assessment, and evaluation*. New York: Walker.

Dunst, C. (1980). *A clinical and educational manual for use with the Uzgiris-Hunt scales of infant psychological development*. Baltimore, MD: University Park Press.

Dunst, C. (1981). *Infant learning*. Hinghan, MA: Teaching Resources.

Dunst, C. (1983). Piagetian approaches to infant assessment. *Topics in Early Childhood Special Education*, **3** (1), 44–62.

Eheart, B. K. (1982). Mother-child interaction with nonretarded and mentally retarded preschoolers. *American Journal of Mental Deficiency*, **87**, 20–25.

Fagan, J. (1978). Infant recognition memory and early cognitive ability: Empirical, theoretical, and remedial considerations. In F. Minifie and L. Lloyd (Eds.), *Communicative and cognitive abilities-early behavioral assessments*. Baltimore, MD: University Park Press.

Fagan, J., & McGarth, S. (1981). Infant recognition memory and later intelligence. *Intelligence*, **5**, 121–130.

Fagan, J., & Singer, L. (1982). Infant recognition memory as a measure of intelligence. In L. P. Lipsitt (Ed.), *Advances in infancy research* (Vol. 2) (pp. 31–78). Norwalk, NJ: Ablex.

Fantz, R. (1961). The origins of form perception. *Scientific American*, **204**, 66–72.

Fantz, R. (1963). Pattern vision in newborn infants.

Field, T. (1977). Effects of early separation, interactive deficits and experimental manipulations on infant-mother face-to-face interactions. *Child Development*, **48**, 763–771.

Field, T. (1983). High risk infants "have less fun" during early interactions. *Topics in Early Childhood Special Education*, **3** (1), 77–87.

Foster, M., Berger, M., & McLean, M. (1981). Rethinking a good idea: A reassessment of parent involvement. *Topics in Early Childhood Special Education*, **1** (3), 55–66.

Fraiberg, S. (1971). Intervention in infancy: a program for blind infants. *Journal of the American Academy of Child Psychiatry*, **3**, 381–403.

Frankenburg, W., van Doornick, W., Liddell, T., & Dick, N. (1976). The Denver Prescreening Developmental Questionnaires (PDQ). *Pediatrics*, **57**, 744–753.

Gesell, A. (1940). *The first five years of life*. New York: Harper.

Gesell, A., & Amatruda, C. (1982). *Developmental diagnosis*. New York: Harper & Row.

Goldberg, S., Brachfeld, S., & Divitto, B. (1980). Feeding, fussing and play: parent-infant interaction in the first year as a function of prematurity and perinatal medical problems. In T. Field (Ed.). *High risk infants and children*. New York: Academic Press.

Gould, J. (1981). *The mismeasure of man*. New York: Norton.

Greenberg, R., & Field, T. (1982). Temperament ratings of handicapped infants during classroom, mother, and teacher interactions. *Journal of Pediatric Psychology*, **7**, 387–405.

Hanson, M. (1984). *Atypical infant development*, Baltimore, MD: University Park Press.

Harris, P. (1983). Infant cognition. In M. Haith and J. Campos (Eds.), *Infancy and developmental psychobiology*. New York: Wiley.

Hayden, A., & Haring, N. (1976). Programs for Down's Syndrome children at the University of Washington. In T. D. Tjossen (Ed.), *Intervention strategies for high-risk infants and young children*. Baltimore, MD: University Park Press.

Hedrick, D. L., Prather, E. M., & Tobin, A. R. (1975). *Sequenced inventory of communication development*. Seattle: University of Washington Press.

Honzik, M. (1976). Value and limitations of infant tests: An overview. In M. Lewis (Ed.), *Origins of intelligence: Infancy and early childhood*. New York: Plenum Press.

Johnson, K., & Kopp, C. (1979). *A bibliography of screening and assessment measures for infants*, Los Angeles: Project REACH, UCLA Graduate school of Education.

Kagan, J. (1970). Attention and psychological change in the young child. *Science*, **170**, 826–832.

Kagan, J. (1979). Structure and process in the human infant: The ontogeny of mental representation. In M. Bornstein & W. Kessen (Eds.), *Psychological development from infancy: Image to intention*. Hillsdale, NJ: Erlbaum.

Kagan, J., Kearsley, R., & Zelazo, P. (1978). *Infancy: Its place in human development*. Cambridge MA: Harvard University Press.

Kaye, K. (1982). *The mental and social life of babies*. Chicago: University of Chicago Press.

Keogh, B., & Pullis, M. (1980). Temperament influence in the development of exceptional children. In B. Keogh (Ed.), *Advances in special education* (Vol. 1). Greenwich, CT: JAI Press.

King, W., & Seegmuller, B. (1973). Performance of 14- to 22-month-old black, first born male infants on two tests of cognitive development. *Development Psychology*, **8**, 317–326.

Knoblock, H., & Pasamanick, B. (1974). *Gesell and Amatruda's developmental diagnosis* (3rd. ed.). New York: Harper & Row.

Kogan, K., & Tyler, N., (1973). Mother-child interaction in young physically handicapped children. *American Journal of Mental Deficiency*, **77**, 492–497.

Kopp, C. (1982). The role of theoretical frameworks in the study of at-risk and handicapped children. In D. Bricker (Ed.), *Intervention with at-risk and handicapped infants*. (pp. 13–30). Baltimore, MD: University Park Press.

Kopp, C., Sigman, M., & Parmelee, A. (1974). A longitudinal study of sensorimotor development. *Development Psychology*, **10**, 687–695.

Lamb, M. E., & Campos, J. J. (1982). *Development in infancy*. New York: Random House.

Lewis, M., Fox, N. (1980). Predicting cognitive development from assessments in infancy. In B. Camp (Ed.) *Advances in behavioral pediatrics* (Vol. 1) (pp. 53-67). Greenwich, CT: JAI Press.

Lewis, M., & Rosenblum, L. (Eds.) (1984). *The effect of the infant on its caretakers: The origins of behavior* (Vol. 1). New York: Wiley.

Lewis, M., & Weinraub, M. (1974). Sex of parent x sex of child: socialemotional development. In R. Richart, R. Friedman, & R. Vande Wiele (Eds.), *Sex differences in behavior*. New York: Wiley.

McCall, R. (1979). The development of intellectual functioning in infancy and the prediction of later IQ. In J. D. Osofsky (Ed.), *Handbook of infant development*. New York: Wiley.

McCall, R., Eichorn, D., & Hogarty, P. (1977). Transitions in early mental development. *Monographs of the Society for Research in Child Development*, **42** (3, Serial No. 171).

McCollum, J. (1984). Social interaction between parents and babies: Validation of an intervention model. *Child Care Health and Development*, **10**, 301–315.

McCollum, J., & Stayton, V. (1985). Infant parent interaction: Studies and guidelines based on the SIAI model. *Journal of the Division of Early Childhood*, **2**, 125–135.

Moss, H. (1967). Sex, age, and state as determinants of mother–infant interaction. *Merrill Palmer Quaterly*, **13**, 19–36.

Osofsky, J., & Connors, K. (1979). Mother–infant interaction: An integrative view of a complex system. In J. Osofsky (Ed.), *Handbook of infant development*. New York: Wiley.

Piaget, J. (1952). *The origins of intelligence in children* (M. Cook, Trans.). New York: International Universities Press.

Prechtl, H., & Beintema, D. (1977). The neurological examination of the full-term newborn infant. In *Clinics in Developmental Medicine (No. 63)*. London: Spastics International Medical Publications, Heinemann.

Ramey, C., Farran, C., & Campbell, F. (1979). Predicting IQ from mother-infant interactions. *Child Development*, **50**, 804–814.

Robinson, G., & Robinson, J. (1978). Sensorimotor functions and cognitive development. In M. Snell (Ed.), *Systematic instruction of the moderately and severely handicapped*. Columbus, OH: Charles E. Merrill.

Rose, S., & Wallace, I. (1985). Visual recognition memory: A predictor of later cognitive functioning in preterms, *Child Development*, **56**, 843–852.

Rothbart, M. (1984). Social development. In M. Hanson (Ed.) *Atypical infant development*. Baltimore, MD: University Park Press.

Sameroff, A., & Chandler, M. (1975). Reproductive risk and the continuum of caretaking casualty. In F. D. Horowitz (Ed.), *Review of child development research* (Vol. 4). Chicago: University of Chicago Press.

Sheehan, R. (1982). Infant assessment: A review and identification of emergent trends. In D. Bricker (Ed.), *Intervention with at-risk and handicapped infants: From research to application* (pp. 47–62). Baltimore, MD: University Park Press.

Sheehan, R. (1984). Intervening in early childhood systems: Challenges for intervention and research. In *Essays by the Spencer Fellows*, Vol. I. Pittsburgh, PA: National Academy of Education Press.

Sheehan, R., & Krakow, J. (1981). Describing and comparing infant progress. *Diagnostique*, **7** (2), 76–90.

Sroufe, A. (1978). Attachment and the roots of competence. *Human Nature*, October, 50–57.

Sroufe, A., & Waters, E. (1976). The ontogenesis of smiling and laughter in the first year of life. *Child Development*, **47**, 1326–1344.

Stein, L., Ozdamar, O., Kraus, N., & Paton, J. (1983). Follow-up of infants screened by auditory brainstem response in neonatal intensive care unit. *Journal of Pediatrics*, **103**, 447–453.

Stein, L., Ozdamar, O., & Schabel, M. (1981). Auditory brainstem responses with suspected deaf-blind children. *Ear and Hearing*, **2**, 30–40.

Stein, L., Palmer, P., & Weinberg, B. (1982). Characteristics of a young deaf-blind population. *American Annals of the Deaf*, **127**, 828–837.

Thomas, A., & Chess, S. (1977). *Temperament and development*. New York: Brunner/Mazel.

Tjossem, T. (1976). *Intervention strategies for high-risk infants and young children*. Baltimore, MD: University Park Press.

Tronick E., & Brazelton, T. (1975). Clinical uses of the Brazelton Neonatal Behavioral Assessment. In B. Friedlander, G. Sterritt, & G. Kirk (Eds.), *Exceptional infant* (Vol. 3). New York: Bruner/Mazel.

Uzgiris, I., & Hunt, J. McV. (1975). *Assessment in infancy: Ordinal scales of psychological development*. Urbana: IL: University of Illinois Press.

Vietze, P., Abernathy, S., Ashe, M., & Faulstich, G. (1974). Contigent interaction between mothers and their developmentally delayed infants. In G. Sackett (Ed.), *Observing behavior (Vol. 1): Theory and applications in mental retardation*. Baltimore, MD: University Park Press.

Wachs, T., Francis, J., & McQueston, S. (1979). Psychological dimensions of the infant's physical environment. *Infant Behavior and Development*, **2**, 155–161.

Wachs, T., & Sheehan, R. (1988). *Assessment of developmentally disabled children*. New York: Plenum Press.

Weikart, D., Epstein, A., Schweinhart, L. & Bond, T. (1978). *The Ypsilanti Preschool Curriculum Demonstration Project: Preschool years and longitudinal results*. Ypsilanti, MI.: High/Scope Educational Research Foundation.

Yang, R. (1979). Early infant assessment: An overview. In J. Osofsky (Ed.), *Handbook of infant development*. New York: Wiley.

Yarrow, L., Rubenstein, J., & Pedersen, F. (1975). *Infant and environment: Early cognitive and motivational development*. New York: Halsted Press.

Zelazo, P. (1979). Reactivity to perceptual-cognitive events: Application for infant assessment. In R. Kearsley & I. Sigel (Eds.), *Infants at risk: Assessment of cognitive functioning*. Hillsdale, NJ: Erlbaum.

Zelazo, P. (1982). Alternative assessment procedures for handicapped infants and toddlers: Theoretical and practical issues. In D. Bricker (Ed.), *Intervention with at-risk and handicapped infants*. Baltimore, MD: University Park Press.

Efficacy of Early Intervention

CARL J. DUNST, SCOTT W. SNYDER AND MARGARET MANKINEN

Western Carolina Center

Abstract—The early intervention literature is examined in terms of both state-of-the-art knowledge and state of practices in the field. A paradigmatic framework, which emphasizes a causal analysis perspective, is used to review and critique efficacy research. *Efficacy* is defined as the extent to which specific dimensions of intervention (specificity) rather than competing explanations (nonspuriousness) showed a discernible relationship (dependence) to the dependent measures. A total of 105 studies divided into 14 groups differing in degree of causal inference were critically examined. Eleven major conclusions regarding efficacy are made based on the available data. The state of practice section proposes 11 questions that program administrators and direct service staff might consider in determining the degree to which their own programs operate for an information base that reflects state-of-the-art knowledge. The chapter concludes with a series of 14 recommendations for direct service, research, and policy.

INTRODUCTION

The term *early intervention* has been broadly used to describe efforts designed to prevent or ameliorate developmental or behavioral problems resulting from environmental or biological influences, or both. Early intervention is a term that encompasses a wide range of experimental, educational, and therapeutic treatments, training procedures, and supportive experiences. The extent to which early intervention and other forms of early provision of support are effective in preventing or circumventing the adverse effects of environmental or biological factors in parent, family, and child functioning is the major focus of this review.

A recent paper by Bush and White (1983) identified 64 previous reviews of early intervention efficacy research. Over 10 other reviews have been published since these investigators attempted to integrate the data from the already available early intervention efficacy reviews (e.g., Bailey & Bricker, 1984; Bricker, Bailey, & Bruder, 1984; Dunst, 1986; Halpern, 1984; Honig, 1983; Palmer & Anderson, 1981; Powell, 1982; Ramey, Sparling, Bryant, & Wasik, 1982; Reynolds, Egan & Lerner, 1983; White & Casto, 1985). Considering these recent efforts it might be asked "Why another review?"

Taken together, most previous reviews have analyzed efficacy studies from the standpoint of "Does early intervention work?" without sufficient consideration of the causal or conditional relationships among the independent (intervention), mediational (child, family, etc.), and dependent (outcome) variables and the broader-based contexts in which early intervention occurs. That is, many reviews have addressed the efficacy question in a binary fashion (effective vs. not effective) and have not considered the manner in which other variables interact with the interventions in producing differential effects. Moreover, most previous reviews have failed to consider the role of early intervention in the broader-based ecology of the family and the ecosystems (neighborhood, church, etc.) in which the family is embedded (Bronfenbrenner, 1979).

The present review builds upon previous efforts (e.g., Bricker et al., 1984; Dunst, 1986; Halpern, 1984; Powell, 1982) but differs in a number of important ways. First, broader-based definitions of both early intervention and efficacy are employed. A social systems definition of early intervention is offered as a foundation for identifying the manner in which components of early intervention either individually, or in aggregation, affect changes in the dependent measure(s). Second, a conceptual framework is proposed that permits clearer specification of the relationships among those variables affecting changes in the outcome measures. This framework allows greater specificity in terms of the myriad of factors (both intervention and nonintervention) that affect parent, family, and child functioning. Third, to the extent possible, efficacy is examined in terms of specifiable dimensions of intervention that are related to changes on the outcome measure(s). Fourth, the efficacy of early intervention is examined in terms of its broad-based impacts on parents and families as well as the child. That is, an explicit effort is made to go beyond child progress as the sole indicator of program success toward more ecologically relevant and valid outcome measures.

Following definitions, discussions, and a rationale for the above points, the literature is examined in terms of both state-of-the-art knowledge and state of practice regarding early intervention. The state-of-the-art section examines studies that have investigated factors known to affect child, parent, and family functioning, including both intervention and nonintervention related variables. The state-of-practice section considers the extent to which methods and guidelines for intervention are consistent with our knowledge base concerning the best practices in the field. The paper concludes with a discussion of the limitations of our review and the implications of our findings for research, service delivery, and policy.

Definition of Terms

Early Intervention

Early intervention has generally been defined either at the level of program involvement (i.e., involved vs. not involved) or in terms of the provision of a certain therapeutic or educational treatment. Denhoff (1981) used the term to refer to "programs of enrichment designed to provide developmentally appropriate activities to babies and toddlers who have or who are at risk for a variety of conditions" (p. 32). Bricker, Bailey, and Bruder (1984) defined early intervention as efforts aimed at eliminating existing or anticipated deficits in children during the first 36 months using therapeutic or educational interventions. Caldwell, Bradley, and Elardo (1975) used the term to refer to the manner in which a quality environment facilitates optimal child development.

The above definitions, which are typical of the field, clearly reflect a child-focused emphasis with no explicit acknowledgement or other influences that affect behavior and development. Dunst (1985) recently proposed a social systems definition of early intervention that does consider these broader-based issues. He defined early intervention as the "provision of support to families of infants and young children from members of informal and formal social support networks that impact both *directly* and *indirectly* upon parent, family, and child functioning" (p. 179). Stated differently, early intervention can be thought of as the aggregation of the many different types of help, assistance, services, and so forth provided to families by individuals and groups. In this chapter, two broad categories of intervention will be analyzed: formal intervention provided by an early intervention program (hereafter referred to as *early intervention*) and informal intervention provided by relatives, friends, neighbors, the church, and so forth (hereafter referred to as *social support*).

The above social systems definition of intervention recognizes the fact that early intervention, broadly conceived, includes a wide array of environmental influences that are likely to affect behavior and development. Also addressed by Dunst (1985) is the fact that variables in addition to "early intervention" and "social support" influence parent, family, and child functioning, and therefore require explicit attention as part of documentation of the impact of early intervention. Such attention is especially crucial with regard to conditional relationships between intervention and other independent variables. This broader-based conceptualization of early intervention will be employed in this chapter as a basis for discerning the efficacy of early intervention and other forms of support on parent, family, and child functioning.

Efficacy

The term *efficacy* has generally been used to refer to the extent to which (a) a particular treatment (intervention) is effective in producing either immediate or long-term outcomes and (b) the effects can be attributed to the intervention and not extraneous factors. In this chapter, we use a multidimensional definition of efficacy that places the notion of effectiveness on a continuum that allows discernment of different types and degrees of causal inference regarding the effectiveness of early intervention. Efficacy will be defined as the extent to which provision of early intervention and social support produces positive influences in parent, family, or child functioning in a manner that rules out competing explanations for observed effects. This definition includes three implicit dimensions of efficacy that require comment. The dimensions are dependence, specificity, and nonspuriousness. *Dependence* refers to the degree to which there is a *functional relationship* between the independent and dependent variables. *Specificity* refers to the degree to which there are specific, *identifiable dimensions* of intervention that bear a discernable dependence (relationship) to the dependent variable. *Nonspuriousness* refers to the degree to which factors other than the intervention can be ruled out as principal sources of influence on the dependent variable. Thus, to the extent that specific dimensions of intervention rather than competing explanations show an identifiable relationship to the dependent variable, an intervention may be considered efficacious.

Two other comments need to be made about this definition of efficacy. First, the definition, together with its implicit dimensions, includes those requirements that are generally taken as necessary for causal inferences to be made about the relationship between independent and dependent variables (Cohen & Cohen, 1983; Cook & Campbell, 1979; Kenny, 1979). Second, the definition allows for different degrees of causal inference depending upon how well the requirements are met. Figure 1 graphically shows the relationship between dependence, specificity, and spuriousness. A study that is highly specific regarding the *independent variables* that bear a strong discernible relationship to the *dependent variable(s)* where there are no spurious factors influencing the outcome permits the greatest degree of causal inference. However, in the social and behavioral sciences causal inference is generally a relative rather than an absolute concept (Baltes, Reese & Nesselroade, 1977; Kenny, 1979), and an infinite number of possible types and levels of inference are possible. For example, in a study that examines the effects of participation versus

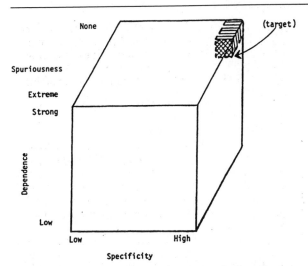

FIGURE 1. Graphic representation of the three dimensions of efficacy.

no participation in early intervention with subjects randomly assigned to treatment and control conditions, dependence and nonspuriousness would be high but specificity low. This set of conditions simply restricts the types of inferences that can be made; in this instance that the intervention was efficacious but that those aspects of the intervention that produced the effects are not discernible.

Dependent Measures

The efficacy of early intervention has been primarily gauged using child progress as the principal measure of program effectiveness (see Dunst & Rheingrover, 1981; Simeonsson et al., 1982; Zigler & Balla, 1982). Bronfenbrenner (1979) noted that the focus on child outcomes as the principal index of program efficacy has resulted in an ecologically restricted view of the goals and purposes of early intervention. Social systems theory suggests the use of both broader-based measures of program effectiveness as well as more ecologically relevant outcome measures (see especially Bronfenbrenner, 1979, chapter 8). A number of investigators have either proposed or employed such expansive measures (Bronfenbrenner, 1979; Dunst, 1986; Lazar & Darlington, 1982; Zigler & Balla, 1982). These include personal (parent) well-being and coping; family integrity; parental attitudes, aspirations, and expectations toward self and child; parent self-concepts and locus-of-control; different dimensions of parent-child interactions (e.g., parenting styles and balance-of-power) (Bronfenbrenner, 1979); child behavior and development (social and adaptive competence, physical health, emotional and motivational development, and engagement levels) (Bailey, Harms, & Clifford, 1983; McWilliam, Trivette, & Dunst, 1985); school-age characteristics of the children (retention in grade, special education vs. regular

class placement); institutional avoidance; child attitudes, values, and aspirations; and community acceptance. To the extent possible, we evaluate the studies reviewed in this chapter in terms of as many broad-based impacts as possible.

Children Served

Four, nonmutually exclusive groups of children are typically served by early intervention programs: those at risk due to environmental factors (e.g., poor conditions of rearing), those at risk due to biological factors (e.g., Down's syndrome), those at risk due to medically-related factors (e.g., prematurity), and those at risk due to family or systemic factors (e.g., parental alcohol or drug abuse).

Children at risk due to environmental factors are youngsters from low SES poverty backgrounds whose conditions of rearing are considered less than optimal. Interventions focus primarily on supplemental enrichment designed to affect changes in intellectual functioning and subsequent school-age performance. The biologically at-risk group is the most heterogeneous, and includes youngsters with diverse handicapping conditions, including cerebral palsy, sensory impairments (blindness, deafness), spina bifida, genetic disorders (e.g., Down's syndrome), brain damage, and mental retardation due to unknown prenatal influences. Interventions with this group tend to focus on enhancement of a wide array of developmental and behavioral competencies (gross motor, language, social-adaptive, cognitive, etc.) designed to reduce the adverse effects of the biological impairments. The medically at-risk group includes children who are low birthweight or premature. Interventions tend to focus on provision of supplemental sensory stimulation designed to facilitate responsiveness to the animate and inanimate environment. The systemic group includes children at risk for abuse, children of an alcohol or drug dependent parent, children of teenage mothers, and parents of children who are retarded or handicapped themselves. Interventions with this group tend to focus on changes in parent and family functioning which in turn is expected to have positive influences on child functioning.

The above is an oversimplification of the types of children served by early intervention programs as well as the types of treatments that the children are provided. The point that needs to be made however is that there are different groups of children with different characteristics being provided different types of interventions as part of their participation in different early intervention programs. The question that needs to be asked is "Do all these differences influence the extent to which the interventions are likely to be effective?" To the extent possible, our review includes a discussion of the manner in which differences in child characteristics affect the nature of the conclusions that can be made about the efficacy of early intervention.

Types of Interventions

A complete description of the types of interventions evaluated in the separate investigations included in our review is beyond the scope of this chapter. Some general information about the interventions is necessary, however, in order to appreciate the types of treatments provided.

Of the 105 studies, 61 or 58% had some type of parental involvement component. The four major types of intervention were cognitive ($N = 60$ [57%]), behavioral ($N = 26$ [25%]), sensory stimulation ($N = 12$ [11%]), and medical, physical, or occupational therapy ($N = 4$ [4%]). Only nine studies (9%) evaluated the extent to which provision of support affected child, parent, or family functioning. Eleven other studies (10%) evaluated the effectiveness of some other types of interventions. The majority of interventions reported within the studies were heterogeneous for treatment type (e.g., cognitive and behavioral treatment combinations).

Taken together, the studies included in this review and analysis covered a wide variety of treatment types. Moreover, even for studies that employed similar theoretical frameworks (e.g., cognitive), there was considerable variability with regard to the manner in which the interventions were conceptualized and implemented. Because of the variability in the treatment types, no attempt was made to contrast the different intervention procedures in order to discern relative efficacy. Rather, we focused on the analysis of the studies based on a set of criteria which permitted logical groupings of studies based on the extent to which certain methodological considerations were addressed as part of the investigations. These are discussed next.

A Paradigmatic Conceptualization of Early Intervention

There is no theory of early intervention, and indeed, for the most part, early intervention has been conceptualized and implemented in an atheoretical manner. Dunst (1986) has argued that the atheoretical nature of early intervention research has resulted in the adoption of a number of assumptions about early intervention that are not entirely tenable and in some cases are faulty. Inasmuch as theories, models, and paradigms are necessary in order to provide a systematic framework for studying the relationship among variables (Baltes et al., 1977; Reese & Overton, 1970), the need for a conceptual framework for conducting and analyzing efficacy studies is clearly indicated.

A simple but useful paradigm for discerning the effects of early intervention is $B = f(A)$ where B is the dependent or outcome variable, A is the independent or treatment variable, and the relationship between the variables is of the form B varies as a function (f) of A. To state this paradigm in intervention terms, changes in parent, family, or child functioning (B) are related to,

vary as a function of, or are otherwise influenced by an intervention (A).

The core paradigm, $B = f(A)$, although useful, needs to be expanded to include variables in addition to A if the full range of influences on B are to be explicated (Baltes et al., 1977; Longstreth, 1968). Accordingly, an expanded paradigm that takes into consideration a wider range of variables affecting B would read: $B = f(I, S, F, C, O. X)$, where I is an early intervention characteristics category (age of entry, intensity of involvement, degree of parent involvement, etc.), S is a social support characteristics category (size of network, degree of helpfulness, reciprocity, etc.), F is a family characteristics category (SES, age, parental attitudes, etc.), C is a child characteristic category (age, level of retardation, temperament, etc.), O is an other explanatory variable category (policy decisions, competency-level of the intervenor, etc.), and X is a set of competing characteristics which pose threats to internal validity (see Cook & Campbell, 1979). By no means do these variables constitute an exhaustive list. They only serve to illustrate the myriad of influences that impact upon parent, family, and child functioning (see especially Bronfenbrenner, 1979; Dunst, 1985).

Following Baltes (1973), our expanded paradigm may be taken one step further and be expressed in terms of the optimization of development. It can be written as: Changes in $B = f(I, S, F, C, O, X)$, where the paradigm now acknowledges the fact that manipulation of the variables on the right side of the equation should produce changes in the level, magnitude, value, and so forth of B. Consistent with our definition of efficacy, the paradigm provides a basis for discerning the relationship among variables; that is, the manner in which formal early intervention (I) and social support (S) affect parent, family, and child functioning in relationship to other variables that are also known to affect behavioral and developmental outcomes (F, C, O, X).

Causal Analysis

Halpern (1984) has argued that inadequacies in causal modeling have in some instances contributed to the inability to document the effectiveness of early intervention. The $B = f(A)$ paradigm provides a useful framework for investigating the causal relationships among variables since identification of causal linkages is an explicit objective of explanatory scientific research. Causal linkages (dependencies) may be either proximal or distal. Proximal influences are ones in which A causes B in a clearly identifiable fashion. Distal influences are ones in which A causes B through C where C functions as a mediating variable.

While complete explication of the relationship among variables is the goal of science, in a practical sense causal inference is relative rather than absolute (Baltes et al., 1977). There is never likely to be the "definitive" study of the efficacy of early intervention, and although the $B = f(A)$ paradigm does imply a cause-effect relationship, the paradigm actually states only that some discernible relationship can be explicated between different variables. Consequently, degree of causal inference needs to be considered along a continuum where explication is the goal but where discerning a noncausal or indirect relationship may in some instances be all that can be expected. It is for this reason that efficacy cannot be treated as an either-or notion but one that varies in type, degree, and kind.

Conditional Relationships

The notion of unconditional and conditional relationships is intricately related to causal analysis. An unconditional relationship is one that holds true in *all* cases and instances. Whatever the form or degree of the relationship, it remains the same regardless of child diagnosis, parental locus of control, SES, and so forth. That is, the relationship between A and B is the same for different treatments, different groups of children, and so forth. In analysis of variance terms, unconditional relationships are referred to as main effects.

Conditional relationships are ones that hold true in only *certain* cases and instances. The relationship between A and B is said to depend upon a third factor (C) where the form and degree of relationship between A and B differs at different levels of C. Thus the B = f (A) relationship may be quite different from home versus center based intervention, environmentally versus biologically at-risk infants, low vs. middle SES families, and so forth. That is, the relationship between A and B is different depending upon types of treatments, children, settings, and so forth. In analysis of variance terms, conditional relationships are referred to as interaction effects.

Complete explication of the relationship among variables requires adequate tests of conditional relationships. In our Changes in B = f(I, S, F, C, O, X) paradigm, tests of conditional relationships between I and S, and F, C, O, and X are necessary in order to discern whether I and S have general (unconditional) or interactive (conditional) effects on B.

Validity Threats

Cook and Campbell (1979) provide an extensive discussion of the manner in which the validity of causal inferences is threatened by factors which have not been adequately considered in the design and implementation of intervention studies. First, the extent to which intervention and treatment related variables may be implicated as causes for changes in B is determined, in part, by the experimental or statistical control of competing explanations. Adequate control over alternative interpretations is referred to as the *internal validity* of an experiment (Cook & Campbell, 1979). Thus, in our basic paradigm Changes in B = f(I, S, F, C, O, X), the ability to conclude that I had main, interactional, or

transactional effects in B not only requires that the conditional relationships between I, S, F, C, and O be analyzed, but that there be adequate control over the X variables which affect spuriousness. Threats to internal validity include history, maturation, testing, instrumentation, regression, selection, and attrition as well as other factors (see Cook & Campbell, 1979).

A second type of validity threat has to do with the types of inferences that can be made about covariation based on statistical tests of significance. This is referred to as *statistical validity* (Cook & Campbell, 1979). Threats to statistical validity include low statistical power, violations of assumptions of statistical tests, unreliability of the dependent measures, inconsistencies in implementation of the treatment, and factors (S, F, C, O) other than the treatment (I) that influence changes in B. The latter condition produces an inflated error term which reduces the probability of documenting program impact when statistical analyses are performed (see especially Dunst, 1985, 1986).

A third type of validity, and one especially important with regard to early intervention, is *construct validity*. To the extent that different but conceptually similar interventions have similar effects, and conceptually different interventions have divergent (differential) effects, the notion of intervention is said to have construct validity. A study with a high degree of construct validity is one in which there is (a) considerable specificity with regard to those dimensions of the intervention that produce changes in B and (b) explicit tests of conditional relationships between these dimensions and other explanatory variables.

A fourth type of validity is referred to as *external validity* (Bracht & Glass, 1968; Cook & Campbell, 1979). External validity refers to the extent to which generalizations about the intervention can be made across persons (intervenors and children/families), settings, and dependent measures.

> The best way known (to design a study with a high degree of external validity) is to specify as explicitly as possible the potential domain of observations to which one would like to generalize and then to obtain a representative sample from it (Baltes et al., 1977, p. 49).

In intervention research, however, randomized selection is generally not possible, and external validity is typically addressed through tests of conditional relationships that involve the domain (e.g., different subgroups of children) to which one would like to generalize.

As noted by Cook and Campbell (1979), internal and statistical validity are interrelated as are construct and external validity. Control over threats to internal validity reduces variance due to extraneous factors whereas control over threats to statistical validity reduces error variance, both of which increase the probability of statements of causal inference. Establishing the construct validity of similar or different interventions increases specificity with regard to the parameters of intervention that have main or differential effects, and control over threats to external validity permits generalization to be made about which types and forms of intervention will work with what persons, in which settings, and have what effects.

Summary

In this section we have come the long way around to the point that the extent to which early intervention is efficacious depends on the simultaneous attention to various aspects of the conduct of an efficacy study. A causal analysis model of efficacy was proposed as a basis for evaluating the degree to which cause-effect inferences can be made regarding the impact of both early intervention and social support on parent, family, and child functioning. This model was placed within a paradigmatic framework that permitted (a) specification of factors affecting behavioral and developmental change, (b) analysis of the extent to which treatments interact with other explanatory factors, and (c) control for validity threats. We believe that our paradigmatic conceptualization and emphasis on causal analysis provides the type of framework necessary for adequate evaluation of the impact of early intervention. We now use this framework as a basis for discerning (within the constraints of the narrative descriptions provided in research reports) the extent to which statements about causal inference can be made regarding early intervention and other forms of support.

State of the Art

The purpose of this section is to review the literature in terms of the *types* of causal inferences that can be made about the efficacy of early intervention. Major emphasis is placed on specifying *degree* of inference while avoiding the dichotomy effective versus not effective. Moreover, an attempt is made to be as specific as possible about the myriad factors that affect parent, family, and child functioning. However, because there are over 100 studies included in our review, extensive study-by-study analysis is beyond the scope of this chapter. Consequently, we analyzed the studies using a causal analysis categorization in order to glean information regarding the extent to which causal inferences can be made about those factors affecting changes in the dependent measures. The major criterion for inclusion of a study in our review was that the interventions began between birth and three years of age for the majority of children in the programs. In instances where there were multiple reports of the same program or investigation, we included the most up-to-date one or the report that was most complete in terms of the description and analysis of the variables most germane to our paradigmatic framework.

In order to make sense out of the efficacy literature, a classification scheme was used that organized studies

into one of three categories of causal inference: low, low to moderate, and moderate to high. Assignment of studies to these categories was based on specific characteristics of the investigations, including: (a) the degree of specificity of early intervention-related variables, (b) assessment of the impact of other forms of support, (c) adequacy of control of family and child characteristics, including tests of conditional relationships, (d) how well threats to internal validity (spuriousness) were assessed and controlled, (e) the ecological relevance of the dependent measures, and (f) the degree of dependence between the independent and dependent variables. Each of these factors were rated on a five-point scale in order to provide a quantitative basis for discerning the overall degree of causal inference (see Appendix for a description of the rating scales). The five study dimensions were independently rated by two scores for all 105 studies. The percentages of agreement were as follows: specificity (89%), social support (96%), child and family characteristics (90%), internal validity (96%), dependent measures (95%), and dependence (89%).

Specificity was rated in terms of the extent to which specific intervention related factors (age of entry, length of involvement, degree or type of parental involvement, theoretical bases, etc.) were examined in relationship to changes in the dependent measures. Social support was rated in terms of the extent to which other types of "interventions" (formal and informal) were assessed in terms of their contributions to changes in the dependent measures. Family and child characteristics were rated in terms of the extent to which adequate descriptive information was provided about the program participants and the extent to which conditional relationships were examined between child, family, and intervention-related variables. Internal validity was rated in terms of the degree to which competing explanations might account for observed changes in the dependent measure. Dependent measures were rated in terms of the extent to which broad-based outcomes were employed and the outcomes had ecological validity. Dependence was rated in terms of the degree to which there was a functional relationship between the intervention and outcome measures. Studies rated highly on *all* dimensions provide the greatest degree of causal inference and those rated low the least amount of causal inference.

Our classification scheme resulted in 14 separate groups of studies within the three causal inference categories. This scheme is shown graphically in Figure 2. The 14 groups are roughly ordered on a continuum from low to high causal inference. We now turn to the description of the analyses used to assign individual studies to the separate groups and causal categories.

Low Causal Inference

The studies that are included in this category generally permit the lowest degree of causal inference, but nonetheless permit certain statements to be made regarding

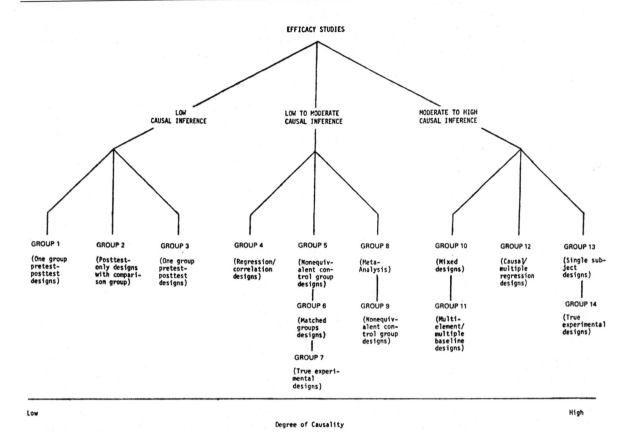

FIGURE 2. Graphic representation of the 14 groups of studies according to degree of causal inference. (NOTES.—See the text for a description of the characteristics of the studies within groups that were used for judging the relative degrees of causal inference. Studies that employed similar research designs but which were judged differently varied according to how well the criteria for the five study dimensions were met—See Tables 1, 2, and 3.)

the relationships between the independent and dependent variables. Table 1 shows selected characteristics of the studies as well as the ratings each received on the six dimensions permitting causal inference. Overall, the studies received low ratings on the seven study dimensions. Differences in individual groups of studies, however, do permit some inferences regarding the differential effects of early intervention. It was possible to discern three major subgroups of studies within this category.

Group I

Taken together, the 13 studies included in this category are ones that are rated the lowest on all six dimensions of the study characteristics (see Table 1). All of the studies used pre-experimental pretest-posttest designs (Cook & Campbell, 1979). A test or measurement was obtained (O_1), the subjects provided an intervention (I), and then at a later time a posttest measurement was taken (O_2). The major assumption of this design is that

gains or changes between O_1 and O_2 are due primarily to the treatment (I).

A number of studies included only biologically at-risk children (Bagnato & Neisworth, 1980; Ford, 1978; Jelinek & Flamboe, 1979; Rottman, 1979; Safford, Gregg Schneider & Sewell, 1976; Wiedar & Hicks, 1970; Wolery & Dyk, 1985; Zeitlin, 1981); several other studies included both biologically and environmentally at-risk children (Hutinger, 1978; Kaplan & Atkins, 1978; Shearer & Shearer, 1972); and one study included biologically, environmentally, and medically at-risk children (Nielsen et al., 1975). Table 1 shows the diagnosis of the children included in each individual study.

Specificity. All of the studies defined the interventions at the level of program involvement. Some studies provided descriptive information regarding the types, frequency, form, and so forth of the interventions, but none attempted to assess the extent to which specific

265

TABLE 1

Studies That Permitted Low Causal Inference

Study	Child Characteristics[a]		Intervention Characteristics[b]				Study Characteristics[c]					
	Risk Category	Child Diagnosis	Theoretical Focus	Intervention Type	Intervention Target	Outcome Measure	Specificity	Social Support	Child & Family Characteristics	Internal Validity	Dependent Measure	Dependence
GROUP 1:												
Bagnato & Neisworth (1980)	N	NS	N	N	G,S,C,M,L	IQ,GD	1	1	1	1	1	1
Ford (1978)	B	DS,CP	N	C,B,P	G,S,C,M,B,L	GD	1	2	2	2	1	1
Hutinger (1978)	E,B	NS	N	C,M,P,S	G,S,C,M,L,A	LA,FF,PS,HS,GD	1	2	1	2	1	1
Jelinek & Flamboe (1979)	E,M,B	NS	N	C,P	G,S,C,M,L,A	IQ,FF,AP,GD	1	2	1	1	2	1
Kaplan & Atkins (1978)	E,M,B	DS,CP,VI,MI,OT	N	C,P	G,M,L,A	2	2	2	1	1	1	1
Neilsen et al. (1975)	E,M,B	DS,CP,PM,MI,AU	C	C,B,P	G,M,L,A,Y	IQ,GD	1	1	2	2	2	1
Revill & Blunden (1979)	N	NS	N	C,P	C,M,L,S,A	GD	1	1	1	1	1	1
Rottman (1979)	B	VI	N	C,P	G,S,C,M,B,L,A	SF	1	1	1	2	2	1
Safford et al. (1976)	M,B	CP,MI,OT	N	Y	Y	IQ,MO,LA	1	1	1	1	1	1
Shearer & Shearer (1972)	E,M,B	DS,VI,HI,MI,OT	N	C	C,S,C,M,L,A	IQ,GD	1	1	1	1	1	1
Wiedar & Hicks (1970)	B	CP,MI	N	C,P,C	G,S,C,M,P	SF,FF,GD	2	3	1	1	2	1
Wolery & Dyk (1985)	NS	NS	N	C,P	G	IQ,GD	2	1	1	2	1	1
Zeitlin (1981)	E,B	VI,MI,OT	C	C,P,O	G,P	LA,SF,GD	2	2	1	1	2	1
GROUP 2:												
Adelson & Fraiberg (1974)	B	VI	C	C,P,Y	G,S,C,M,A,Y	GD	1	3	2	1	1	2
Hanson & Schwartz (1978)	B	DS	N	C,P	G	GD	1	1	3	1	1	2
Hayden & Dmitriev (1975)	B	DS	N	C,P	G,S,C,M,L,A	GD	1	1	2	1	1	2
Hayden & Haring (1977)	B	DS	N	C,P	G,S,C,M,L,A	GD	1	1	2	1	1	2
Zausmer et al. (1972)	B	DS	N	C,P,Y	M,L,A,Y,O,P	MD	1	1	1	1	1	2
GROUP 3:												
Bagnato & Neisworth (1985)	B,O	NS	N	P,O	G,S,C,M,L,A	GD	3	1	3	3	2	1
Bailey & Bricker (1985)	E,B	NS	N	C,P	G	IQ,GD,FF	1	1	3	1	3	1
Barna et al. (1980)	E,B	DS,CP,VI,OT	N	C,P	G	GD	2	2	3	1	1	2
Bricker & Sheehan (1981)	E,M,B	DS,CP,VI,HI,PM,MI,OT	N	D,P,S	G,S,C,M,L,A,O,P	IQ,GD	1	2	3	2	1	2
Clunies-Ross (1979)	B	DS	N	C,B,P	G,S,C,M,B,L,A,O	GD	2	1	2	1	1	2
Goodman et al. (1984)	E,B	AU,EN,NS	N	C,P	G	GD	1	2	3	2	1	2
Gordon (1977)	E,B	CP,MI,OT	C	C	G,S,C,M,L,A,O	LA	1	1	3	1	1	2
Hewitt et al. (1983)	E,B	DS,NS	N	C,P	G,S,C,M,L,A	GD	1	1	3	1	1	2
Macy et al. (1983)	E,B	NS	N	C,P	G	AP,GD	1	1	2	2	2	2
Mahoney & Snow (1983)	B	DS	C	C,B,P	L	IQ,LA,GD	1	1	2	1	1	2
Shapiro et al. (1977)	E,B	NS	C	C,P	G	GD	1	1	3	2	1	2

[a] *Risk Category*: E = Environmental, M = Medical, B = Biological, O = Other, N = Nonspecified. *Child Diagnosis*: DS = Down's Syndrome, CP = Cerebral palsied, VI = Visually impaired, PM = Premature/low birthweight, MI = Motor impairment, AU = Autistic, EN = Environmental, OT = Other, NS = Not specified.

[b] *Theoretical Focus*: T = Theoretical basis stated, C = Conceptual basis stated; N = No theoretical or conceptual basis stated. *Intervention Type*: C = Cognitive, B = Behavioral, M = Medical, S = Social support, Y = Sensory stimulation, O = Other, N = Not stated, P = Parent involvement. *Intervention Target*: G = General development, S = Social development, C = Cognitive development, M = Physical/motor development, L = Communication/language development, A = Adaptive functioning, B = Behavioral/operant, Y = Sensory, O = Other child development, P = Parent/family functioning. (Note: For those studies which provided insufficient information for determining the intervention target, the target was inferred from the outcome measure(s) used in the study.) *Outcome Measure*: IQ = Intellectual functioning, PI = Piagetian/cognitive functioning, MD = Motor development, LA = Language development, GD = Global development, SF = Social functioning, OB = Operant behavior, AP = Academic performance, HS = Child health status, PS = Parenting skills, SS = Social support, FF = Family functioning.

[c] Each study characteristic was rated on a five point scale (see Appendix) where 1 = little or no concern for the study dimension and 5 = considerable concern/attention to the study dimension.

aspects of the interventions were related to the dependent measures. As noted by Dunst (1986), defining the interventions at the level of program involvement implicity assumes that (a) the amount of intervention is the same for *all* program participants and (b) that all children, regardless of their particular at-risk status, benefit equally from participation in the early intervention program. Neither assumption is entirely tenable. Moreover, in none of the studies was there a single, operationally defined treatment. Rather, the interventions consisted of a variety of parent and/or child-level interventions that were generally provided concurrently to the target populations. Consequently, outcomes are confounded with the different treatments, and thus are threats to construct validity (Cook & Campbell, 1979).

Social support. A number of studies considered the possibility that provision or mediation of support to the families by the program might impact upon parent, family, and child functioning (Ford, 1978; Hutinger, 1978; Jelinek & Flamboe, 1979; Kaplan & Atkins, 1978; Wiedar & Hicks, 1970; Zeitlin, 1981), but only one study specifically examined the manner in which parent behavior was influenced by the support services (Wiedar & Hicks, 1970). None of the studies considered the extent to which provision of formal or informal support from persons or agencies outside the early intervention program might have impacted upon parent, family, and child functioning.

Child and family characteristics. The possibility that child or family characteristics might influence changes in the dependent measures was not assessed in any of the studies. Moreover, basic descriptive information about the children and families was often not provided. None of the studies included tests of conditional relationships in order to assess the extent to which there may have been differential influences of the early interventions. Thus, little can be inferred about which types of children and families with what types of characteristics were most or least likely to benefit from participation in the early intervention programs.

Internal validity. The majority of studies fared poorly in terms of control over competing explanations for pretest-posttest differences (see especially Dunst, 1986; Dunst & Rheingrover, 1981). *History* cannot be ruled out because any number of events other than the treatment may have affected pretest-posttest differences (e.g., other forms of support affecting child behavior: see Cochran and Brassard, 1979; Dunst, 1985). *Maturation* is an especially strong rival explanation. On the average, the time between the pretests and posttests was over 6 months. This is ample time for biological changes to be manifested, especially since the majority of subjects were infants, and maturational changes are more rapid during the first 2 years of life. In a number of studies, the methods used to assess progress either statistically or methodologically attempted to control maturational (age) effects (Bagnato & Neisworth, 1980; Jelinek & Flamboe, 1979; Zeitlin, 1981), and consequently permit greater assurance that maturation is a less plausible explanation for observed differences.

Neither testing or instrumentation were adequately controlled in the majority of studies. *Testing* is a potential problem in almost all the studies because the activities that constituted the interventions were the items

from the test used to measure progress. Consequently, a test-training effect cannot be dismissed as a factor contributing to observed differences between the pre- and post-tests. *Instrumentation* is a problem in nearly all the studies because the persons administering the outcome measures were the same persons doing the interventions. Thus, their awareness of the purposes of the study, increased familiarity with the children, and/or test experience gained between the measurement occasions may have affected pretest-posttest differences that had little to do with the interventions.

Dependent measures. In all instances, child progress was used as the only or primary measure of program success. The specific measures of child progress included developmental quotients, developmental rates, developmental ages, and behavioral ratings. All of the studies reported that the children made significant progress from the pretest to posttest, and that the amount of progress was generally greater than would have been expected without provision of services from the early intervention program. This conclusion was based either on statistical analysis of the pretest-posttest differences (Hutinger, 1978; Jelinek & Flamboe, 1979; Neilsen et al., 1975; Rottman, 1979; Shearer & Shearer, 1972; Wiedar & Hicks, 1970; Zeitlin, 1981) or analysis by inspection (Bagnato & Neisworth, 1980; Ford, 1978: Kaplan & Atkins, 1978; Safford et al., 1976). Only one study specifically assessed parental behaviors (Wiedar & Hicks, 1970). The investigators reported several differences in maternal attitudes between the pretest and posttest.

Dependence. The extent to which there were functional relationships between the independent and dependent variables cannot be directly determined in any of the studies. All of the interventions were defined at the level of program involvement, and thus specify conditions where participation "loosely" provided opportunities for affecting behavior change. However, the manner in which these opportunities mediated or caused change were not readily apparent. Consequently, no discernible causal relationships can explicitly be specified, and the types of inference that can be made are quite limited. The major conclusion that can be made about the findings from these studies is that participants in the early intervention programs generally show significant developmental progress, statistically speaking, but that the factors associated with the nature of relationships between early intervention and the observed changes are not directly discernible.

GROUP 2

The five studies in this group all used pre-experimental nonequivalent groups posttest-only designs. In

267

these studies, the treatments were provided, and then on an ex post facto basis, a comparison group was located for the purpose of establishing the effects of the intervention. All the studies included biologically at-risk children. The subjects in Adelson and Fraiberg (1974) study were visually impaired children. All of the other studies included children with Down's syndrome.

Specificity. In all the studies in this group, the interventions were defined at the level of program involvement. Both child- and parent-level services were offered, but no attempt was made to specify the parameters of involvement. Consequently, the assumption was made that all participants received similar "levels" of treatment, and that the degree, amount, and type of involvement was the same for all the children and families.

Social support. Only Adelson and Fraiberg (1974) explicitly recognized the influence of other forms of support in affecting child progress, and the extent to which parent-level needs might influence provision of facilitative child-level experiences. However, no explicit attempt was made to consider the impact of these factors. None of the studies recognized or assessed the potential contributions of extraprogram forms of support (informal or formal).

Child and family characteristics. A partial control over threats to internal validity when using a pre-experimental, nonequivalent groups posttest-only design is the systematic establishment of the fact that the different groups are similar to begin with in terms of important child and family characteristics. A number of studies provided descriptive information about the children and families, but none included comparative analyses on these background variables as a basis for establishing the similarity of the groups. None of the studies included tests of conditional relationships, and consequently it cannot be determined if the effects reported varied as a function of child or family characteristics, or other variables.

Internal validity. The extent to which differences between the experimental and contrast groups can be attributed to the interventions is questionable for two major reasons. The strongest rival explanation is history. Because the subjects in the nonintervention groups were tested in some cases 10 or more years before the intervention groups, the observed differences may be due simply to cohort effects (Baltes et al., 1977). Evidence for this interpretation comes from a study by Connolly (1979) who found that during the past 50 years the IQs of Down's syndrome children have tended to increase somewhat linearly even without the benefits of early intervention. Inasmuch as all but one study included Down's syndrome infants as subjects, this threat is especially strong. The second most plausible explanation for the observed differences is selection. Since the subjects were not assigned to groups on a random basis, there is no assurance that the groups were in fact similar on important explanatory variables. For instance, if the parents of the intervention group specifically sought out services whereas the control group subjects did not, differential selection could account for the observed differences. Dunst (1986) and Dunst and Rheingrover (1981) discuss other threats to the internal validity of Group 2 type studies.

Dependent measures. The dependent measures in the Group 2 studies included the age of attainment of fine motor and gross motor landmarks (Adelson & Fraiberg, 1974; Hanson & Schwarz, 1978; Zausmer, Pueschel & Shea, 1972), developmental ages, and rates of development. All of the investigators concluded that the experimental subjects' development was advanced relative to the contrast group. None of the studies employed family-level measures or more ecologically relevant measures of program success.

Dependence. All of the investigations received low ratings in terms of dependence inasmuch as the interventions were defined at the level of program involvement and thus the factors that were related to group differences are not readily apparent. Based on information provided in the reports of the studies, there is no way to draw direct causal inferences about what exactly it was that produced the observed changes. The major conclusion that can be made about the findings from these studies is that participants in the early intervention programs generally showed rates and patterns of development that reflect some advantage over nonparticipants but that the factors that are related to group differences are not directly discernible.

GROUP 3

The 11 Group 3 studies used pre-experimental pretest-posttest designs, but where several attempts were made to assess the manner in which outcomes differed as a function of other variables. This increased the types of causal inferences that could be made about those factors that affected observed changes. Table 1 shows the ratings that the studies received on the six study characteristics. Two of the studies included only biologically at-risk Down's syndrome infants (Clunies-Ross, 1979; Mahoney & Snow, 1983), one study included biologically and medically at-risk infants (Bagnato & Neisworth, 1985), while all the remaining studies included both biologically and environmentally at-risk infants.

Specificity. The extent to which age of entry affected pretest-posttest differences was examined in two studies (Barna, Bidder, Gray, Clements, & Gardner, 1980; Clunies-Ross, 1979). Both investigations reported that overall rates of development did not differ as a function of entry age, although this finding must be interpreted with caution. First, neither study "tested" for an age effect using test occasion (pretest-posttest) by age of entry repeated measures analysis of variance design. Visual inspection of the graph in the Clunies-Ross (1979) report shows what appears to be an interaction between the treatment variables. Second, the method used by Barna et al. (1980) to determine the effects of age of entry on amount of progress is highly questionable. Gains in mental age (MA) between the pretest and posttests were used as the dependent measure without taking into consideration either the children's entry levels of development nor the amount of time between the test occasions (range = 5 to 25 months). Given the above problems, it is difficult to draw any firm conclusions about the extent to which age of entry may have been related to developmental change. However, Clunies-Ross (1979) did find that the level of performance of an early entry group (less than 12 months) was much greater than for those children entering after 24 months of age. That is, although it cannot be determined whether or not the amount of progress made by the children per month in the program differed as a function of age of entry, the degree of delay was much greater for children who entered after their second birthday.

Social support. The potential contributions of social support on parent, family, and child functioning was recognized in a number of investigations, but no explicit attempt was made to assess the degree to which observed differences may have been affected by provisions of outside program support.

Child and family characteristics. Taken together, the Group 3 studies generally provided adequate information about the diagnostic and developmental characteristics of the children, and most of the studies assessed the differential relationships between child characteristics and effects of the interventions. Only one study provided adequate information on the parents and families (Bricker & Sheehan, 1981).

The extent to which pretest-posttest differences varied as a function of diagnostic group was assessed in three studies. Barna et al. (1980) found considerable differences in amount of child progress depending upon the diagnosis of the children. Environmentally at-risk children manifested the highest rate of development, whereas cerebral palsied and visually impaired children showed the slowest rates of development. The rates of development of Down's syndrome infants and children with developmental delays of unknown etiology were

about the same but much lower than that for the environmentally at-risk group. Hewitt, Newcombe and Bidder (1983) and Bagnato and Neisworth (1985) also reported differential influences of early intervention depending upon diagnosis. However, only Bagnato and Neisworth actually conducted the appropriate type of statistical analysis that permitted inferences to be made about conditional relationships. Bagnato and Neisworth found that interdisciplinary intervention with acquired brain injured infants was more efficanious compared to such interventions with infants with cogenital brain damage.

Several investigations examined the extent to which degree of severity affected child progress. Bricker and Sheehan (1981) and Bailey and Bricker (1985) examined pretest-posttest differences for five subgroups of children (normal, at-risk, mild, moderate, and severe) on a number of dependent measures, and found that although differences were generally statistically significant, amount of progress covaried with group membership. The less severe the degree of impairment the more progress that was likely to be made. Gordon (1977) examined the amount of progress of three groups of children differing in their degree of severity: low, median, and high. Preliminary analyses found no significant differences between the three groups on either child (chronological age, sex, diagnosis, motor dysfunctions, sensory impairments) or family (SES, race) characteristics. Gordon did find differential effects in terms of child progress (i.e., the less severe the impairment, the more progress).

Macy, Solomon, Schoen, and Galey (1983) examined the pretest-posttest difference for three groups of children (mild/at-risk, moderate, and severely handicapped), and found "generally consistent treatment effects across the range of handicap involvement" (p. 448). However, as was the case with the Barna et al. (1980) and Hewitt et al. (1983) studies, inferences about conditional and unconditional relationships in this study was based on visual inspection of the data and not appropriate statistical analyses.

Goodman, Cecil and Barker (1984) found no differential treatment effects for different diagnostic groups, although level of intellectual functioning at the pretest assessment was significantly correlated with posttest scores. The less handicapped the child at the pretest, the higher the child's IQ was at the posttest. Neither child sex or SES was correlated with amount of child progress.

Both Mahoney and Snow (1983) and Shapiro, Gordon & Neiditch (1977) assessed the degree to which initial levels of developmental functioning affected pretest-posttest differences. In both studies, MA at program entry was significantly correlated with amount of child progress. Higher functioning children were more likely to demonstrate the greatest amount of progress. This is another way of saying that less delayed youngsters were more likely to make the greatest developmental progress.

Internal validity. The same threats to validity discussed for the Group 1 studies apply here as well, most notably history, maturation, testing, and instrumentation. Taken together, the Group 3 studies generally did a poor job of controlling for validity threats.

Dependent measures. The primary measure of program success used in these studies was child progress. Rates of development, developmental ages, developmental quotients, and behavior ratings were employed as outcome measures. All the studies reported significant gains in pretest-posttest performance based on either statistical analysis of the data (Bricker & Sheehan, 1981; Goodman et al., 1984; Hewitt et al., 1983; Macy et al., 1983; Mahoney & Snow, 1983; Shapiro et al., 1977) or visual inspection of the patterns of findings (Barna et al., 1980; Clunies-Ross, 1979; Gordon, 1977). Only Bailey and Bricker (1985) reported descriptive outcomes regarding parental satisfaction and program cost.

Dependence. Taken together, the relationship between the intervention-related and dependent variables are defined at a global and nonspecific level. For the studies that did examine age of entry as a mediating variable, the most that can be said is that early entry provides earlier opportunities for affecting behavior change, but that it is not possible to discern the manner in which early entry is functionally related to observed changes. The major conclusion that can be made about the findings from these studies is that participants in the early intervention programs generally show significant developmental progress, statistically speaking, and (a) progress can be expected to vary as a function of diagnosis and degree and severity but (b) the extent to which early intervention related factors are associated with the observed changes is not directly discernible.

Low to Moderate Causal Inference

The studies included in this category generally permit stronger statements (inferences) to be made about cause-effects relationships between the independent and dependent variables. Table 2 shows the ratings that each of the studies received on the six dimensions of the study characteristics. Greater degree of causal inference are possible because increased attention was paid to important aspects of the studies which increased the extent to which the factors related to observed changes could be discerned.

Group 4

The five studies in this group differ from all the preceding investigations in one important respect. In contrast to asking the question "Did early intervention or

other types of treatments have a positive effect on parent, family, or child functioning?", the question that was posed was "What factors are related to significant changes in child functioning?" This type of study is instructive from a causal analysis perspective. To the extent that manipulatable factors are related to desired outcomes [B = f(A)], this suggests the manner in which changes in A will affect changes in B.

One methodological point about the studies in this group. Unlike studies to be discussed later in our review (Group 12) which used theoretical, conceptual, and/or causal model for discerning relationships between the independent and dependent variables, the Group 4 studies were carried out with little concern for the manner in which there might be some priority ordering in terms of the cumulative contributions of different sets of variables.

The Group 4 studies included biologically at-risk (Bricker & Dow, 1980; Simeonsson & Huntington, 1981), environmentally at-risk (Murray, 1977), and both biologically and environmentally at-risk (Brassell, 1974, 1977) children.

Specificity. Bricker and Dow (1980) specifically examined the extent to which both intervention and nonintervention related variables affected program success. The amount of progress made by 40 severely handicapped children participating in a center-based early intervention program was related to seven predictor variables: length of enrollment in the program, child sex, degree of parental involvement, program attendance, mother's employment status (working vs. nonworking), age at which the pretest data were collected, and the child's developmental levels of performance at the time of the pretest. The dependent measures were the four Uniform Performance Assessment System (UPAS) developmental domains: preacademic, communication, gross motor, and social/self-help. Separate multiple regression analyses were performed for each developmental area as well as for an overall measure of developmental status. Order of entry of the predictor variables into each analysis was done in a stepwise manner without regard to any a priori predictions about the relative importance of the independent variables; that is, the order of entry was dictated entirely by which variable accounted for the largest proportion of the variance, the second largest proportion, and so on.

For all five dependent measures, developmental status at the pretest was the best predictor of posttest scores. Children with initially higher scores were the same individuals who made the most progress. Thus, progress was differentially affected by the developmental status of the children. Age of the child at the beginning of the study was the second best predictor, accounting for a significant amount of variance on all but the preacademic subscale. Children who began receiving early intervention at a young age were the same individuals who made the most progress. This

TABLE 2

Studies That Permitted Low to Moderate Causal Inference

| Study | Child Characteristics[a] | | Intervention Characteristics[b] | | | | Study Characteristics[c] | | | | | |
	Risk Category	Child Diagnosis	Theoretical Focus	Intervention Type	Intervention Target	Outcome Measure	Specificity	Social Support	Child & Family Characteristics	Internal Validity	Dependent Measure	Dependence
GROUP 4:												
Brassell (1974)	E,B,	NS	N	C,P	G,S,C,M, B,L,A,Y	IQ	2	1	4	2	1	2
Brassell (1977)	E,B	NS	N	C,P	G,S,C,M, B,L,A,Y	GD	2	1	4	2	1	2
Bricker & Dow (1980)	E,M,B	NS	C	C,P	G,S,C,M, L,A	GD	4	1	3	2	1	2
Murray (1977)	E	EN	N	C,P	G	IQ	3	1	4	2	1	2
Simeonsson & Huntingdon (1981)	B	NS	C	O	O	SF,GD	1	1	4	2	1	2
GROUP 5:												
Brassell & Dunst (1978)	E,B	NS	C	C,P	C	PI	1	1	3	3	1	3
Brinkworth (1973)	B	DS	C	P,Y	S,M,Y,O	GD	1	1	2	3	1	2
Brinkworth (1975)	B	DS	C	C,P,Y	G,C,M,L,Y	GD	1	1	1	2	1	2
Connolly & Russell (1976)	B	DS	N	C,P	G,S,C,M, L,A,Y	GD	1	1	3	3	1	3
Cunningham et al. (1982)	B	DS	N	C,P	G	GD,FF	1	1	4	3	2	3
Dunst et al. (1983)	E,M,B	NS	C	C,G,P,S,Y	ALL	IQ,SF,GD	1	4	4	3	4	3
Leib et al. (1980)	M	PM	N	Y	Y	IQ,HS	3	1	4	3	3	3
Lovaas (1982)	B	AU	N	C,B,P	S,B,L,A	AP	4	1	3	3	3	4
Ludlow & Allen (1979)	B	DS	N	C,P	G,S,C,M, L,A,P	IQ,FF,AP, GD	1	1	3	3	3	3
Peniston (1972)	E,M,B	NS	N	C,B,P	G,S,C,M, B,	IQ	1	1	1	3	1	2
Piper & Pless (1980)	B	DS	N	C,P	G	GD	1	1	3	3	3	3
GROUP 6:												
Aronson & Fallstrom (1977)	B	DS	N	C	G,S,C,M, L,A,Y	GD	3	1	2	3	1	3
Bidder et al. (1975)	B	DS	N	C,B,P	G,S,M,B, L,A,P	GD	1	1	2	3	1	3
Bromwich & Parmelee (1979)	M	PM	C	C,P	S,C,L	IQ,SF,PS	1	4	3	3	3	2
Carlsen (1975)	B	CP	N	P	M,L	IQ	1	1	2	4	1	2
Chee et al. (1978)	B	CP	N	Y	M,Y	MD,HS	1	1	1	3	1	3
Harris (1981)	B	DS	N	O	M	MD,GD	3	1	2	4	1	1
Ottenbacher et al. (1981)	B	CP,MI	N	Y	M,Y	MD, HS	2	1	3	4	1	2
Sandow & Clarke (1978)	E,B	DS,CP,NS, EN	N	C,P	G,S,L,A	IQ	3	2	3	3	1	1
Sandow et al. (1981)	E,B	DS,CP,NS, EN	N	C,P	G,S,L,A	IQ	3	2	4	3	1	2
Sellick & Over (1980)	B	CP	N	Y	M,Y	GD	1	1	1	4	1	1
GROUP 7:												
Kantner et al. (1976)	B	DS	N	Y	Y	MD,GD	1	1	1	3	1	3
Kelly (1982)	B	NS	C	B,P	O	SF	1	1	2	3	3	4
Sandler et al. (1983)	B	NS	N	B,P	O	SF,FF,GD	3	2	1	3	3	3
Scherzer et al. (1976)	B	CP	N	P,O	M	MD,SF,HS ,GD	1	1	4	3	1	3
Wright & Nicholson (1973)	B	CP	N	O	M	MD,HS	1	2	3	3	1	2
GROUP 8[a]:												
Ottenbacher & Peterson (1985)	—	—	—	—	—	—	2	1	1	5	1	2
Snyder & Sheehan (1985)	—	—	—	—	—	—	3	2	3	3	1	3
White (1984)	—	—	—	—	—	—	3	1	2	2	1	3
White & Casto (1985)	—	—	—	—	—	—	3	1	2	2	1	3
White et al. (1985)	—	—	—	—	—	—	2	1	1	5	1	3
GROUP 9:												
Bayley et al. (1971)	B	DS	N	O	L,O	IQ,SF,GD	3	1	3	3	1	3
Dunst (in press)	E,B	DS	C	O	O	PI	2	1	2	3	1	3
Hunt et al. (1976)	E	EN	C	O	O	PI	4	1	3	3	1	3
Paraskevopoulos & Hunt	E	EN	C	O	O	PI	3	1	3	3	1	3
Stedman & Eichorn (1964)	B	DS	N	O	O	SF,HS,GD	2	1	2	3	1	3

Notes: See Table 1 for definitions of the coding scheme for the child and intervention characteristics dimensions. See Appendix for the rating scales used to assess the study characteristics dimensions.

[a]Neither the child or intervention characteristics dimensions were rated for the Group 8 studies since these investigations involved secondary analyses of previously conducted studies. The study characteristics were rated in terms of the extent to which the meta-analysis investigations and not the primary studies assessed each dimension.

suggests that "early may be better" in terms of the age of provision of early intervention services. Length of program involvement was significantly related to overall progress of the children. Children receiving early intervention services for a longer period of time made the greatest developmental gains.

Social support. None of the studies examined the extent to which formal or informal support may have affected observed changes. Indirect measures of intrafamily support (SES, income) were related to the dependent measures in a number of studies. These findings are described next in the child and family characteristics section.

Child and family characteristics. The majority of studies in this group examined the extent to which child and family characteristics affected child functioning. Brassell (1974) found that amount of progress made during a 10 month intervention period was significantly related to the number of behavioral barriers (e.g., stereotypic behavior) manifested by the children; the more barriers, the less progress. Simeonsson and Huntington (1981) as well found child temperament and child motivational variables to be significantly related to child progress. Brassell (1977) found that the degree of mental retardation and degree of motor impairment were significantly related to amount of child progress; the more severe the degree of delay or impairment, the less progress that was likely to be made. The most consistent finding in all studies was that developmental status at the beginning of intervention was the best indicator of amount of progress (Brassell, 1974; Bricker & Dow, 1980; Simeonsson & Huntington, 1981). The higher the level of functioning at program entry, the more progress the child was likely to make.

In addition to child factors, family characteristics were found to be significantly related to child functioning in a number of studies. Brassell (1974) found that maternal responsiveness, family income, parental education levels, and family size were significantly related to amount of child progress. Similarly, in a subsequent study Brassell (1977) found that age and education level as well as other SES-related measures were significantly related to child progress. Murray (1977), in an analysis of the Consortium of Longitudinal Studies (Lazar & Darlington, 1982) data from 11 separate investigations, found that long-term effects on child progress were significantly related to family SES and size and maternal educational level.

Internal validity. The major threat to the validity of these studies has to do primarily with the manner in which data analysis proceeded. Three of the five studies used multiple regression analysis to discern the nature of the relationships between the independent and dependent variable. Control over validity threats is generally accomplished through procedures that statistically remove the variance associated with factors that constitute competing explanations before the effects of the intervention variables are assessed (see Cohen & Cohen, 1983, chap. 10). For example, age of entry into a program may be a factor associated (mediated) by parental interest levels, child health, and so on. If this is the case, and those factors are not controlled, we may implicate one variable for the observed changes when in fact it was another set of variables that "caused" the change. Inasmuch as none of the studies considered this possibility, threats to internal validity are generally not adequately controlled.

Dependent measures. Child progress was used as the only measure of program success in the studies.

Dependence. Taken together, the five Group 4 studies demonstrated that amount of child progress covaried with a number of intervention, family, and child variables. However, because none of the studies employed cause-effect conceptual frameworks, the manner in which the independent variables might be related to the dependent measures is not readily apparent. The major conclusion that can be made from these studies is that the amount of progress manifested by the participants in the early intervention programs was affected by both intervention (age of program entry and length of involvement) and nonintervention (child and family characteristics) factors, suggesting that degree of efficacy is differentially influenced by a number of variables.

Group 5

The 11 studies in this group used quasi-experimental nonequivalent control group designs where pretest similarities in the experimental and control groups were explicitly tested (Connolly & Russell, 1976; Ludlow & Allen, 1979; Piper and Pless, 1980) or differences in the group were statistically controlled (Brassell & Dunst, 1978; Brinkworth, 1973, 1975; Peniston, 1972). In these studies, intact treatment groups and control groups were compared to one another for the purposes of establishing the effects of the intervention. The different studies included biologically at-risk Down's syndrome infants (Brinkworth, 1973, 1975; Connolly & Russell, 1976; Cunningham, Aumonier, & Sloper, 1982; Ludlow & Allen, 1979; Piper & Pless, 1980), biologically at-risk autistic children (Lovaas, 1982), heterogeneously formed groups of biologically and environmentally at-risk children (Brassell & Dunst, 1978; Dunst, Vance, & Gallagher, 1983; Peniston, 1972), and medically at-risk infants (Leib, Benfield & Guidubaldi, 1980).

Specificity. Although the majority of Group 5 studies provided a considerable amount of information about the general nature of the treatments, only two studies specified in detail the parameters of the interventions. Leib et al. (1980) provided the preterm infants in their experimental group supplemental visual, tactile, and vestibular experiences that were operationally defined in terms of the amount and form of stimulation. Lovaas (1982) used "level of intensity" of treatment for distinguishing between the two groups in his study, where specifiable behavioral treatments were provided to the subjects in both groups.

Social support. Only one study considered the possibility that informal or formal provision of support in addition to the intervention might have affected differences between groups. Dunst et al. (1983) found that parental well-being, parent attitudes, family integrity, and parent perceptions of child functioning were significantly related to degree of social support (Dunst, Jenkins, & Trivette, 1984) available to the family. However, the manner in which there was an interaction between the intervention and social support was not assessed.

Child and family characteristics. A number of studies provided background information about the children and families (Brassell & Dunst, 1978; Connolly & Russell, 1976; Dunst et al., 1983; Leib et al., 1980; Lovaas, 1982; Ludlow & Allen, 1979; Piper & Pless, 1980), and several investigations did test for conditional relationships between the different sets of independent variables. Leib et al. (1980) assessed the differential effects of intervention separately for boys and girls but found no main or interaction effects for sex.

Cunningham et al. (1982) compared the rate of development of three groups of Down's syndrome infants provided intervention by psychologists and public health nurses, and found no differences in the children's rate of development. It was concluded that the backgrounds of the intervenors was not a factor in affecting behavior change.

Dunst et al. (1983) examined the rates and patterns of mental, motor, and social-adaptive performance of 10 subgroups of handicapped infants and found that although all but one group of infants made consistent progress from birth to 3 years of age, there was considerable variability in the patterns of growth manifested by the children. For example, comparisons between an environmentally at-risk and medically at-risk group found that patterns of mental and social-adaptive performance were very much alike for both groups but that the subjects' motor development diverged considerably.

Internal validity. Three validity threats (*instrumentation*, *regression*, and *selection*) are major confounding factors in these particular quasi-experimental nonequivalent control group design studies. Instrumentation is a plausible explanation for observed differences between groups in nearly all the studies because the persons testing the children were apparently aware of which subjects were in the intervention and comparison groups. In addition, the test administrators were generally the same persons doing the interventions, and consequently their increased familiarity with the children may have affected the manner in which they assessed performance.

Regression may be a factor that affected differences between groups in the large majority of studies. Because subjects were not assigned randomly to treatment and comparison groups, the possibility exists that uniform regression in the experimental and control groups did not occur. This is especially likely to be the case in those instances where the experimental subjects were selected on the basis of their lower scores (relative to the contrast group). Where this was the case one would expect the treatment group to score higher when retested due simply to regression artifacts.

In any study that uses a nonequivalent control group design, the major threat to internal validity is selection inasmuch as pre-existing group differences rather than the interventions may be the principal factor for observed differences. This possibility was considered in almost all the investigations, and explicit attempts made to rule out selection as a threat. Brassell and Dunst (1978), Connolly and Russell (1976), Leib et al. (1980), Lovaas (1982), Ludlow and Allen (1979), and Piper and Pless (1980) established the fact that the families and/or children were similar on a host of characteristics prior to provision of the treatments. In several studies (Brassell & Dunst, 1978; Brinkworth, 1973; Leib et al., 1980; Peniston, 1972), analysis of covariance was used as a basis for statistically removing any pre-existing differences between groups. Although equivalence of groups cannot entirely be established on the basis of "no differences" on the pretest measures or be statistically eliminated using analysis of covariance (Reichardt, 1979), it is at least a step in the right direction, especially when the same findings are replicated across studies as is the case for the Group 4 investigations.

Dependent measures. Child progress was used as the primary measure of progam success in the majority of studies. The specific indices included developmental quotients, developmental ages, behavioral ratings, and the ages of acquisition of gross motor, communication, and social-adaptive landmarks. Several studies employed broader-based measures in addition to child progress. Dunst et al. (1983) used measures of parental, family, and child functioning outcomes as indices of program success. Leib et al. (1980) used infant temperament, nutritional intake and weight gain as well as child developmental progress as outcome measures, although significant group differences were found only in terms of child progress. Lovaas (1982) used school placement (regular vs. special education) as the primary measure of progress success. Piper and Pless (1980) used several maternal behaviors as outcome measures. Taken together, the Group 5 studies employed broader and much more ecologically relevant measures for determining progress success.

All the investigators except for Piper and Pless (1980) reported significant differences between the experimental and control groups on one or more of the dependent measures. The lack of significant findings in the Piper and Pless (1980) study is due, in part, to the extremely short duration and low level of intensity of the intervention (see Bricker et al., 1984; Dunst, 1986 for a discussion of the conceptual and methodological problems of this study).

Dependence. Except for the Lovaas (1982) study, all the other investigations used distal treatment measures as independent variables. The interventions, and social support in the Dunst et al. (1983) study, were defined at a level which permits only indirect or mediational statements to be made concerning the effects which the interventions had in producing observed differences between groups. The major conclusion that can be made from these studies is that participants in the early intervention programs demonstrated greater progress (relative to comparison groups) which appears related, in part, to the interventions although the exact nature of the causal factors related to the observed differences is not directly discernible.

Group 6

The major purpose of the nine Group 6 studies was to determine the extent to which participants in early intervention programs made more developmental progress relative to control group subjects. Each of the studies used matched groups designs where subjects in the experimental and control groups were equated on family and/or child characteristics prior to the provision of the treatment program. The matching process was used in order to reduce the possibility that selection might be a threat to the internal validity of the studies. The subjects in the studies included biologically at-risk (Aronson & Fallstrom, 1977; Bidder, Bryant, & Gray, 1975; Carlsen, 1975; Chee, Kreutzberg & Clark, 1978; Harris, 1981; Ottenbacher, Short, & Watson, 1981; Sandow & Clarke, 1978; Sandow, Clarke, Cox & Stewart, 1981; Sellick & Over, 1980) and medically at-risk (Bromwich & Parmelee, 1979) infants.

Specificity. A number of studies investigated the extent to which specific dimensions of the interventions affected differences between groups. Length of treatment was evaluated in two studies with Down's syndrome children as subjects (Aronson & Fallstrom, 1977;

Harris, 1981). Harris (1981) provided the treatment (therapy) to the experimental subjects in her study three times a week over a 9-week period. She found little evidence to support the contention that the intervention was efficacious. In contrast, Aronson and Fallstrom (1977), who provided the subjects in their study twice a week intervention for 18 months, found significant differences between groups beginning 6 months after initiation of the intervention program.

Sandow and her colleagues (Sandow & Clarke, 1978; Sandow et al., 1981) found a rather interesting relationship involving intensity of intervention. Comparisons of severely handicapped preschoolers visited in their home every other week versus every 8 weeks found that the more intensively visited group made more progress during the first year of the intervention program, but that the trend reversed during the second year of the program. Sandow argued that these results could be accounted for by increased parent dependence upon the home visiting staff who intervened more frequently whereas the parents in the less intensively visited group became more independently able to provide the types of experiences that were of benefit to the children.

Social support. The potential impact of intraprogram and outside program support was recognized in several studies (Bromwich & Parmelee, 1979; Sandow & Clarke, 1978; Sandow et al., 1981); however, only Bromwich and Parmelee (1979) attempted to assess the impact of support. These investigators found that lack of intrafamily support tended to have a negative effect upon parent functioning, and that the interventions for these parents was more likely to be considered unsuccessful. (This finding provides converging evidence for the results reported above for the Dunst and Leet, 1985, study where parental commitment and interest in early intervention varied as a function of how well more basic family needs were being met.)

Child and family characteristics. There were several studies that examined the degree to which child or family characteristics affected program success. Ottenbacher et al. (1981) found that child age and degree of spasticity were significantly correlated with child progress. Age was negatively correlated with gross motor gains; the younger the age at onset of the intervention, the more progress was likely to be made. Degree of spasticity was also correlated with child progress; the less spasticity the more progress.

Sandow et al. (1981) examined the extent to which SES influenced child progress among severely handicapped preschoolers, but found no differential influences related to social class. The investigators did find, however, that child level of functioning differentially affected parental expectations and needs. Parents with children who were moderately retarded tended to view the intervention process in terms of what could be accomplished to affect child performance. In contrast, parents of profoundly retarded children tended to see success in terms of the types of assistance the program could provide in order to ease the demands of rearing the handicapped youngster.

Internal validity. The major threat to the internal validity of matched group studies is selection (see especially Cook & Campbell, 1979, pp. 178–182). Because groups are not formed based on randomization, differences between groups could be due to differences among subjects rather than the intervention. A partial control over selection artifacts is the matching (blocking) of subjects on background variables (sex, age, diagnosis, SES, etc.) and then the random assigning of the subjects to experimental and control conditions. This was done in four studies (Carlsen, 1975: Harris, 1981; Ottenbacher et al., 1981; Sellick & Over, 1980). Further control over this threat is possible through either multifactor analysis of variance that includes the blocking variables as main and interaction effects or analysis of covariance that partials out the effects of the blocking variables. Neither was done in any study.

Dependent measures. Only Bromwich and Parmelee (1979) used other than child progress data as a measure of program success. The results showed that the intervention group had higher HOME scores compared to the control group. There were no differences between groups on any of the child progress measures used to determine program success.

The three studies that investigated the effects of comprehensive home-based or center-based early intervention services all used child progress as the primary measure of program success. Aronson and Fallstrom (1977) found that the experimental group made significantly more developmental progress compared to the control group. Bidder et al. (1975) found that the experimental group attained higher developmental ages than the control group for two developmental areas (hearing/speech and performance). Sandow et al. (1981), who assessed the effects of a 3 year intervention program, found no differences between the two experimental groups who received different levels of intervention, but that both groups attained higher levels of performance compared to a control group.

Several studies examined the effects of sensory/vestibular stimulation on the gross motor, fine motor, and reflex development of cerebral palsied preschoolers. Chee et al. (1978) and Ottenbacher et al. (1981) found significant differences between groups on all the dependent measures. Sellick and Over (1980), in contrast, found no differences between groups on any of their dependent measures. These contradictory findings are difficult to explain since differences in the subject's ages, nature of the treatments, outcome measures, and methods of analysis make interpretation problematic.

The two studies that examined the effects of facilitative therapy on the gross, fine, and mental development of Down's syndrome and cerebral palsied infants showed very little improvement in the experimental subjects relative to the control subjects. Harris (1981) found no significant differences between groups on either the Bayley mental motor scale or the Peabody motor scale. Carlsen (1975) found significant differences in only one of four developmental areas (gross motor). Tentatively, the results of these two studies suggest that traditional physical and occupational therapy approaches are not effective treatment strategies.

Dependence. The findings from this set of studies suggest rather complex relationships among the independent and dependent variables. Intensity of involvement was found to be an important dimension of intervention in center-based programs (Aronson & Fallstrom, 1977) but less important in home-based programs (Sandow et al., 1981). Child characteristics were found to be very important in terms of the amount of progress the subjects were likely to make; the more severe the children's problems, the less progress. Contrasts between the types of treatments evaluated showed broad-based, comprehensive treatments to be more effective than narrowly focused therapeutic interventions. The major conclusion that can be made from these studies is that the amount of progress made by the experimental subjects is greater than that for the control subjects but only in instances where the treatment is broad-based in nature.

GROUP 7

The five Group 7 studies were all designed to assess the effectiveness of provision of services to biologically impaired preschoolers. All the investigations used true experimental designs where subjects were randomly assigned to treatment and control conditions. The subjects in the different studies included Down's syndrome (Kantner, Clark, Allen & Chase, 1976) and cerebral palsied (Scherzer, Mike & Ilson, 1976; Wright & Nicholson, 1973) infants, and infants with nonspecified handicapping conditions (Kelly, 1982; Sandler, Coren & Thurman, 1983).

Specificity. Sandler et al. (1983) were the only investigators who examined specific dimensions of the treatment program. Their study examined the manner in which parental data keeping in the experimental group (data keeping vs. no data keeping) affected parent and child functioning compared to a control group. Both experimental groups participated in "a series of four 2-hour small group training sessions, followed by four individual training sessions" (p. 356). Several differences were found between the experimental versus control groups on both mother and child outcomes, but only a few differences were found between the two experimental groups.

Social support. Only Sandler et al. (1983) recognized the possible effects of provision of support to the experimental groups by the program, and indeed the intervention was, in part, designed to mediate knowledge and skill acquisition in this area. None of the investigators acknowledged the possibility that outside program support might have had an impact upon child and parent functioning.

Child and family characteristics. Scherzer et al. (1976) found that both child age and severity of impairment were significantly correlated with child progress. Older children showed higher levels of performance while more severely impaired children made less developmental progress. Kelly (1982) stratified her subjects by child age but did not assess the effects of this child variable. None of the studies examined the manner in which family characteristics may have influenced program success.

Internal validity. A number of factors pose threats to the internal validity of these studies. One major confounding factor is selection. In several studies it was clearly the case that despite the randomization process used to assign subjects to experimental and control conditions, the groups were not equated on child and/or family variables (Kelly, 1982); differences in subject characteristics made similarities between groups highly unlikely (Sandler et al., 1983); or extremely small sample sizes and lack of description of the subjects made it impossible to establish similarities between groups (Kantner et al., 1976). Instrumentation is a major problem in several studies because the persons conducting the investigations were the same persons taking measurements on the experimental and control subjects (Kantner et al., 1976; Kelly, 1982). Attrition is a problem in the Wright and Nicholson (1973) study because of the differential loss of subjects in the experimental and control conditions. The various problems with these studies, especially in light of the fact that no attempt was made to control for these factors methodologically or statistically, makes it difficult to rule out these variables as possibly affecting differences between groups.

Dependent measures. Child progress was used as the measure of program success in most of the studies (Kantner et al., 1976; Sandler et al., 1983; Scherzer et al., 1976; Wright & Nicholson, 1973). All but Wright and Nicholson (1973) reported differences between groups, favoring the experimental group in all cases. However, neither Kantner et al. (1976) or Scherzer et

al. (1976) performed statistical analyses to establish the fact that the differences were statistically significant. Kelly (1982) measured program success in terms of styles of parent-child interactions and Sandler et al. (1983) assessed the extent to which parent functioning was affected by the treatment program. Both investigators found significant differences between groups. Kelly (1982) found increases in positive and decreases in negative parent styles of interaction among her experimental subjects. Sandler et al. (1983) found significant improvement in their experimental subjects' knowledge of behavioral principles and styles of maternal interactions.

Dependence. In those cases where significant differences were found between the experimental and control groups, and where alternative explanations for observed differences can be ruled out, the results may be taken as evidence that it was primarily the treatment (intervention) that produced the positive effects. Nonetheless, the majority of treatments were defined in a manner that suggest primarily their mediational and not causal influence. The major conclusion that can be made about these studies is that experimental subjects generally showed improvements in their rates of development compared to control subjects, and that the differences between groups are attributable to the interventions although the dimensions of the treatments accounting for the differences are mediational rather than causal in nature.

GROUP 8

The studies included in this group involved the meta-analysis of previously conducted studies (Ottenbacher & Peterson, 1985; Snyder & Sheehan, 1985; White, 1984; White & Casto, 1985; White, Mastropieri, & Casto, 1985). Meta-analysis is a procedure for taking the results from different studies conducted for the same purpose (e.g., documenting the efficacy of early intervention), quantifying substantive and methodological characteristics of the studies (e.g., research design, family characteristics), converting the findings vis à vis numeric results to a common metric (effect size), and then discerning the aggregated effects of the studies in combination. Given certain methodological provisos (see e.g., Snyder, 1985), meta-analysis can provide the type of information necessary to document the effects of early intervention.

The five investigations differed in terms of the number of studies included in their analyses. Snyder and Sheehan's (1985) study included eight previously conducted investigations. Ottenbacher and Peterson's (1985) study included 38 studies. White (1984) and White and Casto's (1985) studies included 162 investigations. White, Mastropieri, and Casto's (1985) study included the analysis of 21 federally funded Handicapped Children's Early Education Program (HCEEP) projects which meet certain criteria that permitted them to be judged as exemplary programs with proven effectiveness. The different studies included in the analyses employed pre-experimental, quasi-experimental, and to a small degree, true experimental designs. The subjects in the various studies included in the meta-analyses were biologically, medically, and environmentally at-risk infants.

Specificity. The extent to which specific types or dimensions of early intervention were related to efficacy was examined in a number of studies. Snyder and Sheehan (1985) found that programs that used Piagetian-based approaches produced the greatest program effects followed by behaviorally oriented intervention programs. These investigators also found that more structured programs tended to produce greater effects. White and Casto (1985) also found that degree of program structure was an important variable related to effectiveness.

Neither White (1984) nor White and Casto (1985) found that degree of parental involvement was related to program efficacy, although this finding must be interpreted with caution. A recent meta-analysis by Medway (1984) found that type of parent involvement was related to differential effectiveness. Behavioral training procedures produced the greatest effect whereas parent effectiveness training (PET) produced the smallest effect. Because White (1984) and White and Casto (1985) failed to recognize the fact that different types of parent involvement might produce different effects, their conclusion might be in artifact of their method of defining and assessing the impact of parent involvement.

Age of program entry as an intervention variable was examined by White (1984) and White and Casto (1985). The investigators concluded that early entry did not necessarily result in greater effects compared to later entry, but again this conclusion must be interpreted with caution. Age of entry is likely to be influenced by a host of factors that were not considered as part of the analysis (e.g., more severely impaired children being identified earlier and thus enrolled earlier). Likewise, White's (1984) conclusion that neither intensity or duration of treatment are important explanatory variables must be considered cautiously since in all probability children who receive "more" intervention are likely to be those most impaired and consequently will make the least progress.

Social support. None of the studies assessed the manner in which social support may have contributed to observed effects, although Snyder and Sheehan (1985) found a moderate relationship between intrafamily financial support and program effectiveness.

Child and family characteristics. None of the meta-analyses included descriptive information about the families. Snyder and Sheehan (1985) reported some information about severity of the children's impairments. White (1984) assessed the effects of several child and family variables but did not report the results. Perhaps most regrettable was the fact that conditional relationships were not evaluated, especially in the White (1984) and White and Casto (1985) reports, since sufficient data were available to perform second and higher-order interaction analyses.

Internal validity. Meta-analyses can be particularly problematic in terms of threats to internal validity since the extent to which extraneous variables are controlled in the original studies bear directly on the interpretability of the meta-analysis results. Threats to the internal validity of these studies is particularly apparent given the fact that the majority of original studies employed pre-experimental and quasi-experimental designs.

Partial control over threats to internal validity is possible if certain design and study characteristics are analyzed and their effects determined. White et al. (1985) attempted to do this and found that results were hopelessly confounded with the failure to provide adequate control of other variables that were likely to represent alternative explanations for observed effects. Ottenbacher and Peterson (1985) examined the relationship between both design characteristics and threats to internal validity and study outcomes (effect sizes), and found that larger effect sizes were significantly related to weaker types of designs and minimal control over threats to internal validity.

Dependent measures. The primary measures of program success was child progress. The major problem posed by these studies is that effect sizes for quite different dependent measures as well as multiple measures from the same studies were pooled in determining the efficacy of the interventions. As noted by Hedges and Becker (1986), the conduct of a meta-analysis requires that the dependent measures from the different studies reflect a single or unitary construct. To the extent that different outcome measures can be considered a unifying measure of efficacy, the aggregation of results from different studies is appropriate. Ottenbacher and Peterson (1985) found that child change scores were relatively even for different developmental areas and that developmental progress was uniform for standardized versus nonstandardized outcomes measurement tools. These findings suggest that, at least for the dependent measure included in the studies in the Ottenbacher and Peterson (1985) investigation, aggregation of the data for different outcome measures was appropriate.

Dependence. To the extent that a meta-analysis conforms to rigorous methodological and statistical criteria, the procedure represents a valuable tool for making statements regarding causal inference. However, Snyder (1985) recently found that the structural characteristics of meta-analytical data sets often violate basic assumptions, and consequently make the analytic strategy problematic in terms of drawing causal inferences. He argues that at this point meta-analysis should be used primarily as a tool for identifying trends in data sets which can then be empirically tested in more rigorously conducted investigations. The major conclusion that can be made from these studies is that certain intervention-related variables (program type, degree of structure, intensity of treatment) emerge as important factors related to the amount of progress that program participants are likely to demonstrates, although positive results are likely to be confounded with design characteristics.

Group 9

The Group 9 studies are ones that investigated the extent to which different conditions of rearing affected child development. Broadly speaking, these studies contrasted the manner in which environments that afforded different learning opportunities had positive or negative effects upon developmental outcomes. The studies included in this group are ones that employed variations of quasi-experimental nonequivalent groups designs. Intact groups differing in rearing conditions were compared to one another for the purpose of discerning the manner in which the learning environment, broadly conceived, affected behavior change.

Some of the earliest condition-of-rearing studies compared home-reared nonretarded infants with nonretarded infants who for a variety of social and economic reasons were placed in institutional settings. These particular types of studies are not included here (see Clarke & Clarke, 1974, and Robinson & Robinson, 1976, for reviews of these studies). Our review is restricted to studies that compared the effects of differing conditions of rearing with biologically at-risk infants (e.g., Dunst, in press; Stedman & Eichorn, 1964) and studies that assessed the effects of deliberate attempts to improve rearing conditions as a means to affect developmental and behavioral change. The latter studies have been conducted with environmentally at-risk infants (see e.g., Hunt, 1976, 1980) and biologically impaired infants (Dunst, in press).

Specificity. The studies in this group have treated the interventions at a number of different levels of specificity. First, there is the obvious institutional verses noninstitutional dimension. Second, the effects that different child-to-adult caregiver ratios have had on child behavior have been examined (e.g., Paraskevopoulos & Hunt, 1971). Third, deliberate variations in institutional care have occurred in an effort to determine their enhancing qualities (e.g., Hunt, Mohandessi, Ghodssi & Akiyama, 1976). These explicit attempts to define the treatment variables in a number of different ways provide a basis for experimentally assessing how different intervention and nonintervention factors affect child growth and development.

Social support. The manner in which social support and other forms of intervention may have affected observed changes was not assessed in any of the studies.

Child and family characteristics. There is a considerable body of evidence indicating that both child and family characteristics influence decisions about institutional placement (see Robinson & Robinson, 1976); however, the manner in which child- and family-level variables may have influenced observed effects was not assessed in any of the studies. A few studies did attempt to determine whether or not the family backgrounds of the children were similar in order to rule out these variables as factors that may have been related to observed changes.

Internal validity. Conditions of rearing studies are ones in which history is deliberately allowed to vary naturally or be experimentally manipulated in order to assess its effects. The primary threats to internal validity in these studies is selection since groups were not randomly assigned to different treatment conditions. Instrumentation may be a problem in a number of studies since the investigator, who tested the children, were aware of the purposes of the studies.

Dependent measures. Child progress was the only measure of progress success used in the studies. Developmental ages, developmental quotients, and age of acquisition of developmental landmarks were the outcome measures.

The results of the studies that involved comparisons of institutionalized versus noninstitutionalized care all found that home reared children manifested higher levels of mental and language development, suggesting that condition of rearing influenced the development of the children. Stedman and Eichorn (1964) found debilitating effects of institutional placement even for a group of infants who participated in a special enrichment program within the institution. Bayley, Rhodes, Gooch & Marcus (1971), who followed the same subjects in the Stedman and Eichorn study until the children were 8 years of age, found that the home reared children functioned at higher levels of mental, motor, and social development on nearly all outcome measures at 2, 5, 6, and 8 years of age. However, when the institutionalized sample was involved in an intensive language training program beginning when the children were between 5 and 6 years of age, a number of the differences between groups dissipated. The latter finding strongly suggests the potent influence of the environment on development, and indicates that even the debilitating effects of institutional rearing can be overcome as late as 6 years of age.

Hunt (1976, 1980; Hunt et al., 1976) compared the ages of acquisition of sensorimotor landmarks for different groups of environmentally at-risk institutionalized infants where the different subgroups were provided different types of learning experiences. The results clearly showed that the infants who received different types of enrichment experiences attained sensorimotor landmarks at earlier ages than did a comparison group.

The extent to which home-based environmentally and biologically at-risk infants enrolled in early intervention programs acquire sensorimotor landmarks at earlier ages compared to different nonintervention institutionalized and noninstitutionalized infants was examined in a number of studies. Hunt (1980) found that environmentally at-risk infants enrolled in an early intervention program acquired sensorimotor landmarks at earlier ages than did a middle-class group who did not receive supplemental learning experiences. Dunst (in press) found that both home-reared Down's syndrome infants and a heterogeneously formed group of home-reared biologically impaired infants attained developmental landmarks at earlier ages compared to institutionalized environmentally at-risk and institutionalized biologically at-risk children who did not receive any supplemental enrichment.

Dependence. Defining the independent variable in terms of differing conditions of rearing provides very little specific information about these factors that foster or impede development. Thus, although specificity is greater than most of the preceding studies, the Group 9 investigations received moderate ratings on the dependence dimension. The major conclusions that can be made about these studies is that conditions of rearing as well as variations in learning experiences within settings can accelerate rates of sensorimotor and intellectual development, and that environmentally and biologically at-risk infants rates of development can be significantly enhanced as a function of both participation in early intervention programs and rearing conditions.

Moderate to High Causal Inference

The final groups of studies are ones in which greater degrees of causal inference are possible. This is the case because of the manner in which the studies were conducted (methodologically, conceptually, etc.). Each study specifically examined the extent to which different variables and factors affected changes in parent, family, or child functioning in a way that permitted causal inferences to be made at an increased level of certainty. Table 3 summarizes the characteristics of these studies.

GROUP 10

The major purpose of the five Group 10 studies was to determine the manner in which different mediating variables affected a number of different aspects of child and family functioning. The Group 10 studies were grounded in theoretical and conceptual frameworks where direct causal inferences were specific aims of the investigations. The subjects in the various studies included environmentally at-risk (Eisenstadt & Powell, 1980; Gutelius & Kirch, 1975) and environmentally and biologically at-risk (Dunst & Leet, 1985; Maisto & German, 1979, 1981) children.

Specificity. Maisto and German (1979) conducted one of the few studies that considered the possibility that higher-order interactions between intervention and nonintervention variables might affect program success. Entry age (< 11 months vs > 11 months), child sex, and degree of retardation (retarded vs nonretarded) were examined in relationship to Bayley Scale DQ (Developmental Quotient) scores across four evaluation periods, each 3 months apart. A significant age of entry × degree of severity × evaluation period interaction showed that the nonretarded subjects' DQ scores remained high ($M = 92$ to 94) and stable across all four evaluation periods and did not differ as a function of entry age. However, for the retarded subjects, the early entry group attained progressively higher DQ scores across the four evaluation periods whereas the late entry group did not. Thus, it would seem that at least for biologically at-risk infants, the amount of gains likely to be demonstrated that as a function of entry age, and the common wisdom and "early is better" may hold true for this group of infants.

Social support. The manner in which social support affected family and parent functioning was assessed in three studies. Dunst and Leet (1985) examined the extent to which family-level needs were related to parental time, energy, and personal investment necessary to carry out home-based early intervention prescriptions for their developmentally delayed children. The independent measure of support was the Family Resource Scale. This scale measures the extent to which different types of resources are available to a family. The results showed that the extent to which parents had the time, energy, and personal investment to intervene with their children was strongly related to adequacy of family resources. The more adequate the resources, the more likely there was a commitment to and involvement in the intervention process.

Both Eisenstadt and Powell (1980) and Gutelius and Kirsch (1975) found strong relationships between provision of informal suport and intervention-related outcomes. Eisenstadt and Powell (1980) reported several different types of relationship between adequacy of

TABLE 3

Studies That Permitted Moderate to High Causal Inference

| Study | Child Characteristics[a] | | Intervention Characteristics[b] | | | | Study Characteristics[c] | | | | | |
	Risk Category	Child Diagnosis	Theoretical Focus	Intervention Type	Intervention Target	Outcome Measure	Specificity	Social Support	Child & Family Characteristics	Internal Validity	Dependent Measure	Dependence
GROUP 10:												
Dunst & Leet (1985)	E,M,B	NS	C	O	O	SF,FF	1	5	3	3	4	4
Eisenstadt & Powell (1980)	E	EN	T	P,S	P	SF,FF	2	5	3	3	4	4
Gutelius & Kirsch (1975)	E	EN	N	C,M,P	G,O,P	IQ,SF	3	5	3	3	1	3
Maisto & German (1979)	E,M,B	NS	N	C,B,P	G,S,C,M,B,L,A,O	IQ,LA	4	1	3	4	1	3
Maisto & German (1981)	E,M,B	NS	C	C,B,P	G,S,C,M,B,L,A,O	IQ,MD,LA,SF	3	1	4	4	4	3
GROUP 11:												
Barrera et al. (1976)	B	NS	N	C,P,S,Y	S,C,M,L,A,P	GD	2	3	3	4	1	4
Brassell & Dunst (1975a)	E,B	NS	C	C,P	O	I	2	1	3	4	1	4
Brassell & Dunst (1975b)	E,B	NS	C	C,P	O	I	2	1	3	4	1	4
Dunst (1974)	B	NS	C	C,P	O	I	2	1	3	3	1	4
Horton (1971)	B	HI	N	P,O	GL	LA	2	3	1	4	1	3
Hutinger (1978)	E,B	NS	N	C,M,P,S	G,S,C,M,L,A	LA,GD	2	3	1	3	1	3
GROUP 12:												
Crnic, Greenberg et al. (1983b)	M	PM	T	—[a]	—[a]	SF,FF,SS	—	5	5	4	5	4
Dunst & Trivette (1984)	E,B	NS	T	S	P	SF,SS,FF	3	5	4	3	5	4
Dunst et al. (in press)	E,B	NS	T	S	P	IQ,SF,SS	3	5	4	4	5	4
Vadasy et al. (1985)	N	NS	C	S	P	SF,SS,FF	3	3	3	2	4	3
GROUP 13:												
Brinker & Lewis (1982)	B	DS,NS	C	C,B	B,L,O	OB	5	1	1	5	1	5
Cyrulik-Jacobs et al. (1975)	B	CP	N	B	B,L	OB	5	1	2	5	1	5
Dunst et al. (1985)	B	NS	C	B	B	OB	5	1	2	5	3	5
Friedlander et al. (1967)	B	NS	C	B	B,L	OB	5	1	1	5	1	5
Glenn (1983)	B	NS	N	B	B,L	OB	5	1	2	5	1	5
Hanson (1985)	M,B	NS	M	C,B,P,S	G,S,C,B,L,P	OB	3	3	3	3	3	3
Laub & Dunst (1974)	B	NS	C	C,B	B,L	OB	5	1	1	4	1	5
LeLaurin (1985)	M,B	DS,CP,PM,OT	C	C,B	G	OB	3	1	3	3	1	3
Moran & Whitman (1985)	M,B,O,N	CP,PM,OT	C	B,P	B	SF,OB	5	1	3	4	4	4
Ramey et al. (1972)	E	OT	C	B	B,L	OB	5	1	1	5	1	5
Ramey et al. (1976)	E	OT	C	B	S,M,B,L,O	OB	5	1	1	4	1	4
Solkoff & Cotton (1975)	M	PM	N	B	B	OB	5	1	2	4	1	4
Utley et al. (1983)	B	NS	N	B	B,Y	OB	5	1	1	5	1	5
Watson (1972)	N	OT	C	B	B	OB	5	1	1	5	1	5
GROUP 14:												
Cappleman et al. (1982)	E,M	EN	C	C,P	S,C,L	IQ	3	3	4	4	2	3
Field et al. (1980)	E,M	PM,EM	N	C,P	C,P,O	IQ,HS,FF,SF	3	3	3	4	3	4
Garber & Heber (1981)	E	EN	N	C,P	G,S,C,L,J,O	IQ	3	2	2	4	1	3
Lazar & Darlington (1982)	E	EN	N	C[b]	C,L	IQ,LA,SF,AP,FF	4	2	5	4	5	3
Ramey & Haskins (1981)	E	EN	C	C	C,S,L	IQ,PS,FF	4	3	4	5	4	4
Ramey et al. (1985a,b)	E	EN	T	C,P	C,S,L	IQ,PS	4	3	4	5	4	4

NOTES: See Table 1 for definitions of the coding scheme for the child and intervention characteristics dimensions. See Appendix for the rating scales used to assess the study characteristics dimensions.

[a] The Crnic et al. (1983) study assessed the effects of provision of support to infants and their families but who were not in an early intervention program.

[b] The Lazar and Darlington study included the analysis of 11 separate early intervention programs that, taken together, used primarily cognitive-based intervention procedures.

informal support and parent participation in an early intervention program. For example, mothers who had weak informal social support networks were not likely to attend program activities that had socializing value, and mothers with strong informal social support networks were more likely to establish supportive ties with similar program participants. Gutelius and Kirsch (1975) found that informal provision of support provided by staff to parents of environmentally at-risk children was significantly related to the amount of progress made by the children. The investigators argued that the "frequent family contacts with the staff provided to the (experimental) group enhanced feelings of their own worth and of the value of their infants, and that this new dignity was also an important factor in the favorable findings for their children" (p. 387).

Child and family characteristics. Sigel (1985) has recently compiled a convincing body of evidence which indicates that parental belief systems (attitudes, values, self-concepts, etc.) have both direct and indirect influences on child behavior and development. Maisto and German (1981) recently examined the extent to which maternal locus of control among parents of handicapped infants enrolled in an early intervention program affected child outcomes. A significant amount of variance in developmental gains beyond that attributable to SES and maternal education level was accounted for by locus of control; that is, children were more likely to make greater progress if their mothers had internal locus of control.

Internal validity. Taken together, the Group 10 studies generally did an adequate job of controlling for validity threats. This was primarily accomplished by testing for effects that otherwise would have proved to be confounding. Moreover, in studies where the aim is not confirmation or disconfirmation of the benefits of a particular treatment but rather the demonstration of specific types of relationships between the independent and dependent variables, the factors that typically are threats to internal validity attain the status of independent variables in the type of studies included in this group.

Dependent measures. A broad range of child, parent, and family-level outcomes were used as dependent measures in a number of studies. Child indices of program success included developmental quotients, developmental gain scores, and developmental levels. Parent and family efficacy measures included well-being, family integrity, parental attitudes and expectations, and parental perceptions of child functioning. In addition, program utilization and commitment to parent involvement were employed as measures of efficacy. Taken together, these studies provide considerable evidence that different aspects of early intervention and social support, as well as family characteristics, influence parent, family, and child functioning in a manner that permits greater degree of causal inference.

Dependence. Examination of Table 3 shows that the studies in this group were generally rated adequate on this causal inference dimension. This is the case because it was generally possible to make more explicit causal inferences about the functional relationship between the independent and dependent measures. The major conclusions that can be made from these studies is that a host of intervention (age of entry), social support (adequacy of family resources, provision of informal support) and family (locus-of-control, SES, education level) characteristics affect child, parent, and family functioning as part of participation in early intervention programs, including parental commitment to the intervention process and child progress.

GROUP 11

The six studies in this group employed quasi-experimental designs that used the subjects as their own controls for establishing the efficacy of the interventions. In several investigations, changes in specific developmental and behavioral areas were compared against gains made in areas for which no intervenion was provided for purposes of establishing the effects of the treatments (Barrera et al., 1976; Dunst, 1974; Horton, 1971; Hutinger, 1978). In the Brassell and Dunst (1975a, 1975b) studies, comparisons of progress during an intervention period were compared against changes during nonintervention periods as a basis for establishing the effects of the treatment. The majority of studies included biologically at-risk infants (Barrera et al., 1976; Dunst, 1974; Horton, 1971) or biologically and environmentally at-risk children (Brassell & Dunst, 1975a, 1975b; Hutinger, 1978).

Specificity. None of the studies examined the extent to which different dimensions of the interventions may have been related to program success. However, because the interventions were targeted to affect specific changes in specific areas of functioning, greater degrees of specificity are apparent relative to the studies included in the preceding groups.

Social support. None of the studies examined the extent to which informal or formal support may have influenced the observed changes, although the importance of provision of support was explicitly recognized by several investigators (Barrera et al., 1976; Horton, 1971; Hutinger, 1978).

Child and family characteristics. Several studies provided background information regarding the characteristics of the children (Brassell & Dunst, 1975b; Dunst, 1974) or both the children and families (Barrera et al., 1976; Brassell & Dunst, 1975a); however, none of the studies evaluated the extent to which child or family characteristics may have influenced behavior change. None of the studies assessed the extent to which there were conditional relationships among the independent variables.

Internal validity. Overall, the Group 11 studies adequately controlled the majority of validity threats and thus yielded generally interpretable findings. In several studies, testing may be a problem in as much as the intervention activities were the items on the criterion measures used to assess the efficacy of the treatments. Consequently, test training may be confounded with any genuine intervention effects. Likewise, *instrumentation* artifacts could be confounded with the interventions since the persons administering the outcome measures were often the same persons conducting the studies. *Regression* is perhaps the most plausible threat to internal validity because the interventions were provided in areas in which the subjects were generally most delayed, and a second testing would almost certainly show the average gains to be greater in the intervention areas independent of the treatments. The findings from the Barrera et al. (1976) study illustrate this possibility. The developmental areas in which the interventions were provided included those domains in which the subjects were most delayed (clinically selected) and randomly selected domains (experimentally selected). Significant development progress was found only in those areas for which the children were initially most delayed.

Dependent measures. Child progress was used in all the studies as the primary measure of program success. Developmental gains and developmental quotients were the two indices of child progress that were used in the various studies. None of the studies used factors other than child progress as measures of program effectiveness. All of the investigators reported significant changes in child performance relative to progress in the nonintervention areas.

Dependence. Taken together, the Group 11 studies fare much better than all the previous studies in terms of cause-effect inferences. This is the case because the treatments used to affect behavior change were specific sets of intervention techniques and activities that were designed to enhance or facilitate the acquisition of specific types of developmental competencies. Nonetheless, there was some variability in terms of the extent to which a functional relationship can be implicated between the interventions and outcomes, and consequently there are some differences in the studies in terms of ratings for this study dimension (see Table 3). The major conclusion that can be made from these studies is that amount of progress made by the participants in the early intervention programs appeared directly related to the particular types of learning experiences provided them, and that the progress made by the children was significantly greater compared to developmental changes manifested in behavioral domains for which no interventions were provided.

GROUP 12

The major purpose of the Group 12 studies was to determine the extent to which different types of social support affected parent, family, and the child functioning in households with prechool age children. These studies were grounded in by both ecological and social network theory (e.g., Bronfenbrenner, 1979; Cochran & Brassard, 1979; Mitchell & Trickett, 1980; Powell, 1982). A sizeable body of literature indicates that social support has powerful mediational influences on personal and familial well-being (Bott, 1971; Dean & Lin, 1977; McCubbin et al., 1980; Mitchell & Trickett, 1980). There is a growing body of evidence which indicates that social support both directly and indirectly influences attitudes toward parenting (Crnic, Greenberg, Ragozin, Robinson, & Basham, 1983b), styles of parent-child interaction (Crnic, Friedrich, & Greenberg, 1983a; Crockenberg, 1981; Embry, 1980; Giovanoni & Billingsley, 1970; Hetherington, Cox, & Cox, 1976, 1978), parental expectations and aspirations for their children (Lazar & Darlington, 1982), and child behavior and development (Crnic, Friedrich, & Greenberg 1983a; Crockenberg, 1981). The studies reviewed here included medically at-risk (Crnic et al., 1983b), and biologically and environmentally at-risk (Dunst & Trivette, 1984; Dunst, Trivette, & Cross, 1986) children, and nonspecified handicapping conditions (Vadasy, Fewell, Meyer, & Greenberg, 1985).

Specificity. In the Dunst et al. (1986) study, early intervention was measured in terms of the number of services provided by the early intervention program to the (a) child and (b) parents and siblings (see Dunst, 1982, 1985). Three different categories of child services and five different categories of family services were potentially available. Amount of participation was not found to be significantly related to parent, family, or child functioning.

Social support. Crnic et al. (1983b) found that social support (intimate, friendship, & community) affected general life satisfaction, satisfaction with parenting, and the behavioral characteristics of both the mothers and their infants. Moreover, their findings showed differential impacts between the independent and outcome measures. For example, general life satisfaction was primarily influenced by intimate and community support and an interaction between stress and support, whereas maternal sensitivity to their infants cues as well as the clarity of the infant's cues were related only to maternal stress levels.

Dunst et al. (1986), using hierarchical multiple regression analyses by sets, found that social support accounted for significant amounts of variance beyond that attributable to a series of background variables (family and child characteristics) in parental well-being, time demands, parental overprotection, parental perceptions of child functioning, parent-child interactions, and child progress. (The mediational relationships between social support and the various measures of parent, family, and child functioning have been replicated across eight separate studies: see Dunst & Trivette, 1987.) A number of interactions were found between social support and child and family characteristics. For example, child progress was found to be greatest for children from high SES/income families whose parents reported being more satisfied with their sources of social support. Similarly, predictions about the adult living arrangements of the child were influenced by a combination of support satisfaction and child characteristics. Parents indicated, for older children, that their offspring would live in less restricted environments if the respondents also reported being more satisfied with their sources of social support. (See Dunst et al., 1986, for a complete description of these findings.)

Child and family characteristics. Contrary to common wisdom, Dunst et al. (1986) found that neither child diagnosis nor level of retardation were significantly related to parental well-being. Other than the social support variables, family SES and income were the only other variables significantly related to personal well-being (Dunst & Trivette, 1984). The same findings were found for excessive time demands placed upon the parents by the child. In contrast, negative attitudes toward the child as well as family integrity were not related to social support but were related to the child's level of retardation. Overall, family characteristics (SES and income) accounted for significant amounts of variance in time demands, family integrity, family opportunities, financial problems, and child progress. Child diagnosis accounted for significant amounts of variance in attitude toward child, family integrity, perceptions of child functioning, and child progress. These findings, together with those the social support analyses, indicate that a host of factors impinge upon parent, family, and child functioning, although there are differential effects in terms of the manner in which the various factors are related to the different outcomes.

Internal validity. In these studies, those factors that would typically be treated as threats to internal validity are ones that are treated as independent variables and their effects specifically assessed as part of the study. Consequently, these studies methodologically as well as statistically provided adequate control over the majority of validity threats.

Dependent measures. The dependent measures included personal well-being, personal time demands, attitudes toward the child, family integrity, and parents' perceptions of their child's behavior, parental expectations for their child, selected characteristics of parent-child interactions, and child progress. The broad-based nature of the dependent measures used in these studies as well as the ecological relevance of the outcome measures provided considerable evidence that social support can have powerful mediational influence on parent, family, and child functioning.

Dependence. All of the factors found to be related to the outcomes in these studies were mediational in nature. For example, although social support was found to be related to a host of outcomes, the most that can be discerned is that support provides some basis for affecting changes in other behaviors which in turn influences the outcome either directly or indirectly. The major conclusion that can be made about these studies is that social support has positive mediational influences on parent, family, and child functioning beyond that attributable to other explanatory variables.

GROUP 13

The major purpose of the Group 13 studies was to determine the extent to which operant conditioning procedures could be used to affect the acquisition of response-contingent behavior. All of the studies used single-subject research designs to establish the efficacy of the operant conditioning procedures. The studies were conducted with biologically at-risk (Brinker & Lewis, 1982; Cyrulik-Jacobs, Shapira, & Jones, 1975; Dunst, Cushing, & Vance, 1985; Friedlander, McCarthy, & Soferenko, 1967; Glenn, 1983; Hanson, 1985; Laub & Dunst, 1974; Utley, Duncan, Strain & Scanlon, 1983; Watson, 1972), environmentally at-risk (Moran & Whitman, 1985; Ramey, Hieger & Klisz, 1972; Ramey, Starr, Pallas, Whitten, & Reed, 1976), medically at-risk (Solkoff & Cotton, 1975), and heterogeneously formed groups (LeLaurin, 1985) of infants.

Specificity. In operant conditioning studies, the presentation of a rewarding stimulus is made contingent upon a specified response emitted by the infant. Consequently, there is a high degree of specificity in terms of the intervention process, and the majority of studies included here receive the highest ratings on this study dimension. The types of behaviors that were conditioned as operants in these studies included head turning, vocalizations, leg kicking, visual attention, manual manipulation, gross motor movements, and play behaviors. Inasmuch as different types of behavior have been conditioned with different groups of children, the operant conditioning intervention approach can be considered to have high construct validity.

Social support. None of the studies considered the manner in which provisions of support might enhance opportunities for acquisition of response-contingent behavior. Dunst et al. (1985), however, proposed a social systems framework for determining the first-, second-, and higher-order effects of operant learning upon child and parent behavior.

Child and family characteristics. Studies with non-retarded infants have demonstrated that child behavior characteristics (e.g., attentiveness and temperament) differentially affect rates of operant learning (Dunst & Lingerfelt, 1985; Hayes, Ewy, & Watson, 1982; Krafchuk, Sameroff, & Bakow, 1976). Only one Group 13 study (Moran & Whitman, 1985) considered the manner in which child and family characteristics influenced the infants acquisition of operant behavior. Aggregation of the findings for the various studies do suggest that to some degree initial levels of functioning affect the ease of operant learning; the more handicapped, the more time that was necessary before learning was demonstrated.

Internal validity. Single-subject studies generally do an excellent job of controlling for threats to internal validity. Generally the major threats in these types of studies are maturation and history, although both factors can be easily dismissed as causes for observed changes. The majority of studies included here were all conducted in 2 weeks or less, and the stable baselines obtained in each study rules out these factors as possibly influencing the results.

Dependent measures. The principal dependent measures in the majority of studies were the number of operant responses manifested during the conditioning phase relative to baseline and extinction phases. Only Dunst et al. (1985) and Moran and Whitman (1985) assessed the manner in which parent behaviors were affected as outcome measures.

Dependence. In contrast to all other studies reviewed thus far, the Group 13 investigations provide the strongest evidence for a functional relationship between the independent and dependent variables. Taken together, the results from the various studies demonstrate that contingent responding affects the acquisition of operant behavior. The major conclusion that can be drawn from these studies is that acquisition of response-contingent behavior can be facilitated quite rapidly among both handicapped and developmentally at-risk infants in instances where operant conditioning procedures are employed as a form of early intervention.

GROUP 14

The studies included in this group assessed the effects of early intervention with environmentally at-risk infants and older preschoolers (Garber & Heber, 1981; Lazar & Darlington, 1982; Ramey & Haskins, 1981; Ramey et al., 1985a, b) and medically/environmentally at-risk infants (Cappleman, Thompson, De Remer-Sullivan, King & Sturm 1982; Field, Widmayer, Stringer & Ignatoff, 1980). The Lazar and Darlington (1982) study, unlike the other investigations was an evaluation of 11 separate early intervention programs. Moreover, 9 of

the 11 programs included in the Lazar and Darlington study were actually carried out with older preschoolers and not with infants. We have nonetheless chosen to include this particular study here because it illustrates the manner in which a well conceptualized and conducted evaluation can shed considerable light on the efficacy issue.

All of the studies included both experimental and control groups; however, random assignment to treatment conditions differed among the investigations. Garber and Heber (1981), Ramey and Haskins (1981), and Ramey et al. (1985a, b) exercised the most control over random assignment to treatment conditions; Cappleman et al. (1982) and Field et al. (1980) exercised somewhat less control. The 11 Lazar and Darlington (1982) studies varied in terms of degree of random assignment. For the most part, however, the experimental and control groups in the various studies appeared to be generally equated on most explanatory variables that might influence the results.

Specificity. Ramey et al. (1985a,b; Ramey & Bryant, 1982) examined a number of studies, including those in Group 14, in terms of intensity of treatment (amount of time that the programs had *direct* contact with the project participants) and found strong evidence for an intensity effect. Ramey et al. (1985a) concluded that "Programs that have many hours and years of contact with the families and particularly many hours of contact with the children are likely to have the most positive effects on childrens' intellectual outcome" (p. 84). In terms of intensity of treatment, Garber and Heber's (1981) project was the most intense; the Ramey and Haskins' (1981) project the second most intense; the Ramey et al. (1985a,b) project the third most intense; and the Cappleman et al. (1982) and Field et al. (1980) projects and all the projects in the Lazar and Darlington (1982) study the least intense. At least in terms of IQ differences between the experimental and control groups, the data from these studies support the intensity hypothesis.

In addition to intensity of intervention, Ramey et al. (1985a,b) found that a child/parent education focused approach to intervention was more effective than simply parent education alone.

Social support. Nearly all the studies in this group were carried out with low SES families with limited financial, physical, medical, and so forth resources. In addition to the "educational treatments" provided to the children and parents, a number of programs engaged in extensive efforts designed to mediate provision of support from both the programs and other social agencies. There were, however, no explicit attempts to evaluate the impact of these efforts. Moreover, none of the programs considered the manner in which informal support might have affected behavior change.

Child and family characteristics. To the extent that subjects were randomly assigned to treatment conditions, effects due to child and family characteristics should be minimized. This was the case in the Cappleman et al. (1982), Garber and Heber (1981), and Ramey and Haskin (1981) studies. Lazar and Darlington (1982) recognized this as a problem in their investigation, and their analyses included an assessment of the differential and conditional relationships involving child and family characteristics. Their data provided "no evidence that early education differentially affected boys versus girls, children from one-parent versus two-parent homes, or children with different levels of pretest IQ scores, mother's education, or number of siblings" (p. 57).

Field et al. (1980) included a number of comparison groups in her study in order to assess the effects of child and family characteristics. There were few differences between the experimental and control groups, and differences that were found were all explained by differences in maternal age (teenage mothers vs. adult mothers).

Internal validity. Taken together, the Group 14 studies generally did a good job of control over threats to internal validity. To the extent that the subjects in the experimental and control groups were equated and not differentially treated other than factors involving the interventions, factors that might possibly influence the results would be minimized. This was the case in nearly all the investigations.

Dependent measures. The primary measures of program success in the Garber and Heber (1981) study was child progress. Experimental subjects were found to score significantly higher than control subjects beginning around 2 years of age and continuing up to age 5. The dependent measures in the Ramey and Haskins (1981) study included child progress, maternal styles of interaction, school age performance, and child social interaction skills. Experimental subjects performed significantly higher than control subjects on all these measures at the majority of age levels tested.

Both Cappleman et al. (1982) and Field et al. (1980) found significant differences favoring their intervention groups on their child outcome measures, including developmental gains by the children (both studies) and infant weight gain, infant size, infant temperament, maternal styles of interactions, and maternal attitudes and expectations (Field et al., 1980).

Lazar and Darlington (1982) employed particularly ecologically relevant outcome measures. In addition to child IQ scores, these investigators used retention in grade; special education versus regular classroom placement; child attitudes, values, career aspirations, and self-concepts; school performance; and parental attitudes, values, satisfaction, and aspirations for child; as measures of the efficacy of early intervention. They found significant differences on nearly all outcome measures favoring the experimental subjects.

Dependence. Together, the studies included in this group provide perhaps the most convincing evidence that early intervention with environmentally and medically at-risk children is efficacious. The investigations were generally conducted in a manner that permits causal inferences to be made regarding the fact that the interventions were the primary factor that accounts for the differences between groups. What cannot be discerned is the specific aspect of the interventions that accounted for the observed differences, since these were multiple treatment effects. The major conclusion that can be made from these studies is that participation in an early intervention program for environmentally and medically at-risk infants produces both immediate and long-term effects, and that these effects appear directly related to the interventions although the exact nature of what aspects of the interventions produced the effects cannot be discerned.

Summary and Conclusions

This state-of-the-art review and analysis examined the manner in which intervention and nonintervention factors affected child, parent, and family functioning among at-risk infants participating in early intervention programs. Fourteen groups of studies were included in our analysis. Studies within groups were similar in terms of one or more characteristics (research design, purpose, types of analysis, etc.), and may be considered a series of "same-type" study replications. The separate groups of studies were analyzed using a paradigmatic framework that was designed to assess the degree to which causal inferences could be made regarding factors affecting changes in child and family behavior and functioning.

Our analysis presents a rather mixed picture of the efficacy of early intervention. Any conclusions that can be made must be considered tentative and conditional, and considerable caution is warranted in terms of definitive statements about the efficacy of early intervention. With regard to the main focus of review, it must be explicitly stated that there is insufficient evidence at this time to conclude that there are cause-effect relationships between the interventions and outcomes observed in the various studies examined in this chapter. Nonetheless, it is possible to draw a number of conclusions from our review.

The following major conclusions can be made:

1. The large majority of children who participate in early intervention programs make developmental progress and manifest behavior change across time, although the extent to which the interventions are responsible for observed effects is difficult to ascertain.

2. The most convincing evidence regarding the efficacy of early intervention comes from studies of environmentally at-risk infants and young children. We still do not have a sufficient number of studies that have adequately established the efficacy of early intervention with biologically at-risk infants.

3. Cognitively and behaviorally oriented programs tend to produce the greatest effects, although this finding may be confounded with treatment duration since these types of programs tended to be carried out over extended periods of time.

4. There is very little evidence to support the contention that therapeutic-type interventions (physical and occupational therapy) affect changes in child progress, although this finding may be confounded with treatment duration since most of these efficacy studies tended to be carried out as short-term investigations.

5. There are a number of intervention-related variables (age of entry, intensity and duration of treatment) that emerge as being important covariates of program effectiveness; however, these variables tend to have conditional effects. For example, intensity of involvement appears important in center-based programs with minimal parent involvement but is less important in home-based programs where parents function as "teachers" of their own children.

6. Both informal and formal provision of support from the intervention programs as well as from outside sources has strong mediational effects in parent and family functioning and to a lesser degree in child functioning.

7. The rates of progress made by children with differing diagnoses appears to be relatively uniform but that rates of progress differ considerably as a function of severity of impairment; the more severe the child's impairments, the smaller the amount of progress is demonstrated.

8. One of the best indicators of the amount of progress a child is likely to make as a result of participation in an early intervention program is entry level performance. Higher functioning children are more likely to demonstrate the greatest amount of progress.

9. Degree of child progress is also likely to be influenced by child characteristics as well, including behavioral problems, temperament, and degree of motivation.

10. Parent and family characteristics, including education level, locus-of-control, SES, income, and family size, are likely to influence child progress, although this is more likely to be found true in programs serving heterogeneously formed groups of at-risk infants as opposed to just environmentally at-risk children.

11. The evidence regarding the efficacy of early intervention with biologically at-risk infants is based almost solely on child progress data. In contrast, the evidence documenting the effectiveness of early intervention with environmentally at-risk infants is derived from broader-based measures of child, parent, and family functioning.

All of the above conclusions, tentative as they are, must be qualified even further for at least the following reasons:

1. There is considerable variability in the quality of studies both within and across groups so that the degree of confidence about causal inferences must be considered relative rather than absolute.

2. We suspect that there is a considerable publication bias in the studies included in our review since studies that report positive findings are more likely to appear in the literature.

3. Given the complexity of the nature of intervention research, and given the fact that the majority of evidence is based on main effects analyses, it is highly questionable whether or not the findings from the various studies convey an accurate picture of the complex relationships among the host of variables that affect child, parent, and family functioning.

4. Very few studies tested for the types of conditional relationships that would increase the degree to which causal inferences might be made about the relationships among variables.

5, The ecological relevance of many of the interventions evaluated in the studies included in our review may be questioned for a number of reasons, including the type of interventions and the validity of the outcome measures.

6. The differences between the experimental and control groups in many of the studies are very small in magnitude, and often smaller than the standard error of measurement reported for the test instrument used as the dependent measure.

7. The lack of use of regression/causal analysis designs in a large majority of studies limits the types of inferences and conclusions that can be made about the relative impact of intervention and nonintervention factors.

State of Practice

To the best of our knowledge, there are no national survey data available to discern the manner in which practices in the field are consistent with state-of-the-art knowledge. What evidence we do have would suggest that state of practice is not keeping pace with our ever expanding knowledge base. For instance, in White et al.'s (1985) review of 21 federally funded Handicapped Children's Early Education Program (HCEEP) projects considered exemplary programs with proven effectiveness, they found these programs and their evaluation efforts fraught with methodological problems that made interpretation of their efficacy data difficult at best. In addition, our review of several sets of standards which a number of states have established as criteria for the state of practice for programs serving handicapped preschoolers and their families finds many recommendations inconsistent with what our knowledge base suggests should be best practices. Moreover, our analysis of data from one state found a large number of inconsistencies in terms of what the standards established as accepted practice, and what services were provided by state-funded early childhood education programs. In most instances, the state standards established certain foci for the provision of services but actual services did not conform to these standards.

Evidence concerning the lack of information about early intervention practices comes from a survey recently conducted by Spence and Trohanis (1985). These investigators gathered information about several dimensions of early childhood special education services from all 50 states, six trust territories, and the District of Columbia. A total of 52 respondents (91%) reported that services to children under 6 years of age were either mandated or allowed through permissive legislation. (Thirty-seven states/jurisdictions, or 65%, indicated that services to children birth to 3 years of age were either mandated or allowed through permissive legislation.) Thirty-four (60%) of the respondents indicated that their states/jurisdictions had some type of rules and regulations governing early childhood special education programs, but only 18 (32%) indicated that they had specific guidelines for provision of early intervention services. Only four (7%) respondents indicated that efficacy data were being collected to document program effectiveness.

Given the lack of information about state of practice, and rather than speculate about practices in the field, we propose a series of questions that program administrators and direct service staff might consider in assessing the degree to which their own programs operate from an information base that reflects state-of-the-art knowledge. Powell (1982) offers a series of similar type questions designed to bridge the gap between program policy and program practice.

1. Programs that have explicitly stated philosophical and conceptual orientations are more likely to be successful because program goals, objectives, and activities are logically derived and consistent with program "beliefs" (Dunst, 1982): Does the program have a philosophy about children and families that guides the development, implementation, and evaluation of program practices?

2. The lack of a theoretical or causal model for understanding the relationships between the intervention (treatment) and outcome measures is a factor often associated with the failure to establish program effectiveness (Halpern, 1984): Does the program explicitly identify the components of their interventions, and the manner in which the treatment variables are expected to "cause" changes in the outcome measure(s)?

3. Programs that employ broader-based, systems approaches to conceptualizing and implementing early intervention services are more likely to recognize and assess the first-, second-, and higher-order effects of the treatment efforts (Bronfenbrenner, 1979): Does the program view its efforts within the broader contexts of

the family and community, and the manner in which child-level and family-level interventions will impact upon child, parent, family, and community functioning?

4. Programs that use deficit approaches to intervention with children and families are likely to alienate program participants. In contrast, programs that employ proactive models that focus on strengths, and building upon them, are more likely to be received with enthusiasm (Cochran & Woolever, 1983; Dunst, 1985; Stoneman, 1985): Does the program, and its activities, take a positive stance toward children and families and focus on building upon strengths rather than only correcting deficits?

5. Programs that view parent and family involvement in terms of activities designed to meet individual needs rather than as a preselected set of expectations are more likely to be successful (Foster, Berger, & McLean, 1981; Winton & Turnbull, 1981): Does the program tailor its activities to the individualized needs of family members rather than "fit" the children and their parents to predetermined activities?

6. Even the better designed and implemented early intervention programs account for only about 10% of the variance in the outcome measures (Halpern, 1984): Is the program realistic in terms of expectations for changes in child performance resulting from the interventions?

7. As our analysis of the efficacy literature documented, progress by children in early intervention programs is likely to vary as a function of a number of intervention and nonintervention related variables (diagnosis, severity of impairment, age of entry, intensity, and duration of treatment): Does the program take these factors into consideration in terms of expectations established for determining program effectiveness?

8. The extent to which a family has the time, energy, and personal investment to be part of the intervention process with their child is dependent upon the adequacy and degree of support available to them (Dunst & Leet, 1987): Does the program take into consideration existing time demands on the family before asking them to assume additional responsibilities as part of participation in the intervention program?

9. The extent to which a family has a strong and supportive social network will likely influence personal well-being and family integrity which in turn will influence the manner in which a parent successfully adapts to their child's special needs (Crnic, Friedrich & Greenberg, 1983a; Dunst, 1985): Does the program provide or facilitate adequate provisions of support in order to maintain and enhance personal and familial well-being?

10. Programs for families of young children are more likely to be successful to the extent that program activities support and strengthen family functioning and family decision-making rather than replace or supplant parental authority (Hobbs, 1975: Hobbs et al., 1984;

Stoneman, 1985): Do the activities of the program support, empower, and strengthen families as part of their participation?

11. Programs are more likely to document program effectiveness if they obtain broad-based measures of child, parent, and family functioning (Dunst, 1986; Zigler & Balla, 1982): Does the program measure the impact of its services on the child, parents, and family in order to discern the broad-based effects of early intervention efforts?

Recommendations

We conclude our review and analysis with 14 general recommendations for direct service, research, and policy.

1. There is clearly a need to identify and employ conceptual and theoretical frameworks to guide provision of services (direct service), assess the effectiveness of early intervention (research), and establish "tried and tested" approaches (policy).

2. There is a need for both program administrators and direct service personnel to establish the "parameters" of their early intervention efforts as a basis for developing, implementing, and evaluating provision of services to at-risk infants and their families. The series of 11 questions posed in the State-of-practice section should be useful as a framework for defining these parameters.

3. An increasing amount of evidence points to the fact that broad-based, systems approaches to early intervention are most likely to be responsive to, and meet the needs of, at-risk infants and their families. The field of early intervention would benefit immensely if programs adopted and embraced approaches to intervention that recognized the broader-based contexts in which families function and thus their needs arise.

4. We are witnessing a shift away from activity-based toward needs-based approaches to early intervention, which is being recognized as the most efficient approach to provision of services. A needs-based approach to early intervention bases provision of services on the individualized needs of children and families rather than requiring family members to participate in specific program activities.

5. To be relevant and useful to direct service staff, efficacy research must not only attempt to answer the question "Does early intervention work?" but also ask questions that permit the identification of "alterable" factors associated with program success so that direct service efforts can manipulate these variables as interventions. It is therefore necessary to increase the specificity at which we define intervention-related variables in order to identify these factors.

6. Theory must guide efficacy research if we are to make both practical and scientific advances in the field of early intervention. It will only be possible to discern the manner in which interventions affect child, parent,

and family functioning when testable theories guide our research efforts.

8. In order to discern the impact of early intervention and other forms of support, and be assured that it was the "treatments" that affected observed changes, we must use the most rigorous experimental designs possible. Outcome research, or experimental evaluation, must strive toward the highest scientific standards if our knowledge base about the efficacy of early intervention practices is to be discerned.

8. Explanatory efficacy research will become closer to being a scientific endeavor when attempts are made to isolate the myriad of factors that affect child, parent, and family functioning. Our paradigmatic framework, or some other explanatory model, should be useful as a framework for structuring the design and implementation of an efficacy study.

9. Advances in explanatory research are likely to become a reality only when we move away from main effects studies toward investigations that permit tests of conditional relationships among the independent variables.

10. Future integrative reviews are likely to be useful only if they as well are guided by theory which suggests the independent, mediational, and dependent variables that should be examined and the manner in which data interpretation and analysis should proceed.

11. Because sample sizes in individual early intervention programs are likely to be too small for the types of proposed analyses, it will be necessary to pool data across programs. In order to do so, there must be policy and procedures that establish a common data collection protocol that programs both within (state policy) and across (federal policy) states would use as part of their program evaluation requirements.

12. In order to reap the benefits from data pooled across programs, both state and federal agencies must establish policy and procedures that would allocate the time and resources (human, financial, etc.) necessary to compile and analyze the data for both programmatic and research purposes.

13. The conduct of a national survey of state-level standards for early intervention programs is recommended in order to establish similarities and differences across states and determine the manner in which standards are consistent with state-of-the-art knowledge.

14. The conduct of a national survey of federally-funded, state-funded, and privately-funded early intervention programs is recommended in order to (a) establish the extent to which practices in the field are similar and different across and within states, and (b) practices are consistent with state-of-the-art knowledge.

References

Adelson, E., & Fraiberg, S. (1974). Gross motor development in infants blind from birth. *Child Development,* **45,** 114–126.

Aronson, M., & Fallstrom, K. (1977). Immediate and long-term effects of developmental training in children with Down's syndrome. *Developmental Medicine and Child Neurology, 19*, 489–494.

Bagnato, S., & Neisworth, J. (1980). The intervention efficiency index: An approach to preschool program accountability. *Exceptional Children, 46*, 264–269.

Bagnato, S. J., & Neisworth, J. T. (1985). Efficacy of interdisciplinary assessment and treatment for infants and preschoolers with congenital and acquired brain injury. *Analysis and Intervention in Developmental Disabilities, 5*, 81–102.

Bailey, D., Harms, T., & Clifford, R. (1983). Matching changes in preschool environments to desired changes in child behavior. *Journal of the Division for Early Childhood, 7*, 61–68.

Bailey, E. J., & Bricker, D. (1984). The efficacy of early intervention for severely handicapped infants and young children. *Topics in Early Childhood Special Education, 4*(3), 30–51.

Bailey, E. J., & Bricker, D. (1985). Evaluation of a three-year early intervention demonstration project. *Topics in Early Childhood Special Education, 5*(2), 52–65.

Baltes, P. B. (1973). Prototypical paradigms and questions in life-span research on development and aging. *Gerontologist 13*, 458–467.

Baltes, P., Reese, H., & Nesselroade, J. (1977). *Life-span developmental psychology: Introduction to research methods*. Monterey, CA: Brooks/Cole.

Barna, S., Bidder, R., Gray, O., Clements, J., & Gardner, S. (1980). The progress of developmentally delayed children in a home-training scheme. *Child: Care, Health and Development, 6*, 157–154.

Barrera, M. E. C., Routh, D. K., Parr, C. A., Johnson, N. M., Arendshorst, D. S., Goolsby, E. L., & Schroeder, S. R. (1976). Early intervention with biologically handicapped infants and young children: A preliminary study with each child as his own control. In T. Tjossem (Ed.), *Intervention strategies for high risk infants and young children* (pp. 610–627). Baltimore: University Park Press.

Bayley, N., Rhodes, L., Gooch, B., & Marcus, M. (1971). Environmental factors in the development of institutionalized children. In S. Hellmuth (Ed.), *Exceptional infant: Vol. 2, Studies in subnormalities* (pp. 450–472). New York: Brunner/Mazel.

Bidder, R., Bryant, G., & Gray, D. (1975). Benefits to Down's Syndrome children through training their mothers. *Archives of Diseases in Childhood, 50*, 383–386.

Bott, E. (1971). *Family and social networks*. London: Tavistock Publications.

Bracht, G., & Glass, G. (1968). The external validity of experiments. *American Educational Research Journal, 5*, 437–474.

Brassell, W. R. (1974, June). *Early intervention with organically damaged and high-risk infants*. Paper presented at the meeting of the American Association on Mental Deficiency, Toronto, Canada.

Brassell, W. R. (1977). Intervention with handicapped infants: Correlates of progress. *Mental Retardation, 15*, 18–22.

Brassell, W. R. & Dunst, C. J. (1975a). Cognitive intervention by parents of impaired infants. *Mental Retardation, 13*, 42.

Brassell, W. R., & Dunst, C. J. (1975b). Facilitating cognitive development in impaired infants. In C. J. Dunst (Ed.), *Trends in early intervention services: Methods, models, and evaluation* (pp. 142–153). Arlington, Va: Department of Human Resources.

Brassell, W. R., & Dunst, C. J. (1978). Fostering the object construct: Large scale intervention with handicapped infants. *American Journal of Mental Deficiency, 82*, 507–510.

Bricker, D., Bailey, E., & Bruder, M. (1984). The efficacy of early intervention and the handicapped infant. In M. Wolraich & D. Routh (Eds.), *Advances in developmental and behavioral pediatrics* (Vol. 5) (pp. 373–423). Greenwich, CN: JAI Press.

Bricker, D., & Dow, D. (1980). Early intervention with the young severely handicapped child. *Journal of the Association for the Severely Handicapped, 5*, 130–142.

Bricker, D., & Sheehan, R. (1981). Effectiveness of an early intervention program as indexed by measures of child change. *Journal of the Division for Early Childhood, 4*, 11–27.

Brinker, R. P., & Lewis, M. (1982). Discovering the competent handicapped infant: A process approach to assessment and intervention. *Topics in Early Childhood Special Education, 2*(2), 1–16.

Brinkworth, R. (1973). The unfinished child: Effects of early home training on the mongol infant. In A. D. Clarke & A. N. Clarke (Eds.), *Mental retardation and behavioral research* (pp. 213–222). London: Churchill Livingstone.

Brinkworth, R. (1975). The unfinished child: Early treatment and training for the infant with Down's syndrome. *Royal Society Health Journal, 95*, 73–78.

Bronfenbrenner, U. (1979). *The ecology of human development*. Cambridge: Harvard University Press.

Bromwich, R. M., & Parmelee, A. H. (1979). An intervention program for pre-term infants. In T. M. Field (Ed.), *Infants born at risk* (pp. 389–411). New York: Spectrum.

Bush, D. W., & White, K. R. (1983). *The efficacy of early intervention: What can be learned from previous reviews of the literature?* Paper presented at the meeting of the Rocky Mountain Psychological Assocation, Snowbird, UT.

Caldwell, B., Bradley, R., & Elardo, R. (1975). Early stimulation. In J. Wortis (Ed.), *Mental retardation and developmental disabilities: An annual review* (Vol. 7, pp. 128–181). New York: Brunner/Mazel.

Cappleman, M. W., Thompson, Jr., R. J., DeRemer-Sullivan, P. A., King, A. A., & Sturm, J. M. (1982). Effectiveness of a home-based intervention program with infants of adolescent mothers. *Child Psychiatry and Human Development, 13*, 55–65.

Carlsen, P. N. (1975). Comparison of two occupational therapy approaches for treating the young cerebral-palsied child. *American Journal of Occupational Therapy, 5*, 267–272.

Chee, F., Kreutzberg, J., & Clark, D. (1978). Semicircular canal stimulation in cerebral palsied children. *Physical Therapy, 58*, 1071–1075.

Clarke, A. M., & Clarke, A. D. B. (1974). *Mental deficiency: The changing outlook*. New York: The Free Press.

Clunies-Ross, G. (1979). Accelerating the development of Down's syndrome infants and young children. *Journal of Special Education, 13*, 169–177.

Cochran, M., & Brassard, J. (1979). Child development and personal social networks. *Child Development, 50*, 601–616.

Cochran, M., & Woolever, F. (1983). Beyond the deficit model: The empowerment of parents with information and informal supports. In I. E. Sigel & L. M. Laosa (Eds.),

Changing families (pp. 225–245). Princeton, NJ: Educational Testing Service.

Cohen, J., & Cohen, P. (1983). *Applied multiple regression/correlation analysis for the behavioral sciences* (2nd Ed.). Hillsdale, N.J.: Erlbaum.

Connolly, B., & Russell, F. (1976). Interdisciplinary early intervention program. *Physical Therapy, 56*, 155–157.

Connolly, J. (1979). Intelligence levels in Down's syndrome children. *American Journal of Mental Deficiency, 83*, 193–196.

Cook, T., & Campbell, D. T. (1979). *Quasi-experimentaion: Design and analysis issues for field settings*. Chicago: Rand McNally.

Crnic, K., Friedrich, W., & Greenberg, M. (1983a). Adaptation of families with mentally retarded children: A model of stress, coping, and family ecology. *American Journal of Mental Deficiency, 88*, 125–138.

Crnic, K. A., Greenberg, M. T., Ragozin, A. S., Robinson, N. M., & Basham, R. B. (1983b). Effects of stress and social support on mothers and premature and full-term infants. *Child Development, 54*, 209–217.

Crockenberg, S. (1981). Infant irritability, mother responsiveness, and social influences on the security of infant-mother attachment. *Child Development, 52*, 857–865.

Cunningham, C. C., Aumonier, M. E., & Sloper, P. (1982). Health visitor support for families with Down's syndrome infants. *Child: Care, Health, and Development, 8*, 1–19.

Cyrulik-Jacobs, A., Shapira, Y., & Jones, M. H. (1975). Application of an automatic operant response procedure to the study of auditory perception and processing ability of neurologically-impaired infants. In B. Z. Friedlander, G. M. Sterritt, & G. E. Kirk (Eds.) *Exceptional infant: Vol. 3. Assessment and intervention* (pp. 109–123). New York; Brunner/Mazel.

Dean, A., & Lin, M. (1977). Stress-buffering role of social support. *Journal of Nervous and Mental Disease, 165*, 403–417.

Denhoff, E. (1981). Current status of infant stimulation or enrichment programs for children with developmental disabilities. *Pediatrics, 67*(1), 32–37.

Dunst, C. J. (1974). *Patterns of cognitive skill acquisitions in developmentally delayed infants*. Paper presented at the meeting of the American Association on Mental Deficiency, Toronto.

Dunst, C. J. (1982). Theoretical bases and pragmatic considerations in infant curriculum construction. In J. Anderson (Ed.), *Curricula for high-risk and handicapped infants* (pp. 13–23). Chapel Hill, NC: Technical Assistance Development System.

Dunst, C. J. (1985)). Rethinking early intervention. *Analysis and Intervention in Developmental Disabilities, 5*, 165–201.

Dunst, C. J. (1986). Overview of the efficacy of early intervention programs: Methodological and conceptual considerations. In L. Bickman & D. Weatherford (Eds.), *Evaluating early intervention programs for severely handicapped children and their families* (pp. 79–147). Austin, TX: PRO-ED.

Dunst, C. J. (in press). Sensorimotor development of Down's syndrome infants. In D. Cichetti & L. Beeghly (Eds.), *Down's syndrome: The developmental perspective*. Cambridge, MA: Harvard University Press.

Dunst, C. J., Cushing, P. J., & Vance, S. D. (1985). Response-contingent learning in profoundly handicapped infants: A social systems perspective. *Analysis and Intervention in Developmental Disabilities, 5*, 7–21.

Dunst, C. J., Jenkins, V., & Trivette, C. M. (1984). Family Support Scale: Reliability and validity. *Journal of Individual, Family and Community Wellness, 1*(4), 45–52.

Dunst, C. J., & Leet, H. E. (1985). *Family resource scale: reliability and validity*. Unpublished manuscript, Western Carolina Center, Family, Infant and Preschool Program, Morganton, NC.

Dunst, C. J., Lee, H. E. (1987). Measuring the adequacy of resources in households with young children. *Child: Care, Health and Development, 13*, 111–125.

Dunst, C. J., & Lingerfelt, B. (1985). Maternal ratings of temperament and operant learning in two- to three-month-old infants. *Child Development, 56*, 555–563.

Dunst, C. J., & Rheingrover, R. M. (1981). Analysis of the efficacy of infant intervention programs for handicapped children. *Evaluation and Program Planning, 4*, 287–323.

Dunst, C. J., & Trivette, C. M. (1984). *Differential influences of social support on mentally retarded children and their families*. Paper presented at the meeting of the American Psychological Association, Toronto, Canada.

Dunst, C. J., & Trivette, C. M. (1987). *Social support and positive functioning in families of developing at-risk preschoolers*. Paper presented at the biennial meeting of the Society for Research in Child Development, Baltimore.

Dunst, C. J., Trivette, C. M., & Cross, A. H. (1986). Mediating influences of social support: Personal, family, and child outcomes. *American Journal of Mental Deficiency*.

Dunst, C. J., & Vance, S. D. & Gallagher, J. L. (1983). *Differential efficacy of early intervention with handicapped infants*. Paper presented at the annual meeting of the Council for Exceptional Children, Detroit.

Eisenstadt, J. W., & Powell, D. R. (1980). *Parent characteristics and the utilization of a parent–child program*. Unpublished manuscript, Purdue University, Department of Child Development and Family Studies, West Lafayette, IN.

Embry, L. (1980). Family support for handicapped preschool children at risk for abuse. *New Directions for Exceptional Children, 4*, 29–58.

Field, T., Widmayer, S., Stringer, S., & Ignatoff, E. (1980). Teenage, lowerclass, black mothers and their preterm infants: An intervention and developmental follow-up. *Child Development, 51*, 426–436.

Ford, J. (1978). A multidisciplinary approach to early intervention strategies for the education of the developmentally handicapped 0–3 year old: A pilot study. *Australian Journal of Mental Retardation, 5*, 26–29.

Foster, M., Berger, M., & McLean, M. (1981). Rethinking a good idea: A reassessment of parent involvement. *Topics in Early Childhood Special Education, 1*(3), 55–65.

Friedlander, B. Z., McCarthy, J. J., & Soferenko, A. Z. (1967). Automated psychological evaluation with severely retarded institutionalized infants. *American Journal of Mental Deficiency, 71*, 909–919.

Garber, H. L., & Heber, R. (1981). The efficacy of early intervention with family rehabilitation. In M. S. Begab, H. C. Haywood, & H. L. Garber, *Psychosocial influences in retarded performance: Vol. 2. Strategies for improving competence* (pp. 71–88). Baltimore: University Park Press.

Giovanoni, J. & Billingsley, A. (1970). Child neglect among the poor: A study of parental adequacy in families of three ethnic groups. *Child Welfare, 49*, 196–204.

Glenn, S. M. (1983). The application of an automated system for the assessment of profound mentally handicapped children. *International Journal of Rehabilitation Research,* **6**(3), 358–360.

Goodman, J. F., Cecil, H. S., & Barker, W. F. (1984). Early intervention with retarded children: Some encouraging results. *Developmental Medicine and Child Neurology,* **26**, 47–55.

Gordon, R. (1977). *Study of impact of early developmental program on multihandicapped young children and their families.* New York: New York University Medical Center Infant School Program. (ERIC Document Reproduction Service No. ED 149 563).

Gutelius, M. F., & Kirsh, A. D. (1975). Factors promoting success in infant education. *American Journal of Public Health,* **65**, 384–387.

Halpern, R. (1984). Lack of effects for home-based early intervention? Some possible explanations. *American Journal of Orthopsychiatry,* **54**(1), 33–42.

Hanson, M. J. (1985). An analysis of the effects of early intervention services for infants and toddlers with moderate and severe handicaps. *Topics in Early Childhood Special Education,* **5**(2), 36–51.

Hanson, M., & Schwartz, T. (1978). Results of a longitudinal intervention program for Down's syndrome infants and their families. *Education and Training of the Mentally Retarded,* **13**, 403–407.

Harris, S. R. (1981). Effects of neurodevelopmental therapy on motor performance of infants with Down's syndrome. *Developmental Medicine and Child Neurology,* **23**, 477–483.

Hayden, A., & Dmitriev, V. (1975). The multidisciplinary preschool program for Down's syndrome children at the University of Washington Model Preschool Center. In B. Friedlander, G. Sterritt, & G. Kirk (Eds.), *Exceptional infant: Vol. 3, Assessment and intervention* (pp. 193–221). New York: Brunner/Mazel.

Hayden, A., & Haring, N. (1977). The acceleration and maintenance of developmental gains in Down's syndrome school-aged children. In P. Mittler (Ed.), *Research to practice in mental retardation: Vol. 1. Care and intervention* (pp. 129–141). Baltimore: University Park Press.

Hayes, L. A., Ewy, R. D., & Watson, J. S. (1982). Attention as a predictor of learning in infants. *Journal of Experimental Child Psychology,* **34**, 38–45.

Hedges, L., & Becker, B. (1986). The meta-analysis of research on gender differences. In J. Hyde & M. Linn (Eds.), *The psychology of gender: Progress through meta-analysis.* Baltimore: Johns Hopkins University Press.

Hetherington, E., Cox. M., & Cox, R. (1976). Divorced fathers. *Family Coordinator,* **25**, 427–428.

Hetherington, E., Cox, M., & Cox, R. (1978). The aftermath of divorce. In J. Stevens & M. Mathews (Eds.), *Mother-child, father-child relations* (pp. 149–176). Washington, DC: National Association for the Education on Young Children.

Hewitt, K. E., Newcombe, R. G., & Bidder, R. T. (1983). Profiles of skill gain in delayed infants and young children. *Child: Care, Health and Development,* **9**, 127–135.

Hobbs, N. (1975). *The futures of children.* San Francisco: Jossey-Bass.

Hobbs, N., Dokeck, P. R., Hoover-Dempsey, K. V., Moroney, R. M., Shayne, M. W., & Weeks, K. H. (1984). *Strengthening families.* San Francisco: Jossey-Bass.

Honig, A. S. (1983). Evaluation of infant/toddler intervention programs. *Studies in Educational Evaluation,* **8**, 305–316.

Horton, K. (1971, July). *Early amplification and language learning.* Paper presented at the meeting of the Academy of Rehabilitative Audiology, Winter Park, CO.

Horton, K. B. (1974, May). *Early intervention for hearing impaired infants and young children.* Paper presented at the National Conference on Early Intervention with High Risk Infants and Young Children, Chapel Hill, NC.

Hunt, J. McV. (1976). The utility of ordinal scales inspired by Piaget's observations. *Merrill-Palmer Quarterly,* **22**, 31–45.

Hunt, J. McV. (1980). Implications of plasticity and hierarchical achievements for the assessment of development and risk of mental retardation. In D. B. Sawin, R. C. Hawkins, L. O. Walker, & J. H. Penticuff (Eds.), *Exceptional infant: Vol. 4. Psychosocial risks in infant-environment transactions* (pp. 7–54). New York: Brunner/Mazel.

Hunt, J. McV., Mohandessi, K., Ghodssi, M., & Akiyama, M. (1976). The psychological development of orphanage-reared infants: Interventions with outcomes (Tehran). *Genetic Psychology Monographs,* **94**, 177–226.

Hutinger, P. (1978). *Program performance report for handicapped children's early education program: Macomb 0–3 regional project.* Macomb, IL: Western Illinois University. (ERIC Document Reproduction Service No. ED 184 278)

Jelinek, J., & Flamboe, T. (1979). *The Wyoming infant stimulation program.* Laramie, WY: WISP Project. (ERIC Document Reproduction Service No. ED 171 090)

Kantner, R. M., Clark, D. L., Allen, L. C., & Chase, M. F. (1976). Effects of vestibular stimulation on nystagmus response and motor performance in the developmentally delayed infant. *Physical Therapy,* **56**, 414–417.

Kaplan, M., & Atkins, J. (1978). *Model services for handicapped infants.* (ERIC Document Reproduction Service No. 175 174)

Kelly, J. F. (1982). Effects of intervention on caregiver-infant interaction when the infant is handicapped. *Journal of the Division for Early Childhood,* **5**, 53–63.

Kenny, D. A. (1979). *Correlation and causality.* New York: Wiley.

Krafchuk, E., Sameroff, A., & Bakow, H. (1976). *Newborn temperament and operant head turning.* Paper presented at the Southeast Regional Meeting of the Society for Research in Child Development, Nashville.

Laub, K. W., & Dunst, C. J. (1974). *Effects of non-imitative and imitative adult vocalizing on a developmentally delayed infant's rate of vocalization.* Paper presented at the meeting of the North Carolina Speech and Hearing Association, Durham.

Lazar, I., & Darlington, R. (1982). Lasting effects of early education: A report from the consortium for longitudinal studies. *Monographs of the Society for Research in Child Development,* **47** (2–3, Serial No. 195).

Leib, S. A. Benfield, G., & Guidubaldi, J. (1980). Effects of early intervention and stimulation on the preterm infant. *Pediatrics,* **66**, 83–90.

LeLaurin, K. (1985). The experimental analysis of the effects of early intervention with normal, at-risk, and handicapped children under age three. *Analysis and Intervention in Developmental Disabilities,* **5**, 103–124.

Longstreth, L. E. (1968). *Psychological development of the child.* New York: Ronald Press.

Lovaas, O. I. (1982, August). *An overview of the young autism project*. Paper presented at the meeting of the American Psychological Association, Washington, DC.

Ludlow, J., & Allen, L. (1979). The effects of early intervention and preschool stimulus on the development of the Down's syndrome child. *Journal of Mental Deficiency Research, 23,* 29–44.

Macy, D. J., Solomon, G. S., Schoen, M., Galey, G. S. (1983). The DEBT project: Early intervention for handicapped children and their parents. *Exceptionl Children, 49,* 447–448.

Mahoney, G., & Snow, K. (1983). The relationship of sensorimotor functioning to children's response to early language training. *Mental Retardation, 21,* 248–254.

Maisto, A. A. & German, M. L. (1979). Variables related to progress in a parent-infant training program for high-risk infants. *Journal of Pediatric Psychology, 4,* 409–419.

Maisto, A. A. & German, M. L. (1981). Maternal locus of control and developmental gain demonstrated by high risk infants: A longitudinal analysis. *Journal of Psychology, 109,* 213–221.

McCubbin, H., Joy, C., Cauble, A. E., Comeau, J., Patterson, J., & Needle, R. (1980). Family stress and coping: A decade review. *Journal of Marriage and the Family, 42,* 855–871.

McWilliam, R. A., Trivette, C. M. & Dunst, C. J. (1985). Behavior engagement as an outcome measure of early intervention program efficacy. *Analysis and Intervention in Developmental Disabilities, 5,* 59–71.

Medway, F. J. (1984). *Parent education: Where from? Where to?* Paper presented at the meeting of the American Psychological Association, Toronto.

Mitchell, R. E., & Trickett, E. J. (1980). Task force report: Social networks as mediators of social support. *Community Mental Health Journal, 16,* 27–43.

Moran, D. R., & Whitman, T. L. (1985). The multiple effects of a play-oriented parent training program for mothers of developmentally delayed children. *Analysis and Intervention in Developmental Disabilities, 5,* 47–70.

Murray, H. W. (1977). *Early intervention in the context of family characteristics*. Denver, CO: Education Commission of the States. (ERIC Document Reproduction Service No. ED 145 956)

Nielsen, G., Collings, S., Meisel, J., Lowry, M., Engh, H., & Johnson, D. (1975). An intervention program for atypical infants. In B. Friedlander, G. Sterritt, & Kirk (Eds.), *Exceptional infant: Vol. 3. Assessment and intervention* (pp. 222–244). New York: Brunner/Mazel.

Ottenbacher, K., & Petersen, P. (1985). The efficacy of early intervention programs for children with organic impairment: A quantitative review. *Evaluation and Program Planning. 8,* 135–146.

Ottenbacher, K., Short, M. A., & Watson, P. J. (1981). The effects of a clinically applied program of vestibular stimulation on the neuromotor performance of children with severe developmental disability. *Physical and Occupational Therapy in Pediatrics, 1*(3), 1–11.

Palmer, F. H., & Anderson, L. W. (1981). Early intervention treatments that have been tried, documented, and assessed. In M. J. Begab, H. C. Haywood, & H. L. Garber (Eds.), *Psychosocial influences in retarded performance: Vol. 2. Strategies for improving competence* (pp. 45–68). Baltimore: University Park Press.

Paraskevopoulos, J., & Hunt, J. McV. (1971). Object construction and imitation under differing conditions of rearing. *Journal of Genetic Psychology, 119,* 301–321.

Peniston, E. (1972). *An evaluation of the Portage Project*. Unpublished manuscript, The Portage Project, Portage Wisconsin. (Data presented in Shearer, M., & Shearer, D. The Portage Project: A model for early childhood education. *Exceptional Children, 26,* 210–217.)

Piper, M., & Pless, I. (1980). Early intervention for infants with Down's syndrome: A controlled trial. *Pediatrics, 65,* 463–468.

Powell, D. R. (1982). From child to parent: Changing conceptions of early childhood intervention. *Annals of the American Academy of Political and Social Sciences, 461,* 135–144.

Ramey, C. T. & Bryant, D. M. (1982). Evidence for prevention of developmental retardation during infancy. *Journal of the Division for Early Childhood, 5,* 73–78.

Ramey, C. T., Bryant, D., Sparling, J. J., & Wasik, B. H. (1985a). Educational interventions to enhance intellectual development. In S. Harel & N. Anastasiow, (Eds.), *The at-risk infant* (pp. 75–85). Baltimore: Brookes.

Ramey, C. T., Bryant, D. M., Sparling, J. J., & Wasik, B. H. (1985b). Project CARE: A comparison of two early intervention strategies to prevent retarded development. *Topics in Early Childhood Special Education, 5*(2), 12–25.

Ramey, C. T., & Haskins, R. (1981). The causes and treatment of school failure: insights from the Carolina Abecedarian Project. In M. Begab, H. Haywood, & H. Garber (Eds.), *Psychosocial influences in retarded performance* (Vol. 2, pp. 89–112). Baltimore: University Park Press.

Ramey, C. T., Hieger, L., & Klisz, D. (1972). Synchronous reinforcement of vocal responses in failure-to-thrive infants. *Child Development, 43,* 1449–1455.

Ramey, C. T., Sparling, J. J., Bryant, D. M., & Wasik, B. H. (1982). Primary prevention of developmental retardation during infancy. *Prevention in Human Services, 1*(4), 61–83.

Ramey, C. T., Starr, R. H., Pallas, J., Whitten, C. F., & Reed, V. (1976). Nutrition, response-contingent stimulation, and the maternal deprivation syndrome: Results of an early intervention program. *Merrill-Palmer Quarterly, 21*(1), 45–52.

Reese, H. W., & Overton, W. F. (1970). Models of development and theories of development. In L. R. Goulet & R. B. Baltes (Eds.), *Life-span developmental psychology* (pp. 116–145). New York: Academic Press.

Reichardt, C. S. (1979). *The design and analysis of the non-equivalent group quasi-experiment*. Unpublished doctoral dissertation, Northwestern University, Chicago.

Revill, S., & Blunden, R. (1979). A home training service for preschool developmentally handicapped children. *Behavioural Research and Therapy, 17,* 207–214.

Reynolds, L., Egan, R., Lerner, J. (1983). Efficacy of early intervention on preacademic deficits: A review of the literature. *Topics in Early Childhood Special Education, 3*(3), 47–56.

Robinson, N. M., & Robinson, H. B. (1976). *The mentally retarded child: A psychological approach* (2nd ed.). New York: McGraw-Hill.

Rottman, C. (1979). *Project Outreach for the infant program for visually impaired: Final performance report 1978–79*. Mason, MI: Ingham Intermediate School District. (ERIC Document Reproduction Service No. ED 181 645).

Safford, P., Gregg, L., Schneider, G., & Sewell, J. (1976). A stimulation program for young sensory-impaired, multi-handicapped children. *Education and Training of the Mentally Retarded, 11*, 12–17.

Sandler, A., Coren, A., Thurman, S. K. (1983). A training program for parents of handicapped preschool children: Effects upon mother, father, child. *Exceptional Children, 49*, 355–358.

Sandow, S., & Clarke, A. D. (1978). Home intervention with parents of severely subnormal pre-school children: An interim report. *Child: Care, Health and Development, 4*, 29–39.

Sandow, S. A., Clarke, A. D. B., Cox, M. V., & Stewart, F. L. (1981). Home intervention with parents of severely subnormal pre-school children: A final report. *Child: Care, Health and Development, 7*, 135–144.

Scherzer, A. L., Mike, V., & Ilson, J. (1976). Physical therapy as a determinant of change in the cerebral palsied infant. *Pediatrics, 58*, 47–52.

Sellick, K., & Over, R. (1980). Effects of vestibular stimulation on motor development of cerebral-palsied children. *Developmental Medicine and Child Neurology, 22*, 476–483.

Shapiro, L., Gordon, R., & Neiditch, C. (1977). Documenting change in young multiply handicapped children in a rehabilitation center. *Journal of Special Education, 11*, 243–257.

Shearer, M., & Shearer, D. (1972). The Portage Project: A model for early childhood education. *Exceptional Children, 36*, 210–217.

Sigel, I. E. (1985). *Parental belief systems: The psychological consequences for children.* Hillsdale, NJ: Lawrence Erlbaum.

Simeonsson, R. J., Cooper, D. H., & Scheiner, A. P. (1982). A review and analysis of the effectiveness of early intervention programs. *Pediatrics, 69*, 635–641.

Simeonsson, R. J., & Huntingdon, G. S. (1981). *Correlates of developmental progress in handicapped infants and children.* Unpublished manuscript, The University of North Carolina at Chapel Hill, Carolina Institute for Research on Early Education of the Handicapped, Chapel Hill, NC.

Snyder, S. (1985). *Meta-analysis and intervention literature: Issues of data structure.* Unpublished doctoral dissertation, Purdue University, Lafayette, IN.

Snyder, S., & Sheehan, R. (1985). Integrating research in early childhood special education: The use of meta-analysis. *Diagnostique, 9*(1).

Soboloff, H. R. (1981). Early intervention—Fact or fiction? *Developmental Medicine and Neurology, 23*, 261–266.

Solkoff, N., & Cotton, C. (1975). Contingency awareness in premature infants. *Perceptual and Motor Skills, 41*, 709–710.

Spence, K., & Trohanis, P. (1985). Status in states of early childhood special education across twelve dimensions. In *There ought to be a law? Ensuring state-wide services to disabled and at-risk infants and toddlers.* Washington, DC: National Center for Clinical Infant Programs.

Stedman, D. J., & Eichorn, D. H. (1964). A comparison of the growth and development of institutionalized and home-reared mongoloids during infancy and early childhood. *American Journal of Mental Deficiency, 69*, 391–401.

Stoneman, Z. (1985). Family involvement in early childhood special education programs. In N. H. Fallen & W. Umansky (Eds.), *Young children with special needs* (2nd ed., pp. 441–469). Columbus, OH: Charles E. Merrill.

Utley, B., Duncan, D., Strain, P., & Scanlon, K. (1983). Effects of contingent and non-contingent visual stimulation on visual fixation in multiply handicapped children. *TASH Journal, 8*, 29–42.

Vadasy, P. F., Fewell, R. R., Meyer, D. J., & Greenberg, M. T. (1985). Supporting fathers of handicapped young children: Preliminary findings of program effects. *Analysis and Intervention in Developmental Disablities, 5*, 125–137.

Watson, J. S. (1972). Smiling, cooing, and "The Game". *Merrill-Palmer Quarterly, 18*, 4, 323–340.

Weinraub, M., & Wol, B. M. (1983). Effects of stress and social supports on mother-child interactions in single- and two-parent families. *Child Development, 54*, 1297–1311.

White, K. (1984). *An integrative review of early intervention efficacy research.* Unpublished manuscript, University of Utah, Provo.

White, K., & Casto, G. (1985). An integrative review of early intervention efficacy studies with at-risk children: Implications for the handicapped. *Analysis and Intervention in Developmental Disabilities, 5*, 177–201.

White, K. R., Mastropieri, M., & Casto, G. (1985). The efficacy of early intervention for handicapped children: An analysis of special education early childhood projects approved by the joint dissemination review panel. *Journal of the Division of Early Childhood.*

Wiedar, D., & Hicks, J. (1970). *Evaluation of an early intervention program for neurologically impaired children and their families.* Jamaica, NY: United Cerebral Palsy of Queens. (ERIC Document Reproduction Service No. ED 050 533).

Winton, P. J., & Turnbull, A. P. (1981). Parent involvement as viewed by parents of preschool handicapped children. *Topics in Early Childhood Special Education, 1*(3), 11–19.

Wolery, M. & Dyk, L. (1985). The evaluation of two levels of a center based early intervention projects. *Topics in Early Childhood Special Education, 5*(2), 66–77.

Wright, T., & Nicholson, J. (1973). Physiotherapy for the spastic child: An evolution. *Developmental Medicine and Child Neurology, 15*, 146–163.

Zausmer, E., Pueschel, S., & Shea, A (1972). A sensory-motor stimulation program for the young child with Down's syndrome: Preliminary report. *MCH Exchange, 11*, 1–4.

Zeitlin, S. (1981). Learning through coping: An effective preschool program. *Journal of the Division of Early Education, 4*, 53–61.

Zigler, E., & Balla, D. (1982). Selecting outcome variables in evaluation of early childhood special education programs. *Topics in Early Childhood Special Education, 1*(4), 11–22.

APPENDIX

Rating Scales Used for Analysis of the Efficacy Studies

Specificity: The extent to which the efficacy of early intervention was assessed in terms of specific dimensions of the intervention.

1	2	3	4	5
Efficacy assessed dichotomously; no attempt made to relate specific program dimensions to program success	Limited attempts made to determine which dimensions of the treatment were related to program success	Program success assessed in terms of highly specific dimensions of the intervention		

Social Support: The extent to which the effects of informal or formal support were assessed in terms of their impact on the dependent measures.

1	2	3	4	5
Potential impact of provision of support not addressed at all; no acknowledgement of influences external to treatment	Potential influences of external support recognized but not evaluated	Impact of the provision of support was specifically assessed		

Family and Child Characteristics: The extent to which the efficacy of early intervention was assessed in relationship to different family and child characteristics.

1	2	3	4	5
Little or no information provided about child or family characteristics; no conditional relationships assessed	Basic information about child and family characteristics provided; no test of conditional relationships	Child and family characteristics specified and assessed, conditional relationships evaluated		

Internal Validity: The extent to which competing explanations for observed changes were adequately controlled either methodologically or statistically.

1	2	3	4	5
No attention or acknowledgment of alternative explanations for observed changes; minimal or no control over threats to the validity of the findings	Control of at least two validity threats attempted, however, may be inadequate for one or more reasons; no attempt made to rule out competing explanations or qualify findings	Adequate control of validity threats; specific efforts made to rule out or methodologically/statistically eliminate competing explanations		

Dependent Measures: The extent to which broad based and ecologically relevant outcome measures were used as measures of program success.

1	2	3	4	5
Program success based entirely on child progress data; no broader based measures of program success used	Program success measured in terms of child and family outcomes; ecological relevance limited or questionable	Broad-based child and family measures used; program success measures have strong ecological validity		

Dependence: The extent to which there was a functional relationship between the independent and dependent measures.

1	2	3	4	5
Relationship between the independent and dependent variables are entirely distal in nature	Relationship between the independent and dependent variables are mediational in nature; causal modeling permits a conceptual explanation of the cause-effect relationship	Relationship between the independent and dependent variables are proximal; nature of the relationship permits isolation of the causal factors		

Families of Young Handicapped Children

JAMES J. GALLAGHER AND MARIE BRISTOL

University of North Carolina

Abstract—This chapter reviews the impact of the handicapped child upon the family, the role expectations of family members coping with handicapped children, the effects of increased stress on the family unit, and the effectiveness of various parent intervention programs. The Hill Model which focuses on the combination of nature of the stressor, available resources, and perceived parental perceptions leading to stress adaptation is used to organize the literature review. Special emphasis is placed on the role of the father and single parent in adaptation to the handicapped child. Recommendations include a call for a diverse menu of services for families, stronger programs of professional training to work with families, and more effectively designed research with a longitudinal prospective.

INTRODUCTION

The purpose of this chapter is to explore those factors that influence the family's adaptation to having a handicapped child. This chapter will review the impact of a handicapped child upon the family, the role expectations of family members in coping with handicapped children, the effects of increased stress on the family unit, and the effectiveness of various parent intervention programs. Finally, we will suggest some future research and service directions that appear to emerge from this review. One theme of the chapter is that the handicapped child is a member of a complex social system and we must understand the parameters of that system if we are to be effective in helping the child adapt.

The building of a more significant parent/professional partnership has been at the heart of early education programs for handicapped children. Turnbull and Turnbull (1978) list some reasons for the enhancement of the parental role in educational programs for the handicapped:

1. The experimental evidence that parents can influence positively the development of their children through teaching them at home.

2. The encouraging results of early intervention in ameliorating some of the developmental deficits associated with moderate and severe handicaps.

3. The success of parents in bringing litigation to establish the educational rights of their children.

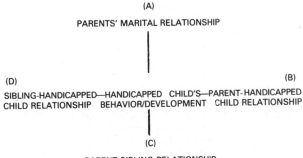

FIGURE 1

Note: From "Siblings of Handicapped Children: A developmental Perspective on Family Interactions" by P. Vadasy, R. Fewell, D. Meyer, & G. Schell, 1984, *Family Relations*, **33**, 155–167.

4. Federal legislation, notably PL 94–142, that sets forth clear standards for parental involvement in the educational process.

Figure 1 indicates the key relationships that surround and influence the child with a handicap. Until recently, only the core of the model in Figure 1, the behavior and the development of the handicapped child, has been studied extensively. Now we have begun to explore the surrounding relationships within the family system (Bristol & Gallagher, 1982). Even these relationships are not comprehensive. As Belsky (1980) pointed out, there are intergenerational factors influencing the parents' behaviors and roles. There are also the larger cultural groups to which the family owes loyalty, such as extended family and friends, the church, social clubs, and those social policies that influence the family system either directly or through the other systems with which the family comes in contact.

Impact of a Moderate to Severely Handicapped Child on the Family

The first bits of clinical evidence regarding the initial impact of a handicapped child on the family came mainly through personal testimony and clinical case studies that reported a range of potential emotions from anger, despair, guilt, and often courage (e.g., Turnbull & Turnbull, 1985). These individual reports, by implication, indicated the range of reaction that such an event may create, but the role of the investigator is to seek patterns beyond individual cases, and research must be conducted through more systematic investigations.

Farber (1959) was one of the first investigators to separate different kinds of stress that were created by the discovery of a handicapped child in the family. One common pattern seems to be a grief reaction that stems from the symbolic death of the "normal child" that had been expected. It is not uncommon for prospective parents to look forward eagerly to the child who is normal and responsive in every respect, and to think about the stages that that child will go through on its way to adulthood. The realization that their youngster has been born with problems that will be chronic and continuing begins a grieving process that parallels the grief in the family of the child who has actually died.

This is quite a different reaction from the family response to the continued demands for care that are presented by the moderate to severely handicapped child. Beckman (1983) found that it was the unusual care-giving demands that seem to represent the predominant source of problems or stress in the family.

Farber (1975) has pointed out that the presence of a handicapped child often represents a developmental delay in family evolution as well. He has defined the character of the crisis faced by families with mentally retarded children as an arrest in the family life cycle whereby (a) family development is slowed and (b) family roles are thrown out of synchronization with the cohort of families who would ordinarily define the characteristic family development sequence.

This loss of synchrony may be particularly evident at certain points in time across the lifespan of the family. MacKeith (1973) identified four major crisis periods in the maturing family development patterns in families with handicapped children. The first crisis occurs when the parent becomes aware that their child is handicapped; the second when the child begins receiving services; the third crisis is identified when the child leaves home and school; and the fourth, when the aging parent can no longer care for the handicapped offspring.

In contrast to the normal family's progressive evolution where the child is first an infant requiring constant care, then a preschooler, then in elementary school, then secondary school, then out of the home at work, or in postsecondary school training, then married, and then with his or her own children, the presence of a moderate to severely handicapped child markedly delays or fixates the family, taking it out of the normal sequence. This disjunction does not allow easy communication between families with a handicapped child and families of nonhandicapped children who ordinarily would be at similar family developmental levels. It has been suggested that it is this disjunction in family development that places the family with a handicapped child in awkward social relationships with other families with

whom they would normally have a close and continuing relationship.

Families with moderately to severely handicapped children have many problems in common, regardless of the specific nature of the handicapping condition. These problems seem to increase the likelihood of, but not ensure, a maladaptive response from the family which the professional community is expected to counteract. Five problems that appear to weaken the family's solidarity, and that require special attention from the researcher and the service provider (Gallagher, 1983) are that:

1. The child has lessened ability to form reciprocal and mutual reinforcing transactions with parents.

2. The handicapped child's greater dependency needs force the caretakers within the family to spend more time and effort coping with the child's needs.

3. There is the danger of a lessening of mutually reinforcing social interactions with other adults and children within the extended family, friends, and neighbors.

4. Families must cope with the symbolic death of their aspirations and hopes.

5. Many varied family structures must cope with these problems.

These increased needs call upon modified behavior on the part of family members.

Roles of Family Members

Role of the Father

Until the mid-1970s, the father had remained a mysterious and shadowy figure in the background of the family unit with the handicapped child. Most of the attempts to provide support services for families were focused on the mother. Since many of the personnel who provide such support services were also women, the father often found himself in a circle of women when seeking support for the child or for himself.

The role that the father plays in families with handicapped children may be contrasted with the masculine role played in the traditional family. Clarke-Stewart (1979) summed up the role of father in a traditional family as follows:

> Fathers have traditionally been portrayed as the family's task leader, breadwinner, and disciplinarian. While he does still usually provide economic support for the family and he does share in the control and management of the child with the mother, the father's role clearly extends beyond these functions. As well as being the child's playmate in physical games, he also offers emotional and practical support to the mother that enables her to fulfill her role as sensitive stimulator. He provides enriching variety and contrast for the child and promotes the child's awareness that there are interesting and responsive people outside of the mother-child dyad. (p. 217)

Parke (1979) also identified the role of playmate as a clearly evident one for fathers. This is one role in which fathers may have difficulty in carrying out with physically handicapped children. Many fathers appear to fear that they will hurt their child if they engage in typical roughhousing kinds of behavior or do not know how to adapt games or other play activities to fit the child's limited abilities. The Kennedy Foundation has recently developed a program of adapted games and sports specifically for use by families with young handicapped children (Shriver, in press).

Lamb (1976) complained that the father's role in the family was actually devalued by the fact that social scientists tended to ignore him in their studies. He pointed out that the father's role has gained importance with the realization that the number of actual mother-child interactions was not as great as generally assumed, and that the amount of time spent together was a poor predictor of the infant's relationship with either parent.

One of the most widely accepted propositions in the field of child development is that the American father has been less attentive to his children than is true of fathers in other cultures. MacKey and Day (1979) embarked on a major cross-cultural study comparing observations of father/mother child interaction in communities in Spain, Mexico, Japan, Ireland, and the United States (primarily the state of Virginia). All of the observations were conducted during daylight hours in places of public access and with equal access by gender. The observations occurred in time intervals when adult males would be expected to be available to children, that is, sabbaths, holidays, festival days, resting times, and so forth

The data failed to support the proposition that American males behave differently toward their children in these settings.

> The data offered here do show that U.S. men were with their children substantially when they could be, and that the men did respond to their children rather actively when they were present. On balance, there is no compelling reason to assume paternal deprivation on the part of American men toward their children. Until contrary data are available, the burden concerning adequacy of the American male as "father" shifts to those charging negligence. (p. 297)

There is little doubt that the presence of a handicapped child has a substantial impact on the father. Cummings (1976) found that fathers of mentally retarded children were more depressed and had lower self-esteem when compared with fathers of either chronically ill or healthy children. Tallman (1965) believed that fathers of severely retarded children were especially vulnerable to social stigma and extrafamilial influences. The coping behavior of the mother may in fact be reflecting the relationship of the mother with the father in the family. A poor mother-child relationship may reflect a lack of support from the father (Pedersen, 1976).

Tavormina, Ball, Dunn, Luscomb, and Taylor (1977) noted four major parental styles in adapting to the crisis of having a handicapped child. These roles involve the differential behavior of the father in each instance. In the first style, the father emotionally divorces himself from the child, leaving the care of the child entirely up to the mother, and involves himself in outside activities such as his job or other social organizations. The second style is characterized by the parents jointly rejecting the child, who is often institutionalized as a result. The third adaptation style occurs when the parents make the child the center of their universe, subordinating all of their own desires and pleasures and those of siblings to the service of this handicapped child. The fourth style is identifiable when the parents join in mutual support of the child and each other, while maintaining a sense of their own identity and semblance of a normal family life.

What role do fathers actually play in the family with a handicapped child? Using a family responsibility scale that details 20 different roles in the family, Gallagher, Cross, and Scharfman (1981) identified patterns of predominant roles in families designated as successful by professionals in coping with their handicapped children. The role allocations in such families seem to parallel the expected roles in families without handicapped children. That is, the predominant father role appeared to be that of provider, protector, and home maintenance person, whereas the mother's major role appeared to be that of nurturance and child care. Many other roles were shared by both parents as, for example, social host. Both mothers and fathers agreed that more father involvement would seem desirable in the family. There seems to be a problem in clearly identifying a proper set of actions for the father in these families that can be accepted by the father and respected by the mother.

Gallagher, Scharfman, and Bristol (1984) compared 50 pairs of parents of moderately to severely handicapped preschool children with 83 families of parents of preschool nonhandicapped children on the division of responsibilities in the family. A somewhat surprising result of this comparison was the very close relationships between the division of responsibilities in the families with nonhandicapped and handicapped children. In this study, both sets of families showed a predominant male responsibility for home maintenance, protection, and for being the provider, while mothers showed traditional domestic responsibilities for food preparation, home maintenance, social planning, and a variety of child care responsibilities. Contrary to expectations, the families with handicapped children did not reveal a stronger role played by the father in such families. Kamoravsky's (1962) concept of *balanced exchange* would predict that stress on one family member (in this case, the mother) will result in greater support by the other family members, but that was not found here. It is possible that support services for their child such as day-care centers for handicapped children might be providing the type of support that makes it unnecessary for the fathers to change or make more intense their patterns of family participation.

Role of the Mother

It is clear that the roles played in the family are complementary. There are tasks that must be done, and if one partner will not do them then the other partner, or someone else in the immediate or extended family, will have to assume them. The mother's role in families with handicapped children seems to be to take care of those tasks not handled by the father, and that turns out to be quite a few tasks. In the study of "successful families" Gallagher et al. (1981) noted many mothers with strong ego control and determination to see themselves through this difficult situation.

Akerly (1975) impressionistically noted a similar pattern through the identification of the characteristics of the "invulnerable parent." She described this parent (mother!) as having stubbornly resisted being engulfed by the handicap, as regarding herself as a positive element in her child's life, as a person who has informed herself about the nature of her child's handicap, and who undertakes an objective, realistic, somewhat distant, yet compassionate approach to her child.

Although traditional patterns of maternal behavior, nurturance, and child care seem to be present in many families of handicapped children, Patterson and McCubbin (1984) suggested that an *androgynous* role orientation was associated with lower reports of distress in families of nonhandicapped children where the husband was absent for long periods of time. Such an androgynous pattern, where the mother is able to assume aspects of both the traditional male and female roles, may have important implications for coping in one-parent families of handicapped children or in two-parent families where the father is only minimally involved.

One of the significant concerns of many child development specialists is what a handicapping condition might do to the normal establishment of *attachment* between the child and mother. Bowlby (1969) proposed four phases of attachment. In the first phase the infant is differentiating inanimate from animate objects in the environment at about 3 months of age. The second phase is the differentiation of the mother and others close to the infant for special contact and proximity seeking. The third phase, near the first year of life, is marked by the child knowing the mother in her absence and recognizing her voice from a distance, thus establishing a mother-object constancy. The fourth phase involves a relationship of trust established between mother and child that allows the child to see the mother depart without untoward anxiety. This phase takes a long time, often not completed until ages 4 or 5.

The question is whether handicapped children, with their reduced responsiveness, in many instances, can move through these attachment phases, particularly the fourth phase. Blacher (1984) points out that children with gross physical deformities may be particularly at risk for parental rejection and limited attachment. Despite this, studies indicate that most parents are observed to be warm and responsive to their handicapped children and, by implication, show attachment to the child (Bristol, 1985).

One particular consequence of nonattachment may well be the increase in child abuse noted in families with a handicapped child. Belsky (1980) maintained that abusive behavior is triggered only if in-family distress is present and there is an absence of secondary or social networks to provide support.

Silverman and Hill (1967) suggested that the allocation of the roles played by husbands and wives in the family can best be understood through a *family development theory*. In this theory, before there are children in the family, the tasks are seen to be alloted evenly between husband and wife. When there are children, the husband becomes involved with his work and is less available for home tasks while the wife has an increased participation in all but major male tasks. When the children are grown the tasks are once again equalized. A cross-cultural study using 731 families from Detroit and 500 families from Belgium supported this view. Apparently this theory also explains the results of the limited shared roles obtained with the families of handicapped and nonhandicapped preschoolers noted above. Clearly further research needs to examine the further ramifications of maternal employment on this developmental sequence in families of handicapped children.

Siblings

Just as professionals were slow in recognizing the interactive factors in which the handicapped child impacted upon the parents, so are we limited in our appreciation of the role played by the siblings in the family. A literature review by Vadasy, Fewell, Meyer, and Schell (1984) revealed increased vulnerability of the siblings to stress and other problems. Simeonsson and Bailey (in press) believe that the type of handicapped condition, per se, has little to do with sibling reaction, but that younger and closer age-spaced siblings seem to have more difficulty adjusting. An asynchrony in the orderly progression of the family through its developmental stages predicts larger sibling maladjustment, as well as does increased parental stress.

It appears that siblings play different roles in the family depending upon their age and sex. Farber (1960) found that daughters who interacted frequently with their retarded siblings were higher in role tension. Breslau, Weitzman, and Messinger (1981) studied 239 families of disabled patients with a wide age range (3–18) and found that older sisters were under more stress than older brothers. Vadasy et al. (1984) in their review, also suggest that the "sister of a handicapped child appears to be most vulnerable."

Simeonsson and Bailey (in press) point out in their literature review that the assumption that siblings are inevitably affected negatively by the presence of a handicapped child is incorrect. Mates (1982) found siblings of autistic children scored in the normal range on measures of adjustment and self-concept. Other studies support the notion that the sibling reaction to the presence of a handicapped child, in many cases, is not negative. A number of positive results, in terms of better family relationships, may emerge (Breslau, 1982; Taylor, 1980). When siblings were given direct responsibility for the care of the handicapped child's siblings, they tended to express satisfaction (Chinitz, 1981; Schreibman, O'Neill, & Koegel, 1983), particularly when the results of their efforts helped the handicapped child.

Separation and Divorce in Families of Handicapped Children

As we discuss family roles, the image of a nuclear family, having two children with a father employed and a mother at home taking care of the household, comes easily to mind. As both the numbers of mothers employed outside the home and the numbers of single-parent families increase dramatically, the traditional family configuration becomes less and less common. Whether the presence of a handicapped child further compounds this situation by "causing a disproportionate number of failed marriages and a higher prevalence of single parents in this group is the subject of a continuing controversy.

In a review of studies of the father's role in these families, Price-Bonham and Addison (1978) conclude that the rate of divorce in families of retarded children is three times the national average. On the other hand, Darling and Darling (1982) in their review of studies of the effect of children with birth defects on family life conclude that "the divorce rate among parents of spina bifida children is about the same as that of the general population". This sentiment is echoed even more unequivocally by Wikler, Haack, and Intagliata (1984), who reviewed different studies and concluded that "When social class is held constant, no significant difference has been found between the divorce rate of parents of normal children and that of parents of children with developmental disabilities". Is the teacher of young handicapped children more apt to be working with separated or divorced families, or is the prevalence of marital dissolution about what would be expected for the nonhandicapped population?

Prevalence rates for marital dissolution given across the seven major statistical studies cited in the above reviews range from an English study finding a rate of 8.6% (5 of 58 families of spina bifida patients with both parents alive and child living at home, Dorner, 1975) to 49% of families in an American study of children with meningomyelocele (Kolin, Scherzer, New, & Garfield,

1971). The midrange is represented by another American study reporting a prevalence rate of 26.6% (Martin, 1975).

A review of the major published statistical studies cited by Price-Bonham and Addison (1978), Darling and Darling (1982), and Wikler et al. (1984) reveals a variety of methodological problems both in studies indicating higher prevalence of marital dissolution and in those indicating no differences from families of nonhandicapped children.

Comparison across studies is hampered by differences in ages of children and type of handicap studied. Other methodological problems include:

1. Anecdotal accounts cited as evidence for prevalence rates.

2. Lack of clarity as to whether the studies include both divorced and separated families in their category of marital breakdown or whether percentages are restricted to divorced families only; in the latter case, marital dissolution in Black families and lower income families of both races will be seriously underestimated because these families are more likely to be permanently separated rather than divorced (Tew, Laurence, Payne, & Rawnsley, 1977; Roesel & Lawlis, 1983; Dorner, 1975).

3. Sweeping conclusions frequently drawn from small and sometimes biased samples (Kolin et al., 1971 ($N = 13$); Martin, 1975 ($N = 34$); Davis & McKay, 1973 ($N = 28$)).

4. Effects of race, social class, and child age, factors known to affect prevalence of divorce in the general population, are often ignored (Martin, 1975).

5. Although data on families of nonhandicapped children show a divorce and separation rate that approximately doubles from children's preschool to school-age years, control for or analysis by child age is generally lacking (only the Roesel & Lawlis, 1983, study analyzed for the effect of child age). The results of this study which found no effect for child age, race, or maternal or paternal education are surprising, since these factors have been shown to affect dramatically prevalence rates of divorce in the general population.

6. Comparative data for families of nonhandicapped children are often entirely lacking, confounded by social class or racial differences, or inappropriate. For example, prevalence (total cumulative number of divorces over time) in families of handicapped children is inappropriately compared with incidence (total *new* divorces in a given year) for families of nonhandicapped children (Davis & McKay, 1973).

In recent research at the Carolina Institute for Research on Early Education of the Handicapped (Bristol, Schopler, & McConnaughey, 1984), the prevalence of separation and divorce in a cohort of 399 families of autistic and communication -handicapped children age 5 or younger was compared with a sample of 8,882 families of children 5 years or younger drawn from the 5% Public Use 1980 North Carolina census data, and with a similar subsample of 6,767 families of children under 5 drawn from a sample of one in every 1,000 families from the national U.S. Census data. (Data had been collected from the families of handicapped children at the time the children were referred for evaluation for autism, but before they received specialized services for autistic children.)

For the total group, prevalence rate for the autistic and communication-impaired young children was 14% compared with 7% for the North Carolina sample of families of young children and 8% for the U.S. sample of similar families. Analyses by parental educational level and income level across groups revealed that the greatest risk is for Black, low income families with low educational levels. In a subanalysis which restricted the autistic or communication-impaired sample to families all of whose children were under 5 (*N* = 213) to make them most comparable to census data, the marital dissolution rate for the handicapped group was approximately 50% higher than that for the census groups for Caucasian families and almost double the North Carolina Census rate for similar Black families.

Since these data reflect preintervention status, it is not clear whether the prevalence rate could have been reduced by earlier specific intervention or whether an intervention program could slow the rate of marital dissolution. It may be that these are the families that would have broken up later anyway and the added stress of the handicapped child only hastened the process. In any case, if intervention were to make a difference, it would have to be early, since these cases of marital dissolution all occurred before the handicapped child was 6 years old.

Another sample of 1,050 families of children under 5 served through a statewide developmental day program for children with a range of handicapping conditions, most of them involving some degree of retardation, was also surveyed. The marital dissolution rate for this group of families of young children was 17%, suggesting that the comparatively high rates found in the above handicapped sample were not peculiar to autism or autistic-like disorders.

What conclusions can we draw regarding impact on marriage of the presence of young, handicapped children? Our data indicate that if samples are of adequate size and appropriate comparison samples are used, families of at least some handicapped children, especially American families, are at greater risk for marital breakdown when their children are young, than are families of young, nonhandicapped children.

Keeping in mind the methodological limitations of most of these studies, it does appear that marital breakdown may be more likely to occur in families which were experiencing personal or financial difficulty before the birth of the child (Darling & Darling, 1982), in those in which the child was conceived premaritally (Tew et al., 1977), in those in which the care of a defective child is not a shared value (Bristol, 1984), or in those (see below) where the demands of the handicapped child

outstrip the available resources of the family and the services found in the community.

Single-Parent Families of Handicapped Children

Single parents represent a large segment of the families of handicapped children. Of the 1,050 families surveyed in a free, statewide program for developmentally disabled children, 41% were headed by a single parent, including those who were separated, divorced, never married, or widowed (Bristol, 1984). The limited research done with single-parent families of handicapped children indicates that they experience a variety of stresses, some of which are similar to those described for two-parent families (Gallagher, Beckman, & Cross, 1983). These include stresses in child care (Beckman, 1983; Cohen, 1982), finances (Bristol, in press-b), and establishing a social life and a social network (Wikler, 1979). In a survey of needs (Wikler, 1979), single parents with retarded children listed respite care as their greatest need, financial needs second, and personal/social needs third. Clinical accounts (Wikler et al., 1984) also describe the triple stigma borne by many single parents of retarded children: those of having a mentally retarded child, of being divorced, and, in many cases where child support is not forthcoming, the additional stigma of being a welfare recipient.

The limited systematic research done with these families indicates that single parents may experience more problems in coping with their children than parents in two-parent families (Beckman, 1983; Holroyd, 1974). However, lack of control for differences in maternal education in these studies may favor the two-parent families in the comparison.

In a comparison of in-home ratings of quality of parenting in two-parent and single-parent families (Bristol, in press-b), single parents were rated lower than two-parent families of handicapped children ages 2–10. When differences in maternal education were statistically corrected, however, group differences disappeared. In future research, it is important to distinguish the effects of father absence per se from differences in social class.

The very real stress experienced by these families, however, is reflected in the fact that single-parent families may be more apt to institutionalize their handicapped offspring than are two-parent families (Appell & Tisdall, 1968; Graliker, Koch, & Hendersen, 1965).

Bristol (in press-b) reviews research findings regarding six issues that should be addressed in future research studies and assessment protocols with single parents of handicapped children. She concludes that: (a) blanket assumptions regarding no father involvement in single-parent families and high father involvement in two-parent families are misleading; (b) persons other than parents contribute significantly to child rearing in these families and should be included in research and assessment descriptions of child rearing environments; (c) research on single parents should control for type of single parenthood (e.g., never married vs. separated or divorced); (d) control for socioeconomic differences between two-parent and single-parent families is critical in designing research and interpreting assessment results; (e) coping with single parenthood is a process that changes and must be measured over time; and (f) the deficit model of "broken homes" is not useful or constructive.

It should be noted, however, that in spite of indications of higher rates of marital breakdown, and acknowledgement of stresses in these families, the clearest finding across all studies is that the majority of families remain together and are coping well with their young handicapped children (see below). What factors, then, enable some families to cope successfully with their young handicapped children while others are overwhelmed by the stress?

Adaptation in Families of Handicapped Children

With few exceptions, most earlier research on families of handicapped children assessed the negative effects of these children on their families. Problems in adaptation and family crises such as divorce or marital problems (see above), depression (Bradshaw & Lawton, 1978; Burden, 1980), and institutionalization (DeMyer & Goldberg, 1983; Lotter, 1978) in these families have been documented.

On the other hand, there is also both research and clinical evidence that most families of handicapped children adapt successfully to the presence and care of a developmentally disabled child and are functioning well in spite of the increased demands (Akerley, 1975; Bristol, 1984; Darling, 1979; Gallagher et al., 1981).

Our own research has been guided by a conceptual framework which focuses on healthy family adaptation to handicapped children. The results of representative studies from our own research and that of others will be used to illustrate both a conceptual model of successful adaptation and the specific factors related to successful outcomes for families of handicapped children.

Family Adaptation to Stress: the Double ABCX Model

There is a growing body of research which helps to explain how families cope with acute or chronic stress, whether the stress is a general life change, physical illness, the stress of military separation, or a natural disaster such as a tornado (Cohen & Lazarus, 1978; Hill, 1958; McCubbin, 1979; Olson & McCubbin, 1983).

It is apparent that no stressful event or stressor, including the presence or care of a handicapped child, invariably causes a family crisis. Hill (1949, 1958) proposed a classic ABCX theory of family stress in which the characteristics of the stressor event (A), the family's internal crisis-meeting resources (B), and the family's

definition of the stressor (C) contribute to the prevention or precipitation of a family crisis (X). The ABCX Model has been further developed conceptually by Burr (1973), Hansen and Johnson (1979), and McCubbin and Patterson (1981, 1983) to deal also with postcrisis adaptation.

The expand Hill's original ABCX theory, McCubbin and Patterson (1981, 1983) proposed a Double ABCX or Family Adjustment and Adaptation Response Model (FAAR). To the original ABCX model, the Double ABCX model adds the pile-up of other family stresses which make adaptation more difficult (aA); the social and psychological resources (bB), and coping strategies (BC) which the family uses in managing potential crisis situations; the meaning the family assigns to the event (cC); and the range of both positive and negative outcomes possible.

The Double ABCX model was chosen as a conceptual framework for the present review because: (a) its emphasis on adaptation over time is consistent with a recognition of the changing developmental status of the child and the family, (b) it is an ecological model which recognizes the social and contextual nature of adaptation over time, (c) it provides for assessment of active coping as well as passive support, (d) it addresses the possibility that healthy adaptation rather than pathology may characterize the family's response to stress, and (e) it has been empirically demonstrated to be applicable to adaptation in families of handicapped children.

Empirical Support for the Double ABCX Model and Adaptation in Families of Handicapped Children

Although dyadic and triadic studies of parent-child and child-child interaction continue to be important in family research, there has been increasing recognition of the necessity for more complex models of family functioning (Bronfenbrenner, 1979; Turnbull, Brotherson, & Summers, 1985).

To test the validity of the Double ABCX framework as a conceptual framework for research on adaptation in families of handicapped children, the model was adapted for use in a study of healthy adaptation in families of autistic and communication-handicapped children (Bristol, 1982; in press-a). The study empirically tested the contribution of characteristics of the handicapped child to healthy family adaptation in the context of the family's other stresses and the resources and beliefs the family brought to the adaptation process. Specifically, the study tested the contribution to healthy family adaptation of severity of handicap (A), the pile-up of other stresses (aA), family cohesion (B), social support (bB), externalization of Blame (C), the definition of handicap as a family crisis (cC), and patterns of coping (BC). Healthy adaptation was measured by the number and frequency of maternal depressive symptoms, an in-home interviewer rating of general family adaptation, and maternal report of marital adjustment.

Whether these variables predicted successful family adaptation was tested using canonical correlation; this is the multivariate equivalent of a multiple regression equation used when you have more than one outcome measure. A canonical correlation of predictor variables with adaptation criteria, when adjusted (Lawley, 1959) for the number of variables in relationship to subjects, yielded a significant canonical correlation (0.67, $p < 0.01$) (Bristol, 1984). This indicated that the ABCX model significantly predicted healthy adaptation in these families of developmentally disabled children. The overall model also significantly predicted substantial amounts of the variance in the individual criteria: about one-third of the variance in maternal depressive symptoms, and more than half of the variance in marital adjustment, and in the in-home rating of family adaptation. The model, as adapted for this study, appears to be an appropriate one for reviewing factors related to successful adaptation in families of handicapped children.

The extent to which representative research supports the contributions of characteristics of the handicapped child (A), resources (B), and beliefs (C) to adaptation in families of young handicapped children (X) will be reviewed below.

(A) Contributions of the Stressor (The Handicapped Child) To Stress or Adaptation

Type of handicap. Although there is not universal agreement on this topic (Tew et al., 1977), it appears that family stress or adaptation varies as a function of the type of the child's handicap, if subject groups are clearly defined and large enough to make such comparisons meaningful. Some types of handicaps such as mental retardation (Cummings, Bayley, & Rie, 1966) and autism seem to be particularly stressful for families. Holroyd and McArthur (1976) found greater stress reported by mothers in families of autistic children than in families of Down's syndrome or psychiatric outpatient children. It also appears that there may be a characteristic pattern of stress associated with autism. Stress profiles from parents of autistic children in North Carolina were similar to those collected from parents of autistic children in California, and differed from those of Down's syndrome and psychiatric outpatient children (Bristol & Schopler, 1983, 1984). In a comparison of mothers of autistic, retarded, and normal older children (Donovan, 1985), parents in both handicapped groups reported more stress than the parents of the nonhandicapped sample and mothers of autistic children were more stressed than those of retarded children.

Although knowledge of effect of type of handicap is important for establishing priorities for support services, more specific intervention strategies are likely to be derived from knowledge of specific behaviors or aspects of a particular handicap which are most stressful. With this knowledge, specific behaviors can be given higher priority for intervention in the limited time available.

Severity of handicap. Result of studies assessing the impact of severity of handicap on family functioning are mixed, with some authors finding no effect for severity (Martin, 1975; Tew et al., 1977), and others finding a definite, if sometimes unexpected effect (Bristol & Schopler, 1984). In a study of families of autistic and communication-handicapped children assessed after the children were referred, but before the child was officially diagnosed, marginally normal children had a more negative effect on marital adjustment than those children who were more retarded and more obviously handicapped (Bristol, in press-a; Bristol & Schopler, 1984). Schopler and Reichler (1972) also found that parents of more mildly handicapped autistic children were less accurate in predicting their child's developmental level and, especially, their future prospects. This is consistent with findings by McCubbin, Cauble, and Patterson (1982) in their studies of general family stress unrelated to handicapping conditions. These authors point out that ambiguity increases the risk of family crisis by engendering disagreements both within and outside the family regarding what the proper course of action should be. Early diagnosis dispels this ambiguity by clarifying the fact that the child is indeed handicapped and is in need of special intervention. This may help prevent disagreements regarding whether the child is handicapped from damaging the marital relationship or lessening support from extended family members or others. This is an hypothesis based on clinical observation which can be tested empirically.

Child age. Among other specific child characteristics which have been related to better adaptation is child age (with parents of younger children expressing less stress than parents of older children, Bristol, 1979; Bristol & Schopler, 1984; Donovan, 1985; Farber, 1959). Expected effects for birth order were not found (Bristol & Schopler, 1984). Among the reasons for reduced stress during the earlier years are (a) the smaller size and potentially greater social acceptability and manageability of the child, (b) some lack of knowledge or denial of the permanence of the child's handicap, (c) greater optimism for the future and, in most cases, (d) the reality that services for young handicapped children may be better and more readily available than those for older children and adolescents (Bristol & Schopler, 1983; Donovan, 1985). It is interesting to note that professionals may tend to overestimate the stress associated with the birth and diagnosis of the child and underestimate parental stress later in the development of the handicapped child.

Child gender. As in studies of nonhandicapped children (Hetherington, 1981), girls have been found to be less stressful than boys in studies of severely retarded children (Farber, 1959), of behavior-disordered children (Patterson, 1980), and of autistic children (Bristol, 1979; Bristol & Schopler, 1984). The more adverse effect for boys may be related to intrinsic differences in boys such as larger physical size, greater irritability, less social responsiveness, and more difficult caretaking, as suggested by Bell (1968) for nonhandicapped children. An alternative cultural expectations explanation was proposed by Farber (1959) for retarded children. He suggested that, at least in lower socioeconomic class families, parents have higher career expectations for males than for females. Mothers of girls in the Bristol (1979; Bristol & Schopler, 1984) study, in fact, commented that girls could be taught to cook and do housekeeping and appeared less distressed that their daughters might not find competitive employment. Although there has been an evolution in parental attitudes toward female career roles, among these largely rural, mostly lower-middle or lower socioeconomic status families, parents persisted in having higher career expectations for boys than for girls and, consequently, experienced more stress when their handicapped child was a boy.

Specific child behaviors and stress. Since fixed child characteristics such as age and sex cannot be changed, the predictive value of specific child characteristics amenable to intervention was assessed for families of autistic children (Bristol, 1979; Bristol & Schopler, 1984). In fact, approximately three-quarters of the variance in reported maternal and family stress problems as measured by the Holroyd Questionnaire on Resources and Stress could be predicted on the basis of characteristics of the children and their environments. These characteristics included difficulty of the children's personality characteristics such as their management problems, their social obtrusiveness, their degree of dependency and need for assistance in self-help skills, and the perceived adequacy of the children's activities, services, and prospects for independent living (Bristol & Schopler, 1984). The stress predicted was independent of socioeconomic status, the mother's age, or birth order of the child and was comparable in Black and white families.

Similar findings for families of children with a variety of other handicaps were found by Beckman (1983). She found that higher levels of parental stress were associated with a more difficult child temperament, less social responsiveness, more stereotypic behavior patterns, a slower rate of progress, and the presence of additional or unusual caretaking demands which alone accounted for the majority of variance in reported parental stress. Once the handicap is diagnosed, then, so that ambiguity of handicap is not itself a source of disagreement, it appears that families with "easier," less dependent children and more adequate services (see below) will be more able to cope successfully. Fortunately, most of the particular child characteristics related to stress are those that, within limits, can be improved through intervention.

The pile-up of other stresses or hardships has also been found significantly to predict adaptation in families of developmentally disabled children both in terms of the magnitude of other stresses (Bristol, 1984) and hardships such as lost maternal employment opportunities directly attributable to the child's handicap (Bristol & Schopler, 1983).

Whether the family will adapt successfully to the handicapped child, however, does not depend on characteristics of the child or pile-up of other stresses alone.

(B) Psychological and Social Resources and Adaptation

McCubbin and Patterson (1982) define resources for family adaptation as "the psychological, social, interpersonal, and material characteristics of individual members, the family unit, and the community that may be brought into play in reducing tension, managing conflicts, and, in general, meeting demands and needs". For a more complete review of resources and adaptation for families of handicapped children see Bristol (1984), and Gallagher et al. (1983).

Although research on stress in the general population (Rabkin & Struening, 1976) has revealed a number of personal or pychological factors which facilitate coping with stress, limited research in this area has been down with families of handicapped children. For the general population, it has been found that social class, intelligence, adaptability, age, income, occupation, and previous experience with similar stresses help to facilitate successful adaptation. Gallagher et al. (1981) found that the mother's ego strength and self-confidence were among variables associated with successful adaptation to the home care of moderately to severely handicapped preschool children. Rosenberg & Robinson (1984) conclude that lack of education, financial stresses, long working hours, limited intellectual ability, or chronic illness may negatively affect the mother's ability to care for a handicapped child. Reisinger, Ora, and Frangia (1976) found that mothers from lower socioeconomic classes were less able or willing to learn to intervene with their behavior problem children.

Other studies suggest less consistent findings. Korn, Chess, and Fernandez (1978) in their follow-up of rubella babies, found the least stress in the lowest and highest occupational classes and the most stress in middle range occupations. Similarly, low social class families of autistic children (Bristol, 1985) often expressed less distress over their child's handicap, apparently because the child's limited occupational prospects were not seen as deviant. According to the concept of a relative deprivation, a son working in a sheltered workshop was better off than a neighbor's son "let go at the mill".

Other researchers have found no relationship between psychological and demographic variables and adaptation (Bradshaw & Lawton, 1978), or else different relationships, depending on the outcome variables measured (Bristol, 1984). These mixed findings highlight the importance for future research of measuring demographic characteristics in a uniform way, of assessing multiple rather than single indicators of adaptation, and of choosing as measures of adaptation those that are least biased toward middle or upper social status to avoid confounding the stress of the handicapped child per se with the stress of limited financial resources. The very real effect of financial constraints, however, cannot be discounted if they do, in fact, distract or detract from the mother's ability to deal with her child's needs (Ramey, Mills, Campbell, & O'Brien, 1975) or if they independently exacerbate the stress of having a handicapped child.

Informal social support and successful adaptation.
One of the most important resources families draw upon is that called *informal social support*. In a widely accepted definition, Cobb (1976) describes social support as information leading a person to believe that he or she is cared for and loved, esteemed and valued, and part of a network of mutual communication and obligation. Although there continue to be differences of opinion regarding the mechanism through which social support operates, research with the general population has linked adequacy of social support to a variety of positive adaptations such as reduction in complications of pregnancy (Nuckolls, Cassel, & Kaplan, 1972), reduced use of steroids in the treatment of asthma (de Araujo, van Arsdel, Holmes, & Dudley, 1973), reduction in incidence of angina pectoris (Medalie, et al., 1973), and even reduced risk of death (Berkman & Syme, 1979).

Problems in accessing social support for families of handicapped children have been found by a number of authors (Davis & McKay, 1973; Friedrich & Friedrich, 1981) and problems for single-parent mothers may be particularly acute. In a comparison of single mothers with and without retarded children, Wikler (1979) found that about a third of the single mothers of retarded children were extremely isolated socially with almost no contact with either formal or informal networks.

Kazak and Marvin (1984) pursued the issue as to whether having a handicapped child changed the perceptions of the parents and also modified the social network and social supports that the family might have. They found the social support networks of the parents of handicapped children were smaller than those of the comparison group. Families of the handicapped children had significantly more *dense networks*, that is, people in

that social network were more likely to interact with one another. The families with handicapped children also had significantly greater *boundary density* than the comparison group, that is, the mothers and fathers of handicapped children had much greater overlapping network membership than was the case in comparison group families. Finally, they reported that many of the mothers present suffered from parental "burnout" and, as a result, often felt less competent as mothers.

The lack of such social support has been related to harsh or abusive parenting (Bittner & Newberger, 1981; Garbarino, 1977). More importantly, the presence of such social support has been shown to be related to positive attitudes toward the child and greater life satisfaction, and to positively affect maternal-child interaction in families with premature and full-term infants (Crnic, Friedrich, & Greenberg, 1983).

A series of three studies (Bristol, 1985a) indicated the relationships between perceived adequacy of informal social support and stress and adaptation in parents of developmentally disabled children. Each study included a self-rating of adequacy of support from spouse, children, maternal and paternal relatives, friends, and other parents of developmentally disabled children, derived from the Carolina Parent Support Scale (CPSS). Two of the studies also included self-assessment measures of stress. The third included self-assessments plus in-home interviewer ratings of quality of parenting.

The first study of 40 mothers of autistic children demonstrated that mothers with higher levels of perceived support, especially from spouse, the mother's relatives, and other parents of handicapped children, reported fewer coping problems. Adequacy of social support also discriminated highest and lowest stress mothers within the group otherwise comparable on severity of child handicap and sociodemographic variables.

The second study replicated the inverse relationship between adequacy of social support and a shorter measure of stress with 160 additional parents of autistic and autistic-like children. Findings on a subset of 49 of these parents also showed no significant correlation between social support ratings and a measure of social desirability.

In the third study of 45 additional mothers, perceived adequacy of social support was related not only to maternal reports of depression and marital adjustment, but also to an in-home rating of quality of parenting. Social support was more strongly related to the in-home rating of family adaptation than was severity of the child's handicap. The strongest relationship found with the home rating of quality of parenting was the perceived adequacy of the support from the child's father ($r = 0.65$).

On the basis of these studies, it appears that informal social support affects not only maternal feelings, but also the mother's interaction with her handicapped or at risk child. The particular importance of the father's support has been found in a number of studies (Beckman, 1983; Bristol, 1985; Bristol & Gallagher, in press;

Gallagher et al., 1981; Friedrich, 1979). Mothers of children who reported more adequate support from their spouses reported fewer depressive symptoms, happier marriages, and received higher scores from raters on acceptance and quality of parenting (Bristol & Schopler, 1984).

Formal support and successful adaptation. There is an assumption among persons involved in formal intervention services that formal services, in addition to promoting child progress (see below), also reduce stress and increase adaptation in families. There are poignant accounts and some research evidence, however, that indicate that at least some kinds of services for some families of handicapped children actually increase stress (Schopler & Loftin, 1969; Turnbull & Blacher-Dixon, 1980; Turnbull & Turnbull, 1978; Turnbull & Winton, 1984).

Among the coping strategies found most helpful by mothers of autistic children in reducing stress, two of those rated most helpful were "Learning how to help my child improve" and "Believing that my child's program has my family's best interests in mind." In a similar vein, in a series of studies, mothers identified their child's intervention program as their most helpful source of support, even before their spouse (Bristol, 1982). Furthermore, in a study by Suelzle and Keenan (1981), parents indicated that their most frequent source of help at all ages was school personnel.

High quality, appropriate formal services, then, can contribute not only to child gain, but to successful family adaptation to handicapped children. Inadequate or inappropriate services, however, may increase family stress.

Coping strategies. Discussion of support networks often seems to imply a rather passive role for families in dealing with stress. As McCubbin (1979) has pointed out, however, there is much that parents can do to cope actively with stress. These coping responses—which include both actions designed to change the stressful situation and actions or beliefs required to tolerate, ignore, or minimize the stressful situation—are important determinants of a family's ability to endure stress over time. In a study of mothers of autistic children (Bristol, 1984), mothers indicated which of 45 specific coping responses on a modified Coping Health Inventory for Parents (McCubbin & Patterson, 1981) they used to cope with the stress of their handicapped child and indicated how helpful they perceived each to be.

The most helpful coping strategies used by at least two-thirds of the families were (in decreasing order of helpfulness): (a) believing that the child's intervention program had their family's best interests at heart, (b) learning how to help their children improve, (c) believing in God, (d) talking over personal feelings and

concerns with their spouses, (e) building closer relationships with spouses, (f) trying to maintain a stable family life, (g) developing themselves as persons, (h) telling themselves that they had many things to be thankful for, (i) doing things with their children, and (j) believing that their children will get better. Among the least helpful were eating (worry about becoming overweight presumably compounded the original stress), and allowing themselves to get angry. Parents remarked that although it felt good to let off steam, they subsequently felt guilty for their impatience or lack of tolerance.

To determine if patterns of coping responses were related to better family adaptation, the relationship of the three coping factor scores to the interviewer rating of adaptation was then assessed. Higher scores on all three factors (i.e., more coping strategies and/or greater utility of various strategies) were significantly related to more favorable interviewer ratings. Coping scores for mothers of autistic children on these three factors were comparable to those reported by Nevin and McCubbin (1979) for mothers of children with cystic fibrosis. Apparently, coping with a handicapped child may elicit similar levels of coping regardless of type of handicap, at least before any specific training or intervention. In keeping with McCubbin's (1979) contention that active coping strategies go beyond the passive receipt of support, in the prediction of in-home ratings of family adaptation, coping scores contributed significantly to the prediction even after the variance attributable to social support was accounted for (Bristol, 1984).

Child characteristics, informal, and formal support, and coping strategies alone do not explain how some families cope so successfully. Another major mediator of stress is the ideology (Turnbull et al., 1985) or subjective beliefs (element C in the ABCX model) the family holds regarding having a handicapped child.

It should be noted that four of the top ten coping strategies referred to subjective beliefs rather than actions. We are just beginning to appreciate the extent to which such subjective beliefs affect functioning in families of handicapped children.

(C) Family Definition of the Stressful Event

As Hill (1958) points out, stressors become crises depending upon the definition the family makes of them. He cites three possible definitions of the crisis-precipitating event: the objective definition of an impartial observer, the cultural definition of the community, and the subjective definition of the family, and concludes that the most relevant in precipitating a family crisis is the subjective definition. He further noted that if the blame for the stressful event can be placed outside the family, the stress may solidify rather than disorganize the family. A tornado is a stressful event but one not likely to precipitate a family crisis since the source of blame, he suggested, is outside the family. Lavelle and Keogh (1980) draw similar conclusions in their review of expectations and attributions of parents of handicapped children.

In contrast, work by Affleck and his associates (Affleck, Allen, McGrade, & McQueeney, 1982) suggests that mothers of either developmentally disabled or severely at-risk infants who blamed themselves for the infant's condition reported less mood disturbance than mothers who blamed others.

Although the concept of self-blame or guilt in families of disabled children has received considerable clinical attention, there are relatively few systematic data relating such subjective definitions to family outcomes. In research with mothers of autistic children (Bristol & Schopler, 1984), mothers who blamed themselves for their child's condition were more depressed, less happily married, and were rated by in-home interviewers as providing poorer quality of parenting for the child. Mothers who defined having a handicapped child as a family catastrophe were also rated as providing a poorer quality of parenting by raters "blind" to the self-assessment.

It does appear, however, that finding some broader meaning for the child's condition is related to better family functioning for both families of children with cystic fibrosis (Venters, 1982), and families of children with malignant diseases (Chodoff, Friedman, & Hamburg, 1964). The importance of personal belief in God has been found by a number of authors (Bristol, 1984; Gallagher et al., 1981).

Rosenberg & Robinson (1984) found that subjective beliefs affected competency of parents in an early intervention training program. Mothers' beliefs that they could effectively facilitate their child's development was the strongest predictor of both maternal teaching skills and child progress. Subjective beliefs appear to influence both family stress and adaptation to the child, and the actual quality of parent-child interaction and home environment. Measurement of parents' beliefs regarding their ability to influence child outcome (DeVellis et al., 1985) may be important measures of efficacy of early intervention.

The majority of parents of young handicapped children, then, through the use of resources, active coping strategies, and subjective beliefs are able to mediate the stress of their child and adapt successfully to the very real demands of their difficult situations. It is a process that continues over time and, to be fully understood, must be measured over time. Keogh and Bernheimer (1985) presented findings regarding a follow-up study of 35 preschool developmentally disabled children at about 6 years of age. They concluded that the behavioral and adjustment problems of developmentally disabled children are not outgrown but resulted in continuing, and often increasing, stress for parents and families, particularly during transition periods (i.e., school placement). Unfortunately, little research to date has studied such adaptation over time.

Family Intervention

Wolery and Bailey (1985) have noted some reasons that are widely accepted as calling for family intervention services:

> Families with handicapped children experience high levels of stress and may need professional support. Families may not know how to interact appropriately with their children.
>
> Families may not perceive themselves as having control over their future and need information regarding rights and service options. (pp. 120–121)

These are reasons why family intervention is needed, but do not describe how such services are delivered. They are delivered in a wide variety of program designs. There are a wide variety of types of family intervention including parent training, respite care, psychotherapy, and even legislative initiatives to encourage parental participation in policy making.

Perhaps the most common model of intervention is parent training. Baker (1984) described differing parent training models, each of which has some data assessing program capabilities. Some of the more common settings are described below.

Clinic- or School-Based Training. A series of meetings may be held at a clinic or school providing the parents with the opportunity to learn techniques to use with their children, coteaching or teaching their child with videotype replay and comment, and so forth.

Home-Based Training. Regular home visits are conducted over an extended period of time. This approach is particularly used in rural areas where travel is difficult for parents, or with disadvantaged families where such service delivery is the only option to no treatment at all.

Simulated Home Training. A model home is set up near the treatment facility so that the families can stay for a few days and try out their training in a home-like setting.

Group Training. These groups can receive curriculum with minilectures and the members can be supportive of one another. This type of program seems to be more amenable to research and observation. Self-help skills, setting behavioral objectives, contingent reinforcement and other techniques can become the core of such programs.

Therapy. Another program intervention involves the delivery of therapeutic counseling to the parents. Parent counseling can generally be divided into two major strategies. The first attempts to deal with the emotions and attitudes of the parents and their feelings about the parent-child relationship while the second focuses on preparing the parents to change child behaviors and parent-child interactions.

Respite care. One of the alternatives to parent training programs is the respite care programs which provide child care services for the handicapped child while the parents have a brief time or short weekend vacation away from the constant care demands of their handicapped child.

Siblings. The general success obtained through working with parents and peers have encouraged the use of siblings as potential teachers for handicapped children. Generally, siblings are taught basic behavior-shaping skills and given practice under supervision (Schreibman et al., 1983; Weinrott, 1974).

Parent power and legislative intervention. The Education for All Handicapped Children law (PL 94-142) and its successfor (PL 98-199) have made an attempt to empower parents and give them an important role to play in their child's education. In PL 90-538, the Handicapped Children's Early Education Act, approved centers serving preschool handicapped children were given funds to demonstrate the exemplary nature of their programs (DeWeerd, 1979). One of the conditions for receiving these funds was that they had to include "parents in the operation and evaluation of the projects". Four types of parental activity were noted in the regulations for PL 90-538: (a) planning, development, operation and evaluation of project; (b) parent training; (c) participation in the educational and therapeutic components of the project; (d) dissemination of information about the project.

Efficacy of Family Intervention

There has been increasing interest, but limited research, on the effectiveness of providing assistance to families. The emphasis has been on the delivery of such services, and this has resulted in a thin research literature on efficacy of family intervention programs.

Methodological issues. There are many serious methodological problems in trying to assess the effectiveness of training programs for parents. Since most of these assessments are executed in the framework of an ongoing clinical program, there is little opportunity for the evaluator or researcher to design the program in order to yield more definitive results. The most common flaws are in the *research design, sampling, measurement indices,* and the *lack of theoretical input.*

Actually, the experimental model most in favor by traditional researchers is unavailable to these programs. The randomized experiment-control design which would have some parents receive no treatment in the control group is now considered unethical. Treatment cannot be withheld from people in need and there are limits to which some type of placebo treatment can be considered.

In terms of sampling one must first consider the parents who are not in the program. Why aren't they participating? Are they less well-organized or motivated? Not all parents at a given treatment center will necessarily participate in a program either. One program (Baker, Clark, & Yasuda, 1981) invited 74 families with a moderate to severely retarded child to participate in group parent training but only 18 joined, and those 18 parents were more educated and more involved in school activities than those who did not join. Also, most studies are done in only one geographic spot or center with obvious generalization limitations to other staff, other places or other program efforts. The final problem with the samples in these studies is that they are often very small, making it more difficult for the study to yield significant or powerful results.

The results of other studies are limited by the choice of variables to measure. Some programs may use child improvement, for example, as a measure for parent program success, not always an appropriate choice since severely handicapped children may show little movement even if parents learn a great deal. Others will rely upon parent opinion of success, without corroborating evidence and the measuring instruments themselves often have limited validity and reliability.

Most of the research or program evaluation has paid little or no attention to psychological or sociological theory. There needs to be a much greater linkage between the empirical studies and the available theories. Farber (in press) has pointed out one problem with the absence of such theory. Many of our treatment strategies presuppose a Companionship Family Model, which stresses the primacy of mutuality and reciprocity between husband and wife, when, in fact, a Pluralistic Family Model, which stresses the fulfillment of each family member, may be a more predominant model in modern society.

> . . . if in contemporary society the Pluralistic Model predominates over the Companionship Family, then introducing a multitude of additional burdens maybe counterproductive for achieving a desirable level of nurturance. The family paradigms of the policy makers thus may not correspond with those models that guide the family life of the people to whom they are supposed to apply. (Farber, in press)

In part, because of the above issues, the literature on family intervention efficacy is mixed.

Behavior training. The evidence for positive outcomes of the behavioral approach appears to be quite strong. There is little doubt that parents can be taught specific skills that they can use with their handicapped children.

The evaluation of the utility of training of mothers to work with their own autistic children was shown to be superior to direct instruction by professional staff (Koegel, Schreibman, Britten, Burke, & O'Neill, 1981). Such training can also increase parent skills and decrease inappropriate and bizarre behaviors (Marcus, Lansing, Andrews, & Schopler, 1978). It also results in the generalization of treatment gains to other settings and maintainance of gain over time (Lovaas, Koegel, Simmons, & Long, 1973; Short, 1984).

A broad-based family-focused intervention program was found to have reduced the rate of institutionalization from one-fifth to one-tenth that reported for similar populations of autistic children (Schopler, Mesibov, & Baker, 1982).

Table 1 presents a summary by Baker (1984) of studies of parent training divided by type of research design. Those studies using a *single group pre-post design* generally reported gains in child behavior, parent knowledge, and skills. The studies with a *no training control group* also reported significant gains in knowledge and in child behavior in most studies. The type of training did not seem to be critical since various types of training showed gains in the *studies with two or more experimental groups.*

Baker (1984) comments:

> There is compelling evidence that parents who have participated in training increase their knowledge of teaching principles and their skill in applying these with their child. The question arises whether gains in parent knowledge and skills are specific to training program content or derive from nonspecific factors such as trainer's attention and encouragement. (p. 344)

Baker concluded, however, on the basis of further study (Baker & Brightman, in press) that the gains parents made *were* related to the specific training they received.

One of the most important questions to be posed regarding the long-term effect of parental training programs is the issue of instructional *generalization.* Does the training that is received get utilized in a different setting? This would indicate that the parents have mastered the techniques so well that they are now able to use it more broadly in caring for their children.

Forehand and Atkeson (1977) reviewed an extensive literature on four types of generalization as follows:

1. *Temporal Generality*—The maintenance of treatment effects following termination of treatment.

2. *Setting Generality*—The occurrence of treatment effects in settings other than the therapeutic one.

3. *Behavioral Generality*—Changes in behaviors not targeted for treatment.

4. *Sibling Generality*—Changes in the behaviors of the treated child's sibling.

There appears to be some evidence for temporal generality and this appears to be particularly true if a gradual "fading" of the treatment is used, or if there is a major follow-up program involved as part of the treatment (see Patterson, 1974). In the range of studies reviewed, there is much variance in the results of maintaining treatment effects over time.

In the case of setting generality most of the research investigated the transfer of skills from the clinic to home, or from home to school. There is a range of results again but some evidence that transfer can take place and that some training methods can be used to enhance the transfer.

There is only minimal support to demonstrate decreases in nontreated target behaviors after treatment of specific targeted behaviors. The evidence for behavioral generality is quite limited.

There appears to be sibling generality without a clear picture as to the process which allows it to occur. Whether it is the parents applying the behavioral skills from the treated child to the sibling or whether there is reduced need for sibling misbehavior with the treatment of the target child, or whether other options have to be considered, remains open in the absence of more definitive research.

Therapy. There are a number of approaches falling under the general heading of parent counseling or therapy. Parent Effectiveness Training (PET) is one of the most popular approaches using the strategy of focusing on feelings. Rinn and Markle (1977) summarized the available literature on PET. These authors complained about the lack of methodological rigor and inadequate design but then concluded: "Nonetheless, the data available on PET for review do *not* support the assumption that Parent Effectiveness Training is effective" (p. 105).

While treatment in the form of psychotherapy may occasionally be needed, as it is in the general population, the vast majority of parents with handicapped children are not pathological (Bristol & Schopler, 1984; Cantwell, Baker, & Rutter, 1978). Furthermore, psychotherapy for either autistic child or parent has not seemed to change the child's status significantly (Wing, 1976).

There is some research that indicates that appropriate intervention through the use of father support groups (Fewell, 1983; Meyer, Vadasy, Fewell, & Schell, in press) results in reductions in stress for both fathers and for their wives, who did not participate in the program.

Respite care. Joyce and Singer (1983) reported that such a program provided emotional relief, was of more benefit to families with recently disabled children than families with long-term disabled children, and tended to encourage the parents to maintain the handicapped child in the family and not institutionalize him or her.

The use of parents as teachers or therapists depends upon their willingness to participate in this fashion and

TABLE 1

Studies of Training with Parents of Developmentally Disabled Children

Authors	N	Child Diagnosis: age (years)	Program	Measures	Results	Results; follow-up (FU)
1. Single group pre-post						
Baker & McCurry, 1983	20	Mentally retarded; 9.2	School-based for low SES (6 half days)	Parent knowledge (Behavioral Vignettes Test), skills, & home teaching	Significant improve pre-post on all measures	Home teaching not maintained; 6-month FU
Feldman, Manella, Apodaca, & Varni, 1982	4	Spina bifida; 8	9 group meetings	Knowledge, child skills; marital inventories	Multiple baseline: significant gains on both; no change marital adjustment	Continued child gain; maintenance of knowledge; 3-month FU
Feldman, Manella, & Varni, 1983	4	Physically handicapped; 4–10	10 group meetings, single parents	Knowledge, child skills	Multiple baseline: significant gains on both	None
Harris, Wolchik, & Weitz, 1981	11	Autistic; 3.9	10 group meetings and 6 home visits	Language skill hierarchy	Significant improvement pre-post; No change pre-1 to pre-2	Continued progress; 2-, 4- & 13-month FU
Rose, 1974b	33	Mentally retarded; 3–8	7–10 small group meetings and home visits	Parent frequency counts	82% modified 1 or more child behavior to their satisfaction	20 of 21 maintained gains; 3–6 month FU
Salzinger, Feldman, & Portnoy, 1970	15	Brain injured; 3–12	Individual or group training	Success of child program	8 fully or partially carried out program and produced change	None
Sebba, 1981	5	Profoundly mentally retarded with multiple handicaps	28 individual sessions	Bailey Scales of Infant Development	No significant improvement pre-post	None
Uditsky & MacDonald, 1981	64	Developmentally delayed	8 group and home visits; 3-month tapered FU	Interview post vs. 3-month, 1-year, or 2-year FU		Cross-sectional design; 3 FU groups similar, 75% or more in each condition maintained or improved target behavior
II. Studies with a no-training control group						
Bidder, Bryant, & Gray, 1975	16	Mentally retarded, Down's syndrome; 1–3	12 group meetings	Griffiths Mental Development Scales	T > C on Language and Performance Scales	None
Brightman, Ambrose, & Baker, 1980	16	Mentally retarded; 2.5–13	School-based, 3 or more days	Parent knowledge, skill; home teaching	Trained > matched comparison group on all	None
Clements, Evans, Jones, Osborne, & Upton, 1982	20	Mentally handicapped; 6.5	Biweekly home visits for 18 months (Portage model)	Reynell Developmental Language Scales	T improved significantly, but T = C; note: T, C not randomly assigned	None
Diament & Colletti, 1978	22	Learning disabled; 7	8 group meetings, groups of 5, 6	Observing mother-child play, parent ratings. Adjective Checklist (ACL)	T > C Mother praise-child attend and ACL conduct; T = C parent ratings	Maintained gains; 3-month FU
Hirsch & Walder, 1969	30	Severely disturbed and mentally retarded;	9 group meetings	Knowledge, behavior rating; anxiety–depression	T > C on knowledge, behavior rating; no change in anxiety, depression	None

TABLE 1 *(continued)*

Studies of Training with Parents of Developmentally Disabled Children

Authors	N	Child Diagnosis: age (years)	Program	Measures	Results	Results; follow-up (FU)
Prieto-Bayard & Baker, in press	20	Mentally retarded; 6.7	10 group meetings in Spanish with child group	Parent knowledge, skills; home teaching; child self-help, behavior problem	T significant gain on all; T > C except for teaching skill and self-help	Home teaching gains only partly maintained; 6-month FU
Sandler, Coren, & Thurman, 1983	21	Mentally retarded; 3.8	4 group and 4 individual meetings	Parent-child interaction; knowledge, attitude; Dvp checklist	T > C interaction and knowledge; no change on attitude and child development checklist	None
III. Studies with two or more experimental groups						
Baker & Brightman, in press	15	Mentally retarded; 5.7	Group training (N = 8) or advocacy (N = 7)	Teaching knowledge, skill; advocacy knowledge, skill	Generally, each group improved on measures specific to its training	None
Baker & Heifetz, 1976; Baker, Heifetz, & Murphy, 1980; Heifetz, 1977	160	Mentally retarded; 7.2	Training by manuals (N = 32), phone consultation (N = 32), groups (N = 32), groups and visits (N = 32), or no training (N = 32)	Parent knowledge; child self-help skills	Training conditions had equivalent outcome, but each surpassed controls	Parent-child gains maintained; further teaching equal across conditions; 1-year FU
Brightman, Baker, Clark, & Ambrose, 1982	66	Mentally retarded; 6	Individual (N = 16), group (N = 37), or control (N = 13)	Parent knowledge, skills; self-help, behavior problems	I = G > C except self-help (I = G = C)	Home teaching; I = G; 6-month FU
Hudson, 1982	40	Mentally retarded; 0.3–3.5	Group training: Didactic (D), D with behavioral principles, D with modeling and role play, or control (N = 10@)	Parent knowledge and skill; home tasks completed; Denver Developmental Screening Test (DDST)	Knowledge, DDST, T > C, D = DB = DM; skills, DM > C; home tasks DM > D = DB	None
O'Dell, Flynn, & Benlolo, 1977	40	Mentally retarded; 8.2	Group training after pretraining (N = 14), placebo pretraining (N = 13), or no pretraining (N = 13)	Parent knowledge, skills; attitudes; home implementation	Outcome did not differ on any measure across pretraining conditions	Conditions not different in implementation; 1-month FU
Sandow & Clarke, 1978	32	Severely mentally retarded; 2.5	2 years' home visits, bi-weekly (N = 16) or bi-monthly (N = 16)	Cattell Infant IQ	Biweekly, rise in year 1 and then decrement; bi-monthly, opposite	None
Tavormina, 1975; Tavormina, Hampson, & Luscomb, 1976	51	Mentally retarded; 6.7	Behavioral (N = 19) vs. reflective (N = 19) vs. control (N = 13)	Hereford Parent Attitude Scale; Behavior observation, parent ratings; Missouri Behavior Problem Checklist	B > R > C on Hereford causation scale, behav. obs. and par. ratings; B = R > C on several sub-scales of BPC	Assessed satisfaction with training; B > R; 1-year FU

Note: From "Intervention with Families with Young Severely Handicapped Children" by B. Baker. In *Severely Handicapped Young Children and Their Families* (pp. 319–376), by J. Blacher (Ed.), 1984, Orlando, FL: Academic Press.

their aptitude for learning the necessary skills to carry out the interactions effectively. Some mothers seem to respond better to respite care, or time away from their handicapped child, rather than increasing the intensity of their interaction with their handicapped child through becoming an aide in a special education program (Winton & Turnbull, 1981).

Sibling training. There is a limited literature on the effectiveness of sibling training but what there is is encouraging. Training allows siblings to interact more constructively with their handicapped brother or sister and the siblings often feel good about their own competencies and their contribution to the family. As Powell and Ogle (1985) point out: "It is not for every sibling, and siblings should not be forced to participate in an intervention program. Properly instituted though, a sibling teaching program can be rewarding" (p.141).

The general efficacy of professional assistance to various members of the family seems to be supported, but the range of response to any particular program suggests that many different types of programs may be necessary to provide comprehensive service.

Legislative intervention. Hocutt and Wiegerink (1983) studied 23 of these demonstration programs and found that the predominant parent activity in these centers was the receipt of information from professionals, and the training of parents to work with children at home assisting in the execution of the educational or therapeutic program. The professionals apparently did not wish parents to be participating in the policy- or decision-making aspects of the program even though parents who did participate in this element of the program showed the most satisfaction with the program itself.

Conclusions on Family Intervention

The limited conclusions that can be drawn from the literature on family intervention have been spelled out by Wiegerink, Hocutt, Posante-Loro, & Bristol (1980):

> Although parental involvement has been found to be generally linked with positive findings in child performance, parent satisfaction, and program success, to what extent this is a correlational versus a cause and effect relationship is not known. To date there has not been sufficient study of the methods of parental involvement that may cause increases in child progress, parent satisfaction, and program success. (p. 81)

Casto and Lewis (1984) reported on the results of a meta-analysis on child development variables comparing programs for early intervention which had parental involvement as a major factor in the intervention with programs that had little or no parental participation in

the program. They found no differences in effect sizes for child developmental variables in the two different types of programs. Since these results differ from those reported in Table 1, there would need to be some explanation for these differing results.

In the first place, the meta-analysis of Casto and Lewis included as outcome variables only child characteristics and did not explore whether the parent training programs created a difference in the attitudes or feelings of the parents themselves. In addition, Casto and Lewis pointed out that virtually all of their data came from samples of disadvantaged, rather than handicapped children. In those programs where the children were handicapped, moderate or severely handicapped children probably could not have been expected to progress much on IQ test scores, regardless of the potential success that the parent program might have in easing the stresses or pressures on the parents themselves. Nevertheless, analyses such as those by Casto and Lewis should raise a caution flag against any automatic assumption of the virtues of parental training for the young child.

The difference in these findings from Casto and Lewis (1984) and Baker (1984), therefore, may be attributed to the use of different types of child progress measures across studies, or the fact that many of the most dramatic efficacy data for parental involvement are found in single subject studies, which had not been included in meta-analyses.

Baker (1984) concluded his review with some implications for intervening with families of severely handicapped children:

1. A primary concern must be choosing specific child behaviors to modify and monitor the progress of these. Not unexpectedly, child gains have been shown to be less as the level of handicap is greater . . . it must be focused in its intervention and measurement.

2. It is likely that the most helpful program for parents will be integrated with the child's ongoing school and draw on related professionals for consultation about objectives.

3. Although intervention with children should be focused on specific skills, intervention with parents might be productively broadened. Parents of severely handicapped children are likely to need more support and information than those where the disability is milder.

4. Families should have a choice about their level of involvement. There must not only be greater services but also greater options. Simply because persons suddenly find themselves in the role of parents of a handicapped child does not mean they should be required to participate a half-day every week in a school program or any other involvement. (pp. 365–366)

Future Issues and Recommendations

If we are to profit from our past experiences as documented in this review, then several steps need to be taken. The following recommendations represent the authors' view of what needs to be done.

The nature of success

We need to go beyond the simple research question, "Do parent programs succeed?" The answer is clearly "Yes, for some parents, in some types of programs, under certain kinds of conditions." The better question to ask is, "What are the conditions under which success occurs for certain parents?" We must be careful to define "success" as well. The answer to the question of the conditions for success will allow us to plan more targeted and differentiated programs.

Recommendation

There is a clear need to build additional sophistication in program evaluation. That need can be met in the following ways:

1. There should be inservice training of existing service personnel in the basic procedures and design of program evaluation so that program directors can avoid the more obvious design problems in meeting their own evaluation requirements.

2. There needs to be systematic support of efforts to develop more satisfactory models and instruments related to program evaluation. This implies the continued support and encouragement of research groups or centers towards instrument development, since they have the needed expertise to provide more creative answers to evaluation design.

One of the limitations of the existing research literature is an inability to identify precisely the specific elements of the treatment process that are creating positive effects. A careful study of the process of the treatment could provide confidence that it was the key factor in parental or family changes that are noted (Wiegerink & Comfort-Smith, in press).

Family diversity

The diversity of families with young handicapped children is well-documented in the current review. Their needs, values, and interests stretch over an enormous spectrum. In order to be of maximum help, then, professionals must design programs to fit that diversity. Not every mother can be a teacher to her child; not every father should become a surrogate mother.

Recommendations

The great diversity of family needs and resources calls for a program that will make available a menu of services to meet those needs. This, in turn, means that agencies that provide support for service programs must include in their guidelines the approval of such a strategy so that the service personnel do not believe that they have to follow a single pattern of service delivery (for example,

fostering parent involvement whether the parents want it or not).

Conceptual framework needs

We need to find conceptual frameworks that help us to organize our family programs more effectively. The Hill-McCubbin model noted in this review helps us to think about the issue of parental stress in a productive way. We need similar models for treatment or therapy (Turnbull et al., 1985) so that we don't find ourselves grasping at alternatives with no good or justifiable reason.

The work with families seems to be one of the most justifiable foci of our work with moderately to severely handicapped children. If we are seeking *alterable variables*, factors we can productively change, then the family is clearly one set of such variables, sometimes easier to modify than the intellectual development of a severely retarded child. While we should not neglect child progress, we must view the family as a social unit needing comprehensive assistance.

Recommendation

The general lack of conceptual frameworks in service programs for families reflects the preoccupation of the service delivery personnel with the immediate needs of their clientele. Larger conceptual models usually emerge from the work of academically oriented personnel, often social scientists whose interests proceed along these lines. This means we should provide the opportunity for interaction between the practitioners and the social scientists through conferences designed to encourage interaction on model building. Financial support should be available to encourage social scientists to undertake the task of developing a model, or of applying existing models from their own disciplines to this special interest area.

The family being a dynamic system, we must entertain the possibility that positive changes in one element or member of the family can result in negative consequences in other members. Thus, an increase in positive mother-handicapped child interactions could result in poorer mother-sibling relationships. We must try to capture the entire family system if we can as opposed to individuals or dyadic relationships.

Longitudinal perspective

Almost totally lacking in the current research, and strongly needed, is a longitudinal perspective. The study of families over time will enable us to look at possible problems that arise at major transition points, such as when the child begins public school. Such research will help us determine whether the later years of parenting bring a different set of problems requiring different levels and types of assistance.

Recommendation

Few people would argue against the importance of longitudinal data, therefore its absence must mean that the supportive conditions necessary for the generation of such data are not present.

Longitudinal studies in this case do not necessarily mean following a child into adulthood, but rather a study of the family over key transitional periods in their lives, that is, from preschool to public school programs, or from school to postschool activities. Serious attempts to collect longitudinal data require a long-term commitment together with an organization that can support such an effort. The Early Childhood Research Centers, funded by OSEP, is one example of organizations that are carrying out such longitudinal studies.

Alternative family patterns

The one-parent family is an obvious concern, yet little systematic research has been done that identifies the familial, economic, and social resources necessary for successful adaptation to the presence of a handicapped child in such families. We must look beyond the nuclear middle-class family as the sole focus of our efforts. We should also investigate the effects of social changes such as maternal employment on the family with handicapped children.

Recommendation

Specific research studies and demonstration programs should be supported that focus on alternative family patterns so that we increase our knowledge and skills with such family patterns.

Personnel preparation

Personnel preparation programs should include working with families as an integral part of preparing early intervention personnel. Similarly, multidisciplinary (or transdisciplinary) training will help to encourage a broader family perspective as opposed to the more traditional educational focus on the child alone.

Recommendation

Since the current interest in families of handicapped children is a relatively new thrust in various professions, it is likely that there are many professionals now at work who have been trained prior to this emphasis. It also means that many existing training programs may still not have adequate components of training that would focus upon the family as an interest area. Three specific strategies should be employed: (a) A major program of inservice training should be supported that would allow existing practitioners to learn new skills in how to interact professionally with the families; (b) new requirements should be made upon existing training programs

to urge them to provide systematic experiences with families through the choice of practicum settings that stress multidisciplinary family emphases, or the design of research studies with a similar focus; (c) upgrading the skills of professors who are responsible for administering the graduate training programs would be an additional positive element in an overall training program.

These recommendations require that additional resources be made available and a commitment on the part of existing funding agencies to pursue the development of a more sophisticated support system to undergird service delivery to families of handicapped children. This means planning to provide long-term support in research, instrument development, leadership training, inservice training, and dissemination.

References

Affleck, G., Allen, D., McGrade, B., & McQueeney, M. (1982). Maternal causal attributions at hospital discharge of high-risk infants. *American Journal of Mental Deficiency*, **86**(6), 575–580.

Akerley, M. (1975). The invulnerable parent. *Journal of Autism and Childhood Schizophrenia*, **5**, 275–281.

Appell, M. A., & Tisdall, W. (1968). Factors differentiating institutionalized from non-institutionalized referred retardates. *American Journal of Mental Deficiency*, **73**, 424–432.

Baker, B. (1984). Intervention with families with young severely handicapped children. In J. Blacher (Ed.), *Severely handicapped young children and their families* (pp. 319–376). Orlando, FL: Academic Press.

Baker, B. L., & Brightman, R. P. (in press). Training parents of retarded children: Program specific outcomes. *Journal of Behavior Therapy and Experimental Psychiatry*.

Baker, B. L., Clark, D. B., & Yasuda, P. M. (1981). Predictors of success in parent training. In P. Mittler (Ed.), *Frontiers of knowledge in mental retardation*. Baltimore: University Park Press.

Beckman, P. B. (1983). Characteristics of handicapped infants: A study of the relationship between child characteristics and stress as reported by mothers. *American Journal of Mental Deficiency*, **88**, 150–156.

Bell, R. (1968). A reinterpretation of the direction of effects in studies of socialization. *Psychological Review*, **75**, 81–95.

Belsky, J. (1980). Child maltreatment: An ecological integration. *American Psychologist*, **5**, 320–335.

Berkman, L. F., & Syme, S. L. (1979). Social networks, host resistance, and mortality: A nine-year follow-up study of Alameda County residents. *American Journal of Epidemiology*, **109**(2), 186–204.

Bittner, S., & Newberger, E. H. (1981). Pediatric understanding of child abuse and neglect. *Pediatrics in Review*, **2**(7), 197–207.

Blacher, J. (1984). A dynamic perspective on the impact of a severely handicapped child on the family. In J. Blacher (Ed.), *Severely handicapped young children and their families* (pp. 1–50). Orlando, FL: Academic Press.

Bowlby, J. (1969). *Attachment, Vol. 1: Attachment and loss.* New York: Basic Books.

Bradshaw, J., & Lawton, D. (1978). Tracing the causes of stress in families with handicapped children. *British Journal of Social Work*, **8**, 181–192.

Breslau, N. (1982). The psychological study of chronically ill and disabled children: Are healthy siblings appropriate controls? *Journal of Abnormal Child Psychology*, **11**, 379–391.

Breslau, N., Weitzman, M., & Messinger, K. (1981). Psychological functioning of siblings of disabled children. *Pediatrics*, **67**, 344–353.

Bristol, M. M. (1979). *Maternal coping with autistic children: The effect of child characteristics and interpersonal support.* Unpublished doctoral dissertation, University of North Carolina at Chapel Hill.

Bristol, M. M. (1982). *The home care of developmentally disabled children: The double ABCX model and successful coping.* Paper presented at the NICHHD Lake Wilderness Conference on the Impact of Residential Settings on the Retarded, Seattle, WA.

Bristol, M. M. (1984a). *Families of developmentally disabled children: Healthy adaptation and the double ABC model.* Paper presented at the Family Systems and Health Preconference Workshop, National Council on Family Relations, San Francisco, CA.

Bristol, M. M. (1984b). Family resources and successful adaptation to autistic children. In E. Schopler & G. Mesibov (Eds.). *The effects of autism on the family* (pp. 289–309). New York: Plenum Press.

Bristol, M. M. (1985a). *A series of studies of social support, stress, and adaptation in families of developmentally disabled children.* Paper presented at the Biennial Meeting of the Society for Research in Child Development, Toronto, Ontario.

Bristol, M. M. (1985b). Designing programs for young developmentally disabled children: A family systems approach to autism. *Remedial and Special Education*, **4**(6), 46–53.

Bristol, M. M. (in press-a). The home care of developmentally disabled children: Some empirical support for a conceptual model of successful coping with family stress. In P. Vietze & S. Landesman-Dwyer (Eds.), Living with Retarded People. *Monographs of the American Association on Mental Deficiency*. Washington: American Association on Mental Deficiency.

Bristol, M. M. (in press-b). Issues in the assessment of single-parent families. *Journal of the Division of Early Childhood*.

Bristol, M. M., & Gallagher, J. J. (1982). A family focus for intervention. In C. Ramey & P. Trohanis (Eds.), *Finding and educating the high-risk and handicapped infant*. Baltimore: University Park Press.

Bristol, M. M., & Gallagher, J. J. (in press). Research on fathers of young handicapped children: Evolution, review, and some future directions. In P. Vietze & J. J. Gallagher (Eds.), *Family adaptation to handicapped children*, Baltimore, MD: Paul H. Brookes.

Bristol, M., & Schopler, E. (1983). *The ABCX model: predicting successful family adaptation to developmentally disabled children.* Carolina Institute for Research on Early Education for the Handicapped, University of North Carolina at Chapel Hill, Chapel Hill, NC.

Bristol, M. M., & Schopler, E. (1984). A developmental perspective on stress and coping in families of autistic children. In J. Blacher (Ed.), *Families of severely handicapped children: Review of research*. New York: Academic Press.

Bristol, M., Schopler, E., & McConnaughey, R. (1984). *The prevalence of divorce in families of preschool children and nonhandicapped children.* Paper presented at the National Handicapped Children's Early Education Program/DEC Conference, Washington, DC.

Bronfenbrenner, U. (1979). Contexts of child rearing—Problems and prospects. *American Psychologist*, **34**(10), 844–850.

Burden, R. L. (1980). Measuring the effects of stress on the mothers of handicapped infants: Must depression always follow? *Child: Care, Health and Development*, **6**, 111–125.

Burr, W. (1973). *Theory construction and the sociology of the family*. New York.

Cantwell, D. P., Baker, L., & Rutter, M. (1978). Family factors in the syndrome of infantile autism. In M. Rutter & E. Schopler (Eds.), *Autism: A reappraisal of concepts and treatments*. New York: Plenum Press.

Casto, G., & Lewis, A. (1984). Parent involvement in infant and preschool programs. *Journal of the Division for Early Childhood*, **9**(1), 49–56.

Chinitz, S. P. (1981). A sibling group for brothers and sisters of handicapped children. *Children Today*, 21–23.

Chodoff, P., Friedman, S. B., & Hamburg, D. A. (1964). Stress, defenses, and coping behavior: Observations in parents of children with malignant disease. *American Journal of Psychiatry*, **120**, 743–749.

Clarke-Stewart, K. (1979). The family drama of a child development. In B. Brazleton & V. Vaughn (Eds.), *The family: Setting priorities*. New York: Science & Medicine.

Cobb, S. (1976). Social support as a moderator of life stress. *Psychosomatic Medicine*, **38**(5), 300–314.

Cohen, S. (1982). Supporting families through respite care. *Rehabilitation Literature*, **43**, 1–2, 7–11.

Cohen, F., & Lazarus, R. (1979). Coping with the stresses of illness. In G. Stone, F. Cohen, & N. Adler, & Associates (Eds.), *Health Psychology—A Handbook*. San Francisco: Jossey-Bass.

Crnic, K., Friedrich, W., & Greenberg, M. (1983). Adaptation of families with mentally retarded children: A model of stress, coping, and family ecology. *American Journal of Mental Deficiency*, **88**(2), 125–138.

Cummings, S. (1976). The impact of the child's deficiency on the father: A study of fathers of mentally retarded and of chronically ill children. *American Journal of Orthopsychiatry*, **46**, 246–255.

Cummings, S., Bayley, H. C., & Rie, H. E. (1966). Effects of the child's deficiency on the mother: A study of mothers of mentally retarded, chronically ill, and neurotic children. *American Journal of Orthopsychiatry*, **36**, 595–608.

Darling, R. B. (1979). *Families against society: A study of reactions to children with birth defects*. Beverly Hills and London: Sage.

Darling, R. B., & Darling, J. (1982). *Children who are different: Meeting the challenges of birth defects in society*. St Louis: C. V. Mosby.

Davis, M., & McKay, D. N. (1973). Mentally subnormal children and their families. *Lancet*, **ii**(7835), 974–975.

deAraujo, G., van Arsdel, P. P., Holmes, T. H., & Dudley, D. L. (1973). Life change, coping ability and chronic intrinsic asthma. *Journal of Psychosomatic Research*, **17**, 359–363.

DeMyer, M., & Goldberg, P. (1983). Family needs of the autistic adolescent. In E. Schopler & G. B. Mesibov (Eds.), *Autism in adolescents and adults*. New York: Plenum Press.

DeVellis, R. F., DeVellis, B. E., Rivicki, D. A., Lurie, S. J., Runyan, D. K., & Bristol, M. (1985). Development and validation of the child improvements locus of control (CILC) scales. *Journal of Clinical and Social Psychology*, **3**, 308–325.

DeWeerd, J. (1979). *Handicapped children's early education program*. Washington, DC: U.S. Department of Education, Special Education Programs.

Donovan, A. (1985). *Maternal perception of family stress and ways of coping with adolescents: A comparison study of mothers with autistic, mentally retarded and nonhandicapped adolescents*. Unpublished doctoral dissertation. University of North Carolina at Chapel Hill.

Dorner, S. (1975). The relationship of psychical handicap to stress in families with an adolescent with spina bifida. *Developmental Medicine and Child Neurology*, **17**, 765–776.

Farber, B. (1959). Effects of a severely mentally retarded child on family integration. *Monographs of the Society for Research in Child Development*, **24**(2) (Serial No. 71).

Farber, B. (1960). Family organization and crisis: Maintenance of integration in families with a severely mentally retarded child. *Monographs of the Society for Research in Child Development*, **75**.

Farber, B. (1975). Family adaptation to severely mentally retarded children. In M. Begab & S. Richardson (Eds.), *The mentally retarded and society: A social science perspective*. Baltimore: University Park Press.

Farber, B. (in press). Historical contexts of research on families with mentally retarded members. In P. Vietze & J. Gallagher (Eds.), *Family adaptation to handicapped children*. Baltimore, MD: Paul H. Brookes.

Fewell, R. R. (1983). *Supporting extended family members: Summary of research findings*. Paper presented at the 107th Meeting of the American Association for Mental Deficiency, Dallas, TX.

Forehand, R., & Atkeson, B. M. (1977). Generality of treatment effects with parents as therapists: A review of assessment and implementation procedures. *Behavior Therapy*, **8**, 575–593.

Friedrich, W. (1979). Predictors of the coping behavior of mothers of handicapped children. *Journal of Consulting and Clinical Psychology*, **47**(6), 1140–1141.

Friedrich, W. N., & Friedrich, W. L. (1981). Psychosocial assets of handicapped and nonhandicapped children. *American Journal of Mental Deficiency*, **85**(5), 551–553.

Gallagher, J. J. (1983). The Carolina Institute for Research: Early education for the handicapped. *Journal of the Division for Early Childhood*, **7**, 18–24.

Gallagher, J. J., Beckman, P., & Cross, A. H. (1983). Families of handicapped children: Sources of stress and its amelioration. *Exceptional Children*, **50**(1), 10–19.

Gallagher, J. J., Cross, A. H., & Scharfman, W. (1981). Parental adaptation to a young handicapped child: The father's role. *Journal of the Division for Early Childhood*, **3**, 3–14.

Gallagher, J. J., Scharfman, W., & Bristol, M. (1984). The division of responsibilities in families with preschool handicapped and nonhandicapped children. *Journal of Division for Early Childhood*, **8**(1), 3–11.

Garbarino, J. (1977). Human ecology of child maltreatment: A conceptual model for research. *Journal of Marriage and the Family*, **39**, 721–735.

Graliker, B., Koch, R., & Hendersen, M. (1965). A study of factors influencing placement of retarded children in a state residential institution. *American Journal of Mental Deficiency*, **69**, 553–559.

Hansen, D. A., & Johnson, J. A. (1979). Rethinking family stress theory: Definitional aspects. In W. R. Burr, R. Hill, F. I. Nye, & I. Reiss (Eds.), *Contemporary theories about the family, Vol. 1, Research-based theories* (pp. 582–603). New York: The Free Press.

Hetherington, E. M. (1981). Children and divorce. In R. Henderson (Ed.), *Parent-child interaction: Theory, research and prospects*. New York: Academic Press.

Hill, R. (1949). *Families under stress: Adjustment to the crisis of war separation and reunion*. New York: Harper.

Hill, R. (1958). Social stresses on the family. *Social Casework*, **39**, 139–150.

Hocutt, A., & Wiegerink, R. (1983). Perspectives on parent involvement in preschool programs in handicapped children. In R. Haskins & D. Adams (Eds.), *Parent education and public policy* (pp. 211–229). Norwood, NJ: Ablex.

Holroyd, J. (1974). The questionnaire on resources and stress: An instrument to measure family response to a handicapped member. *Journal of Community Psychology*, **2**, 92–94.

Holyroyd, J., & McArthur, D. (1976). Mental retardation and stress on the parents: A contrast between Down's syndrome and childhood autism. *American Journal of Mental Deficiency*, **80**(4), 431–436.

Joyce, K., & Singer, M. (1983). Respite care services: An evaluation of the perceptions of parents and workers. *Rehabilitation Literature*, **44**(9–10), 270–274.

Kamoravsky, M. (1962). *Blue collar marriage*. New York: Random House.

Kazak, A. & Marvin, R. (1984). Differences, difficulties, and adaptation: Stress and social networks in families with a handicapped child. *Family Relations*, **33**, 67–77.

Keogh, B., & Bernheimer, R. (1985). Stress and accommodation in families of developmentally delayed children. *Biannual Meeting Society for Research in Child Development*, **5**, 470. (Abstract).

Koegel, R. L., Schreibman, L., Britten, K. R., Burke, J. C., & O'Neill, R. E. (1981). A comparison of parent training to direct child treatment. In R. L. Koegel, A. Rincover, & A. L. Egel (Eds.), *Educating and understanding autistic children* (pp. 260–279). San Diego, CA: College-Hill.

Kolin, I. S., Scherzer, A. L., New, B., & Garfield, M. (1971). Studies of the school-age child with meningomyelocele: Social and emotional adaptation. *Pediatrics*, **78**(6), 1013–1019.

Korn, S. J., Chess, S., & Fernandez, P. (1978). The impact of children's physical handicaps on marital quality and family interaction. In R. M. Lerner & Y. B. Spanier (Eds.), *Child influences on marital and family interaction: A life span perspective*. New York: Academic Press.

Lamb, M. E. (1976). The role of the father: An overview. In M. Lamb (Ed.), *The role of the father in child development*. New York: Wiley.

Lavelle, N., & Keogh, B. K. (1980). Expectations and attributions of parents of handicapped children. In J. J. Gallagher (Ed.), *New directions for exceptional children* (Vol. 4). San Francisco: Jossey-Bass.

Lawley, D. N. (1959). Tests of significance in canonical analysis. *Biometrika*, **46**.

Lotter, V. (1978). Follow-up studies. In M. Rutter & E. Schopler (Ed.), *Autism: A reappraisal of concepts and treatment* (pp. 475–596). New York: Plenum Press.

Lovaas, O. I., Koegel, R., Simmons, J. L., & Long, J. S. (1973). Some generalizations and follow up measures on autistic children in behavior therapy. *Journal of Applied Behavior Analysis*, **6**, 131–165.

MacKeith, R. (1973). The feelings and behavior of parents of handicapped children. *Developmental Medicine and Child Neurology*, **15**, 524–527.

MacKey, W., & Day, R. (1979). Some indicators of fathering behaviors in the United States: A cross-cultural examination of adult male-child interaction. *Journal of Marriage and the Family*, **41**(2), 287–298.

Marcus, L., Lansing, M., Andrews, C., & Schopler, E. (1978). Improvement of teaching effectiveness in parents of autistic children. *Journal of American Academy of Child Psychiatry*, **17**, 625–639.

Martin, P. (1975). Marital breakdown in families of children with spina bifida cystica. *Developmental Medicine and Child Neurology*, **17**, 757–764.

Mates, T. E. (1982). *Siblings of autistic children: Their adjustment and performance at home and in school as a function of their sex and family size*. Unpublished doctoral dissertation, University of North Carolina at Chapel Hill.

McCubbin, H. (1979). Integrating coping behavior in family stress theory. *Journal of Marriage and the Family*, **41**, 237–244.

McCubbin, H. I., Cauble, A. E., & Patterson, J. M. (Eds.). (1982). *Family stress, coping, and social support*. Springfield, IL: Charles C. Thomas.

McCubbin, H. I., & Patterson, J. (1981). *Systematic assessment of family stress, resources and coping*. St. Paul, MN: Family Stress Project, University of Minnesota.

McCubbin, H. I., & Patterson, J. M. (1982). Family adaptation to crises. In H. McCubbin, A. Cauble, & J. Patterson (Eds.), *Family stress, coping, and social support* (pp. 26–47). Springfield, IL: Charles C. Thomas.

McCubbin, H., Sussman, M., & Patterson, J. (1983). *Social stress and the family*. New York: Haworth Press.

Medalie, J. H., Snyder, M., Gruen, J. J., Neufeld, H. N., Goldcourt, U., & Riss, E. (1973). Angina pectoris among 10,000 men: 5-year incidence and univariate analysis. *American Journal of Medicine*, **55**, 583–594.

Meyer, D. J., Vadasy, P. F., Fewell, R. R., & Schnell, G. (in press). *A handbook for the fathers program*. Seattle: University of Washington Press.

Nevin, R. S. & McCubbin, H. I. (1979). *Parental coping with physical handicaps: Social policy implications*. Paper presented at the National Council on Family Relations annual meeting, Boston, MA.

Nuckolls, K. B., Cassel, J., & Kaplan, B. H. (1972). Psychosocial assets, life crisis and the prognosis of pregnancy. *American Journal of Epidemiology*, **95**, 431–441.

Olson, D. H., & McCubbin, H. I. (1983). *Families: What makes them work*. Beverly Hills, CA: Sage.

Parke, R. (1979). Perspectives on father-infant interaction. In J. Osofsky (Ed.), *Handbook of infant development*. New York: Wiley.

Patterson, G. R. (1974). Intervention for boys with conduct problems. Multiple settings, treatments, and criteria. *Journal of Consulting and Clinical Psychology*, **42**, 471–481.

Patterson, G. (1980). Mothers: The unacknowledged victims. *Monographs of the Society for Research in Child Development*. Serial No. 186.

Patterson, J., & McCubbin, A. (1984). Gender roles and coping. *Journal of Marriage and the Family*, **47**, 52–66.

Pedersen, F. (1976). Does research on children reared in father-absent families yield information on father influence? *The Family Coordinator*, **4**, 459–463.

Powell, T., & Ogle, P. (1985). *Brothers and sisters: A special part of exceptional families*. Baltimore, MD: Paul H. Brookes.

Price-Bonham, S., & Addison, S. (1978). Families and mentally retarded children: Emphasis on the father. *The Family Coordinator*, **27**(3), 221–230.

Rabkin, J., & Struening, E. (1976). Life events, stress and illness. *Science*, **194**(4269), 1013–1060.

Ramey, C. T., Mills, P., Campbell, F. A., & O'Brien, C. (1975). Infant's home environments: A comparison of high-risk families and families from the general population. *American Journal of Mental Deficiency*, **80**, 40–42.

Reisinger, J. J., Ora, J. P., & Frangia, G. W. (1976). Parents as change-agents for their children: A review. *Journal of Consulting Psychology*, **4**, 108–123.

Rinn, R. C., & Markle, A. (1977). Parent effectiveness training: A review. *Psychological Reports*, **41**, 95–109.

Roesel, R., & Lawlis, G. F. (1983). Divorce in families of genetically handicapped/mentally retarded individuals. *The American Journal of Family Therapy*, **11**, 45–50.

Rosenberg, S., & Robinson, C. (1984). *Factors predicting parent participation in early childhood programs*. Presentation at Conference on Comprehensive Approaches to Disabled and At-Risk Infants, Toddlers, and their Families, Washington, DC.

Schopler, E., & Loftin, J. M. (1969). Thought disorders in parents of psychotic children: A function of text anxiety. *Archives of General Psychiatry*, **20**(2), 174–181.

Schopler, E., & Mesibov, G., & Baker, A. (1982). Evaluation of treatment for autistic children and their parents. *Journal of the American Academy of Child Psychiatry*, **21**(3), 262–267.

Schopler, E., Reichler, R. J. (1972). How well do parents understand their psychotic child? *Journal of Autism and Childhood Schizophrenia*, **2**, 387–400.

Schreibman, L., O'Neill, R. E., & Koegel, R. L. (1983). Behavioral training for siblings of autistic children. *Journal of Applied Behavior Analysis*, **16**, 129–138.

Short, A. (1984). Short-term treatment outcomes using parents as cotherapists for their own autistic children. *Journal of Child Psychology and Psychiatry and Allied Disciplines*, **25**, 443–458.

Shriver, E. K. (in press). *Let's play to grow*. Washington, DC: J. P. Kennedy Foundation.

Silverman, W., & Hill, R. (1967). Task allocation in marriage in the U.S. and Belgium. *Journal of Marriage and the Family*, **29**, 353–359.

Simeonsson, R. J., & Bailey, D. B. (in press). Siblings of handicapped children. In J. Gallagher & P. Vietze (Eds.), *Research directions in families with handicapped children*. Baltimore: Paul H. Brookes.

Suelzle, M., & Keenan, V. (1981). Changes in family support networks over the life cycle of mentally retarded persons. *American Journal of Mental Deficiency*, **86**, 267–274.

Tallman, I. (1965). Spousal role differentiation and the socialization of severely retarded children. *Journal of Marriage and the Family*, **27**, 37–42.

Tavormina, J. B., Ball, N. J., Dunn, R. C., Luscomb, B., & Taylor, J. R. (1977). *Psychosocial effects of raising a physically handicapped child on parents*. Unpublished manuscript, University of Virginia.

Taylor, S. C. (1980). The effect of chronic childhood illnesses upon well siblings. *Maternal-Child Nursing Journal*, **9**, 109–116.

Tew, B. J., Laurence, K. M., Payne, H., & Rawnsley, K. (1977). *British Journal of Psychiatry*, **131**, 79–82.

Turnbull, A. P., & Blacher-Dixon, J. (1980). Preschool mainstreaming: Impact on parents. In J. Gallagher (Ed.), *New directions for exceptional children* (Vol. 1). San Francisco: Jossey-Bass.

Turnbull, A. P., Brotherson, M. J., & Summers, J. A. (1985). The impact of deinstitutionalization on families: A family system approach. In R. H. Bryininks (Eds.), *Living and learning in the least restrictive environment*. New York: Brooks.

Turnbull, A. P., & Turnbull, H. R. (1982). Parent involvement in the education of handicapped children: A critique. *Mental Retardation*, **20**, 115–122.

Turnbull, H. R., & Turnbull, A. P. (1978). *Free appropriate public education: Law and implementation*. Denver, CO: Love.

Turnbull, H. R., & Turnbull, A. P. (Ed.). (1985). *Parents speak out: Then and now* (2nd ed.). Columbus, OH: Charles E. Merrill.

Turnbull, A. P., & Winton, P. J. (1984). Parent involvement policy and practice: Current research and implications for families of young severely handicapped children. In J. Blacher (Ed.), *Severely handicapped young children and their families* (pp. 367–395). Orlando, FL: Academic Press.

Vadasy, P., Fewell, R., Meyer, D., & Schell, G. (1984). Siblings of handicapped children: A developmental perspective on family interactions. *Family Relations*, **33**, 155–167.

Venters, M. (1982). Familial coping with chronic and severe illness: The case of cystic fibrosis. In H. McCubbin (Ed.), *Family stress, coping and social support*. Springfield, IL: Charles C. Thomas.

Weinrott, M. R. (1974). A training program in behavior modification for siblings of the retarded. *American Journal of Orthopsychiatry*, **44**, 362–375.

Wiegerink, R., & Comfort-Smith, M. (in press). Parent involvement as a means of support for families of children with special needs. In S. Kagan, D. Powell, H. Weiss, B. Weissbourd, & E. Zigler (Eds.), *Family support: The state of the art*. New Haven, CT: Yale University Press.

Wiegerink, R., Hocutt, A., Posante-Loro, R., & Bristol, M. (1980). New directions for exceptional children. In J. Gallagher (Ed.), *Ecology of exceptional children*. San Francisco: Jossey-Bass.

Wikler, L. (1979). *Single parents of mentally retarded children: A neglected population*. Paper presented at a meeting of the American Association of Mental Deficiency, Miami, FL.

Wikler, L., Haack, J., & Intagliata, J. (1984). Bearing the burden alone? Helping divorced mothers of children with developmental disabilities. *In families with handicapped members: The Family therapy collection*. Rockville, MD: Aspen Systems Corporation.

Wing, L. (1976). The principles of remedial education for autistic children. In L. Wing (Ed.), *Early childhood autism* (2nd ed.). Oxford: Pergamon Press.

Winton, P., & Turnbull, A. (1981). Parent involvement as viewed by parents of preschool handicapped children. *Topics in Early Childhood Special Education*, **1**(3), 11–19.

Wolery, M., & Bailey, D. (1985). *Early childhood education of the handicapped: Review of the literature*. Charleston, WV: West Virginia State Department of Education.

Personnel Preparation: Handicapped Infants

DIANE BRICKER AND KRISTINE SLENTZ

University of Oregon

Abstract—A review of literature pertinent to the preparation of educational personnel to work with handicapped infants and their families is presented. This review is supplemented by a discussion of the results of a nationally conducted survey of Early Childhood/Special Education (ECH/SE) training programs. From these data seven major issues surrounding preparation of personnel to work with handicapped infants are identified and examined. Finally, a set of research and policy recommendations for preparing ECH/SE personnel are offered.

INTRODUCTION

When compared with preservice programs that prepare personnel to work with school-age children, personnel preparation programs particularly designed to graduate individuals with expertise to work with infant populations are new endeavors. This recency is reflected by an absence of empirical work in the area. Indeed, even written program descriptions and discussions of issues and philosophical orientations are limited. For many people the existence of any training program specifically geared to prepare teachers, therapists, and others to intervene in the lives of infants and their families is suspect or undesirable.

Our "reading" both of nonprofessionals and many professional colleagues suggests that they tend to consider intervention with infants suspect for two reasons. First, many people wonder about the learning capabilities of infants. Such questioning comes not so much from the perspective that infants cannot learn, but rather from concern about the nature of what infants learn and how that body of knowledge and skills can be influenced during infancy. Our guess is that many, and perhaps most, people believe that infants learn to sit, walk, talk, and play when they are ready to do so and not before. That is, the maturation of the nervous system rather than intervention efforts dictates when and how the infant acquires new behavior. Parents often feel that factors beyond their control account for their own infant's growth and development, particularly if the child is ill (DeVellis et al. 1985).

A second reason many people may be suspicious about intervening with infants is the tendency for the intervention process to be rather invasive to family functioning. The bonding and attachment between the infant, the mother, and other family members is subject to disruption if outsiders become involved in daily familial interactions. Poorly conceived and/or hastily implemented intervention efforts may damage the fabric of family life and cause disruptions that are difficult to mend and to overcome.

Given that consciously or unconsciously many people resist the idea of intervention during the period of infancy, what has stimulated growth in programs for infants and attendant efforts to prepare personnel to operate these programs? We believe the answer lies in the historical development and convergence of several important trends. These evolving trends are forcing a reevaluation of widely held views on the impact of early experience, the survival of at-risk and handicapped infants, and the need for specialization in education.

Impact of Early Experience

The importance of early experience for the infant and child seems to be based on a widely held premise that early experience is essential to later development because continuity exists between early behavior and subsequent behavior. It is the "as the twig is bent so grows the tree" philosophy. The notion of continuity is fundamental to prevention and early intervention efforts. Continuity suggests some basic consistency to intellectual and personality variables in the development of the child into an adult. The infant who begins as a placid, easy-going baby is expected to, most likely, develop into a relaxed adult. It is not uncommon to hear an individual's parents comment that, "John has been that way since he was a baby." Most people seem to hold the belief that there is a strong relationship between personality and intellectual functioning of the child and the type of adult the child becomes.

Ramey and Baker-Ward (1982) have indicated that since the Second World War a belief in the primacy of early experience has been the pervasive model for viewing and interpreting normal and atypical development. However, prior to this time the prevalent view

319

was that of the primacy of the genetic contribution or predeterminism.

The concept of predeterminism is based on the belief that development is genetically determined. Developmental rate and outcomes are seen to be exclusively controlled by maturation. This position became popular in the 1900s and according to Hunt (1961) has its modern roots in the Darwinian theory of natural selection. An early advocate of predeterminism was Francis Galton whose writing suggests that physical traits and mental abilities are largely inherited. In an edited volume on the topic of individual differences, Galton's reprinted article entitled "Classification of Men According To Their Natural Gifts" argued that people come with mental abilities which are normally distributed and which are relatively resistant to training (Galton, 1961); some are born with great gifts while others, whom Galton labeled as "idiots and imbeciles," have little ability (1961). This view was consonant with the notion of the constancy of the IQ held by a number of influential educators and psychologists at the turn of the century (Hunt, 1961).

An associated corollary of the position of the heritability of mental abilities was that the environment had little impact on the developing child. Those believing in predeterminism argued that the infant came genetically well-equipped or poorly equipped and thus the environment could do little to counter or enhance the youngster's developmental outcome. Interestingly, investigators supporting the predeterminism position during this early period failed to recognize, or perhaps refused to acknowledge, that those children who tended to perform well came from adequate homes while those children who did poorly tended to reside in poverty circumstances. Holding the view that environmental stimulation produced minimal change provided little hope that intervention during the early years could affect the ultimate path of the child.

Thus, no reason existed for providing early schooling (for that matter any schooling) to intellectually or otherwise handicapped persons. Rather, the most appropriate solution was to remove those individuals from society and provide them with custodial care (Wolfensberger, 1969). The custodial care solution clearly obviated any need for interventionists trained to provide preventative or remedial services.

Given the apparent strength of the predeterminism position, what factors were responsible for the development of the position in which the major determinant of individual differences shifted from genetic contribution to a belief in the primacy of the environment? In approximately four decades we have witnessed a dramatic change in the view of environmental influences and the primacy of early experience.

A number of factors appear to be responsible for the shifting view toward the importance of environmental impact on a child's welfare and away from the primacy of early experience. These factors include: (a) other philosophical positions; (b) psychoanalytic influences,

(c) animal research on the impact of early experience, and (d) reanalysis of environmental impact on humans. (For a detailed discussion of these factors see Bricker, 1986.) The impact of this latter factor has been particularly powerful; however, during the 1970s several questions emerged that suggested a reinterpretation of the primacy of early experience might be needed. First, a number of investigators had found essentially no correlation between the scores infants obtained on intelligence tests before age 2 and scores obtained in later developmental periods. Honzik, MacFarlane, and Allen (1963) reported for a group of 252 children who were tested periodically between 21 months and 18 years that predictions became increasingly poor as the time interval between tests increased. The lack of predictive validity between performance on intelligence tests before age 2 and at adolescence called into question the continuity between early and late forms of behavior and further suggested that the infant's early environment, whether adaptive or maladaptive, can be offset by subsequent intervening variables (McCall, 1979).

In addition, the animal and human research that appeared to provide evidence of the impact of early environmental enrichment or deprivation was reexamined. In a number of instances it was found that what appeared to be permanent effects of early experience could be eliminated with subsequent intervention. For example, it was found that monkeys undergoing social deprivation—if the deprivation were not too extreme—could develop into normal adults after spending time with nonisolate monkeys (Harlow & Harlow, 1966). In a cross-cultural study, Kagan and Klein (1973) reported that infants raised in a remote Indian village in Guatemala appeared listless, fearful, and quiet. When the performances of such infants were compared to American infants along a number of dimensions, 3 months developmental retardation was generally evidenced by the Guatemalan infants. However, according to Kagan and Klein (1973), by 11 years of age the children of the village conducted themselves in responsible ways, meeting the demands of their society in a competent and acceptable manner. Further, these children were able to perform a number of cognitive tasks similarly to patterns shown by middle-class American children.

Even in situations where great deprivation is experienced, many reports exist that suggest the resiliency of children and the reversibility of early effects (see for example, Mason, 1963). Clarke and Clarke (1976), present a number of remarkable case studies in which children made near-miraculous recoveries from situations in which they had experienced extreme forms of deprivation. Also, Dennis and Najarian (1963) found that significant retardation during the first year of life in institutionalized infants did not necessarily predict that these children would perform poorly at age 6. A final source of information causing questioning of the primacy of early experience has come from early intervention efforts. In some notable cases the experimental children who participated in early intervention programs did not show superior performances to controls (Blatt & Garfunkel, 1969) or initial differences in favor of the experimental children dissipated over time. According to Clarke and Clarke (1977), Kirk's work was one such project in which the initial superior performances of the children attending a preschool program were lost after the control children completed one year of school. The Clarkes contended that the outcome of the Kirk study (1958) accurately predicted the "washout" effects reported for the Headstart programs (Ramey & Baker-Ward, 1982). And thus, for many "experts," the Headstart programs became the target of arguments against short-term and nonecologically based approaches to the war on poverty (Bronfenbrenner, 1975).

The previous discussion has reflected the shifting perspectives on the impact of early experience for understanding today's view of early experience held by a number of theoreticians, researchers, and interventionists (see, for example, Clarke & Clarke, 1976; Kagan, Kearsley, & Zelazo, 1978; McCall, 1979; Pick, 1978; and Ramey & Baker-Ward, 1982). These contemporary views include: (a) early experience is important, (b) subsequent experience is also important, (c) an enriched early experience does not protect the child from subsequent poor environments, and (d) a deprived early environment does not have to doom the child to retardation or maladaptive functioning if corrective action is taken (e.g., child's environment changes in positive ways). This set of assumptions, if correct, provides early interventionists with a useful perspective in which early experience is seen as but one link in the chain of growth and development. However, given the assurance of a reasonable environment, the better an infant or young child's beginnings, the more likely is future success. An associated corollary is that individuals specifically trained to understand and appreciate the period of infancy are better equipped to develop and implement effective intervention approaches.

Survival of At-Risk Infants

As Kopp (1983) points out, the infant mortality rate has dropped dramatically during the past 100 years. As medical science becomes more sophisticated, smaller and sicker infants are surviving, creating dilemmas and necessitating decisions about optimal care for these often tiny, fragile newborns.

Initially, early care of the biologically at-risk infant (most often the preterm infant) was provided by obstetricians. Gradually, care for the preterm and sick infant was shifted to the new speciality area of pediatrics. Today care of the biologically at-risk infant is primarily handled by neonatalogists who are trained specifically to care for distressed newborns. Most major medical facilities have Neonatal Intensive Care Units (NICU) which are designed to provide special medical care and contain sophisticated equipment to monitor and maintain distressed newborns. NICUs are generally staffed with a cadre of neonatologists and specially trained nurses. Hospitals that do not have NICUs often refer newborns with serious problems to a metropolitan or regional medical facility that does have a NICU.

With the advent of NICUs, and increased medical knowledge which permits successful management of smaller and sicker newborns, two issues have taken on growing importance. The first issue concerns the ethics involved in the saving and maintenance of severely impaired newborns and the second issue concerns the type of care or stimulation that will maximize biological and psychological growth in biologically at-risk infants.

The first issue requires serious consideration by medical and educational personnel as well as society in general. At least two factors need to be confronted. First, what is the quality of life of these infants saved through the heroic efforts of the medical community? In many cases there appears to be little relationship between the state of the infant during the early months and subsequent developmental outcomes. As Sigman, Cohen, and Forsythe (1981) note, the "prediction from early medical complications to later mental performance is poor" (p. 313). As these investigators suggest, the great plasticity in the early stages of development, taken in tandem with the significant impact possible from the caregiving environment, can lead to considerable fluidity in the subsequent repertoires displayed by biologically at-risk infants. Thus we are currently in a poor position to make sound judgments about the developmental outcomes of biologically at-risk infants.

A second factor associated with the care and increasing survival rate of the biologically at-risk infant is the cost. A report published by the U.S. Congress's Office of Technology Assessment (Budetti, Barrand, McManus, & Heinen, 1981) indicated that in 1978 the cost ranged from $1,800 to $40,000 per at-risk infant. An analysis examining cost by birthweight indicated that the average cost for infants less than 1,000 grams (under 3 pounds) was $22,508 and the cost per survivor was $46,340. As the birthweight increases, the cost per survivor decreases. As significant as these costs appear, they probably do not reflect the expense of similar care in a NICU today. Thus we are clearly saving more infants but the cost is reaching astronomical proportions.

The second major issue that has been raised by the increasing survival rate of the biologically at-risk infant concerns the form of care or stimulation provided the infant once the baby's medical status becomes stable. During the 1960s and 1970s a variety of intervention strategies for biologically at-risk infants were undertaken. Cornell and Gottfried (1976) have classified these as two basic types. One strategy entails designing interventions to counteract presumed sensory deficits; for example, providing additional auditory (e.g., heartbeat), or movement (e.g., rocking) stimulation. The other strategy is to provide the preterm infant with "extraordinary" stimulation; for example, extra handling, talking, and/or auditory/visual stimulation. In an analysis of the impact of these various intervention strategies on the biologically at-risk infant Cornell and Gottfried (1976) concluded:

> In summary, the most pervasive trend involves what may be generally described as motor development. The performance of stimulated or experimental-group infants tended to exceed that of control-group infants on measures of sensorimotor and motor skills, as well as muscle tone. (p. 37)

However, these authors caution against drawing generalizations because of the diversity of the populations, treatments, and measures employed in the investigations.

From the original work that focused on stimulation of the preterm or at-risk infant evolved a perspective which changed the focus from the infant to the infant-caregiver relationship (Barnard, 1976). The importance of the early environment provided by the caregiver became increasingly clear to researchers and practitioners and an increasing number of programs have been developed to encourage and enhance the attachment of the parent to the infant (Barnard, 1976).

Much of the underlying rationale for the increased attention to bonding was stimulated by the work of Klaus and Kennell and their colleagues (Klaus & Kennell, 1976). These investigators argued that shortly after birth there was a critical and heightened period for establishing maternal attachment. Delivering a preterm and/or sick infant who was subsequently removed to a NICU separated mother and infant during this period, thus impacting maternal-infant bonding. Many intervention programs conducted in NICUs attempted to attenuate the disruption, thus impacting maternal and infant bonding less significantly. Studies of early maternal-infant separation have generally not focused on the possible negative or long-term impact on maternal-child relationships (Kopp, 1983). This is not to indicate, as Ramey, Zeskind, and Hunter (1981) remark, that having a premature or sick infant is not a significant event; rather it is to suggest that when separation occurs the outcomes are not uniformly predictable.

A number of longitudinal studies of at-risk infants (primarily preterms) have been conducted. Four of the more ambitious are the San Francisco study (Hunt, 1981). Springfield study (Field, Dempsey, & Shuman, 1981), Staten Island study (Caputo, Goldstein, & Taub, 1981) and Los Angeles study (Sigman, Cohen, & Forsythe, 1981). The outcomes of these four longitudinal studies to date have been analyzed by Sameroff (1981) who reports that in three of the four studies, "The single most potent factor influencing developmental outcome turns out to be the cultural environment of the child, as expressed in socioeconomic status and parental educational level" (p. 392). Further, Sameroff notes that, "No single factor, either birth weight alone or

accompanying physical problems, clearly predicts a specific developmental outcome" (p. 392).

None the less, when considering preterm infants or infants having other conditions placing them at risk as a group, the outcomes are less positive than for well, full-term infants. This finding has served as a basic rationale for continuing to develop early intervention programs for at-risk infants both during their stay in the NICU and after discharge.

In spite of our inability to predict those at-risk infants who will thrive and those who will not and the equivocal outcomes of intervention efforts (Cornell & Gottfried, 1976; Gibson & Fields, 1984; Kopp, 1983), a number of researchers and clinicians see value in offering early intervention programs to infants at risk. Taft (1981) indicates two reasons in support of intervention programs: first, the considerable plasticity of the nervous system during the early developmental periods and second, many of the positive outcomes of intervention have not yet been measured. Support for infant intervention programs indicates an implicit need for trained infant interventionists.

Contemporary intervention approaches for at-risk infants are designed to be conducted in the NICU, following discharge of the infant, or both. Current NICU intervention programs differ in target populations, period of intervention, staffing, service delivery systems, and intervention goals (Sweet, 1982).

Most NICUs have established criteria for determining the population to be served or to isolate selected subgroups of infants (e.g., those at extreme risk). Programs also vary in terms of when or for how long they intervene with the target population. Some states, such as Florida and California, provide developmental assessment during the first year for infants meeting certain risk criteria (Sweet, 1982).

Some intervention programs are conducted by the nursing staff, some by social workers, and some by specially trained educators (Cole & Gilkerson, 1982). Those conducted in the NICU are largely in the form of assisting the parent, when possible, to provide the infant with appropriate stimulation. In addition, support groups for parents are often available. Once the infant is discharged the program may provide home visitation, a center where the family can bring the infant, or both. The nature of these programs is generally to assist parents in coping with their infants, many of whom may be irritable and difficult during the first weeks at home. Offering such programs requires expertise and training in a number of areas not generally covered by traditional personnel preparation programs.

Specialization in Education

Modern education has undergone significant change since the one-room school. From our perspective one of the prominent changes has been the move toward increasing specialization of instructional personnel. Although the move toward specialization has occurred in regular education (e.g., elementary teachers, middle school math and science teachers, high school biology teachers), it is exemplified in special education, the very nomenclature of which reflects specialization.

Examining the evolution of special education dramatically reflects the increasing move toward specialization. The first "special" classes were developed in the late 1800s primarily in large urban areas (Sarason & Doris, 1969). One might be safe in thinking that these early classes contained an array of children who had a variety of different problems which produced retardation in terms of academic expectations for the youngsters' particular chronological age. One might further surmise that many of these children were difficult to manage, although at this time the more seriously retarded and disturbed children were institutionalized in large residential facilities with little thought about their educational and/or therapeutic needs (Wolfensberger, 1969).

After the Second World War, two major events occurred that stimulated growth in programs for exceptional children (Kirk, 1978): "First, a number of states that previously had not supported programs of special education in the public schools passed laws to subsidize such programs . . . The second major impetus was the parent movement" (p. 6). As the number of programs increased, programs were initiated to serve those children labeled as learning disabled, behaviorally disordered and language impaired. With the passage of PL 94–142 in the mid-1970s a major move was begun to serve the more severely impaired student in public school programs. This law required local public school districts to provide appropriate educational programs for all school-age children. The advent of public school programs to serve this seriously disabled group required that state systems of higher education and private universities and colleges develop personnel preparation programs to staff these new programs adequately. With the development of new training programs and areas has come the attendant need for states to develop certification standards against which newly prepared professionals can be evaluated.

A theme pervading the changes described above is the need for personnel trained for specific disorders and age groups. Early on it seemed that a consensus developed in the professional community to the effect that instructional personnel prepared to teach and manage children in regular education did not have the necessary information base or management skills for dealing with children who have specific learning difficulties. This perspective required the development of special personnel preparation programs.

In addition to feeling that training needs are different for regular and special educators, many professionals believe training should vary for different age groups. Teachers prepared to work with high school populations are generally not considered appropriately prepared for

teaching primary-age children. Such feelings are generally true for the therapies as well. For example, programs have been developed to train pediatric physical therapists, or speech/language pathologists to work primarily with adult stroke victims.

Beginning in the early 1970s programs were developed for preschool-age handicapped children (Bricker & Carlson, 1981). The success of these early programs in conjunction with the passage of legislation in many states requiring programs for handicapped 3-, 4-, and 5-year-olds has resulted in the development of a number of training programs specifically designed to prepare personnel for working with handicapped preschoolers (Cohen, Semmes & Guralnick, 1979).

The 1970s and 80s have brought increased specialization in education, as programs have been developed for low-incidence groups like autistic, orthopedically impaired, and multiply handicapped persons. In addition, programs for at-risk and handicapped infants are being created, and at the other end of the age continuum more programs for the post-high school severely handicapped person are evident. Since the 1950s the educational enterprise has been expanded to include the age range from birth to 18 years and there are now even school programs available for pregnant teenagers and for severely handicapped youth over 18 years of age. The range of disabilities has expanded to include all handicapping conditions and gifted students. With this expansion has come an associated need for personnel specifically prepared to meet the needs of this array of students. The information base and management skills necessary effectively to educate such diverse groups of children differ considerably. This variability, in turn, demands personnel preparation programs specifically designed to offer the relevant content and management skills for particular populations of children. This move toward increasing specialization appears to explain, in part, the advent of training programs to serve infant populations in spite of widely held beliefs that the period of infancy is neither responsive to, nor appropriate for, intervention.

Overview*

The field of early intervention has grown significantly during the past two decades. Moving from a few isolated programs in the late 1960s–early 1970s, there now exists a well-established network of federally, state, and locally supported programs for handicapped children under school age. Associated personnel preparation programs, curriculum development, assessment-evaluation strategies, and general knowledge about effective procedures have been developed during this period for older preschool children. As the field has become

---

* This chapter was written before the passage of P.L. 99–457 and thus some of the content does not reflect changes brought about through enactment of this legislation.

increasingly confident about its ability to work effectively with the 3- to 5-year-old handicapped child, concern has begun to encompass the birth to 2 population. Increasingly this concern is being translated into the development of intervention programs for the at-risk and handicapped infant. Adding fuel to this movement has been the recent federal legislation (PL 99–457) and fiscal support focused on the birth to 2 population (e.g., Office of Special Education and Rehabilitative Services, Division of Personnel Preparation funds for training programs specifically designed for the birth to age 2). The federal emphasis will likely provide legitimacy to the development and provision of services to at-risk and handicapped infants and we are likely to experience a surge in the growth of programs for at-risk and handicapped infants. The development of early intervention programs for the birth to 2 population is to be encouraged; however, currently it appears that the development of such programs may be occurring without the necessary preplanning in terms of curricular content, evaluation, and most importantly, without adequately prepared personnel. This last statement is based on the assumption that programs and personnel who work with the birth to 2 population should have different information and skills than personnel who serve preschool and school-age children. This assumption will be addressed in a later section of this chapter.

Currently both federal and state legislation addressing the birth to 5 population is in flux. Some states, such as Oregon, have expanded their mandate for severely handicapped infants and preschool children while others, such as Idaho, have enacted new, more restrictive laws curtailing services to the birth to 5 population. Smith (1984) reports, "While several states have enacted laws over the past twenty years mandating early intervention, an almost equal number have repealed mandates" (p. 34).

Not only is there extreme variation in the age and disability groups serviced, but states also vary considerably in their definition of preschool handicapped children, which is critical in determining who is eligible to receive services. The more restrictive the definition, the more easily children can be denied services. Lessen and Rose (1980) report of the 44 state consultants who responded to a survey, that 7 states had specific definitions, 14 states used existing categorical definitions, 4 states used miscellaneous criteria, 19 states had no current guidelines. State standards and regulations for certifying teachers of preschool handicapped children also vary (O'Connell, 1983).

One might assume that state educational policies closely reflect federal policy; however, Noel, Burke, and Valdivieso (1985) argue that state and local procedures often compromise the intent of federal policy. The implementation of federal policy at the state level appears to be determined, in part, by the availability of necessary resources, public opinion, and interpretation of nonspecific federal mandates. Thus, different interpretation and implementation of federal policy does occur across states.

The U.S. Congress has never appropriated the necessary funds for states to implement the mandates of PL 94–142 completely; thus states have been required to provide much of their own financial support for the law's implementation. As Noel, Burke, and Valdivieso (1985) note, "Differences in state educational policies largely reflect the general wealth of an individual state, the strength of its commitment to the handicapped, and its available resources" (p. 27). Further, in PL 94–142, educational services for the 3 to 5 age group are encouraged but not mandated, unless by state law, and the birth to 2 group is not mentioned. PL 98–199 has now extended the age to require state plans to "address the special education and related service needs of all handicapped children from birth through five years of age . . ." (PL 98–199, 97 stat. 1366). Although the federal government has now extended national policy to cover all handicapped children birth to 21 years, not all state policies have kept pace.

The recency of the comprehensive federal interest in the birth to 5 age group and the reluctance and lack of resources at state levels to implement programs for this population has clearly impacted service delivery for the handicapped young at the community level. Several serious barriers exist to the implementation of programs for the birth to 5 population.

First, states either do not have adequate guidelines or the interpretation of the established guidelines is debated. Programs may be faced with ambiguity concerning mandates, or worse, may have to adhere to inappropriate interpretation of state and federal law. On the state level there may be disagreement about which agency is responsible for providing services, or two agencies may overlap in the provision of services, causing conflict or other problems at the local level. Interagency collaboration continues to be a serious problem for early intervention programs and the families they serve.

Second, local programs are chronically underfunded if they are dependent entirely on state and/or local support. This problem becomes particularly acute when local programs are not receiving adequate funds even to meet established state guidelines.

Third, adequately trained personnel and instructional resources are often not available. Programs may be staffed by individuals either poorly prepared or untrained to work with a specific disability or age group. In addition, resources for assisting in selecting evaluation and curricular materials may be unavailable at the local level and states often cannot or do not provide adequate technical assistance.

Finally, programs for handicapped infants and young children are developed and maintained through a variety of agencies: (a) public schools with local, district, and state support; (b) other state-supported agencies such as mental health, human services: (c) national non-profit organizations such as United Cerebal Palsy; and

(d) federally supported programs such as Headstart and the Handicapped Children's Early Education Program. Support and regulations for these programs can vary considerably along many dimensions, introducing one more source of inconsistency.

In spite of the problems facing the area of Early Childhood/Special Education, programs for infants and young children continue to grow. A network of programs has been established and personnel are beginning to recognize the need for consistency in services and the need for adequate communication at the local, state, and federal level.

The lengthy introduction and overview sections have been formulated to serve as a foundation to assist the reader in appreciation of the major purposes to be addressed in this chapter. The goals are to: (a) provide a useful synthesis of available research on preparation of personnel to serve handicapped infants and their families, (b) discuss the findings of a national survey to determine the status of current personnel preparation programs training personnel to work with handicapped infants, (c) discuss the major issues pertinent to personnel preparation programs for the birth to 3 population, and (d) generate a set of recommendations designed to motivate and direct policy and research into preparation of personnel to work with handicapped infants.

Definitions

Prior to a review of the literature, clarification of essential terms is helpful. No claim is made that the definitions provided below are shared by all or even a majority of professionals working with handicapped infants and young children. As indicated above, little consensus exists in the area of personnel preparation for the handicapped infant, or in the field of Early Childhood/Special Education (ECH/SE), for that matter. Given no consensus, we have attempted to develop definitions and parameters specifically for the purpose of aiding the reader in understanding the issues raised in this chapter.

The reader may have noted a lack of clarity in the introductory section as to whether statements were applied to the birth to 2 population, the 3 to 5 population, or the entire range from birth to 5 years. Just what age range does ECH/SE cover? For the purposes of this chapter, ECH/SE will refer to the birth to 5 year population and those individuals specifically trained to deliver services to this age population and their families. Within the ECH/SE area, a distinction will be made between the birth to 2 and the 3 to 5 age range. The focus of this chapter is the birth to 2 range, and handicapped infants are those whose developmental age ranges from birth to approximately 3 years of age. Unfortunately, the literature and many personnel preparation programs fail to make a distinction between the birth to 2 and 3-to 5-year-old populations. It is unclear whether distinctions between these groups are seen as unimportant, or whether it is an oversight. Our position is that the birth

to 2 group should be seen as distinct from the older preschool-age population.

We believe the distinction between the under 3 and over 3 year groups is justified for several reasons. First, models of service delivery tend to be different. Older children are usually served in center-based classroom programs that involve groups of children. Infants are frequently served at home or, when served in a center, an individual or small group approach is adopted (Bricker, 1986; Guralnick & Bricker, 1987). Second, as suggested by the service delivery models, greater individual attention is required for increasingly younger infants or the more severely impaired (this distinction is discussed below). Third, development during the birth to 2 and 3 to 5 age ranges is different. Thus the content of intervention should reflect these dissimilarities. Fourth, although the involvement of the family is important for all young children, it appears to be more critical for the infant. Thus, managing adults may be as important for personnel working with the birth to 2 population as is working with the infant.

Separation of the birth to 2 and 3 to 5 populations requires addressing the issue of whether that separation should be based on chronological or developmental age. In general, we believe the distinction should be made on developmental age for the population of children under age 6 years. Thus children who are between chronological ages 3 through 5 years but function developmentally below age 3 should be considered as part of the birth to 2 population. For example, a 4-year-old severely retarded child who is functioning at a 9 month level should be seen as a member of the birth to 2 group. However, using this classification scheme, a 6-year-old multiply-handicapped child who also may be functioning at a 9 month level would not be included in the birth to 2 group. Although admittedly an arbitrary distinction, we believe it is inappropriate to include children over age 6 in a birth to 2 group primarily because of the specific instructional content. Toys and activities (e.g., rattles and peek-a-boo) appropriate to the period of infancy, we believe, are inappropriate for children whose chronological age exceeds 5 years. Thus, for the severely impaired child age 6 and over other types of materials and activities should be employed for training.

One last definitional issue surrounding the target population is the distinction between handicapped and at-risk. For our purposes, *handicapped* refers to documented existence of an organic condition or pathology that interferes with the infant's growth and development and/or an obvious delay in the infant's acquisition of developmental milestones even though no specific cause can be determined. This definition has advantages because it includes Down's syndrome infants who are functioning within normal limits as well as infants who are obviously delayed but have no discernable etiology. *At-risk infants* are those whose subsequent development is suspect for medical or environmental reasons. This definition would include, for example, infants of teenage, diabetic, or alcoholic mothers, and/or infants who spend significant time in a newborn intensive care unit because of low birthweight, prematurity, or respiratory distress. Increasingly, at-risk populations are being included in infant intervention programs. We believe that it is important to distinguish these two groups when possible.

The intent of this chapter is to integrate available research findings on personnel preparation for handicapped infants. Training programs can be divided into two major types: preservice and inservice. The focus here is on preservice programs, which are defined as formal undergraduate or graduate programs of studies meeting the following criteria. The program of studies has a definite focus on at-risk and handicapped infants or young children. Program trainees are required to take multiple courses in the area of infancy and early childhood. Required practica are taken in programs specifically for infants and young children. Upon graduation, the expectation is that the trainee will seek employment in programs focused on infants and young children. Although we have argued that the birth to 2 and 3 to 5 populations should be seen as separate groups, descriptions of many personnel preparation programs unfortunately do not make this distinction. Unless specifically noted, descriptions and discussions of programs are inclusive of the birth to 5 age range.

Related disciplines (e.g., therapies, allied health) and subspecialities of ECH/SE (e.g., research and evaluation) are not addressed in this chapter. Length restrictions for the chapter limit the discussion of personnel preparation to the discipline of early childhood special education. Also, literature on personnel preparation for the allied health disciplines tends not to focus on the birth to 2-year population, which is the stated topic of this chapter. Similarly, personnel preparation of early childhood educators (e.g., Headstart and other mainstreamed preschool settings) has been excluded since their target population does not include birth to 2-year-olds with special needs.

Review of the Literature

A review of the literature in the area of personnel preparation for early childhood special educators reveals a surprisingly sparse information base in comparison to the breadth and depth of publications available relevant to other aspects of early intervention. The major bibliographic sources for this literature review were ERIC databases Resources in Education (RIE) and Current Index to Journals in Education (CIJE). A computerized search was conducted using these two sources from 1974 through 1984, including 11 descriptors: preparation/training of early childhood specialists/educators, infant intervention, infant specialists, birth to 3 specialists, interdisciplinary/transdisciplinary training of infant interventionists, enhancement of infant development, training/educating infants, team approach to early intervention, early intervention specialists, parent education/training, and interactional approach to parents and infants. Of the 140 "hits" procured from the computer search, fewer than 10 were relevant to the topic of personnel preparation. The vast majority of documents abstracted addressed early intervention program models, assessment and evaluation, curricular approaches, typical and atypical child development, and parent involvement/intervention.

In addition to the ERIC database, the authors conducted a comprehensive search of journals in the area of ECH/SE, that is, *Journal of the Division of Early Childhood, Exceptional Children,* and *Topics in Early Childhood Special Education,* from 1977 to 1985. Finally, a number of handbooks and similar documents describing components of personnel preparation in ECH/SE were included in the literature review and reference list. From thousands of publications on early intervention, relatively few were found to be appropriate to personnel preparation for ECH/SE populations.

Hutinger (1981) suggests that early intervention's interest in personnel preparation is quite recent compared to the field's investment in direct intervention activities. A recent advent of interest in personnel preparation may account for the relative lack of published information on the subject in the ECH/SE literature. The absence of an available information base on personnel preparation may also stimulate legitimate concern about the field's commitment to providing resources to aspiring and practicing ECH/SE professionals. Hopefully, this chapter will serve to emphasize the importance of personnel preparation efforts in quality intervention and research in ECH/SE.

The literature on personnel preparation for this chapter has been organized for review around four major content themes. First, information on mandated services for the ECH/SE population is presented. Second, development in the areas of certification and endorsement and the availability of preservice training programs for early childhood special educators nationwide is briefly delineated. Third, a variety of preservice training models is compared and contrasted with the goal of identifying trends and commonalities. Last, a number of models for inservice and volunteer training is described.

Mandated Services

States that have passed laws or instituted regulations for handicapped infants and preschool-age children have generally employed two strategies. Some states have chosen to lower the school age for handicapped children, making preschool children eligible to receive services. The rules and regulations governing school-age children have been expanded to include younger children and infants. Other states have chosen to establish a new authority with rules and regulations specific to preschool-age handicapped populations (Smith, 1979). Even so, few states require that all handicapped children between birth to 5 years receive services (see Table 1). Rather, most states have statutes that mandate services only to identified subgroups of children (e.g., hearing-impaired, visually impaired). Less than half of the states mandate services for all handicapped children 3 to 5 years, and far fewer states have any mandatory programs for the birth to 2 populations (O'Connell, 1983; Smith, 1984).

Table 1

Age of Mandated Services for 57 States/Territories

States/ Territories	Age of Mandated Services						
	0–3	0–5	2–5	3–5	4–5	5	none
Frequency	2	12	1	12	4	16	10
Percentage	3	21	1	21	7	28	18

Data taken From *National Directory of Early Childhood Special Education Services (1984)* by N. Carran, 1984, National Consortium of State Education Agencies and Early Childhood/ Special Education Coordinators.

A 1984 report disseminated by the National Consortium of State Education Agencies and Early Childhood/ Special Education Coordinators (Carran, 1984) provides some useful data which illustrate this point. The survey conducted by this group obtained information from six territories/trusts, 50 states and the District of Columbia. A mailed questionnaire posed a series of relevant questions and sought a variety of information on services and standards for preschool-age handicapped children including: age of mandated and permissive services, certification requirements, and standards for delivering services.

Results of this survey are contained in Table 1 which indicates the age at which the 57 states/territories mandate services to children ages birth to 5 years. Collapsing categories from Table 1 reveals that 18% of the states/ territories have no mandated services for the birth to 5 age group, 35% mandate services for only 4- and 5-year-olds, 22% mandate services for 2- to 5-year-olds and an additional 21% mandate services from birth to 5 years. As children become older, more states/territories mandate services; however, 10 states/territories still mandate no services for this population.

Although the statistics reported in Table 1 continue to change, it seems apparent that this nation lacks a consistent and comprehensive policy to provide guidance in establishing mandated services to this population.

Trends in Certification and Training

Certification and endorsement requirements for ECH/SE have a direct impact on the development and operation of personnel preparation programs. State-regulated certification or endorsement establishes standards which early interventionists must meet in order to become practicing professionals. However, major disparities exist between requirements for certification and the availability of preservice training nationwide and

within individual states (Hirshoren & Umansky, 1977; Stile, Abernathy, Pettibone, & Wachtel, 1984).

Given the assumption that the birth to 2 age group has unique service needs, there are few consistent policies or guidelines to provide structure for the preparation of personnel to work with the birth to 2 population. An early study, published in 1977, found that 12 states required certification or endorsement of ECH/SE teachers, and 5 states were in the process of developing ECH/SE certification standards (Hirshoren & Umansky, 1977). More recent surveys reflect a number of changes in certification and endorsement requirements across the nation. For example, O'Connell (1983) found that 18 states required certification for teachers working with preprimary special needs populations, which is on increase of 6 states over the 12 states reported by Hirshoren and Umansky (1977). O'Connell's 1983 survey found 12 states to be developing ECH/SE certification standards, and 21 states with no certification in operation or under development.

A study which investigated both certification and training of early childhood special educators (Stile et al., 1984) further documents the trend for states to certify ECH/SE teachers. Stile et al. (1984) found that 20 states required a specialized endorsement or certification for preprimary special education teachers, and 10 additional states required a combination of special education and early childhood training for certification/ endorsement. Interestingly, these data are somewhat discrepant with those published in the National Directory of ECH/SE Services compiled by the National Consortium of State Education Agency Early Childhood/Special Education Coordinators (Carran, 1984). Eighteen states/territories were reported to require ECH/SE certification, while 36 did not. Three respondents provided no information.

Although the trends described above seem to indicate an increase in the number of states requiring a specialized, hybrid certification for early childhood special educators, Stile et al. (1984) found the increase to be less rapid than predicted by Hirshoren and Umansky in 1977. In addition, four states which had reported requiring ECH/SE certification/endorsement in 1977 no longer reported having ECH/SE certification requirements in 1983. A number of states have allowed teachers in existing intervention programs to be "grandfathered" or granted temporary certification under newly devised certification standards, (Anderson & Black, 1981). Such practices further compromise the consistency of standards for ECH/SE professionals. Although interesting in their own right, these data become even more intriguing when compared with the data on mandated services. Many states which mandate services for handicapped preschoolers do not require certification of ECH/SE professionals, and some states require certification without mandating services.

Discrepancies between data reported by Carran (1984) and those reported by Stile et al. (1984) may be due to actual differences in the database at the times surveys were completed, or may reflect inconsistent responses from individual states and/or differences in interpretation of the questions asked. A further limitation is the lack of distinction between infant (0–2 years) and preschool (3–5 years) populations for certification and endorsement. Nevertheless, certification standards in ECH/SE represent the most appropriate guidelines available for the preparation of infant specialists, and have therefore been included in the discussion. Similarly, the following description of trends in ECH/SE preservice training is based primarily on data which do not distinguish between infant and preschool populations.

Trends in preservice training in the area of ECH/SE indicate a fluctuation in the number of available training programs, and a lack of coordination between state certification guidelines and university training programs. In Hirshoren and Umansky's 1977 survey, 10 of the 12 states requiring certification for ECH/SE also reported preservice training programs designed to prepare personnel for early childhood special education positions. In addition, the same survey reported the existence of ECH/SE preservice training programs in 24 states that did not certify teachers of preprimary children with special needs. Two states which required certification reported having no preservice training programs. Hirshoren and Umansky (1977) projected that the lack of coordination between State Education Agencies (SEAs) and university trained programs, evidenced by discrepancies between certification and training, would improve as more services were mandated for preschool handicapped children.

Six years later, a total of 27 states reported having preservice training programs for ECH/SE (Stile et al., 1984), a decrease from the 34 states reporting preservice training programs six years earlier (Hirshoren & Umansky, 1977). Seventeen of the states reporting ECH/SE preservice training programs in 1983 also reported ECH/SE certification requirements, an increase from 10 states having both in 1977. However, also in 1984, the National Consortium of SEAs and ECH/SE Coordinators (Carran, 1984) found 44 states that reported providing perservice training in early childhood special education. Eighteen states reported personnel preparation in the area of ECH/SE as a state priority.

The discrepancies in data reporting the availability of preservice training in ECH/SE may reflect differences in the intensity and duration of various programs. Mallory (1983) reports that the U.S. Office of Special Education, Division of Personnel Preparation funds over 100 programs that have early childhood components. A review of published descriptions, however, reveals that the nature of specific components varies drastically from site to site. (See survey data that follow.) Such variability may cause survey data to differ depending upon the exact wording and interpretation of the questions asked.

The implications of poor coordination between certification and training guidelines in ECH/SE predict a number of unfortunate outcomes. First, personnel may be poorly prepared in terms of content and strategies required to work effectively with handicapped infants or preschool children. Second, personnel prepared to work with school-age children may be inappropriately assigned to programs that service preschool populations. Conversely, graduates of specialized ECH/SE preservice training programs may not meet certifications standards for public school employment in states which do not certify in ECH/SE but mandate services for the preschool population.

Professionals working in programs for infants, toddlers, and preschoolers with special needs often indicate feeling unprepared for the range of tasks they are expected to perform. Gorelick (1978), in a survey of 93 infant interventionists, found that although 60% of infant personnel surveyed held graduate degrees, only a few program coordinators or teachers of infants and toddlers had academic backgrounds in child development. Seventy-five percent of the respondents in the Gorelick (1978) survey favored a specialized credential for early childhood programs serving either delayed or nondelayed infants and toddlers. A survey of program staff in 49 Handicapped Children's Early Education Program (HCEEP) sites (Zeitlin, duVerglas, & Windhover, 1982) found a variety of backgrounds among direct intervention staff serving the birth to 3 population. Of the 181 respondents, 151 (83%) indicated the need for additional training in order to work effectively with infants. In addition, Mallory (1983) pointed out the difficulty of placing interns with experienced staff, when the staff operating programs are underprepared. Although Mallory (1983) discussed the positive aspects of creativity and flexibility of training possible in the absence of certification standards, these advantages appear to be outweighed by the disadvantage of inconsistencies in training and nationwide certification, both to children in the ECH/SE population and the professionals who serve them. The uniqueness of handicapped infants and young children and the necessary focus on the family as an intervention target require that personnel working with this group receive specialized training if intervention programs are to be maximally effective.

Figure 1 presents a map of the United States and a list of trusts/territories, indicating which states/territories have mandated services, which have certification requirements, and which have established guidelines. These data were garnered from the National Consortium of SEAs and ECH/SE Coordinators (Carran, 1984). One might expect to see a strong relationship between mandated services, guidelines, and certification. However, a review of Figure 1 suggests inconsistent rather than consistent patterns exist. Only 10 states/territories have mandated services, certification requirements, and guidelines. Fourteen states/territories have mandated services and guidelines; five have mandated services and certification, three have certification and guidelines but no mandated services; eighteen have only mandated services, and seven indicate

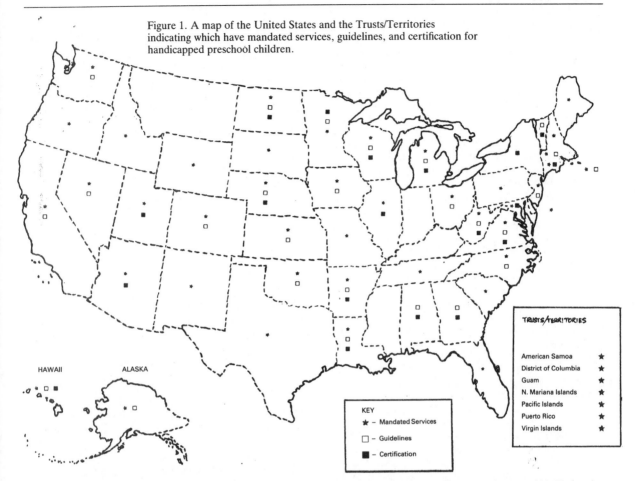

Figure 1. A map of the United States and the Trusts/Territories indicating which have mandated services, guidelines, and certification for handicapped preschool children.

HAWAII

ALASKA

TRUSTS/TERRITORIES

American Samoa	★
District of Columbia	★
Guam	★
N. Mariana Islands	★
Pacific Islands	★
Puerto Rico	★
Virgin Islands	★

KEY
★ – Mandated Services
☐ – Guidelines
■ – Certification

Note. Data taken from *National Directory of Early Childhood Special Education Services (1984)* by N. Carran, 1984, National Consortium of State Education Agency Early Childhood/Special Education Coordinators.

they have no mandated services, guidelines, or certification.

The information presented in this section on certification, mandated services, and guidelines for the ECH/SE area leads to the inescapable conclusion that currently there exists a crazy quilt pattern which makes isolating trends difficult. Nevertheless some tentative observations seem appropriate. First, in spite of significant resistance, we detect a gradual move by state legislatures toward the adoption of certification for the ECH/SE population. Concomitantly, we see the state departments of education being forced to develop and issue appropriate standards for ECH/SE certification and for intervention programs. Finally, we perceive a need for leadership by appropriate federal agencies to establish some consistency in terms of certification requirements and program standards. An obvious caveat with any suggestion of federal leadership is the need for ongoing research to provide the data with which to evaluate and revise adopted standards.

Preservice Training Efforts

Preservice training programs in ECH/SE are available at the graduate and undergraduate levels. These preservice programs vary in terms of numbers of academic hours ranging from a single course designed specifically to remedy the lack of interdisciplinary training for professionals dealing with handicapped young children (Freund, Casey, & Bradley, 1982), to two full semesters (Hutinger & Swartz, 1979), to one calendar year or more (Rosenthal, 1980) of specialized training.

The audiences and training foci among ECH/SE preservice training programs described in the literature are equally variable (Jackson, 1979). Training may be categorical or noncategorical, although in recent years the trend has been toward less categorical programs of personnel preparation (Blackhurst, 1981). Preservice training may be designed to produce direct interventionists

(Hutinger & Swartz, 1979; Blackhurst, 1981) consultants and trainers (Rosenthal, 1980), (or both Geik, Gilkerson, & Sponseller, 1982). Preservice training programs in ECH/SE prepare specialists with a range of foci from disadvantaged and at-risk infants, toddlers, and their families (Rosenthal, 1980) to hearing- and language-impaired preschoolers (Smith, 1979), and youngsters with orthopedic and neurological impairments (Blackhurst, 1981).

Despite the existing variety in ECH/SE preservice training audiences, foci, and content, there are also evident a number of emerging common factors. The brief overview which follows is intended as an introduction to the more specific data presented in the next section on survey results. Perhaps the most consistent approach to ECH/SE preservice training since the mid-1970s has been a competency-based model (Jackson, 1979). This approach requires students to demonstrate proficiency in a prespecified set of skills prior to graduation (cf. Geik et al., 1982; Hutinger, 1981; Mallory, 1983). The competency-based model of preservice training attempts to impose uniform minimum standards of performance across all graduates of a specific program. As early as 1977, Miller had analyzed descriptions of 15 preservice training programs to determine the nature of required competencies (Miller, 1976–77). Classroom performance fell into the areas of general competence, assessment and curriculum planning, teaching, evaluation, and parent involvement. Bricker and Iacino (1977) added the categories of ability to synthesize transdisciplinary inputs and willingness to serve as a trainer of staff and parents. More recently, Zeitlin et al. (1982) suggested competencies in the areas of child development, family involvement, program implementation, assessment, and administration as guidelines for preparation of infant interventionists. Fewell (1983) proposed the additional competencies of environmental assessment and arrangement, and program evaluation.

A second consistent trend in ECH/SE preservice training evident in published descriptions is a clinically based model. The majority of program descriptions specify practicum or field placement requirements that are considered critical to successful program completion (cf. Mallory, 1983; Geik et al., 1982; Rosenthal, 1980; Hutinger, 1981). Direct experience with the target population is cited by Bricker and Iacino (1977) as a necessary prerequisite to successful teaching in early intervention settings, particularly those serving severely impaired youngsters. Practicum-based programs also provide necessary opportunities for trainees to practice new behaviors, integrate skills, and develop professional attitudes in the context of applied roles (Walker-McCollum, 1982).

An examination of course content described in the literature shows a number of consistent themes which reflect the hybrid nature of ECH/SE (Stile et al., 1984). Many programs present the content and sequence of normal child development as a basis for contrasting and understanding various handicapping conditions. There

has more recently appeared an ecological theme (cf. Geik et al., 1982; Hutinger, 1981; Mallory, 1983) that emphasizes knowledge and skills in the areas of parent involvement, adult education, family dynamics, community integration, and systems approaches. An interdisciplinary focus has become evident in competencies, coursework, and field experiences. This focus aims to train students for roles as educational synthesizers (Bricker, 1976; Fewell, 1983), team collaborators (Geik et al., 1982), and liaisons between interdisciplinary teams and other professionals (Allen, 1978), as well as using professionals from other disciplines to train ECH/SE personnel (cf. Rosenthal, 1980; Freund et al., 1982; Hutinger, 1981). Early childhood/special educators may be trained by special educators, child development specialists, health and medical personnel, psychologists, social workers, educators, or any combination thereof, depending on the specific training program and its focus.

Geik et al. (1982) present a thoughtful discussion of issues raised by current ECH/SE training practices. The analysis of these researchers indicates a need for careful management of students involved in field placements as members of interdisciplinary teams and/or parent/family interventionists. Close supervision is desirable to permit students to learn and practice important new skills without taking on roles for which they may be yet unprepared. In addition, Geik et al.'s (1982) discussion points to the need for ongoing training opportunities, either available to part-time students or on an inservice basis, to address the needs of practicing professionals in ECH/SE.

Inservice and Volunteer Training Programs

The availability of ongoing training for ECH/SE professionals practicing in the field varies considerably from location to location. Staff development and inservice training have been identified as factors that positively influence retention of professionals working with handicapped preschool children in rural areas. Moore (1981) reported that opportunities for additional training for infant educators working in health care settings are possible through university programs, on-the-job training and professional exchanges. One might surmise that urban settings, where specialized health care services for newborns are typically located, would offer a richer array of staff development and inservice opportunities than would rural settings. The provision of inservice training to rural area professionals often requires organization and transportation of training materials and personnel, and arrangement of training schedules to meet the needs of working trainees (Davis & Porter, 1981).

Inservice program models described in the literature are at least as diverse as the preservice models described above. Programs range in length and format from 3- to 5-day workshops (Flynn, 1981), to 2-week summer institutes (McDermott & Ivy, 1981), to 9 months of weekly participation (Davis & Porter, 1981). Programs may be primarily didactically oriented or incorporate field work, consultation, and follow-up. Some programs of inservice training emphasize evaluation of participant performance and satisfaction (cf. Davis & Porter, 1981) or follow-up of participants at later dates (Flynn, 1981); others do not.

Training for those working with the ECH/SE population is often geared specifically toward professionals such as administrators, special educators, therapists (Flynn, 1981; Davis & Porter, 1981), paraprofessionals (Kelly & Havlick, 1982), or even volunteers (Galey, Garner, Pillans, & Solomon, 1981).

The content of inservice training for ECH/SE personnel appears to vary according to the professional level of the audience. Davis and Porter (1981) describe a program designed to refine professional skills in the areas of measurement, normal and abnormal infant and child development, educational programming and curricular development, parent training, and community liaison work. Special topics, for example, interdisciplinary team collaboration, are also available to professionals through inservice training (Flynn, 1981). Paraprofessionals are trained in Kansas by the state Department of Education to be facilitators for district personnel making use of paraprofessionals in special education classrooms (Kelly & Havlick, 1982). Content includes general skills of understanding characteristics of special education students, interpersonal skills, and skills for working with children. Volunteers have been trained to screen young children for handicaps and be knowledgeable about available services (Galey et al., 1981).

A specialized area of inservice training in ECH/SE is that provided to parents of very young handicapped children. Parents are often responsible for daily implementation of habilitative programs, especially with the birth to 3 population (Filler, 1983). As primary interventionists, parents need to acquire many of the skills required of ECH/SE professionals and paraprofessionals although they most often operate as volunteers. A review of published descriptions of model ECH/SE service programs reveals that most programs offer some sort of parent training (Walker, Slentz, & Bricker, 1985). Parents are commonly trained to understand their child's diagnosis and its effect on development and functioning, to implement specific educational programs, and to monitor the child's progress. Of recent advent and less frequently reported are efforts to have skilled parents become trainers for other parents (Walker et al., 1985).

Inservice programs described in the literature tend to be individualized and oriented strongly around the needs of participants. McDermott and Ivy (1981) conducted a needs assessment of both the program and individual participants designed to generate individual training goals and objectives. A similar, systems-oriented approach is used by Davis and Porter (1981) to meet the needs of a wide variety of rural professionals and the agencies for which they work. It is of interest to note that the cost of inservice training is rarely mentioned in published descriptions. Our experience has been that unless the training is grant funded there is usually some cost involved for participants or the employing agency.

A review of training for ECH/SE professionals, both preservice and inservice, evidences a number of disparities as well as a number of similarities. Professionals interested in quality personnel preparation are well advised to consider building upon the existing factors in common among programs, toward the end of identifying those courses, competencies, and field experiences necessary to comprise minimal standards for new ECH/SE professionals.

The Survey

The lack of available information on preservice training programs in ECH/SE prompted us to conduct a nationwide survey. Our hope was to compile current data on ECH/SE preservice training programs as a complement to the literature review and a basis for discussion of issues. The survey was developed at the University of Oregon and consisted of 22 questions addressing the areas of: identifying information about the respondents, program content and emphasis, program structure and format, funding, follow-up of trainees, state certification requirements, and conceptually oriented position statements.

Two sources were combined to generate an initial mailing list for the national survey. The first and most extensive source was a directory of Office of Special Education and Rehabilitative Services (OSERS) funded personnel preparation programs specified as having early childhood components. The second listing contained names of participants from a conference addressing ECH/SE personnel preparation issues held at George Washington University in September, 1984.

A total of 181 names was obtained by combining the two listings described above. Adjustments for known duplications of respondents from the same institutions and/or academic departments within institutions reduced the final mailing list to 131. Of the 131 questionnaires mailed, 65 were returned, constituting a response rate of 50%. Of the returned questionnaires, 43 were found to be appropriate for analysis while 22 were determined to be inappropriate for analysis because respondents were only tangentially involved in personnel preparation for ECH/SE. Follow-up letters were sent only to those people on the list who were known to the authors to be associated directly with ECH/SE preservice training programs. The less than enthusiastic overall return rate may reflect the inclusion on the mailing list of many others who were only indirectly or marginally involved with ECH/SE personnel preparation, and therefore did not bother to complete and return the survey.

The 43 completed questionnaries were coded individually and analyzed as a group for each of the 22 questions. Analyses consisted primarily of frequency distributions, ranges, and measures of central tendency. Responses to some items are reported qualitatively rather than in quantitative terms, either because the questions were difficult to tabulate in a concise manner (e.g., the various roles for which the trainees are prepared) or because more complete data were provided by the literature review (e.g., certification requirements).

Prior to reporting actual results of the survey, it is important to consider the limitations of the data presented. First, reliance on the OSERS directory of federally funded training programs with early childhood components for the mailing list does little to guarantee a representative sample of personnel preparation efforts nationwide. One must wonder how the survey results may have differed if nonfederally funded ECH/SE personnel preparation programs were included as well as programs operated by allied health professionals (e.g., physical therapy). In addition, the relatively low return rate prompts cautious interpretation of reported results.

The Respondents

The 43 questionnaries analyzed represented 32 states and Washington, DC, distributed geographically as follows: six from the Eastern states, nine from the Midwest, eight from Western states, and nine from Southern states. Five questionnaires were returned from California, three from Illinois and Pennsylvania, and two from Connecticut, Massachusetts, Minnesota, District of Columbia, Louisiana, and Wisconsin. The remaining 20 surveys came from 20 individual states. The survey results thus cover all areas of the country with more Southern schools reporting than any other region.

The majority of respondents reported holding professional positions with primary emphasis in the area of ECH/SE. Thirty-seven percent of the sample held ECH/SE academic positions in combination with ECH/SE program directorships (e.g., HCEEP demonstration projects, DPP training grants). Twenty-three percent of respondents held special education positions, and 11% reported holding early childhood positions.

Although ECH/SE was most often reported as the primary area of professional responsibility, 72% of the respondents were operating within departments of Special Education. Sixteen percent of the sample was from child study departments and the remainder were subsumed under education, educational psychology and counseling, or graduate school programs. Small institutions tended to report less specialized departmental structures, accounting for special education operating within general education or graduate school programs. The majority of special education departments responding is likely due, at least in part, to the use of the OSERS directory as the mailing list.

Almost all questionnaires (90%) were completed by professionals directly involved in the training of

ECH/SE students. The few who reported being indirectly involved managed field work or training programs for school-age children. Those directly involved with preservice training cited a number of specific training responsibilities: coordination, supervisor and advising, program direction, and teaching. Thirty percent of the sample reported filling only one role, most often instruction. Two thirds of the respondents performed duties for multiple roles, the most frequent combination being teaching, supervising, and advising.

To summarize, the data for the survey results contained in the following pages were generated primarily by ECH/SE professionals working in special education departments in universities and colleges of various sizes. The vast majority of respondents were directly involved in preservice teacher training activities.

Position Statements

The responses of the 43 respondents described above were combined with an additional 22 questionnaires for analysis of four position statements ($N = 65$). The additional 22 surveys were completed by professionals from other disciplines only tangentially involved with ECH/SE preservice training, and were therefore inappropriate for analysis of program structure and content information. The position statement question was analyzed for all respondents, however, and response patterns were consistent for ECH/SE and other professionals.

Survey respondents were asked to agree or disagree with the following statements:

1. Individuals who work with at-risk and handicapped infants and their families require information and skills different from personnel working with the 3–5 age group and training programs should reflect these differences.

2. The primary focus of intervention with the birth to 3 population should be the primary caregiver(s) and family members and training programs should reflect this emphasis.

3. Since intervening with infants and their families requires professional maturity and judgment, training programs should require extensive practical experience.

4. Intervening with infants and their families often requires coordination of many disciplines and agencies, and training programs should reflect this need.

Respondents were overwhelmingly (89%) in agreement with the first statement, suggesting the need for a distinction in training procedures and content between the birth to 2 and 3- to 5-year-old populations. There were two disagreements, and five responses were equivocal or questionable in nature (e.g., marking on the dividing line between agree and disagree; comments without marking agreement or disagreement).

The second statement, designating the caretaker as the primary focus of intervention, elicited the most disagreement and comment. While a majority of respondents (78%) agreed with the statement, 14% disagreed entirely, and 7% of the responses were equivocal or questionable. Comments written in the margins led us to believe that the question was unclear to some readers. Those respondents who disagreed seemed to interpret the position as advocating the primary focus of intervention on the caregiver at the expense of attention to infants and toddlers. The intent of the statement was to suggest a shift of focus from professionals to caregivers as interventionists with the infant population. It is therefore unclear if the disagreements are contentions with the position statement or misinterpretations of the meaning.

There were only two disagreements out of the 65 responses to the statement advocating extensive field-based experience as a component of preservice training. Responses were in unanimous agreement with the final position statement which addressed training in coordination of input from many disciplines. Practical experience in interdisciplinary settings was endorsed by our sample, at least philosophically, as desirable practice in preservice training.

Responses to the four position statements posed by the survey indicate that, for the most part, professionals appear to share selected basic assumptions about ECH/SE preservice training programs. There was concern voiced, however, that a shift in intervention focus to caregivers should not be undertaken at the expense of the infants themselves.

Program Structure

The survey included questions designed to explore program resources, levels of training, and funding. Seventy-four percent of the respondents indicated their programs were federally funded and the sole reported source of federal funds was OSERS Division of Personnel Preparation. Responses to the survey were received from first year programs and programs that had been in operation for 15 years. The mean length of time all programs reported having trained students was 6.75 years. Eleven programs had been operating for 3 years or less, 11 for 4 to 6 years, and 14 for 7 to 10 years. Seven programs had been training students for over 10 years.

Questionnaires returned represented training programs at all levels: associates, bachelor's, master's, doctoral, postdoctoral and inservice training. Only one program was reported for postdoctoral and one for associate level degree. Master's programs were most frequently reported, with 90% of respondents describing programs leading to master's degrees. The high frequency of master's level programs may reflect a preference of OSERS to fund training at the graduate level. Many programs operated training programs at more than one level, the most frequent combinations being master's and doctoral degrees, and master's degree and inservice training programs. Doctoral degree programs

were offered by 51% of the sample, and inservice training programs by 47% of the sample. All possible combinations of levels of training were reported (e.g., all levels bachelor's through doctoral, plus inservice; bachelor's, master's, inservice).

The single program which reported training students for associates degrees had 49 students in 1983–84 and 59 students in 1984–85. Bachelor's level programs ($N = 11$) reported from one to 53 students with a mean of 17 students enrolled in 1983–84 and 20 students enrolled in 1984–85. As might be expected, master's level programs ($N = 37$) were somewhat smaller, with a mean of 15 students enrolled per program in 1983–84 and 18 students enrolled per program in 1984–85. The range of students enrolled in master's level programs was quite wide, however, with a low of 2 students and a high of 65 students. Programs reporting a large number of master's level students specified having part-time as well as full-time trainees.

Doctoral level training programs ($N = 21$) enrolled still fewer students, with a range from one to 25 trainees. The mean number of enrolled doctoral students per program was four students for 1983–84 and five students for 1984–85. The trend for smaller programs at higher levels of training is clear, although it is impossible to tell from these data whether or not the number of students in ECH/SE programs is increasing over time.

The number of faculty resources reported to be available to individual programs varied greatly. The range of answers led us to suspect that the questions themselves may have been unclear. As reported, the number of ECH/SE faculty ranged from one to 14, with a mean of 2.5 per program. Eighty-eight percent of the respondents reported having three or fewer specialized ECH/SE staff members. The number of associated faculty involved in ECH/SE training programs was reported to range from zero to 27 faculty members. Again, our failure to clearly operationalize the role of associated faculty may have resulted in various interpretations of the question. Seventy-seven percent of respondents reported having six or fewer associated faculty members.

The survey returns represented a heterogeneous group of programs in terms of number of years of training activities, level of training offered, and the number of students enrolled. Faculty resources available to programs also appeared to vary greatly but, as indicated above, the range of responses may have reflected differences in interpretation of the questions rather than true differences in numbers of participating faculty.

Program Content

A number of questions on the survey were designed to collect information on the content of ECH/SE training across programs. Although this particular sample of respondents generally agreed that training should be different for infants and toddlers than for preschoolers, 77% of the programs described a combined training approach that encompassed birth to 5-year-olds. Few programs (12%) in this sample provided a specialized training focus on the infant population.

Most ECH/SE training programs (95%) in this sample reported their program content emphasized handicapped children. Seven programs (16%) reported a focus on both handicapped and at-risk populations. An additional 18 programs (51%) included handicapped, at-risk, and normal youngsters in content emphasis. It appears that the primary focus of ECH/SE programs is indeed the special education population, but that at-risk and normal children are also being included in the content emphases of many programs.

The preservice training programs represented in the survey sample were preparing students for multiple professional roles. Although classroom teacher was the role most often reported (84%) as a training target, 77% of programs were training students to be parent educators. A majority of programs included training for roles of team collaborators (67%), infant specialists (65%), and facilitator/consultants (65%). Less frequently cited training targets were program developers (49%), advocate (46%), and program evaluator (37%). Almost all training programs reported preparing students to fill a variety of roles simultaneously.

Ninety-two percent of reporting programs specified the fulfillment of competencies as requirements for graduation. Students were required to meet competency requirements in the general areas of coursework (knowledge) and practica or field experience (skills), although the specific competencies provided and the evaluation of students' performance were quite variable across responding programs.

The total number of credit hours required for graduation varied predictably with the level of training. At the bachelor's level, the total number of required quarter credit hours ranged from 120 to 150, with a mean of 129 credits. Of the total number of hours required for graduation, an average of 35 hours were reported in specific ECH/SE content, with a range from 6 to 63 ECH/SE hours required. Master's level students were required to complete a mean total of 38 quarter credit hours for graduation with a mean of 21 hours of ECH/SE coursework. As might be expected, at the undergraduate level, ECH/SE coursework comprised proportionately less of the total program (27%) than at the master's level, where specialized ECH/SE coursework accounted for over half of all required hours. Although bachelor's level programs reported requiring more ECH/SE hours in absolute terms than did master's programs (an average of 35 versus 21 ECH/SE hours), one might expect the graduate level material to be more sophisticated, and contain more in-depth and technical content. Doctoral level programs were generally reported to be individually tailored to each student's background, experience, and career goals.

Requirements for practica or field-based experiences were reported in all bachelor programs and all but two master's programs. The number of practicum hours

required ranged from zero to 19, with a mean of 10 field-based hours required for the bachelor's level and 7 hours for the graduate level. The question on practica may also have been interpreted differently by different respondents and a number of data were missing, rendering the reported data suspect. Some respondents appeared to report the number of clock hours instead of credit hours required, inflating the mean number of practicum hours for bachelor's level programs. What is clear is that most ECH/SE training programs require practical experience, but perhaps not to the extent indicated by the sample's overwhelming agreement with the third position statement.

Practica sites reported student placement options ranging from University Affiliated Facilities to public schools and a number of public and privately funded agencies. Public school special education classrooms were the most frequently reported practica sites, followed closely by state and local agency programs. Since many states do not serve preschool children with handicaps in the public schools, it is not surprising to find that the state and local agencies providing services for children also provide training sites for preparation of ECH/SE personnel. University-based service delivery and demonstration models ranked third in this sample as training sites, followed by hospital settings and private agencies. Responses to our survey indicated a variety of practica and field placements accessible to students in training, although individual programs reported operating within restraints of available local settings.

A majority of programs reported the availability of departmental resources from outside special education. The respondents in our sample reported an average of three other departments in which students took coursework or practica directly related to their preparation as ECH/SE professionals at the master's level. At the master's and bachelor's levels, the most frequently reported extradepartmental resource was elementary education, while doctoral programs most often made use of psychology department coursework. In bachelor's and master's programs, departments of psychology and family and child development were cited most frequently, following elementary education. Doctoral students were reported most often to make use of resources in departments of medicine, communication disorders, family and child development, social work and counseling/educational psychology, in addition to psychology.

Respondents to our survey reported preparing students for a number of employment opportunities. Almost half (49%) of the ECH/SE programs in the survey sample reported preparing students to take jobs as any one of the following: teachers, infant specialists, parent/family interventionists, or program coordinators. Two programs were training therapists, in addition to the above positions. The remaining 22 programs reported training students for various but less diverse combinations of professional positions.

Ninety-five percent of the programs responding to the questionnaire conducted follow-up surveys of students after graduation. An average of 81% of ECH/SE program graduates were employed in the area of ECH/SE and twice as many graduates were reported to be working as preprimary classroom teachers than in any other professional position. Program coordinator was cited as the next most frequently held position, followed by infant specialists and home/parent trainers. Fewer graduates were reported to hold jobs as teacher consultants, child care providers, primary teachers, aides, and therapists.

Although over 60% of the programs in our sample operated in states without certification for ECH/SE teachers, 75% of the programs reported offering a course of studies which satisfied existing state certification standards. The requirements most often satisfied were for a general special education certification/endorsement for teachers of kindergarten through 12th grade.

In summary, the survey results on program content were fairly consistent with the literature reviewed. Both sources indicated that preservice programs in ECH/SE tend to be offered at the graduate level housed primarily in departments of special education; although other departments and disciplines are frequently involved in the students' training. The ECH/SE training programs prepare students for a variety of general and specialized roles through a combination of coursework and practica experience. Follow-up data indicate most trainees find positions in programs serving handicapped infants and children.

Synthesis of Issues

Our review of pertinent literature in conjunction with an analysis of the survey outcomes permits the identification of a number of major issues that require attention if progress is to be made toward the development of more effective personnel preparation programs focused on the birth to 2 population. These issues include: (a) training specializations for personnel working with handicapped infants, (b) focus of intervention efforts, (c) maturity and professional judgment, (d) coordination of efforts, (e) generalist versus a specialist role, (f) competency and certification requirements, (g) how and by whom personnel should be trained.

Training Specializations for Personnel Working with Handicapped Infants

Respondents to the survey were in agreement that training to prepare personnel to work with handicapped infants should differ from that provided for personnel who are planning to work with older preschool handicapped children (e.g., 3- to 5-year-olds). This philosophical or conceptual agreement is particularly interesting given that personnel training program descriptions offered on the questionnaire as well as in the literature often do not clearly delineate the training

efforts between the two populations. That is, few programs appear to indicate systematic course, practica, or competency differences for the birth to 2 versus the 3- to 5-year-old populations. We cannot be sure whether this is an oversight or whether a distinction in training between birth to 2-year-olds and 3- to 5-year-olds does not exist. Our sense is that, except for the few programs particularly designed to address the birth to 2 population, most training personnel do not make an explicit distinction between the two groups in terms of the didactic and practical coursework offered students. Currently there appears to be a significant discrepancy between many trainers' philosophical positions and the training approaches found in most institutions of higher education. Nevertheless, we believe a number of reasons exist for making training distinctions for the birth to 2 population.

Without belaboring the obvious, the content of instruction will differ for the birth to 2 population. Development that occurs during the early periods is significantly different from, for example, what 4-year-olds do. Knowledge about early responses and how they change over time is critical. Certainly personnel can be knowledgeable about both the birth to 2 and 3- to 5-year periods, but having information only about the 3- to 5-year period is insufficient when dealing with handicapped infants.

In addition to being conversant about the content of early development, the interventionist must develop skills in different instructional formats for the birth to 2 age group. Much of the instruction or stimulation is provided to an infant individually by an adult; little group participation or learning is expected until the infant is well into the second year. Then too, many interventionists find that the more structured approaches that have been successful with older children fare less well when applied to infants. Forcing an infant to remain in a specific location and to complete specific activities may lead to crying, inattention and even fatigue. More profitable approaches appear to capitalize on the infant's motivation and self-generated activity.

A third reason to consider training differences for the birth to 2 population is the intervention setting. Often services are delivered in the hospital, home, or in "baby groups" that meet in centers (Bricker, Bailey, & Bruder, 1984; Filler, 1984). These settings, as opposed to the more traditional classroom programs, may require the interventionist to have a different set of skills as well as a different information base. Again, we emphasize that personnel working with older populations may also be equipped to deliver services to handicapped infants if they are able to expand their information and skill base properly to accommodate the needs of the younger population.

Although serving the 3- to 5-year population requires teamwork between the professionals involved with the family, serving the handicapped infant may require considerably more team collaboration. Often during the first year, procedures are underway to determine the infant's problems and to acquire appropriate services. Significant collaboration between involved professionals may be required to determine an accurate diagnosis and to specify the critical educational goals for the infant and the family. The significant need for the team collaboration may suggest differences in training emphasis for the birth to 2 and 3 to 5 age groups.

We believe (and as indicated by the survey results, many of our colleagues share the position) that for the reasons enumerated above, personnel preparation programs should be specifically designed to understand and accommodate the needs of handicapped infants and their families. It seems possible that training programs currently focused on the 3 to 5 age group could be expanded to provide trainees the necessary information and skills to work effectively with handicapped infants. What appears equally clear to us is that current training programs that are focused on the preschool population are not adequately preparing their graduates to work effectively with a younger population.

Focus of Intervention Efforts

Although some survey respondents (14%) indicated they felt the focus of intervention efforts should be divided between the caregiver and the infant, the majority of respondents indicated the primary focus should be the caregiver. A number of philosophical and practical reasons exist for this position.

Except in unusual situations, most infant programs are able to provide only a few hours of intervention per week. If intervention efforts are reserved for these brief periods, progress may be slow. If the caregiver, who spends considerably more time with the infant, is assisted in learning how to manage and stimulate the infant effectively, then intervention time is expanded considerably.

A second reason for focusing training on the caregiver is the positive impact on caregivers of learning how to manage and intervene effectively with their handicapped infants. It seems important psychologically to help caregivers feel that they can successfully manage and assist their disabled infant if both initial and subsequent interactions are to be strengthened and maintained. Rather than caregivers becoming dependent upon professionals to assist their infant, it seems more useful to assist the caregiver in developing the necessary expertise to be able to work with the professional. We are not arguing that the professional is unimportant or unnecessary but rather that the approach be shifted so the caregiver becomes the primary intervention agent when possible. Although more severe handicaps may require relatively more direct professional intervention, parents of handicapped infants still need to feel they are in control of their infant's life and can be instrumental in selecting and reaching the family-determined goals and values.

A third reason for focusing training on caregivers is the impact of outside influences on the family unit. If

training is directed primarily to the infant, little effort may be expended toward understanding the dynamics of the family system, that is, the reciprocal impact of family members and community influences. Focusing on the caregiver should assist the interventionist in acquiring a more accurate perception of the family's functioning, which in turn permits intervention efforts with infants that enhance family functioning rather than destroy it.

Although the handicapped infant is the focus of our concern, intervention efforts that benefit the infant at the expense of the caregiver and/or other family members most likely will be short-lived. Interventionists who wonder why parents fail to follow through on home programs or complete assigned tasks should ask themselves how integrally the parents were involved in the setting of those particular goals or the selection of those particular activities. Further, interventionists should ask what impact the suggested activities for the infant are likely to have on the functioning of the family unit. Focusing intervention efforts on caregivers should provide the infant with more intervention time, enhance the parent-infant interaction, and improve family functioning.

The changing training focus from infant to caregiver or, perhaps better said, the caregiver-infant dyad has significant implications for preservice and inservice personnel preparation programs. Our perusal of the competency information and program descriptions provided by many ECH/SE training programs suggests there exists little emphasis on preparing graduates to work with adults. At most, programs offer one course in parent/family involvement and practica sites used by training programs do not appear to emphasize the inclusion of caregivers in meaningful ways.

If instructional faculties believe, as they indicated in our survey, that caregivers should be an important focus of training, then personnel preparation programs should change to reflect this emphasis. Specifically, programs should offer more coursework relevant to parent/caregiver involvement and communication/management skills with adult populations. Practica sites should also reflect this emphasis and parents and family members included as an integral part of their infant's intervention team.

Maturity and Professional Judgment

Of the 43 respondents indicating that their institution had preservice ECH/SE personnel preparation programs, 11 indicated they had undergraduate programs in this area. Thus, superimposed upon the traditional baccalaureate requirement, programs required in the neighborhood of 35 additional hours to receive a degree in child development or ECH/SE. These undergraduate programs raise an important issue: can adequate practical training occur at the undergraduate level to provide the trainee maturity and professional judgment? Indeed this same question might be raised for those graduate programs which indicate they require as few as 3 practicum hours.

Conducting business in a classroom program where presumably ongoing structure and administrative supervision are available may be far different than functioning in homes or other less traditional intervention settings (e.g., hospitals). Inexperienced interventionists may be able to function effectively in a classroom where the daily schedule is set, where conversations with parents tend to center on the program, and where other resources are readily available should a problem arise. Inexperienced interventionists may fare less will—as may their clients—if they are delivering services in the home, where no particular structure has been generated and where other resources may not be readily available. How well can an interventionist with limited practical experience manage parents who have recently learned their infant is severely handicapped? Will the inexperienced interventionist have the maturity and professional judgment to support the family and make an appropriate referral if necessary, or will the family suffer because the interventionist is, in effect, learning as he or she goes along? How well can the inexperienced interventionist deal with irate parents who insist the private physician has conducted an inappropriate procedure on their infant? Some infant/parent specialists have wondered about the necessity of infant interventionists having support and counseling skills to better prepare them for dealing with difficult emotion-laden situations. Even referral to other professionals requires judgment and tact often not available to the inexperienced interventionist.

Synthesis of available information suggests that many professionals believe personnel preparation programs should be prepared to provide their trainees with extensive practical experience with handicapped infants and their families. Prior to being certified as equipped to function as an infant specialist (i.e., granted a degree), the trainee should have had extensive supervised experience in delivering services to handicapped infants and their families in order to assure that maturity and professional judgment has been acquired to protect the family as well as the interventionist.

Coordination of Efforts

As we have remarked earlier, the identification and development of intervention procedures for handicapped infants may require more coordination of disciplines and agencies than required for other populations. As the literature review indicated, there currently exists an uncoordinated effort to service the birth to 2 population. Until the recent passage of PL 99–457, there has not been a federal initiative to serve the under-3 population. States and local communities have developed a variety of approaches to serve this population using mental health, public health, education, and private agencies to meet the handicapped infant's need. In most states a variety of groups and agencies has splintered

responsibilities for this population. Unless this pattern of uncoordinated efforts is reversed and legislative mandates for coordination are forthcoming, most likely the infant interventionist will be faced with the ongoing need for considerable coordination across disciplines and agencies.

Personnel preparation programs should be geared, in part, to assist their trainees in understanding local, state, and federal service patterns, and in managing the multiplicity of agencies in the infants' and families' best interest. Further, the importance of future developments to infuse some standards and consistency of services delivered should be impressed on trainees so that they can become active advocates for changes in the current systems.

In addition to a variety of agencies serving the birth to 2 population, often a variety of professionals are involved in program implementation. Infants identified early are often those who are severely and multiply disabled. The severity of their problems may require that a broad range of professionals such as physicians, communication specialists, psychologists, educators, and physical therapists be included in the diagnostic and program development stages. Further, many high-risk and handicapped infants have serious medical problems that require specific intervention for survival and maintenance (e.g., special feeding techniques, mechanical ventilation). Initially the family's primary requirements may be assistance from medical personnel to manage their infant. These health maintenance needs often require that attention to other goals and objectives wait until the infant's medical condition is stabilized.

As indicated above, the fragile medical status and/or serious birth defects of some infants require the coordination of input from the many professionals involved with the development and implementation of the habilitation plans. Successful coordination of efforts by health, allied health, and educational personnel can be accomplished if each discipline recognizes the other's value. No physician, physical therapist, or ECH/SE specialist has the knowledge and expertise to develop and implement a comprehensive plan for seriously disabled infants who may, for example, have seizures, hypotonicity, and cognitive deficits. The physician is necessary to develop a treatment plan for controlling the seizures, the physical therapist is necessary to design a set of exercises to counter the hypotonicity, and the ECH/SE specialist is necessary to evolve a systematic set of curricular activities to address the infant's cognitive deficits. Each professional is essential to the development of a comprehensive treatment plan and the expertise of each should be mutually recognized.

As well as recognizing the importance of other disciplines, it is essential for professionals to recognize the need to coordinate their multiple inputs into a cohesive plan of action for infants and their families. Without the coordination of efforts, various treatments and intervention regimens may work at cross purposes.

In preparing personnel to work with the birth to 2 population, training programs should emphasize the mutual need for the inclusion of health, allied health, and educational personnel in the development of appropriate intervention plans for handicapped infants. In addition, assisting students in the acquisition of skills for the coordination of multiple inputs should be emphasized.

Generalist versus Specialist Role

Given that there is a legitimate area of intervention focused on handicapped infants, should interventionists be generalists or specialists? The philosophical stance and subsequent program emphasis evolving from conceptual positions does and will have significant impact on the information and skills the trainee will garner from training programs. The content and instructional strategies adopted by trainees will determine in large part how services are delivered to infants and their families. Consequently, whether the trainee should be prepared to function as a generalist or a specialist becomes an issue. By *generalist* we believe that most trainers mean the person is knowledgeable about a number of areas including: child development, parent involvement, counseling, intervention strategies, and evaluation. The generalist role is to coordinate input from a variety of professionals such as physical therapists, social workers, communication specialists, and pediatricians, into a cohesive and practical intervention plan. On the other hand, the *specialist* role dictates the person functions in a manner similar to other specialists (e.g., occupational therapist, physical therapist) with knowledge about infancy being the specific area of expertise. In this capacity the infant specialist offers input consistent with the manner other specialists offer information.

A number of factors have an impact on whether training programs prepare individuals to be specialists or generalists. Some of these factors weigh toward preparation of ECH/SE as specialist while others do not. Programs located in rural areas may be required to serve infants having a range of problems and disabilities. In small towns and remote areas, a cadre of medical, allied health, and educational specialists may be inaccessible, requiring that the interventionist in an early intervention program take on a generalist role. At best, infants and families may have intermittent contact with specialists with the consequences that the program interventionist must formulate and implement instructional and treatment programs with minimal assistance from other specialists. Although clearly not ideal, this situation is often reality for program personnel located in rural areas and argues for the preparation of ECH/SE as generalist.

Another factor having an indirect impact on the training of generalists is the issue of territoriality. Members of some disciplines may perceive ECH/SE personnel who function as generalists to be engaging in activities that should be managed by other disciplines. For example, infant specialists who are willing to work on range of motion with motorically disabled infants may be perceived by physical therapists as stepping into another discipline's area of expertise. Such perceptions, whether correct or not, hinder the development of cooperative efforts between professionals and require thoughtful preparation of personnel who function as generalist.

Conversely, providing appropriate programming to some specific populations may argue for the preparation of specialist. Techniques for working with low-incidence groups such as the visually impaired, hearing-impaired, deaf-blind, and autistic populations are often idiosyncratic to a specific population (e.g., mobility training) and require specialized training. The specialized nature of the training mitigates against becoming knowledgeable about and skillful with more than one of these populations. The practicality of becoming a generalist with a variety of low-incidence populations should be thoughtfully considered.

A review of intervention programs (cf., Bricker, Bailey, & Bruder, 1984) suggests that programs currently use both approaches but the majority appear to use their ECH/SE personnel as generalists who are responsible for seeking and coordinating input from specialists. Our hunch is that in most cases the ECH/SE personnel will continue to accept the role as generalist because of the nature of their training and because other professionals—except in programs using a transdisciplinary approach—do not have the time or inclination to function in a coordinator's role.

Competency and Certification Requirements

Sensibly there should be a close relationship between competencies targeted by training programs and subsequent certification requirements. That is, meeting program performance and coursework requirements should permit certification. In 18 states/territories, the ECH/SE certification standards have been developed and therefore training programs can design their offerings to meet established requirements. However, in 36 states/territories, no ECH/SE certification is currently available. Further, in 27 states/territories, no guidelines or standards exist for the delivery of services to preschool handicapped populations. These data (Carran, 1984) make clear that considerable variability exists in standards and certification requirements.

Given the absence of ECH/SE certification and standards in many states/territories, deriving program competencies may become idiosyncratic to specific training programs. The idiosyncratic nature of programs may have been further reinforced because so few program descriptions appear in the literature.

The majority of respondents (92%) indicated their personnel preparation programs are competency-based. Interestingly, although wording varies, some consistent training targets/competencies emerge including: (a) knowledge of typical (normal) child development, (b) knowledge of atypical (abnormal) child development, (c) assessment (developmental and behavioral) skills, (d) individual program development skills, (e) intervention (teaching strategies) skills, (f) data collection and individual program monitoring skills, (g) parent training and family involvement skills. Beyond these agreed upon areas, many programs include other, apparently more idiosyncratic competencies, such as professionalism, program administration, training others, program evaluation, research, interpersonal communication, and specializations (e.g., feeding, cued speech).

The listing of competencies, often an important first step, does not address a number of important issues. First, are the listed competencies essential to the effective functioning of ECH/SE personnel? What accounts for the variability in competencies across programs? Is there a relationship between program competencies and existing certification requirements? Who determines or determined existing ECH/SE certification requirements, and how?

To our knowledge, no empirical work exists to help answer these questions. Currently it appears that program competencies and certification requirements are derived by expert assumption. Attempts to develop some uniformity of expectation for ECH/SE personnel might lead to the development of useful and pertinent program competencies and certification requirements.

How and By Whom Personnel Should be Trained

A final issue generated from the survey results and literature review is focused on determining how and by whom personnel intervening with handicapped infants should be trained. While educators tend to feel and assume that intervention is their domain and thus their responsibility, in many states medical personnel and agencies have traditionally dealt with populations under age 3 and public schools have not. Determination of where to house programs for the birth to 3 population, and the constitution of training staff, will have a significant impact on how personnel are trained to manage this population.

Some authorities (e.g., Hobbs, 1975) have argued that the public schools are the only institutions equipped to be responsible administratively and programmatically for the education (taken in the broadest sense) of handicapped populations. To establish parallel systems of sufficient size would be difficult and wasteful. Critics of this position fear that placement of infants into public school programs will lead to these youngsters being handled like small school-age children. That is, the infant will be expected to attend daily classes and be regimented into structured programs conducted by personnel who have little understanding of an infant's needs.

As indicated above, a number of professionals from medical and other allied health fields have voiced concern over the content and approaches adopted for infant intervention programs. Some of these professionals have stated that the birth to 3 population should remain under the egis of medical personnel. They fear programs that they believe treat infants like miniature preschoolers and turn parents into instructional agents. They believe such approaches are unhealthy for both the infant and the family. In particular, many health professionals see placement of infant programs under the public schools' egis inevitably leading to highly structured academic programs even for the youngest infant. These professionals believe that approaches that emphasize parent-infant interactions to promote parental-infant comfort and control are to be preferred to approaches which turn parents into didactic task masters with their infants. Futher, they believe that infants need considerable time to explore their social and physical environment on the infants' own terms rather than through highly structured and forced intervention régimes.

Conversely, many educationally oriented professionals are concerned about the nature of infant intervention programs that are designed and directed by medical and allied health specialists. This concern often derives from experiences in which the educator has seen intervention programs developed by allied health professionals that appear to focus primarily on the infants' medical needs and disregard their educational needs. For example, programs implemented by physical therapists for motor-impaired infants tend to emphasize work in the motor area to the exclusion of assisting the infant in acquiring social, cognitive, and self-help skills. Of course, many physical therapists are concerned about the general development of impaired infants and design programs that reflect more global intervention targets.

There exists a potential tug-of-war between educational and allied health professionals over who will serve at-risk and impaired infants and where these programs will be executed. Such a conflict serves no one's best interest, least of all the infants. Ample precedent of cooperative and joint efforts between these camps exists (Goldberg & Divitto, 1983; Thornton & Frankenburg, 1983; Waldstein, Gilderman, Taylor-Hershel, Prestridge & Anderson, 1982). A number of real examples of how educational and allied health personnel can work together to design and implement infant programs are available. Placing the birth to 2 population under the authority of the public schools or in medical facilities does not have to result in the development of inappropriate programs.

The location of the program is unimportant if participating infants and caregivers are offered appropriate content generated by the joint efforts of medical, allied health, and educational specialists. However, the location of intervention programs may have a significant impact on the type of training, who does it, and the

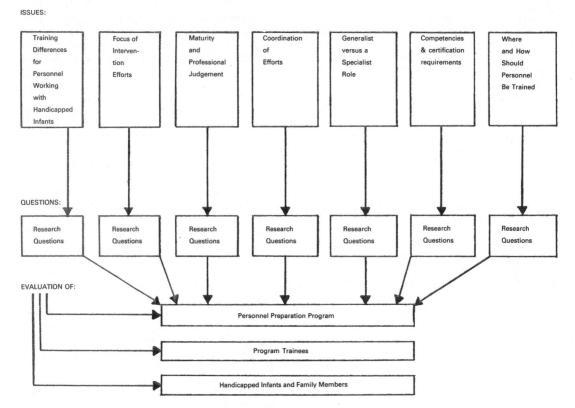

ISSUES:

| Training Differences for Personnel Working with Handicapped Infants | Focus of Intervention Efforts | Maturity and Professional Judgement | Coordination of Efforts | Generalist versus a Specialist Role | Competencies & certification requirements | Where and How Should Personnel Be Trained |

QUESTIONS:

| Research Questions | Research Questions | Research Questions | Research Questions | Research Questions | Research Questions | Research Questions |

EVALUATION OF:

| Personnel Preparation Program |

| Program Trainees |

| Handicapped Infants and Family Members |

Figure 2. Schematic of overall research recommendations for personnel preparation program focused on handicapped infants.

required credentials. A number of intervention programs have been initiated in hospital settings for infants assigned to NICUs. A number of these programs are operated by medical personnel and some by combinations of child development specialists, and allied health professionals. A few of these programs employ special educators who work in conjunction with allied health professionals. Other programs are housed in public schools and these employ educational and allied health specialists.

Although some significant overlap may occur, the information and skills required to operate a program for organically impaired infants in a NICU may be different from those required to operate an infant group for Down's syndrome babies. Should training for interventionists assigned to hospital NICU programs for disabled infants differ from that of home-based programs operated by local public schools? Time and energy are required to examine these issues thoughtfully and arrive at some conclusion that will assist the field in making sound judgments about who should train professionals to work with handicapped infants. Most likely, a variety of training options should be available. Included in these options should be professionals from a number of relevant disciplines in order to develop and deliver the most appropriate services to handicapped infants and their families.

Summary

This section may have been unsatisfactory for the reader who expected that some resolution surrounding major issues was forthcoming. Unfortunately, the state of the art does not permit solutions. However, we are hopeful that the articulation and synthesis of the major issues will assist in moving toward such resolutions.

Research Recommendations

Generally, research conducted on personnel preparation is exceedingly sparse. The reasons for this unfortunate state of affairs are numerous. First, attempting to control all the relevant variables that produce an effective versus ineffective interventionist is impossible. For example, entry criteria are general and thus students enter programs with significantly different backgrounds. Second, the quality of the training programs may vary from time to time as a function of faculty expertise or motivation, student commitment and/or availability of appropriate resources (e.g., practica sites). Third, selection of criteria for determining success can be difficult. An effective interventionist may accept a position in a program whose philosophical orientation interferes with the delivery of appropriate services. Fourth, other factors apart from the quality of the training may impact performance, for example, illness or serious personal difficulties. Attempting to tease apart program factors from extraneous factors is often impossible and seriously compromises evaluation of training efforts.

Although training programs tend to have required courses and practica, there is usually some variation within and beyond the requirements. For example, some students may actively seek additional appropriate coursework or practica that significantly enhances their expertise. The final quality of the personnel may be more a function of their own motivation than the quality of the training program. Another significant difficulty is the generally small number of trainees involved in a program per year. Programs with large numbers tend to be in urban centers and many of these students are part-time and often take considerable time to complete their degrees. Consequently, most programs have small numbers for a basis on which to answer questions. For example, the University of Oregon program usually has 8 master's students per year. Consolidating this group of students over time to enhance the numbers becomes tricky because of programmatic changes (e.g., courses, instructors, supervisors, and practica changes).

Finally, most personnel preparation programs do not have adequate funds to conduct well-controlled research. The best most programs can do is to evaluate students' performance in courses, practica and/or competencies; seek feedback from students; and to conduct follow-up questionnaires upon students' graduation. Although providing some information, such evaluations are quite limited in terms of assessing the impact of the program on the trainee and the trainee's impact on infants and families.

Figure 2 provides an overall schematic of the research recommendations offered for personnel preparation. This figure was designed to provide a general evaluative format and to generate more specific questions. The general or overall questions concern: (a) the differences between programs, (b) how those differences may or may not impact trainees' on-the-job performance, and (c) how trainees' performance impacts the infant and family members.

Table 2 presents a series of three research questions generated for each of the seven issue areas. Again, the general nature of these questions is similar, beginning with determining if differences exist in programs and if so, do these differences produce differences in trainees' on-the-job performance and subsequently, do these trainee differences have differential impact on infants and family members. In effect, the three questions generated for each issue constitute our research recommendations for the area of personnel preparation for handicapped infants.

The apparent redundancy of research questions posed in Table 2 is pertinent to the overall structure, not the specific content. The structural redundancy emphasizes the importance of attempting to establish program differences and similarities, to examine the impact of the differences on trainees and to measure how infants and families are subsequently effected. When the research questions are restated to reflect the content pertinent to a major issue, the redundancy disappears. For example, measuring the impact on infants and families in terms of differences in coordination of efforts will likely differ from questions of where and how personnel should be trained.

The specific research goals generated for the seven major issues are comprehensive and if undertaken would constitute a huge investment of time and other resources. More realistically, the posed questions or modifications and expansions of them should be addressed in phases. Hopefully, addressing selected questions in specific areas would lead to the systematic generation of information that would permit the development of more useful approaches to subsequent questions and areas.

TABLE 2

List of Specific Research Questions for Each
Major Issue Area

ISSUE 1: Training differences for personnel working with handicapped infants

1. Can didactic and practica differences be delineated between training program for birth to 2 and 3 to 5 populations?
2. Do training program differences impact trainees' on-the-job- performance?
3. Do trainees' performance differences impact children and families?

ISSUE 2: Focus of intervention efforts

1. Can differences be delineated in programs that focus on preparing personnel to intervene with adults with those that focus on intervening with infants?
2. Do training foci produce differences in trainees' on-the-job performance?
3. Do different training foci effect infants and/or parents differently?

ISSUE 3: Maturity and professional judgment

1. Can differences be delineated in amount and type of practical experience offered by programs to their trainees?
2. Do practical training differences impact trainees' on-the-job performance?
3. Do practical training differences impact infant and family performances?

ISSUE 4: Coordination of efforts

1. Do training programs have differential emphasis on coordination across disciplines/agencies?
2. Do training differences impact trainees' on-the-job performance?
3. Do training differences impact infants and families differentially?

ISSUE 5: Generalist versus a specialist role

1. Do training programs differ in their preparation of trainees as generalists or specialists?
2. Do training differences impact trainees' on-the-job performance?
3. Do training differences impact infants and families differently?

ISSUE 6: Competencies and certification requirements

1. Do training programs differ in required competencies; and do state certification requirements differ?
2. Do competency differences and certification differences impact trainees' on-the-job performance?
3. Do differences in competencies and certification requirements impact infants and families differently?

ISSUE 7: Where and how should personnel be trained

1. Can training programs be delineated by faculty expertise and orientation?
2. Do training differences impact trainees' on-the-job performance?
3. Do training differences differently impact infants and families?

Policy Recommendations

Our synthesis of the research, the results of our survey, and the insights garnered from our experience leads us to offer three policy recommendations. First, we recommend that the appropriate federal agencies associated with research programs establish the study of personnel preparation as a priority area. Our sense is that little emphasis has been placed on studying how to prepare quality personnel. The lack of investigative work in this area may be, in part, the result of little emphasis or tangible support for conducting relevant studies in personnel preparation. Establishing priorities and providing funds particularly earmarked for study in this area may attract competent investigators to study relevant dimensions of personnel preparation for the birth to 3 population.

A second policy recommendation is the need to encourage and support research directed toward solving some of the difficult design and methodology problems encountered when attempting to investigate factors associated with personnel preparation. As discussed above, investigators are faced with small, heterogeneous populations, and often adequate controls are unavailable. Studies directed at developing method/design alternatives are needed and should be encouraged by establishing such methodological work as a priority.

Our third and final recommendation flows naturally from the others and is the need for some consistent longitudinal funding for investigation of questions such as those posed in Table 2. Establishing a consistent support base would encourage investigators to become involved in the area of personnel preparation. Further, a consistent support base might facilitate collaborative efforts or at least complementary efforts between investigators.

Without consistent support in terms of established priorities and available monies, a future review of research conducted on personnel preparation efforts for handicapped infants will most likely yield a scant outcome similar to that reported in this chapter.

Summary

This chapter has reviewed the literature on the preparation of personnel to work with handicapped infants and their families. For the most part, little information on programs was uncovered and we found no empirical studies of the impact of preparation programs on their trainees or on the populations served by programs' graduates.

To garner additional information, a national survey of ECH/SE personnel preparation programs was conducted. The survey outcomes have significant limitations in that the respondents were selected from a list of project directors who had received training grants from OSERS and from a list of individuals who attended an invitational conference on personnel preparation at George Washington University. A second limitation is the return rate of the survey which was only 50%. Nevertheless, the descriptive information provided by the survey does offer some suggestive trends for this sample of programs. In particular, most are master's degree programs housed in departments of special education. Most programs include coursework and practica focused on acquiring information and skills pertinent to handicapped infants, children, and their families. Most programs have an associated set of competencies, but how programs assure acquisition of these skills is generally unclear.

The respondents' reactions to the set of four assumptions on the (a) presumed difference between the birth to 2 and 3 to 5 age groups, (b) training focus on the caregivers as the primary intervention agent, (c) need for extended practical experience, and (d) need for the acquisition and coordination of disciplines and agencies were uniform and positive. Interestingly, these assumptions did not always appear to be represented in the program descriptions provided by the respondents (e.g., some programs require few practicum hours, most programs fail to distinguish between the under three and over three populations). Such discrepancies suggest to us that the field of ECH/SE would benefit from increased thought and dialogue focused on the philosophical, conceptual, and practical requirements of training programs.

An analysis of the literature and the survey results assisted in identifying seven major issues including:

- Training specializations for personnel working with handicapped infants

- Focus of intervention efforts
- Maturity and professional judgment
- Coordination of efforts
- Generalist versus a specialist role
- Competencies, certification requirements
- How and by whom personnel should be trained.

A discussion of these issues illuminates the need for applied research in the area of personnel preparation for individuals working with handicapped infants and their families.

The major research recommendations suggested are the conduct of investigations centered on three basic questions appropriate to each of the seven identified issues. These questions are: identification of program differences with respect to a particular issue (e.g., program competencies), determining the impact of the identified differences on programs' trainees, and determining trainees' impact on infants and families.

Finally, during the lengthy review process established for the chapters included in this volume, an issue surfaced which we had not addressed: the need for leadership in the area of personnel preparation for the birth to 2 population. Most state legislatures and state agent personnel have shown considerable reluctance in developing services for the handicapped population under 3. Equal or greater reluctance has been evidenced in the development of appropriate credentials for the personnel who work with this population. We believe that resistance encountered at local and state levels places a burden on the federal government to provide leadership in this area.

The federal government has at least three mechanisms to provide the necessary leadership to help assure personnel preparation programs are graduating quality personnel. First, OSERS' Special Education Program (SEP) could issue guidelines for personnel preparation applications that enforce the development of quality training programs. In June, 1985, a paper compiled by the Higher Education Consortium for Special Education (1984), describing indicators of quality doctoral programs, was disseminated by the SEP's Division of Personnel Preparation. Such efforts are to be applauded and other similar efforts encouraged. Second, the panels assembled by SEP to review personnel preparation applications should be composed of individuals with demonstrated expertise in specific areas. Training grants focused on the preparation of infant specialists should be reviewed by panel members who are knowledgeable about the field of infancy and, when possible, have trained personnel in this area. Finally, the federal government could provide leadership through the passage of additional legislation that mandates services be extended to the birth to 2 population. In concert with this legislation should be additional regulation encouraging or requiring states to develop certification or credentials specifically for personnel working with the birth to 2 population. Employing these and other similar strategies should assist in establishing a professional commitment and responsibility to providing quality services to the birth to 2 population.

References

Allen, K. (1978). The early childhood education specialist (ECES). In K. Allen, V. Holm, & R. Schiefelbusch (Eds.), *Early intervention—A team approach* (pp. 287–306). Baltimore, MD: University Park Press.

Anderson, J., & Black, T. (1981). *Special education mandated from birth*. Chapel Hill, NC: University of North Carolina, Technical Assistance Development System (TADS).

Barnard, K. (1976). Nursing: High risk infants. In T. Tjossem (Ed.), *Intervention strategies for high risk infants and young children* (pp. 703–725). Baltimore, MD: University Park Press.

Blackhurst, E. (1981). Noncategorical teacher preparation: Problems and promises. *Exceptional Children*, **48**(3), 197–205.

Blatt, B., & Garfunkel, F. (1969). *The educability of intelligence*. Washington, DC: The Council for Exceptional Children.

Bricker, D. (1976). Educational synthesizer. In M. Thomas (Ed.), *Hey, don't forget about me!* (pp. 84–97). Reston, VA: The Council for Exceptional Children.

Bricker, D. (1986). An analysis of early intervention programs: Attendant issues and future directions. In B. Blatt & R. Morris (Eds.), *Special education research and trends* (pp. 28–65). New York: Scott, Foresman.

Bricker, D., Bailey, E., & Bruder, M. (1984). The efficacy of early intervention and the handicapped infant: A wise or wasted resource? *Advances in Behavioral Pediatrics* (Vol. V), Greenwich, CT: JAI Press.

Bricker, D., & Carlson, L. (1981). Issues in early language intervention. In R. Schiefelbusch & D. Bricker (Eds.), *Early language: Acquisition and intervention* (pp. 477–517). Baltimore, MD: University Park Press.

Bricker, D., & Iacino, R. (1977). Early intervention with severely/profoundly handicapped children. In E. Sontag, J. Smith, & N. Certo (Eds.), *Educational programming for the severely and profoundly handicapped* (pp. 166–176). Reston, VA: The Council for Exceptional Children.

Bronfenbrenner, U. (1975). Is early intervention effective? In B. Friedlander, G. Sterritt, & G. Kirk (Eds.), *Exceptional infant* (Vol. 3, pp. 449–475). New York: Brunner/Mazel.

Budetti, P., Barrand, N., McManus, P., & Heinen, L. (1981). *The implications of cost-effectiveness analyses of medical technology. Case study #10: The cost and effectiveness of neonatal intensive care*. Washington, DC: Office of Technology Assessment.

Caputo, D., Goldstein, K., & Taub, H. (1981). Neonatal compromise and later psychological development: A 10 year longitudinal study. In S. Friedman & M. Sigman (Eds.), *Preterm birth and psychological development* (pp. 353–386). New York: Academic Press.

Carran, N. (1984). *National directory of early childhood special education services (1984)*. National Consortium of State Education Agency Early Childhood/Special Education Coordinators. Des Moines, IA: Department of Public Instruction.

Clarke, A., & Clarke, A. (1976). *Early experience: Myth and evidence*. New York: The Free Press.

Clarke, A., & Clarke, A. (1977). Prospects for prevention and amelioration of mental retardation: A guest editorial. *American Journal of Mental Deficiency*, **81**, 523–533.

Cohen, S., Semmes, M., & Guralnick, M. (1979). Public Law 94–142 and the education of preschool handicapped children. *Exceptional Children*, **45**, 279–285.

Cole, J., & Gilkerson, L. (1982). Developmental consultation: The role of the parent/infant education in a hospital/community coordinated program for high risk premature infants. In A. Waldstein (Ed.), *Issues in neonatal care* (pp. 107–122). Seattle, WA: WESTAR/TADS.

Cornell, E., & Gottfried, A. (1976). Intervention with premature human infants. *Child Development*, **47**, 31–39.

Davis, J., & Porter, M. (1981). An inservice training program for rural area professionals concerned with early childhood special education. In B. Smith-Dickson (Ed.), *Making it work in rural areas: Training, recruiting and retaining personnel in rural areas* (pp. 19–36). Macomb, IL: HCEEP Rural Network Monographs.

Dennis, W., & Najarian, P. (1963). Development under environmental handicap. In W. Dennis (Ed.), *Readings in child psychology* (pp. 315–331). Englewood Cliffs, NJ: Prentice-Hall.

DeVellis, R., DeVellis, B., Rivicki, D., Lurie, S., Runyan, D., & Bristol, M. (1985). Development and validation of the Child Improvement Locus of Control (CILC) Scales. *Journal of Social and Clinical Psychology*, 3, 308–325.

Fewell, R. (1983). The team approach to infant education. In S. Garwood & R. Fewell (Eds.), *Educating handicapped infants* (pp. 299–322). Rockville, MD: Aspen.

Field, T., Dempsey, J., & Shuman, H. (1981). Developmental follow-up of pre- and postterm infants. In S. Friedman & M. Sigman (Eds.), *Preterm birth and psychological development* (pp. 299–312). New York: Academic Press.

Filler, J. (1983). Service models for handicapped infants. In G. Garwood & R. Fewell (Eds.), *Educating handicapped infants* (pp. 369–386). Rockville, MD: Aspen.

Flynn, M. (1981). Focus on training: Training interdisciplinary teams for preschool programs. In R. Sexton (Ed.), *Project Sunrise: The annual Montana symposium on early education and the exceptional child* (pp. 66–74). Billings, MT: Eastern Montana College, Institute for Rehabilitative Services.

Freund, J., Casey, P., & Bradley, R. (1982). A special education course with pediatric components. *Exceptional Children*, **48**(4), 348–351.

Galey, G., Garner, D., Pillans, D., & Solomon, G. (1981). Training rural volunteers to deliver services to handicapped infants: The D.O.T.S. approach. In B. Smith-Dickson (Ed.), *Making it work in rural areas: Training, recruiting, and retaining personnel in rural areas* (pp. 37–45). Macomb, IL: HCEEP Rural Network Monographs.

Galton, F. (1961). Classification of men according to their natural gifts. In J. Jenkins & D. Paterson (Eds.), *Studies in individual differences* (pp. 1–16). New York: Appleton-Century-Crofts.

Geik, I., Gilkerson, K., & Sponseller, D. (1982). An early intervention training model. *Journal for the Division of Early Childhood*, **5**, 42–52.

Gibson, D., & Fields, D. (1984). Early stimulation programs for Down's syndrome: An effectiveness inventory. In M. Wolraich (Ed.), *Advances in behavioral and developmental pediatrics* (Vol. 5, pp. 331–371). Greenwich, CN: JAI Press.

Goldberg, S., & DiVitto, B. (1983). *Born too soon: Preterm birth and early development*. New York: Freeman.

Gorelick, M. (1978). *Survey of staff preparation for infant/toddler development programs*. (ERIC Document Reproduction Service No. 171389).

Guralnick, M., & Bricker, D. (1987). The effectiveness of early intervention for children with cognitive and general developmental delays. In M. Guralnick & F. Bennett (Eds.), *The effectiveness of early intervention*. New York: Academic Press.

Harlow, H., & Harlow, M. (1966). Learning to love. *American Scientist*, **54**, 244–272.

Higher Education Consortium for Special Education (1984). *Indicators of quality in special educational doctoral programs*. Washington, DC: HECSE.

Hirshoren, A., & Umansky, W. (1977). Certification for teachers of preschool handicapped children. *Exceptional Children*, **44**, 191–193.

Hobbs, N. (Ed.) (1975). *Issues in the classification of children* (2 vols.). San Francisco: Jossey Bass.

Honzik, M., MacFarlane, J., & Allen, L. (1963). The stability of mental test performance. In W. Dennis (Ed.), *Readings in child psychology* (pp. 223–232). Englewood Cliffs, NJ: Prentice-Hall.

Hunt, J. (1961). *Intelligence and experience*. New York: Ronald Press.

Hunt, J. (1981). Predicting intellectual disorders in childhood for preterm infants with birthweights below 1501 gm. In S. Friedman & M. Sigman (Eds.), *Preterm birth and psychological development* (pp. 329–351). New York: Academic Press.

Hutinger, P. (1981). Approach for training early childhood teachers: WIU 0–6 early childhood handicapped personnel training project. In B. Smith-Dickson (Ed.), *Making it work in rural areas: Training, recruiting and retaining personnel in rural areas* (pp. 11–18). Macomb, IL: HCEEP Rural Network Monographs.

Hutinger, P., & Swartz, S. (1979). An interdisciplinary model for early childhood handicapped teachers. *The Teacher Educator*, **14**(3), 6–10.

Jackson, E. (1979). Current status of personnel training for early intervention programs. In K. Schuster, & S. McBride, (Eds.), *Early Intervention of Developmental Disabilities. A report on the Conference on Early Intervention of Developmental Disabilities* (May 18 & 19, 1979, Nashville, IN) (pp. 25–55). Bloomington, IN: Early Childhood Unit, Developmental Training Center, Indiana University.

Kagan, J., Kearsley, R., & Zelazo, P. (1978). *Infancy: Its place in human development*. Cambridge, MA: Harvard University Press.

Kagan, J., & Klein, R. (1973). Cross-cultural perspectives on early development. *American Psychologist*, **28**, 947–961.

Kelly, P., & Havlick, L. (1982). A statewide network for training special education paraprofessionals. *Exceptional Children*, **48**(6), 535.

Kirk, S. (1958). *Early education of the mentally retarded*. Urbana, IL: University of Illinois Press.

Kirk, S. (1978). The federal role in special education: Historical perspectives. *UCLA Education*, **20**, 5–11.

Klaus, M., & Kennell, J. (1976). *Maternal-infant bonding*. St. Louis: Mosby.

Kopp, C. (1982). The role of theoretical frameworks in the study of at-risk and handicapped young children. In D. Bricker (Ed.), *Intervention with at-risk and handicapped infants* (pp. 13–30). Baltimore, MD: University Park Press.

Kopp, C. (1983). Risk factors in development. In M. Haith & J. Campos (Eds.), *Infancy and the biology of development*. Vol. 2 from P. Mussen (Ed.). *Manual of child psychology*. New York: Wiley.

Lessen, E., & Rose, T. (1980). State definitions of preschool handicapped populations. *Exceptional Children*, **46**, 467–469.

Mallory, B. (1983). The preparation of early childhood special educators: A model program. *Journal for the Division of Early Childhood*, **7**, 32–40.

Mason, M. (1963). Learning to speak after years of silence. In W. Dennis (Ed.), *Readings in child psychology* (2nd ed.) (pp. 201–210). Englewood Cliffs, NJ: Prentice-Hall.

McCall, R. (1979). The development of intellectual functioning in infancy and the prediction of later IQ. In J. Osofsky (Ed.), *Handbook of infant development* (pp. 707–741). New York: Wiley.

McDermott, S., & Ivy, E. (1981). *Personnel preparation: Training specialists to work with young hearing impaired children and their families*. (Paper presented at the annual International Convention of the Council for Exceptional Children, New York.)

Miller, P. (1976–1977). Teacher competencies in early education of the handicapped. In P. Miller (Ed.) *Models for Training Teachers of Early Education for the Handicapped*. Reston, VA: The Council for Exceptional Children.

Moore, S. (1981). Competency skill level of the professional working with infants: Where and how are skills acquired? In D. Gilderman, D. Taylor-Hershel, S. Presridge, & J. Anderson (Eds.), *The health care/education relationship: Services for infants with special needs and their families* (pp. 92–98). Seattle, WA: WESTAR.

Noel, M., Burke, P., & Valdivieso, C. (1985). Educational policy and several mental retardation. In D. Bricker & J. Filler (Eds.), *The severely mentally retarded: Research to practice* (pp. 12–35). Reston, VA: The Council for Exceptional Children.

O'Connell, J. (1983). Education of handicapped preschoolers: A national survey for services and personnel requirements. *Exceptional Children*, **49**(6), 538–543.

Pick, A. (1978). Discussion summary: Early assessment. In F. Minifie & L. Lloyd (Eds.), *Communicative and cognitive abilities—Early behavioral assessment* (pp. 107–114). Baltimore, MD: University Park Press.

Ramey, C., & Baker-Ward, L. (1982). Psychosocial retardation and the early experience paradigm. In D. Bricker (Ed.), *Intervention with at-risk and handicapped infants* (pp. 269–289). Baltimore, MD: University Park Press.

Ramey, C., Zeskind, P., & Hunter, R. (1981). Biomedical and psychosocial interventions for preterm infants. In S. Friedman & M. Sigman (Eds.), *Preterm birth and psychological development* (pp. 395–415). New York: Academic Press.

Rosenthal, M. (1980). Developing leadership roles for inte-

grated early childhood programs in Israel. *Young Children*, **35**(3), 21–26.

Sameroff, A. (1981). Longitudinal studies of preterm infants: A review of chapters 17–20. In S. Friedman & M. Sigman (Eds.), *Preterm birth and psychological development* (pp. 387–393). New York: Academic Press.

Sarason, S., & Doris, J. (1969). *Psychological problems in mental deficiency*. New York, Harper & Row.

Sigman, M., Cohen, S., & Forsythe, A. (1981). The relation of early infant measures to later development. In S. Friedman & M. Sigman (Eds.), *Preterm birth and psychological development* (pp. 313–327). New York: Academic Press.

Smith, B. (1984). Expanding the federal role in serving young special needs children. *Topics in Early Childhood Special Education*, **4**(1), 33–42.

Smith, J. (Ed.) (1979). *A consumer's guide to personnel preparation programs: Thirty projects/a conspectus*. Albuquerque, NM: University of New Mexico.

Stile, S., Abernathy, S., Pettibone, T., & Wachtel, W. (1984). Training and certification for early childhood special education personnel: A six-year follow-up study. *Journal for the Division of Early Childhood*, **8**(1), 69–73.

Sweet, N. (1982). New faces and approaches in the intensive care nursery: The roles of the developmental/educational specialist. In A. Waldstein (Ed.), *Issues in neonatal care* (pp. 61–81). Seattle, WA: WESTAR/TADS.

Taft, L. (1981). Intervention programs for infants with cerebral palsy: A clinician's view. In C. Brown (Ed.), *Infants at risk*. (Pediatric Round Table Series 5), Princeton, NJ: Johnson & Johnson Baby Products.

Thornton, S. & Frankenburg, W. (Eds.) (1983). *Child health care communications: Enhancing interactions among professionals, parents and children* (Pediatric Roundtable 8). Shellman, N. J.: Johnson & Johnson Baby Products.

Waldstein, A., Gilderman, D., Taylor-Hershel, D., Prestridge, S., & Anderson, J. (1982). *Issues in neonatal care*. Chapel Hill, N.C.:TADS.

Walker, B., Slentz, K., & Bricker, D. (1985). *Parent involvement in early intervention*. Rehabilitation Research Review, National Rehabilitation Information Center, Washington, DC: The Catholic University of America.

Walker-McCollum, J. (1982). Teaching teachers to teach: A framework for preservice program planning. *Journal of the Division of Early Childhood*, **6**, 52–59.

Wolfensberger, W. (1969). The origin and nature of our institutional models. In R. Kugel & W. Wolfensberger (Eds.), *Changing patterns in residential services for the mentally retarded* (pp. 59–171). Washington, DC: President's Committee on Mental Retardation.

Zeitlin, S., duVerglas, G., & Windhover, R. (1982). *Basic competencies for personnel in early intervention programs: Guidelines for development*. Monmouth, OR: WESTAR.

Author Index

Subject Index